CORINNE TRANG

ESSENTIALS OF
ASIAN CUISINE

FUNDAMENTALS AND FAVORITE RECIPES

BLACK-AND-WHITE PHOTOGRAPHS BY CORINNE TRANG

COLOR PHOTOGRAPHS BY CHRISTOPHER HIRSHEIMER

SIMON & SCHUSTER
New York   London   Toronto   Sydney   Singapore

SIMON & SCHUSTER
Rockefeller Center
1230 Avenue of the Americas
New York, NY 10020

For information about special discounts for bulk purchases,
please contact Simon & Schuster Special Sales:
1-800-456-6798 or business@simonandschuster.com

Designed by Toby Fox

Manufactured in the United States of America

10   9   8   7   6   5   4   3   2   1

Library of Congress Cataloging-in-Publication Data

Trang, Corinne.
   Essentials of Asian cuisine : fundamentals and favorite recipes / Corinne Trang;
black-and-white photographs by Corinne Trang; color photographs by
Christopher Hirsheimer.
      p.   cm.
   Includes bibliographical references and index.
   1. Cookery, Asian.   I. Title.
LTX724.5.A1 T73   2003
641.595—dc21   2002030490

ISBN 0-7432-0312-7

FRONTISPIECE: PUSO, RICE BOILED IN A HAND-
WOVEN COCONUT LEAF POUCH, IS A POPULAR SNACK
SOLD BY STREET HAWKERS IN THE PHILIPPINES.

To my husband,

Michael McDonough,

who was my reader,

best friend, partner,

and unwavering supporter

during the creation

of this book

ACKNOWLEDGMENTS

THIS BOOK would not have been possible without the support and encouragement of family, friends, and fellow professionals. I owe a great deal of gratitude to my husband, Michael McDonough, who has always encouraged me to write about the foods and cultures I love most. We talked and debated endless hours over meals prepared at home or foods sampled at restaurants or during our travels; many of those debates are remembered here. I am also very thankful to my agent, Angela Miller, of The Miller Agency, who believed in me and in this project the minute she read my proposal. Once again, I was blessed to have Sydny Weinberg Miner as my editor at Simon & Schuster. Her directions were as crucial for the project as they were for my previous book, *Authentic Vietnamese Cooking: Food from a Family Table* (1999). Thank you, Kate Nowell-Smith, Anthony Wing Kosner, David Russo, and Mary Vidal for reading the words, for your constructive criticism, and for your questions, which I hope have been answered. My hat goes off to Virginia McRae, copy editor; and Jonathon Brodman, production editor, who scrutinized every single word, phrase, and punctuation mark; and to Nancy Wolff, index editor, who cross-referenced page numbers to recipe titles or descriptions. Thank you, Jim Thiel, production supervisor; and Laura Holmes, assistant editor, for your input. My thanks also go to publicists Victoria Meyer and Aileen Boyle for launching the book.

My creative team once again rose to the occasion. Thank you, Christopher Hirsheimer, for your beautiful color food photography. It is as balanced as the flavors of Asia, bold and subtle, all in the same shot. Thank you, photo editors María Millán and Rosa Vilá of Imágenes LLC, for the use of your beautiful Day 1 Studio. Thank you, Kathleen Hackett, for your participation during the photo shoot. And thank you, Toby Fox, art director and designer, who worked on my previous book, for turning double-spaced manuscript pages and photos into a beautiful, elegant book.

While creating this book, I have crossed paths with many food and travel professionals who deserve recognition and my sincere thanks and appreciation for sharing their knowledge and for giving me their precious time. In no particular order they are:

In Bali: Ibu Wayan, Cafe Wayan; Ketut Suardana, Puri Bagus Villa Resorts and Cooking School; and Linda Garland, Environmental Bamboo Foundation. In Cambodia: Gilbert Madhavan, Thomas Meier, and Shanker Rajoo, Raffles International, Hotel Le Royal, Phnom Penh; Eric Simard, Accor, Phnom Penh; and Ronald Sathianathan, Raffles International, Grand Hotel d'Angkor, Siem Reap. In Japan: Elizabeth Andoh, A Taste of Culture Japanese Arts Program, Tokyo;

Mark Simon and Antoine Chahwan, Four Seasons Hotel, Tokyo; Masuhiro Fukaya, Sakae Soy Sauce Brewing; Taeko Fujii, Urasenke International Association, Kyoto; Ogawa Michi, Women's Association of Kyoto; Ken Shimizu, Ryokan Yoshi-Ima; and Takako Yamatari and Hiroko Tayama, interpreters. In Korea: Sophie Park, interpreter; Chae Won Hwa, Panyaro Institute for the Way of Tea, Seoul; Han Jung Hae, Han Jung Hae's Cooking Academy, Seoul; Yeon Sook Son, Jeong Sook Son, and Bokhi Chang, Son's Korean Home Culture, Seoul; Hyo-Ju Ahn, Sun-Hee Lee, and Anna Han, The Shilla, Seoul; Kwang-Ho Yoo and Jan Yoo, Hotel Lotte Pusan; J. O. Lee and Hyeong Gyun Lee, Hotel Hyundai, Kyongju; Seung Seok Yang, Kyongju World Culture Expo 2000; Chong-Bae Kim, Deuk-Pyo Ahn, and In-Sook Lee, Korea National Tourism Organization, Seoul. In the Philippines: Joy A. Wassmer, Neil M. Rumbaoa, and Gene S. Delprado, Shangri-La, Manila; Merle Rivera, Ding R. Rodenas, and Gael Moureau, Shangri-La, Cebu; Remedios A. Raymundo, Southeast Travel Corp; Larry J. Cruz, LJC Restaurant Group; Glenda R. Barretto, Via Mare Catering Services Inc.; Jessica R. Avila, Tiya Nena's Cooking School and Restaurant; Helen O. Genaldo, interpreter; Georgitta "Beng" Pimentel-Puyat; Nora Villanueva Daza; and Jacqueline Lasne. In Hong Kong: Patsy Chan, Shangri-La, Kowloon; Kelly Sum, Shangri-La, Central; Peter Randall and Mandy Lo, Hong Kong Tourist Association in Hong Kong. In Thailand: Sompon Nabnian, Chiang Mai Thai Cookery School; Michael J. Kemp, Derek Watanabe, Vemporn Ratsameejam "Nui," Sangway Sapma, and Lee Sutton, The Regent Chiang Mai; and Somrith Haikham, interpreter. In Vietnam: Didier Corlou, Richard Kaldor, and Marc Bégassat, Sofitel Metropole Hanoi; and Serge Rigodin, Christophe Pairaud, and Phoeung Sakal, Sofitel Plaza Saigon.

There are others in the United States whom I wish to thank: Deok-Soo Ahn, Kwang-Ho Kang, and Gregory M. Kelly, Korea National Tourism Organization; Lilibeth Bishop and Diana Shen Budiman, Hong Kong Tourist Association; Etsuko Kawasaki and Marian Goldberg, Japan National Tourist Organization; Sari Freeman, Sari Freeman Associates; Romdoul Kim, The Royal Embassy of Cambodia; Marion Darby, Shangri-La Hotel and Resorts; Joon Han Lee, Ing Soo Park, and Michael J. King, Asiana Airlines; August E. Whitcomb, Cathay Pacific; and Ken Fish and Ashley Isaacs, Absolute Asia.

I also want to thank Dr. Julio Aramberi and Francis McFadden, department director, for welcoming me as a visiting faculty member of the Culinary Arts program at Drexel University. They have given me a forum in which to share with others what I am most passionate about, food and travel, and it is a pleasure to be teaching in such a wonderful learning environment.

To my parents, Nhu Minh and Marie-Jeanne "Minou" Trang, who taught me about food and culture. You have given me the best of both worlds, and I have spent the last thirty years or so deciphering what it all might mean. To my international family—scattered throughout Europe, Asia, and North America—thank you for giving me a purpose in life. I didn't make it to all the family reunions, but I love you all very much.

Thank you all very much from the bottom of my heart.

CONTENTS

THE RICE FROM THE PADDIES OF
THE REGENT CHIANG MAI IN
NORTHERN THAILAND IS
HARVESTED TWICE A YEAR.

ESSENTIALS OF
ASIAN CUISINE

INTRODUCTION

GROWING UP among wonderful home cooks in the kitchens of Southeast Asia, the expatriate Chinese communities in Paris, and traditional provincial cooks in the Loire Valley of France; then expanding my circle to include chefs and restaurateurs throughout Europe, the United States, China, and East Asia, I came to see continuities between and among the great cuisines of the East that could be expressed in Western terms. This book is intended to explore those continuities. In seeking out the basic principles of China's regional kitchens, I believe it is possible to establish a way of bringing to life all of the great cuisines of Asia for any cook who cares to learn.

Western cooks are easily intimidated by Asian cooking. Ingredients seem alien, techniques unfamiliar, and languages impenetrable, even to professionals well versed in international cookery. It needn't be that way. Perhaps because I came to know both Eastern and Western cooking naturally, absorbing them as I grew up, the connections have always seemed obvious, the techniques manageable, the language issues inconsequential.

The more one looks at the cuisines of Asia, the more one realizes that they are closer than not to what we know in the West. Historically, trade routes and land bridges linked Europe, Southwest Asia, India, and Southeast Asia. For example, the Indonesian island of Java had for centuries closer ties to the

IN THAILAND, FRUIT AND VEGETABLES ARE CARVED INTO BEAUTIFUL SCULPTURES. THIS ROSE WAS ONCE A CARROT.

cultures of Iran and, by inference, Rome than to China, which was only a few hundred miles to the north. The Dutch, English, Portuguese, French, and Spanish had as much influence as the Chinese, and the ingredients and cooking styles reflect these circumstances. Many of the most central ingredients to the cooking of China itself are of Western origin, having come by way of war and trade. Corn, peanuts, sesame seeds, potatoes, pumpkins, tomatoes, and chili peppers were transplanted from Western Europe and the Americas. Indeed, for centuries the Philippines had closer ties to Spain, Mexico, and to the United States than it did to neighboring China.

The most important lesson I took from French cuisine was its notion of structure in cooking. When one learns the "architecture" of a cuisine, the rest will follow. (Indeed, France's first chef and one of its most important culinary pioneers, Marie-Antoine Carême, was an amateur architect!) Despite the fact that there are dozens of preparation and cooking techniques, hundreds of ingredients, and thousands of traditional Asian dishes, I believe strongly that the basics of Asian cuisine can be gleaned through an understanding of Chinese cooking, and that Southeast Asian and East Asian cooking can be seen as an extension of the Chinese kitchen, colored by local traditions and Western influences. This book is intended to set down what I feel are the fundamentals that bind all Asian cuisines, to provide a way of seeing and understanding what may have at one point seemed inscrutable to the average Western cook. *Essentials of Asian Cuisine* contains references to both Asian and Western cooking techniques, ingredients, culinary history, and cultural context, but it is not intended as a scholarly work. Rather, I hope that the enthusiastic cook will use it as a handy tool, and find it as much in sync with today's kitchens, supermarkets, and other culinary resources as with the culinary cultures it embodies.

The basics and organizing principles of Asian cuisines can be learned. The book includes, for example, a discussion of *feng shui*, the overarching principle in living a harmonious life that extends to cooking harmoniously, as well as the principle of *yin yang*, the art of balanced opposites that is central to Asian cuisine. There are brief overviews of Eastern culinary histories and cultures, so that the reader may better understand how foods evolved over time, and the whys and wherefores of ingredients and techniques.

Fusion, which is a basic principle of all world cooking, is a subject of much interest to many contemporary chefs. In the best sense, fusion means that ingredients and techniques, flavors and textures, backnotes and overtones develop and evolve as cultures rub up against one another and people move around. This notion has held true for the peoples of Asia for millennia. Asia's history is the story of migration, displacement, population shift, colonization, and empire. Partly out of a need to survive, partly out of a need to belong, and out of a need to accept, foods are fused. And out of all these needs, wonderful dishes evolve (the best of these having developed slowly), both through trial and error and for well-thought-out reasons. Also in the best tradition, flavors and combinations of foods are understood through the process of creating a meal, rather than simply as discrete items. Fusion is not a fad; it is an essential process in the evolution of human culture, and the cooking of Asia demonstrates this wonderfully. It is hoped that this book may provide some insight into the processes and aid cooks who are interested in the use of unfamiliar ingredients.

A caveat and an aspiration: It is important to keep in mind that this book is intended as a guide to cooking principles and not an exhaustive compendium. It points the way but does not describe every culinary nook and cranny along the way. It encourages personal discovery and experiment based on understanding.

While I have touched on what I believe are the principal historical cuisines of Asia, I have not gone into great depth relative to the cooking of a few countries. This is because as political boundaries have changed, cultural connections have remained intact, and cooking traditions do not acknowledge political borders. Laotian cooking largely reflects the principles of Vietnamese and Cambodian cooking, for example. Burmese cooking reflects that of Thailand. Malaysia was, for centuries, tied to the traditions of Sumatra, Java, and the rest of Indonesia. And—with author's emphasis—the cooking of vast and ancient India is best seen as a separate subject entirely.

Nonetheless, where Indian influences are felt, they have been included and described. And in the cases of Laos, Burma, and Malaysia, a few recipes have been included to illustrate the particular color and tone of their national cooking.

Every recipe in this book stands on its own, so that the reader may simply select an item on impulse. At the same time, the book can be approached as a pleasurable course of study. In addition to hundreds of recipes, there are also sections on essential ingredients, equipment and technique, food rituals, seasonal menus, and mail-order sources. From there, I encourage the adventurous cook to relax into improvisation and experimentation. In time, the essentials of Asian cooking will seem a potential part of any culinary foray. Opportunities for your own brand of fusion will arise. I hope my Asian kitchen will become part of your own.

Corinne Trang
New York, 2003

ESSENTIAL INGREDIENTS:
the asian pantry

I

N THIS CHAPTER you will find the ingredients I consider essential for making Asian foods in general and the recipes in this book in particular. Some, like fish sauce, are widely used, appearing in many Southeast Asian cuisines. Others are specific to one culture, such as the bonito flakes used in Japanese cooking.

Although I love to spend hours perusing the aisles of Asian markets, I do not always have time for that luxury. For this reason there are always a few essentials in my cupboard: Chinese light soy sauce, Japanese dark soy sauce, fish sauce, Chinese white rice vinegar, canola or grapeseed oil, and sesame oil. I make sure that garlic, ginger, and scallion are in the refrigerator, and replenished weekly. I refrigerate air-cured meats such as Chinese sweet pork sausage, liver sausage, and duck legs, double-wrapped in foil and stored in a plastic bag. In my freezer I keep dried shrimp, dried squid, dried tiger lilies, and plenty of homemade chicken stock. Dry ingredients include rice, wheat and egg noodles, shiitake mushrooms, and five-spice powder. Preserved vegetables such as Tientsin cabbage (sold in ceramic jars), Swatow mustard cabbage (packed in plastic pouches with brine), and preserved daikon strips are also staples in my kitchen. With just a few of these you can make any number of quick, humble meals in a pinch.

Beyond these basics, shopping in Asian markets or online catalogues can

BAMBOO SHOOTS ARE COMMON
INGREDIENTS IN ASIAN COOKERY.

be a way to learn more about the cuisines. The variety can be downright intimidating at first, but it can also be an adventure. If you see something that piques your curiosity, try it. The more you eat the particular ingredient, and try it in different ways, the more you will feel relaxed and even excited about it.

Here's a good exercise for people who are shy about grabbing strange things when shopping for food: choose five so-called "exotic" ingredients and cook with them for a month using them in the recipes in this book. Don't just try them once and stop. The next month select five more ingredients and repeat the process. By doing this, you will eventually get to know more exotic ingredients than you could have imagined. You will also be sensitized to their attributes, and use them appropriately. I am convinced that short of traveling to the country whose cooking you are learning, this is the best and simplest way to learn about a cuisine and its underlying culture.

The following are ingredients that are readily available in the West through various sources. I have also listed them by general type and mentioned brands that I particularly like. (Feel free, however, to try other brands.) These products are carried by Chinese, Southeast Asian, Korean, Filipino, Japanese, and other ethnic markets, and can also be mail-ordered via the Internet or other sources. (See mail-order sources, page 563.)

OILS

WHEN BUYING OILS remember that they have a limited shelf life and do go stale. Buy oil in small quantities, and store it in a cool, dark place. If the original container is not airtight, transfer the contents to one that is. Do not open too many bottles at a time: you will not be able to finish them before they go bad. Make it a point to finish your oil within about three months time. (You can also use pork fat in stir-frying or braising dishes. For a long time the Chinese and Southeast Asians did just that, since oil was a luxury item that only a few could afford. Many people still use pork fat instead of oil, feeling that it gives their food a richer flavor.)

canola oil: This is my everyday cooking oil. It has the same healthful benefits as olive oil but is also prone to smoking and burning if the heat is too high for too long. When stir-frying, however, things happen rather quickly, and the ingredients are usually added before the oil has a chance to burn. Canola oil is at its best when used over medium to low heat.

chili oil: You can make chili oil by infusing grapeseed oil with dried whole red chilies or flakes over medium-low heat for a few minutes, then straining the mixture, or you can buy it in Chinese and Southeast Asian markets. Orange-red in color, this spicy item is delicious drizzled over noodle dishes (soups or stir-fries) just before serving.

coconut oil: I have never bought coconut oil because it is easily made at home. Gently boil down coconut cream (page 77) until the milk evaporates and all that is left is a rich clear oil. One cup of coconut cream makes about ¼ cup oil when cooked down over medium heat. This oil is richer than peanut oil, but it is especially delicious when used in making Thai curries.

grapeseed oil: A mild-flavored oil, this has the same healthful benefits as canola and olive oils, but can take high-heat cooking better. It is perfect for stir-frying and deep-frying.

palm oil: In Southeast Asia, the palm tree is used for making both palm sugar and oil. The oil is used in cooking, cosmetics, and other products. Use it in cooking as you would any other vegetable oil.

peanut oil: Also known as ground nut oil, this oil has a deep flavor and can sometimes taste and feel a bit heavy. The Chinese love groundnut oil and use it in a lot of their cook-ing. Personally, I find it a bit overwhelming at times. If you wish to use this oil for deep-frying, try mixing it with a bit of grapeseed oil for a more subtle flavor.

sesame oil: Extracted from sesame seeds, and at times roasted for a more pronounced flavor, sesame oil has a strong nutty flavor note. It should be used sparingly because its pungent flavor will go a very long way. Look for Amoy or Kadoya 100 percent pure sesame oil. Spicy sesame oil (labeled "hot sesame oil") is also available, but you can also use regular sesame oil in combination with chili oil, adjusting the intensity to your liking.

SOY SAUCES AND OTHER SOYBEAN PRODUCTS

LIKE OILS, soy products are better when fresh, so do not buy them in bulk. Keep them in a cool, dark place, or refrigerate them, as is necessary in the case of hoisin sauce, fermented bean curd, and miso once the jars are opened.

chinese light soy sauce: A basic seasoning in Chinese cooking, in this particular sauce "light" refers to its fluidity, not its dietetic characteristics. Lighter and saltier than Chinese thick soy sauce, it is made from fermented soy beans, wheat, and yeast, and sometimes labeled "thin" soy sauce. Strict vegetarian Southeast Asian Buddhist monks use this soy sauce for seasoning instead of fish sauce. While China's Pearl River Bridge brand (look for the French word clair, meaning "clear" or "light") is consistently good, the less salty and more balanced Wan Ja Shan brand from Taiwan is my favorite.

chinese thick soy sauce: Also known as "dark" soy sauce, this is less salty, sweeter, and thicker than Chinese thin or light soy sauce, because of the inclusion of molasses. A natural colorant, it imparts a deep reddish-brown hue to foods. It is generally used in small quantities and usually in combination with Chinese thin soy sauce. My favorite brand is Koon Chun, which comes in a jar. The Pearl River Bridge brand is also good but not as rich. Its label will have the French word épais, meaning "thick." If you are unsure of what you are buying, flip the bottle upside down and then back up. If the sauce sticks to the sides of the bottle for a while and is a thick dark amber color, then you have found thick soy sauce. If it speeds down the bottle on the return, it is the thin type.

hoisin sauce: A sweet thick bean sauce, with a near paste consistency, this is made primarily from fermented soy beans, vinegar, sugar, and garlic. Its deep rich flavor is the basis for the Chinese barbecued ribs. It is also used by the Vietnamese to flavor rice noodle soups or peanut sauce. Keep refrigerated. The Koon Chun brand is consistently good.

indonesian sweet soy sauce: Thick, dark, and sweetened with palm sugar, this soy sauce, called *kecap manis*, is like syrup. It is labeled "sweet" soy sauce; look for the ABC brand.

japanese dark soy sauce: The Japanese use dark soy sauce for everyday cooking. It is made of equal amounts of soybean and wheat. When I traveled to Japan, I was amazed at what artisanal soy sauce, brewed from whole soybeans in 100-year-old oak barrels, tasted like. It had all the complexities of a great wine. Kikkoman, the most popular of all Japanese soy sauces in the United States or abroad, is very different from the authentic artisanal item. Much less expensive, it is made from processed rather than whole soybeans, and brewed for four months, instead of the traditional year or so. Inevitably, it has a different, less developed character.

After trying several commercially produced dark soy sauces, I settled upon the Ninben brand. The so-called "seasoning" soy sauce by Ninben (with bonito and kelp extract) is also delicious. Both types are rich in flavor and perfect when employed in any of the Japanese recipes here. For more information on artisanal Japanese soy sauce, see pp. 466–67.

korean dark soy sauce: This is similar in flavor to that of the Japanese dark soy sauce; the two are interchangeable. For more information see page 93.

mushroom soy sauce: The Vietnamese, Cambodians, and Thai are very fond of this soy sauce, which is flavored with straw mushroom essence and often used in marinades for a more concentrated flavor. Its thickness is somewhere between that of the Chinese light and thick soy sauces. Look for the Pearl River Bridge brand.

tamari sauce: A Japanese product made from soybeans with no trace of wheat. It is the preferred soy sauce for dipping raw fish.

fermented bean curd: Small cubes of strongly scented pasty curd that tastes of wine must. The three main types are white (actually tan in color); red (from the use of red food coloring); and spicy, flavored with red chili. Fermented bean curd is usually flavored with rice wine. The Shanghainese red bean curd, flavored with red rice and Shaoxing rice wine by Harvest Superlucky Food Co., is really delicious. It comes in a tan ceramic jar with two panda bears carved on the side and a bamboo branch section carved on the lid. Keep refrigerated.

miso: Miso paste is made from fermented soybeans and rice. There are dozens of types but the most common are white, red, and black miso. They can be purchased in Korean and Japanese markets. For more information on miso, see page 66.

toenjang: This is the Korean version of the Japanese miso paste. A bit chunky, it is used as a base for soups or braised dishes or spread on grilled foods such as the classic bulgogi. It is sold in plastic tubs or jars and is reddish-yellow in color.

SEAFOOD SAUCES AND PASTES

anchovy sauce: Chinese anchovy or shrimp sauces are light gray thick liquids or loose pastes and are fluid compared to the Southeast Asian Thai or Indonesian shrimp pastes (see below). They are also lighter in color and less pungent. A good brand is Koon Chun.

bagoong sauce: The Filipinos make *bagoong* from tiny anchovies and shrimp. A loose, grayish, opaque thick liquid, it has chunks of the fish or shrimp in it. A good substitute for this sauce is Chinese anchovy sauce.

fish sauce: This sauce is an indispensable seasoning in Southeast Asia. The best versions are made with special select anchovies. The anchovies are layered with salt in wood barrels and fermented for about three months; the juices are then extracted and poured back into the barrel. After another six months, the juices are again extracted. This, the first pressing, is quite pungent and the most expensive version, and is generally bottled and used as a table condiment. The second and third pressings are less pungent and used in everyday cooking. Consistently good Vietnamese and Thai brands are Double Parrot, Oyster, and Tiparos, the last-named being the mildest of all and perhaps a good one to start with if you are unfamiliar with this product. The Filipino types can be good, but I find them to be generally saltier than other types.

oyster sauce: This thick brown sauce is made from dried oyster extract, sugar, water, salt, and cornstarch. Add it sparingly to stir-fries or braised dishes, as its flavor is quite strong; it is often diluted with chicken stock. It is also drizzled straight from the bottle over steamed greens such as Chinese broccoli. A good brand is Lee Kum Kee.

prahoc: This Cambodian sauce is made with mud fish, grey featherback, or gourami. Fermented with rice and salt, it has a strong and, frankly, offensive smell. When added to foods it takes on a rather pleasant character, however, and many people develop quite a taste for it. *Prahoc* is also used in Thai and Laotian dishes where it is called *plara* or *padek*, respectively. A Vietnamese version exists as well, made from shrimp, but it is not nearly as strong or pungent. This sauce is indispensable in Cambodian cooking, largely defining the cuisine. For more information see page 76.

shrimp paste: Thai and Indonesian foods would not be complete without shrimp paste, called *kepi* and *terasi*, respectively. The Thai version is a condensed soft paste with a rich purple hue to its dark gray tone. It is sold in plastic tubs. The Indonesian or Malaysian versions are generally preroasted and sold in rectangular blocks. They are also drier and darker in color and are generally sliced rather than scooped. In the recipes in this book I call for spoon measurements, because these are consistent with Western cooking methods. For rough equivalents, you can think of a ⅛-inch slice of Indonesian shrimp paste as equal to 1 teaspoon of Thai shrimp paste. Use sparingly, as this item is pungent. The best brands are the Thai P. Prateep Thong, and Blachen or Balachan from Malaysia. These have the same degree of intensity and can be used interchangeably.

WINES AND OTHER LIQUIDS

I DO NOT like to use "cooking" wines when cooking either Western or Eastern foods. They are often seasoned with salt and sugar and sometimes flavored with spices, predetermining the flavor of the dish. I only use unseasoned wines or spirits, meaning those types that are drinkable. This way I can better control the flavors of the foods I cook.

shaoxing wine (also spelled Shao Hsing): Brewed in the eastern Chinese city of Shaoxing, this amber-colored rice wine is made from fermented sticky rice, millet, and yeast. Found in Chinese wine shops and drunk at room temperature, chilled, or warm, it has an alcohol

Bagoong is a cloudy, chunky fish or shrimp sauce with a strong aroma similar to that of the Cambodian prahoc.

percent (200 proof) alcohol made from fermented sticky rice is white and crystal clear. Use it to flambé drunken shrimp or battered and deep-fried banana, for example. Vodka with the same level of alcohol is a good substitute.

sake: Sake is white in color or crystal clear and has the same alcohol level (or less) as Chinese rice wine. There are many types of Japanese sake to choose from. For cooking, I usually get a filtered sake in the medium-price range. Some sakes are unfiltered and cloudy; these are usually rather expensive and reserved for drinking.

mirin: This is simply sweetened sake. It is delicious added to marinades, dipping sauces, or dressings.

coconut water: Southeast Asians collect the coconut water, or juice, from fresh, young green coconuts for cooking. Mildly sweet, it is used as the base for Vietnamese caramelized pork shank (pp. 458–59). While you can find canned young coconut water, I suggest you try to get fresh coconut from an Asian market and extract the water. You will recognize the young coconut not by its green skin (which has been removed) but by its skinless white spongy shell, cylinder-shaped with a conical top. Do not confuse

content of 13 to 18 percent. (Dry sherry makes a good substitute if your wine shop does not sell Shaoxing wine.) Presented in a beautiful celadon ceramic "bottle gourd" shaped vessel, the Pagoda brand is good. Look for a gold label that says Shao Hsing Hua Tiao Chiew (18 per-

cent) in black. It usually has a red ribbon. You should also try the wine sold in the celadon ceramic round bottle with a red label reading Tart-Pie Nuehong (13 percent). These are the wines I use for making drunken chicken (page 486).

rice alcohol: This distilled 100

this coconut water with coconut milk.

VINEGARS

VINEGARS, like any condiment, have a shelf life. I like to buy them in small quantities and finish them up over a span of three to five months. The longer you keep a bottle of vinegar open, the less intense and fresh its flavor will be. While you may be tempted to use Western type red or white wine vinegars, these make for poor substitutes in Asian cooking, altering the flavors of your foods drastically. Store vinegar in a cool, dark place.

chinese black vinegar: A strongly flavored vinegar made of fermented "glutinous rice" (sometimes millet, sorghum, or wheat), salt, and water, it is actually dark brown in color. While its deep rich color and somewhat malty flavor bears some resemblance to Italian balsamic vinegar, Chinese black vinegar is definitely more acidic. Look for the Chinkiang Vinegar label.

white rice vinegar: A clean-tasting white vinegar, this is crystal clear and perfect for pickling ginger or vegetables. Rice vinegar is widely available in Asian markets, but you can substitute regular white vine-gar diluted with water (4 to 1 part water). In Asia, vinegar is always combined with sugar to counter-balance the acidity. My favorite Chinese brands are Narcissus and Swatow.

coconut vinegar: When the Fil-ipinos talk about vinegar in generic terms, they mean coconut vinegar. This is made from coconut palm sap and, occasionally, coconut water (pp. 10–11) that has been exposed to air for some time and soured. Some versions are seasoned with herbs; look for plain coconut vine-gar, which is cloudy white in color and bottled under the Sukang Iloco, Sarap, and UFC brands. Coconut vinegar has a lower acidity content than most other Asian vinegars, but Chinese white rice vinegar is a good substitute.

japanese seasoned rice vinegar: The Japanese often use a mildly sea-soned (salt and sugar) rice vinegar. It is perfectly suited for salad dress-ings and making sushi rice. This vinegar is light amber in color. A great brand is Marukan.

PASTES, SAUCES, AND CONCENTRATES

BECAUSE these condiments lose their flavor over time and eventually spoil, buy pastes and sauces in small quantities and get more only as nec-essary. Be sure to use a clean utensil to scoop them from the jar. Utensils with other food on them, or uten-sils that have been on your plate or in your mouth, can introduce bac-teria into the paste and spoil it.

hot mustard paste: Chinese hot mustard is available in powdered or paste form. The Oriental Mascot and Assi brands make good pastes; the S&B brand offers the powder. If using powder, add a teaspoon or so of water for every 2 tablespoons of powder. The Koreans also use this mustard.

koch'ujang: This is a Korean hot chili paste used as a base for dip-ping sauces, soups, and stews. Made from red chilies, fermented soybean paste, and sticky rice flour, it is deep red in color. Look for the Choripong brand.

sesame paste: Made from pureed sesame seeds, this oily tan paste is used for flavoring cold noodle dishes such as the Shanghainese thin egg noodles (page 30). Some-times the dense paste settles at the bottom of the jar, separating from its oil, which sits at the top. Simply stir the layers back together (if the item is very separated, or if you need an exceptionally smooth paste, you may want to use a food processor). Look for the Lan Chi brand. Southwest and Central Asian (Near and Middle Eastern) cultures also use this paste in their cuisine.

thai curry paste: Excellent commercial green (very spicy), red (spicy), or yellow (mildly spicy) curry pastes are made with chilies, lemongrass, and galangal, among many other exotic herbs. If you do not have time to make your own, look for the Mae Ploy brand, which is especially good.

wasabi paste: Made from the "Japanese horseradish," this is available in tubes. I recommend you buy the fresh root when available, or the powdered form (add 1 teaspoon or so of water for every 2 tablespoons of powder); in a pinch, this paste makes a good substitute.

chili and garlic sauce: While nearly all available brands have the same chili and garlic ingredients, some are preserved in oil, others in vinegar; some are salty, others have a subtle sweetness to them. Try several types. Many brands are good, but the most recognizable types are made by Huy Fong Foods. The green-capped clear bottle reveals a bright red sauce, either smooth (*Sriracha*) or chunky (*Sambal Oelek*).

fermented black bean and gar-lic sauce: I encourage you to make your own fermented black bean and garlic sauce (page 86), but there are commercially prepared, ready-to-use versions available. Look for the Lee Kum Kee brand.

sweet chili sauce: This Thai spicy, sweet, and slightly tangy sauce resembles a relish or chutney made of chilies and garlic. It's sold in glass bottles; look for the Mae Ploy brand. It is often used as a dipping or basting sauce for grilled or deep-fried foods and is especially good with deep-fried fish.

tamarind: The tamarind fruit is shaped like a broad bean pod. It is brown in color and its pod is dry and breaks easily. The sour and subtly sweet pulp is contained within the pod, and surrounds easily removable seeds. You can buy fresh pods, or packaged pulp (with or without seeds).

tamarind concentrate: If you do not wish to make your own tamarind extract using fresh tamarind (page 75), tamarind concentrate is commercially available. It is rather intense, more so than if you make your own, so add it gradually to any dish requiring the product, tasting as you go. The Por Kwan, Tamcon, and Garden Queen brands are all equally good.

DRIED SEEDS, POWDERS, AND OTHER ITEMS

DRIED ITEMS such as spices, herbs, and beans should be kept in a dark, cool place and in airtight containers to retain freshness. Dried ingredients that are stored properly can, in many instances, keep indefinitely.

annatto seeds: These mild-flavored, tiny red seeds are added to dishes primarily for coloring. Rather than add them directly to the dish, you can also soak them in hot water for 30 minutes and strain the beautiful red liquid. Use ¼ cup seeds with 2 cups water (or less if you want a more concentrated color).

lotus seeds: These are small off-white seeds of the fibrous aquatic lotus plant. Soak the dried seeds in water (for at least 12 hours, or overnight) until tender prior to using in any recipe. (I stay away from canned versions; they taste mostly of salt and the metal can.) The seeds are used in desserts and savory dishes.

sesame seeds: These seeds are white or black and have a mild nutty flavor. The black seeds are used as is. The white ones need to be roasted in a dry nonstick pan over medium heat until golden, to concentrate the flavor. You can purchase ready-to-use toasted sesame seeds. The seeds are often used as garnish, or sprinkled on battered food prior to deep-frying, or processed into pastes.

five-spice powder: This Chinese spice blend of fennel seeds, star anise, licorice root, cloves, Szechwan peppercorn, and cinnamon is often added to marinades for meat. Because its flavor is quite pungent, it is used sparingly. There are generally more than five spices, but the name is said to come from the fact that the pungent notes represent the five Chinese flavors—salty, bitter, sour, spicy, and sweet—which correspond to the five natural elements—water, fire, wood, metal, and earth.

haeng lei **powder:** This powder is sometimes available in Thai markets, but you can easily make it at home. In its simplest form it can be made by mixing together equal parts of coriander, cumin, turmeric, and mace powder. Store in a jar in a cool, dark place. For the best results grind the spices fresh when you need them.

indian curry powder: This powder contains spices such as turmeric (from which it gets its vibrant yellow color), cumin seeds, coriander seeds, fennel seeds, star anise, cinnamon, and cloves. It has more in-gredients than *haeng lei* powder (see above) but is often used as a substitute.

sansho **powder:** A Japanese seasoning made from the seed pods of a prickly ash tree. *Sansho* has a mildly hot character, like black pepper, and is used as a last-minute flavor enhancer. It is especially nice sprinkled on soups.

shichimi togorashi **powder:** The Japanese *shichimi togorashi* translates as "seven-flavor spice." It is especially wonderful sprinkled over a steamy bowl of Japanese noodle soup. Like Chinese five-spice powder, the exact ingredients differ from manufacturer to manufacturer. Depending on the mix, it might include mandarin peel, and/or hemp, sesame, poppy, rape, and mustard seeds. Red chili powder is always included and it is generally held that at least six other ingredients are required to make the mix.

turmeric powder: This powder is very mild in flavor and is used as an orangey-yellow coloring agent for foods. It is also used to give Indian Madras curry powder its vibrant deep yellow color. See also the section below on fresh herbs (page 21) for more information on turmeric.

cassia bark: This is related to cin-namon but is mild and sweeter. It is particularly well suited for Chinese and Southeast Asian cuisines, which are complex in flavor and benefit from its particular characteristics. Believed to aid blood circulation and digestion, it is added to soups and stews. If using common cinnamon (indigenous to Sri Lanka) as a substitute, cut the quantity by half.

chinese red chilies: These dried red chilies tend to appear slightly faded in color. They are hot and are used particularly in Western Szechwan regional cuisine. You can also use them for Southeast Asian recipes, but I generally like to dry my own Thai chilies, which are hotter and have a slightly different character.

ginseng: A cure-all and believed to be an aphrodisiac and blood cleanser, this root is most often available dried, in capsules, in powder, and in extract (or paste) form. For cooking purposes use the whole dried roots or fresh ones preserved in brandy. Korean and American ginseng are reputed to be of superior quality.

korean coarse red pepper powder: Korean chilies are bright deep red in color, and are very hot. The chilies, which are two to three times the size of Thai chilies, are most often used dried. Look for the Wang brand.

korean fine red pepper powder: The base to any good *kimchi* (often used in combination with the coarse version), this item is indispensible. Look for the Wang brand.

korean red pepper threads: These are used to garnish *kimchi* and numerous other dishes. Look for the Wang brand.

star anise: Originally from China, star anise, as the name suggests, looks like a star. It tastes a bit like licorice and is used in sweet and savory dishes alike. It is available through spice merchants and Asian markets. A good substitute is anise seed.

szechwan peppercorn: This tiny reddish-brown berry comes from a bush that is related to the prickly ash tree (see *sansho* powder, page 13), and appears to be opening as if it were blossoming. It is not a peppercorn in the true sense and is not related to black or white pepper. Its woodsy aroma is responsible for the distinct flavor character of the cuisine of Szechwan, where the spice originated. When eaten, it gives a numbing rather than spicy hot sensation to the palate. It is sold in clear plastic bags sometimes labeled "dried red pepper," and is one of the spices used in the Chinese five-spice powder.

tangerine peel: Soaked in water, dried tangerine peel can be added to stocks, soups, and stews, and to savory or sweet dishes alike. It gives a nice citrus flavor to food. Once softened in water, scrape any pith off the peel prior to adding to recipes.

DRIED NUTS, FLOWER BUDS, AND FUNGI

candlenuts: Candlenuts, which resemble macadamia nuts in size and richness, are native to Malaysia and are used widely in Indonesian cuisine. Raw, the nuts are toxic. They are roasted to crack the shell open, then crushed and stir-fried with other spices until cooked through. You can find these sold already shelled, or you can substitute macadamia nuts, which are more readily available, but much more expensive.

ginkgo nuts: These small nuts are delicious roasted, boiled, steamed, and added to savory or sweet dishes. When cooked they have a light green hue. The Koreans are especially fond of them.

pine nuts: Pine nuts are widely used in both Italian and Korean cooking. They are most often imported either from China, these being roundish in shape, or Italy, these being long, and a bit more costly. About ¼ inch long, they are delicious lightly toasted in a dry skillet. The Koreans love to grind them to a fine powder and add them to any number of savory and sweet dishes.

tiger lilies: Also called golden needles or lily buds, they are used in stir-fries, soups, and stews, imparting a unique floral scent. When choosing them, make sure they are 2 to 3 inches long and light golden rather than dark brown, as the dark ones have been sitting on the shelf for much too long. Soak them to soften before using. The Chinese use them as a tonic that is believed to treat coughs.

black mushrooms: Most commonly known as shiitakes, these mushrooms have a more concentrated aroma when dried than when fresh. (In fact, the two hardly resemble one another.) The majority of Chinese dishes include the dried form; the Southeast Asians, especially the Vietnamese with their long Chinese history, love these dried mushrooms as well. The Japanese enjoy both dry and fresh shiitakes. There are many different varieties, the best being thick and pale in color. Soak to rehydrate and soften them prior to stir-frying, steaming, or adding to stews or soups. Fresh shiitakes are very subtle in flavor and so they do not replace the intense flavor of the dried shiitakes. In a pinch, however, they make a good substitute.

cloud ear: Also known as tree ear (it grows on tree trunks), this mushroom is dark brown to black in color and is sold dried. When rehydrated in water, it turns a rich translucent dark brown. Cloud ears are close to being flavorless, and as such their main function is to add texture to stir-fried dishes or stuffings.

wood ear: A close cousin to the cloud ear (it also grows on tree trunks), it is thicker in texture and brown in color with a fuzzy, beige underside. Usually there are hard knobs that need to be removed. The cloud ear is just about knob-free and more delicate by comparison.

white "snow" fungus: These resemble small yellowish-white sponges, and are used in both savory and sweet dishes. Close to flavorless, this fungus is employed for its gelatinous crunchy texture and its ability to absorb flavors. I like to set them in an almond jelly, the beautiful flower-like fungus making for a lovely presentation. Soak until soft and cut off any hard knobs prior to using.

CEBUAN DRIED-FISH MARKET, THE PHILIPPINES

DRIED SEAFOOD

AS A general rule all dried seafood must be soaked until rehydrated and softened prior to using. While some is packaged and sold in Asian markets, the best-quality dried seafood is purchased by weight at Chinese dried herbal and seafood specialty shops. Store in a cool, dark place. I often wrap dried seafood individually by type in a double layer of aluminum foil and keep it in the freezer.

abalone: A fairly expensive item, this can be found in several sizes in Chinese medicine and dried seafood shops. It must be soaked overnight or up to twenty-four hours until completely rehydrated.

fish: There are too many types of fish dried whole, in chunks, fillets, or strips to mention here. After soaking in water until softened, they can be deep-fried and eaten with rice, or shredded and used as garnishes, or sliced and added to stir-fries, stews, or soups. Having been sun-dried, these fish items have a concentrated flavor. Like all dried seafood and fermented seafood products, dried fish can be an acquired taste.

oysters: Available in several sizes and prices, oysters are sun-dried. Their concentrated flavor is used to enhance soups and stews. Soaked until soft, they are sometimes dipped in batter and deep-fried. Depending on the size, they should soak for thirty minutes to several hours.

scallop: One of the most expensive dried seafood items, *conpoy*, as it is also known, is delicious. It can be used as a stuffing, or shredded and used as a garnish for simple vegetable dishes. It is also added to rice porridges. Depending on the size, it should be soaked for thirty minutes or several hours; overnight soaking does not hurt.

shrimp: Used to season a variety of dishes, dried shrimp add a chewy texture and distinct flavor, so use them sparingly. They should be meaty, thin-shelled, vibrant orange in color, and slightly springy to the touch. Avoid dried flaky ones. Dried shrimp are available in different sizes and can be kept in the refrigerator or freezer.

shrimp chips: Made primarily of ground shrimp and egg whites, shrimp chips are round, hard, and translucent. Some are colored green and red for a more festive appearance. When deep-fried, they triple in volume and are crispy and as light as air. They are perfect served as a party food or served with salad, grilled meats, or steamed meat pâtés. Often used as an accompaniment or color note with Asian dishes, the best come from Indonesia.

squid: Like dried shrimp, these are used to season and add texture to a variety of dishes. They are very pungent, so use them sparingly. They come in several sizes, but I prefer squid that weigh about two ounces, so I can use them whole. They can also be toasted over an open flame, shredded, and eaten as a snack.

DRIED SEA VEGETABLES

THOSE who think of the use of sea vegetables (or seaweeds as they are often unappetizingly termed) as being Japanese may be surprised to learn that the Chinese have been cultivating sea vegetables for millennia. Mostly consumed as medicinal foods, sea vegetables have evolved into a part of the daily diet. Sea vegetables imported from Japan are best and can be purchased in Japanese or Korean markets. The Chinese have nori and other types of sea vegetables such as moss, but of a lesser quality, because there is a lack of attention to detail in processing. Store in a dry, cool, dark place. For more information on sea vegetables see the chapter "Vegetables and Herbs," page 304.

agar-agar: Agar-agar is employed in making desserts throughout Asia. The gum is harvested from dried and bleached red sea vegetables, then processed into translucent white stick, strip, or powder forms. Once placed in boiling water it dissolves and turns into jelly. The Japanese, who discovered this item and call it *kanten*, also eat it as part of a sea vegetable salad.

konbu: This is the primary sea vegetable used in making the Japanese stock called *dashi*. It comes in strips or chips and is dark green in color. It can also be eaten sliced and added to soups or deep-fried. Once rehydrated it has a thick slippery texture.

nori (laver): Sold in large sheets, strips, or small individually packaged items, nori is dark green in color and is used to wrap food such as Japanese sushi. It is also julienned and used as a garnish. The Chinese sometimes add it to soups.

wakame: Mostly added to *miso* soups, *wakame* is occasionally used in making sea vegetable salads as well. It has a slippery and delicate texture.

AIR-CURED MEATS AND PRESERVED EGGS

IF YOU have access to a Chinese butcher in a Chinatown near you, you'll want to buy air-cured meats from him. Meats found hanging behind the meat counter are usually of much better quality than the commercially packaged types.

chinese sweet pork sausage: At the butcher shop, these are strung in pairs. The commercial types are usually sold eight to ten per package. Look for vibrant red-colored sausages. If the color is dull do not buy them; this is a sign of spoilage. Each link measures about 6 inches long and ½ inch in diameter. Links have visible pork fat chunks, but most of the sausage should be meat (70 percent lean). Sweet and savory, they add a tremendous amount of flavor to stir-fried rice.

chinese liver sausage: Made with either pork or duck liver, these are dark brown in color, and sweet and savory. Buy them strung in pairs at the butcher's or buy them packaged (eight to ten links per package). Each link measures about 6 inches long and ½ inch in diameter. These are absolutely delicious in stir-fried rice.

duck legs and thighs: Like all Asian dried meats, these are also best purchased from a butcher. They are added to any number of dishes for a sweet and savory note and slightly chewy texture. I especially love these duck legs or thighs when they are employed as the flavor base of a rich egg noodle soup.

smithfield ham and shoulders: A very good substitute for Yunnan ham, whole air-cured hams and shoulders are found at Chinese butcher shops. I buy the shoulder because it is much smaller than the ham, and it fits in my refrigerator without taking up too much room. (It will last for months.) Soak the shoulder in water for twenty-four hours, drain, and repeat the process one more time. This softens the meat and gets rid of the excess salt. Keep refrigerated, wrapped in a cotton towel. Because it is rather salty, you should always try to cut this meat paper thin. This will give a delicate flavor and texture to any dish you are adding it to. This ham is also available sliced into ½-inch steaks.

salted duck eggs: This Chinese specialty is also enjoyed throughout Southeast Asia. Boiled, they are eaten halved with the shell on and scooped out small portions at a time; their salty flavor is often enjoyed with rice porridge. The bright orange yolk is the "moon" in Chinese moon cakes, made during the Autumn Moon Festival. You'll recognize these eggs by the black ash that covers their shells when they are sold in shops. Homemade salted duck (or chicken) eggs are easily made. Boil ½ cup salt with a quart of water. Once the salt is dissolved, allow the water to cool completely. Place the eggs in a container and pour the salted water on top to cover. Place in a dark, cool place for a month, and refrigerate thereafter. To eat, hard-boil the eggs first.

thousand-year-old eggs: Preserved for about 100 days, this Chinese egg specialty is an acquired taste. For some, the visual aspect of a translucent, blackish-brown, white and jelly-like greenish yolk is too much to take. But the flavor, which has a mild fermented character, is quite delicious. Like the salted egg, it is eaten in small bites; sometimes sugar is sprinkled on top. I prefer them combined with salty egg, chopped and sprinkled over a bowl of plain rice porridge. These do not need to be cooked prior to eating (keep refrigerated).

PRESERVED VEGETABLES

OFTEN SOLD both in bulk in Asian markets as well as in small packaged quantities, these salty items are often sold without printed preparation instructions. Rinse all preserved vegetables in water several times prior to using. Once the package is opened, refrigerate any unused portion.

swatow mustard cabbage: A specialty of southern China, this sweet, savory, and tangy preserved cabbage is not only enjoyed by Chinese but by Thai cooks as well. Thinly sliced, it is added to stir-fries and soups.

szechwan cabbage: This looks like a shriveled green vegetable ball covered in a spicy red pepper paste and salted. It is thinly sliced and most often added to stir-fries and soups. Like the Swatow mustard cabbage, it should be well rinsed prior to using.

DRIED, FRESH, AND FRIED BEAN CURD PRODUCTS

fresh tofu: Firm, medium-firm, soft, and silken tofu are the four varieties of fresh tofu cakes. They are available by the piece or packaged in one-pound containers. The ones sold from buckets by street vendors in Chinatowns are usually extraordinarily good.

fried tofu: Rectangular, square, and triangular pieces of fried tofu are commercially available. Deep-fry these to reheat and recrisp them.

pressed tofu: These are sold cut in rectangular ½-inch-thick slices in small plastic bags, usually four to six per pack. Some are plain, others have been seasoned with soy sauce and sometimes with five-spice powder and are dark brown in color. Thinly sliced along their width they are added to stir-fries such as *pad Thai*, soups, and stews.

tofu skins: These yellow skins are sold in flat, fresh, frozen, or dried sheets or sticks. The sheets are used as spring roll wrappers and steamed, then deep- or pan-fried. The sticks, which look like folded sheets, are used for braised dishes. Both types need to be soaked in water until pliable prior to using in any recipe.

DRIED LEGUMES AND WRAPPING LEAVES

azuki red beans: These tiny red beans are boiled for sweet soups or made into paste for buns or sticky rice dumplings. Commercial red bean paste is available, but it is easy to make your own (see page 513), which will be free of any tinned flavor.

peeled split mung beans: Rather than buy dried whole green mung beans (unpeeled yellow mung beans), choose peeled ones, which come either whole or split and are bright yellow. Soaked prior to cooking, they are used in both sweet and savory foods.

bamboo leaves: These dried, long and narrow leaves with pointy ends are sold in bundles and impart a wonderful flavor to foods. Soaked until pliable, bamboo leaves are used to wrap foods that are then boiled or steamed. Sometimes you can find frozen bamboo leaves, which are even better than the dried version, imparting an even more pronounced perfume to foods.

banana leaves: Look for these in the frozen food sections of Southeast Asian markets. Used to wrap savory or sweet food items, they lend a subtle flavor to foods and make for a beautiful presentation.

lotus leaves: Like bamboo leaves, lotus leaves are dried and sold in folded bundles. These rather large leaves are soaked until pliable and used to wrap foods.

pandan leaves: These narrow leaves are used as a natural green food colorant that imparts a delicious butterscotch-like flavor to both sweet and savory foods. Used in Southeast Asia, these leaves have no substitute.

FRESH HERBS AND OTHER SEASONING

cilantro: This is also known as coriander (strictly, this term refers not only to the greens but also to the seeds and plant as a whole) or Chinese parsley. Although you will most often use the leaves, the stems are also full of flavor, and you can include them when making soups or steaming rice. (Trim off the part of the stem closest to the root.) When choosing cilantro, make sure the leaves are bright green. If they are dull, they are beyond their

FRESH INGREDIENTS in Asia are not only necessary because of the lack of refrigeration but are preferred. Many recipes assume the use of fresh items, and people go to the market three times daily on average. This is especially true in parts of China and Southeast Asia where the high cost of electricity makes refrigerators unaffordable and the climate is too warm for shelf storage. In the more modernized parts of Korea and Japan, refrigeration is common, but fresh ingredients are a cultural preference.

Refrigeration is generally not a problem in the United States of course, but I prefer to buy fresh vegetables, herbs, seafood, and meat whenever possible. The idea of refrigerating vegetables or fruit, especially, has little appeal, and certain items such as tomatoes are rendered flavorless by refrigeration. Time permitting, there is a sensual pleasure to marketing, especially in the soft light of early morning. The hustle and bustle of New York City's or San Francisco's Chinatowns can be just as intense as that of the Asian markets of China, Cambodia, Vietnam, Thailand, the Philippines, Korea, and Japan, and the early morning also affords the strategic advantage of wide selection, smaller crowds, and calmer merchants. Midday or late afternoon marketing in Chinatown, by contrast, will require perseverance and patience, because not many vendors will take the time to explain what the ingredients are or how they are used. Indeed, many street vendors in the very dense streets of Chinatown seem to know very little English except that required for the simplest commerce.

For those of you who do not have access to Chinatown's open-air markets and street vendors, I recommend organic food markets, the organic food section of your local markets, specialty shops, or when possible, a local farmers' market.

prime. I often pinch off a single leaf and taste it to be sure.

curry leaves: Sold in plastic bags, these small, dried sweet leaves impart a lemony and curry-like essence. They are most often added to spice pastes, soups, or braised dishes.

galangal: Also known as lesser ginger, this pungent rhizome has a translucent yellow skin. Its flavor is unique and there is no substitute for it. (For a different yet delicious flavor, use ginger if you cannot find galangal.) It is common in Southeast Asian cuisines, except that of the Philippines. While fresh is best, it is not always available. Frozen pieces are the next best thing. Dried

LOTUS FLOWERS MAKE FOR A BEAUTIFUL PRESENTATION. THEIR LARGE LEAVES ARE USED TO WRAP FOODS FOR COOKING.

forms are weak in character, but in a pinch they will do.

garlic: This common item is a fundamental building block of Chinese, Korean, and Southeast Asian cuisines. Its presence in a dish can be increased or decreased depending on when it is harvested, its type, its freshness, and how it is prepared. When I buy garlic, I look for spring garlic heads with small cloves because they tend to be sweeter. The larger cloves tend to have a bitter sprout inside, which should be removed. Garlic appears in almost every savory dish, especially meat dishes, in part because of its health benefits. It lowers cholesterol and is believed to cleanse the blood.

ginger: An important flavor ingredient in Asian cuisine, ginger is readily available. Two types are common. Young ginger has a nearly translucent thin yellow and pink skin and is incredibly tender; it can be preserved in salt brine, candied, or used in cooking. Mature ginger, with a dull yellow, thicker skin, is more fibrous and should be cut against the grain for use in savory dishes. Ginger is considered therapeutic for stomachaches and seafood poisoning.

kaffir lime leaves: Available fresh, frozen, or dried, these leaves are used to flavor stews and soups. They lend a somewhat flowery, bitter flavor to foods. While there is no real substitute for kaffir lime leaves, you can use lime peel for a different yet still bitter note.

lemongrass: Also known as citronella, lemongrass is used widely in Southeast Asian cuisine. Its unique tangy flavor complements a wide range of dishes, from soups to stir-fries to stews and even desserts. It is a grass and will always look very fibrous and fairly dry. Remove the outer leaves and dark green leafy tops before using. The bulb, which is the lower, creamy white part, can be crushed, ground, and sliced. Fresh or frozen lemongrass is best, as the dried versions have lost their flavor.

salam leaves: These small, oval-shaped, pointy green leaves are widely used in Indonesian cooking, lending a subtle sour flavor to any number of dishes. Related to cassia, the fresh leaves turn brown when dried. Toast dried leaves lightly to release their essence prior to adding to the desired recipe. Bay leaves are not good substitutes, so if you cannot find salam leaves, omit them altogether. Found in Southeast Asian markets.

saw leaves: These long and narrow leaves have serrated edges, hence the name. The taste is similar to that of cilantro but more pronounced. They are also widely used in South American cuisines.

scallions: Also known as green onion and spring onion, this is an important herb in Asian cooking. Select thin and tender rather than thick and fibrous scallions. Found in virtually any market.

shallot: When Southeast Asians say red onion, what they really mean is shallot. This sweet pungent onion-like bulb is particularly well suited for Southeast Asian foods. Try to select firm bulbs with a nice reddish color. Found in virtually any market.

shiso leaves: These heart-shaped leaves with serrated edges are especially enjoyed in Japanese and Korean cuisine. They come in two color shades, green and purple, and have a concentrated mustard-like character; when you bite into them you feel a sudden, intense, pungent rush. They are also known as perilla leaves. While both are eaten raw, the purple ones are also added to pickled plums, lending their beautiful color to the fruit.

thai basil: Also known as holy basil, this herb has a very distinct lemony and licorice-like flavor; its narrow green leaves have a subtle purple hue, especially near the stem. It is a main ingredient in Southeast Asian dishes, with the exception of Filipino foods. Italian basil is not a substitute. If you can't find Thai basil, skip it altogether.

thai chilies: These are the most commonly used in Southeast Asian cuisines. They should be seeded, as the seeds are overpoweringly hot and lack subtlety. The heat of these chilies can be overwhelming, so use them sparingly. In the Philippines this chili is known as the finger chili for its small, pinky-finger size.

turmeric: Harvested from the curcuma rhizome, turmeric resembles both ginger and galangal in shape, but is so subtle in flavor that it is used primarily for its deep orangey-yellow color. While it is available fresh or frozen, it is more readily available in dry powdered form. If you can find fresh turmeric, use it. It has a much nicer color and does have a nice flavor, however subtle it may be.

vietnamese coriander: This herb has pointy narrow leaves and a very distinctive flavor. It has no real substitute, so make a real effort to find this herb. If all else fails, use cilantro for a different but still authentic flavor.

wasabi: Also known as "Japanese horseradish," it is not technically horseradish, however it may look, taste, and feel like it. Fresh, it is finely grated and its light green pulp is used as a paste in Japanese cooking. It is most commonly combined with soy sauce as a dipping sauce for raw fish (sashimi) or for eating plain soba noodles.

FRESH FRUITS AND VEGETABLES

asian eggplant: Long, narrow, and light purple in color, this is also known as Japanese eggplant.

pea eggplant: Tiny and green like peas, this eggplant is slightly bitter and enjoyed through Southeast Asia. Added to spicy dipping sauce, it has a wonderfully firm texture.

thai eggplant: Round and about the size of a Ping-Pong ball, this white- and green-streaked eggplant is full of tiny seeds. With its very pleasant tender, yet firm, texture, it is quartered or halved and added to stews such as curries.

bamboo shoots: Fresh bamboo shoots are easier to find today than ever. Covered in their green or light brown leaves, or sheaths, they are easy to prepare. Many of the fresh bamboo shoots found in the United States are imported from South America. If you cannot find these, use frozen or canned whole shoots. Bamboo absorbs flavor easily and so the more it is broken down by being sliced or julienned, the more it will absorb the flavor of the tin if canned. Buy the whole shoots, and prior to using them, blanch them in boiling water. When using fresh or frozen shoots, peel the leaves, then trim the shoot so it is even in shape. It should look like a cone. Slice the shoot as directed, blanching a few minutes in boiling water to get rid of the natural toxins (depending on the species, some shoots have higher toxin contents than others), and add to the recipe. Fresh bamboo shoots have a wonderful texture and flavor and tend to be creamy-white in color as opposed to the yellowish shoots from the can. In Japanese markets you can sometimes find fresh shoots that have already been boiled and are vacuum packed or sold in loose pieces. These are also excellent choices. The canned version of anything should always be your last resort.

bitter melon: This lumpy, light green cucumber-like gourd is full of quinine; the Chinese and Southeast Asians eat it for its medicinal properties. To offset its bitterness it is often combined with pork and shrimp. Be sure to remove the spongy core and seeds from the center prior to stuffing or adding to soups or stir-fries.

bok choy: White- or green-stemmed, this green leafy cabbage is widely available all year round. Choose small tender stems and leaves rather than large fibrous ones. Unfortunately many organic vegetable markets seem to offer these grown to a large size, and it can be difficult to find small ones. The most tender bok choy comes from Chinese vendors. Also try baby bok choy, which has a sweet flavor. Sold as a specialty item, it has more leaf than stem.

carambola: Also known as star fruit, this distinctively shaped fruit is yellow to light green in color and, as the name suggests, the cut pieces are shaped somewhat like a star. It is eaten as a fruit when sweet and ripe (yellow to golden yellow), and as a vegetable when unripe (green to light green). When unripe, its tangy flavor is an excellent complement to sweet grilled meat; as such, it is often part of the "table salad" that accompanies many Vietnamese dishes.

chinese broccoli: With firm thick stems and large leaves, this dark green vegetable is especially well liked by Chinese cooks. Best stir-fried or steamed, it is far superior to Western-style broccoli, which can have a slight ammoniated taste and mushy texture when overcooked.

fuzzy melon: A mild-tasting light green gourd, this vegetable is named for its fuzzy or hairy skin. Peel before cooking, or simply scrub off the fuzz. Fuzzy melon is added to soups, braised dishes, or stir-fries, and, when cut into rings, it can be stuffed. Remove the core prior to cooking.

green papaya: Sometimes called pawpaw, green papaya is large and round or oblong in shape. It has a dark green skin with light green flesh. The white small round seeds in the center must be discarded. Unlike its sweet red-fleshed cousin, it has a subtle bitterness. Very crunchy, it is especially enjoyed when julienned as a salad, or sliced and added to soups.

green mango: Prepared the same way as green papaya, this fruit is used as a vegetable in salads. In Southeast Asia, it is not unusual to thinly slice this sour fruit and dip it in pure fish sauce before eating it as a delicious snack.

lotus root: A beautiful stem, lotus root is tan in color with a pinkish hue. The roundish cross-section reveals small holes, which hold the seeds. Widely used as a vegetable, freshly sliced lotus root is most often employed in stir-fries or soups. During the Chinese New Year, lotus root slices are sugar coated and sold as candy, often packaged alongside sugar-coated lotus seeds, water chestnuts, and winter melon chunks. The fresh lotus root is best, of course, but in a pinch dried slices may be used. Unpeeled, the fresh root will last up to two weeks refrigerated. Dried slices will last indefinitely stored in a cool dark place; soak in water until completely softened prior to using.

mung bean sprouts: The sprouts have small yellow heads with a thin green skin and a white stem, about 1½ inches long. If these are not available, you can use soybean sprouts, which have larger yellow

heads with a similar size white stem.

napa cabbage: Also called celery cabbage or Chinese cabbage, this vegetable has creamy-white, yellowish-green leaves and is available in most supermarkets. It has a sweet flavor and can be added to soups, stews, and stir-fries. Look for small tender cabbage rather than large fibrous ones.

pea shoots: Also known as pea pod leaves, these are small green and incredibly tender round leaves. They are best when stir-fried but can be added to brothy soups.

rape seed oil cabbage: Known as choy sum, this leafy green vegetable with thin, somewhat stringy stems is often added to noodle soups. It is also delicious stir-fried.

water chestnut: Technically this is a corm. It is grown on rice paddies, and, when bought fresh, is often covered with a bit of mud. Fresh water chestnuts are about the size of regular large chestnuts and are round with a spike in the center. Their brown skins are peeled off to reveal a beautiful crispy, sweet, and juicy white flesh. The texture is a combination of starchy potato and crisp, firm, Asian pear. Water chestnuts can be eaten raw as a fruit, or chopped and added to fillings for dumplings or spring rolls. They are

sold in Chinese and Southeast Asian markets. Canned water chestnuts should be your last resort. If these are your only option, blanch them in boiling water to get rid of any tin flavor.

water spinach: This leafy green vegetable grows on both wet and dry land. Available throughout the year, it is widely eaten by the Chinese and Southeast Asians. There are two types of water spinach: one is light green in color with large leaves and thick stems; the other is dark green with narrow leaves and slim stems. The latter is the least preferred but widely eaten nonetheless.

winter melon: These melons have dark green skins with pale green flesh and are mildly sweet. They are available in Chinatowns, mostly sold in large wedges, as a whole winter melon can weigh several pounds. Remove the skin and seeds, then slice and add to soups. Once cooked, the flesh turns a beautiful translucent color. The most famous dish using this vegetable is Chinese winter melon and ham soup. Winter melon is never eaten raw.

yard-long beans: Also known as Asian beans or long beans, these can reach three yards in length. Two types exist: one, light green, thick, and smooth; another, dark green and less smooth. The latter is the preferred because it is the crunchiest and sweeter of the two.

FRESH BLOSSOMS AND FUNGI

banana bud: Hanging at the end of banana clumps, these purplish buds are harvested just as the fruit has formed. Widely used as a vegetable in Southeast Asia, the purplish outer leaves and tiny banana buds are removed, revealing a creamy-white center. Thinly sliced, it is soaked in lemon water to keep it from darkening, then tossed in a dressing and eaten as a refreshing salad.

enokitake mushrooms: These tiny, delicate, white-headed mushrooms with long thin stalks are delicious added to soups.

shiitake mushrooms: These are now readily available in virtually any market as a fresh item. Use them especially for Japanese or Korean foods. Chinese and Southeast Asians prefer the dried form, which is much more concentrated in flavor. There is, however, a thick meaty type of shiitake that is now available fresh. Its flavor is very concentrated, almost as much as the dried form. Its cap is thick and round, and brown with whitish streaks. Discard the stems of fresh shiitakes, as they tend to be woody.

CANNED VEGETABLES AND FUNGI

bamboo shoots: Two varieties of bamboo shoots, spring and winter types, are available canned year round. The young winter shoots are best because they are the most tender. They are available whole, shredded, sliced, or chopped, but I recommend buying only the whole ones because they will absorb less tin flavor from the can than the other processed types. Blanch for several minutes in boiling water before using. Ma Ling is a consistently good brand.

straw mushrooms: Available only canned, straw mushrooms are very delicate in flavor and tender in texture. They come unpeeled and look like tiny brown eggs, or peeled, with small dark brown caps and short, stubby, creamy-white stems. Peeled straw mushrooms are great for delicate soups, while the unpeeled ones are perfect for braising with heavier sauces.

coconut milk: You can make fresh coconut milk (page 77) or buy unsweetened canned coconut milk. When opening the can you will notice that the top layer is rather thick. This is the cream, the milk being directly below. The cream can be reserved to make coconut oil (page 77) or can be mixed back into the milk for a richer, thicker coconut milk. There are many different products on the market but the Chaokoh brand is very good.

RICE FLOUR AND OTHER STARCHES

rice flour: Sometimes labeled rice powder, it is made from milled long-grain rice and used to make all sorts of fresh and dried noodles, crêpes, dumplings, and buns. (It is also used in Chinese cosmetics, giving the skin a porcelain white look, which is much appreciated by the Chinese.) Thailand's Erawan (Three Elephant) brand is excellent.

sticky "glutinous" rice flour: Sometimes labeled glutinous rice powder, this is made from sticky short-grain rice and is also referred to both as sweet rice flour and glutinous rice flour, although there is no trace of gluten in it. The pastries and other sweets made with this flour tend to have a pleasantly chewy yet tender texture. Thailand's Erawan (Three Elephant) brand is excellent.

toasted rice flour: Toasted rice flour is used as a binder for Vietnamese fresh shrimp paste on sugar cane or any kind of Southeast Asian seafood ball or meatball. Not only does it add an interesting texture (especially when homemade, as this version is slightly coarser than any commercial flour), but a smoky flavor as well. This flour is easy to make. Toast sticky short-grain rice in a dry nonstick pan over medium heat until rich golden brown, shaking the pan occasionally so as not to burn the grains. In a clean spice or coffee grinder, grind the grains to a powder consistency, and sift the rice flour through a very fine sieve. Return whatever ground rice is left behind to the grinder and process it again, until fine. Repeat this process until all of the powder passes through the fine sieve. Store it in a jar away from the light (I refrigerate mine), and use it within six months for best flavor. The commercial D&D Golden Bell brand is good, but I encourage you to make your own. One and a half cups sticky rice grains will yield about 1 cup toasted ground rice flour.

jelly sticks: Dried jelly sticks are made with agar-agar (page 16). They are sliced into squiggly shapes and made in various colors, usually green, red, and clear. Rehydrated in water, they are added to sweet coconut drinks or soups. Like tapioca pearls, they have almost no flavor, but lend a wonderfully tender but firm texture to many Asian desserts. I like the Double Parrot brand.

BANANA BLOSSOMS AND LEAVES ARE USED IN SOUTHEAST ASIAN COOKING.

panko: The Japanese use *panko*, fine white breadcrumbs, for breading deep-fried foods such as tempura. *Panko* give an especially crunchy texture to foods. You can also make deep-fried chicken cutlets, coating the pieces with flour and egg, then *panko*, for a crisper texture. The Oriental Mascot brand is very good.

potato starch: Like tapioca starch or cornstarch, this is used as a thickening agent for sauces, and added to batters, meatballs, and doughs for a springy and tender consistency. As it is stickier than the other two starches, you need only half of the quantity usually called for when using tapioca or cornstarch. Like other thickening agents, potato starch needs to be diluted with a bit of water prior to being added to sauces or soups to prevent its lumping up. I like to use this starch specifically for making meatballs. The D&D Golden Bell and Katakuriko brands are excellent.

sago pearls: Made from the sago palm, they look like and are used in the same manner as tapioca pearls (see below).

sweet potato starch: Sweet potato starch is a thickening or binding agent employed in sauces and soups and for adding texture to fillings or to meatballs. Use as you would regular potato starch, but use half of the amount of cornstarch or tapioca starch. The Golden Buffalo brand is very good.

tapioca pearls: Made from tapioca starch, these are used in Asian desserts such as tapioca and coconut soup. They come in different sizes, ranging from BB pellets to the pearls. I prefer the BB-pellet size for its delicate texture. They are also available in a variety of pastel colors, including green, pink, and yellow, for festive occasions. You can make your own tapioca pearls by mixing tapioca starch with water to form a stiff dough, which you hand shape into small round pellets or pearls.

tapioca starch: This is used widely in everyday Asian cooking as a thickening agent for sauces and soups, and for sprinkling over morsels of fish or meat prior to frying or stir-frying. I prefer it to cornstarch because it gives better results. It is a natural product extracted from the cassava (also called yucca or manioc) root, which is cultivated in tropical areas, including South America and Asia. I also add it to homemade ice cream to prevent the ice cream from melting too fast (an excellent trick!). Tapioca starch gives a beautiful sheen to sauces and soups. I use the Erawan (Three Elephant) brand from Thailand. If you cannot find tapioca starch, cornstarch makes an acceptable substitute.

wheat starch: This is not to be confused with wheat flour, which contains gluten. Wheat starch, used to make Chinese crystal shrimp dumplings (*haar gao*), is free of gluten. It is sold in pure form, or premixed with potato, tapioca, or cornstarch. The last-named is an "instant" version, and all you need to do is mix the contents with hot water and make the filling of the dumpling (omitting any starch ingredient called for in the recipe, because it would be redundant). Dough made with wheat starch turns shiny and translucent when steamed, revealing the shrimp dumpling filling's beautiful colors.

It has a slightly chewy yet tender texture and is soft to the touch. The D&D Golden Bell brand is very good.

RICE GRAINS

RICE is sold both with its bran on and with it polished off. This milling process is as important in determining rice type and character as the specific variety. Red and brown types have the bran intact; because the bran is the most complete part of the grain in terms of nutrition and vitamins, these rices retain more nutrients. Most Asians prefer the less pronounced flavor and texture of polished white rice, however, using it as kind of neutral palette for other flavors and textures. Grain in general is referred to as *fan* in the Chinese system of foods; this is part of a duality that contrasts *tsai*, or vegetable, and fish or animal proteins against grains. The *fan tsai* system is unique in world cooking and forms the basis of almost all Chinese and most other Asian cuisines. The assumption here is that when supplemented by all sorts of *tsai* side dishes, the white rice is plenty nutritious.

Rice should not be kept for longer than six months or it will go stale. If it is not part of your daily diet, buy it in small quantities. Most rice comes in five-, ten-, and twenty-five-pound bags. A ten-pound bag is a good size for a family of two or three people, but if you eat rice very rarely, choose a five-pound bag. Although the instructions on some rice bags say not to rinse the rice before cooking, it is necessary to attain the perfect texture.

For the best texture, cook the rice in a Chinese sand pot (also called a clay pot) that is glazed on the inside and unglazed on the outside. It may take a couple of tries before you get familiar with this ancient cooking vessel, but the results will be well worth it. Modern electric rice cookers with warming cycles are my least favorite way to prepare rice. They do an okay job, and the warming cycle is a nice convenience, but this feature dries the rice when used over a period of a few hours or more, and the resulting grains are flavorless. If you feel you need an electric cooker, buy the simplest one, with no warming cycle.

bhutanese red rice: This nutty red short-grain rice is nutritious, but stronger in flavor and coarser than white rice. If you are concerned about not getting enough nutrition from your meal (especially if you are a strict vegetarian), then you may prefer this red rice, which has its germ intact, has more nutrients, and is more filling.

black sticky "glutinous" rice: This sticky rice, sometimes referred to as "forbidden rice," is unpolished and used in making sweets. Sold in long-grain or short-grain form it is brownish-black (although some are pure black). Cooked, it turns a beautiful purple hue, and is enjoyed throughout Southeast Asia in sweet food items. The Thai Rice King is a good brand.

broken rice: During processing some rice grains are fractured, and the product is sold as broken rice, which is the least expensive of all Asian rice. Recently available in the United States, it is considered rare and somewhat exotic, and therefore is more expensive than any other rice here. Broken rice is delicate in that it looks no bigger than couscous or fine bulgur, a grain used to make the classic Middle Eastern dish *tabouleh*. Broken rice is just as delicious as any other rice; the only difference is that the grains are not whole.

brown rice: Long- or short-grain brown rice is rice in its purest form. It has not been milled and the rice bran—the most nutritious part of the grain—still remains. While in Japan I discovered that some Japanese who prefer white rice (because it is "clean") now buy vitamins to add to the rice cooker as the grain boils in the belief that the vitamins make white rice as nutritious as the brown variety. It is unlikely, however, that the steamed vitamins have much potency.

kalijira rice: The grains of this rice are the tiniest of all rice grains in the world. Although they are no bigger than broken rice, these grains, native to India, are whole and are often referred to as prince rice. Their flavor is pure and the delicate grains make for a beautiful presentation. When cooked, the grains are fluffy and stay separate much like jasmine rice. I especially like to use this rice when serving a vegetarian dinner; and sometimes I flavor it with herbs.

long-grain rice; jasmine long-grain rice: Long-grain rice is the daily staple rice of China, Southeast Asia, and India's southern region. Thin and firm, it is translucent when raw, and opaque, tender, fluffy, and separate when cooked. (Do not confuse this rice with northern Indian basmati rice, which is much thinner, longer, and firmer than regular long-grain rice.) Jasmine-scented long-grain rice is my favorite, giving off a most fragrant and flowery perfume as it gently boils. If you can only find unscented long-grain rice but would love to add some flavor, add to the pot a few slices of ginger, fried garlic, cilantro, lemongrass, mint, or any herbs you like. I sometimes add herbs to my jasmine rice for an even more pronounced flavor. The Erawan (Three Elephant) brand is excellent.

short-grain rice: Sold both as "short-grain" and "sushi" rice, this rice is translucent when raw; when cooked it is opaque and its texture is somewhere between that of long-grain rice and that of sticky ("glutinous") rice. It also tends to clump together, which makes it easy to pick up with chopsticks. This is an everyday rice for Japanese and Koreans, who use it as a basis for meals, and as the rice element in sushi. The Chinese use it specifically for making *jook* (rice porridge). Excellent brands are the Japanese Hikari Imperial Quality and the Korean Assi.

medium-grain rice: The Japanese and Koreans enjoy both medium-grain and short-grain rice, which can be interchanged at a meal. (For making sushi use short-grain rice.) The grains are fatter and shorter than that of long-grain rice, but as fat as and slightly longer than short-grain rice. When raw they are translucent and when cooked they are opaque. While medium-grain rice has a good amount of stickiness, it is fairly dry. It is a very good substitute for the javanica rice used in Indonesian foods. One of my favorite brands is Kakuho Rose Extra Fancy Select, a premium quality rice cultivated in California, which is very easy to find. Some Japanese claim that it is better than some of the best Japanese rice on the market.

white sticky ("glutinous") rice: Eaten mostly as a dessert item, sticky rice is eaten all over Southeast Asia, Japan, and Korea. In Thailand, especially in the north, it is often eaten as a staple, replacing jasmine rice during meals. When you go into a Thai restaurant or home, they'll ask if you prefer sticky rice or jasmine rice. Look for the Oriental Mascot brand.

RICE NOODLES, RICE PAPERS, AND STARCH NOODLES

DRIED RICE vermicelli, sticks, and papers are used widely in all Asian culinary cultures. They may seem daunting to those who are new to the subject, because they appear in many forms and the packages often have no cooking instructions. The main principle here is similar to that of Italian pasta: thin varieties require less cooking time and are better with light ingredients and flavors; thicker varieties require a bit more time and generally accompany heavier ingredients and flavors.

An important difference between Asian and Western noodles when it comes to the specifics of preparation is that most Asian products must be soaked in water until pliable (about thirty minutes) prior to using. With the exception of the rice papers (which are only soaked), once softened, rice vermicelli and sticks are cooked in lightly boiling water for no more than five seconds (not minutes) until tender, yet firm. Added to individual bowls, stock is usually ladled over the noodles for soup. It is critical that you soak the dried noodles. If you try to cook them after the Western fashion by adding them dry to a pot of boiling water, you will never be able to control the speed at which they cook. (It can be a disaster!) Do as all Asians do; soak, then cook briefly. When using these items with stir-fries, use the technique specified in the individual recipe. The best brand on the market is the Erawan (Three Elephant) brand, which is available at Chinese and

Southeast Asian markets or through mail-order sources.

Fresh Asian rice noodles and sheets are especially delicious. Like the dry varieties, they require very minimal "cooking" (oftentimes they are just dipped in hot water to heat them quickly, as they are already cooked; or they are added as is to stir-fries or steamed dishes). Fresh noodles and related items are available in Chinatown from street vendors specializing in noodles and tofu, and from Chinese or Southeast Asian markets.

dried rice vermicelli: Like all rice noodles, dried vermicelli is made of rice flour, salt, and water. Perhaps the thinnest vermicelli made, it is almost always part of the Vietnamese table salad served to wrap grilled meats, seafood, and other foods such as spring rolls. It also appears in Thai foods such as mi krob. The Chinese use a version of rice vermicelli that is firmer than the Vietnamese or Thai versions. Theirs are especially suited for noodle soups.

dried rice sticks: Dried rice sticks are flat and come in three sizes: S (small), M (medium), and L (large). They are used in soups or in stir-fries such as the classic pad Thai.

dried rice papers: Made from the pith of the rice flour tree (a shrub), or rice flour, salt, and water, once shaped, the papers are left to air-dry on bamboo mats, giving them a cross-hatched pattern. Before you use the rice papers, be sure to soak them in water until they are soft and pliable. Do not throw the whole stack of papers in the water at once: separate the papers and soak only two to four at a time. Take the papers out of the package only as you are ready to soak them, leaving the rest inside the package. (Once the paper has contact with air, it dries out and curls up.)

Rice papers are extraordinarily brittle and you will break some (if they're not already broken). When I set out to make rolls, I make sure I have two packages of rice papers on hand, using one for backup. When buying rice papers make sure you inspect them through the clear package, selecting the one with the least visible broken papers. These sheets come in several sizes of rounds, but I use six- to eight-inch rounds for making Vietnamese summer rolls and the triangular shapes for making Vietnamese spring rolls. The Cambodians use these, as well, for their versions of the Vietnamese specialties.

fresh rice sheets: These are found in Chinese and Southeast Asian markets or sold by street vendors. Sheets are oiled and folded. When fresh they are easily pliable and at their best. Once they have been refrigerated they are no longer pliable enough to make certain dishes like cheung fan guen (page 262). Instead, thinly slice the folded sheets crosswise into strands and drop them in boiling water for a few seconds to separate them. Added to fragrant broth, they also make for delicious noodle soups.

fresh rice vermicelli: Fresh rice vermicelli is slightly thicker than the dried and ultra-thin vermicelli. It is sometimes served with curries or with grilled meats and shredded vegetables.

fresh silver pin noodles: Silver pin noodles are made primarily of rice flour, wheat starch, and tapioca starch. They look a bit like thick white worms (the Chinese actually call these "rat-tail" noodles). Tapered at both ends, each pin is no longer than 2 inches long and is about ⅛ inch in diameter at the center, which is the thickest part. They are sold in one-pound bags by street vendors or found in Chinese or Southeast Asian markets.

mung bean noodles: Also known as cellophane noodles, mung bean threads are dried, as thin as vermicelli, and white in color. When cooked, they turn transparent. They are not particularly flavorful but have the ability to absorb flavors. For this reason they are often used in fillings for dumplings and spring rolls. These noodles must be soaked in water until pliable prior to cooking. They are available at Asian markets.

potato starch noodles: The Koreans use these to make their classic stir-fried noodles dish, *chap chae*. While slightly thicker than mung bean threads, they are grayish in appearance and turn translucent when cooked. Slippery, they have a neutral flavor but absorb a great deal of flavor from whatever they are cooked with. They are available in Korean and Japanese markets.

EGG AND WHEAT NOODLES AND WRAPPERS

DRIED WHEAT and egg noodles are produced by many manufacturers. Try any of them, as they are generally all pretty good. You can choose from regular wheat and egg noodles, available in vermicelli, round, or thin to thick flat varieties. Chinese egg noodles flavored with bits of crab, shrimp, and vegetables are delicious. They can be found in Chinese, Korean, and Japanese markets.

wheat noodles: Chinese *mien* (flat Shanghai noodles) or Japanese *udon* (flat linguini-like wheat noodles) can be found fresh in the refrigerated section or dried in the dried noodle section of Asian markets. In Chinatown they can be purchased from the street vendors who also sell homemade tofu. In Chinese markets they are packaged by the pound in plastic bags and sold as "Shanghai noodles," which can also refer to thin, round types—luckily you can see through the package.

wheat vermicelli: Popularly known as *somen* in Japanese, these are sold dried in Asian markets. The Japanese love these, especially in cold noodle dishes or light brothy soups. When rice vermicelli is not available, you can use these noodles as a substitute for making *bun tom nuong xa* (page 223), boiling them, then shocking them in cold water.

soba noodles: Made from buckwheat flour, these are found mostly dried and occasionally fresh-frozen in Japanese markets. They have a nutty flavor and complement poultry dishes especially well.

cha soba noodles: Made from buckwheat flour and *matcha* (powdered green tea), these noodles are not only nutty in flavor but have a delicious bitter note. They are wonderful topped with a mushroom stir-fry or any poultry or seafood stir-fry. They also make tasty cold noodle dishes.

ramen noodles: Thin flat egg noodles, these are shaped into square portions and deep-fried. Originally Chinese noodles, they are now mostly associated with Japanese cuisine. These cook very quickly, simply being boiled and added to soups. (I have also used them for stir-fries.) These "instant noodles" are sold stacked about eight portions high in a clear plastic bag in Chinese markets. The Japanese usually sell them individually as convenience food with broth seasoning packages included.

thin egg "shanghai" noodles: These egg noodles are a favorite among Chinese cooks. Semi-fresh, the curly thin round egg noodles are perfect for making double-fried egg noodles or adding to soups. They are sold in one-pound plastic bags by street vendors or Chinese or Vietnamese markets. Thin egg noodles are the type used in making Shanghainese cold noodles.

wonton noodles: These fresh thin egg noodles are rather dull yellow in color. When serving wontons in broth, wonton noodles are boiled for a couple of minutes in water and added to a bowl, topped with wontons and hot broth for a heartier meal. They are sold fresh by street vendors or are available in the refrigerated section of Chinese or Southeast Asian markets. Four bundled portions are sold in one-pound bags.

thick round egg noodles: Fresh round egg noodles, sold in one-pound plastic bags, are found in Chinese and Southeast Asian markets or sold by street vendors. Made with wheat flour and egg, they are like thick spaghetti and are used to make Chinese *lo mien* (page 237) or Thai *khao soi* (pp. 240–41), for example. Blanch these in water for about two minutes prior to adding to a recipe. (This will get rid of some of the yellow food coloring.) You can also deep-fry these straight from the bag. This crunchy noodle is a traditional topping for the *khao soi*.

egg roll wrappers: Chinese egg roll wrappers are square and are basically an enlarged version of the wonton wrapper. These are the types of wrappers used by Chinese-American take-out restaurants for deep-fried egg rolls. Look for the Dynasty brand.

spring roll wrappers: Chinese spring roll wrappers are made with all-purpose wheat flour, tapioca starch, and water. Paper thin, they are available as square or round items and are employed in making the very delicate Chinese spring rolls (pp. 272–73), Filipino fried *lumpia* (pp. 276–77), and Thai fried *paw piah taud* or fresh *paw piah saud* (pp. 274–75). TYJ Spring Roll Pastry from Singapore is an excellent brand. They measure eight inches square and can be easily cut in half for making bite-size triangular patties. Four-inch square wrappers are also available. Precooked, they can be steamed to soften for making fresh rolls or fried for a crispy texture.

wonton wrappers: Square or round (for making *siu mai*), they are made with egg, wheat flour, and water. Measuring 2½ inches square (or in diameter), the wrappers are available fresh in Asian markets. They can be frozen and are ideal for making all sorts of dumplings, including *siu mai* or wontons. There are several commercial brands of wonton wrappers, so be sure to choose one that is paper thin. Wheat egg-free wrappers are also available. Use round wheat wrappers for making Chinese *jaozi* (potstickers), *siu mai* (open dumplings), or the Korean *mandu kuk* (dumpling soup).

EQUIPMENT
AND TECHNIQUES:
the basics

MY FAVORITE—and indispensable—pieces of kitchen equipment for preparing Asian food are the humble traditional implements I buy inexpensively in Chinatown. They include clay pots, woks, bamboo steamers, and Chinese cleavers—the essentials of any Asian kitchen.

If you are comfortable with the equipment you have always used, then continue using it. If you would like to experiment with new equipment, then the few items I have listed above can be purchased for about seventy-five U.S. dollars (total) and will last virtually forever with the few tips I give in this chapter.

You will find that each recipe in this book not only has approximate cooking times but, more important, visual descriptions at each step. We all have different equipment and stoves with particular burners, ovens, and broilers. All have different intensities of heat depending on the manufacturer, not to mention the fact that some are gas and others are electric powered. Altitude above sea level also affects cooling times. Pots, pans, and cutlery perform differently, depending on their materials and how well they are made, not to mention how they are used. What all this means is that you simply must have a feel for your equipment.

For these reasons, in each of my recipes I try to give you descriptions of the food as it is taken from one stage to another in the cooking process. At the

HANDMADE KNIVES HONED BY THE MASTER AT THE ARITSUGU CO. SHOP IN KYOTO, JAPAN same time approximate cooking times are, in my opinion, the only truthful way to tell you how long the process will take. I suggest that you rely on your five senses as much as any strict sense of time when you are cooking.

Listed below are some of my favorite pots and pans, cooking vessels, and implements, and several of the cooking techniques that I employ when preparing Asian foods. While you can benefit and learn from these, if you prefer your equipment and techniques, then I encourage you to keep doing what you love, as long as the end result is to your liking. (See mail-order sources on page 563 for purchasing Asian cooking equipment.)

EQUIPMENT

bamboo steamers: Bamboo steamers are usually set over woks one-third filled with water. They work well and only require rinsing with running hot water after each use. Food should not touch the bamboo rack directly. Traditionally, a few lettuce leaves or a plate is set on the steaming rack to hold the food. Cheesecloth is an adequate substitute. Stainless-steel steamer pots are perfect for steaming larger food items such as lobsters or crabs, or you can buy a steaming basket to fit into a stockpot.

chopsticks: Chopsticks, traditionally made of bamboo, are also made of ivory, plastic, or lacquered wood for everyday use; or the more expensive gold, silver, or jade for special occasions. I recommend old-fashioned bamboo chopsticks for their versatility and their heat resistance. Unlike plastic, they do not melt. Chopsticks are used in China, where they were invented, and in Japan, Korea, and Vietnam. In Thailand they are used only for eating noodle soups; otherwise, spoons and forks are the norm. In Cambodia and Indonesia, fingers are believed to make food taste better, but forks are used to eat noodles or fried rice dishes. The Filipinos use Western utensils. Long chopsticks are generally used for stir-frying or deep-frying, while shorter ones are better for mixing batters, sauces, or marinades, or for eating.

To use chopsticks properly, it is important to relax your hand (left or right): (1) Rest the thicker upper part of a chopstick in the web between the thumb and forefinger of your hand, and rest the lower, thinner part on your fourth finger, which should be slightly bent. (2) Hold the thicker, upper part of the second chopstick between the tip of your thumb and the inside of the second knuckle of the forefinger. (3) Move the top (second) chopstick up and down with the help of your forefinger and middle finger to pick up morsels of food.

clay pots: Also referred to as sand pots, these are made of a combination of clay and sand. They come in all sizes, small to large, with single or double handles, and are sold with lids. Beautiful to see and hold, they have glazed interiors (most often brown, but sometimes black or dark blue) and unglazed sandy white exteriors. Because they are fragile, clay pots are sometimes encased in wire frames, which protect and distribute the heat evenly over the surface. Clay pots are used to cook rice, soups, or stews, and they make a beautiful presentation vessel at the table.

When new, a clay pot may have an unpleasant odor, which comes from its not having been baked or cured fully. So it is a good idea to soak it for several hours, even overnight, drain, and air-dry it. Then fill it with water and place it over a low flame, gradually increasing the heat to medium, and let the water boil until reduced by half. You can also fill it with water and place it in a 250° to 275°F oven until the water is reduced. This gets rid of some of the odor, but not necessarily all of it. Do not be alarmed. The smell will not be imparted to the food, and once you really start cooking with the pot, the odor will eventually disappear.

Be sure you never place a cold, empty pot over direct heat (it must have liquid or some ingredients in it), and never put a hot pot on a very cold surface. Either can crack the pot. Also, remember to start at a low temperature and increase the heat gradually. For example, braising, a common clay-pot cooking method, is traditionally done over low to medium heat.

Clay pots are meant to be used over an open flame, so a gas stove is preferable. Electric stoves are not particularly well suited to these pots, but if this is your only option, place a heat diffuser on the electric element first.

As the pot is used over time, the outside will darken in color. Some hairline cracks may appear eventually, but as long as the glazed interior is not cracked, the pot can still be used. Clay pots can be used successfully in ovens, again starting with low heat and increasing it gradually. This technique is most appropriate for braised dishes.

After cooking, clean the pot with salt and hot water. Gently rub the salt against the glazed surface, picking up any residue (without scratching the cooking surface), and rinse the pot under running hot water. If cooking residue is particularly stubborn, try boiling it out by filling the pot with water and gradually bringing it to a boil over medium heat. Always fill the pot with hot water after you have cooked in it to start degreasing the pot or removing any sticking bits.

cleavers: There are three main Asian cleaver sizes: the small one, with a blade two inches wide, is used for carving meats and slicing vegetables. The large and heavy one has a blade measuring four inches wide and is thicker; it is used for splitting bones. The medium-size cleaver, with a three-inch-wide blade, is the most versatile. Acting as a multipurpose tool that is perfect for any type of slicing, chopping, and crushing, it can even chop through poultry bones. If there is any Chinese cleaver you should invest in, it is a medium-size one, which costs about fifteen dollars.

dowel: I use a light-weight dowel to roll out doughs. The dowel used by Chinese dumpling makers measures ¾ inch in diameter by 14¼ inches long and can be purchased in Asian food markets or at a hardware store. At hardware stores they tend to be longer; just ask the vendor to cut it to a manageable length.

You can also use the blade of a Chinese cleaver to flatten, as opposed to roll out, the dough into disks. If using the cleaver technique, be sure to lightly oil the side of the blade to prevent the dough from sticking to it as you hit it against a flat surface. Be sure not to over-oil the blade, for it can slip and injure you. Apply the oil lightly with a paper towel for better results.

You can also use a water glass with straight sides, or even a rolling pin if you feel more comfortable. All will work, but my personal preference is the light-weight dowel.

Once I have made a perfect ball from a piece of dough, I flatten it slightly against a lightly floured surface with the palm of my hand. I place the dowel in the center of the dough, and using the palm of my hand to guide the dowel, roll it in one direction, turn the dough clock- or counterclock wise, and roll it again to form a disk. In addition to the dowel, you can also use a pasta machine or a Mexican tortilla press; this will make the task of shaping dough into wonton or dumpling skins easier and cut the time in half.

flat strainer: Flat strainers have a long bamboo handle and are sold in Asian markets. They come in several sizes and shapes. They are useful not only for deep-frying but for cooking noodles, keeping them from falling loosely into the oil or boiling water.

mortar and pestle: If you are going to use the mortar-and-pestle grinding method, make sure you have a mortar that is especially wide and a pestle that is heavy. The Thai make an especially good mortar and pestle from green granite. If you can find one, get the large size. This is necessary not only to accommodate ingredients but to ensure that the pestle has adequate room to grind. Electric mini-grinders are also fine. The only items I do not grind too often are onions and shallots, which quickly turn to mush. This is all right if you are frying the paste that you are making. Otherwise, you are better off mincing onions and shallots with a cleaver.

nonstick pan: A nonstick skillet or pan is especially good to have on hand. It can be used not only for stir-frying but also for making crêpes or omelettes. If the weather does not permit barbecuing, I lightly oil my nonstick skillet and home-grill meats and seafood. Be careful not to use metal utensils, as they will scratch and destroy the nonstick surface. Use only a wooden or plastic spatula and wooden chopsticks. While it is costly, I recommend an All-Clad nonstick pan, which has not one but three layers of excellent nonstick material.

sauté pan: This pan is perfect for sautéing (stir-frying) or pan-frying. If you have an electric stove, you will probably be better off using this pan instead of a wok. For health reasons be sure to use a stainless steel pan as opposed to aluminum.

steamer racks: Metal steamer

racks that are set at the bottom of woks or pots can hold odd-shaped plates (such as oval ones used for steaming fish). Put the plate on the rack set inside the wok, cover with the wok's lid, and steam.

spatula and ladle: I find that an Asian spatula (which usually comes with the purchase of a wok) or a ladle is useful for scooping out stir-fried ingredients from a wok. I always have both on hand.

sticky rice steamer: This is essentially a woven bamboo conical basket set over a metal pot, specifically made to steam sticky rice. Another way to steam sticky rice is to cover a bamboo rack with cheesecloth and spread the sticky rice on top. Cover with the lid and steam.

woks: Used for stir-frying, deep-frying, or steaming, woks are made of spun metal such as carbon steel, stainless steel, or aluminum. Extremely thin cast-iron woks are common in Asia but difficult to find in the West. The most popular wok in the United States is made of carbon steel and is available in several sizes. The most functional ones measure about fourteen inches across, wide enough to steam a whole fish. Because stovetops are not made to accommodate round-bottomed vessels, woks usually

Cebuan cooking pots are used for preparing soups and rice and for braising meat or seafood.

come with a diffuser (or rim collar). The narrow side of the diffuser should sit directly over the flame, and the wider side should support the wok.

If you have an electric stove or hot plate, you should cook in a flat-bottomed wok. These are made by American manufacturers and are usually nonstick. Or, you may prefer to use a sauté pan.

When you first get your wok, you must wash it with an abrasive cleanser and hot soapy water to remove the factory's light machine oil. Repeat this process several times until you are satisfied that it is thoroughly clean. Then apply a thin layer of vegetable oil on the cooking surface with a paper towel prior to stir-frying.

With every use, your wok will darken. This is normal, as it is curing like a cast iron skillet. The more the wok cures, the better the food tastes. Also, curing creates a nonstick surface.

To wash your wok, simply sprinkle a layer of table salt across the cooking surface. When the salt has picked up the cooking residue (i.e., turned dark), use a paper towel to lightly rub the wok in a circular motion, removing any unwanted residue. Rinse under running hot water, or boiling water, and heat the wok immediately to dry it completely and prevent rusting.

COOKING TECHNIQUES

ATTENTION to detail and fresh ingredients are critical factors in the preparation of all the Asian cuisines as they largely determine the success of a dish in flavor, texture, and presentation. In planning menus, always remember that the flavors—deriving from the style of cutting and proportion of ingredients can be sharp or mild, salty or sweet, bitter or sour, or a combination of all these, and must always be well balanced.

braising (stewing): In Asia, braised dishes are often referred to as slow-cooked dishes because they are cooked on a low (simmer) to a medium-low (gentle boil) heat. Generally, fatty fish, dark poultry meat, and red meats are prepared this way, the fat moisturizing the lean parts throughout the cooking process and ensuring the meat will be tender. Braising can take thirty minutes or several hours, depending on what is being braised. Because braising is a gentle cooking process it should be done in a heavy-bottomed pot or clay pot. Always cover the pot with a lid while braising to seal in the moisture.

broiling: When broiling fish or poultry or anything, be sure not to place the food directly under the broiler flames. Place the rack in the middle (midway up or midway down) of your oven. Preheat the broiler for twenty minutes, and proceed with the recipe.

mis-en-place: This is a French term, which basically means "to put in place." When cooking you should always organize your ingredients in the order in which you will be using them from the time you prep them, to the time you cook them, to the time you present them. This is a good habit, as important as cleaning your work surface after each task.

stir-frying (sautéing): Stir-frying is the most important technique you will ever use in Asian cooking. All the ingredients are cut up in bite-size morsels and stir-fried in a wok over high heat. Because you are cooking over high heat a spatula and ladle (such as the ones often included in the package when buying a wok) are used to toss the food around continuously so as not to burn it but cook it evenly. Stir-frying is best achieved over an open flame and in a wok. The success of the stir-fry is not only based on your cooking vessel but also on the power of your range. Standard ranges have an average of 8,000 BTU to 13,000 BTU per burner; this is hardly enough heat to wok properly, and chances are you will collect water from your vegetables when stir-frying them. To prevent too much moisture from collecting, be sure that your vegetables are drained completely after washing them. You may want to spin them in a salad spinner before proceeding with your recipe. Also be sure that you see smoke come off the wok prior to putting anything in it. Upon contact the wok should, as if talking to you, give you a good strong sizzling report and spit back some small amounts of oil.

CUTTING TECHNIQUES

BEFORE slicing anything, the single most important thing you can do is to practice holding a cleaver. The cleaver should always slice perpendicular to the cutting board, with the knuckles of the free hand guiding the blade through each cut. When slicing, make sure the sharp edge of the cleaver does not rise above your knuckles, or the blade's return could result in serious injury. If you do not feel comfortable with a cleaver, use your favorite knife.

julienning (shredding): The food to be julienned must sit flat against the cutting board. For example, in the case of a carrot, cut it in half lengthwise and lay the cut side on the board to stabilize the carrot. It is now safe to slice the carrot into thin planks. Collect the planks and slice them lengthwise into long thin strings or matchsticks. Another good trick is to use a peeler to make paper-thin slices; then stack the slices and slice them lengthwise into long threads. There are three types of julienne: fine, matchstick (or *allumette*), and *batonnet* (the thickest). In Asia a julienne is generally really fine. In this book, ginger is assumed to be finely julienned, or threadlike, unless I call specifically for matchsticks.

chopping and mincing: For chopping or mincing boneless meats or vegetables, the motion is in the wrist. As you grip the handle of your cleaver, the awkwardness of the position will allow your wrist to move up and down while the blade falls naturally of its own weight onto the food. I use one cleaver, although some cooks use two, one in each hand, to go faster. During chopping, the food will scatter around the chopping board. Just gather it back to the center by scooping it up with the side of the blade.

chopping through bones: Hold the cleaver with your thumb pressed against the side of the blade and your other fingers grasping the upper half part (closest to the blade) of the handle. Your thumb will steady the blade while you move your forearm up and down in clean, firm strokes. This technique will allow you to chop through fish and poultry bones successfully and cleanly. If you are uneasy about it, hit a wooden mallet against the flat top of the blade after you have properly positioned it against whatever you are cutting. (In this technique, lifting the blade is not necessary.)

Never use a medium-weight cleaver to chop through heavy beef, veal, or pork bones. The blade will turn, causing you to lose control of the cleaver. Instead, use a heavier bone cleaver, or ask your butcher to take care of this task. When chopping through bones, any movement must be firm, decisive, and clean so the bones do not splinter and you do not damage the cleaver or injure yourself.

diagonal slicing: Hold the food at an angle of about 60 degrees against the blade of the cleaver (or knife) and slice.

freezing and slicing: Unless you have a professional slicing machine at home, a good way to slice any meat or lemongrass paper thin, for example, is to freeze the ingredient for about twenty minutes then use a sharp blade to thinly slice against the grain or fiber.

MISCELLANEOUS TECHNIQUES

barbecuing: When barbecuing do not use too much charcoal; a little will go a long way. Rather than use lighting fluid, which has a strong chemical smell that can be imparted to the food, use a lighting chimney. Place some paper at the bottom of the unit and top with charcoal.

Light the paper with a match and when the charcoal is lit place it in the barbecue pit. Place the grill on top and wait until the flames have subsided and the charcoal turns red with white ashes (embers). Your grill is now ready to receive any meat, seafood, or vegetable. Be sure to clean your grill after each use.

cleaning squid: Insert your thumb and index finger into the body (mantle) of the squid to pull out the head and as many innards as you can. The innards should be discarded along with the plastic-like center bone (or cartilage). Run your fingers inside the body, pulling out any remaining tissue, or cut the body open and scrape it off. Peel off and discard the skin from the body. Cut the tentacles above the eyes, squeeze out the hard inner structure (beak), and discard along with the eyes. Both body and tentacles are edible. If you're squeamish, your fishmonger can do this for you.

flavor layering: Many cooks tell you not to color the onions or garlic when stir-frying, but this is a matter of some debate and interpretation. The garlic and onions are often the first ingredients to be stir-fried. To release their essence and sugar, stir-fry them until golden. Do not, however, allow the garlic and onions to become dark brown, for

that is a sign that the natural sugars are burning, lending a bitter rather than sweet note to the food. A rich golden color is acceptable; anything beyond it is not. After the garlic and onions are stir-fried, and depending on the recipe, add the spice pastes or powders and stir-fry them until they become a shade darker. This is to toast the paste, releasing its fragrance for the next step, which can be adding the stock, proteins, or vegetables. This is the base (or foundation) upon which you build a dish, and in many cases it is done one layer of flavor at a time. If you add everything at the same time, you will rob the dish of its true complex character. Always think about developing the layers when cooking any food.

marinating: There are certain factors to consider when marinating:

1. Marinades penetrate seafood, poultry, and meat at different rates.

2. Refrigeration slows down the penetration.

3. Marinating at room temperature speeds the penetration.

4. The character of the marinade, salty, sour, or sweet, will affect the rates of penetration in different foods.

5. Marinades should be well balanced, particularly in terms of their salt and sweet content.

6. When marinating shrimp with their shells on, marinate about an hour more and be sure to rub the marinade between the shell and the flesh.

7. When marinating chicken with its skin on, take a skewer and poke holes through the skin and into the flesh so the marinade penetrates better.

8. If the protein items are sliced thin, they will require less marinating time than if sliced thick (i.e., the more you break down the protein, the more absorbent it will become).

seeding chilies: You can seed a chili without opening it completely, ensuring that you can easily make it into perfectly round or diagonal slices. It's a simple process: slice the very top of the stem end open crosswise, then roll the chili between your thumb and index fingers. The seeds will "crawl" out. If you have sensitive skin, wear thin surgical gloves so you can still feel what you are doing. And always keep your fingers away from your eyes, and wash your hands thoroughly when you're finished.

selecting offal or innards: When buying chicken or duck hearts and gizzards (for example), look for a bright reddish color and a firm texture. Whenever possible, use only fresh innards, as frozen ones lose some texture, taste, and color.

skimming stocks: When making stock, you will need to leave some fat in the pot to get a flavorful stock. At the end of the simmering process, however, you can skim off as much fat as you desire. Here are three techniques that work well: (1) Lower a ladle so it floats on top of the stock. Angle the ladle just enough to let only the fat seep in, then discard it. Do this in small batches rather than all at once to ensure that you do not take any of the stock along with the fat. This technique can easily be used with stews and sauces as well. (2) Hold a thick paper towel at each of two corners with your fingertips, then lower it so that it floats and covers the entire surface of the stock. Then lift the towel. You will notice that the fat clings to it. Discard the fat-laden paper towel and repeat as necessary. Eventually the towel will come away with no fat. (3) Refrigerate the stock for at least six hours, then remove the solid mass of fat that has formed on the surface and discard it.

soaking: Dried ingredients such as beans, rice sticks, cellophane noodles, shiitake mushrooms, seafood, some dried or preserved vegetables, and some meat must be soaked prior to using. Soaking is done to rehydrate the dried ingredients, making them pliable (as in the case of noodles), or soft (as in the case of mushrooms and seafood), or to remove excess salt (as in the case of Smithfield ham). Although the recipes in this book give you specific minimum soaking times, you can soak the items overnight and not damage them. Dried ingredients such as Chinese sweet pork sausage, liver sausage, or duck legs or thighs do not require soaking.

FUNDAMENTALS:
an overview

N EARLY ALL ASIAN food shows a significant Chinese influence. Notwithstanding the effects of Indian (which is a distinct cuisine), Western colonial, and Central Asian frontier cultures, the structure or "architecture" of the food throughout the continent reflects the thousands of years of Chinese military, political, mercantile, intellectual, and cultural influences. China is to Asia what Rome was to Europe: the civilizer, the empire builder, the consolidator. And as Rome—with its imperial aspirations, leisured intellectual classes, and access to the resources of a continent—took Europe out of Bronze Age cookery and into ideas of structure, exotica, culinary cross-referencing, use of nonlocal ingredients, spicing, and other tenets of modern cuisine, so China performed a similar role in Asia. The ruling classes of China valued gastronomy as more than survival, as an expression of its civilization, as an art. The key, therefore, to the fundamentals of Asian gastronomy is Chinese cooking.

Not that it ends there. The cultures of Cambodia, Indonesia, Japan, Korea, the Philippines, Thailand, and Vietnam—which, along with China, are the focus of this book—are remarkable in their own right. Japan, for example, can rightly be thought of as having evolved a distinct national cuisine, largely based on subtlety and understatement, a minimalist sense of refinement, and emphasis on artful presentation. Thailand, too, has a highly developed

THE BAYON, A FOUR-SIDED FIGURE, WAS BUILT IN THE TWELFTH CENTURY C.E. IT IS PART OF THE GREATER TEMPLE COMPLEX AND ANCIENT CITY OF ANGKOR, CAMBODIA, BUILT FROM THE NINTH TO THE THIRTEENTH CENTURY C.E. OTHER FAMOUS TEMPLES WITHIN THE COMPLEX INCLUDE BANTEAI SREI, TA PROHM, AND ANGKOR WAT.

kitchen, where the ingredients and techniques of India and China overlap, finding expression in a highly developed, complex gastronomic culture. Korea has evolved certain critical parts of Chinese cooking, especially its preservation techniques, these manifested in the remarkable culture of kimchi. Indonesia, an archipelago with thousands of islands, finds itself in the center of millennia-old trade routes, pathways of European imperial conquest and religious colonization. Its cuisine reflects these influences, blending them with strong indigenous ingredient traditions. The Philippines—another island chain—reflects the doubly powerful pervasive Chinese influence, and the four-centuries-long Spanish colonial presence, melded with regional ingredients and cooking techniques. Vietnam and, to a certain extent, Cambodia manifest themselves as cultural crossroads between East and West, particularly of their colonial conquerors, China and France. Ironically perhaps, torn by war, they have united the culinary arts of two of the greatest gastronomic cultures on earth, pointing the way to the future of cooking: preserve your traditions, but incorporate the new.

Having been raised in both Eastern and Western cooking cultures, I have noticed that it is easy for Western cooks—even quite serious ones—to hold one of two erroneous ideas about Asian food. One is that all Asian food is the same, that is, all Chinese; the other is that Asian cuisines are too divergent and complex, too culturally diverse and distant from Western models, ever to master. Both of these reflect half-truths, but the truth lies in a middle path. Chinese cuisine has a conceptual structure that can be understood quite readily in Western terms; the differences and complexities of other non-Chinese facets of Asian culinary culture are comprehensible through it. For those just learning about Asian food, ingredients and facets of the cuisine may seem unfamiliar, preparation techniques may vary, emphasis on one component or another of a meal may be surprising. What unites Asian food, however, is a learnable, logical, and quite elegant set of organizing principles. When you have come to know them, you can proceed at your own pace, enjoying what can be anything from a few favorite dishes in your repertoire to a lifelong adventure of culinary discovery.

The key to Chinese cooking is threefold:

1. A STRUCTURED BALANCE OF OPPOSITES IN FOOD: rooted in the philosophical principles of yin yang, it is the idea that all ingredients must be blended harmoniously, and tasted separately, while coming together on the palate.

2. FIVE PRINCIPAL FLAVOR NOTES—salty, bitter, sour, spicy, and sweet—are present in every meal. A further expression of yin yang thinking and the effort of experimentation over millennia, this idea finds expression in a rather formal approach to food, comparable to the rigor of French cooking in the West. This system points to food being used as medicine: ingredients are evaluated for more than flavor alone; balance in the diet makes for physiological and mental health.

3. GRAINS—rice for the most part, and wheat in the northern regions—are at the center of Asian culture and

at the center of the meal. Holding enormous importance in the cuisine by Western standards, rice is understood as part of a larger relationship (the *fan tsai* principle) between grains and their accompanying vegetable, seafood, poultry, and meat complements.

These principles have not only united Chinese cuisine across centuries and thousands of miles but spread to the countries of Southeast Asia and Pacific Asia as well. They form the basis for nearly all Asian cooking, and are as much present in a bowl of Indonesian *nasi goreng* as they are in a Korean *kimchi*, a Japanese tempura, or a Thai *tom yam gung*, for example. By mastering these principles and a few simple cooking techniques, and evolving a sense of Asian ingredients, I believe, a cook can work comfortably with any Asian cuisine and be confident preparing any recipe in this book.

BALANCED OPPOSITES: YIN YANG

THE YIN YANG principle posits all existence as the interaction and balance of two basic opposing forces of the universe. Evolving in China from the fourth century B.C.E. forward, it was rooted in Taoism's connection to nature and Buddhism's

search for enlightenment. (Scholars see parallels elsewhere in the ancient world: the Greek notion of "humors," the *sardi-garmi* principle of Iran and Afghanistan, and similar ancient Indian belief systems.) *Yin yang* essentially advocates a view of the world, indeed the universe, as harmonious. This harmony is observable in nature and can be experienced by living in a balanced way. The individual can literally take the harmony of the universe inside himself or herself through food that is balanced according to the *yin yang* principle.

Yin embodies female, dark, and cold forces; *yang* embodies male, bright, and hot forces. The moon is the symbol of *yin*, for example; the sun is the symbol of *yang*. This duality is all-pervasive and has acquired a specific application to food. The necessity to maintain a balance in the body and in the diet between *yin* and *yang* is a fundamental principle, often unspoken, which underlies the planning of meals for the Chinese. This system is also understood as the "hot-cold" food system, in which *yin* foods, those which have a cooling effect, include watery items such as vegetables, fruits, certain seafoods and animal proteins, and foods of

mild flavor. *Yang* foods, representing strength and heat, include other seafood and animal proteins, herbs, and hot spices. These foods form a culinary spectrum, from extremely hot to warm to neutral to cool to extremely cold.

THE FIVE FLAVOR NOTES

IN A SYSTEM that further parallels other ancient cultures, the yin yang, hot-cold food system is further expressed through five flavor notes—salty, bitter, sour, spicy, and sweet—that correspond to the five elements—water, fire, wood, metal, earth. This again reflects a millennia-old belief system in which five elements or aspects are present in everything and everyone. They are necessary for life, and good physical and spiritual health can be achieved through their balance. Expressed in terms of food, this system can be understood as follows: water corresponds to salty and black; fire corresponds to bitter and red; wood corresponds to sour and green; metal corresponds to spicy and white; and earth corresponds to sweet, subtle, yellow, orange, and brown. The system is perhaps too complex to be discussed in depth here, but the gist of it is that elements represent or correspond to the physicality and functions of the internal organs and form the basis for organizing the medicinal, or life-balancing, properties of food. It is also used as the conceptual foundation for acupuncture, for example.

THE BALANCED MEAL:
FAN TSAI

ONE OF THE unique aspects of Chinese cooking and the Asian cuisines it has influenced is that the basic principles of culinary organization are the same in all meals and at all strata of society. Thus, the humblest peasant cook and the most exalted chef at court shared the same goal of harmony and balance in cooking. Every cook will therefore plan a meal around balancing *fan* (grains and rice) with *tsai* (vegetables and meat). A harmonious, refined symmetry of ingredients is as common to the simplest snack as it is to the wedding feast.

Of the two food groups, *fan* is fundamental and indispensable, and is considered primary. *Tsai* is secondary. Without *fan* one cannot be nourished; without *tsai* the meal is simply less tasty. Overindulgence in food and drink is discouraged as unbalanced and unhealthful. Waste is anathema. The proper amount of

consumption is, as Chinese parents have said to their children for millennia, *chi fen pao* or "70 percent full." Chinese folklore is full of stories told to children about the negative consequences of waste. My brothers and I were always told: "Finish your rice or your future mate will have a pockmarked face."

In modern Chinese cuisine we can observe and experience the world as it once was. Chinese cooking principles date back to ancient times, before scientific methods, before medicine was understood as a subject separate from food, and when direct observation of nature was the only means of understanding human existence. Asian foods exhibit all of the strength and weaknesses of a culture that evolved through trial and error, observation of the natural world, and empirical models that evolved over time. Perhaps the most important lesson to be gleaned from this body of knowledge is that as the modern world feels more and more separated from nature, Asian cooking can provide a possible pathway back to connectedness. On a practical level, the system helps any cook understand and critique his or her own work, for every recipe and every meal should have a sense of

balance and some relation to the five notes, and should be based on grains served with complementary items.

CONSCIOUS COOKING:
FENG SHUI

FENG SHUI has enjoyed a revival in the West of late. Evolved from ideas about balance and harmony in architecture, landscape, and interior design, the term means "wind and water," and implies that any environment has to be properly aligned and in harmony with the four cardinal points of the compass, or the four winds. In its most extreme manifestation it involves assigning values to every corner of a room, house, garden, or tomb; adjusting the axis of entry or exit, the furnishings, and so forth; and "correcting" deficiencies by "redirecting energy" through the use of symbolic objects. My husband, an architect with an interest in the subject, likes to say that *feng shui* simply means paying enlightened attention to every part of your personal environment and making sure that you feel good about it. After having worked with *feng shui* masters and written on the subject as it applies to cooking, I have concluded the following: the most important aspect of the *feng shui* kitchen is your own presence in the moment.

I have written that food preparation can be an expression of caring and of love for others. It can also be deeply rewarding for the cook, and for me it is a kind of meditative act. I like to think of this as experiencing the five senses through conscious food preparation, comprising techniques Asian cooks have used for thousands of years.

sight: In addition to the obvious functions of helping you navigate the kitchen and work with your utensils, your eyes can also tell you how your dish is coming along. When stir-frying, the subtle liquification of the oil just before it smokes indicates it is ready to receive the ingredients. When making a coconut flan, the beautiful golden color and clear aspect of the caramel indicate that it is sweet while a dark brown, somewhat opaque aspect indicates that it has been cooked for too long and will be bitter. When grilling shrimp, look for the flesh to turn pink and opaque halfway through before turning it over. When it's completely opaque and pink, but still vibrant in color, take it off the heat. Depending on the type of shrimp, further cooking could make it too firm or mealy and dull the color.

sound: Food speaks. My clay pot "sings" to me when I am cooking rice. When the rice and water come to their first gentle boil, the pot's lid rattles, and I know the rice is halfway through its cooking process. At that point I lift the lid once to stop the boil, replacing it immediately, turning down the heat, and allowing the rice to absorb the remaining moisture through its finish. Listen for a loud sizzling noise when stir-frying ingredients—this will ensure that the items will be crisp and firm. A strong, sharp sizzle says, "I'm ready to take on the food." Anything less, and your stir-fry will be soggy.

smell: Most foods smell like essences of themselves when they're ready to eat. Garlic, mushrooms, tomatoes, and meat release their perfumes as they finish cooking. Cooking smells can guide you through the transformation of each ingredient. Take any food, whether vegetables or animal protein. When you first smell a vegetable or animal protein, it should smell fresh. When it comes into contact with the heat, its natural essences are released. When cooking garlic or onions, for example, their natural sugars are released through chemical transformation, and they soon smell sugary.

When they have overstayed their welcome, they start smelling burned.

touch: When choosing food at market and when cooking, touch the food. A gentle squeeze can tell you whether fruit is ripe or vegetables are fresh. Meat becomes firm to the touch as it cooks through, fish becomes tender; vegetables and starches soften. Many great cooks consider the tactile sensation of handling food one of the greatest joys of cooking. When steaming carp, I touch it at the end of the steaming process. If the flesh is firm and springs back, it needs more cooking; if the flesh gives under light pressure without falling apart, the fish is perfectly done.

taste: Even the best recipe cannot guide you as much as your taste buds. Tasting as you go is critical. If at all possible, always taste your ingredients before you use them. Taste your food as it cooks. Taste your finished dish before it is served. This is not only to correct for seasoning; it is also to ensure that all the ingredients have come together. When I am making a dish such as caramelized pork shank, in which there is great play between the various flavor notes, especially in critical sweet, savory, and spicy notes, it is impor-

I cannot overemphasize the importance of this sensualist approach. It is for me the core of my cooking. It is the only way to be intimately connected to your food, and the only way to really learn how to cook. Structure and organization of your ingredients and cooking sequence are important, of course, but always remember, especially as you become more experienced, your five senses are the ultimate guide. In the *feng shui* of Asian foods, multiple notes must be balanced and the refinement of the dish is critical. Echoing my husband's view of the art, you must pay attention to and be comfortable with all points in the process.

CHINA: LINCHPIN OF THE EAST

TO GET at the complexity of Asian cooking, the key is an understanding of the central role of Chinese influence in Asia. China is part of the largest continent on earth, the site of extraordinary diversity in plant and animal life, experiencing near arctic to tropical and subtropical climates, and possessing vast mountain ranges, high plateaus, and mighty rivers that fall across lowlands toward thousands of miles of

tant that I taste several times during the preparation process. The type of ginger I use can make a difference. Young, juicy, bright-colored ginger is spicier than more mature, dull, yellow ginger, so I take that into account when adding ginger to the pot. Similarly, Chinese dried red chilies are spicy, but less so than dried Thai chilies. Different types of fish sauces differ in salt intensity; some taste more of salt than fish, so I compensate with the amount of caramel I use. By proceeding in this way, tasting and adjusting as I go, I can be confident that the dish will be as it should be when served.

varied coastline. Chinese cuisine reflects this diversity, having filtered it through thousands of years of culinary development, racial, religious, and cultural diversity, and numerous foreign influences.

For our purposes the subject of Chinese cooking will be considered through four main categories: north, south, east, and west; or Beijing (Peking), Guangzhou (Canton), Shanghai, and Szechwan, respectively. Each of these has numerous internal differences, subtle variations, and items that break the very rules that define them. Some developments are unique enough that they may be considered separate cuisines, as is the case when considering Fujian (Fukien) in relation to Canton; or superior cuisines, as is the case when considering Shandong (Shantung) in relation to Beijing. Despite these differences, China had, for a period some scholars date back as far as 2000 B.C.E., a penchant for refined cuisines. Chinese intellectual and political leaders had, more than any other ancient civilization, a pronounced interest in and dedication to the culinary arts, connecting them, as we have seen, not only to satisfying hunger, but to notions of health and the very nature of existence.

The power of this idea was enormous, and it spread through commerce, exploration, and war throughout the Asian continent. Thai cooking shows a powerful connection to the cooking of Szechwan, for example, the two peoples being racially related. Southeast Asia in general reflects the influence not of the immediately adjacent provinces of southern China but of the Mongol invaders from the north, who also exerted historical influences there. Japan took critical clues in terms of ingredients and philosophy from trade with eastern and northeastern China, as did Korea. Cooks in the Philippines include the Chinese kitchen among their influences. Indonesia has a significant number of Chinese among its population who continue to influence cooking technique and ingredient preference.

This flow of ideas and techniques was never only outward. China was invaded in the north by Mongols, who brought a taste for beef, and the Manchus, who brought components of Islamic food culture. Japan occupied large sections of China for periods, as did a once imperial Tibet. In more peaceful times, China's rulers sent explorers westward, along what we now remember as the "Spice Routes," traveling thousands of miles, reaching·Persia, Turkey, the greater Middle East, and North Africa, crossing the Balkans, and trekking even to Rome. Others were dispatched south, into India, with its similarly long history, diverse cultures, and varied climates; others into mountainous Southeast Asia. Still others, it is now believed, traveled east by ship, well into the Pacific. Each brought back new ingredients, new ideas for cooking; these were absorbed by the chefs at court and eventually by the population as a whole. Sesame seeds, for example, reached China this way, as did refined sugar, coconut, jackfruit, and even MSG, to name only a few foods.

In addition to internal and regional invasion and voluntary exploration, China has absorbed items from external European military invasion and colonization as well. The English, Spanish, French, Dutch, and Portuguese had long and powerful colonial presences throughout Asia. To a lesser extent, there were German, American, and Russian influences as well. Much of Filipino culture comes from Spanish culture; Vietnam and Cambodia have clear French tendencies; Macao served as a gateway for things Portuguese, and the Dutch presence is still felt in Indonesia. Potatoes, chilies, yams, tomatoes, and corn all came to China this way. As the twenty-first century dawns, the influences of globalization, including international trade, modern electronic communications, and corporate economics remain to be seen. Still, over four thousand years China has absorbed and fused it all, remaining the Middle Kingdom, the center of Asia's culinary world.

northern or beijing cuisine: For many centuries Beijing has been China's seat of government as well as its intellectual and cultural center. Home to the Forbidden City, it was the seat of the nearly four-hundred-year rule of the Manchus, the last dynasty to rule China before Communism. Chefs from all over China migrated to the capital, and it was for centuries home to some of the finest restaurants and most elegant dishes in the world. Beijing also became the center of cooking instruction, where chefs practicing China's other regional schools of cooking established themselves, setting up restaurants there.

Although rice is the main staple in most of China, peoples in the north are more likely to eat other starches, saving the rice for special occasions. Wheat is their primary crop, with sorghum, millet, and potatoes being cultivated as well. All sorts of noodles and breads are made, including deep-fried scallion pancakes, various wheat noodle dishes (stir-fried or in broth), and vegetable and pork dumplings with wheat-flour skins. The antecedent of the dumplings now enjoyed worldwide in Chinese restaurants, these are boiled or steamed, and dipped in a gingery and vinegary soy sauce mixture before eating. Historically, Beijing was invaded by the Mongols and Manchus and eventually absorbed their culinary traditions. Primitive beef barbecues and lamb cooking were transformed into sophisticated dishes, but the nineteenth-century Peking duck is perhaps the city's most famous contribution to gastronomy. An exquisite three-course dish, it represents a particular level of refinement seldom achieved in any cuisine.

Many people hold that Shandong, a province just south of Beijing, is actually the heart of the region's cooking traditions. Home of Confucius, one of China's first epicures and father of the region's sophisticated cuisine, Shandong cooking dates back over two millennia. Suf-fice it to say that the cooks of the imperial palace had to please emperors who sometimes requested new dishes every day, relying on hundreds of cooks, year in and year out. They also had to prepare elaborate court banquets, where each of several successive refined and exotic dishes had to both complement and out-do the last. Whether you consider Beijing proper or the surrounding provinces the font of all things culinary in the north, the city certainly had to pull and mix and fuse dishes for centuries in a role befitting its imperial stature. Aside from Peking duck, Westerners may also know Tientsin or white (napa) preserved cabbage, and Tsingtao beer, both of which also come from the north.

southern or cantonese cuisine: Cantonese food is by far the best-known Chinese cuisine in the West. This is due to the fact that over the past several hundred years Canton and its surrounding province of Guangdong and neighboring Guangxi have been the major source of emigration out of the country. This has not always worked to the advantage of the cuisine's reputation, however, as a lot of the dishes originated in the poorest, most rural, and least developed areas, or—in the case of *chop suey*—were just thrown together stir-fried leftovers. Having experienced these basic dishes, Westerners may be surprised to learn that in China, Cantonese chefs have had a status not dissimilar to that of French chefs in the West.

Canton, along with the other major southern city, Fukien, has a tropical climate in which virtually anything will grow in abundance. Two rice crops—as opposed to the one in most of China—grow each year, and a multitude of plant-based foods are supplemented by plentiful meat and fowl. Historically known as merchants and adventurous seafarers, people from throughout the region enjoy a long, bountiful coastline, and many have access to extremely fresh fish and seafood items. The Cantonese in particular have a reputation for culinary eccentricity as well as sophistication; their chefs prepare snake, shark's fins, abalone, and dried seafoods, cat (wild and domesticated), tiny buntings (also known as rice paddy birds), and worms. These dishes are delicacies and not eaten every day, however, and, in general, the food can be said to rely on extreme freshness and very little spicing. Soy sauce, oil, and

garlic, and little else are most often employed, and many dishes are stir-fried or steamed, as the Cantonese prefer quick cooking methods, exposing the foods to as little heat as possible. Food prepared in this way retains its natural texture and flavor, rather than being radically transformed, as occurs in slow-cooked preparations. While they may not have invented dumplings, the Cantonese offer several hundred variations on the theme, usually served in their *dim sum* restaurants.

The Hakka, a displaced people from China's north who eventually settled in the southern regions, practice the art of peasant dishes raised to high cuisine. These are often of humble, labor-intensive origin, and require multiple cooking techniques and long cooking times. Salt-baked chicken, for example, began as a meal prepared outdoors, baked in a hole in the ground. It has now evolved into a refined kitchen preparation.

Chiu Chow is also an important culinary region of the south (and where my father's parents were born). It is known for both fresh and preserved mustard cabbage specialties. Closely related in culinary terms is the city of Fukien, whose food is sometimes considered a separate

cuisine, and whose cooks prepare rice noodle soups much like those appreciated in Vietnam. Fukien lies in the southeast corner of China, close to Taiwan, to which it has close links through emigration. I include it in the southern region because its climate is closer to that of Canton than that of Shanghai, for example. Fukienese cooking also includes shredded fish, shredded pork, *popia* (delicate crêpes, used in Shanghai for making spring rolls), and special bean curd skins filled with meat and vegetables.

Hong Kong is known as an international food capital, and it is perhaps in this wealthy cosmopolitan metropolis that the best Cantonese cuisine can be sampled. Hong Kong's chefs are also known for their restless ability to fuse various of China's cuisines with those of the West. One of my greatest pleasures when visiting the city, however, is to drop into a *dai pai dong*, a small, inexpensive, often loud and crowded eatery where I can join the unembarrassed patrons gleefully slurping away at their simple bowls of noodle soup. I have also enjoyed a spectacular meal in the Lei Yue Mun district in Kowloon, where the ritual is to select your own fresh items from a local fisherman at the dock, carry them to your dining spot of choice, and have them prepared immediately by the chef. I once selected a medley of fresh seafoods and ate it lightly steamed or stir-fried in the Cantonese fashion, with only a subtle hint of black bean and garlic sauce or with pungent ginger and scallions. I remember the meal to this day.

eastern or shanghainese cuisine: Shanghai is unique among China's cities, having been a major commercial center and Chinese port city for hundreds of years and occupied by the Western powers during the twentieth century. It served as a sort of Asian New York, London, and Paris rolled into one, complete with corruption, armed insurrection, and extraordinary cuisine. Surrounded by fertile plains and some of antiquity's most developed canal systems, its environs were considered China's garden spot. The city is known for its seafood dishes, including two specialties employing yellow eel and hairy crab, the latter enjoyed steamed, and valued for sweet roe that is reminiscent of caviar. Among other regional eastern cities, Yangchow (Yangzhou) has particular historical importance, for it was here that Marco Polo experienced

China's varied cuisines, declaring the city to be the most spectacular in the world. Fried rice may have originated in Yangchow, but its most famous dish is lion's head, a ginger- and tangerine-flavored pork meatball casserole cooked with cabbage. Shaoxing (Shao-hsing) is another eastern city of note, famous, especially, for its rice wine. Shaoxing wine is used in lightly cured and raw seafood or steamed poultry dishes such as Shanghainese drunken prawns, crabs, or chicken. Shanghai's cuisine, in particular, is rich, oily, and sweet, and includes special red-cooked dishes, which employ a lot of soy sauce mixed, again, with Shaoxing wine. Other robustly flavored items from the region include a vinegar and soy sauce dip fragrant with ginger and served with special crab-and-pork soup dumplings. The same dipping sauce also accompanies deep-fried Shanghainese spring rolls.

western or szechwanese cuisine: Szechwan, the largest of all of China's provinces, lies on the west central high plateau. The province is rather hot and humid and is known for its spicy food and the use of Szechwan "peppercorn," a spice that distinguishes its cuisine from

all other regional cuisines of China. This is supplemented by chilies brought to the region by seventeenth-century Spanish and Portuguese traders. Despite the strong, hot chilies in their cuisine, Szechwanese cooks are known for their ability to balance all five flavor notes within a single dish, particularly in the capital of Chengdu (Chengtu). Examples of Szechwanese food include hot and sour soup, and *ma po dofu*, a spiced tofu and pork-flavored dish. The province's preserved vegetables are also very spicy; some of the best examples are chili-laden cabbages. The Szechwanese are also famous for their smoked meats. Yunnan, which is southwest of Szechwan but still considered part of western Chinese culinary tradition, is home to the famous Yunnan ham (often incorrectly referred to as Hunan ham), a salt- and air-cured ham used as a flavor enhancer in many dishes. Unlike the foods of neighboring Szechwan, Yunnan food is not particularly spicy but is very fragrant, as seen in winter melon and ham soup, for example.

JAPAN

JAPAN is an island nation that lies five hundred miles east of China and one hundred miles from Korea, and is surrounded by the East China Sea and the Japan Sea. A land with several active volcanos and high mountains, it experiences both hot summers and severe winters. Japan was historically influenced by Chinese culture (filtered through Korea), a powerful connection to the sea and fishing cultures, and a strong sense of its own cultural and aesthetic identity. Japan was closed to the rest of the world for significant parts of its history, remaining in virtual isolation until the mid-nineteenth century, when the West intervened militarily, forcing Japan into international trade and leading to a period of military expansionism.

Japan has an assortment of culinary influences, transformed over the centuries into a cuisine uniquely Japanese. Vegetarian Buddhist monks had significant influence on the culinary culture, as did the highest manifestations of its imperial court cooking, centered in the old capital of Kyoto. Developing out of the highly ritualized tea ceremony, the cuisine, known as *kaiseki*, features elaborately minimal presentation of bite-size items (a single baby fish on a special platter, for example). *Shojin-ryori* is a traditional Zen Buddhist meal, presented in the same fashion as any Japanese meal (several small dishes of various food items with a broth for sipping and rice) but all vegetarian. The sixteenth century Portuguese brought techniques that developed into wheat flour–dredged and deep-fried morsels known as tempura. The relatively recent presence of beef in their diet is, in large part, due to the influence of European cultures, and other dishes categorized under *nabemono* (foods that are essentially "dropped and retrieved"), which are represented by such famous specialties as *shabu-shabu* (beef hot pot) and *sukiyaki* (shallow-cooked beef). Japanese noodles in general have been an influence of the Chinese.

The Japanese have a strong preference for raw seafood, served as sushi and sashimi. "Sushi quality" fish has been frozen rock solid to kill any worms or bacteria, then thawed before being precisely sliced. Sea vegetables such as *wakame*, *konbu*, and processed agar-agar are most often used in creating salads, or added to soups or stir-fries. The cuisine is seasonal, in terms of both items served and aesthetics: carrot may be carved into a red maple leaf and served with classic autumn dishes to recall the colors of turning leaves. Occasionally meat items are served raw as well; chicken sashimi is offered in some restaurants. The Japanese penchant for exotica is strongly mirrored in food culture, too: still living, raw lobsters being consumed at table, for example.

Aesthetics in Japanese food is not simply the artful presentation of dishes. Rather, it is an expression of an aesthetic system called *wabi sabi*. Somewhat difficult to understand with a non-Japanese set of values, it is rooted in Zen Buddhism and describes a worldview that holds steady, even as the Japanese absorb outside influences. More broadly, it manifests as an impulse to perfect what is absorbed, rather than to create new forms. As pervasive as Greek notions of ideal beauty in the West, for example, it advocates a refined and minimalist sense of nature and humanity's place in it. *Wabi sabi* permeates Japanese life, finding expression in everything from meditative rock gardens to evocative *haiku* poetry, to the ritualized tea ceremony, to food preparation. No Japanese food item would be presented without consideration for its appearance and its effect on the diner, for example.

Elizabeth Andoh, an American

lecturer who has lived in Japan for decades, has said that "Japanese food looks so beautiful you're afraid to dig in." A bowl of rice in Japan is never a plain bowl of unornamented rice. The bowl and its underplatter are selected for visual effect, and the rice is visually enhanced with a colorful garnish such as sesame seeds, or *matcha*, a green tea powder, for example. Whether you are eating in a Japanese restaurant or at home, the same concept holds true: beauty, especially as it reflects, embodies, or complements nature, is an integral part of life.

KOREA

KOREA juts dramatically from the Asian landmass, southward into the Yellow Sea. Known as "the land of morning calm," the peninsula's sheer eastern coastal cliffs rise to rocky peaks of the Ta'aebaek mountain range, then fall to the western and southern plains, where the land seems to come apart at its edges, fracturing into more than 3,000 islands. Hot summers and cold, dry winters are balanced by exquisite springs and autumns. Rivers and streams abound, spilling like watery necklaces across the land.

The Korean people are descended from the Mongols, who occupied the peninsula at various points in history. They have a stronger preference for beef dishes than seen in many other parts of Asia; these are enjoyed on special occasions. Such dishes include numerous barbecue items such as *bulgogi* and *kalbi gui* served with *kimchi*, often served in special restaurants with grills built into the table so that diners can cook in a comfortable setting. Imperial Korean foods include *kujolp'an* (nine-sectioned dish), an array of colorful julienned vegetables, seafood, and meat delicately rolled in small crêpes; and *shinsollo*, an equally colorful, slow-cooked hot pot. At outdoor markets, you can pull up to street-side food stalls to sample such classics as *chap chae*, translucent potato starch noodles stir-fried with vegetables and shredded beef; *p'ajon*, a sizzling scallion pancake; or *bim-bim pap*, a classic rice, vegetable, and meat dish seasoned with a pungent chili paste and nutty sesame oil. With these dishes, you can drink roasted rice water.

Kimchi, the traditional staple of preserved vegetables and fish, always accompanies meals. Robust and complex in its flavors, the dish exists in hundreds of variations, ranging from napa cabbage, daikon, and spring onions, to baby crabs, shrimp, and squid. *Kimchi* evolved from Chinese techniques, using salt and other spices as preservatives and flavoring agents, and matured as part of the national cuisine about five hundred years ago, when chilies (brought by the Spanish) were introduced into the mix. In addition to being served as a side dish, *kimchi* is added to soups, stews, and stir-fries.

Korean food also mirrors certain aspects of Japanese food (the Japanese occupied the country for periods of time) and includes simple versions of raw fish sushi and sashimi, for example, and, occasionally, raw pork liver items as well. The Japanese tendency toward minimalism and refinement is also present, although it is mediated by Korea's own sense of identity and different history. A unique expression of these is the tendency to display five critical colors in many circumstances, reaching even to the level of ingredient selection in food. *Shinsollo*, for example, uses color-selected foods such as bell pepper (green), egg white (white), carrot (considered to be in the red family), shiitake mushrooms (black), and egg yolk (yellow); representing the five elements—wood, metal, fire, water, and earth—that originated in the Chinese *yin yang* principle.

SOUTHEAST ASIA

THE MOUNTAINOUS, river-raked, and somewhat inaccessible geography of mainland Southeast Asia is such that ancient patterns of northern Asian civilization lagged there to a certain extent. By contrast, its southern, insular reaches are fingers of land and island archipelagos that reach from the Bay of Bengal to the Pacific Ocean and extend into the Indian Ocean and the Java and South China seas; this facilitated ancient patterns of east-west trade. The northernmost regions were strongly influenced by China. The racial stock of Vietnam, for example, has much in common with the same Yue peoples associated with Canton, and with the Mongols, who conquered China hundreds of years ago. Similarly, the Thai have connections to the peoples of Szechwanese high plains. The southern portions of the region had much to do with east-west trade routes connecting Southwest Asia, especially Persia, India, and the amalgam of island states now known as Indonesia. The Philippines, lying several hundred miles east of the Asian mainland,

KALAMANSI AND FINGER (OR THAI) CHILIES ARE OFTEN USED IN THE COOKING OF BICOL, THE PHILIPPINES.

were also somewhat isolated from the continent's evolution, their largest outside influence the result of colonization by Spain.

Empires existed within the region, however, notably the Malay, Annamese, and Thai. Little is known about the early Malay or Srivijaya kingdoms, save that they comprised Malaysia and much of what is now modern Indonesia and parts of the southern Philippines. Contact between the area and China was not established until relatively late (the fifth century), but Indian influence flourished there for about a thousand years, and there is some evidence that its sailors reached as far west as the coast of Africa. Taking most of its religious and cultural clues from the Indian subcontinent and Southwest Asia, the legacy of the Malay empire includes the enormous influence of Islam in the area, as well as lasting connections to Indian culinary cultures. From the ninth to the fourteenth centuries, the classical civilization of the Annamese or Khmer comprised much of what is now Thailand, Cambodia, and central Vietnam, manifested in the extraordinary Angkor Wat in the Cambodian highlands of Siem Reap, and the cuisine of the imperial capital of Hue in Vietnam. The Thai empire, reaching from Burma in the west to what is now Laos in the east, flourished from the fifteenth century to the nineteenth century. Because its ruling classes were, like the Chinese, interested in gastronomy as an expression of their sophistication and stature, its cuisine is complex and highly structured.

The cuisine of Southeast Asia employs raw-ingredient dishes and the marked influence, principally, of Indian cuisines, and Chinese cuisines in terms of methodology, as well as the legacies of Dutch, English, French, and Portuguese colonization. Having emerged in a rainy subtropical climate, the most important ingredients unifying the area are the coconut, which is used in all of these countries; rice, which is a basic food everywhere; and strong spices and herbs, especially garlic, ginger, lemongrass, and chili. Despite the commonalities, however, the skillful use of condiments by inventive cooks over the centuries makes each of these countries gastronomically distinct.

THE PHILIPPINES

A TROPICAL ISLAND nation, the Philippines comprise two large and numerous smaller island groups lying about five hundred miles southeast of the Asian continental landmass. Colonized briefly by the Chinese in the eleventh century, and historically visited by Chinese, Indian, and other merchants, the character of the modern nation was cast by the Spanish military conquest of the islands in the late 1500s. Spain dominated the country for four hundred years, using it as a production base for sugar and other agricultural crops, and as a trading port of some significance within Spain's global empire. The United States won the country from Spain in the late nineteenth century and eventually granted it independence after World War II.

Filipino food is quite different from that of the rest of Southeast Asia in that the intense herbal notes and spicing are largely absent from their food, with the exception of Bicol food, where the use of coconut and finger chilies is pervasive. Garlic, onion, and ginger compose the foundation of Filipino cuisine. A blend of Spanish colonial cooking mixed with the traditional foods of the indigenous people, it enjoys regional variations, but is, in general, a simple, hearty cuisine. Exotic foods are often used in this cuisine, including grilled chicken offal, and insects, such as rice paddy crickets.

The Filipinos are a warm people, quick to smile, and in touch with a sense that life is to be enjoyed. Remembering the half-century of American cultural domination, as well as Japanese military occupation in the mid-twentieth century, they have adopted and adapted the ways of outsiders to a certain extent. Jessica R. Avila, a restaurateur and cooking instructor on the resort island of Cebu, prepared a delicate sour soup called *sinigang*, which she served to me in a young coconut shell. She explained that "the lightness and delicate presentation in the dish is a direct influence of the Japanese." She recounted additional centuries-long influences on the cuisine, including, by her account, Islamic Malaysian, Catholic Spanish, Buddhist Chinese, and modern secular American influences.

The Chinese influence is obvious in the national dish, *pancit*, a noodle dish often served on birthdays and at weddings, and *lumpia*, a fried spring roll. From the Malays they have the pork blood stew called *dinuguan baboy*, meat and intestines cooked in blood and vinegar. *Kinilaw* is a modern version of a Filipino dish derived from the Caribbean Spanish *ceviche*. Originally part of a fisherman's rite in which freshly caught fish were vinegar-dipped and eaten raw, *kinilaw* is now prepared with coconut vinegar and *kalamansi* juice, with red chilies and green mango adding color. *Sinigang* is a sour soup that appears throughout Southeast Asia, but here it is distinctive in its use of *kamias*, a small sour fruit resembling *carambola*. Spanish-influenced chicken or pork *adobo* is eaten everywhere, seasoned with Filipino fish sauce known as *patis* (similar to Thai *nam pla*, Vietnamese *nuoc mam*, or Cambodian *tuk trey*) and, uniquely, brown sugar.

INDONESIA

AN ISLAND archipelago located off the Southeast Asian mainland in the Indian and Pacific oceans, Indonesia sits between China and Australia. It is the largest and most populous nation in Southeast Asia, comprising thousands of islands that range from the international, predominantly Hindu resort island of Bali, to the main, predominantly Muslim island of Java (with the capital city of Jakarta), to Sumatra, parts of Borneo and New Guinea, and numerous other islands. In its early history, what is now modern Indonesia was pulled to the west, to India and Persia, rather than China. It was also a draw for Near Eastern and Indian trade through the rest of Southeast Asia, in whose cuisines the spicy, curried Indian influences are felt to this day. Chinese traders visited the islands with increasing frequency from the sixth century onward, seeking trade and safe harbors for their long, adventurous sea journeys. For centuries Indonesia was a part of the Malay empire and, after the advent of Indian Hinduism, also saw the influence of Buddhism. From the thirteenth century to today, Islam has been ascendant, and Indonesia is now the largest Muslim

nation on earth. In the early seventeenth century Indonesia was cruelly subjugated by the Dutch. The British and French also had interests there during the Napoleonic wars of the nineteenth century; they were eventually supplanted by the returning Dutch, who persisted into the twentieth century. The country was occupied by the Japanese during World War II, and gained its independence after the war's end.

Despite the diverse religious and cultural influences of its history, Indonesian cuisine is relatively consistent. Largely defined by the use of coconut, cooking throughout the archipelago employs the fruit as a vegetable, main course, ingredient, cooking fat, relish, fruit, and beverage. Despite the inevitable influence of Dutch colonization, a significant Chinese population, and trade with the Near East and Portugal, Indonesia still can boast of a unique cuisine.

Rijsttafel, a Dutch word meaning "rice table," is formalized as an almost endless procession of beautifully arranged, carefully organized dishes, ranging from sweet to sour, mild to very spicy, cold to hot. Nationally popular is *nasi goreng*, or fried rice, which originated in China. The Indonesian version is sometimes served with a pan-fried egg on top and perhaps some grilled skewered meat, satay, on the side. One of the most essential elements of an Indonesian meal is *sambal*, sauces that can be used in the kitchen or at the table. Few Indonesian meals are served without *gado gado*, an interesting *mélange* of raw and cooked vegetables and *tempeh* (a coarse tofu cake) with a spicy peanut and coconut sauce.

THAILAND

WITH BURMA and India to the west, Malaysia to the south, Cambodia to the southeast, and Laos to the east, Thailand (formerly Siam) offers one of the most exotic cuisines in the world. Thai food is complex, rice-, rice noodle-, and coconut-based, with a counterbalanced array of sweet, spicy, salty, sour, and bitter flavors occurring in dishes throughout a meal. There is a strong Indian influence, especially in the use of spices, and particularly curries. The Chinese influence, too, can be seen in the use of woks, bamboo steamers, and cooking techniques in general, as well as stir-fries such as Chinese sweet pork sausage fried rice, for example. The Thai use chopsticks to eat noodle soups in the Chinese fashion; their fingers to eat sticky rice with dipping sauces in the Indian fashion; and a fork and spoon to eat many other dishes in the Western fashion.

Thai chilies (finger chilies), palm sugar, galangal (lesser ginger), kaffir lime leaves, and lemongrass are used in dishes such as *tom yam gung* (spicy sour shrimp soup), and rice noodle stir-fries such as *pad Thai*, a dish now familiar in the West using dried shrimp, shredded egg, peanuts, pressed tofu, mung bean sprouts, lime juice, sugar, and spices.

Despite their name, Thai curries are markedly different from Indian versions, and include red, green, and yellow curry pastes that are the backbone of the cuisine. *Haeng lei* powder is similar to Indian curry powder, and is used in some curries. These versions omit the coconut milk often used with the pastes. It is also combined with a red curry paste for making the egg noodle soup called *khao soi*, a complex but balanced egg noodle and seafood or meat soup.

Bangkok is perhaps more famous for its temples than its cuisine, but its floating market is a noteworthy curiosity, with fresh produce and snacks sold by boat vendors. Street vendors also offer freshly prepared noodles, dumplings, fried foods, grilled foods, soups and sweets, available all day and night.

Chiang Mai, arguably the culinary capital of Thailand, is located at the foothills of the northern Mae Rim mountains. The magnificent Buddhist Doi Su Thep temple dominates and to a certain extent defines Chiang Mai. (Buddhism was spread from here across mainland Southeast Asia and into southern China.) Street hawkers line the climbing path to the temple, displaying all sorts of food, including meatballs, chicken, sweet sticky rice cakes, and fried bananas. These are bought initially as symbolic offerings to Buddha, then eaten. As an interesting aside, Thai food carvings, vegetables and fruit made into floral garnishes and decorative serving vessels, have an international reputation for elaborate artistic excellence.

CAMBODIA

SOME WESTERN (and indeed, Eastern) food scholars discount Cambodia's culinary heritage, assuming it is, like that of Laos, an offshoot of Vietnamese, or, perhaps, Thai cooking. Cambodia was, however—until its precipitous collapse in the twelfth century—the seat of a large, prosperous empire. Indeed, the only imperial court cooking in Vietnam is that of the Annamese or Khmer, who had sophisticated kitchens in what is now Hue. There is evidence that the massive effort required to construct the civilization's most lasting monument, the temple city of Angkor Wat, may have bankrupted the empire and rendered the area a vassal state of Thailand for centuries. Like Vietnam and Laos, Cambodia was also colonized by the French in the nineteenth and twentieth centuries, after which it was occupied by the Japanese, granted its independence, then plunged into a genocidal civil war, the effects of which are still being felt to this day.

Like Thailand's, much of Cambodia's culture stems from that of India, including its Hindu-Buddhist belief system. Seventy percent of the country is jungle, but rice, maize, vegetables, fruit, and tropical nuts all grow plentifully in the lowlands to the south. Salt, which has enormous importance in subtropical lands, is extracted from the sea near Kampot, on the Gulf of Thailand.

While pork, chicken, and small birds are part of their diet, fish—both saltwater and particularly freshwater varieties—is the most important Cambodian dietary protein. Cambodia's most important contribution to the culinary world is a pungent fermented fish paste called *prahoc*. Cambodian cooking at its base evidences both Indian spicing and Chinese rice- and stir-fry-based cooking, and, as such, echoes the cooking of much of Southeast Asia. There are enough differences, however, to justify treating it as a separate development here.

Cambodian cooking is savory, sweet, and spicy, but not nearly as sweet and spicy as Thai cuisine. *Prahoc* is used in such dishes as *pleah saiko* (raw beef salad), where it adds a curiously subtle fermented note. *Kroeung*, an herbal paste made of lemongrass, galangal, and other herbs is the basis for the fragrant and succulent steamed freshwater fish and coconut custard specialty called *amok*. Sour and acid notes from lime juice and tamarind extract are widely present in the cuisine. Ginger is also employed in copious quantities when stir-frying chicken or pork, to aid digestion as well as add a refreshing finish to the dish.

VIETNAM

SITTING LIKE a pearl necklace along the eastern edge of Southeast Asia, Vietnam is bounded by the Gulf of Tonkin to the north, the South China Sea to the east, the Gulf of Thailand to the south, and Laos and Cambodia to the west. Geographically a spine of steep mountains that fall to plains and to the sea, the country has been a crossroads of civilizations for centuries, resulting in both the tumult and diversity associated with its long history. The Viet (also Yue-Viet) were an ancient race who, over the centuries, mixed with more than fifty other ethnic groups to form the country's modern racial stock.

Chinese cooking is an enormous and lasting influence, more directly here, perhaps, than elsewhere in Southeast Asia. The pervasive use of woks and chopsticks, as well as cooking methods such as stir-frying and deep-frying, can be traced from southern China, especially the Red River delta. Specialties such as beef and rice noodle soups known as *pho*, and spring rolls called *nem ran* (or *cha gio* in the South), and *mi xao don do bien*, crispy egg noodles topped with a seafood stir-fry, were all direct influences. The pronounced use of beef can be traced directly to the twelfth-century invasions of the Mongols, who remain an important racial type in the north to this day.

The Cambodian, or Khmer (Annamese), empire extended from Thailand to the coast of central Vietnam in the eighth to twelfth centuries, contributing to the development of an imperial Vietnamese cuisine. Its primary gastronomical contribution was to combine traditional Chinese-influenced northern and indigenous southern Vietnamese cuisines, producing a refined hybrid suitable for noble families of Hue. In essence, this presented as an array of bite-size morsels, delicately styled, not unlike Cantonese *dim sum*. The Khmer also provided a conduit for other Southwest Asian and Indian influences, notably mild Indian curry powders. To this day, India's spicy cuisine is most purely felt in the south, where sea trading routes, the Gulf of Thailand, and the delta cultures of the Mekong River have fused to form a distinctive regional cuisine.

France colonized and dominated Vietnam culturally from the nineteenth to the mid-twentieth century. French culinary influence can be seen in the use of baked breads such as *banh mi* (baguette), certain desserts such as *banh gan*, essentially crème caramel made with coconut milk instead of cow's milk, and beverages such as *ca phe*, a sweet, strong version of *café au lait*, made with condensed milk.

Vietnam may be one of the world's finest examples of fused cuisines, hybridized versions of ancient and modern taste cultures, Eastern and Western cooking techniques, ingredients, menu styles, and structure. Variations are subtle, never coarse. Ingredient substitutions are intelligent and evolved, never extravagant or employed solely for effect. Dishes are greater than the sum of their parts, and in this way, closer to the art of cuisine than the theatrics of what passes for "fused" dishes in much international contemporary restaurant cooking. Ironically, perhaps, this poor, war-torn, bedeviled country has set the bar very high, indeed.

A CLOSING NOTE

ASIA IS SO VAST, variations in its cuisines so numerous, internal and external influences so complex, that it is difficult to claim that any one recipe is "definitive." Recipes can be authentic, however, reflecting traditions, respecting structures, and using proper ingredients in proper proportions. Complete is another word I do not readily associate with descriptions of a cuisine. The idea that any listing of recipes could make for a complete embodiment of a cuisine is preposterous. It would take volumes to describe virtually any cuisine, and even then it would not be complete, simply because cuisines are constantly evolving. This has been historically true in Asia, where history has gathered almost all the nations of the earth in some form or another, where all extremes of the human condition have been lived out among the billions of her people, and where the culinary melting pot has been boiling for thousands of years. And it has never been more generally true in our ever-shrinking, more closely knit world. That is the joy, the mystery, and the adventure of cooking.

And on that note . . . *chi fen!* (eat rice!).

1

CONDIMENTS

TECHNICALLY, condiments are any foodstuff of pronounced flavor used to season or heighten the natural flavor of foods, aid digestion, stimulate the appetite, or preserve food. They can be used as accompaniments (table condiments) or ingredients (kitchen condiments). While they appear in virtually every cuisine, in Asia they hold enormous importance in cooking, and loom large in the structured systems of food preparation, nutritional balance, and medicinal properties. As evolved in Chinese cuisine, five general condiment types—extracts, pastes, marinades, dipping sauces, and garnishes—aid in balancing the five principal flavor notes—sweet, salty, bitter, sour, and spicy (see "Fundamentals" chapter,

page 43)—required at each meal. This "five plus five" approach has spread outward from China, progressing throughout Asia in regional influences and localized ingredients, evolving into something closer to a class of specialized dishes than the salt and pepper, ketchup, and mustard we commonly use in the West. (In fact, salt and pepper, as we know them, are largely absent from the traditional Asian table.) The traditional Chinese use of condiments has almost nothing in common with the mild mustard, and sweet plum ("duck") sauces commonly served in Chinese-American restaurants, and applied to any food served. These are Americanized variations on sauces originating in Canton, from which I tend to stay away. I also find the use of artificial MSG, in either home or restaurant cooking, unnecessary. Reputed to improve food's flavor by opening the taste buds (small amounts of MSG occur naturally in many foods), the chemical compound MSG often points to either unquestioned force of habit or an unsophisticated kitchen. When food is fresh and properly prepared, MSG can be eliminated completely or replaced by a pinch of sea salt.

Indian, Western colonial, and other condiment influences (which

are obvious in southern, sea-based trade route areas) are largely absent in Asian cooking, or relegated to minor influences. The one important exception is curry pastes. Having developed outside of Chinese traditions, these spicy, pungent pastes have become fully integrated into national culinary identities in Thailand, Cambodia, Vietnam, and Indonesia. The spicy, complex Thai noodle curry soup called *khao soi* (pp. 240–41) employs chicken and egg noodles with a combination of *haeng lei* powder (similar to Indian curry powder) and red curry paste as a base.

Condiments are often used with rice as the basis for a quick, simple meal. Preserved Tientsin cabbage (a salty preserved item) over a bowl of rice porridge is a meal in China. In Japan or Korea this tradition is expressed in dishes such as rice served with pickled vegetables, be it *tsukemono* or *kimchi*, respectively. In Indonesia, the use of extremely hot peppers in rice—hot to the point of diners weeping at table—has evolved into something like a national obsession. Condiments are the basis for traditional Asian "fast food." The closest thing I can think of in French tradition is *moutarde, lard, et baguette*, the "mustard and cured pork fat sandwich" *maman* gives to her kids in a pinch. The Asian dishes are more evolved and better balanced nutritionally, however, probably because at certain points in China's history they were all her vast peasantry had to eat.

Condiments also act as psychological enhancements in dining. Dipping morsels of grilled meat into a spicy, herbal, soy sauce dip just before eating reinforces a perception of freshness in the food. Also, your guests do not take the ritual and structure of the meal for granted; they, too, take meaningful part in the last moments of its preparation.

THE FIVE CONDIMENT TYPES: EXTRACTS, PASTES, MARINADES, DIPPING SAUCES, AND GARNISHES

EXTRACTS

EXTRACTS ARE essentially highly concentrated fluids taken from a single flavor-bearing item, the most familiar examples in the West probably being vanilla or almond extracts used in baking. In Asia, however, extracts are part of everyday food preparation. In China, ginger extract is a juice concentrate, ground and filtered through a fine-grain filter such as cheesecloth or mesh sieve. It is used to make a delicate steamed ginger-milk custard popular in Hong Kong (page 528) and reappears, for example, in Japan, as the basis for a salad dressing. More broadly, these concentrates can range from Cambodian fish extract *tuk prahoc*, made from fermented fish (page 76), to concentrated tamarind extract (page 75), used in Southeast Asia to give a tangy note to pastes, marinades, sauces, and soups. Other examples include annatto seed water ("Essential Ingredients," page 12), a natural food coloring made from steeping the essentially tasteless seeds in water until it turns red, and coconut milk extracted from desiccated coconut meat (page 77).

I remember going to a market in Thailand where a woman making coconut milk caught my attention. Sitting on a wooden stool, cleaver in hand, she split a brown coconut, reserving its rich juice in a bowl. Using the stool's specially outfitted serrated-tipped arm, she took each coconut half and rocked it back and forth until the meat was completely grated into the same bowl as an extremely fine pulp. Conjuring up memories from my childhood, the aroma made me want to reach for the pulp and eat it on the spot (the final product is worth waiting for, however). Water was then added to the pulp and juice, the mixture was allowed to sit, then strained through cheesecloth, let sit again, then skimmed of its cream (reserved for making coconut oil, page 77). The result was the very best coconut milk possible. Fresh, rich, and naturally sweet, it is something that gives distinctive flavor to many home-cooked Thai dishes. For the Western cook who has neither stool nor time, canned unsweetened coconut milk (not cream) is a fine substitute.

PASTES

PASTES ARE ALSO concentrates, thick, silky, or coarse rather than fluid, and typically contain one or more ingredients. Along with marinades and dipping sauces, they may be the single biggest open secret of successful Asian food preparation. Examples of pastes are Chinese lotus paste, red bean paste, and black bean paste, made, respectively, from lotus seeds, azuki red beans (also used in Japan), and black beans, cooked in water with sugar. These are most often used in making sweet snacks and so are covered in the "Sweets and Drinks" chapter (page 508). Fermented black beans (soybeans that are yellowish green before they oxidize and turn black— not to be confused with the black beans used for making sweets) and garlic paste, salty and sometimes flavored with ginger extract, is also used by the Chinese and is a delicious complement to seafood dishes.

The Chinese fermented bean curd called fu yu is also a soybean product and a salty note; it is a bit of an acquired taste. Like other Chinese preserved items, it started as survival food, and was eventually adopted into the cuisine as a condiment and an ingredient in many dishes. Sold in jars, it has the look of aged cheese, as well as a concentrated and intense flavor. Eaten alone, it is almost unbearably strong, and for this reason tiny portions at a time are eaten with a plain bowl of rice porridge. If you serve it, be sure to suggest that guests try it in moderation first, then build up to whatever level they are comfortable with. When used as a seasoning, however, it adds subtle notes to dishes such as Cantonese roast pork (page 454), or stir-fried water spinach or pea shoots (pp. 324–25).

The Japanese also developed preserved soybean pastes. These are more central to the cuisine than perhaps anywhere else in Asia and have been developed into a minor art form. In Japan, miso—of which over a hundred variations exist, from coarse to smooth, and sweet to salty—is as common as soy sauce. Among the more familiar types is shiromiso, so-called "white," but actually yellowish-tan in color and somewhat sweet in flavor. It is a good all-purpose soybean paste for flavoring soups or creating salad dressing, and the type I like to use most often. It is great for tossing with green beans (page 102), for example. Akamiso is reddish-brown, salty, and robust in flavor and used to marinate meats, including beef sirloin (page 479), prior to being grilled. While the previous pastes are made of soybeans mixed with rice, the third most popular variety, mamemiso, is made solely of soybeans. Another darker variety of rice-free paste is called kuromiso (black miso). It is so intense in flavor that it is often combined with other soybean pastes and added to soups or used in cooking meatless dishes. Hatchomiso is a type of mamemiso that is salty and strong in flavor and is used in braised dishes such as Japanese braised pork (pp. 468–69). While not as well known as the Japanese miso, Korean soybean paste also has a long history. Known as toenjang (also daenchang), these tan-colored soybean pastes are added to soups and stews. As a table condiment, toenjang complements the popular bulgogi, grilled or broiled beef (page 480). Wrapped in a lettuce leaf with a dab of this pungent fermented soybean paste, bulgogi is rich, salty, and refreshing all at the same time.

In Southeast Asia, more exotic herbs are used in making pastes, notably lemongrass and galangal, often combined with garlic. Lemongrass and garlic are so often used in Vietnamese cooking that a paste of the two can be made in quantities to last for a week. Freezing it means it will always be at hand for quick stir-fries or marinades. More elaborate pastes are used in Indonesia and Cambodia, notably base gede (page 80) and kroeung (page 78) respectively. They typically contain garlic, shallots, galangal (also known as lesser ginger), chilies, lemongrass, turmeric, and other ingredients. With slight regional variations, especially in the Indonesian spice pastes which use kencur (a pungent root), candlenuts, and shrimp paste, these herbal pastes more than enhance a multitude of seafood, poultry, and meat dishes, turning them into vibrant foods both from a visual and flavor point of view. Thailand is known for its curry pastes, which combine both dried spices and fresh herbs. While there are many existing curry pastes (page 82), including regional ones, the three most popular generic types are red, green, and yellow.

Shrimp paste is another important ingredient in Southeast Asian cuisines. While the Filipino version, known as *bagoong*, is sold as a somewhat loose mixture in bottles (you can see tiny shrimp floating in the sauce), the Thai sell their smooth, dark purplish-brown paste, *kepi*, in a plastic tub. The Indonesians (and Malaysians) sell theirs, *terasi*, in rectangular blocks wrapped in several layers of paper to minimize the paste's strong odors. The Thai and Indonesian versions are readily available in Southeast Asian markets the world over and all are available through mail-order sources. These basic pastes are, in turn, the basis for still more complex pastes, in which garlic, chilies, shallots, and other ingredients are stir-fried in oil.

Some pastes have regional variations that depend on the availability of ingredients locally. Aside from the emphasis on hotter, spicier fla-vors in the south, an ingredient or two might also be eliminated or adjusted for use with fish, chicken, or beef. In Bali, where the use of pastes is highly developed, palm sugar is used for pastes with goat dishes, while the acidic tamarind extract is employed when preparing fish (page 399). Sugar subtly lifts the flavor of the gamey Balinese goat (page 484), while the tamarind cuts the oil in the fish. This is an example of the refinement and sophistication of cuisines that have evolved for millennia through numerous cultures.

Pastes are sometimes used in a manner similar to marinades in that they are often rubbed on or into a food prior to cooking, the idea being to infuse the ingredient with additional flavor or otherwise adjust it. Often pastes are added to liquids. Soy sauce or fish sauce is used to dilute and salt; oil is used to increase adhesion. Pastes can also be fried in a small amount of oil in which poultry, meats, or seafood with vegetables may be stir-fried.

One of my most persistent memories of Asian cities is impromptu strolls through the outdoor food markets that seem to appear around nearly every corner. I think especially of the wonderful aromas of meat and seafood grilling, fragrant with herbs and spices, all ready for purchase. These delicious bite-size finger foods are rubbed with pastes or marinated, skewered, then cooked over wood coals. Quick, requiring little effort, and offering enormous amounts of flavor, grilled lemongrass skewered shrimp (page 223) in Vietnam and Cebuan grilled whole fish in the Philippines come to mind. People toiling away in tiny food stalls, preparing wonderful food, are as much a part of the Asian landscape as pagoda-style roofs in China, and twice as enchanting.

MARINADES

MARINADES ARE most often flavored liquids in which meat, poultry, and seafood are soaked for a period of time. Essential to many Asian cuisines, they can also be any harried cook's lifesaver. When you are short on time, or do not want to prepare an elaborate meal, many marinades give you all five flavor notes—salty, sweet, bitter, sour, and spicy—considered essential in Asian cooking. A classic Chinese marinade for any grilled meat uses soy sauce and vegetable or sesame oil as its base, counterbalanced with sugar or honey, infused with garlic and ginger, and spiced with chili flakes (or ground black or white pepper). Sometimes Shaoxing wine is added to the mix to round out and unify the flavors. Fairly mild, it complements rather than overwhelms the flavor of the main ingredient. This allows a simple marinated and grilled poultry such as chicken, for example, to be a complete meal. And, because the principles are so simple, in learning one classic or fundamental marinade, and understanding timing (page 40), you lay the groundwork for learning many more.

When I go food shopping I always stock up on ingredients that can quickly become part of a marinated dish (not just two stalks of lemongrass, but a dozen). I am never out of garlic, ginger, chilies, and scallions. Five-spice powder, a Chinese kitchen condiment also used in Vietnamese cooking, is within arm's reach; so are soy sauce, fish sauce, and sugar. With these basics and a variety of oils, any cook can explore many of the cuisines of Asia with nothing more than a small bowl, a knife, and a fork for stirring. And because so many marinades keep well, even if I set out to make a simple Chinese ginger and garlic soy sauce marinade (page 84), I make enough to set aside in the re-

frigerator for future use. This pays off when I'm traveling, and my husband is more than appreciative when all he has to do is marinate and grill some meat for a superb meal.

Many marinades are the foundation of Asian meat-, poultry-, and fish-based stir-fries, no more complicated than mixing soy sauce, sugar, and tapioca starch. They prepare the food for the wok, imparting a rich flavor, making for a perfect main dish, to be complemented by simple vegetables. Several of the pastes described above can also be used as marinades, simply by being diluted with soy sauce or fish sauce sufficient to liquefy and to impart additional flavors to the food.

In Japan, marinating is more akin to sequential dipping. The marinades serving as basting liquids. In a typical *yakimono* (grilled foods) eatery, skewered morsels of chicken and other popular items such as octopus and sardines are dipped in a sauce, then set on the grill for a few seconds, then dipped again, and so on, until cooked all the way through. This marinating-at-the-speed-of-light style makes for tasty but less assertive flavors. While the Japanese may have a more delicate approach to marinating, they serve their grilled skewered foods with a

dipping sauce on the side, which is similar to the cooking marinade in character and flavor. Subtlety is key.

In Korea, *bulgogi* (page 480), a national dish, is marinated in soy sauce, scallions, garlic, and sesame oil prior to being grilled (restaurant-style), or stir-fried (home-style). Served with the ubiquitous preserved spicy cabbage called *baechu kimchi* (page 359), fresh lettuce leaves to wrap the morsels in, and chunky fermented soybean paste or spicy vinegar sauce (page 93) to dip in, it is delicious.

In Vietnam, marinades often incorporate lemongrass and garlic paste into fish sauce, sugar, and oil (page 83). This simple recipe is a universal marinade for poultry, meat, and seafood alike, especially chicken, pork, shrimp, and squid. In Cambodia, where the food is related to that of its neighboring countries to some degree, mushroom-flavored soy sauce (also popular in Vietnam and Thailand), garlic, and black pepper are used to marinate small birds such as quail, a roadside item.

In Indonesia, *base gede* (see "Pastes," pp. 65–67) can be used as a marinade, as in *bebek betutu* (pp. 502–3), a duck covered in a spice paste and wrapped in banana or similar leaves. After marinating for several hours, the bundle is smoked for twelve hours in rice husks. I had the pleasure of seeing this dish prepared in a hamlet outside of Ubud in Bali. An esteemed local cook and his daughter were involved in the preparation for days and, having been singled out as representing the best of culinary tradition in his region, had been selected to prepare this duck for the president hundreds of miles away in Jakarta. I was honored, of course, that he would prepare it for me, but even as I marveled at the final results, I noted that the marinade was actually quite straightforward.

In the Philippines, marinades show Chinese and Spanish influence. They have special items not unlike *ceviche*, raw seafood such as fish, shrimp, squid, or scallops cured in acidic liquid such as lime juice. One such raw fish dish is called *kinilaw*, or, depending on the region, *kilawin*; it is marinated in coconut vinegar, *kalamansi* juice (a tiny green citrus fruit no bigger than a pinball), sliced shallots or onions, and ginger. In the southern Bicol region, where the people love spicy, rich foods, coconut milk is added to the mix along with hot finger (Thai) chilies. Marinated for about twenty minutes, the fish or seafood

A TAKE-OUT FOOD SHOP IN KYOTO OFFERS MANY GRILLED ITEMS.

of choice is then served in the marinating liquid. I enjoyed these dishes on recent trips to the Philippines and have included recipes using mackerel (page 404), scallops, or octopus in the "Fish and Seafood" chapter (page 374).

A word on marinating times: a whole chicken should marinate for six to eight hours; a duck can go overnight. If cut up into thighs, drumsticks, wings, and breast sections, limit the marinating times to two to four hours. If you poke holes in the meat it will take flavor more quickly. If cubed, an hour or so is all you need. The principle is: the more the bird is broken down the more quickly it will absorb, and that's true for beef, pork, or any meat as well. Marinating cubed meat overnight would be disastrous, resulting in overly salted food. Even though generally tougher, whole cuts of meat should still be limited to not much more than twenty-four hours (depending on the size), with pork being the most fragile and beef the least. Cubed meats should be limited to about two hours if bite-size.

Seafood, from the more fragile fish to the tougher (in terms of withstanding marinating times) mollusks, with crustaceans in between, is generally more delicate than any poultry or meat. Limit it to no more than two hours. Marinating times also depend on size and type when it comes to seafood. For example, firm blue tiger shrimp can stand marinating for much longer than tender gray shrimp. And like meat and poultry, the larger the pieces, the longer they can hold up to the marinade.

Another consideration is marinating at room temperature versus marinating in a refrigerator. Refrigeration generally slows down the absorption process, and marination can take twice as long. My "Marinating Tips" (page 40) in the "Equipment and Techniques" chapter (page 33) will give you a better sense of how to proceed.

DIPPING SAUCES

ENJOYING DIPPING sauces is a big part of any Asian meal. This can be as simple as dipping a piece of chicken in chili-garlic sauce from the jar, or out-of-the bottle soy sauce, or it can be as elaborate as preparing an herb-infused soy sauce to accompany deep-fried tofu or steamed rice noodles. Special little divided dishes of chili paste and spicy yellow mustard (not the Western version) are presented in authentic Chinese restaurants and used to flavor roasted chicken, fried egg rolls, dumplings, and other similar items. Other sauces are made specifically to accompany particular dishes. Peanut sauce intensified with curry and shrimp pastes is served with Thai *sate* (page 98); another more delicate version is diluted with ginger-infused chicken stock and balanced with lime juice, a wonderful complement to Cambodian or Vietnamese summer rolls. Herbal and spice-infused soy sauces can be found in Chinese, Japanese, and Korean restaurants, too. Examples can be as simple as *wasabi* (so-called "Japanese horseradish") and soy sauce combinations for eating raw fish in both Japanese and Korean restaurants, to hoisin sauce straight from the jar, smeared on delicate flour pancakes for rolling Chinese

crispy Peking duck skin, julienned cucumber, and shredded scallions. Vinegar and sugar-based dipping sauces are favored by Filipinos; they seem to love sweet flavors in general.

Because dipping sauces play an important role in Asian cuisines, it should be noted that many foods accompanied by these sauces are often intentionally lightly seasoned, so that when dipped to individual taste they are not overly seasoned. Chinese or Vietnamese boiled or steamed chicken dipped in an oil-based ginger, garlic, scallion, and salt dip (page 104), and Thai spring rolls (pp. 274–75) dipped in a sweet chili sauce (sold commercially), or fresh chili slices in vinegar are good examples. Eaten alone, these foods would seem bland and be regarded as culinary errors ("Only one note!" as my father might admonish). Eaten with their appropriate condiment dipping sauces, however, they really are little wonders.

Balance is everything here, and the finishing touches are so much part of the meal that you often must anticipate the pairing of sauces and other items before starting to cook. Examples abound: Thai *taud man*, or fish cakes (page 407), are always served with a sweet rice vinegar–based spicy cucumber relish (page 350) pungent with shallots and enriched with crushed peanuts. Indonesian steamed prawns are served with sweet soy sauce enhanced with freshly sliced hot chilies. Filipino lumpia (their version of spring rolls; pp. 276–77) would not be complete without a brown sugar-based coconut vinegar dipping sauce (page 96). And Japanese sashimi is always served with a combination of soy sauce (or more properly tamari) and wasabi.

GARNISHES

GARNISHES ARE essentially leaves, flowers, herbs, or other similar color and texture items used to enhance food visually and lift the palate with a final flavor note. Unlike in the West, where they are often thought of as mere discardable decoration, in Asia garnishes are ingredients: integral to a dish, adding volume, color, and texture while enhancing its flavor, enhancing it in every way.

In Western cooking, garnishes are specifically chosen for their digestive, palate cleansing, or breath-freshening properties. Parsley often accompanies garlic-flavored dishes, for example, and mint is served with strong-tasting lamb. While this practice is preserved in very sophisticated Western kitchens, in lesser ones garnishes are flavorless or worse. In Asian cooking, however, the opposite is true. Garnishes are food, and all the principles surrounding their selection, freshness, preparation, and use apply. Simply put, if your Thai basil garnish is not as fresh as the chicken in your chicken soup, you have messed up.

Aside from the fresh items mentioned above, Asian, and more specifically Southeast Asian, garnishes also include fried savories. For example, shallots are thinly sliced, then fried and drained and sprinkled on top of many foods, adding a sweet flavor and crispy texture. Ginger, julienned into delicate strands, is deep-fried until it is crisp and its color becomes brighter. Its mildly piquant flavor is perfect for fish and seafood dishes. When finely chopped garlic is fried and reserved in its frying oil, it adds a nutty flavor to noodle soups. Scallions sliced, fried, and reserved in their frying oil add a sweet note to a simple bowl of rice or rice noodle dish with grilled meat or seafood.

While these fried garnishes are simple to prepare, it is important to know a few basics. First, use medium heat and be careful not to burn or brown the ingredients. You want to bring out their natural sugars and stop there. Once they reach a rich golden color, they must be taken off the heat. Think of making a caramel sauce: the more concentrated and darker the sugar syrup gets, the more bitter the flavor becomes, until it is inedible. The same principle applies to fried herbs: gentle and light are the watchwords. Use a mild-flavored oil such as grapeseed or canola oil so as not to mask the flavor of the herbs. Transfer garlic and scallion oils to heat-proof jars. Drain shallots and ginger on paper towels. A hint: shallot and ginger oils are not served with crispy shallot or ginger, but they can be reserved to flavor a stir-fry.

Garnishes can also be used to transform the humble into the spectacular. Citrus fruit skins (zests) such as lime, for example, can be finely grated as quick, colorful garnishes. Sprinkled atop a simple Chinese soy sauce–roasted chicken they are transforming, lifting and subtly complementing the richness of the bird while adding color. The same principle can be applied to more complex flavorings, such as five-spice roasted squab (page 500), barbecued pork ribs (page 454), or fish dishes such as fried pomfret (page 394).

Herbs, when used as garnishes,

can be thought of as a special sub-class of condiments in Asian cooking. While the basic structures were inherited from China, the tradition has flowered profoundly in Southeast Asia, where herbs often take the place of vegetables. It is customary, for example, to add freshly torn cilantro, Thai basil, and other leaves to Vietnamese noodle soups (pho). These are used in such quantities that they are basically ingredients as well as a garnish, both essential to the texture of the dish, and allowing/requiring personal adjustment and participation on the part of the individual diner. Timing in this tradition is also important. The herbs' essential oils are released just as they are added to the soup, while the still steaming broth lightly "cooks" the herb and releases its fragrance.

Herb preparation techniques vary. Fresh herbs can be stir-fried quickly at high temperature with small amounts of oil and used as part of meat or fish dishes, as in the wonderful northern Vietnamese fried fish dish called cha ca (pp. 396–97) accompanied by dill, Thai basil, and cilantro. In fish dishes such as Chinese steamed sea bass, julienned ginger, scallions, and shiitakes are scattered across the length of the fish, then steamed.

In the case of Korean, Japanese, and Filipino cuisine, herbs are used sparingly as garnishes. In the Philippines, the occasional sprig of parsley is as popular as it is in the West. In Japan and Korea, cooks place special emphasis on presentation, individual food items are traditionally placed in separate small bowls or plates and garnished lightly with thinly sliced scallion and toasted sesame seeds. The Japanese also love to add finely chopped blanched daikon leaves (or whatever is available), julienned nori (laver), shiso leaf, or a sprinkle of matcha (green tea powder) atop their bowl of rice. These provide both color and texture in equal measure.

To be completely fair, I have to note an exception to nearly all I have written above. Consider the case of the completely inedible garnish. It occurs ironically (and quite deliberately) in one of the most refined styles of Asian food preparation, Japanese kaiseki. In Kyoto, where I was enjoying kaiseki—dishes once served to nobility and the wealthy—I was served small dishes that were beautifully, I have to admit, decorated with maple leaves and other flora unique to some specific geography or seasonal tradition I knew little about. Short of

being a horticulturist versed in exotics, I quickly learned that there is simply no way to navigate these items as a novice. (One is not informed of the niceties of "edible versus inedible" in these circumstances; one asks or abstains.) I have unending respect and enthusiasm for the kaiseki tradition, and see it as the extraordinary exception that makes the rule. In everyday eating, however, such disregard for the simple pleasures of the palate is counter to much of what I hold dear in cooking.

As a traveler in the exalted and the humble both, my advice in such matters is: When using beautiful leaves or flowers from the garden or elsewhere, be sure that they are not toxic and are organic or pesticide free, and inform your guests as to your intentions in serving them. In common practice, however, there is a simpler way: use leaves that are normally used in cooking. Wonderful, fragrant items such as kaffir lime leaves, cilantro, saw leaf, or shiso—virtually any fresh Asian herb—can enhance the plate as well as the palate. Or as the many Chinese mothers have said for millennia, "Eat your vegetables."

CONDIMENTS AT HOME AND WHEN DINING OUT

PRACTICALLY SPEAKING, one of the things that most strongly recommends the use of Asian extracts, pastes, marinades, dipping sauces, and garnishes in home cooking is their ease of preparation and use. They can be made ahead of time, refrigerated for a week or so, frozen for a few weeks, or kept longer if you use canning procedures. You'll find this chapter especially useful in a pinch, when you only have thirty minutes or less to prepare a meal. I often place meat such as pork chops in a lemongrass, garlic, fish sauce, and sugar marinade that morning, so that when I come home in the evening, all I need to do is grill them while my rice is cooking. Having a jar of dipping sauce is also helpful. It will change a steamed chicken into something elegant. Accordingly I have organized my condiment recipes in one chapter in deference to busy working persons. Any steamed, grilled, roasted, broiled, or deep-fried poultry, meat, seafood, or vegetable will be transformed with many of the dipping sauces included here.

One closing note on dining with condiments at Chinese banquets, in formal circumstances, and other situations: in Amy Tan's book *Joy Luck Club* (and the film that followed) the Chinese cook says to her guests in a most humble manner that her food is just okay, perhaps not worth eating. It was, of course, masterful; she is just being polite in a most Asian fashion. The would-be non-Asian son-in-law mistakenly takes her remarks to mean that more seasoning (before tasting) is necessary and pours (not shakes) soy sauce over a perfectly prepared steamed fish, mortifying the cook and guests alike. It nearly costs him his impending marriage.

In the case of elaborately prepared or presented meals, always taste food before seasoning. Never season a dish shared by all, but season your own serving. Remember that individual dishes are often accompanied by their own specific seasonings. When multiple seasonings are offered with a dish (as they often are with soups), remember to try a bit of each, aiming to achieve a balance. Even humble rice is not exempt: most Asians would hesitate to drizzle soy sauce over their bowl of white rice or fried rice. When served with rice, dishes are prepared so as to offer a rich and rounded dining experience. The rice is intended as a neutral white canvas upon which a multitude of flavors are introduced. Finally, if you are unfamiliar with or have a question about something served to you, do not be afraid to ask.

GINGER EXTRACT

MAKES ABOUT 1½ CUPS

1 pound fresh GINGER, peeled

GINGER, CULTIVATED since ancient times, was one of the most highly valued exotic spices imported by the Roman Empire, where it was used principally as a medicinal herb. It has been in continuous use in the West for hundreds of years, notably in making such classics as ginger-snaps and all sorts of spiced cakes. When very young, the rhizome is tender and pale yellow, with a translucent skin that has a beautiful pink hue. In its early stages it is spicier and juicier than its aged, dark yellowish-to-tan man-ifestation, which also tends to be more fibrous and less pungent. Ginger is strong in flavor. It evolved in Asia as both a complement to fish (it cuts fishy tastes and is believed to prevent seafood poisoning), and a flavoring agent for otherwise bland ingredient combinations. The Japanese like to pickle young ginger (page 355) and serve it with sushi and sashimi. The Chinese use the extract described here to make sweet steamed ginger milk custard (page 528). You can also use this extract for salad dressings, dipping sauces, marinades—anywhere you need a concentrated flavor without the volume or texture of the rhizome.

It is preferable to use young ginger for this extract, but mature ginger will do. Depending on the ginger you pick, you may have more or less of the juice called for in this recipe.

Coarsely chop the ginger, transfer it to a mini food processor, and pulse to a fine paste. (Or finely grate the ginger.) Working in batches, place the ginger pulp in a fine sieve. Press the pulp against the sides of the sieve with the back of a spoon to ex-tract the juice. Do it several times until the solids become very dry. You can also place the pulp in a double layer of cheesecloth, twist-ing the cloth tightly to extract the juices. (You can also use a juicer.) Discard the solids and transfer the extracted juice to a jar. This keeps well for several days refrigerated. You can also divide the juice to fill sections of an ice-cube tray and freeze it for up to 3 months. Place the tray in a sealed plastic freezer bag to prevent freezer burn.

TAMARIND EXTRACT

MAKES ABOUT 2 CUPS

8 ounces fresh or packaged
TAMARIND PULP

T HE TAMARIND TREE is an evergreen native to Africa. Its edible fruit, resembling a long, brittle brown bean, is cultivated for its sour yet mildly sweet pulp. The pulp, light to dark brown in color, surrounds dark brown seeds that can be roasted and eaten. The leaves are also occasionally used in cooking. According to *The Oxford Companion to Food* by Alan Davidson (Oxford; 1999), since prehistoric times, it has been grown in India, where it was used as a souring agent in braised dishes such as curries and chutneys. Also known as Indian date, tamarind has been a commodity on Asian spice trade routes for millennia, and is popular as a cooking ingredient throughout Southeast Asia. Although its principal use is to flavor savory dishes, it is also enjoyed as a sweet snack, as in Thailand and the Philippines, where the raw pulp is candied or simply sprinkled with sugar.

Tamarind has a very distinctive flavor in which there is no real substitute. In a pinch, however, where you have to settle for its souring properties alone, lemons or limes are fine. The flavors will be different; the desired dish will still have its characteristic sour note. If time is a problem and you want to skip making your own extract, buy tamarind concentrate. It is labeled "Concentrated Cooking Tamarind" and is imported from Thailand.

WHILE FRESH TAMARIND PODS are occasionally available in Asian and Latino markets, it is more likely that you will find the harvested pulp packed tightly into blocks. Some brands offer pure pulp; others contain seeds and, occasionally, fibers. These fibers are undesirable but can be easily removed (see recipe). Either version can be made into extract. Although I buy the packaged pulp, when I find fresh tamarind pods at the market I buy them in quantity. (They are great for any number of recipes, and keep for several weeks.) If you are adventurous, crack the pod open and snack on the fresh pulp. Basically sour, it has a mildly sweet note.

Bring 2 cups water to a boil in a small saucepan over high heat. Remove from heat. Place the tamarind in a large bowl and pour the hot water over it, loosening the paste with a fork to soften it. Allow to rest, occasionally stirring, until a thick brown sauce is formed, about 30 minutes. Pass the mixture through a fine sieve and with the back of a spoon press the extract through. Discard the solids and transfer the extract to a jar. Keeps for up to a week refrigerated. You can also divide the juice to fill sections of an ice-cube tray and freeze it for up to 3 months. Place the tray in a sealed plastic freezer bag to prevent freezer burn.

TUK PRAHOC
FISH EXTRACT

MAKES ABOUT 1 CUP

¼ cup PRAHOC

P RESERVED FISH, *prahoc* (also spelled *prawhohk*), is perhaps the most important seasoning in Cambodian cuisine. In the United States, most types are imported from Thailand or Vietnam and packed in glass jars. Although the best *prahoc* is made of fish fillets only, most available brands have some tiny fish bones as well. Several types of fish are used in making *prahoc*, including mud fish, grey featherback, or gouramy. Mixed with ground rice and salt, the fish are left to ferment for months. During the fermentation process the fish breaks down, becoming very pungent and giving off an unpleasant aroma stronger than any shrimp paste or fish sauce on the market. You may think it has spoiled, but that strong odor is inherent to the fermentation process. (Think of the strongest French cheese you have ever experienced, then triple its intensity!) A small jar of this fish extract will go a long way and keep for months. While you do not have to refrigerate *prahoc*, as with most packaged pastes or sauces, I do. The chill reduces the fierce smell. Once the jar is opened, be sure to place it in well-sealed double plastic bags prior to storing it. *Prahoc* is not used directly from the jar. A couple of tablespoons are added to boiling water for several minutes. Then the juice is extracted, leaving the solids—including those nasty bones—behind. The extracted juice, called *tuk prahoc*, is what you use in cooking. Once made, the juice can be kept refrigerated for a week or so.

MY HUSBAND is very adventurous when it comes to eating, and my kitchen produces all sorts of cooking smells, from grilling sardines (he complained that the oily aroma lingered for weeks), to boiling *prahoc,* where he instructs me to "close all the closet doors, and open all the windows" while I prepare it. He calls it tear gas! Strangely enough, when the *prahoc* juice is used in a recipe such as the Cambodian raw beef salad (page 470), it takes on a whole new characteristic and, while rounding out the flavors, becomes almost sweet. It is definitely an acquired taste, but if you like fish sauce and shrimp paste, you will eventually enjoy *tuk prahoc,* too.

Bring 1 cup water to a boil in a small saucepan over high heat. Reduce heat to medium-low, add the *prahoc*, and gently boil for about 10 minutes. At this point the fish will have broken down and the water will be cloudy. Pour the mixture through a fine mesh sieve and into a bowl. Use the back of a spoon to press the fish against the sieve and extract the juices, but be careful not to let any tiny fish bones through in the process. Just to be sure all bones were held back, pass the extract one more time through a sieve lined with cheesecloth. Allow to cool and transfer to a jar or use as directed in recipes.

FRESH COCONUT MILK

MAKES ABOUT 1 QUART

1 BROWN COCONUT

COCONUT IS THE SINGLE most commonly used fruit in Southeast Asian savory and sweet food preparations, and you will use significant amounts of coconut milk when making Thai and Vietnamese curries and other stewed or braised dishes. (The Chinese use coconut less often, but they love a good sweet coconut tapioca soup [page 517] on occasion.) When shopping, buy a brown, hard, and somewhat hairy coconut. Shake it to make sure that there is natural water inside. Be sure that the shell is intact (free of cracks) and that the three "eyes" on top are not moldy. When you are at home, pierce the eyes and taste the coconut water. If it is sweet, then proceed with the recipe. If it is sour, throw the coconut away; it is spoiled. Once made, fresh coconut milk should be used immediately or refrigerated. Even when refrigerated, however, the coconut milk should be used that day. (In a pinch, use canned unsweetened coconut milk.)

Green coconut, which has a tender smooth skin and a very thin amount of meat, is not used for making milk. It is used for the tremendous amount of sweet water it carries, which is not a substitute for fresh coconut milk.

IF YOU HAVE a hard time cracking the coconut open and separating the meat from the shell, after emptying it of its natural juice, place the coconut in a 350°F oven until it cracks, about 15 minutes. This should make it easier to get the meat out.

1. With the back of a cleaver, carefully crack the coconut shell all around, and place over a large bowl to collect the natural juice. Pull the halves apart. Pry the meat out and peel the brown skin. Place the coconut meat in a food processor and finely shred. Transfer the shredded meat to the bowl containing the juice. Bring 3 cups of water to a boil over high heat. Pour the water over the shredded coconut and stir. Allow the coconut pulp to settle down and steep for 30 minutes. Pour the liquids through a fine mesh sieve, pressing the pulp against it to extract the milk. You can also transfer the pulp to a clean cotton kitchen towel and twist to extract the milk.

2. Pour the coconut milk into a large glass measuring cup and wait for the rich cream to rise to the top, and the milk to settle beneath. Separate the two if you wish and use the cream to make oil; use the milk to make savory and sweet dishes alike. The cream and milk can also remain together if you wish to have a rich milk for cooking.

3. To make coconut oil, gently boil the coconut cream over medium heat until the milk solids evaporate, leaving behind the oil.

KROEUNG
FRESH HERBAL PASTE

MAKES ABOUT ¾ CUP

2 LEMONGRASS STALKS, root ends trimmed, outer leaves and tough green tops removed, and 6-inch-long inner bulbs chopped

1 ounce GALANGAL, peeled and chopped

½ ounce fresh TURMERIC, peeled and chopped; or ½ teaspoon TURMERIC POWDER

6 large GARLIC CLOVES, crushed and peeled

1 large SHALLOT, peeled and chopped

4 KAFFIR LIME LEAVES, ribs removed; or zest of 1 LIME

½ teaspoon KOSHER SALT

KROEUNG, SOMETIMES spelled kreuang, is a versatile Cambodian herbal paste consisting of lemongrass, kaffir lime leaves, galangal, and turmeric. It is used to flavor marinades and soups, such as the spicy beef soup (pp. 150–51), and is rubbed on skewered meats for grilling. Exotic herbs such as the ones mentioned here are available fresh or frozen at Asian markets, sometimes at your local supermarkets, or through mail-order sources (page 563).

Although you can make this paste using dried ingredients, do so as your very last resort; herbs lose a great deal of flavor when dried. Fresh or frozen herbs are best. While turmeric powder is used mainly as a deep yellow coloring agent, fresh turmeric has a wonderfully sour-sweet flavor. Kaffir lime leaves have a very distinct bitter flavor, which, in absolutely authentic cooking, is irreplaceable. You can, however, use lime zest as a substitute. While the zest does not have the same flavor as kaffir lime leaves, it does have a slight bitter flavor that works well in interpretative adaptations.

Place the lemongrass, galangal, turmeric, garlic, shallot, lime leaves or zest, and salt in the bowl of a mini food processor and pulse until the ingredients form a fine paste. If you have trouble processing the ingredients evenly, add some water, a tablespoon at a time, but try not to use more than about 2 tablespoons of water. This paste will keep about 3 days refrigerated.

Variation: Stir-fry the paste in ⅓ cup vegetable oil over medium heat until fragrant and slightly darker, 5 to 7 minutes. Transfer to a heat-proof jar along with the cooking oil, and refrigerate for a week or so.

KAFFIR LIME, *Citrus hystrix,* is a member of the citrus family. Known as *makrut* in Thailand, and *jeruk purut* in Indonesia, it is widely used in Southeast Asian cuisines. Small, dark green to yellow, and knobby-round in shape, it is used mostly for its zest because the quantity of its juice is minimal. The leaves are widely used in cooking, giving a curiously pleasant bitter note to foods. Somewhat comparable in use to bay leaves in the West, Kaffir lime leaves are as prevalent an ingredient in Asia. The fragrant dark green, oval-round leaves are naturally connected by their stems in pairs, forming a figure 8. "Kaffir" is of Arabic origin, meaning "nonbeliever." The Kaffir lime may have originated in Africa and traveled to Southeast Asia with Islam, by way of the Malays.

SAMBAL TERASI
SPICY FERMENTED
SHRIMP PASTE

MAKES ABOUT ¾ CUP

⅓ cup VEGETABLE OIL

4 large SHALLOTS, peeled and minced

6 medium to large GARLIC CLOVES, peeled and minced

6 SCALLIONS, root and dark green ends trimmed, and 6-inch stalks minced

12 THAI CHILIES, stemmed, seeded (optional), and minced

1 tablespoon INDONESIAN or THAI SHRIMP PASTE

THE PASTE *SAMBAL TERASI* includes a good amount of tiny hot chilies and shrimp paste. This paste is "fierce," as my husband would say. Indonesian cooks say, "If your eyes do not water, the food is not good." You get the idea. When making *sambal terasi*, you will probably need to open the windows just to breathe. The fiery chilies may make your throat scratchy, and you will want the pungent smell of the Indonesian shrimp paste, *terasi*, to dissipate. Is it worth it? Definitely. Although you may be put off by the preparation process, *terasi* is tasty and people tend to acquire a taste for it rather quickly. (Try serving Indonesian fried rice with crab [page 212]; you will understand.) There is plenty of oil and salt in this paste, which helps to preserve the ingredients while refrigerated.

Heat the oil in a saucepan or wok over medium heat. Add and stir-fry the shallots, garlic, scallions, and chilies until fragrant and lightly golden, 5 to 7 minutes. Add the shrimp paste, breaking it up with a fork, and fry until dark, about 5 minutes. Transfer the whole thing, including all of the oil, to a heat-proof jar and refrigerate until needed. It keeps for a week or so.

BASE GEDE
BASIC SPICE PASTE

MAKES ABOUT 1½ CUPS

1 tablespoon CORIANDER SEEDS

1 teaspoon BLACK PEPPERCORNS

4 CANDLENUTS

½ teaspoon grated NUTMEG

2 LEMONGRASS STALKS, root ends
trimmed, outer leaves and tough
green top removed, and 6-inch-
long inner bulbs chopped

1 ounce GALANGAL, peeled and
chopped

1 ounce KENCUR root, peeled and
chopped (optional)

1 ounce TURMERIC, peeled and
chopped; or ½ teaspoon
TURMERIC POWDER

1 ounce fresh GINGER, peeled and
chopped (add for meats)

7 THAI CHILIES, stemmed and
seeded

4 medium SHALLOTS, peeled and
chopped

4 large GARLIC CLOVES, crushed
and peeled

¼ cup TAMARIND EXTRACT
(add for seafood)

½ cup VEGETABLE OIL

1 tablespoon INDONESIAN or
THAI SHRIMP PASTE

2 tablespoons PALM SUGAR (omit
for seafood)

I N BALINESE COOKING, *base gede* is your basic spice paste. A combination of dried and fresh ingredients, including coriander seeds, candlenuts, nutmeg, galangal, lemongrass, shrimp paste, and palm sugar, it is used to season a wide range of poultry, meat, and seafood items. There exists, however, a slight variation in the paste for each item. For example, when preparing seafood, tamarind extract, with its oil-cutting citrus note, is added. When preparing strong-flavored meats such as beef or goat, ginger is included to tame the aroma of the meat as it cooks. With poultry, neither of these two ingredients are included. *Base gede* is widely used to flavor braised dishes and stir-fries, or rubbed on morsels as a marinade prior to grilling. The following recipe is based on a few I've tried. The only caveat is that fresh turmeric, which does have a mild flavor in addition to the vibrant orange color it imparts, is not always available; neither are candlenuts, or *kencur*, a root also known as lesser galangal. If you cannot find these three items, feel free to substitute turmeric powder and macadamia nuts, omitting the *kencur* altogether (it has no substitute). The galangal, which you can get in Asian markets or through mail-order sources, lends plenty of exotic flavor to the paste.

Using a mortar and pestle or small food processor, grind the coriander seeds, peppercorns, candlenuts, and nutmeg to form a fine powder. Add the lemongrass, galangal, *kencur*, turmeric, ginger (if using), chilies, shallots, garlic, and tamarind extract (if using), and process to a slightly grainy paste. Heat the oil in a saucepan or wok over medium heat. Add and stir-fry the paste until fragrant and slightly browned, about 5 minutes. Add the shrimp paste and palm sugar and continue to stir-fry until well combined and darker by two shades, but not burned, 3 to 5 minutes more. Transfer the paste, including all of the oil, to a heat-proof jar and refrigerate until needed. It keeps for about a week.

A Balinese woman goes to market.

THAI RED OR GREEN
CURRY PASTE

MAKES ABOUT 2 CUPS

20 to 25 red or green THAI CHILIES
(choose one color), stemmed,
seeded, and minced

5 large GARLIC CLOVES, crushed,
peeled, and minced

3 large SHALLOTS, peeled and
minced

2 LEMONGRASS STALKS, root ends
trimmed, outer leaves and tough
green tops removed, and 6-inch-
long inner bulbs finely ground

Zest of 1 LIME (KAFFIR LIME
preferably), finely grated

1 ounce GALANGAL, peeled and
minced

1 ounce CILANTRO root or stems,
minced

1 tablespoon THAI SHRIMP PASTE

1 tablespoon freshly ground
CORIANDER SEEDS

½ teaspoon freshly ground CUMIN
SEEDS

Freshly ground WHITE PEPPER

KOSHER SALT

EXCELLENT-QUALITY Thai red and green curry pastes are available in Southeast Asian markets under the brand name of Mae Ploy, but as with many foodstuffs, freshly made versions taste even better. This paste is mostly simple prep work, done prior to grinding the ingredients in a mortar and pestle. The paste evolves through the pounding and crushing process, continuing until the flavors are well combined and the ingredients broken down to form a uniform paste. This paste keeps about a week when refrigerated and topped with about ⅛ inch of vegetable oil. Fry the paste only when you are ready to make your curried dish. This recipe is good for 2 to 3 coconut curries, depending on how spicy you like them.

When selecting your mortar and pestle, be sure it is heavy, and specifically bottom heavy. When you pound, the mortar should not budge. My favorite types are made of green granite and come from Thailand. Also make sure that the mortar is wide enough, so that your ingredients can be crushed against its sides.

Place the chilies, garlic, shallots, lemongrass, lime zest, galangal, cilantro, and shrimp paste in a mortar and pound with the pestle to form a paste. Add the ground coriander, cumin seeds, white pepper, and salt, and continue to pound until all the ingredients are evenly distributed and you have a homogenous paste. (You can also use a mini food processor.)

THERE ARE MANY different kinds of coconut curry. In India, where the dish originated, curry powder is used in making coconut curries that are generally served over basmati rice in the north, and jasmine rice in the south. In Vietnam, the same curry powder is used as the basis for coconut curries served with a rice flour–based French baguette. Thai curries, made with pastes, are the spiciest of all curries, and are often served over jasmine rice in the south and sticky rice in the north. From the northern region of Chiang Mai—arguably the culinary capital of Thailand—comes *khao soi* (pp. 240–41), a vibrantly flavored soup of boiled egg noodles, served in a spicy, tangy-sweet curried coconut broth, and garnished with crispy fried noodles.

Soba Noodles with Three Mushrooms (page 248)

TOFU-ASPARAGUS QUENELLES AND BUTTERNUT SQUASH (PAGE 367)

TOFU-ASPARAGUS QUENELLES AND BUTTERNUT SQUASH

SERVES 4 TO 6

1 pound firm TOFU, cut into
½-inch-thick slices
4 young ASPARAGUS SPEARS,
peeled if necessary and thinly
sliced into rounds
8 small fresh SHIITAKE
MUSHROOMS, stemmed, caps
julienned or finely chopped
1½ pounds BUTTERNUT SQUASH,
peeled, seeded, and sliced into
½-inch-thick wedges, then
halved crosswise; you should
have approximately 18 pieces
2 cups KONBU DASHI (pp. 124–25)
½ cup MIRIN
4 tablespoons JAPANESE DARK
SOY SAUCE
1 teaspoon SESAME OIL
Freshly ground BLACK PEPPER
1 tablespoon TAPIOCA STARCH
or CORNSTARCH

ONE OF MY FAVORITE combinations is tofu and acorn squash or pumpkin. At Omen, a wonderful Japanese restaurant in the heart of SoHo, I first tasted soft tofu mixed with green asparagus chunks, steamed in an acorn squash and served with a thickened silky dashi-based sauce. An absolute winner. On my way to Kyoto I experienced a similar dish. Pumpkin was sliced into small wedges and steamed, then served alongside tofu served in thickened dashi. I liked the pumpkin because it was sweeter than the acorn squash, and I love the tofu mixed with asparagus. Back home in New York, I created this vegetarian dish of sliced bright orange butternut squash and tofu quenelles in a slightly thickened broth served in a shallow bowl.

1. Place a double layer of paper towels on a plate and arrange the tofu slices in a single layer on top. Cover with a double layer of paper towels and refrigerate overnight. Check every 4 to 6 hours to change any drenched towel.

2. Place a wok filled halfway with water over high heat. Place a two-tier bamboo steaming rack with a lid inside the wok.

3. Mash the tofu in a bowl and thoroughly mix in the asparagus and shiitakes. Divide the tofu mixture into 12 equal portions and shape into oblong pieces. Place these on a plate. Place the butternut squash wedges on a separate plate. When the bamboo rack is filled with steam, place the tofu plate on one rack and the butternut squash on the other. Secure the lid. Steam until the tofu is heated through and the squash is very tender, about 10 minutes. Divide the tofu quenelles among individual plates along with an equal amount of butternut squash wedges.

4. Bring the stock, mirin, soy sauce, and sesame oil to a boil over high heat. Reduce the heat to low. Dilute the tapioca starch with 2 tablespoons of water and stir into the stock until it thickens, about 3 minutes. Drizzle an equal amount over each serving of tofu and butternut squash and serve while hot, as an appetizer or a side dish.

MA PO DOFU
BRAISED TOFU WITH PORK

SERVES 4 TO 6

1 tablespoon VEGETABLE OIL

1 large GARLIC CLOVE, crushed, peeled, and minced

1 ounce fresh GINGER, peeled and julienned

2 SCALLIONS, root and dark green ends trimmed, and 6-inch stalks cut into ¼-inch pieces

12 ounces GROUND PORK (70 percent lean)

1 pound firm TOFU cakes, cut crosswise into ½-inch-thick rectangular slices

1 teaspoon CHINESE DARK SOY SAUCE

1 tablespoon CHINESE LIGHT SOY SAUCE

2 teaspoons HOT BEAN PASTE; or CHILI AND GARLIC SAUCE (page 106)

½ cup BASIC CHICKEN STOCK (page 116); or BASIC PORK STOCK (page 118)

1 teaspoon TAPIOCA STARCH or CORNSTARCH

½ teaspoon SZECHWAN PEPPERCORNS

KOSHER SALT

Freshly ground BLACK PEPPER

A SZECHWANESE SPECIALTY believed to be about four hundred years old, *ma po dofu* is a mildly spicy braised tofu dish. Rich with firm tofu and ground or shredded pork, it is fragrant with ginger, garlic, scallions, and chili sauce, and lightly seasoned with soy sauce and chicken stock. Often in Chinese-American restaurants, the tofu is drowned in a heavy brown sauce containing far too much dark soy sauce and cornstarch. I like to season *ma po dofu* with light soy sauce and stain it ever so slightly with the dark soy sauce. Tapioca starch is much more delicate than cornstarch, and a small amount will do.

Hot bean paste is made with preserved soybeans (not to be confused with fermented bean curd) and can be purchased at Chinese or Southeast Asian markets and through mail-order sources (page 563).

1. Heat the oil in a heavy-bottomed pot over medium heat. Stir-fry the garlic, ginger, and scallions until fragrant, about 3 minutes. Add the pork and stir-fry continuously to prevent the pork from lumping, about 5 minutes. The ground meat should be separate and dry. Lower the heat to medium-low and add the tofu, dark and light soy sauces, and hot bean paste.

2. Whisk together the chicken stock and tapioca starch until smooth and add it to the pot, along with the Szechwan peppercorns. Simmer the mixture for 20 minutes, stirring gently once or twice, so as not to break up the tofu too much. Adjust the seasoning with salt and pepper if necessary.

LEGEND HAS IT that *ma po dofu* was created by a woman from Chengdu, the capital of Szechwan, who once greeted an emperor. An able cook, she ferreted around her kitchen and put together a dish using humble ingredients such as tofu and pork. Pleased by the dish, the emperor named it after the cook. Created by an elderly woman with a scarred face, the dish was called *ma po dofu*, or pock-marked grandma's tofu.

Goi Du Du: Green Papaya Salad with Shrimp (page 351)

BAECHU KIMCHI: PICKLED SPICY CABBAGE (PAGE 359)

CHAR SIU: CANTONESE ROAST PORK (PAGE 454)

Adobong Na Manok: Chicken Adobo (PP. 496–97)

DAHN JOOK: EGG RICE PORRIDGE (PP. 194–95)

PHO GA: RICE NOODLE AND CHICKEN SOUP (PP. 228–29)

NUOC MAM TUONG XA GARLIC AND LEMONGRASS MARINADE

MAKES 1¼ CUPS

MAKES 1¼ CUPS

¼ cup PALM SUGAR; or
   GRANULATED SUGAR
⅓ cup FISH SAUCE
2 LEMONGRASS STALKS, root ends
   trimmed, outer leaves and tough
   green tops removed, and 6-inch-
   long inner bulbs finely ground
2 large GARLIC CLOVES, crushed,
   peeled, and minced
1 tablespoon VEGETABLE OIL

ONE OF MY FAVORITE Vietnamese marinades, *nuoc mam tuong xa*, is made with fish sauce, garlic, and lemongrass and sweetened with palm sugar or regular sugar. While it is most popularly used to flavor pork or shrimp prior to grilling or stir-frying, it is also delicious with chicken, beef, squid, or fish.

Whisk together the palm sugar and fish sauce in a bowl until well combined. Stir in the lemongrass, garlic, and oil until evenly distributed.

I'VE SPENT MANY SUMMERS in Paris, where my Asian side of the family lives. This lemongrass and garlic marinade was at the center of our barbecues, where everyone enjoyed cooking together. While some made the marinade, others separated chicken legs into thighs and drumsticks and poked them with metal skewers to allow the marinade to penetrate. Pork chops were cut into ¼-inch-thick slices. They were thin by any standard but these chops packed a lot of flavor. Grilled in just a few minutes, the chops, along with some refreshing cilantro, tender lettuce leaves, thin cucumber slices, shredded carrots, and chili and garlic sauce (page 106), made one delicious baguette sandwich. Others preferred prawns with juicy heads and shells intact. We would devein the shrimp by cutting right through the shell and rubbing the lemongrass and garlic marinade inside and out. The shell not only accentuated the rich flavor of the prawn but kept the flesh from burning on the barbecue. Beef filet mignon, cubed and skewered, was marinated, then sprinkled with crushed peanuts, an excellent accompaniment to deep-flavored meats. All was well thought out, and family and friends enjoyed endless hours of eating slowly to savor every bite.

CHINESE SPICY SOY SAUCE MARINADE

MAKES ABOUT 1 CUP

⅓ cup CHINESE LIGHT SOY SAUCE

1 tablespoon CHINESE DARK THICK
SOY SAUCE

2 tablespoons SHAOXING WINE

¼ cup GRANULATED SUGAR

2 medium to large GARLIC
CLOVES, crushed, peeled, and
minced

2 SCALLIONS, root and dark green
ends trimmed, and 6-inch stalks
minced ·

1 ounce fresh GINGER, peeled and
finely ground

2 or more THAI CHILIES,
stemmed, seeded, and minced

1 tablespoon VEGETABLE OIL

I'VE SPENT MANY summers at my parents' weekend house helping to prepare barbecues, where there are as many versions of this spicy soy sauce marinade as there are cooks. My personal favorite adds Shaoxing wine to round out the flavors and ginger for a refreshing earthy finish. When selecting the wine, I always make sure it is a straightforward Chinese rice wine. I do not use "cooking" wines of any type because they are already seasoned with sugar, salt and sometimes herbs, and I much prefer to be in control of the seasoning. Barbecues are a great family event because everyone gets involved. Men barbecue meats over the hot, smoky, charcoal fire; women prepare refreshing accompaniments such as Vietnamese green papaya salad (page 351), Thai spicy cucumber and shallot salad (page 350), and fragrant jasmine rice (pp. 186–87).

Whisk together the light and dark soy sauces, Shaoxing wine, and sugar in a bowl until the sugar is completely dissolved. Stir in the garlic, scallions, ginger, and chilies until evenly distributed, and stir in the oil. This marinade can be refrigerated for up to a week.

SOY SAUCE is indispensable in Chinese cooking. The terms thin or "light" and thick or "dark" as applied to Chinese soy sauce refer to the fluidity and saltiness of the sauce. One is not a "diet" version of the other. Thin soy sauce, a combination of soybean extract, wheat flour, and salt, is used to season. Thick or "dark" soy sauce, made with soybean extract and molasses, is much less salty, and used mostly as a coloring agent, imparting a reddish-brown hue. It is often used in combination with the salty thin soy sauce. Shaoxing wine, named after the town of its origin, is made from fermented sticky rice. Although it is widely used in cooking, it is also drunk warm, at room temperature, or chilled, like Japanese sake. Several types of Chinese rice wine are used in cooking, according to their alcohol levels. Rice wines that are amber in color and contain 18 percent alcohol are used in everyday cooking and marinades such as this one. They are also used in curing meats, such as Chinese drunken chicken (page 486). Rice wines that are clear white and have 50 or more percent alcohol (generally about 120 to 150 proof) are used to flambée (meaning ignite; essentially to "fire up" or "put a flame to") as in Chinese drunken shrimp (page 405) or Vietnamese *bananes flambées* (page 542).

BASIC SOUTHEAST ASIAN MARINADE

MAKES ABOUT 1½ CUPS

2 LEMONGRASS STALKS, root ends trimmed, outer leaves and tough green tops removed, and 6-inch-long inner bulbs finely ground

2 large GARLIC CLOVES, crushed, peeled, and chopped

2 SCALLIONS, root and dark green ends trimmed, and 6-inch stalks chopped

½ ounce fresh GINGER, peeled and chopped

¼ cup FISH SAUCE

3 tablespoons GRANULATED SUGAR

1 tablespoon VEGETABLE OIL

THIS LEMONGRASS, garlic, and fish sauce marinade is a perfect Southeast Asian marinade. There is nothing easier than rubbing it on such items as chicken, pork, beef, shrimp, squid, or lobster before grilling (indoors or outdoors), pan-frying, roasting, or broiling. Lemongrass, a core ingredient, is a delicious herb used in Asia in all its parts. Even the outer leaves are used to wrap food.

Many Western chefs, having recently discovered lemongrass, use only the creamy-purplish part of the stalk (the inner lower bulb, about 6 inches long). I, like many Southeast Asians, consider the yellowish-green part (the next 3 inches of inner stalk) perfectly useful as well. Its juice and fragrance are slightly less intense but are made acceptable by fine grinding. If you prefer, however, you can reserve the yellowish-green part for flavoring stocks, or making herbal infusions for drinking.

1. Place the lemongrass, garlic, scallions, and ginger in a mini food processor and pulse to a paste-like consistency.

2. Whisk together the fish sauce and sugar in a bowl, until the sugar is completely dissolved. Add the herbal paste and oil and stir to combine thoroughly.

LEMONGRASS AND GARLIC are both widely employed in Vietnamese and other Southeast Asian cuisines. Lemongrass has a citrusy, earthy flavor without the sourness associated with lemons or bitterness of limes, while garlic lends a pungent note. Both are considered cure-alls in Vietnamese herbal medicine (based on Chinese herbal medicine). Among its many benefits, lemongrass is believed to help cure colds and dyspepsia. Garlic is believed to cleanse the blood and help prevent cancer. Because this herbal combination is so popular in Southeast Asian cooking, my Aunt Loan always makes a pure lemongrass and garlic paste in quantities sufficient to last a week, incorporating it in marinades for grilling beef, pork chops, or shrimp, for example. If you wish to make a large batch and keep it for 3 months in the freezer, use 6 to 8 stalks lemongrass and 6 to 8 garlic cloves, and finely grind them in a mini food processor, and freeze.

When grinding lemongrass I find a mini food processor gives me better results than a mortar and pestle. The lemongrass becomes pulpy, making it pleasant on the palate and easy to digest.

SEE TZUP JENG
FERMENTED BLACK BEAN
AND GARLIC SAUCE

MAKES 1¼ CUPS

1 cup fermented BLACK BEANS

2 tablespoons VEGETABLE OIL

3 large GARLIC CLOVES, crushed, peeled, and minced

1 ounce fresh GINGER, peeled and minced

½ cup SHAOXING WINE

2 teaspoons GRANULATED SUGAR

ALTHOUGH SOME VERSIONS of fermented black bean and garlic sauce are sold commercially, the homemade version is by far the best. The difference is, as the expression goes, "like night and day." When homemade, the beans, preserved in salt and sometimes flavored with ginger, break down slightly, giving a distinctive texture and flavor to your recipes. In the store-bought versions the beans have a puree-like consistency. Pungent, this earthy, salty, concentrated black bean and garlic sauce lends itself well to an array of steamed foods such as rich yet delicate carp, clams (page 414), or tofu (page 364). It's a study in contrast of flavors, textures, and colors. One cup will usually last me a couple of weeks refrigerated, as I only use about 2 tablespoons at a time.

Salted black beans, sometimes called fermented or preserved black beans, should be firm but soft to the touch rather than dried up, a sign that it has been stored too long.

1. Place the fermented black beans in a bowl and cover with water to get rid of the excess salt. Drain after 20 minutes.

2. Heat the oil in a saucepan or wok over medium heat. Stir-fry the garlic and ginger until just golden, about 3 minutes. Add the fermented black beans and stir-fry until fragrant, about 2 minutes. Reduce the heat to low, add the Shaoxing wine and the sugar, and continue cooking until the liquid evaporates slightly, 5 to 10 minutes. Transfer the moist beans to a heat-proof jar and allow to cool completely prior to refrigerating.

THE ART OF FERMENTING black beans for use in Chinese cooking goes back to the Han dynasty (206 B.C.E.– 221 C.E.). Most popular in southern Chinese cooking, fermented black beans should not be confused with the black beans eaten in Mexico or the Southwestern United States. Fermented black beans are actually soybeans that have been salted and, through oxidation, have turned from their original yellowish-green color to black. Although some Chinese cooks do not bother rinsing the beans prior to use, I prefer to do so; the process gives food a bold flavor without the excess salt. Either way is correct; it is simply a matter of preference.

TERIYAKI SAUCE

MAKES ABOUT 2 CUPS

1 cup MIRIN

½ cup JAPANESE DARK SOY SAUCE

¼ cup TAMARI SAUCE

1 cup SAKE

3 ounces fresh GINGER, sliced (optional)

5 SCALLIONS, root and dark green ends trimmed, and 6-inch stalks cut into 1½-inch pieces (optional)

2 large GARLIC CLOVES (optional)

PERHAPS THE MOST popular of all Japanese sauces, especially among Westerners, is teriyaki. (The word *teriyaki* can refer both to this sweet soy sauce and to the final dish.) Traditional teriyaki sauce is made with soy sauce, mirin (sweet sake), dry sake, and tamari sauce, but infusing it with aromatics such as ginger, scallions, and garlic gives the sauce extra layers of flavor. I encourage you to try both versions. Many Japanese restaurants offer teriyaki chicken or salmon; oftentimes it is a Western interpretation where the morsels of meat have been cooked in the sauce. This is an unfortunate shortcut, because the sauce was never intended to be used as a marinade or cooked with the meat. In fact, the word *teriyaki* is from *teri*, meaning "gloss" or "luster" and *yaki*, meaning "broiled" or "grilled." In classic practice teriyaki is a glaze drizzled over broiled meat as it comes off the heat, just before it is served.

Japanese soy sauce, *shoyu*, has a cleaner taste than Chinese soy sauce, *see yao*, which has a nutty flavor. I am strict when it comes to soy sauce. Japanese soy sauce is perfect for Japanese and Korean foods, while Chinese soy sauce complements the more complex regional cuisines of China and Southeast Asia.

Bring the mirin, dark soy sauce, tamari, and sake to a gentle boil in a saucepan over medium heat. Reduce the heat to low, and if using, add the ginger, scallion, and garlic. Continue to simmer until reduced by about 15 percent, about 30 minutes.

TERIYAKI IS PERHAPS the first Japanese food I had. Growing up an adventurous kid in a culturally diverse family, I ate everything put in front of me without thinking twice . . . except raw fish. Slippery raw fish slices, chewy octopus tentacles, or popping fish roe were too scary for words. When I was a teenager in Tokyo, watching Japanese businessmen choosing their live lobster from the fish tank one minute, then seeing the lobster served split open with its muscles still vibrating at the table the next, was like watching a Stephen King movie. Needless to say, teriyaki *anything* on the menu was my lifesaver. Today I favor delicately sliced raw fish when I'm ordering in a Japanese restaurant, but my nephews, just like me when I was younger, prefer the more familiar-looking chicken teriyaki.

SPICY SOY SAUCE DIP

MAKES ABOUT 1 CUP

½ cup CHINESE LIGHT SOY SAUCE

¼ cup VEGETABLE OIL

4 SCALLIONS, root and dark green ends trimmed, and 6-inch stalks cut into 1-inch-long pieces and julienned

½ cup CILANTRO LEAVES

2 or more THAI CHILIES, stemmed, seeded, and thinly sliced diagonally

WHEN EATING fried tofu or steamed shrimp in a Chinese restaurant, you will often be served an herbal, mildly spicy dipping sauce on the side. Easily made at home, julienned scallions, cilantro leaves, and thinly sliced red chilies are deep-fried in vegetable oil and added to a cup containing soy sauce. The dip turns any steamed or deep-fried seafood, poultry, or meat into a spectacular rich-flavored dish.

Do not heat up the soy sauce with the oil in a pot. The soy sauce will quickly evaporate and turn into pure salt, as many of my skeptical students find out.

Put the soy sauce in a heat-proof bowl. Heat the oil in a saucepan over medium-high heat and deep-fry the scallions, cilantro, and chilies until just golden, about 2 minutes. (The pot will be full of herbs but there is plenty of oil to cook them all.) Pour the hot oil with the scallions, cilantro, and chilies into the soy sauce and serve as a table condiment. Stir the sauce before dipping morsels.

GINGER-INFUSED
VINEGAR DIPPING SAUCE

MAKES ABOUT 1½ CUPS

½ cup CHINESE LIGHT SOY SAUCE
¾ cup CHINESE BLACK VINEGAR
2 ounces fresh GINGER, peeled and
    julienned lengthwise

I F YOU'VE BEEN to a Shanghainese restaurant and had *siu long bao*, crab-and-pork soup dumplings, they were served with a vinegary soy sauce dip infused with fresh ginger. Reminiscent of better grades of Italian balsamic vinegar in its thickness, Chinese black vinegar provides the sourness and a slight sweetness to this soy sauce dip. The ginger imparts essential flavor and texture, and helps cut the fat of the meat. This sauce is also delicious with Shanghainese spring rolls (pp. 272–73).

A piece of ginger weighing 1 ounce measures 1¼ to 1½ inches long, depending on its diameter. To lend maximum flavor to the vinegar dip, you must julienne the ginger very finely. Each strand should be as thin as thread.

Mix the soy sauce, vinegar, and ginger together in a small bowl and allow the ingredients to steep for 30 minutes prior to serving in individual sauce cups. This sauce will keep refrigerated for weeks.

PONZU
SWEET AND SOUR SOY DIPPING SAUCE

MAKES ABOUT 3 CUPS

Juice of 4 LEMONS
½ cup JAPANESE SEASONED RICE
    VINEGAR
1¼ cups JAPANESE DARK SOY
    SAUCE
¼ cup TAMARI SAUCE
½ cup MIRIN
⅓ cup BONITO FLAKES
6-inch-square piece of KELP, cut in
    6 pieces

THIS SWEET AND SOUR sauce is especially delicious served with *shabu-shabu* (page 160), a Japanese hot pot, and is categorized under Japanese *sunomono*, or vinegared foods. Its sour notes are a perfect complement to tempura, fried battered shrimp or small fish, or vegetables. When making *ponzu*, I like to use Japanese amber rice vinegar, which is seasoned with sugar and salt. A milder vinegar than its Chinese cousin, it complements the acidity of the lemon juice and the saltiness of the soy sauce, beautifully rounding out the flavor rather than sharpening it.

Pour the lemon juice, vinegar, dark soy sauce, tamari, and mirin in a bowl. Add the bonito flakes and kelp and let stand overnight or at least 24 hours. Strain through a fine mesh sieve or cheesecloth and discard the solids. Transfer the liquid to an airtight jar and allow the flavors to develop for at least a month, refrigerated. This sauce gets better with age, but consume it within 6 months.

YAKITORI NO TARE
SWEET SOY SAUCE DIP

MAKES ABOUT 2½ CUPS

CHICKEN BONES, such as 1 neck
  and 2 wings (optional)
1¾ cups JAPANESE DARK SOY
  SAUCE
½ cup TAMARI SAUCE
¾ cup MIRIN
1 cup SAKE
4 to 5 ounces ROCK SUGAR; or
  ⅓ cup or more PURE SUGAR
  CANE crystals

YAKITORI NO TARE, soy sauce sweetened with sugar, is a delicious sauce
served with yakitori, or skewered grilled chicken (page 493). The soy
sauce, tamari, mirin, and sake are simmered with chicken bones for
added flavor. It can be prepared without the bones, and can be served with all
sorts of grilled seafood and meats as well. Since the chicken is intended as a
subtle note, the bones of a few pieces will do.

The Japanese use rock sugar, which gives a nice sheen to the sauce. You
can, however, certainly use pure sugar cane crystals, a more than adequate
substitute. For grilling seafood, such as swordfish (page 401), make the
sauce without the chicken bones.

Place the chicken bones in a saucepan with the soy sauce, tamari,
mirin, sake, and rock sugar. Stir well
and simmer over medium-low heat
until reduced by about 1½ cups, 30
to 45 minutes. Allow to cool and
serve with grilled foods.

TEMPURA DIPPING SAUCE

1¼ cups DASHI (pp. 124–25)
½ cup MIRIN
½ cup JAPANESE DARK SOY SAUCE
3 ounces DAIKON, peeled and
   finely grated
1 to 1½ ounces fresh GINGER,
   peeled and finely grated

IN JAPAN, food almost always comes with a special accompanying sauce. In the case of deep-fried food known as tempura, a sweet and savory sauce, spiced with freshly grated ginger and daikon, helps digest the rich food. This sauce is the same for both the vegetable tempura and seafood tempura (pp. 345 and 417, respectively).

Stir together the *dashi*, mirin, and soy sauce and divide among 4 to 6 bowls. Serve with finely grated daikon and ginger on the side. Instruct your guests to add daikon and ginger to their individual sauce cups just when they are ready to eat the tempura.

CH'O KANJANG
SPICY VINEGAR
DIPPING SAUCE

MAKES ABOUT 1 CUP

½ cup CHINESE WHITE RICE
  VINEGAR

1 ounce fresh GINGER, peeled and
  finely grated; or 2 tablespoons
  GINGER EXTRACT (page 74)

¼ cup KOREAN or JAPANESE DARK
  SOY SAUCE

2 tablespoons GRANULATED SUGAR

1 teaspoon SESAME OIL

1 large GARLIC CLOVE, crushed,
  peeled, and minced

1 SCALLION, root and dark green
  ends trimmed, and 6-inch stalk
  sliced into paper thin rounds or
  minced

½ to 1 teaspoon KOREAN HOT
  CHILI POWDER (optional)

1 teaspoon toasted SESAME SEEDS

SPICY DIPPING SAUCES or dressings such as this vinegary Korean version enliven an array of grilled foods or salads. A favorite treat when dining with friends is a meal at Woo Lae Oak—a well-known Korean restaurant in New York City's SoHo district. We order all sorts of meat and seafood to grill on a built-in hibachi set in the center of our table; the grilled items are always seasoned with the restaurant's version of this spicy, vinegary dipping sauce. While the vinegar cuts the richness of our barbecued foods, the spiciness from the chili lifts the palate with every bite. This recipe is my interpretation of that marvelous sauce; it can be used either as a dip or a salad dressing.

I often serve this vinegary sauce along with the Korean sweet and sour chili dipping sauce (page 105), offering two very different dipping sauces at table. When pairing them like this, however, I generally omit the chili powder mentioned here. If I am undecided about the final touches on the menu, or unsure about my guests' preferences, I also usually refrain from adding the chili powder until just before serving.

Whisk together the rice vinegar, ginger or ginger extract, soy sauce, and sugar in a mixing bowl until the sugar is completely dissolved. Add the sesame oil, garlic, scallion, and chili powder (if using), and allow to stand for at least 1 hour. Pour some sauce in individual sauce dishes and garnish each serving with a sprinkle of toasted sesame seeds.

IN ADDITION to Chinese and Japanese soy sauces, there are two Korean types as well. The dark soy sauce, called *chin kanjang,* has a well-rounded flavor perfectly suited for marinating meats, and for making dressings like the one described in this recipe. The light soy sauce, called *kuk kanjang,* is saltier and reserved for flavoring soups. If you cannot find Korean soy sauce, the Japanese types are good substitutes. Use Japanese dark soy for everyday use, or marinating and cooking. Different brands of soy sauces—even when comparing dark to dark, or light to light—can vary in salt content. For this reason, it is important to taste before using. This will help you in determining final adjustments, such as whether the sauce requires additional sugar for balance.

GYEOJA
MUSTARD DIPPING SAUCE

MAKES ABOUT ½ CUP

⅓ cup CHINESE WHITE RICE
   VINEGAR
2 tablespoons GRANULATED SUGAR
1 teaspoon KOSHER SALT
¼ cup CHINESE HOT MUSTARD
   PASTE

THE KOREANS USE Chinese hot mustard to make this tangy and sweet mustard sauce. I have tried it when served with *kujolp'an*, nine-section dish five-color (see below), an elaborate plate with vibrantly colored foods such as shredded carrots, cucumber, shrimp, mushrooms, beef, watercress, egg yolks and whites (cooked separately), and little pancakes spread with a thin layer of this delicious mustard sauce. It gives the dish yet another layer of color, as well as a real flavor kick. Use it as a replacement for (or accompaniment to) chili paste when you would like a milder, less spicy but still pungent note.

If you cannot find Assi or Chinese Oriental Mascot brand Chinese hot mustard paste, combine 3 tablespoons Colman's English Mustard Powder with 1 tablespoon of water.

Whisk together the vinegar, sugar, and salt in a bowl until the sugar and salt have dissolved completely. Add the mustard and stir until well combined and smooth.

Kujolp'an for special occasions: Bring 1 quart water and 1 tablespoon kosher salt to a boil in a pot over high heat. Blanch 3 medium peeled carrots until just tender, about 5 minutes. Cut into 2-inch-long matchsticks. Remove the stems from 12 large fresh shiitake mushrooms and blanch the caps in the same pot, 1 to 2 minutes. Julienne. Boil 12 small to medium headless and shelled shrimp in the same pot, about 1 minute. Halve and devein. Separate 2 eggs. Lightly oil a nonstick pan set over medium heat. Make a yolk, then a white omelette (do not brown). Julienne. Peel 1 seedless cucumber and cut into 2-inch-long matchsticks. Prepare the spinach (or watercress) and mung bean sprouts (page 326) and *bulgogi* (page 480) recipes. Arrange all ingredients in individual piles on a platter, placing *gyeoja* in a cup, and 2½-inch-diameter Filipino or 24 Indonesian Lumpia Crêpes (page 256 or 257) in the center. Dab a crêpe with *gyeoja* and wrap a tiny amount of one or more items. Enjoy!

SUKAT BAWANG SAWSAWAN
GARLIC VINEGAR
DIPPING SAUCE

MAKES ABOUT ¾ CUP

½ cup COCONUT or CHINESE
   WHITE RICE VINEGAR, or
   CIDER VINEGAR
1 large GARLIC CLOVE, crushed,
   peeled, and minced
FISH SAUCE; or KOSHER SALT (if
   using cider vinegar)
Freshly ground BLACK PEPPER

CULTURALLY, THE FILIPINOS enjoy entertaining in large groups, and when I go to my sister-in-law Melinda's house, I am able to indulge in a wide variety of foods served buffet-style. Pork, beef, shrimp, fish, vegetables, noodles, and egg rolls abound, with all sorts of dipping sauces to accompany them. *Sukat bawang sawsawan*, vinegar and garlic sauce, is often drizzled over individual servings of food to counterbalance the fat in this often very rich cuisine. Sometimes fried egg rolls are dipped in the sauce as well, for the same reason. There are two ways to make the sauce: when using coconut or Chinese white rice vinegar, add *patis*, or fish sauce, to complement the tanginess; when using the fruity cider vinegar, use kosher salt instead. Both versions are delicious. *Sukat bawang sawsawan* keeps for several weeks when well refrigerated.

Mix the vinegar and garlic together in a bowl. Season to taste with fish sauce if using coconut rice vinegar, or kosher salt if using cider vinegar, and pepper. Let the ingredients steep together for at least 30 minutes before serving.

LUMPIA COCONUT VINEGAR DIPPING SAUCE

MAKES ABOUT 2 CUPS

2 tablespoons VEGETABLE OIL

2 large GARLIC CLOVES, crushed, peeled, and thinly sliced lengthwise

⅓ cup CHINESE LIGHT SOY SAUCE

⅓ cup COCONUT or CHINESE WHITE RICE VINEGAR

¼ cup DARK BROWN SUGAR

1 tablespoon TAPIOCA STARCH or CORNSTARCH

LUMPIA (pp. 276–77), fried egg rolls dipped in a sweet, sour, and salty lumpia sauce, are my young nephew Christopher's favorite Filipino food. When they're gone, he pleads "Why?" in desperation. Young or old, nearly everyone sneaks a taste of this thick brown sugar mixture, which my brother William, Christopher's father, describes as "plate-licking good."

1. Heat the oil in a saucepan over medium heat. Stir-fry the garlic until golden and crisp, about 3 minutes. Transfer the garlic to a paper towel–lined plate.

2. Off the heat, add 1 cup water, the soy sauce, vinegar, and brown sugar to the saucepan containing the garlic-flavored oil. Bring the mixture to a gentle boil over medium heat. Lower to a simmer and, stirring constantly, allow the sugar to melt completely, 3 to 5 minutes. Dilute the tapioca or cornstarch with 2 tablespoons water, and add to the saucepan in a steady stream while continuously stirring until the sauce thickens, about 1 minute. Transfer to a serving bowl, garnish with the fried garlic, and serve alongside the lumpia.

SAMBAL KACANG
INDONESIAN
PEANUT DIPPING SAUCE

MAKES ABOUT 2 CUPS

1 tablespoon VEGETABLE OIL

2 large GARLIC CLOVES, crushed, peeled, and minced

1 large SHALLOT, peeled and minced

1 cup roasted unsalted PEANUTS, finely ground (not peanut butter)

1 tablespoon INDONESIAN or THAI SHRIMP PASTE

1 tablespoon PALM SUGAR

3 tablespoons TAMARIND EXTRACT (page 75); or juice of 1 LIME

1 tablespoon INDONESIAN SWEET SOY SAUCE

1 or more teaspoons HOT CHILI POWDER

6 THAI BASIL LEAVES, minced

IN INDONESIA (and Malaysia, where the cuisine is very closely related), peanut sauce is called *sambal kacang* or *bumbu sate*. It is perhaps less herbally complex than Thai peanut sauce, but that is likely because Indonesian meats (e.g., ground duck satay, page 421) are already mixed with herbs. This sauce is also lighter than the Thai version because the coconut milk is omitted altogether. Its principal spicy note comes from ground dried chili peppers, and I recommend making your own chili powder for a fresher flavor.

Store-bought peanut butter is often margarine-based and contains a lot of salt. To obtain a more natural flavor, use unsalted roasted peanuts to make your own peanut butter or powder (for added texture) from scratch.

Heat the oil in a saucepan over medium heat and stir-fry the garlic and shallot until slightly golden, about 5 minutes. Add the peanuts, shrimp paste, and palm sugar and continue to stir-fry until the peanuts darken and release some of their natural oil, about 5 minutes more. Add 1 cup water, the tamarind extract, soy sauce, chili powder, and basil, and continue to boil gently until reduced and thickened, about 20 minutes. Allow to cool, and process in a food processor to a smooth paste.

NAM JIM SATE
THAI PEANUT
DIPPING SAUCE

MAKES ABOUT 2 CUPS

1 tablespoon VEGETABLE OIL

1 to 1½ tablespoons THAI RED CURRY PASTE (page 82); or commercial equivalent

1 tablespoon THAI or INDONESIAN SHRIMP PASTE

2 tablespoons PALM SUGAR

1 cup roasted unsalted PEANUTS, finely ground (not peanut butter)

1 cup unsweetened COCONUT MILK (page 77); or commercial equivalent

3 tablespoons TAMARIND EXTRACT (page 75); or juice of 1 LIME

6 THAI BASIL LEAVES, minced

IT IS PROBABLY fair to say that the Thai are responsible for popularizing satay in the West. While this peanut sauce, or *nam jim sate*, served as an accompaniment to grilled meats, *sate* is very popular in Thailand, the dish satay (i.e., peanut sauce and grilled meats) is popular all over Southeast Asia. What makes this recipe specifically Thai is the use of red curry paste, which lends not only heat but a complex herbal note to the sauce.

Heat the oil in a saucepan over medium heat and stir-fry the curry paste until fragrant, about 2 minutes. Add the shrimp paste and palm sugar, and continue to stir-fry until the shrimp paste slightly darkens and the palm sugar has melted, about 1 minute. Add the peanuts and stir, roasting until slightly darkened, about 2 minutes. Add the coconut milk and tamarind extract or lime juice, and basil, and stir until combined thoroughly. Continue to gently boil until reduced by a third and thickened, about 20 minutes.

Sate: Combine 1½ cups fresh coconut milk (page 77; or commercial equivalent) with ¼ teaspoon turmeric powder and 1 teaspoon fish sauce. Marinate 1 to 1½ pounds thinly sliced beef sirloin or filet mignon, pork tenderloin, or chicken breast. Thread 2 pieces on each of 24 soaked bamboo skewers and grill. If grilling indoors, oil a grill pan and set it over high heat for searing. If grilling outdoors, be sure to wait until the flames have subsided and you have a nice bed of embers. Grill meats until crispy on the edges but still tender on the inside, 1 to 2 minutes per side.

NUOC CHAM DAU PHONG
VIETNAMESE PEANUT
DIPPING SAUCE

MAKES ABOUT 2 CUPS

1 tablespoon VEGETABLE OIL

2 large GARLIC CLOVES, crushed, peeled, and minced

½ cup roasted unsalted PEANUTS, finely ground (not peanut butter) plus 1 tablespoon crushed PEANUTS

1 cup BASIC CHICKEN STOCK (page 116)

½ cup unsweetened COCONUT MILK (page 77); or commercial equivalent

2 tablespoons TAMARIND EXTRACT (page 75); or juice of 1 LIME

2 tablespoons FISH SAUCE

1½ tablespoons HOISIN SAUCE

2 tablespoons PALM SUGAR

2 THAI CHILIES, stemmed, seeded, and minced

¼ cup minced CILANTRO LEAVES

IN VIETNAM, *nuoc cham dau phong*, peanut sauce, is perhaps the lightest I've ever tasted and is delicious with *goi cuon*, summer rolls (pp. 286–87). The secret is chicken stock; it enriches the flavor while lightening the sauce. Palm sugar, hoisin sauce (a Chinese sweet and salty bean paste), fish sauce, and lime juice create a wonderful medley of sweet, salty, sour, and bitter notes, while fresh red chilies lift the palate with their fiery hot character. A small amount of coconut milk rounds out the flavors.

Heat the oil in a saucepan over medium heat and stir-fry the garlic until slightly golden, about 3 minutes. Add the ground peanuts and continue to stir-fry until they darken and release some of their natural oil, about 3 minutes more. Add the chicken stock, coconut milk, tamarind extract, fish sauce, hoisin sauce, palm sugar, and chilies, and continue to gently boil until reduced and thickened, about 20 minutes. Stir in the cilantro, transfer to a dish (or individual ones) and sprinkle with crushed peanuts.

NUOC CHAM
SPICY, SWEET, AND SOUR FISH SAUCE DIP

½ cup GRANULATED SUGAR

¾ cup FISH SAUCE

1 cup LIME or LEMON JUICE (about 3 LIMES or 2 LEMONS)

2 large GARLIC CLOVES, crushed, peeled, and sliced or minced

2 or more THAI CHILIES, stemmed, seeded, and sliced or minced

¼ cup roasted unsalted PEANUTS, finely crushed (optional)

1 large CARROT, peeled and julienned (optional)

NUOC CHAM (also *nuoc mam cham*), a clear, light dipping sauce, is the most important table condiment of Vietnam. It combines fish sauce, lime or lemon juice, garlic, chilies, and sugar in perfect harmony. Its refreshing sweet and spicy character complements dozens of foods, ranging from a simple bowl of rice, which is transformed when drizzled with *nuoc cham*, to a myriad of grilled and deep-fried foods, including grilled lemongrass shrimp (page 223) and spring rolls (pp. 284–85). In Cambodia, where the sauce is called *tuk trey* (also the generic name for the bottled plain fish sauce), it commonly accompanies fried fish (page 394) and a Cambodian version of Vietnamese summer rolls (pp. 286–87).

The northern Vietnamese like their food mild, so they slice the garlic and chili to produce less dominant flavors. The southerners prefer their garlic and chili minced, yielding a more pronounced flavor. The Cambodians like to add crushed peanuts to their sauce for a richer flavor. In the West, Vietnamese restaurants often serve *nuoc cham* with julienned carrots, a way to further sweeten the sauce and give it additional color and texture.

Whisk together the sugar, fish sauce, ⅓ cup water (or more depending on how strong the fish sauce is), and the lime or lemon juice in a bowl until the sugar is completely dissolved. Add the garlic and chili, and let stand for 30 minutes to allow the flavors to come together. Sprinkle with crushed peanuts (if using), or julienned carrot (if using), just before serving.

RADISH AND
GINGER SALAD DRESSING

MAKES ABOUT ¾ CUP

3 tablespoons JAPANESE SEASONED
RICE VINEGAR

2 tablespoons MIRIN

2 tablespoons JAPANESE DARK SOY
SAUCE

2 tablespoons VEGETABLE OIL

½ teaspoon SESAME OIL

1 tablespoon finely grated DAIKON

1 tablespoon finely grated CARROT

1 tablespoon finely grated fresh
GINGER; or 1 to 2 teaspoons
ginger extract (page 74)

1 SCALLION, root and dark green
ends trimmed, and 6-inch stalk
minced

Freshly ground BLACK PEPPER

I ORIGINALLY CAME UP with this dressing at home one summer while serving *yakitori*, grilled chicken (page 493), over a shiitake and *soba* noodle stir-fry (page 248). Since then I have taken to using it as a salad dressing in response to a pet peeve of mine concerning Japanese restaurant salads, which are regularly offered with a mayonnaise-based dressing. A poorly conceived gesture toward what is assumed to be the Western palate, the use of mayonnaise is inappropriately heavy for the delicate raw fish items that often follow. The delicacy of this recipe is more consistent with traditional Japanese cooking technique and culinary philosophy. It more naturally lends itself to raw vegetables: grated radish (or daikon) and ginger give texture and flavor; grated carrot gives sweetness and vibrant color. You can also use this as a table condiment at any Japanese meal where such accompaniments are appropriate.

Whisk together the vinegar, mirin, soy sauce, and vegetable and sesame oils until well combined. Stir in the daikon, carrot, ginger, and scallion. Season with pepper to taste and toss with fresh mesclun or any tender lettuce leaves.

GOMA DARE
SESAME DRESSING

MAKES ABOUT ¾ CUP

¼ cup KELP DASHI (pp. 124–25)

3 tablespoons MIRIN

2 tablespoons JAPANESE DARK SOY
SAUCE

2 teaspoons GRANULATED SUGAR

2 tablespoons SESAME PASTE

1 tablespoon SHIROMISO

1 teaspoon WASABI PASTE

SESAME PASTE is used to create delicious Asian sweet dumpling fillings. Yielding a nutty flavor when roasted, both blond and black sesame pastes are similar in flavor, the colors being derived from the different variety of seeds. Blond sesame seeds are toasted and ground to a paste, and used for flavoring noodle dishes such as Shanghainese cold noodles (page 234), or to make this classic Japanese dressing, which can be used on many foods. I like to toss boiled string beans with this dressing, as they were once served to me in Kyoto, but I have also drizzled it over seared tuna served on top of mesclun greens, for example. While it's not traditional, I love to add shiromiso—literally "white miso" (which is actually yellow)—for a richer flavor. The addition of wasabi—a.k.a. Japanese horseradish or green mustard—makes for a spicy finishing touch.

Sesame paste can be purchased in Asian or Middle Eastern markets, or you can make your own by grinding lightly toasted sesame seeds. Walnuts, hazelnuts, and peanuts can be substituted for sesame seeds for interesting variations on a theme.

Whisk together the dashi, mirin, soy sauce, and sugar in a bowl until the sugar is completely dissolved. Stir in the sesame, shiromiso, and wasabi pastes until well combined and smooth. Keeps well refrigerated, but it's best when freshly made.

DRY SALT DIPS

MAKES UP TO ½ CUP

¼ cup freshly ground SEA SALT (or
  KOSHER SALT)

1½ teaspoons FIVE-SPICE POWDER
  or

2 teaspoons DRIED RED CHILI
  POWDER or

2 tablespoons freshly ground
  BLACK PEPPER

D RY SALT DIPS are commonly used as last-minute seasonings at the table in Chinese and Vietnamese cuisines. They accompany roasted, grilled, or braised poultry or meat dishes and are used to heighten flavors. Chinese roasted squab is sometimes accompanied by a five-spice and salt mixture, while Vietnamese spicy beef stew is deliciously enhanced with a chili-salt dip. Salt and pepper combined in equal amounts make for deliciously well-seasoned deep-fried prawns or squid pieces. Serve about a tablespoon of your preferred flavored salt in individual sauce dishes.

Mix together the salt with either the five-spice powder, chili, or black pepper. Divide among 4 sauce dishes.

SEA SALT is all I use in cooking, no matter what cuisine I cook. *Sel de Guérande* and *fleur de sel* (coarse sea salts and fine sea salts from France's northern Brittany) are moist, less sharp, and more delicate than regular salts. Colored grayish-green by seaweed, they are full of the taste of the sea. French salts are very expensive; a one-pound bag can cost ten to fifteen dollars.

Natural coarse sea salt is also popular in Asian cuisines, and you will have no trouble finding it in Chinese, Korean, and Japanese markets. Asian sea salts are generally less perfectly produced and packaged than French. They have crystals of uneven size and cost five dollars or less for one pound. It is true that the French versions have more seaweed flavor than the Asian versions, but in Asian cooking, where soy sauce or fish sauce is added to most dishes, there is no particular need for such refined salts.

In this book I have called for kosher salt throughout because it is readily available. Feel free to experiment with different salts.

GINGER AND SCALLION SALT DIPPING SAUCE

4 ounces fresh GINGER, peeled and finely grated

12 SCALLIONS, root and dark green ends trimmed, and 6-inch stalks minced

1 tablespoon KOSHER SALT

½ cup VEGETABLE OIL

HEALTHY, SIMPLE, REFRESHING, and delicious is the best way to describe this salty ginger and scallion condiment. I steam or boil unseasoned chicken, cut it up in chunks, and present this sauce as an accompaniment. Just a dab or two makes the food come alive with refreshing, pungent flavors. Served with fragrant jasmine rice, it is a light meal perfect for spring and summer and has been enjoyed this way in traditional Chinese and Vietnamese cuisines for hundreds of years.

Stir together the ginger, scallions, and salt until well combined. Place in a jar and pour the oil on top. Press the ingredients down with the back of a spoon, submerging them in the oil. This mixture keeps about 1 week refrigerated, but is best when consumed freshly made.

Variation: Substitute a tablespoon of fish sauce and a teaspoon of sugar for the salt. You can also add a peeled and minced large garlic clove to the dip for extra flavor.

WALKING DOWN THE STREETS of New York City's Chinatown, my eyes wander from restaurant window to restaurant window. Hanging on hooks are many delicious items, from crispy baby pigs, to roasted ducks and pork butt, to soy sauce chickens, and boiled chickens, too. One of my favorite things to have for lunch is a pile of jasmine rice topped with cut-up boiled chicken served with the delicious thick ginger and scallion salt dip. A dab or two on a piece of chicken breast or thigh, and the boiled meat becomes extraordinary, so simple yet so rich with flavor. Those are the times when I think: so little time for such a great reward.

CH'O KOCH'UJANG
SWEET AND SOUR
CHILI DIPPING SAUCE

MAKES ABOUT 1 CUP

½ cup KOREAN HOT CHILI AND
   BEAN PASTE
¼ cup HONEY
3 tablespoons CHINESE WHITE
   RICE VINEGAR

MY FAVORITE KOREAN chili sauce is this sweet and tangy version, often used for dipping thinly sliced raw fish or grilled meats, or adding to marinades and braised dishes. I have also served it as a condiment for simple pan-fried tofu, which works exceedingly well. You can make a large batch; refrigerated, it will keep for several weeks. I generally make a full cup at a time and use it up over the course of a month or so. The core ingredient, Korean hot chili and bean paste (chilies, bean paste, wheat flour, and salt), can be purchased in Korean markets or through mail-order sources. Choripdong is an excellent brand.

Stir together the chili paste, honey, and vinegar until thoroughly combined. Transfer to a jar and refrigerate up to a month.

SAMBAL OLEK
CHILI AND GARLIC SAUCE

MAKES ABOUT 1 CUP

⅓ cup VEGETABLE OIL
6 to 8 large GARLIC CLOVES,
  crushed, peeled, and minced
2 cups RED THAI CHILIES,
  stemmed, seeded (optional),
  and minced
1 teaspoon KOSHER SALT

IMPORTED FROM ALL OVER Asia, there are dozens of commercially available chili and garlic sauces or pastes. Marketed as *sambal olek* in Indonesia, *sriracha* in Thailand, *tuong ot toi* in Vietnam (look for these national names on Chinese-character-labeled bottles as a key), it can be loose, thick, chunky, or smooth. Some are fried and preserved in oil, others are preserved using salt and vinegar (see variation). The Chinese, in particular, sometimes include fermented soybeans for a deeper flavor. This is a version I like to make for a table condiment, but it can also be added to marinades, pastes, braised dishes, stir-fries, and so forth if you like a spicy note in your food.

You can use this sauce for both Chinese and Southeast Asian foods in general. As composed here, it is very spicy. To make it less so, simply remove the seeds from the chilies.

Heat the oil in a wok or pan over medium heat. Stir-fry the garlic until golden and fragrant, about 3 minutes. Add the chilies and continue to stir-fry until fragrant, about 3 minutes more. Transfer the sauce to a heat-proof jar and allow to cool completely. At this time puree it in a blender if you want a smooth texture. Keep refrigerated.

Variation: Salt and vinegar are great preservatives. Rather than fry the chili and garlic paste, put it in a blender and grind with 1 to 1½ teaspoons kosher salt and ¼ cup white rice vinegar. Transfer the sauce to a jar and refrigerate.

NAM PRIK POW
FRIED BLACK CHILI SAUCE

MAKES ABOUT 1 CUP

¼ cup dried SHRIMP

½ cup VEGETABLE OIL

6 large GARLIC CLOVES, crushed, peeled, and minced

4 large SHALLOTS, peeled and minced

12 or more dried RED CHILI PEPPERS, stemmed, seeded, and finely chopped

2 tablespoons THAI or INDONESIAN SHRIMP PASTE

2 to 3 tablespoons PALM SUGAR

ONE OF MY FAVORITE Thai soups is *tom yam gung*, spicy shrimp soup (page 134), and the reason lies in the use of this fried chili sauce, called *nam prik pow*. A mixture of dried shrimp, shrimp paste, garlic, shallots, and dried chilies, it gives deep spicy, salty, sweet, bitter notes and fermented character to the soup. Because it is very spicy, however, it is often served as a table condiment with the soup, so your guests can add just the amount they wish to their individual bowls. When frying the ingredients, be sure they darken in the pan. Unlike many other fried ingredients in Asian cooking, here you are not looking for a light golden color, but a brown to dark brown color. This sauce can also be used as a dipping sauce for simply prepared—grilled, roasted, or broiled—seafood or meat dishes. But I must admit that it is best in soups with a sour note, such as *tom yam gung*, or the Cambodian-Vietnamese sour fish soup (page 131). I also like it with Chinese or Southeast Asian noodle soups.

You can remove any seeds from the dried chilies if you prefer a less spicy sauce.

Soak the dried shrimp in water to cover for 20 minutes to soften them and get rid of any excess salt. Drain and mince. Heat the oil in a wok or saucepan over medium heat. Stir-fry the garlic and shallots until fragrant, about 3 minutes. Add the chilies, dried shrimp, shrimp paste, and palm sugar and continue to stir-fry until brown, about 5 minutes. Remove from heat, transfer to a heatproof jar, allow to cool completely, and refrigerate.

FRIED GINGER, SCALLIONS, SHALLOTS, OR GARLIC

S ½ TO 1 CUP

1 cup VEGETABLE OIL

4 ounces fresh GINGER, peeled and julienned very finely lengthwise or

12 SCALLIONS, root and dark green ends trimmed, and 6-inch stalks julienned very finely into 1½- to 2-inch-long strands or

12 large SHALLOTS, peeled and thinly sliced

G INGER AND SCALLIONS are some of my favorite garnishes for Asian food. Deep-fried, they not only lend a crunch, but a refreshingly sweet and mild herbal note to any food, especially at the finish. A welcome garnish for foods ranging from a simple pan-fried tofu to grilled sardines, these delicious crispy threads, vibrantly golden yellow and green, also add to the visual impact of your table. Fried shallots are added to Southeast Asian foods for the sweet note they add to all sorts of grilled meats and noodle soups. Garlic or scallion oil is also very popular as a fragrant garnish (see variation).

You can deep-fry cilantro, Thai basil, and all sorts of herbs in the same manner. Leeks are a delicious substitute for scallions. Reserve the fragrant oils in separate jars to use in stir-fries.

Heat the oil in a small pot over medium heat. When the temperature reaches 360° to 375°F, deep-fry either the ginger, scallions, or shallots until golden, not brown, about 3 to 5 minutes. Drain on a paper towel–lined plate. Transfer the solids to a glass jar and refrigerate for up to 3 weeks. (Reserve the oil for stir-frying.)

Variation: To make garlic or scallion oil, heat ½ cup vegetable oil over medium heat. Meanwhile, thinly slice 12 trimmed scallions or mince 12 large peeled garlic cloves. Add either the scallions or garlic to the hot oil and fry until golden (not brown), 3 to 5 minutes. Transfer the scallions or garlic with the frying oil to a heatproof jar. Allow to cool, then refrigerate. This keeps well for up to 3 weeks.

IN PREPARING FRIED GINGER, scallions, shallots, or garlic, all should be crispy, but this does not mean that the darker they are the crispier they will be. If fried until too dark they will turn bitter. The ginger should look like curled-up gold threads, while the scallion should retain its light green color with golden stains here and there. The shallots and garlic should be golden. As with anything that is fried, you should keep a close eye on them. The delicate strands and slices can go dark rather quickly, and you will want to catch them before it is too late.

FRIED TARO CUPS

MAKES 2 TO 4 CUPS

VEGETABLE OIL for deep-frying
2 cups finely shredded or julienned
TARO ROOT

DEEP-FRIED TARO CUPS are often used in Chinese restaurants to serve stir-fried seafoods and vegetables. Consider making them at home, as they are surprisingly easy to prepare and will lend a festive elegance to any stir-fry. You will need two sieves shaped like deep bowls; one needs to fit into the other perfectly, forming a sort of mold. Depending on the size of the sieves, you can make 2 to 4 fried taro cups.

Heat enough vegetable oil for deep-frying in a pot over medium-high heat until it reaches a temperature of 360° to 375°F. Meanwhile, scatter ¼ to ½ of the taro in one of the sieves, spreading it around in a single layer on the inside of the sieve. Place the other sieve so it sits perfectly on top of the scattered taro. (This will prevent the taro from coming up to the surface and floating.) Lower the two sieves with taro sandwiched in between into the hot oil and deep-fry until golden and crisp, about 5 minutes. Remove the taro cup from between the sieves and drain it on a paper towel–lined plate. Repeat the process with the remaining taro.

Variation: Many starchy root vegetables (potatoes and carrots, for example) will work for making cups. Feel free to experiment. You may just decide that the orange color of carrots will make your dish look even more beautiful than a yellowish-white potato.

2

STOCKS,
PALATE
CLEANSERS,
AND STARTER
SOUPS

MAKING A STOCK or broth is fundamental to Asian cooking. A culinary building block in the preparation of many meals, the simplest stock can be the basis for anything from a palate cleanser to an elaborate dish. Asian stocks are not flavor-neutral liquids; they are subtle, well-structured, complex flavor enhancers for stews, stir-fries, sauces, and, of course, soups. While bones, fat, meat, ginger, scallion, onion, and often some sort of radish to gather impurities are at the base of any good Asian meat stock, the variations possible within it and ornaments to it are numerous.

The predominant use of stocks in cooking is, of course, not peculiar to Asia. Wherever there exist highly developed food cultures, a deep understanding of stock as a culinary

building block is present. In France, for example, cooks will reduce a completed stock, achieving a more concentrated liquid called demi-glace or fond, which is used to create rich sauces. The northern Italians use stock to cook the classic rice dish called risotto. Traditional North African cuisines use stocks to create some of the most delicious stewed vegetable and meat dishes. A Moroccan friend demonstrated to me that steaming couscous the traditional way, i.e., over a rich stock, gave her couscous an extra layer of subtle flavor. The way to think of stocks in Asia, however, is to take these examples and imagine a much deeper and broader pattern of use.

Stocks are easy to make if you have patience. Patience is key because the ingredients must simmer, not boil, so that the water can absorb the essence of each ingredient slowly, creating a clear and intensely flavored liquid. A good time to make stock is when you have to be in or near the kitchen for two to three hours, and you have a free burner. If you come home from work and put all your ingredients in a pot, you can make a rich, flavorful stock before you go to bed. Remember that the preparation of stocks evolved in cultures where

cooks could be in the general vicinity of a simmering pot while performing other tasks. This means that while the cooking takes a bit of time, the actual preparation time is only 20 to 30 minutes, plus a few moments for skimming and perhaps adjusting the heat. Strain the stock when it has reduced, and you are done. Time actively expended making the stock is about equal to the time it would take you to go buy canned stock.

You can keep stock in the refrigerator for 3 days, after which it is a very good idea to boil it every other day for up to a week. When I freeze my stock I generally do not keep it more than 3 months (if it lasts that long!). Stocks are also a wonderful way to make use of the extra ingredients you didn't have a chance to cook. Rather than let them go to waste, get creative and make a stock based on my basic vegetable stock recipe (page 126), for example. Stocks are also wonderful "instant warm-ups" during the winter. Heat some up and pour it into mugs. It is always appreciated on cold days.

A word on canned stocks: I recommend that whenever possible you avoid the use of canned stocks in Asian cooking. Most commercially available stocks are Western rather than Asian in style as well as being overly salty. It is also important that you have the ability to flavor your own stocks. Ginger, scallion, and soy or fish sauce, for example, would never be flavoring agents in canned stock, but you need them for a basic Asian stock.

Stocks have long been a favorite among the Chinese and their Asian neighbors. Clear soups (meaning free of rice or noodles) are the most common in Asian cooking and can complement numerous dishes, especially when they are of the lighter, clear broth variety. Their role is to cleanse the palate, provide a different texture, and round out the five flavor notes—salty, sweet, sour, bitter, and spicy—at any given meal. Also all five flavor elements may be present within the stock. They act as a buffer to rich foods, cutting grease, washing down bites of rice and other food tidbits. They also warm the body on a cold day, and if spicy—as they often are in South and Southeast Asian climates—help cool it on warm days.

Palate cleansers are the simplest of all Asian soups. They consist of a clear broth and small amounts of chunky ingredients. Like *trou Normand* or sorbets in Western meals, they serve to refresh the senses and aid digestion. However, Asian palate cleansers are not presented at specific moments in the meal and are not necessarily meant to be consumed all at once. Rather they are sipped throughout the meal, often serving as the only drink at the table. They are served in individual or large communal bowls. Some of my favorites are winter melon and Yunnan ham soup (page 143), my Chinese grandmother's cure-all pork and cilantro soup (page 145), and Korean *kimchi* and tofu soup (page 130). The chunky bits are fun to nibble on between rich courses and give texture to the meal.

In Southeast Asia, there exist "sour soups," as they are often referred to generically. These have distinctive sour notes, from the assertive use of tamarind extract (page 75), lime juice, or other souring agents. *Kamias*, a small lime-green elongated fruit that grows exclusively in the Philippines and is related to and resembles *carambola* (star fruit), is used in Filipino soup cookery. Found in *sinigang*, a Filipino national dish, it is the basis for this sour soup. *Sinigang* can be made with one of several stocks and include a wide array of vegetables or meats.

In Bicol, where they love their foods spicy and rich, hot chilies and coconut milk are added for a delicious *sinigang na isda*, a fish version of the soup (pp. 146–47). In Cambodia and Vietnam, fish and pineapple soup (page 131) soured with lime juice or tamarind extract is absolutely delicious, balanced, as it often is, with just enough heat from a few chilies. Thailand's most famous sour soup is *tom yam gung* (page 134), a spicy shrimp soup also flavored with tamarind extract. In general, the farther south you go, and the more tropical the climate, the more pronounced tangy and spicy elements in the food. In contrast, food in China, Korea, and Japan does not have these intense combinations. Even the Chinese soup known as "hot and sour soup" is more evenly balanced among the five notes (and not particularly sour) in comparison to Southeast Asian sour soups.

Bitter soups are also appreciated in Asian cuisine, although the uninitiated may find they need a little getting used to. In China, bitter melon (also bitter gourd) is eaten primarily for its medicinal properties. Containing quinine, it is believed to strengthen the immune system. (Think a bitter lemon carbonated drink without the sweeteners and carbonation.) The Chinese,

Filipinos, and Vietnamese like to add it to pork broths, stir-fries, and steamed or braised dishes. Other types of bitter soups include Cambodian duck and preserved-lime soup (pp. 140–41), and Korean chicken and ginseng soup (pp. 198–99). Both delicious, they have a cooling effect. Other bitter notes come from the use of fresh herbs, which have both a refreshing character and a subtle bitterness (some more than others). Kaffir lime leaves, used to flavor Thai curried noodle soup (pp. 240–41), are a wonderful example of that pleasant bitter note. Soups also get their bitter undertones from ginger, galangal, and lime (also a souring agent).

Examples of hearty soups, not as brothy but rather full of chunky bits, are Cambodian spicy beef soup (pp. 150–51), and Indonesian chicken and fried potato soup (pp. 136–37). Just shy of stews in texture, they are often meant to be had as complete meals, with a bowl of rice as an accompaniment. These are occasionally thickened with tapioca starch or cornstarch. The most famous is Chinese *suen lat tong*, hot and sour soup (page 127), a Szechwanese specialty. A classic, it has been made popular in the United States through its being offered as a starter in Chi-

nese-American restaurants. A somewhat Americanized version of a Cantonese classic, wonton soup ("Rice, Noodles, Dumplings, and Bread" chapter, pp. 266–67), is equally familiar in the West. Asian soups are never thickened with cream but with starch. Vietnamese crab and asparagus soup (pp. 132–33) is another starch-thickened soup, essentially an interpretation of the French *velouté d'asperges*, but without the cream. (Centuries of living without a major dairy presence have left their culinary mark.) Sweet soups served as snacks tend to be on the thick side as well. Some examples are banana coconut soup (page 517) with tapioca, which is served not only in China but Southeast Asia in general, and legume soups such as Chinese, Korean, and Japanese red bean soup (page 514) and Vietnamese mung bean soup (page 516). These are covered in the "Sweets and Drinks" chapter (page 508).

Many Asian soups have a certain amount of fat. Western cooks, especially in contemporary practice, have an obsession with removing all fat from stocks. In Chinese cookery, however, a layer of glistening fat in a soup, or on any food, is perceived to both add flavor and keep the food hot. When I skim, I judge the

amount of fat left in by the stock's intended use, the season (more during cold winters, less in other seasons), and the guests who will be enjoying the meal.

Serving the soup in an Asian bowl as opposed to a Western-style shallow plate keeps it hot. And I like my soup piping hot. (This is partially personal preference and partially tradition. Heat, as in body heat, is associated with life in Chinese culture.)

Echoes of traditional, family-style meals are seen in the serving of soups in Chinese restaurants where soups are most often brought to the table in a large bowl, then dispensed into individual serving bowls. This tradition reflects the serving of soups in a communal bowl at home: soup is placed at the center of the table with all the other dishes, then taken from the bowl and sipped one little ceramic spoonful at a time. My family still serves special soups this way at festive holiday meals.

Soups play a great part in the most important of all festive meals, Chinese New Year. Generally considered the most important holiday in China and Vietnam, and other parts of Asia, it involves three or more days of feasting. Based on the lunar New Year, it is usually celebrated in either January or February. The Chinese hot pot, *da bin low* (pp. 156–57), is set at the center of the table. Looking like a very large fondue pot—with charcoal (traditionally) or an electric heating element (modern times)—the hot pot vessel contains a simmering ginger-infused chicken broth. Filled with fragrant shiitake mushrooms and greens such as bok choy, napa cabbage, or spinach, the pot is visited again and again by chopstick-wielding diners; each guest cooks raw slices of beef, chicken, shrimp, and fish. The cooked morsels are dipped in condiments such as salty soy and oyster sauces; nutty sesame oil, spicy chili-garlic paste, and sweet hoisin sauce. After all the morsels are gone, cellophane noodles are cooked in the pot, retrieved with some of the very flavorful broth, and enjoyed as the grand finale. This soup ritual is at the core of family and friends sharing a holiday season, reconnecting in a time of renewal. In my family it has traditionally been served on the holiday eve and the first day of the New Year. My husband has grown quite accustomed to the flavors, craving them every once in a while, whether or not it is the New Year.

Similar to the Chinese holiday hot pot is the Japanese dish, or "dipping soup," called *shabu-shabu* (page 160). Tender marbled beef, along with fresh shiitake mushrooms, napa cabbage, and tofu are cooked in the broth, and dipped in *ponzu* sauce (page 90) or sesame dressing (page 102) before eating. In Vietnam, beef is cooked in the same fashion but in a vinegary broth. All these "dipping soups" derive from the Mongolian idea of dipping thinly sliced meats (the Mongols most likely used goat or mutton) and vegetables into a vessel of simmering broth, a practice that evolved in the central northern high plateaus over four hundred years ago.

In this chapter I have focused on a few basic stocks—vegetable, seafood, chicken, pork, and beef—as well as a selection of my favorite palate cleansers and starter soups. I have kept things simple on purpose, allowing for seasoning and spicing the basics to the specifics of any recipe. The beef stock described below, for example, is simply seasoned with salt and pepper and flavored with ginger and onions. By adjusting the seasoning, it can be used to make the Cambodian spicy beef soup or the Korean beef soup. I have also included a few special or more specific stocks, such as Japanese *dashi* (sea vegetable stock), Chinese superior stock, or Southeast Asian beef stock. One stock I always try to have on hand is chicken, because it is light and the most popular stock used in Asia. When I make it, I generally have two stockpots going at the same time, giving me large batches I can store. My personal "stock ritual" is to divide the stock into several one-quart containers and refrigerate some while I keep the rest in the freezer for later use.

BASIC CHICKEN STOCK

MAKES 3 TO 3½ QUARTS

1½ to 2 pounds meaty CHICKEN
BONES, such as carcass, neck,
and wings

2 to 3 ounces fresh GINGER, thinly
sliced lengthwise

5 SCALLIONS, root and dark green
ends trimmed, and 6-inch stalks
halved crosswise and lightly
crushed

1 large YELLOW ONION, peeled

1 teaspoon WHITE or BLACK
PEPPERCORNS

KOSHER SALT

THIS CHICKEN STOCK can be used as a base for several Asian soups.
When making chicken stock use meaty bones. Although some butchers will sell you bones for making stock, I like to buy a whole
chicken, remove and reserve the breast and legs for another use, then make
the stock with the remaining carcass. Because there is enough fat in the
meaty bones, there is no need for the skin, which only adds unnecessary fat
and minimal flavor. When choosing a bird, make sure it is 3 to 3½ pounds so
you get a good amount of meaty bones. Note that Asian stocks are not as
concentrated as French stocks; they are generally more delicate while being
very flavorful. Season lightly so you can augment the seasoning in the recipes
you choose later on.

1. Place the chicken bones in a
stockpot and cover with 5 quarts
water. Add the ginger, scallions,
onion, and peppercorns, and bring
to a boil over high heat. Skim off the
foam, reduce the heat to medium-
low, and season with salt. Simmer,
uncovered, occasionally skimming
off any foam, until the stock is reduced by about 2 quarts, about 3
hours. At this time skim off as much
fat as you desire.

2. Strain the stock, discard the
solids, and use according to the
recipe of your choice. The stock can
be kept up to 3 days in the refrigerator or 3 months in the freezer.

I AM VERY PARTICULAR about my
stocks. Late one winter's evening,
when I first started cooking for my
husband before we were married, I
wanted to make a beautiful dish that
begins with chicken stock. He proudly
reached into his bachelor's pantry and
produced a can of stock, saying, "Just
use this." I explained that the meal—a
very special rice noodle soup with
chicken, dried shrimp, and Asian
greens (pp. 226–27)—was best cooked
with freshly made stock. "The final results rely on the quality of the stock," I
explained. "We need a fresh bird for
the stock." He was a little taken aback.
In fairness, I was sending him into the
snowy dark of night for a chicken. After
a bit of prodding, he went, returning
about a half hour later with the bird. I
prepared my noodle soup and offered it
to him, asking, "Do you taste the difference between canned and freshly made
stock?" Sipping the broth, then pausing
a moment, he smiled and said, "It's day
and night."

SUPERIOR STOCK

MAKES 3 TO 3½ QUARTS

1 to 1½ pounds meaty CHICKEN
BONES, such as the carcass, neck,
and wings

6 ounces SMITHFIELD HAM, thinly
sliced

1 pound lean PORK RIBS

2 to 3 ounces fresh GINGER, thinly
sliced lengthwise

5 SCALLIONS, root and dark green
ends trimmed, and 6-inch stalks
halved crosswise and lightly
crushed

1 large YELLOW ONION, peeled

8 ounces DAIKON, peeled and cut
into 1-inch-thick slices

1 teaspoon WHITE or BLACK
PEPPERCORNS

KOSHER SALT

I N CHINA, superior stock is made for heartier, often more expensive soups such as shark's fin or snake soup. Although Yunnan ham is popular in China, you will more readily find Smithfield ham from Virginia, which is a close cousin, in many Chinese butcher shops or supermarkets in the form of a whole ham or shoulder, or vacuum-packed thick slices. The ham can be shredded and added to soups such as the winter melon and ham soup (page 143), or added to stir-fries for a wonderfully salty note, or steamed with fish (pp. 388–89). Before using this very salty meat in a recipe you must first rinse it well, then place it in a large container and cover it with water. For a shoulder, allow it to soak for twenty-four hours. Change the water, allow it to soak for another twenty-four hours, then drain. (This is absolutely necessary to get rid of the heavy salt content.) Once soaked, the skin and meat are softened, making slicing much easier. I generally buy a whole shoulder, which is about half the size of the whole ham and small enough so that it easily fits in my refrigerator. After each use be sure to wrap the ham in a clean cotton kitchen towel and refrigerate it—a good way to keep it nice and fresh. One shoulder will last at least three months.

1. Place the chicken bones, ham, and pork ribs in a stockpot and cover with 5 quarts water. Add the ginger, scallions, onion, daikon, and peppercorns, and bring to a boil over high heat. Skim off the foam, reduce the heat to medium-low, and season with salt (sparingly; you already have the ham). Simmer, uncovered, occasionally skimming off any foam, until the stock is reduced by about 2 quarts, about 3 hours. At this time skim off as much fat as you desire.

2. Strain the stock, discard the solids, and use according to the recipe of your choice. The stock can be kept up to 3 days in the refrigerator or 3 months in the freezer.

Variation: If you don't have the time to soak the ham overnight, buy a thick slice of ham, which is usually vacuum packed. Bring a pot of water to a boil and blanch the ham slice to get rid of the excess salt, 10 to 15 minutes. Drain the ham and slice it thinly crosswise. Use the ham as directed in the recipe of your choice. I've also made this soup using 3 air-cured duck legs, which are available at Chinese butcher shops. Mildly sweet and salty, these do not require soaking prior to making the stock.

BASIC PORK STOCK

MAKES 3 TO 3½ QUARTS

2 to 2½ pounds meaty PORK RIBS

8 ounces DAIKON, peeled and cut
into 1-inch rounds

2 to 3 ounces fresh GINGER, thinly
sliced lengthwise

5 SCALLIONS, root and dark green
ends trimmed, and 6-inch stalks
halved crosswise and lightly
crushed

1 large YELLOW ONION, peeled

1 teaspoon WHITE or BLACK
PEPPERCORNS

KOSHER SALT

PORK RIBS are the best for making this stock, allowing a flavorful balance between meat, fat, and bone. The fat is skimmed off at the end when the stock has finished reducing. Daikon is used much like an egg-white raft is used to clear French stock, gathering any foam, odd bits, or other impurities that have floated to the surface. The daikon not only helps to clarify the stock, it also imparts a nice earthy note that rounds out the meat flavor. Some people use egg shells for this process, but I find that to be a bit risky. This stock can be used for cooking Asian foods in general.

1. Place the pork ribs in a stockpot and cover with 5 quarts water. Add the daikon, ginger, scallions, onion, and peppercorns, and bring to a boil over high heat. Skim off the foam, reduce the heat to medium-low, and season with salt. Simmer, uncovered, occasionally skimming off any foam, until the stock is reduced by about 2 quarts, about 3 hours. At this time skim off as much fat as you desire.

2. Strain the stock, discard the solids, and use according to the recipe of your choice. The stock can be kept up to 3 days in the refrigerator or 3 months in the freezer.

SOUTHEAST ASIAN
PORK STOCK

MAKES 3 TO 3½ QUARTS

1 medium dried SQUID

2 to 2½ pounds meaty PORK RIBS

8 ounces DAIKON, peeled and cut into 1-inch rounds

4 ounces preserved DAIKON

1 large YELLOW ONION, peeled

2 to 3 ounces fresh GINGER, thinly sliced lengthwise

5 SCALLIONS, root and dark green ends trimmed, 6-inch stalks halved crosswise and lightly crushed

1 teaspoon WHITE or BLACK PEPPERCORNS

3 tablespoons FISH SAUCE

I N SOUTHEAST ASIA, pork broth tends to be more pronounced, with the addition of preserved vegetables and dried seafoods. It is pungent, and at the same time smoky, sweet, and savory. Flavored with dried squid, preserved daikon, and fish sauce, it can be used for virtually any Southeast Asian recipe that calls for pork broth. I use this fragrant stock to make the delicious Saigon rice noodle and ground pork soup with dried shrimp (pp. 226–27), for example. It is, however, too strong for Chinese, Korean, or Japanese foods.

When you char the dried squid, you may find the fishy aroma somewhat offensive. It is strong, but you'll soon forget about it when you taste the beautiful rich stock that comes from its use.

1. Lightly char the squid over an open flame until slightly darkened on both sides, no more than a minute per side, flipping several times so as not to burn it too much. Place the pork ribs in a stockpot, cover with 5 quarts water, and bring to a boil over high heat. Reduce the heat to medium-low and add the squid, daikon, preserved daikon, onion, ginger, scallions, and peppercorns. Skim off any foam and add the fish sauce. Simmer, uncovered, continuing to skim off any foam, until the stock is reduced by about 2 quarts, about 3 hours. At this time skim off as much fat as you desire.

2. Strain the stock, discard the solids (except for the pork ribs), and use according to the recipe of your choice. The stock can be kept up to 3 days in the refrigerator or 3 months in the freezer.

I HATE TO WASTE FOOD, and while it is true that when you make chicken stock using a whole chicken the meat loses its flavor almost completely, with pork a bit of flavor is retained. When I make this stock, I like to reserve the pork meat from the ribs. It is so tender that it shreds very easily, making it perfect for a quick and easy Japanese stir-fried pulled pork recipe (pp. 466–67). Served with rice or noodles, it makes a nearly instant meal.

BASIC BEEF STOCK

2 to 2½ pounds OXTAIL; or BEEF
   SHANK or RIBS

8 ounces DAIKON, peeled and cut
   into 1-inch rounds

2 to 3 ounces fresh GINGER, thinly
   sliced lengthwise

5 SCALLIONS, root and dark green
   ends trimmed, and 6-inch stalks
   halved crosswise and lightly
   crushed

1 large YELLOW ONION, peeled

1 teaspoon WHITE or BLACK
   PEPPERCORNS

KOSHER SALT

WHEN MAKING BEEF STOCK, always use meaty bones with fat, because all three elements—meat, bones, and fat—are needed for a well-rounded stock. Oxtail is perfect, although any meaty bones will do. Oxtails are readily available in most supermarkets, or call your butcher and request them a day or so ahead of time. Blanch the oxtail for several minutes, rinse, and then proceed with the recipe. This process, although not absolutely necessary, is a good way to get rid of tiny bone chips, fat, and blood particles. Otherwise, wait until these impurities surface when making the stock, creating a grayish foam, and remove with a ladle.

Season this stock lightly so you can continue to season in the recipes you choose later on, such as the oxtail and lotus root soup (see variation).

1. Place the beef bones in a stockpot and cover with 5 quarts water. Add the daikon, ginger, scallions, onion, and peppercorns, and bring to a boil over high heat. Skim off the foam, reduce the heat to medium-low, and season with salt. Simmer, uncovered, occasionally skimming off any foam, until the stock is reduced by about 2 quarts, about 3 hours. At this time skim off as much fat as you desire.

2. Strain the stock, discard the solids, and use according to the recipe of your choice. The stock can be kept up to 3 days in the refrigerator or 3 months in the freezer.

Variation: The Chinese occasionally eat beef, and one of the most delicious beef dishes is oxtail and lotus root soup. Make the beef stock using oxtail. Peel and thinly slice 8 ounces fresh lotus root and add it to 8 cups strained beef stock in a pot over medium heat. Shred the meat from the oxtail (about a cup) and add to the pot. Add a tablespoon of Chinese light soy sauce and a teaspoon of sesame oil; adjust the seasoning with freshly ground salt and pepper. Gently boil for 30 minutes. Divide the soup among individual large soup bowls and serve with garlic oil and 2 thinly sliced scallions (white to light green parts only) on the side for garnishing. Serve with individual bowls of jasmine rice on the side.

SOUTHEAST ASIAN BEEF STOCK

MAKES 3 TO 3½ QUARTS

2 to 2½ pounds OXTAIL; or BEEF
    SHANK or RIBS

1 pound DAIKON, peeled and cut
    into large chunks

2 to 3 ounces fresh GINGER, thinly
    sliced lengthwise

5 SCALLIONS, root and dark green
    ends trimmed, and 6-inch stalks
    halved crosswise and lightly
    crushed

1 large YELLOW ONION, peeled
    and studded with 5 CLOVES

5 STAR ANISE

1 piece of CASSIA BARK, 3 to
    4 inches long; or a CINNAMON
    STICK

2 tablespoons GRANULATED SUGAR

1 teaspoon WHITE or BLACK
    PEPPERCORNS

KOSHER SALT

DRIED SPICES are often thought of as the bane of the serious cook's pantry, but they shine in this stock. Southeast Asian beef stock is full of dried aromatics such as cloves, cassia bark (also known as Chinese cinnamon), and star anise, which particularly suit the cuisines of Vietnam and Cambodia, giving them their distinctive warm, sweet, and spicy character. Dishes such as *pho*—Vietnamese Hanoi beef and rice noodle soup (pp. 228–29)—and Cambodian spicy beef soup (pp. 150–51) are especially delicious when made using this aromatic broth.

1. Place the beef bones in a stockpot and cover with 5 quarts water. Add the daikon, ginger, scallions, clove-studded onion, star anise, cassia bark, sugar, and peppercorns, and bring to a boil over high heat. Skim off the foam, reduce the heat to medium-low, and season with salt. Simmer, uncovered, occasionally skimming off any foam, until the stock is reduced by about 2 quarts, about 3 hours. At this time skim off as much fat as you desire.

2. Strain the stock, discard the solids, and use according to the recipe of your choice. The stock can be kept up to 3 days in the refrigerator or 3 months in the freezer.

BASIC LAMB STOCK

MAKES 3 TO 3½ QUARTS

2 to 2½ pounds LAMB BREASTS or
SHANKS, or any meaty LAMB
BONES

1 pound DAIKON, peeled and cut
into large chunks

2 to 3 ounces fresh GINGER, thinly
sliced lengthwise

5 SCALLIONS, root and dark green
ends trimmed, and 6-inch stalks
halved crosswise and lightly
crushed

1 large YELLOW ONION, peeled

1 teaspoon WHITE or BLACK
PEPPERCORNS

KOSHER SALT

THIS LAMB STOCK is perfect for making the Mongolian lamb hot pot (pp. 152–53) or Indonesian curried goat (page 484). It can also be used for making double-cooked five-spice lamb (page 483). Similar to the technique for making pork or beef stock, I like to use meaty bones for making lamb stock. Lamb breasts and shanks are inexpensive and produce a delicious stock. While I call for the more commonly available lamb, you can certainly use goat or mutton if you prefer.

1. Place the lamb bones in a stockpot and cover with 5 quarts water. Add the daikon, ginger, scallions, onion, and peppercorns, and bring to a boil over high heat. Skim off the foam, reduce the heat to medium-low, and season with salt. Simmer, uncovered, occasionally skimming off any foam, until the stock is reduced by about 2 quarts, about 3 hours. At this time skim off as much fat as you desire.

2. Strain the stock, discard the solids, and use according to the recipe of your choice. The stock can be kept up to 3 days in the refrigerator or 3 months in the freezer.

BASIC SHRIMP STOCK

MAKES 3 TO 3½ QUARTS

2 tablespoons VEGETABLE OIL
Heads and shells from 5 or more
   pounds fresh SHRIMP or PRAWNS
2 to 3 ounces fresh GINGER, sliced
   into ⅛-inch-thick slices
   lengthwise and lightly crushed
5 SCALLIONS, root and dark green
   ends trimmed, and 6-inch stalks
   halved crosswise and lightly
   crushed
1 teaspoon WHITE or BLACK
   PEPPERCORNS
KOSHER SALT

WHEN I BUY shrimp or prawns for meals, I like to buy them with their heads and shells intact. When I get home, I remove the heads and the shells and use them to make a rich stock. To get maximum flavor, I stir-fry them in the pot that will be used to make the stock. You can use this for any seafood recipes requiring stock, such as the Korean spicy seafood stew (page 420), or the delicious Thai classic, spicy and sour shrimp soup (page 134).

1. Heat the oil in a stockpot over medium heat. Add the shrimp heads and shells and stir-fry until they turn pink and give off flavor, about 10 minutes. Cover with 5 quarts water and add the ginger, scallions, and peppercorns, and bring to a boil over high heat. Skim off the foam, reduce the heat to medium-low, and season with salt. Simmer, uncovered, occasionally skimming off any foam, until the stock is reduced by about 2 quarts, about 3 hours.

2. Strain the stock, discard the solids, and use according to the recipe of your choice. The stock can be kept up to 3 days in the refrigerator or 3 months in the freezer.

Variation: For fish stock, substitute 2 to 2½ pounds fish heads and bones for the shrimp heads and shells. Omit the stir-frying process in step 1. Simply place all the ingredients in the stockpot and follow the recipe.

For seafood stock, mix crustacean shells, fish heads, and bones.

DASHI
SEA VEGETABLE STOCK

MAKES 1½ TO 2 QUARTS

2 ounces dried KELP (konbu),
wiped clean with a damp towel
2 ounces BONITO FLAKES
(omit if making konbu dashi)

DASHI, OR SEA VEGETABLE stock, is unique to Japan. It is used almost exclusively in Japanese cooking to make sauces, marinades, stir-fries, soups, and many other dishes. The Japanese generally hold that making dashi is the first step on the road to learning their cuisine. Made using konbu, or kelp, and katsuo-bushi—a brown fish stick from which hana-katsuo, or bonito flakes, are made—dashi tastes of the sea. I have included three types of dashi: primary dashi, or ichiban dashi; secondary dashi, or niban dashi; and kelp stock, or konbu dashi, used by Zen Buddhist monks who are strict vegetarians. Like most cultures, the Japanese believe that without a good stock, a meal can only be mediocre. Traditionally, one's abilities as a cook were measured by the quality of one's dashi. Today, however, with more Japanese women working outside the home, the use of instant (packaged) dashi is growing. This is unfortunate when something is as easy to make as dashi, especially konbu dashi.

1. To make ichiban dashi: Place the kelp in a stockpot and pour 2 quarts cold water over it. Bring to a gentle boil over medium heat. Never allow the water to come to a full boil; reduce the heat if necessary or add ¼ cup cold water to the pot. Allow the kelp to rehydrate, softening completely and lending its flavor to the gently boiling water, 10 to 15 minutes. At this point the water should have a green hue. Remove the kelp, increase the heat to high, and bring the stock to a full boil. Reduce the heat to medium and add the bonito flakes. Return to a boil and remove from the heat immediately. Wait 30 to 45 seconds for the flakes to settle at the bottom of the pot. Another option is to remove the pot from the heat after you have removed the kelp, then sprinkle the bonito flakes on top and wait 30 to 45 seconds until they settle to the bottom of the pot. Skim off any foam, then pour through a paper towel–lined strainer set over another pot. Do not discard the solids; instead, use them to make niban dashi, or secondary dashi.

2. To make niban dashi: Place the kelp and bonito flakes used in making the primary stock in step 1 in a stockpot and add 2 quarts cold water. Bring to a gentle boil over medium heat, and reduce by about half, 45 minutes to 1 hour. Skim off any foam, then pour through a paper towel–lined strainer set over another pot. Discard the solids.

3. To make konbu dashi: Place the dried kelp in 2 quarts cold water and let

stand at room temperature for at least 12 hours or overnight (refrigerate, if you wish). Remove the kelp and use the stock for the desired recipe.

———————————————————

HARVESTED MAINLY from the waters surrounding the northern coastal island of Hokkaido, *konbu* is a dark brownish-green leafy sea vegetable. Known as kelp in the West, it is perhaps the most important sea vegetable in the Japanese culinary repertoire. *Konbu* comes in various sizes and is graded according to quality. In Japan, shops generally specialize in one item. In *konbu* shops, you can choose from many sizes, from tiny squares, to larger pieces, to full-length pieces up to several feet in length; these are sometimes reserved for wrapping foods. In reference to grades, prices vary, with the most expensive being from the best waters, most carefully selected, and most beautiful. If using *konbu* to make the simplest, pure kelp *dashi,* I suggest that you use one of the highest quality (i.e., most costly) grades, as this will impart a robust flavor. (In the United States your choices will almost certainly be limited; generally, the most expensive variety costs about ten dollars.) However tempted you may be, do not wash *konbu* before using it or you'll lose a lot of the flavor.

Instead, use a damp towel to wipe it clean. *Konbu* can also be rehydrated and fried or stir-fried and served as a vegetable dish. In fact, rather than throw away the kelp used to make your *dashi,* try sautéing it with some soy sauce, a sprinkle of sugar, and a drizzle of mirin (sweet sake), and enjoy it with a bowl of sushi rice.

BASIC VEGETABLE STOCK

MAKES 3 TO 3½ QUARTS

10 dried medium SHIITAKE
   MUSHROOMS

2 large LEEKS or 6 SCALLIONS, root
   and dark green ends trimmed,
   and 6-inch stalks halved
   crosswise and lightly crushed

5 whole Asian or 3 regular CELERY
   STALKS

6 NAPA CABBAGE LEAVES,
   quartered crosswise

8 ounces DAIKON, peeled and cut
   crosswise into 1-inch-thick
   rounds

4 medium CARROTS, peeled and
   halved crosswise

1 bunch CILANTRO, trimmed,
   stems and leaves intact

2 to 3 ounces fresh GINGER, thinly
   sliced lengthwise

1 teaspoon WHITE or BLACK
   PEPPERCORNS

KOSHER SALT

WHEN I GO to the vegetable market, inevitably I load up with fresh seasonal vegetables. They're often so beautiful that I imagine cooking up great recipes for each one I've carefully selected. Reality sets in once I get home, and I can't possibly eat everything I've bought while it is still good. My "no waste" approach to this bounty is to make a beautiful vegetable stock. Usually my vegetable stock flavors are a bit ad hoc, depending heavily on the vegetables left in the refrigerator, so feel free to experiment with this one (just don't waste your vegetables). The following recipe is one that is especially well suited to vegetarian Asian recipes.

1. Put the shiitakes in a bowl with hot water to cover, then set a plate over the bowl to prevent steam from escaping. Let stand until the mushrooms rehydrate and soften, about 30 minutes (or longer depending on the size of the mushrooms). Squeeze the mushrooms between the palms of your hands to get rid of the excess water. Using a paring knife, remove any hard stems from the mushrooms.

2. Place the mushrooms, leeks or scallions, celery, cabbage, daikon, carrots, cilantro, ginger, and peppercorns in a stockpot, cover with 5 quarts water, and bring to a boil over high heat. Skim off any foam, reduce the heat to low, and season with salt. Simmer, uncovered, occasionally skimming off any foam, until the stock is reduced by 2 quarts, about 3 hours. Taste, and add salt to taste.

3. Strain the stock, discard the solids, and use according to the recipe of your choice. The stock can be kept up to 3 days in the refrigerator or 3 months in the freezer.

SUEN LAT TONG
SOUR HOT SOUP

SERVES 4 TO 6

8 small dried or fresh CLOUD EAR
    MUSHROOMS

16 dried TIGER LILIES

8 cups VEGETABLE STOCK
    (page 126); or SUPERIOR
    STOCK (page 117)

2 tablespoons CHINESE BLACK
    VINEGAR

1 tablespoon SHAOXING WINE

1 tablespoon CHINESE LIGHT SOY
    SAUCE

2 teaspoons CHINESE DARK SOY
    SAUCE

1 to 2 teaspoons GRANULATED
    SUGAR

1 teaspoon SESAME OIL

1 teaspoon CHILI OIL

3 dried whole RED CHILIES

1 small BAMBOO SHOOT, quartered
    lengthwise and julienned

1 ounce fresh GINGER, peeled,
    thinly sliced, and julienned

KOSHER SALT

Freshly ground WHITE or BLACK
    PEPPER

8 ounces firm TOFU, sliced and cut
    into ¼-inch-thick sticks

1 to 2 tablespoons TAPIOCA
    STARCH or CORNSTARCH

2 SCALLIONS, root and dark green
    ends trimmed, and 6-inch stalks
    thinly sliced into rounds

Sour hot soup (also hot and sour soup, depending on the restaurant) is a Szechwanese specialty. Thickened with tapioca starch or cornstarch, it is a satisfying soup that contains the five flavor elements in the form of spicy chili oil, sour rice vinegar, salty soy sauce, bitter rice wine, and sweet sugar. Unfortunately, it has become a perhaps too familiar appetizer in Chinese-American restaurants, often overthickened and lacking in subtlety. While classic versions of *suen lat tong* can include shredded pork, shrimp, or crab, and sometimes duck or pork blood, this vegetarian recipe is quite delicious, and leaves room for other foods served during the meal to follow. Because this soup is thickened, I prefer to serve it at the beginning of a meal rather than throughout the meal as a palate cleanser. In comparison to Southeast Asian sour soups, *suen lat tong* does not have an overly strong sour note; all its flavors are well balanced.

Cloud ear mushrooms are available fresh in Japanese supermarkets and can be used here. Tiger lilies are available in Chinese or Southeast Asian markets. Choose lighter yellowish ones; the dark brown ones have been on the shelf too long. Add more or less tapioca starch, depending on how thick you prefer the soup.

1. Put the cloud ears (if dried) and lilies in separate bowls with hot water to cover, then set a plate over each bowl to prevent steam from escaping. Let stand until they rehydrate and soften, about 30 minutes (or longer depending on their size). Squeeze the cloud ears and lilies between the palms of your hands to get rid of the excess water. Using a paring knife, remove any hard stems, and quarter the cloud ears. Cut off the very hard tip of each lily stem end, then tie them in knots.

2. Bring the stock to a boil in a pot over high heat. Reduce the heat to medium-low and add the vinegar, wine, light and dark soy sauces, sugar, sesame oil, chili oil, chilies, bamboo shoot, ginger, cloud ears, and lily stems. Season with salt and pepper and simmer until heated through, about 15 minutes. Add the tofu. Dilute the tapioca starch with 1 to 2 tablespoons water and stir it into the soup until thickened slightly, 1 to 2 minutes. Ladle the soup in individual bowls and garnish with scallions.

MISO SOUP WITH TOFU AND WAKAME

SERVES 4 TO 6

8 cups KONBU DASHI (pp. 124–25)

¼ cup WAKAME SEA VEGETABLE, soaked in water for 30 minutes and drained

8 ounces firm TOFU, cut into ½-inch cubes

3 or more tablespoons WHITE MISO PASTE

2 SCALLIONS, root and dark green ends trimmed, and 6-inch stalks sliced into thin rounds

THERE ARE MANY different kinds of miso soup, but my favorite is the simple version with cubed tofu and wakame sea vegetable (often referred to as seaweed), which I order as a starter nearly every time I eat sushi in a restaurant. White miso paste (which is actually yellow in color) is the least salty soybean paste available. A combination of white miso and red miso—a saltier brownish-red soybean paste—can also be used to create a richer, more complex flavor (see variation). Because Japanese soybean paste is pungent, I prefer to use konbu dashi as the foundation, giving a delightfully delicate character to the soup. Feel free to use primary or secondary dashi for a stronger flavor, as many Japanese chefs do. Soybean paste soups are also very popular in Korea, where they are called miyok kuk, and oftentimes a dash or two of nutty sesame oil is added as a finishing touch.

Pour all but 1 cup dashi into a pot and bring to a boil over high heat. Reduce the heat to medium-low. Add the wakame and tofu and allow to heat through, 2 to 3 minutes. Whisk together the remaining dashi with the miso paste in a bowl until smooth, stir into the soup, and simmer for 2 minutes more. Ladle the soup into individual bowls and garnish with scallions.

Variations: Try this soup using half white and half red miso paste for a slightly stronger flavor and darker color.

You can add just a few more ingredients to this basic miso soup to create a satisfying meal: 4 to 6 medium julienned fresh shiitake mushroom caps with 2 dozen baby bok choy or spinach leaves; or shucked fresh cherrystone or the smaller Venus clams; or thinly sliced chicken breast. Bring a small pot of water to a boil over high heat and poach a cup of shucked fresh cherrystone or the smaller Venus clams, or 8 ounces of chicken breast thinly sliced against the grain for about 1 minute prior to adding to the miso soup. Add these ingredients at the same time as you would the wakame and tofu.

FRESH AUTUMN MUSHROOM SOUP

SERVES 4 TO 6

8 cups KONBU DASHI (pp. 124–25)

½ cup MIRIN

⅓ cup JAPANESE DARK SOY SAUCE

8 OYSTER MUSHROOM CAPS,
trimmed, cleaned, and halved or
quartered lengthwise

8 medium fresh SHIITAKE
MUSHROOMS, stemmed, caps
julienned

8 fresh small CLOUD EAR
MUSHROOMS, any hard knobs
trimmed

2 SCALLIONS, root and dark green
ends trimmed, and 6-inch stalks
sliced into thin rounds

1½ ounces fresh GINGER, peeled
and grated

3 ounces DAIKON, peeled and
grated

AUTUMN IS THE SEASON for harvesting and eating beautiful wild mushrooms. This particular mushroom soup was served to me at a dinner in Kyoto. It was delicate, a perfect complement to the other dishes: pan-fried fish, egg custard, fu (wheat gluten), and pickled eggplant and daikon. The soup contained wild pine mushrooms (page 317), which are indigenous to Korea and Japan. They are not available in the United States, but you can substitute fresh shiitakes and oyster mushrooms with confidence. Although not as earthy in flavor as their wild cousins, oyster and shiitake mushrooms are also used in Japan for making similarly delicate soups, and for making stir-fries. Fresh shiitake soup is perfect for any Japanese breakfast, lunch, or dinner. Unlike Western meals, Asian meals often tend to be similar throughout the day. The Japanese in particular enjoy a light soup, a bowl of rice, pickled vegetables, fish, and fresh fruit at any meal.

Pour the *dashi* in a stockpot and bring to a boil over high heat. Reduce the heat to medium-low, stir in the mirin and the soy sauce, add the oyster, shiitake, and cloud ear mushrooms, and cook for 3 minutes. Ladle the soup into individual bowls and garnish with some scallions, ginger, and daikon.

BAECHU KUK
PICKLED SPICY CABBAGE
AND TOFU SOUP

SERVES 4 TO 6

12 small dried SHIITAKE
 MUSHROOMS

8 cups VEGETABLE STOCK
 (page 126); or BASIC CHICKEN
 STOCK (page 116)

2 cups drained CABBAGE KIMCHI
 (page 359); or commercial
 equivalent, cut into 1-inch
 pieces

1 ounce fresh GINGER, thinly sliced
 lengthwise

2 tablespoons JAPANESE or KOREAN
 DARK SOY SAUCE

KOSHER SALT

Freshly ground BLACK PEPPER

8 ounces firm TOFU, drained and
 cut into ¾-inch cubes (optional)

2 SCALLIONS, root and dark green
 ends trimmed, and 6-inch stalks
 thinly sliced on the diagonal

KOREANS LIKE TO SERVE their pickled cabbage, kimchi, to make one-dish lunches and also as a table condiment to accompany their meals. Accordingly, kimchi often finds its way into stews or soups such as the one described here. While many Koreans thin the kimchi brine with water to make a simple stock, I prefer to use vegetable or chicken stock for a richer, more flavorful broth. This soup can be served with a bowl of rice on the side or as part of a bigger meal that can include barbecued beef (page 480), and stir-fried spinach and mung bean sprouts (page 326), for example.

The addition of tofu is optional. Some Koreans like to add it for a more satisfying vegetarian soup. Egg or wheat noodles are often added to this soup. Use chicken, pork, beef, or fish stock, with thinly sliced and blanched chicken, pork, or beef, or fish chunks, matching the protein to the stock, for a hearty meal.

1. Put the shiitakes in a bowl with hot water to cover, then set a plate over the bowl to prevent steam from escaping. Let stand until the mushrooms rehydrate and soften, about 30 minutes (or longer depending on the size of the mushrooms). Squeeze the mushrooms between the palms of your hands to get rid of the excess water. Using a paring knife, remove any hard stems from the mushrooms.

2. Place the stock in a pot and bring to boil over high heat. Reduce the heat to medium-low and add the mushrooms, kimchi, and ginger, and season with soy sauce, salt, and pepper. Simmer for 30 minutes, until the stock has absorbed the flavor of each ingredient. Add the tofu, cover with the lid, and continue to sim-mer until the tofu is heated through, about 2 minutes. Ladle the soup into individual bowls and garnish with scallions.

Variation: Spicy pickled cabbage soup with noodles: Bring a pot of water to a boil over high heat and add 8 ounces dried precooked thin noodles. Use chopsticks to untangle the noodles. When the water comes back to a boil, cook the noodles for a minute or two. Drain and divide among individual soup bowls. Blanch 12 ounces thinly sliced chicken breast or pork tenderloin in boiling water until cooked through, 1 to 2 minutes. Divide the meat into 4 equal portions and set atop each noodle serving. Pour the kimchi soup over each serving of noodles, garnish with scallions, and serve hot.

CANH CA CHUA
HOT AND SOUR FISH SOUP

SERVES 4 TO 6

12 ounces COD steaks, skinned and
   cut into bite-size chunks
KOSHER SALT
Freshly ground BLACK PEPPER
8 cups BASIC FISH STOCK
   (page 123)
¼ cup or more TAMARIND
   EXTRACT (page 75)
2 tablespoons FISH SAUCE
7 ounces ripe PINEAPPLE, cut into
   ¼-inch-thick slices, cored, and
   cut into bite-size chunks
1 ripe medium TOMATO, cut into
   8 equal wedges and seeded
2 or more RED THAI CHILIES,
   stemmed, seeded, and sliced thin
   diagonally
10 THAI BASIL LEAVES, julienned
4 SAW LEAVES, julienned; or ⅓ cup
   CILANTRO LEAVES, tightly
   packed
FRIED GARLIC OIL (page 108)

C*ANH CA CHUA* is a Vietnamese hot and sour fish soup. Its variations are popular in Cambodia, where it is called *samlaw m'juu trey*; Indonesia, where it is known as *sayur asam ikan*; and Thailand, where it is referred to as *tom som pla*. It can be oppressively hot and humid in these countries, and this sour soup is enjoyed for the cooling effect from the tangy tamarind and fresh fiery hot chilies. The Vietnamese and Cambodians enjoy the sweetness of pineapple in the soup, while the Indonesians and Thai omit it, adding sugar instead. I like to think of it as a multifunctional soup. Assertive yet not overwhelming, *canh ca chua* can be served to accompany an array of various dishes as a palate cleanser. Full of chunky fish morsels, it can also serve as the fish (and soup!) at a meal. I love hot and sour fish soup with a simple bowl of rice, because its chunky bits make for a light but satisfying meal.

1. Season the fish chunks with salt and pepper on both sides and refrigerate until ready to use.

2. Meanwhile, bring the stock to a boil in a pot over high heat. Reduce the heat to medium-low, add the tamarind, fish sauce, pineapple, tomato, and chilies, and simmer for 10 minutes. Add the seasoned fish chunks, adjust the seasoning, and continue to simmer until the fish is cooked through, 3 to 5 minutes. Ladle into individual soup bowls and garnish with basil, saw leaves, and some fried garlic oil as desired.

Variations: Substitute *prahoc*, fish extract (page 76), for the fish sauce if you wish to make a Cambodian version of this soup.

For the Indonesian or Thai version, omit the pineapple. Add 1 tablespoon sugar to the stock in step 2. Stir-fry a large crushed, peeled, and minced garlic clove, an ounce of peeled and julienned fresh ginger, and a tablespoon of shrimp paste together in a tablespoon of vegetable oil until the ingredients are fragrant and golden, about 5 minutes. Proceed with the recipe, omitting the fish sauce and fried garlic oil.

SUP CUA
HANOI CRAB SOUP

3 STONE CRABS or 2 DUNGENESS
   CRABS

2 cups MUNG BEAN SPROUTS,
   root ends trimmed

1 bunch VIETNAMESE CORIANDER
   or CILANTRO, leaves only

2 tablespoons FISH SAUCE

KOSHER SALT

Freshly ground BLACK PEPPER

2 SCALLIONS, root and dark green
   ends trimmed, and 6-inch stalks
   thinly sliced into rounds

2 THAI CHILIES, stemmed, seeded,
   and sliced crosswise

Juice of 1 LIME

FRIED GARLIC OIL (page 108)

1 LIME, sliced into 4 to 6 wedges

S UP CUA is a brothy northern Vietnamese crab soup that is perfect as a palate cleanser. I was served this version at the Hanoi Metropole, one of the original grand hotels dating back to the turn of the twentieth century, when Vietnam was part of French Indochina. The soup was served as part of a special northern-style meal prepared by chef Didier Corlou, a French national who married a northern Vietnamese woman and has lived in Hanoi for the past ten years. He has a special interest in preserving northern Vietnamese cuisine, which he learned from his in-laws over the years. My meal included fish grilled in bamboo leaves, rice cooked in a special narrow-mouth clay pot (this is inverted and cracked open at the table), and sup cua. I enjoy the recipe because it offers a minor moral lesson: it is a perfect example of how the Vietnamese, like the Chinese, do not waste a thing. The crabs are boiled in a pot of water, which is reserved as the base for the soup.

Stone crabs with black-tipped claws have a sweeter meat than do Dungeness crabs, which tend to be on the salty side. Season accordingly.

1. Scrub the crabs well on both sides, being very careful that you do not get pinched! Bring 1½ quarts water to a boil over high heat and cook the crabs for 15 minutes. Remove the crabs from the cooking liquid. Strain the liquid through a fine mesh sieve into a new pot.

2. Being thorough, open the crabs and remove and reserve all the crab meat. Place an equal amount of crab meat, mung bean sprouts, and Vietnamese coriander in individual soup bowls. Add the fish sauce to the reserved cooking liquid and bring to a boil over high heat. Ladle a generous amount of steaming broth over each serving, and instruct your guests to

adjust the seasoning with fish sauce or salt, and add scallions, fresh chili slices, and fried garlic oil, then squeeze a lime wedge over their individual bowls of soup, as desired.

Variation: For sup cua mang tay, crab and asparagus soup, follow step 1 of the recipe. Omit the mung bean sprouts and Vietnamese coriander leaves. Instead, put 2 cups cooked, drained, and coarsely chopped white or green asparagus, the crabmeat, and crab stock in a pot and bring to a boil over high heat. Reduce the heat to low, add the fish sauce, season with salt and pepper to taste, and allow the flavors to blend, about 10 minutes. Slowly and in a steady stream, stir 2 egg whites into the soup. Mix a tablespoon of tapioca starch (or cornstarch) with 2 tablespoons cold water and stir into the soup. Continue simmering until the soup thickens, about 1 minute more. Ladle the soup into individual soup bowls and garnish each with a generous amount of fresh cilantro leaves. If you find the crab stock too strong and salty, substitute vegetable or chicken stock for it and proceed with the recipe.

CRAB AND ASPARAGUS SOUP is one of my favorite soups. Originating in colonial French Indochina (i.e., mid-1800s to mid-1900s), *sup cua mang tay* is derived from both the classic Hanoi *sup cua* and French *velouté d'asperges* (cream of asparagus soup). The French colonialists living in Vietnam missed their beloved asparagus, trying unsuccessfully to grow it in tropical lands. Craving the delicious spear in all its forms, they finally gave up on growing it altogether and settled for the imported French canned variety. Vietnamese cooks, who saw it as "Western bamboo," created what has become one of their most popular soups. While some chefs puree the soup, I prefer the classic thickened broth with chunks of asparagus and crab for texture.

TOM YAM GUNG
SPICY SHRIMP SOUP

SERVES 4 TO 6

8 cups SHRIMP STOCK (page 123)

¼ cup TAMARIND EXTRACT
  (page 75)

2 tablespoons FISH SAUCE

2 large GARLIC CLOVES, crushed
  and peeled

2 LEMONGRASS STALKS, root
  ends trimmed, outer leaves
  and tough green tops removed,
  and 6-inch-long inner bulbs
  halved crosswise and crushed

1 ounce GALANGAL, thinly sliced
  lengthwise

4 KAFFIR LIME LEAVES, lightly
  crushed

4 red THAI CHILIES

1 ripe medium TOMATO, cut into
  8 equal wedges, seeds removed

12 canned STRAW MUSHROOMS;
  or 4 medium fresh SHIITAKES,
  stems removed, caps quartered

12 medium BLUE TIGER SHRIMP
  (headless optional), peeled and
  deveined

12 large THAI BASIL LEAVES,
  freshly torn; or ⅓ cup tightly
  packed CILANTRO LEAVES

FRIED BLACK CHILI SAUCE
  (page 107)

THIS FAMOUS SPICY shrimp soup is a favorite among people who enjoy Thai food. Fragrant with lemongrass, galangal, kaffir lime leaves, and Thai basil, its sour flavor comes from tamarind. Thai chilies and *nam prik pow*, roasted chili paste, are responsible for its fierce heat, while the shrimp tomalley in the stock lends richness and sweetness to the soup. For a simple lunch serve it with a bowl of jasmine rice on the side, or serve the soup throughout a more elaborate meal. *Tom yam gung* is a national dish in Thailand, and several regional variations exist. Some use tamarind extract as the souring agent; others use lime juice. Some cooks garnish the soup with Thai basil; others use cilantro. The black chili paste, *nam prik pow*, is widely used, lending the soup a delicious smoky quality.

Traditionally straw mushrooms are used in the recipe, but these are only available canned. Prior to using, blanch them for 3 minutes in boiling water to get rid of any tin flavor.

1. Bring the stock, tamarind extract, fish sauce, garlic, lemongrass, galangal, kaffir lime leaves, and chilies to a boil in a pot over high heat. Reduce the heat to medium-low and allow to simmer until the flavors develop, about 20 minutes.

2. Add the tomato wedges and mushrooms and cook for 2 minutes. Add the shrimp and cook for an additional 2 minutes. Ladle the soup into individual bowls, discarding lemongrass, galangal, and kaffir lime leaves in the process. Garnish the soup with fresh Thai basil or cilantro or both, and a small amount of fried black chili sauce. Serve hot.

GAI TONG
CLAY POT—STEAMED
CHICKEN SOUP

SERVES 4

4 dried medium SHIITAKE
MUSHROOMS

2 skinless CHICKEN LEGS, thighs
and drumsticks separated at the
joint (optional)

3 SCALLIONS, root and dark green
ends trimmed, 6-inch stalks
halved and lightly crushed

1 ounce fresh GINGER, thinly sliced
lengthwise

2 tablespoons CHINESE LIGHT SOY
SAUCE or FISH SAUCE

1 tablespoon SHAOXING WINE

KOSHER SALT

Freshly ground BLACK PEPPER

4 sprigs CILANTRO

LIKE MANY COOKS around the world, Chinese chefs and home cooks are experimenting more and more with ingredients from other parts of the world. My Chinese family, having lived in Southeast Asia, where fish sauce is more commonly used than soy sauce, is a perfect example, substituting fish sauce for the more traditional soy sauce. The fish sauce not only salts the soup but gives it a delicious light fermented sealike note.

THIS STEAMED CHICKEN SOUP, *gai tong*, is a chicken and herbal infusion made in a special clay steamer from China's Yixing region, from where the famous brownish-red clay teapots of the same name originate. The pots have a special hollow stem at their center that rises up to the full height of the pot, gathering steam from the boiling water in its sand underpot. Looking something like a short-stemmed, upside-down umbrella sitting on its back, the design actually allows the soup to cook by steaming. The result is the most delicate, clean-tasting chicken broth you will ever have; it makes a perfect palate cleanser. Yixing steam pots are sold in Chinatowns. Conversation pieces and very pretty, they make great presentation vessels.

1. Put the shiitakes in a bowl with hot water to cover, then set a plate over the bowl to prevent steam from escaping. Let stand until the mushrooms rehydrate and soften, about 30 minutes (or longer depending on the size of the mushrooms). Squeeze the mushrooms between the palms of your hands to get rid of the excess water. Using a paring knife, remove any hard stems from the mushrooms and halve or julienne the caps, as you prefer.

2. Fill a sand pot (underpot) ¾ of the way up with water and place the Yixing clay pot on top. (If you do not have this cooking equipment, simply make the soup using the same technique as for making basic chicken stock; page 116). Place the chicken, mushrooms, scallions, and ginger in the clay pot and fill it with 6 cups water; place over medium-low heat. Add the soy or fish sauce and rice wine, season with salt and pepper, and place the lid on top of the clay pot. Steam until the ingredients have released their essence, creating a flavorful broth, about 3 hours. Check the water level in the sand pot every hour to make sure it is not empty. Replenish the water as necessary, being careful not to burn yourself as you pick up the steaming vessel with gloves.

3. Divide the soup, including the chicken, among large individual soup bowls and garnish with cilantro sprigs prior to serving.

SOTO AYAM
CHICKEN AND
POTATO CHIP SOUP

SERVES 4 TO 6

VEGETABLE OIL for deep-frying,
  plus 1 tablespoon

1 large RUSSET or WAXY POTATO,
  peeled, halved lengthwise, and
  cut into ⅛-inch-thick slices
  crosswise

1 large GARLIC CLOVE, crushed,
  peeled, and minced

1 ounce fresh GINGER, peeled and
  minced

1 LEMONGRASS STALK, root
  ends trimmed, outer leaves and
  tough green top removed, and
  6-inch-long inner bulb finely
  ground

4 KAFFIR LIME LEAVES, lightly
  crushed

2 CANDLENUTS, finely crushed

1 teaspoon crushed CORIANDER
  SEEDS

½ ounce fresh TURMERIC, peeled
  and finely grated; or ½ teaspoon
  TURMERIC POWDER

1 to 2 teaspoons INDONESIAN or
  THAI SHRIMP PASTE

KOSHER SALT

Freshly ground BLACK PEPPER

8 cups BASIC CHICKEN STOCK
  (page 116)

12 ounces CHICKEN BREAST, skin
  removed, thinly sliced against
  the grain

1½ cups finely shredded GREEN or
  NAPA CABBAGE

1½ to 2 cups fresh MUNG BEAN
  SPROUTS, root ends trimmed

1 cup CELERY LEAVES

2 to 3 hard-boiled large EGGS,
  shelled and sliced crosswise
  into thin rounds

⅓ cup CILANTRO LEAVES

FRIED SHALLOTS (page 108)

1 SCALLION, root and dark green
  ends trimmed, and 6-inch stalk
  thinly sliced into rounds

1 or 2 THAI CHILIES, stemmed,
  seeded, and thinly sliced
  diagonally

2 LIMES, each cut into 6 to 8
  wedges

INDONESIAN SWEET SOY SAUCE

SOTO AYAM is the first Indonesian soup I ever ate, and it remains one of my favorites. There are several regional versions of this chicken and fried potato soup, notably on the resort island of Bali, where they add cellophane noodles; and in Jakarta, where I learned this version from my Aunt Ny's cook. There it is made without the noodles, the lightest soto ayam I have ever tasted. Because it includes protein, starch, and vegetable, it can be eaten as a full meal. The combined textures of tender chicken, hard-boiled egg slices, crispy homemade potato chips, and crunchy mung bean sprouts are as delightful as the medley of colors—golden-yellow, white, green, and red. Garnished with fresh cilantro, pungent chili, crispy fried shallots, tangy lime juice, and sweet soy sauce, soto ayam's warming yet refreshing characteristics are great for any season.

1. Heat enough vegetable oil for deep-frying in a pot over medium heat. When the oil reaches 360° to 375°F, carefully add the potato slices and fry until golden crisp, 2 to 3 minutes. Drain on paper towels and set aside. Fry the chips one more time for a minute or so to crisp further just before adding to the soup.

2. Heat 1 tablespoon oil in a stockpot over medium-high heat. Add the garlic, ginger, lemongrass, kaffir lime leaves, candlenuts, coriander seeds, turmeric, and shrimp paste, and stir until the mixture becomes a shade darker and is fragrant, 5 to 10 minutes. Pour the chicken stock into the pot and bring to a boil over high heat. Reduce heat to medium-low and continue to simmer for 15 to 20 minutes. Adjust seasoning with salt and pepper. Strain the stock and discard the solids. Return the stock to the pot over medium-low heat, add the chicken, and stir a few times until cooked, about 2 minutes.

3. Meanwhile, place some shredded cabbage, mung bean sprouts, and celery leaves in individual large soup bowls. Ladle the broth with the chicken over each serving and top with some hard-boiled egg slices and fried potatoes. Serve the cilantro leaves, shallots, scallion, chilies, lime wedges, and sweet soy sauce on the side. Instruct your guests to garnish their soups to taste.

Variation: Follow the recipe but add a small package (.7 ounces) of cellophane noodles for an interesting, slippery texture. Place the dried noodles in water to cover until pliable, about 30 minutes. Meanwhile, bring a pot of water to a boil over high heat, then add the noodles, untangling them every so often with chopsticks, until they are cooked (transparent), about 5 minutes. Drain and divide the noodles among individual large soup bowls. Proceed with step 3.

THIS IS A CURIOUS SOUP. The potato chips—a Western influence brought by the Dutch—are a wonderful surprise, adding an element of fun and palate-pleasing taste and texture. If you eliminate the fresh chili slices, you can easily serve the soup to children. (Who wouldn't want to try "potato-chip soup" just once?) Although it may be tempting to use store-bought potato chips, I do not recommend them. If you must, however, try a brand like Cape Cod Potato Chips, i.e., thick-cut, low salt, and extra crispy.

A BALINESE BASKET WEAVER ROLLS UP HER MATERIAL.

BINACOL NA MANOK
CHICKEN AND YOUNG
COCONUT SOUP

SERVES 4 TO 6

1 tablespoon VEGETABLE OIL

3 large GARLIC CLOVES, crushed
and peeled

1 small YELLOW ONION, cut into
thin wedges

1 ounce fresh GINGER, peeled and
julienned

2 fresh whole RED THAI CHILIES;
or 4 dried whole RED CHILIES

6 cups CHICKEN STOCK (page 116)

2 tablespoons FISH SAUCE

KOSHER SALT

Freshly ground BLACK PEPPER

1 young GREEN COCONUT, water
reserved and meat julienned; or
the equivalent frozen or canned
but unsweetened

1 cup julienned fresh GREEN
PAPAYA; or 1 GREEN MANGO,
peeled, pit removed, and
julienned

24 MALUNGGAY LEAVES (if dried,
rehydrate in water first; if frozen,
thaw first)

8 ounces skinless CHICKEN
BREAST, thinly sliced crosswise

2 small vine-ripe TOMATOES, each
cut into 8 wedges and seeded

1 SCALLION, root and dark green
ends trimmed, and 6-inch stalk
cut into 1½-inch pieces and
julienned

I FIRST ATE *binacol* (also spelled *binakol*) on Cebu—an island situated in the southern Visayas region of the Philippines, and noted for its historical importance as a political center and its paradisiacal beauty. It was served at Tiya Nena, one of the best restaurants on the island, which also serves as a cooking school. When I arrived there, my host, chef and owner Jessica Avila, had all sorts of dishes laid out for me, from crab shells (pp. 410–11), to chicken *adobo* (pp. 496–97), to fresh *lumpia* filled with shredded coconut palm heart (pp. 280–81). Although all were exquisitely executed, I especially enjoyed what she calls the "welcome and good-bye soup," a light chicken and coconut soup she served in individual coconut shells. It is traditionally made with *buko* (young green coconut), which contains naturally sweet coconut water, and a very thin and tender layer of somewhat slippery coconut meat. The *buko* water is combined with chicken stock for the broth; the coconut meat is julienned and added as a vegetable in the soup. Coconut water (a.k.a. coconut juice) is subtly sweet, and a perfect complement to the chicken stock, which is seasoned with salty *patis* (fish sauce). What makes Jessica's personal variation on the classic recipe (which is essentially a cross between two classic Filipino soups, *binacol* and *sinigang*) so special is that she adds green papaya or mango, *malunggay* (horseradish leaves), and finger (Thai) chilies to the dish. "The soup is delicate and rich at the same time," notes the inventive chef. "The sourness of the green papaya cuts the fat, while the lightly bitter *malunggay* and spicy chilies lift the palate. I like to use generous amounts of all of these ingredients, except, perhaps, the chilies!"

Young green coconut is available at Asian markets or by mail order. Fresh is preferred, but frozen is a good substitute. *Malunggay* leaves are available dried or frozen at Filipino markets or by mail order.

1. Heat the oil in a stockpot over medium heat. Stir-fry the garlic, onion, ginger, and whole chilies until the garlic and onion turn golden and the mixture becomes fragrant, about 5 minutes. Add the chicken stock and fish sauce, season to taste with salt and pepper, and bring to a boil.

2. Reduce the heat to medium-low and add the coconut water, coconut meat, and green papaya or green mango, and cook until just soft, about 5 minutes. Add the *malunggay* leaves, chicken, and tomatoes. Stir well and simmer until the chicken turns opaque and cooks through,

1 to 2 minutes. Ladle the soup into individual large soup bowls and garnish with scallion.

Variation: If you want to make a classic *binacol*, omit the green papaya or mango, *malunggay* leaves, tomatoes, and chilies.

MATURE COCONUTS ARE USED FOR THEIR MEAT, AND FOR MAKING MILK, CREAM, AND BUTTER.

SAMLAW TIAH
DUCK AND
PRESERVED LIME SOUP

SERVES 4 TO 6

One 3- to 4-pound Long Island
   DUCK
KOSHER SALT
Freshly ground BLACK PEPPER
2 preserved LIMES
1 ounce fresh GINGER, thinly sliced
   lengthwise
1 SCALLION, root and dark green
   ends trimmed, and 6-inch-stalk
   thinly sliced into rounds
FRIED GARLIC OIL (page 108)

SPECIAL ASIAN PRESERVED (or pickled) limes in brine lend an assertive bitter flavor to this rich, gamey duck soup. While this version is
Cambodian, it is strongly related to versions made in China, specifically in the southern region of Chiu Chow, where preserved limes are commonly used in cooking. The Chiu Chow version of this soup (they call it *ling
mown dun ngap*) also contains Shaoxing wine, an amber-colored rice wine that
adds a sweet note and rounds out the flavors. My recipe calls for a whole
duck, which may initially seem like a lot of meat, but by the time you've
skimmed off all the fat and picked the meat from the skin and bones, you'll
find the amount is just right. I like to garnish this soup with scallion and
fried garlic oil for a refreshing and nutty herbal note. *Samlaw tiah* served with
a bowl of rice and some stir-fried leafy greens makes for a wonderful meal.
My mother learned to make it from my grandmother Huong in Phnom
Penh. Grandmother Huong was of Chiu Chow ancestry and had mastered
several variations on the Chinese original. My mother often serves the Cambodian version in summer, when the lime has a welcome cooling effect. We
eat in the early evening, using our chopsticks to pick the meat off the duck,
which sits whole in its tureen in the center of the table. (Reaching in these
informal circumstances is not only polite, it is required!) Ceramic soup
spoons are employed for slurping the tasty broth. My father loves this soup.
It reminds him of his childhood in Phnom Penh and the delicious scents of
my grandmother's kitchen. His favorite part is the small amount of duck fat,
which glistens on the surface of the broth and keeps the duck nice and hot.

There is no substitute for Asian preserved limes in brine, but these are easily found in Asian markets or through mail-order sources (page 563).

1. Place the duck in a stockpot with 4 quarts water. Season with salt and pepper and bring to a boil over high heat. Reduce the heat to medium-low and continue to simmer for 1½ hours.

2. Season with salt and pepper to taste, add the preserved limes and ginger, and continue to simmer, occasionally skimming off the fat, for 1 hour more. The stock should have reduced by about 1½ quarts and the duck should be fork tender.

3. Transfer the whole duck to a tureen or large bowl, and garnish with the scallion and some fried

garlic oil. You can also shred some duck meat and place a portion in large individual soup bowls, then ladle a generous amount of broth over each serving followed by some scallion and fried garlic oil. Leftovers are delicious the next day.

Variation: For the Chiu Chow version, add ¼ cup Shaoxing wine to the pot in the beginning of the recipe.

SUP VIT
DUCK WITH SIX NUTS SOUP

SERVES 4 TO 6

VEGETABLE OIL for deep-frying

3 DUCK LEGS, thighs and
  drumsticks separated

2 tablespoons FISH SAUCE

Juice of 1 young GREEN COCONUT;
  or 2 cups WATER

2 stalks LEMONGRASS, root ends
  trimmed, outer leaves and tough
  green tops removed, and 6-inch
  bulbs bruised

12 medium to large CHESTNUTS,
  shelled and peeled

⅓ cup skinless roasted unsalted
  PEANUTS

⅓ cup roasted unsalted CASHEWS

⅓ cup skinless roasted unsalted
  ALMONDS

12 JUJUBES

KOSHER SALT

Freshly ground BLACK PEPPER

12 fresh LITCHI NUTS, peeled and
  pit removed

THIS IS AN UNUSUAL DISH, WHICH IS MADE using a combination of both soup-making and braising techniques. It is sometimes called *sup* (meaning soup) and other times *tiem* (meaning braised). I've had the pleasure of trying it in a small family-style restaurant in the 36 Streets (French quarter) of Hanoi, and it was absolutely delicious. The rich chestnuts, peanuts, cashews, and almonds were unexpected, yet perfectly suited for the cooler northern climate of Vietnam. (I usually make this in winter, when the richness can be appreciated as a culinary bulwark against the cold.) The jujubes (Chinese red dates) and fresh litchi nuts lend a subtle sweet and floral note to the soup.

Young green coconuts are available in Asian markets. Their green skins have usually been removed, revealing a spongy cylindrical white husk with a slightly conical top. They should be cracked open at the top, held over a bowl, and drained so as not to lose any coconut water. The coconut water should then be strained through a fine mesh sieve to remove any fibers that may have come loose during the "cracking." If you cannot find fresh coconut water, substitute frozen coconut water or spring water for it. I do not recommend canned coconut water, which has been sweetened and often tastes of tin. (Coconut milk is not a substitute for coconut water, also referred to as juice.)

1. Heat enough oil for deep-frying in a pot over medium-high heat to 360°F. Season the duck legs with salt and pepper and deep-fry, in batches if necessary, until golden crisp, 10 to 15 minutes total, turning the duck legs once.

2. Bring the coconut water and 2 quarts water to a boil in a pot over high heat. Reduce the heat to medium-low, add the lemongrass and duck legs, season with fish sauce, and cook for 3 hours. Add the chestnuts, peanuts, cashews, almonds, and jujubes. Adjust seasoning with salt and pepper, and cook until the duck is fork tender and the chestnuts and jujubes are soft, 30 to 45 minutes more. Skim the fat off the top and add the fresh litchi nuts. Serve alone or with rice on the side.

DOENG GWA TONG
WINTER MELON AND
HAM SOUP

SERVES 4 TO 6

6 dried medium SHIITAKE
  MUSHROOMS
8 cups SUPERIOR STOCK
  (page 117)
1 cup shredded HAM from making
  SUPERIOR STOCK
KOSHER SALT
Freshly ground WHITE or BLACK
  PEPPER
6 ounces WINTER MELON, peeled
  and thinly sliced
12 SNOW PEAS
2 SCALLIONS, root and dark green
  ends trimmed, and 6-inch stalks
  thinly sliced diagonally

W INTER MELON SOUP is one of the classic Chinese clear soups. The key to a delicious winter melon soup is superior stock, made with meaty chicken bones and Yunnan or Smithfield ham. The ham used in making the stock is shredded and added to this soup, contributing a beautiful dark pink color that contrasts with the translucent whitish green melon, bright green snow peas, and dark brown mushrooms. Scallion lifts the palate, but you can also add some fried garlic to the soup for a sharper finish and a light roasty note.

1. Put the shiitakes in a bowl with hot water to cover, then set a plate over the bowl to prevent steam from escaping. Let stand until the mushrooms rehydrate and soften, about 30 minutes (or longer depending on the size of the mushrooms). Squeeze the mushrooms between the palms of your hands to get rid of the excess water. Using a paring knife, remove any hard stems from the mushrooms and quarter the caps.

2. Pour the stock in a pot and bring to a boil over high heat. Reduce the heat to medium-low, add the shiitakes and shredded ham, and simmer until the mushrooms are tender and the flavors blend, about 15 minutes. Adjust seasoning with salt and pepper as necessary. Add the winter melon and cook until tender but firm, about 5 minutes. Add the snow peas and cook until tender but firm, about 1 minute. Ladle the soup into large individual soup bowls and garnish with scallions.

FU GWA TONG
PORK AND
BITTER MELON SOUP

SERVES 4 TO 6

8 cups BASIC PORK STOCK
(page 118)
1 cup shredded PORK RIB meat
from the stock (page 118)
1 small BITTER MELON, halved
lengthwise, core removed, and
sliced ¼-inch thick diagonally
2 tablespoons CHINESE LIGHT SOY
SAUCE; or FISH SAUCE
KOSHER SALT
Freshly ground BLACK PEPPER
2 SCALLIONS, root and dark green
ends trimmed, and 6-inch stalks
thinly sliced crosswise

BITTER MELON, fu gwa, is rich in vitamin C and is consumed for its medicinal qualities. A lightish vibrant green, elongated, and bumpy
melon that somewhat resembles a cucumber, it can be found at many
Asian markets. Its distinctive and intense bitterness comes from quinine (the
naturally occurring compound used in making bitter lemon and tonic water
carbonated soft drinks), which is present in the plant. Fu gwa is believed to
strengthen the immune system, aid digestion, and stimulate the appetite. It is
often paired with pork, which buffers its bitterness. This soup is one of the
more traditional ways to prepare fu gwa, but it is also delicious stir-fried with
fermented black bean and garlic paste (page 86), or stuffed with shrimp and
pork and pan-fried (pp. 328–29).

1. Bring the pork stock to a boil in
a pot over high heat. Reduce the
heat to medium-low and add the
shredded pork and bitter melon
slices.

2. Stir in the soy sauce or fish sauce
and add a generous amount of pepper. Simmer, uncovered, until the
melon is fork tender and has lent its
flavor to the broth, about 10 minutes. Adjust the seasoning with salt
and pepper to taste. Ladle the soup
into large individual bowls and garnish with scallions. Serve as a palate
cleanser to be enjoyed throughout
the meal.

Variation: For an equally refreshing
version of this soup without the bitterness, substitute a small, peeled,
seeded cucumber for the bitter
melon.

JU YOOK HEONG CHOY TONG
PORK AND CURE-ALL
CILANTRO SOUP

SERVES 4 TO 6

8 cups BASIC PORK STOCK
(page 118)
12 ounces GROUND PORK
(70 percent lean); or cooked
shredded PORK RIB meat
from making the stock
2 large bunches CILANTRO
(4 ounces or more), trimmed
and coarsely chopped; a few
sprigs reserved for garnish
2 tablespoons CHINESE LIGHT SOY
SAUCE; or FISH SAUCE
KOSHER SALT
Freshly ground BLACK PEPPER

ILANTRO—ALSO KNOWN as Chinese parsley and coriander—is a beautiful bright green herb that is widely used in Asian and South American cuisines. In North America, the word "cilantro" is used to describe only the leaves, while the word "coriander" is used to describe the seeds. Throughout the rest of the world, "coriander" is used to describe both the leaves and the seeds, and, in fact, the herb in all its parts. In Chinese medicine and all other herbal medicines derived from it, cilantro is considered a cure-all. Having a warm, sweet, and lemony character, it is believed to cure loss of appetite, aches and pains, indigestion, and arthritis. It is also reputed to be an aphrodisiac. In this soup, the cilantro—stems and leaves—simmers in the pork broth. The result is a sweet herbal infusion that is both warming and refreshing.

Pork and cilantro soup is a soup for all seasons. My grandmother Huong, my aunts, and my mother made it when someone in the family was feeling under the weather. When my brother William and I were kids, we would often get sick at the same time and have to share a bedroom in a sort of quarantine so we would not contaminate the rest of the house. I remember my mother bringing her version of this steamy Chinese soup to us. The cilantro infusion filled my head and always made me feel better. As an adult, I continue the ritual: when my husband feels under the weather, I make him this soup.

1. Bring the pork stock to a boil in a pot over high heat. Reduce the heat to medium-low and at this time, if using, add the ground pork a little at a time as follows, working in batches as necessary: Place the pork in a ladle. Lower the ladle into the soup and with a pair of chopsticks separate the meat so it is loose and does not cook in large lumps. Release the pork into the stock. Repeat the process until you have added all the pork. Cook for about 10 minutes. If you're using the cooked pork rib meat, add it to the stock and proceed with the recipe.

2. Add the cilantro stems and leaves and soy sauce to the stock, and continue cooking until the cilantro is completely wilted and the broth is infused with its essence, about 20 minutes. Adjust the seasoning with salt and pepper. Ladle the soup into large individual soup bowls and garnish with cilantro sprigs.

SINIGANG NA BABOY
PORK AND
SOUR FRUIT SOUP

SERVES 4 TO 6

8 cups BASIC PORK STOCK
  (page 118)

⅓ to ½ cup TAMARIND EXTRACT
  (page 75)

1 ounce fresh GINGER, peeled and
  julienned

1 small YELLOW ONION, peeled
  and cut into thin wedges

2 medium vine-ripe TOMATOES,
  each cut into 8 wedges and
  seeded

2 tablespoons FISH SAUCE

KOSHER SALT

Freshly ground BLACK PEPPER

12 ounces PORK TENDERLOIN,
  thinly sliced against the grain

2 cups tender LEAFY GREENS, such
  as BABY BOK CHOY or BABY
  SPINACH

6 to 8 YARD-LONG BEANS,
  trimmed and cut into 1-inch
  pieces

2 SCALLIONS, root and dark green
  ends trimmed, and 6-inch stalks
  thinly sliced into rounds

I DON'T THINK there is one country in Southeast Asia that doesn't have some sort of sour soup. In the Philippines, where this soup is considered a national dish, numerous variations exist. (Filipino cooks say, "Anything goes as long as it is sour!") *Sinigang* in the northern Philippines tends to be more pronouncedly sour than in the south, where it is called *tinola*. Technically *sinigang* means to boil with sour fruit or vegetable. The sourness is most often from tamarind, but it can also come from *kamias*, a bright green, somewhat translucent cylindrical fruit about 2 inches long. Growing in clusters, and loosely resembling *carambola*, or star fruit, *kamias* has five rounded longitudinal lobes. It is best suited for *sinigang na isda* (sour fish soup; see variation). *Kamias* is available all year round but rarely found at market. In a wonderful tradition of communal sharing, Filipinos usually collect their *kamias* directly from a *bilimbi* tree (a.k.a. cucumber tree) in their backyard. Once mature, *kamias* do not last long, and are often given to anyone who needs them for making *sinigang* or refreshing salads. (Tamarind is also backyard grown, widely used in cooking, and shared among neighbors when ripe.)

Good substitutes for *kamias* (not available in the United States) are unripe *carambola*, which I use here in the sour fish soup variation. Fresh tamarind pods or packaged tamarind pulp are available at specialty food markets, Asian markets, or through mail-order sources.

1. Bring the pork stock to a boil in a pot over high heat. Lower the heat to medium and add the tamarind extract, ginger, onion, and tomatoes, and cook for 10 minutes.

2. Add the fish sauce, adjust the seasoning with salt and pepper to taste, and add the pork, leafy greens, and yard-long beans. Stir well and simmer until the pork turns opaque and cooks through, 2 to 3 minutes. Ladle the soup into large individual soup bowls and garnish with scallions.

Variation: To make the Bicol rich and spicy fish version called *sinigang na isda*, substitute 6 cups fish stock (page 123) and 2 cups coconut milk (page 77) for the pork stock. Follow the rest of the instructions, adding 3 whole fresh or dried red chilies to the soup. Substitute 12 ounces white fish fillet such as cod (cut into large chunks) for the pork tenderloin, and add it along with a small unripe green *carambola* (star fruit thinly sliced into stars and seeds removed if any) to the soup just before serving. And remember, anything goes as long as it is sour!

IN THE PHILIPPINES, as in other Asian countries, brothy soups are served and enjoyed throughout the meal, and not only as starters. During the meal, *sinigang,* which also serves as a drink, is sipped to cleanse the palate and stimulate the appetite; accordingly, bowls are constantly replenished. Some Filipino cooks say that *sinigang* improves with age. They leave it in the refrigerator for a day or two, letting the flavors blend, then reheat it.

KALBI T'ANG
BEEF SHORT RIB SOUP

SERVES 4 TO 6

8 cups BASIC BEEF STOCK made
   using BEEF SHORT RIBS
   (page 120)
2½ tablespoons KOREAN or
   JAPANESE DARK SOY SAUCE
1½ tablespoons GRANULATED
   SUGAR
1 large GARLIC CLOVE, crushed,
   peeled, and minced
3 SCALLIONS, root and dark green
   ends trimmed, and 6-inch stalks
   thinly sliced into rounds
2 teaspoons toasted SESAME SEEDS
Freshly ground BLACK PEPPER
12 ounces cooked SHORT RIBS
   from the stock, shredded
KOSHER SALT

THE KOREANS ARE PASSIONATE beef eaters. Whether in Korea or in New York's Koreatown, whether in a private home or a restaurant, rarely have I had a Korean meal without beef. It shows up at practically every meal, if not as one of the main dishes, then most definitely as a clear broth. A variation on a much more complex traditional soup (see sidebar), this soup is a common example of the type sipped throughout a meal. Like many subtle clear soups in Korea, it is garnished by individual diners with some thinly sliced scallion and sea salt to taste.

As is the case with many Korean soups, you can also serve it as a light meal by adding thin wheat noodles such as *somen*, and garnishing with thinly sliced scallion and sea salt to taste.

1. Bring the beef stock to a boil in a pot over high heat, then reduce to medium-low. Meanwhile, whisk together the soy sauce and sugar in a bowl until the sugar is completely dissolved. Add the garlic, 2 tablespoons scallions, toasted sesame seeds, and some pepper. Marinate the cooked and shredded short rib meat for 15 minutes.

2. Add the meat to the stock and continue to simmer until heated through and the flavors have developed, about 20 minutes. (Do not pat dry the meat before adding to the stock. Much of the flavor will come from the marinade.) Ladle the soup into large individual bowls and instruct your guests to garnish with the remaining scallions and salt to taste.

A FASCINATING oxtail beef stock is the Korean *kom t'ang*. Milky white, it obtains its color from a slow-cook process. The oxtail simmers in water in huge vats for a minimum of 24 hours. *Kom t'ang* is usually eaten at restaurants specifically set up to make it. When I first had it, I thought it was bland, especially after having had other types of Korean food, which more often than not tends to be spicy. After several tries, I came to appreciate it as a subtle yet rich palate cleanser. Making it in small portions doesn't work. At Komt'ang restaurant in New York City's Koreatown, two large vats full of the stock are kept in plain view at the rear of the dining area. I'm told the stock has never come off the fire; the pots are simply replenished with water every so often.

WANJA T'ANG
MEATBALL AND TOFU SOUP

SERVES 4 TO 6

12 ounces GROUND BEEF
  (70 percent lean)
8 ounces firm TOFU, drained
4 SCALLIONS, root and dark green
  ends trimmed, 2 6-inch stalks
  minced, 2 cut into 1½-inch-long
  pieces crosswise and julienned
1 large GARLIC CLOVE, crushed,
  peeled, and minced
1 tablespoon KOREAN or JAPANESE
  DARK SOY SAUCE
1 teaspoon SESAME OIL
2 teaspoons toasted SESAME SEEDS
8 cups BASIC BEEF STOCK
  (page 120)
KOSHER SALT
Freshly ground BLACK PEPPER

WANJA T'ANG, meatballs in broth, is a popular dish in Korea. Made with a rich beef broth, it not only serves as a soup to cleanse the palate but as a beef dish as well. Simple to make, the small meatballs are a delicious item you can also easily serve to children. Like all soups in Korea, meatball soup is lean: the traditional Korean kitchen skims the fat from soups and uses lean cuts of beef for the meatballs.

The best way to drain the tofu cakes is to cut them into ½-inch-thick slices, place each slice between two double layers of paper towels on a plate, and refrigerate overnight. The next day the towels are laden with the water absorbed from the tofu, and the tofu is ready to be incorporated into your recipe.

1. Mix together the ground beef, tofu, minced scallions, garlic, soy sauce, sesame oil, and sesame seeds in a bowl until thoroughly combined. Shape the mixture into 24 small meatballs.

2. Meanwhile, bring the stock to a boil in a pot over high heat. Reduce the heat to medium and add the meatballs. When the meatballs are cooked through and floating on the surface, about 3 minutes, add the scallions, adjust the seasoning with salt and pepper, and cook for 30 seconds more. Divide the meatballs among large individual soup bowls and ladle broth over each serving.

Variation: If you like crispy meatballs, dip each meatball in a beaten-egg mixture and dredge them in flour. Heat 1 or more tablespoons vegetable oil in a skillet over high heat and pan-fry the meatballs, rolling them around to brown them evenly, about 5 minutes. Eat them as finger food, or served in broth.

SAMLAW MACHOU KROEUNG
SPICY BEEF
AMBROSIA SOUP

SERVES 4 TO 6

4 NEW MEXICO CHILIES

16 CURRY LEAVES (optional)

1 tablespoon VEGETABLE OIL

⅓ cup KROEUNG (page 78)

2 to 3 fresh THAI CHILIES; or dried
  RED CHILIES

8 cups BASIC or SOUTHEAST ASIAN
  BEEF STOCK (page 120 or 121,
  respectively)

⅓ cup TAMARIND EXTRACT
  (page 75)

1 to 2 tablespoons FISH EXTRACT
  (page 76), FISH SAUCE, or
  SHRIMP PASTE

1 or more tablespoons
  GRANULATED SUGAR

1 pound boneless BEEF SHANK
  from making BEEF STOCK,
  shredded; or 1 pound SIRLOIN,
  thinly sliced

12 round THAI EGGPLANTS,
  stemmed and halved; or
  2 JAPANESE EGGPLANTS,
  stemmed and cut into bite-size
  chunks

1 bunch CHINESE or regular
  WATERCRESS, tough stems
  trimmed

KOSHER SALT

Freshly ground BLACK PEPPER

S AMLAW MACHOU KROEUNG can only be described as Southeast Asian am-
brosia. A medley of spicy, sweet, and tangy flavors, it is Khmer food at
its best. What makes this soup distinctive is the subtle play of flavor and
texture derived mainly from an herbal paste called *kroeung*. While the lemongrass and tamarind provide tanginess, the chilies, garlic, and shallots give it
different levels of spiciness, and galangal, toasted curry leaves, and kaffir
lime leaves (or lime zest) lend a subtle bitter note. Perfectly balanced with
the sweetness of beef shank and a small amount of sugar, the flavors are
rounded with Cambodian fermented fish extract, *tuk prahoc*, or shrimp paste.
The beautiful color comes from yellow-orange turmeric and red chilies.
There is nothing timid about this soup; even its aroma is bold. A perfect
complement to *samlaw machou kroeung* is a simple serving of jasmine rice,
which tempers the spicy heat.

Thai eggplants, streaky green and white, are approximately the size of
Ping-Pong or golf balls. Widely used in Southeast Asian cuisine, they are
available in Southeast Asian markets. If you cannot find them, however, Japanese eggplants or tiny Italian eggplants will do. You will also find galangal,
turmeric, and kaffir lime leaves, fresh or frozen, at Asian markets, or over
the Internet.

1. Soak the New Mexico chilies in
water for 30 minutes. Split them
open to remove the seeds and veins.
With a spoon scrape out the pulp.

2. Heat a dry skillet over high heat
and toast the curry leaves until they
crisp or crackle, a few seconds on
each side. Remove from the heat
and set aside.

3. Heat the oil in a heavy-bottomed
pot over medium-high heat and
add the *kroeung* paste, New Mexico
Chili pulp, and whole chilies. Allow

the paste to sizzle while stirring to
prevent it from burning, until it just
darkens, about 2 minutes. Add the
beef stock, tamarind juice, fish extract
(fish sauce, or shrimp paste), and
sugar, and bring to a boil. Reduce the
heat to medium-low, add the beef,
eggplants, and watercress, adjust the
seasoning with salt and pepper, and
cook until the flavors develop, about
15 minutes more. Stir in the toasted
curry leaves and allow their flavor to
render about 5 minutes more. Ladle
the soup into large individual soup
bowls and serve with rice on the side.

THAYCHILIES, ALSO KNOWN AS "FINGER" CHILIES, ARE USED WHOLE OR CHOPPED, WITH OR WITHOUT THE SEEDS, IN MANY SOUTHEAST ASIAN CUISINES.

WHILE GIVING a cooking demonstration at Rhode Island School of Design, in Providence, one day, my hosts and I went to the Four Seasons Cambodian Restaurant in Cranston, Rhode Island, a nearby town with a large Cambodian community. I was very excited because it is difficult to find Cambodian restaurants, let alone authentic Cambodian restaurants, in many parts of the United States. Although the menu had everything from Chinese to Thai and Vietnamese dishes, its Cambodian menu was quite good. *Samlaw machou kroeung* was perhaps the most authentic and delicious Cambodian dish on the menu. With a little encouragement from our table, the chef was good enough to make it spicy, just as he would have in Cambodia.

MENG KU SHUA YANG JOU KUO

MONGOLIAN LAMB HOT POT

SERVES 4 TO 6

12 to 16 dried small to medium
SHIITAKE MUSHROOMS

12 cups BASIC LAMB STOCK
(page 122)

½ pound dried flat WHEAT
NOODLES

1 cup SHAOXING WINE

¼ cup CHINESE WHITE RICE
VINEGAR

⅓ cup SOY SAUCE

¼ cup GRANULATED SUGAR

1 or more tablespoons SESAME
PASTE

1 tablespoon CHILI AND GARLIC
SAUCE (page 106); or
commercial equivalent

2 to 2½ pounds LAMB SHOULDER
OR LEG, thinly sliced against the
grain

3 heads small BABY BOK CHOY; or
1 bunch SPINACH, trimmed and
leaves separated

8 large NAPA CABBAGE LEAVES,
halved lengthwise and cut
crosswise in 1-inch-wide strips

3 SCALLIONS, root and dark green
ends trimmed, and 6-inch stalks
cut into 1½-inch-long pieces
crosswise

NOMADIC TRIBES COLONIZED at various points in their history by Turkish and Chinese rulers, the Mongols reversed the military tables under Genghis Khan and ruled an empire that stretched from Yugoslavia in Europe to all of China in Asia. Originating in the highland plateaus of what is now modern landlocked Mongolia, the Mongols traditionally raised livestock, including the "five animals": sheep, goats, cattle, horses, and camels. They lived on these and other meats (and their dairy products) in the form of simple soups and stews, and boiled, grilled, or roasted dishes. With less than one percent of the land in agricultural production, wheat is the major crop, giving the traditional Mongol kitchen its breads, and, through Chinese influences, its dumplings and noodles. Remembering their humble beginnings, even some modern Mongolian recipes start with phrases like "first kill the goat" (with detailed instructions) and include techniques such as cooking animal carcasses with fire-heated rocks. One of the most important and influential dishes, meng ku shua yang jou kuo, or Mongolian lamb (or mutton) hot pot, dates back four or five hundred years. Originally this may have been a communal celebration of a successful kill that incorporated sharing of the meat. Meat soups, sometimes employing tea as a base, are important in Mongol cooking, but they are exceedingly straightforward. In khar shol (generically, meat or "black" soup—dairy is "white"), meat and bones are boiled in a pot, other ingredients such as potatoes and salt being optional. About a hundred years after its inception among the Mongols, the hot pot was adopted by the Chinese, who called their version da bin low (pp. 156–57). Consistent with Chinese culinary tradition, da bin low evolved as a more refined food, introducing herbal notes such as ginger and scallion, and mutating into a culinary technique as much as a specific recipe. Reflecting China's regional differences and widespread colonial influences in Asia, the dish developed numerous variations. Szechwanese versions, for example, have hot chilies in the broth, the Cantonese introduce seafood, and the Japanese have a more subtle character. In the modern Chinese interpretation of the Mongolian dish, guests dip thin slices of strong-flavored raw lamb in a communal pot of gently boiling lamb broth. This particular recipe—which is akin to a "Mongolian hot pot" you might be served in a contemporary Beijing restaurant—reflects three-hundred-odd years of adaptation and enthusiasm. The dipping sauces use Chinese ingredients, also adjusted for the lamb.

Unlike the Cantonese *da bin low*, in which cellophane noodles are cooked in the broth as a finale to the meal, do not cook the wheat noodles in the broth. The wheat will cloud the broth. Instead, be sure to cook the noodles separately as the recipe suggests.

1. Put the shiitakes in a bowl with hot water to cover, then set a plate over the bowl to prevent steam from escaping. Let stand until the mushrooms rehydrate and soften, about 30 minutes (or longer depending on the size of the mushrooms). Squeeze the mushrooms between the palms of your hands to get rid of the excess water. Using a paring knife, remove any hard stems from the mushrooms and set the caps aside.

2. Bring the stock with the shiitakes to a boil in a pot over high heat. Transfer the stock to a traditional hot pot vessel heated by charcoal, or an electric wok that you can plug in. Always keep the stock at a constant gentle boil. You will need to maintain the charcoal amount if using the traditional vessel, or keep the electric wok on a medium to medium-low setting.

3. Bring a pot of water to a boil over high heat and cook the wheat noodles until tender but firm, about 3 minutes. Drain and shock under cold running water. Drain again and cover with plastic wrap until ready to use.

4. Whisk together the wine, vinegar, soy sauce, and sugar in a bowl, until the sugar is completely dissolved. Stir in the sesame paste and chili and garlic paste until thoroughly combined. Divide the dipping sauce among individual sauce dishes.

5. Arrange the lamb on one communal plate (for everyone to share) or individual plates. Place the bok choy, napa cabbage, and scallions on a second set of individual plates.

6. Encourage your guests to take a slice of raw lamb or vegetable, using chopsticks, and lower the piece into the simmering broth until cooked to the preferred doneness. The morsel is then fished out with chopsticks or small wire strainers and dipped into the dipping sauce. After all the meat and vegetables are finished, the diners put noodles in their bowls and ladle hot broth over them for a delicious noodle soup.

SHINSOLLO
KOREAN "FANCY" HOT POT

SERVES 4 TO 6

8 ounces GROUND BEEF
(70 percent lean)

½ cup TAPIOCA STARCH or
CORNSTARCH

6 large EGGS, 2 separated into
yolks and whites

5 SCALLIONS, dark green tops
and ends trimmed, one 6-inch
stalk minced, four cut into
2-inch-long pieces crosswise

2 medium GARLIC CLOVES,
crushed, peeled, and minced

4 teaspoons KOREAN or JAPANESE
DARK SOY SAUCE

1 teaspoon toasted SESAME SEEDS,
crushed

1 teaspoon SESAME OIL

KOSHER SALT

Freshly ground BLACK PEPPER

4 ounces BEEF LIVER, sliced
diagonally into thin strips

2 tablespoons GINGER EXTRACT
(page 74)

4 ounces WHITE FISH FILLET,
such as FLOUNDER or SOLE,
sliced diagonally into thin flat
strips

4 ounces BEEF EYE OF ROUND,
thinly sliced against the grain,
then shredded

1 small ONION, peeled, halved, and
sliced into thin wedges

8 cups BASIC BEEF BROTH
(page 120)

O F ALL ASIAN CUISINES, *shinsollo* (Korean "fancy" hot pot) is perhaps the most closely related to the Mongolian hot pot. Similar to what is reputed to be both the earliest forms of the recipe and to Mongolian meat cooking today, modern Korean cooks layer the ingredients in the hot pot vessel (also *shinsollo*) with some broth, then serve it. Diners simply pick out the cooked morsels from the pot. Han Jung Ha, director of the cooking academy of the same name in Seoul, notes, "*Shinsollo* was originally served to the emperors, but today it is enjoyed by everyone." Because the dish takes so long to prepare—the ingredients having been precooked in preparation for the hot pot—*shinsollo* is reserved for special occasions and served during *kyoja sang*, a traditional party table where meat, fish, and various vegetables are served in addition to the hot pot. Consistent with many Korean dishes such as *bimbim pap* (pp. 214–15), *chap chae* (page 250), and *kujolp'an* (page 94), and the borrowed Chinese philosophy of balanced opposites known as *yin yang*, the five elements (wood, metal, fire, water, and earth) are represented by colors (green, white, red, black, and yellow, respectively) and appear in the form of color-selected foods such as bell pepper, egg white, carrot (considered to be in the red family), shiitake mushrooms, and egg yolk. This ritualized concern for color in food, incidentally, is echoed in Korean architecture, art, and clothing, as well.

The Korean hot pot vessel is essentially the same as the Japanese *shabu-shabu* vessel; both are derived from the Chinese hot pot vessel, and you can use them interchangeably.

---

1 large CARROT, peeled and cut
into thin 2-inch-long planks

6 large SHIITAKE MUSHROOMS

12 WALNUT HALVES, peeled

24 GINGKO NUTS, shelled

1. Mix together the ground beef, 2 tablespoons of the tapioca starch, 1 egg (beaten), the minced scallion, 1 teaspoon minced garlic, 2 teaspoons soy sauce, ½ teaspoon sesame seeds, sesame oil, and a pinch of salt and pepper in a bowl until thoroughly combined. Heat a well-greased 8- to 10-inch nonstick pan over medium heat, spread half the meat mixture into a thin even layer, and cook until well done, 2 to 3 minutes. Slide onto a plate and allow to cool prior to cutting into approximately 1-inch squares. Form 12 small meatballs with the remaining mixture and pan-fry them in a well-greased nonstick pan over medium heat until cooked through, about 4 minutes total. (Be sure to roll the meatballs around to brown evenly.) Transfer the meatballs to a plate and set aside.

2. Pat dry the liver slices, season with salt and pepper, and sprinkle with 1 tablespoon ginger extract. Place 2 tablespoons tapioca starch in a bowl, and 1 egg (beaten) in another. Dredge each liver slice in the tapioca starch, shaking off any excess, and dip in the egg wash. Heat a well-greased nonstick pan over medium-high heat and pan-fry the liver until well cooked, about 2 minutes per side. Transfer to a plate and set aside. Repeat the same process with the fish, using 2 tablespoons fresh tapioca starch and 1 egg (beaten). Clean the nonstick pan and heat it, well-greased, over medium-high heat. Pan-fry the fish slices until well cooked, about 1 minute per side. Transfer to a plate and set aside.

3. Place the remaining 2 tablespoons tapioca starch in a bowl, and 1 egg (beaten) in another. Using wooden toothpicks, skewer the remaining cut scallions (3 pieces on a single toothpick) crosswise so they are all the same length. Dredge each scallion skewer in the tapioca starch, shaking off any excess, and dip in the egg wash. Heat a well-greased nonstick pan over medium-high heat and pan-fry the scallions until well cooked, about 2 minutes per side. Transfer to a plate and set aside. When cool enough to handle, carefully remove the toothpicks so as not to separate the bound scallions.

4. Whisk the 2 egg yolks until loose. In a well-greased nonstick pan over medium-low heat, cook the yolks into a thin omelette, about 2 minutes. Slide onto a plate and allow to cool. Repeat this process with the 2 egg whites. Slice these into 2-inch-long and ½-inch-wide rectangular strips.

5. Mix together the beef eye of round, onion wedges, and remaining soy sauce, minced garlic, and crushed sesame seeds in a bowl until evenly combined. Spread this mixture in an even layer around the bottom of the hot pot vessel. Working in single uniform layers (overlapping the morsels when necessary), spread the beef squares, liver patties, and fish patties. On top, vertically arrange the carrots, pan-fried scallions, shiitake mushrooms, and egg white and egg yolk strips, overlapping and interchanging them to create a continuous rainbow of the five colors. Pour the beef broth over the ingredients, making sure not to disturb the arrangement. On the outer edge of the vessel, place the meatballs, interchanging them with gingko nuts. Around the chimney pipe, arrange the walnuts with a few more gingko nuts. Heat the hot pot and serve with rice.

DA BIN LOW
CHINESE HOT POT

One .7-ounce package dried
CELLOPHANE NOODLES

12 to 16 dried small to medium
SHIITAKE MUSHROOMS

12 cups BASIC CHICKEN STOCK
(page 116) or SUPERIOR STOCK
(page 117)

8 ounces BEEF EYE OF ROUND,
sliced paper thin against the
grain diagonally

1 skinless CHICKEN BREAST, sliced
paper thin against the grain
diagonally

8 ounces fresh FLOUNDER FILLET,
cut into ¼-inch slices against the
grain diagonally

12 small to medium BLUE TIGER
SHRIMP, heads removed, shelled,
and deveined

4 heads small BABY BOK CHOY; or
1 bunch SPINACH, trimmed and
leaves separated

12 large NAPA CABBAGE LEAVES,
halved lengthwise and cut
crosswise in 1-inch-wide strips

GINGER-INFUSED VINEGAR
DIPPING SAUCE (page 89)

CHILI AND GARLIC SAUCE
(page 106)

CHINESE NEW YEAR would not be a celebration without *da bin low*, or Chinese hot pot (also known as Cantonese steamboat), the traditional fondue served during this holiday since the early 1700s. Plates filled with any combination of meat and seafood are placed around a communal vessel containing ginger-infused chicken stock. A classic hot pot vessel has a built-in underpipe or "chimney" that holds hot charcoals and keeps the stock at a constant gentle boil, allowing the ingredients to be cooked at the table. (You can also use an electric wok for heating the stock in the center of the table if you wish.) Vegetables such as shiitakes, bok choy, and napa cabbage are added to the stock. After all the meats and vegetables have been eaten, softened cellophane noodles are added to the stock until cooked. Everyone takes a serving of noodles with some broth and slurps and sips. Although traditionally reserved for the Chinese New Year celebration, it is a satisfying meal that can be had any time of the year.

While I've listed some of my favorite ingredients, you can add your own. For example, try baby squid, butterflied and halved, clams, pork, lamb, spinach, Swiss chard, or anything similar you might enjoy.

1. Soak the cellophane noodles and shiitakes in two separate bowls of water to cover until rehydrated, about 30 minutes (or longer for the mushrooms, depending on their thickness). Drain and squeeze the noodles and mushrooms to get rid of the excess water. Place the noodles in a bowl and seal with plastic wrap so they do not dry out, and set aside. With a paring knife, remove any stems from the mushrooms and set the caps aside.

2. Bring the stock with the shiitakes to a boil in a pot over high heat. Transfer the stock to a traditional hot pot vessel heated by charcoal, or an electric wok that you can plug in. Always keep the stock at a constant gentle boil. You will need to maintain the charcoal amount if using the traditional vessel, or keep the electric wok on a medium to medium-low setting.

3. You can arrange the ingredients in one of two ways. The more traditional way is to arrange all the raw ingredients on their individual plates for everyone to share. Another way is to arrange a portion of beef, chicken, fish, and shrimp on individual plates and the bok choy and napa cabbage on a second set of individual plates with the cellophane noodles in the center.

4. Encourage your guests to take raw morsels, whether protein or vegetable or both, using chopsticks, and lower the pieces into the simmering broth until cooked. Then each diner will need to fish out the pieces with chopsticks or small wire strainers and dip them in a selection of dipping sauces, including the ones listed in the ingredients list or straight from the bottle (Chinese thin soy sauce or hoisin sauce, for example). After all the meat and vegetables are finished, you can add the cellophane noodles to the broth until cooked, about 5 minutes. Each diner should then fish out and transfer a portion of the cooked noodles into his or her bowl and ladle hot broth over them for a delicious noodle soup.

THE DRAGON DANCE CELEBRATES THE YEAR OF THE DRAGON, LUNAR CALENDAR YEAR 4698, HONG KONG.

BO NHUNG DAM
VIETNAMESE
SOUR BEEF HOT POT

SERVES 4 TO 6

4 ounces dried RICE VERMICELLI

4 to 6 ANCHOVY FILLETS packed in oil, drained

1 tablespoon GRANULATED SUGAR

Juice of 1 LEMON

2 THAI CHILIES, stemmed, seeded, and minced

2 large GARLIC CLOVES, 1 crushed and peeled, 1 minced

1 cup minced ripe PINEAPPLE

8 cups SOUTHEAST ASIAN BEEF STOCK (page 121)

1 or more cups CHINESE WHITE RICE VINEGAR

1 large SHALLOT, peeled and thinly sliced

1 LEMONGRASS STALK, root end trimmed, outer leaves and tough green top removed, and 6-inch inner bulb cut into ¼-inch-thick diagonal slices

Dash of SESAME OIL

2 to 2½ pounds BEEF EYE OF ROUND, thinly sliced against the grain

2 heads BOSTON LETTUCE, trimmed, leaves separated

1 bunch MINT, stems trimmed

1 bunch CILANTRO, stems trimmed

1 bunch THAI BASIL, stems trimmed

VIETNAMESE HOT POT is both related to and different from other Chinese-derived Mongolian hot pots. Like all versions of this dish, it uses broth for cooking the ingredients. Like the Japanese *shabu-shabu*, it uses beef. It also incorporates Southeast Asian traditions, however, including assertive spicing, the use of fruit and fish notes (pineapple and anchovy fillets), fresh herbs, and wrapping of the cooked morsels in lettuce before eating. Unlike other Asian versions, the broth—a combination of vinegar and beef broth in equal amounts—is traditionally not drunk at the end of the meal. I have always thought of this as a bit of a waste, however, and here I use Southeast Asian beef stock—a fragrant, sweet stock used in making the traditional Hanoi rice and beef noodle soup (pp. 228–29) combined with less vinegar than in the traditional recipe.

The pineapple and anchovy dipping sauce is pungent and may be an acquired taste; a dab will go a long way.

1. Place the dried rice vermicelli in a dish with water to cover. Let stand until pliable, about 30 minutes, and drain. Bring a pot of water to a boil over high heat and cook the vermicelli until tender but firm, about 30 seconds. Drain and shock under cold running water. Drain again and set aside, covered with plastic wrap to prevent the vermicelli from drying out.

2. Crush together the anchovies and the 1 teaspoon sugar until smooth. Add the lemon juice, chilies, minced garlic, and pineapple and crush lightly so the sauce is still somewhat chunky. Divide among individual sauce dishes.

3. Bring the stock, vinegar, the remaining sugar, the crushed garlic, shallot, lemongrass, and sesame oil to a boil over high heat. Transfer the stock to a traditional hot pot vessel heated by charcoal, or an electric wok that you can plug in. Always keep the stock at a constant gentle boil. You will need to maintain the charcoal amount if using the traditional vessel, or keep the electric wok on a medium to medium-low setting.

4. Arrange the beef on a communal plate or individual plates, and the lettuce, mint, cilantro, and Thai basil on another communal plate, or individual ones.

5. Encourage your guests to take a slice of raw beef, using chopsticks, and lower it into the simmering broth until cooked to the desired doneness. Each diner will need to fish out the pieces with chopsticks or small wire strainers and place the morsel on a lettuce leaf with some freshly torn herb leaves and a few strands of rice vermicelli. Rolled up, the bundle should be dipped into the anchovy and pineapple sauce prior to taking a bite. After all the meat and vegetables are finished, you can ladle some broth into a bowl and sip.

SHABU-SHABU
JAPANESE BUBBLING
BEEF HOT POT

SERVES 4 TO 6

2 to 2½ pounds prime-quality
MARBLED BEEF, thinly sliced
against the grain

4 SCALLIONS, root and dark green
ends trimmed, and 6-inch stalks
cut into 1½-inch-long pieces
crosswise

12 to 16 small to medium
SHIITAKE MUSHROOMS, stems
removed

8 large NAPA CABBAGE LEAVES,
halved lengthwise and cut
crosswise into 1-inch-wide
strips

6 ounces BAMBOO SHOOTS, halved
lengthwise and thinly sliced

8 ounces firm TOFU, cut into
¾-inch cubes

8 ounces WHEAT GLUTEN CAKES
(pp. 290–91; or commercial
equivalent; optional)

6-inch-square piece of KELP

PONZU SAUCE (page 90)

GOMA DARE (page 102)

*S*HABU-SHABU is the Japanese version of the Chinese hot pot (pp. 156–57) and Mongolian lamb hot pot (pp. 152–53). Compared to the Chinese and Mongolian versions, which are centuries old, Japanese *shabu-shabu* is fairly recent: the Japanese did not eat beef until well into the mid-1800s. Also, in comparison to its older hot-pot cousins—as well as the Vietnamese hot pot (pp. 158–59)—*shabu-shabu* is very subtle in flavor. Here the morsels of beef—often very marbled tender beef such as Kobe (meat from steer fed and massaged with beer)—are boiled in mildly flavored kelp water (not to be confused with very concentrated kelp stock; pp. 124–25), then dipped in either *ponzu* or *goma dare* dipping sauces. (The name *shabu-shabu* comes from the noise the beef makes when swished around in the boiling liquid.) The Japanese will caution you to cook the beef first, then the vegetables, so your water turns into a fragrant broth at the end of the meal, which you can sip. The health-conscious can substitute beef filet mignon, which has less fat, for the marbled beef.

1. Arrange the beef and scallions on one communal plate or individual plates. Place the shiitakes, napa cabbage, and bamboo shoots on a communal plate or individual plates. Place the tofu and wheat gluten, if using, on a communal plate or 4 individual plates.

2. Meanwhile, wipe the kelp with a dampened cloth, cut it into 6 strips, and place it in a pot with 2 quarts water. Bring to a boil over high heat, then remove the kelp. (Hint: The kelp can be reused, since its use here is minimal; refrigerate.) Transfer the liquid to a traditional hot pot vessel heated by charcoal, or an electric wok that you can plug in. Always keep the cooking liquid at a constant gentle boil. You will need to maintain the charcoal amount if using the traditional vessel, or keep the electric wok on a medium to medium-low setting.

3. Encourage your guests to take a slice of beef, vegetable, or other items, using chopsticks, and lower the piece into the simmering broth until cooked to the preferred doneness. The morsel is then fished out with chopsticks or small wire strainers and dipped into the dipping sauce. After all the meat and vegetables are finished, ladle some broth in a bowl and sip.

SOTO BABAT
FRAGRANT BEEF
TRIPE SOUP

SERVES 4 TO 6

1 cup plus 1 tablespoon CHINESE
    WHITE RICE VINEGAR
2½ pounds BEEF HONEYCOMB
    TRIPE
KOSHER SALT
Freshly ground BLACK PEPPER
¼ cup SAMBAL TERASI (page 79)
1 tablespoon CHILI AND GARLIC
    SAUCE (page 106)
2 tablespoons TOMATO PASTE
10 cups BASIC BEEF STOCK
    (page 120)
3 large GARLIC CLOVES, crushed
    and peeled
1 ounce fresh GINGER, peeled and
    finely grated
2 LEMONGRASS STALKS, root ends
    trimmed, outer leaves and tough
    green tops removed, and 6-inch-
    long inner bulbs finely ground
4 KAFFIR LIME LEAVES; or zest of
    1 LIME
6 ounces DAIKON, peeled,
    quartered, and thinly sliced
FRIED SHALLOTS (page 108)

OTO BABAT is a delicious beef tripe soup full of fragrant herbs and spices. While I like my tripe very tender (similar to the way the French and Italians prepare it, cooking it for eight hours or more), this soup traditionally uses tripe that is cooked only for an hour or so, and is a bit chewy. I've adjusted the classic recipe to my liking, splitting the difference in cooking time between Indonesian- and Western-style cooking techniques. Because the cooking time is extended, I have added more stock than might otherwise be used in the traditional recipe. This soup sometimes is paired with a tomato-based sauce called *sambal tomat* for a sweet and spicy note. Meanwhile, if you want to prepare the authentic version, see the variation below.

1. Bring 3 quarts water to a boil in a pot over high heat. Reduce the heat to medium-low, add 1 cup vinegar and the tripe, and season with salt and pepper. Simmer for an hour, drain, and cut the tripe into 1-inch square pieces.

2. In a small saucepan heat the *sambal terasi* over medium heat. Stir in the chili and garlic sauce and tomato paste until well combined and heated thoroughly, about 3 minutes. Remove the spicy tomato paste from the heat.

3. Bring the beef stock to a boil in a pot over high heat. Reduce the heat to medium-low, add the tripe, the remaining vinegar, garlic, ginger, lemongrass, and lime leaves and simmer, partially covered, until the tripe is tender, about 5 hours. Add

the daikon and cook for an additional 15 minutes. Ladle the soup into large individual soup bowls, garnish with fried shallots, and serve with the spicy tomato paste on the side. Instruct your guests to add the paste to taste.

Variation: For an authentic, albeit chewy, version of *soto babat*, follow step 1. When you're ready for step 3, simmer the tripe along with all the other ingredients, including the daikon, until the daikon is cooked through, about 15 minutes. Serve the soup according to the instructions (and get ready to chew your soup!).

3

RICE,

NOODLES,

DUMPLINGS,

AND

BREADS

RICE, NOODLES, DUMPLINGS, AND BREADS are best considered as a single subject in Asian cooking because they share common ingredients, preparation techniques, and historical evolution. The cook who is new to the Asian kitchen may be surprised to learn that breads are relegated to a fairly insignificant role, while rice, often thought of as a side dish in the West, occupies a central role in the East. Deeply ingrained in Asian cultures for millennia and appearing as grain, flour, dough, noodles, bread, beverage, alcoholic drink (both wine and spirit), seasoning, dessert, and more, rice is in many ways Asian cuisine. Noodles, and their ancestral predecessors, dumplings (or boiled dough), appear with significant frequency as well, and the aspiring cook will want to

PREVIOUS SPREAD: A FIELD OF SHORT-GRAIN RICE IN KYONGJU, KOREA

master the fundamentals of selecting and preparing the dozens of different noodle types that are available in markets today. Fresh noodles such as thin or thick, round or flat, rice, wheat, and egg noodles are available all year round in the refrigerated food sections, and in some cases (e.g., Japanese buckwheat noodles) the frozen food sections of Asian markets. All sorts of dried noodles are also available. As complex as the choices among the many types can seem, certain basic rules and assumptions will serve as a guide: for example, as with Italian pasta, thin types go well with light sauces; thick types go well with heavier sauces. As my architect husband might say, "Once you understand the architecture of the food, it is simple." Breads have either indigenously evolved in wheat-growing cultures, such as Mongolia, the northern and far western provinces of China, and cities such as Beijing and Shanghai, or were adapted from European colonial models such as Portuguese, American, and Spanish in the Philippines, and French in Vietnam and Cambodia. In this chapter, I have organized the recipes into rice, wheat, egg, and buckwheat noodle dishes, and mung bean and potato starch–based cellophane noodle dishes.

RICE

IN CHINA, when a mother calls her family to the table, she says, "Chi fen"—eat rice. So essential is the grain that its very name is equated with food and, implicitly, life. Whether as a grain or as flour noodles, sheets, or dough, it occupies a place in Asian kitchens similar to that of wheat in the West: a building block of life. Culturally, however, it looms even larger. Nearly always present in some form or other at meals, it is also an important part of rituals and celebrations. A symbol of prosperity (if you have rice, you have wealth), it is thought of as sacred, an offering to the gods. Its presence in the Asian diet cannot be overstated. Shops in Chinatowns everywhere sport twenty-five-pound bags of rice piled high. Presentation of a complementary bowl of rice when being served in a restaurant is expected. Sweets have a rice base; so do powerful alcoholic drinks. And when my Asian aunts call their families to the table, to this day, whether there is rice or not, they still say, "Chi fen."

Rice has been cultivated all over Asia for millennia. Used as a boiled grain, it is eaten nearly everywhere, except in locales where it is particularly difficult to grow and wheat takes its place as the main crop (as in Mongolia). Westerners are familiar with Asian fried rice dishes, and may have an attraction to flavored rice dishes; Asian cooks tend to think of rice as a blank canvas. It is upon that canvas that a multitude of colorful, flavorful dishes begins. From Chinese red-cooked chicken (pp. 488–89) to Korean braised black cod (page 393), the humble white grain is both a foundation and an integral element.

My father likes to remind me that the subject of rice cultivation and production is as complex as that of grape cultivation and wine production: "The soil, the weather, the experience and tastes of the grower, the care with which the grain is handled, the type of processing, the packaging, the storage—all this and more come into play. And remember, in Asia rice is also used for making wine."

In fact, all rice is one species, divided roughly into three major varietal groups—indica, japonica, and javanica—with dozens and dozens of regional and other variations. Rice in Asian cooking is understood as a neutral-flavored item, used according to its texture and its ability to absorb flavors. Jasmine rice, an

exception, is scented with jasmine leaves and valued for its subtle fragrance. The Asian cook may select the rice most fitting for a meal by its texture, although most simply choose by habit, frankly. For example, long-grain rice is common in everyday use in China and Southeast Asia. The slightly stickier medium and, more predominantly, short-grain rice are preferred in Japan and Korea. Special exceptions include the more filling and chewy sticky short-grain rice preferred in northern Thailand, which is enjoyed with refreshing light dishes such as green papaya salad. Brown rice, it should be noted, is sold with its bran intact (rather than polished off, as in white rice) and is not used much in Asian cultures. (Some Asians refer to it condescendingly as "cattle feed," and are amused by its popularity in the West.) Red rice and black rice also play minor roles. Red is considered an inferior type; black is used in certain sweetened dessert items.

Rice grains in themselves, which have undergone no flavoring process, have only very subtle differences in flavor, and are more apt to be influenced by relative freshness or storage technique. When cooking long-grain rice I sometimes add

fragrance by boiling it in chicken stock with fresh cilantro and fried garlic and ginger. When serving Indian dishes, I use basmati rice cooked with green cardamom, cumin, and clarified butter, as is traditional. At various meals I have offered my father basmati rice, prince rice, medium-grain rice, and sushi rice; and even cooked risotto for him. In the end he says, "The texture and flavor of long-grain jasmine rice is the best in the world," and considers others inferior.

Rice began as a wild grass, most likely in India, where it was slowly brought into domestic production over thousands of years, then spread through trade and war throughout Asia. Light, portable, easy to prepare, easily stored for long periods without spoiling, it was arguably one of the planet's first "fast foods." In certain very remote and still primitive parts of Indonesia where yam- and taro-based cuisines still persist and rice appeared as recently as five hundred years ago, it is still met with some suspicion, a "newfangled" foodstuff supplanting the Bronze Age tuber cultures.

The specifics of rice preparations are as varied as its cultivation. In the most common method of preparation, grains are boiled until the grains are fluffy, tender, and separate, then served as a foundation for simple meals or an accompaniment to complex meals. Rice can also be cooked down to a porridge or gruel, the base of a rice soup (congee or jook in China), and served as breakfast, lunch, dinner, or snack. Rice grains can be toasted and ground to a fine powder, then used as a flavoring binder in making Vietnamese fresh shrimp paste on sugar cane (page 421). Raw rice is also ground into flour for making breads and noodles. As the Chinese say: "A meal without rice is not a meal."

BOILED RICE PREPARATION

BOILED RICE PREPARATION—a basic building block of Asian cooking—is a matter of rinsing the rice, establishing the correct water-to-rice ratio, and getting the temperature right. Some rice package instructions state that you should not rinse rice before cooking, as rinsing ostensibly gets rid of nutrients. Every Asian cook I ever met disregards this advice and gently rinses their rice prior to cooking it.

Rice's texture and fluffiness, its degree of separation, and its stickiness or lack of stickiness are critical.

Like many things in Asian cooking, it is a matter of balance. To get perfectly cooked rice, rinse the rice three times to get rid of most but not all of the starch: put the rice in a medium bowl or use the utensil you will employ for cooking. Add water just to cover, then gently swirl your fingers around in the vessel to release the starch from the grains while draining the water. Repeat, and repeat again. At the third rinse, the water should be ever so slightly cloudy, and you should be able to see every grain through the water. If the water is too cloudy the grains will not be separate and fluffy when cooked. If the water is too clear the rice will be too dry. This may take a bit of practice before you get a feel for it, but it is very important that the water be ever so slightly cloudy, and equally important that you see the rice grains through the water. You then add water and cook the rice in a Chinese clay pot (glazed on the inside; unglazed on the outside). This will give you perfect results every time.

I am sorry to say that many Asian cooks have abandoned their clay pots for the extraordinarily popular electric rice cooker. These work well enough, and are set up to cook the rice nearly perfectly every time.

Everyone in my mother's generation seems to like the convenience of this device, and would never give it up. In my opinion, the rice cooker makes dry rice, especially when the cooker has a warming cycle, which automatically turns on so your rice is warm all day. I still like the look and feel of the clay. It smells great when the rice cooks and the grains are fluffy without being dry or wet. In my estimation there is a romantic aspect to cooking rice in something that has been used for thousands of years.

DECORATION OF BOILED RICE

AFTER MASTERING THE ART of cooking boiled rice, you will want to be at least conversant with the Japanese and Korean tradition of decorating rice. Herbs, leaves, and other such ingredients are typically sprinkled or dusted over a bowl of rice to lend subtle flavor, vary texture, and add color. Edible and inedible flowers are used for aesthetic effect. Julienned shiso leaves add a spicy note. Black sesame seeds add a bit of crunch. Nori (laver) adds a subtle taste of the sea, while matcha (green tea powder) gives a deep but understated bitter note. Individual cooks will also surprise you with their impulses. Japanese tea master Taeko Fujii once prepared shojin-ryori, a delightful vegetarian meal, for me at her home in Kyoto. Rather than throw away the trimmings from her daikon leafy stems, she blanched, chopped, and garnished our bowls of rice with them. I had never seen the minuscule stems used in this way. "I ask myself, why waste anything?" she said. "Even if they are tiny, the humble stems make your rice look beautiful." The impulse was cultural, the interpretation personal, the result memorable.

In Korea, a bowl of rice can be topped with items such as toasted sesame seeds, pine nuts, or thinly sliced scallions. I encourage you to do as the Japanese and Koreans do, adorning your rice with all sorts of understated and colorful toppings. Try julienned or finely diced blanched carrots, green peas, herbs such as cilantro or mint leaves, or thinly sliced jujubes.

RICE PORRIDGES AND SOUPS

CONGEE, OR RICE PORRIDGE, is a thick short-grain rice gruel served in Chinese kitchens the world over. Rice porridge was created as a way of stretching a meal in times of need, when there was not enough rice to go around. Three to four times more water than usual was added during the cooking process so that the rice grains would break down, eventually becoming gruel. A single bowl of rice, which could feed four people when boiled, would feed eight when cooked as a thick soup. The Cantonese call this rice porridge jook, meaning soft rice.

The most popular of all porridges—generically known in the West as congee—is bak jook, white congee (plain rice porridge), often referred to simply as jook. A dish found throughout the historical Chinese sphere of influence in Asia, it technically contains only rice and is made without even the simplest seasonings (including salt).

Jook needs to have a certain amount of stickiness when cooked. While some cooks like to mix long-grain rice and sticky short-grain rice, I prefer to use regular short-grain rice (sushi rice), which has a good amount of stickiness and breaks down beautifully. The result is a porridge that is never too loose, never too gummy, but always a delightfully balanced and refined dish. Other cooks add tapioca starch or cornstarch to thicken their rice porridge, an unnecessary step if the rice is properly selected.

While some enjoy congee for lunch and dinner—or as a midnight snack, as my father does—plain congees are most often eaten for breakfast with one or more side dishes such as scallion omelette, preserved cabbage, fermented bean curd, and pan-fried sweet pork sausage. Congee accompanied this way is light, yet filling enough to hold you over for a more satisfying lunch later on in the day. Because it is light and nutritious, it is eaten as a pick-me-up, or as a mild curative when someone is feeling under the weather, as in Japan.

Congee is also used as food for infants and young children. My grandmother Huong raised her children on it from the time they were babies. In turn, my aunts, my mother, and now my brother William have followed in my grandmother's footsteps. As we got older, my mother added crushed vegetables and finely shredded fish, chicken, and other tasty items such as thinly sliced and sautéed preserved mustard cabbage, developing our palates at the same time. Future generations of my family will no doubt follow in this tradition.

Although congee had a humble beginning, like so many Asian foods it has evolved into a sophisticated

JAVANESE RICE IS A UNIQUE GRAIN WITH A TEXTURE AND APPEARANCE SOME-
WHERE BETWEEN SHORT- AND LONG-GRAIN RICE.

dish. Combinations such as shredded chicken, shiitakes, scallions, and ginger are prepared; sometimes the very expensive and somewhat exotic abalone is added. Perhaps more humble but no less sophisticated are salted egg and thousand-year-old egg congee (page 194), a sa-

vory treat. Fish congee (page 193), sometimes garnished with roasted peanuts, is also delicious. Expensive dried seafood such as scallops, oysters, and sea cucumber can be soaked until softened, thinly sliced or shredded, and added. In addition to exotic ingredients, there are sub-

tle shadings of flavor achieved with ginger, scallion, sea salt, and (depending on where the congee recipe originates) fish sauce, or soy sauce.

Sometimes the rice is roasted in a dry pot until lightly browned, then cooked down with water or stock, producing a nutty flavor. While the possibilities are many, the important thing to remember is that the rice is the most important ingredient and its flavor must shine through. The added ingredients should complement both one another and the rice as pleasant accents. In these "prepared" (as opposed to plain) congees, refinement and balance are key.

In Southeast Asia, where a strong Chinese influence in culture and culinary tradition exists, other varieties of rice soups are also enjoyed. These are prepared much differently than congee. The rice and stock are cooked separately, then combined a few minutes before serving, resulting in a brothy whole grain rice soup. They tend to be more pungent, with exotic flavorings such as fish sauce, shrimp paste, lemongrass, chilies, and Thai basil. In Japan and Korea, a plain bowl of congee—much like a plain bowl of rice—can be garnished with pine nuts, sesame seeds, or thinly sliced pickled daikon. Special congees include Japanese *cha-gayu*, or green tea rice porridge, in which rice is cooked down in green tea rather than water; and Korean sweet porridges such as *hugimjajuk*, sweet black sesame rice porridge (page 518), and *chatjuk*, pine nut rice porridge (page 518), in which rice grains and other ingredients are soaked, finely ground, then cooked down.

I have outlined the congee basics in this chapter, providing both enough information for you to get a grasp of fundamental principles, and encouragement to explore on your own as you master them. Note that as in stir-fried rice dishes, for example, leftovers can make a delicious jook. I have often diced Cantonese roast pork (page 454), or sliced five-spice roasted duck (pp. 500–1) and served it over a bowl of plain congee with some scallions and fried garlic oil (page 108), sprinkled on top for a quick and delicious meal. A plain congee with ginger and scallion salt dip (page 104) stirred in makes for a delicious breakfast with a julienned omelette on top.

STIR-FRIED RICE

STIR-FRIED RICE is a Chinese dish that goes back thousands of years,

evolving out of a basic need to not waste food. Like congee, it is a way to make leftover rice (in this case, plain cooked rice) go further. Unlike white rice dishes, however, and because it often has many flavors and ingredients, it is not quite considered part of a proper meal, and is more likely to be had as a snack or breakfast.

Leftover rice is perfect for the dish. Refrigerated overnight, the plump cooked rice grains harden and dry out, yielding the perfect consistency for stir-fries. Air-cured meats such as Chinese sweet pork sausages or ham can be added, often with preserved vegetables such as mustard cabbage. Fresh vegetables, seafood, and meat work well, as do leftover meat, poultry, crustaceans, and vegetables. There is no rule other than to be sure you use day-old rice. (If you do not follow this simple rule, the grains will become sticky during stir-frying.) In a perfectly balanced stir-fried rice, the rice must shine through, while all other items included in the stir-fry must complement and never overwhelm either its texture or flavor.

In Southeast Asia, Chinese sweet pork sausage is often diced and stir-fried along with the rice. For more pungent and unexpected types of

stir-fried rice, I may use leftover Thai curry chicken (page 499), or Cambodian spicy beef when I have leftover spicy beef soup (page 150). The Philippines have a straightforward stir-fried leftover rice with garlic (pp. 210–11), which is served with deep-fried dried fish and meat jerkies and enjoyed at breakfast. Japanese-style fried rice is also simple, reflecting the subtlety of Japanese cuisine in general. I have enjoyed a version made with brown rice and mushrooms (page 213). For a Korean-style stir-fried rice, you will not want to miss the unique *bimbim pap* (pp. 214–15). This is served in a hot stone bowl with all sorts of vegetables, sometimes including *kimchi*, shredded beef, and a raw egg, mixed with sweet and sour chili sauce (page 105). *Bimbim pap* is absolutely delicious, and unlike any other stir-fried rice in the world.

Indonesia also has unique stir-fried rice dishes called *nasi goreng*, seasoned with pungent *terasi* (shrimp paste) and red hot chilies. I have to say, as delicious as *nasi goreng* is, when I enjoyed it at breakfast in Ubud, Bali, it tasted even better. The glass doors of my hotel terrace were the only thing between me and the rice fields that stretched to the horizon beyond. Luscious green rice plants, like exquisite tall grass, were swaying gracefully in the wind. I could not help reflecting on the fact that all of this beauty was the source of the rice on my breakfast plate. Sweet grains every one, they were served with onions, bright red tomatoes, spicy chili and garlic sauce, sweet Indonesian soy sauce, and a delicious pan-fried egg. When I broke the bright yellow yolk, it was soaked up by the rice, so that every bite was moist and rich.

OTHER RICE-COOKING TECHNIQUES

RICE CAN BE SIMMERED, steamed, or fire-roasted in leaves, techniques that are used throughout Asia and have their roots in China. In the original Chinese tradition, bamboo leaves and lotus leaves are used to wrap sticky rice. The package is then simmered in water for several hours, allowing the rice to pick up the flavor from the leaf and to become sticky enough that it can be sliced. Filled with Chinese sweet pork sausage and salty eggs, these items, called *jeng* (pp. 218–19), are often available from food markets, street vendors, and food carts.

One shop I frequent in New York's Chinatown occasionally sets up sidewalk tables, offering several versions of these "wraps." Others keep them in the refrigerator; still others set them out in baskets near the checkout counter. No matter where you find them, however, you can be sure that any of these delicious, portable rice-based items make for great snacks, light meals, or school lunches.

Southeast Asian cooks also use leaves and other plant parts to cook rice. In Cambodia, Thailand, and Indonesia, for example, bamboo culms (the tall, hollow tubular "stems" of the plant) are used as cooking vessels that lend flavor. Sold by street vendors, the rice-filled culms, cut in approximately two-foot-long sections, roasted over a fire, are arranged upright in baskets for sale. In the Philippines, *puso*, long-grain rice cooked in woven coconut palm leaves, are sold as a quick snack. Here the leaves function both as a cooking utensil and serving platter that is gradually unwoven as you eat the rice within. The Indonesians enjoy rice prepared the same way. In the Mae Rim mountains of Thailand's northern region of Chiang Mai, in the Indian tradition, rice morsels are sometimes eaten with the hands. Once while enjoying a snack at a food stall, I was served sticky rice in a round woven bamboo box. It was explained that small portions are taken and rolled with the fingertips and thumb into bite-size balls. When perfectly round, the translucent sticky rice balls are dipped into a bowl of chicken curry, then eaten. Another memorable rice-based Southeast Asian treat—I have had similar versions in Indonesia and Thailand—is black sticky rice pudding (page 519). The black sticky (also incorrectly referred to as "glutinous") rice turns purple as it cooks. Served at room temperature, it is often finished with a warm sweet and savory coconut milk sauce. It has become one of my favorite afternoon snacks.

In Japan and Korea short-grain rice is wrapped with nori (laver), a sea vegetable sold in dried, paper-thin sheets. (While these are also popular in China, where they are added to soups, I find that the best-quality nori comes from Japan and Korea.) When I'm having a simple lunch in Japan, a humble bowl of rice is often served to me with a package of nori cut into two-inch-wide by one-inch-long strips. Observing the traditional custom, I use my chopsticks to pick up a piece of nori, which I then wrap around a bite-size portion of the short-grain rice. This is a simple and delicious way to enjoy rice with a subtle salty sea vegetable accent.

Nori and rice also appear in Japanese sushi, mostly raw fish and vinegar-flavored rice wrapped in any number of ways—cones, rolls, triangles, and so forth—with nori. Salmon skin handroll (page 217) is one of my favorites, although I enjoy many different kinds, and watching any of them being prepared at the sushi bar seems to make them even better. I especially enjoy watching the preparation of the special semi-sticky short-grain rice particularly suited to sushi. Cooked in huge rice cookers, it is scooped out and layered uniformly in a wooden tub, sprinkled with seasoned rice vinegar, and fanned to cool it down to prevent it from getting soggy. The sushi chefs move quickly, molding bite-size amounts of rice into the palms of their hands with moistened fingers, then topping them with thin slices of raw fish and arranging their creations on lacquer trays for serving.

Sushi is most often associated with Japanese food, of course, but it also exists in Korea. Generally speaking, far fewer Korean varieties exist than Japanese. I have to say, however,

that one chef at the Shilla Hotel in Seoul forever challenged my notion of sophistication in sushi. Chef Hyo-Ju Ahn specializes in making sushi portions that are perfectly sized to the mouth size of the individual guest. He believes that "the delicate lump of rice and fish morsel must be eaten in one single bite for optimum enjoyment. If you must split the morsel in two bites, already half the pleasure is gone." When I dined at his restaurant, he looked at me for a moment, then said, "Your sushi must be exactly 247 grains of rice." I did not count them, of course, but it was especially pleasant eating something sized specifically for me.

NOODLES

WHEN MY HUSBAND and I first went shopping for Asian noodles, he was overwhelmed by the variety of styles and types in the shops, and not a little daunted by the preparation techniques. I assured him that as with Western noodles and pasta, a pathway to understanding existed. Convinced that anyone can get a handle on this seemingly vast but, I assure you, equally rewarding subject, I have outlined my experience and understanding here.

The origins of noodles are unclear, but it is fair to say that the populist "Italy versus China" debate is ultimately rendered trivial when seen in a larger context. Some scholars have noodles originating in Central Asia, others insist on Persia. Some feel that flat doughs, ravioli, or wonton-style foods came first, with noodles evolving from them. This scenario, in particular, proposes that shapeless pieces of dough eventually became dumplings, then evolved into noodles. Other authorities, however, note that noodles were once a large part of Middle Eastern and North African Arabic cultures, where they seem now to be almost completely absent, having given way to couscous (which is actually a hand-rolled pasta). Still others point to the curious absence of almost all noodles in Indian cuisine. It is as if any chain of historical events that might fix the origins of the food—trade routes, military campaigns, cultural exchanges—was broken at some point, and the evidence is therefore inconclusive.

For the cook about to learn how to prepare Asian noodles, however, the debate over origins is less important than the knowledge that Chinese noodles are among the earliest examples of this foodstuff, and that their use spread to other Asian nations, where they took on regional characteristics. By mastering a few Chinese noodle fundamentals, you will be on your way to understanding everything from sweet red-stained crispy Thai *mi krob* (page 222) to delicate Japanese cold *soba* (pp. 244–45) to hearty Filipino *pancit* (page 238). I present wontons and other filled flat noodles, essentially Asian ravioli, under the heading "Dumplings, Spring Rolls, Flat Breads, and Buns" later on (page 177).

The first thing you will notice in an Asian noodle shop is that unlike Italian pasta, most of the noodles are similar in shape (i.e., either thin and vermicelli-like, wide cut like fettuccini, or broad flat sheets, as in a super-wide lasagna), but wildly diverse in their ingredients. Rice, wheat, sorghum, millet, mung bean, corn, buckwheat, soybean, agar-agar (a sea vegetable), and potato noodles are all made in China, and they may be flavored with shrimp, crab, vegetable, and eggs. Almost all forms are available dry, some are precooked, and a few specific ones are offered fresh by street vendors, specialty noodle shops, or in Chinese and Southeast Asian markets. By far the three most

common forms of noodle in China are wheat (predominantly in the north, where it is the principal crop); egg (mostly in the east and south as enjoyed in both Shanghai and Canton); and rice (also in the south, where rice grows in abundance). (See my "Essential Ingredients" chapter for more specifics on noodles, pp. 28–31.) Surprisingly, choosing a type of Asian noodle for a dish is often a matter of preference, and even the Japanese, who tend to be strict in matters of food, interchange types all the time. As with Italian pasta, thick noodles will hold up to meat, whereas thin vermicelli-like noodles do better with vegetables.

The Japanese have never developed rice noodles, preferring the boiled grain instead. You will do well to gain at least a cursory knowledge of Japanese noodles, many of which are sold in Japanese food shops and health food stores. Southeast Asian noodle dishes can be understood as essentially Chinese in nature, altered by local custom, ingredients, and other trade route influences. The Philippines offer noodles that are more cross-cultural in nature with Chinese, Southeast Asian, and Spanish-European influences.

Cooking techniques fall into five main categories: boiling, stir-frying, double-frying, braising, and steaming. Dried rice sticks, also called vermicelli, are popular in China and Southeast Asia; cellophane noodles (mung bean or potato starch) are popular in China and Northeast and Southeast Asia. They are soaked in water until pliable, then boiled for a few seconds to achieve a tender yet firm consistency; similar in texture to the Italian al dente but slightly less so. Other fresh wheat or egg noodles are boiled prior to being added to soups or stir-fries. (Note that Asian egg noodles have a distinctive egg taste, much more so than any Western variety. My students are often very surprised at this, and have to get used to the strong flavor. They also tend to be very yellow because of the inclusion of "yellow color #5.") Some are also double cooked, a technique found in both China and Vietnam. Thin egg noodles are generally boiled for a few minutes, arranged in a single layer to dry, then pan-fried until crisp. These are then flipped like a crêpe and pan-fried on the other side. This results in a pancake-shaped noodle patty, crispy on the outside and soft on the inside. Double-fried noodles are usually topped with a stir-fry of meat, poultry, seafood, and vegetables. My favorite combination, *liang mien hwang* (page 235), or *mi xao don do bien* in Vietnamese, celebrates the bounty of the sea, with scallops, shrimp, and squid, adding tender yet crunchy green snow peas and julienned orange carrots for texture and color. A velvety and rich chicken-stock-based sauce envelops the crispy noodles, transforming their texture in the finished dish.

Hand-rolled noodles, *nen dzem fen* in Chinese, are also known as silver pin noodles (page 220). They are about the width of one's palm and pointy on both ends and are often added to soups or stir-fries. Silver pin noodles are my uncle Ming's specialty. He stir-fries them in his wok with shredded chicken and scallions and stains them ever so slightly with soy sauce. He only makes one batch at a time to prevent them from sticking. Everyone in my family is more than willing to wait for their portion, however, as they probably will be in yours.

Fresh rice sheets, which are available from food carts and noodle shops in Chinatown, can be sliced and stir-fried, or rolled up with ground beef, roast pork, minced shrimp, or scallion, then steamed. My husband's favorite breakfast is *haar cheung* (page 297): rice noodle sheets, stuffed with fresh shrimp, rolled up, steamed in a bamboo steamer over a wok, then drizzled with a spicy scallion and cilantro soy sauce (page 88). We take pleasure in shopping for the noodles, shrimp, and other fresh ingredients in the very early morning, then returning home for a leisurely mid-morning meal, often with a cup of fragrant green tea.

Certain Asian noodles, notably the wheat flour–based, hand-pulled varieties made in northern China, involve special preparation techniques. Basic wheat noodles can be made at home, and often still are. The northern-style hand-stretched noodles are something very different, however: in the hands of a master, the preparation technique approaches a kind of artful choreography of strong arms and flying dough. It goes something like this: First the flour and water are mixed to the appropriate consistency. Allowed to rest for several hours, the dough is then kneaded and repeatedly slammed down to allow the wheat gluten to develop. (A great deal of elasticity in the dough is required for proper texture.) The dough is then rolled into a log, picked up at both ends, and flipped up and down (or swung), while being stretched. It is then folded over, then re-stretched, re-folded, and swung again until the coarse folds become delicate individual strands. The process is repeated many times, with the strands occasionally re-floured lightly to keep them nice and separate. In the hands of a master the stretching and folding process takes about fifteen continuous minutes, and the resulting pulled strands can be anywhere from moderately thick to angel-hair thin. Quite something to see, it takes at least two years of practice to master the technique. In Hong Kong and other cities, noodle shops featuring hand-pulled wheat noodles situate the noodle master in the front window, where his expert pulling, folding, and swinging entice countless passersby to try this special fare.

Noodles were brought to Japan by the Chinese during the Nara period, eighth century C.E. They are known collectively as *menrui*. They evolved from Chinese techniques, eventually developing into distinct varieties and unique dishes. The most important types are *soba* (buckwheat noodles); *udon* (thick round or square wheat noodles); and *somen* (made from wheat dough that has been lightly oiled prior to being transformed into vermicelli). Other types, less known in the West but delicious just the same, are *kishimen* (flat dried wheat noodles) and *hiyamugi* (wheat vermicelli). In general, wheat noodles are made with wheat flour, salt, and water. *Soba* can be made solely from buckwheat flour, but most are made from a combination of buckwheat and wheat flours, rendering the dough less brittle and easier to roll out. Making *soba* at home is a bit difficult because the freshly milled flour required to do the job properly is hard to come by. Very good quality *soba* is available frozen or dried, however, and will do just fine in most instances. (I have listed sources in the mail-order section, page 563.) As with any noodles, Japanese dough is kneaded for a long time to bring out the gluten and achieve proper elasticity. Some cooks add eggs to their dough for a richer flavor, and as a binder.

I have to say that when freshly handmade cold *soba* noodles are properly made and served with a dipping sauce, they are the ambrosial essence of refinement. Honmura An—a Japanese restaurant in the SoHo district of New York City—is famous for its *soba* cuisine. If your timing is right, the noodle chef can be observed in his glass-enclosed noodle kitchen, surrounded by traditional implements. When served, the noodles are arranged on bamboo draining mats set over lacquered boxes to collect any excess water and presented at table. The dipping sauce of mirin, soy sauce, and *dashi* perfectly complements the rich, slightly grainy, and nutty *soba*. One adjusts the sauce with such pungent items as freshly grated daikon and *wasabi* and thinly sliced scallion, dips the fresh noodles, and . . . perfection. When the noodles are finished, the attentive staff takes the cloudy starch-rich cooking liquid from the noodles, heats it, and pours it into the remaining dipping sauce. Guests sip their "instant" broth slowly, enjoying the flavor of the noodles as well as the fragrant sauce, a wonderful finale to the meal.

Beginning after World War II, the original, centuries-old Chinese noodle varieties have again become popular in Japan. Ramen are among the most widely enjoyed. Thin, flat egg noodles, they are precooked (generally fried), dried, and packaged as instant noodles and noodle soups. Ramen also has the odd distinction of being a Chinese noodle commonly assumed to be Japanese. (It bears its original Chinese name, a name now so common in Japanese cooking that it is taken for part of the Japanese language.) One confession concerning ramen: ever the advocate of cooking from scratch with only the freshest ingredients, I have to admit to enjoying the occasional doctored Asian instant noodle soup, especially when it is late or cold or raining, there is little else in the house, and food shopping seems particularly unappealing. The ramen typically included in these soups can be dropped into a pot of boiling water, followed by their packaged seasoning powder. Add sliced leftover meat or seafood and leafy greens, and you have an instantly warming light meal.

Korean noodles include potato starch noodles, called *tang myon*, and wheat noodles, called *kal guksu*. (*Myon* is a word derived from *mien*, the Chinese word for noodles.) Buckwheat noodles, *naeng myon*, are also enjoyed. Unlike the buckwheat *soba*, however, they are made of buckwheat flour and potato starch, with a slightly chewy character, and slightly more subtle flavor. A classic Korean dish, *chap chae*, is composed of stir-fried *tang myon* with meat and all sorts of colorful vegetables, usually accompanied by a bowl of rice and *kimchi* for a light lunch. For the most part, the Koreans think of noodles as snack items, not as the basis for a full meal. Here, as in Japan, the boiled rice grain is the backbone of culinary culture. When first visiting Korea I was surprised to see rice as an accompaniment to noodle dishes at meals. Once when eating in a restaurant I was offered a somewhat hearty dish, wheat noodles in a rich beef broth, and my host went on to order me rice as well. I commented on her two starchy choices, and she chided me gently, saying that a meal without rice is not a proper meal.

In Southeast Asian cooking the predominant noodle varieties are made from ground rice. In Vietnam these include *banh pho* (flat thin rice sticks), used in soups; *banh hoai* (rice vermicelli), often used as a table condiment with herbs and lettuce leaf to wrap meat morsels; *bun tau* (cellophane noodles), added to light brothy soups or chopped and added to spring roll fillings; and *bun* (fresh rice vermicelli), eaten tossed with all sorts of shredded raw vegetables and grilled meats.

In Thailand, fresh rice noodle

A JAPANESE DRIED-NOODLE SHOP OFFERS A WIDE ARRAY OF THIN, THICK, FLAT, AND ROUND WHEAT AND BUCKWHEAT NOODLES.

sheets called *kway tiao* (*k'tieu* in Cambodia) are sliced into thin or wide flat strands and added to soups or stir-fries; *ba mee* (dried egg noodles) are stir-fried or added to soups; *wun sen*, cellophane noodles made of mung bean starch, are used

in making spring roll fillings, or added to light brothy soups. *Mi krob* (page 222), the crispy sweet fried noodle dish popularly offered in Thai restaurants, is made with dried rice vermicelli called *khanom jin* and a sugary and vinegary fish-based sauce. Another almost universally popular Thai noodle dish is *pad Thai* (pp. 224–25). The versions I remember most fondly are the ones I tasted at food stalls in Bangkok. Sitting on a stool set beside his folding table, the vendor stir-fries thin, flat, dried rice stick noodles (*sen mi*), pressed tofu, dried shrimp, and eggs with fresh mung bean sprouts, roasted peanuts, and a fresh squeeze of lime juice. During his work day—usually morning until night—he will prepare dozens of batches. Even when I go to the late-night bazaars, the smell of *pad Thai* lingers in the air, as if to say, "Forget shopping, come and eat!"

In Indonesia, there is a version of the Chinese rice vermicelli *mi fen*, referred to as *bihun*. Egg noodles, however, are the most widely eaten variety. Known as *bakmie*, they are the basis for the popular stir-fried dish known as *bakmie goreng*, stir-fried egg noodles. Rooted in the Chinese tradition of *lo mien*—thick egg noodles with beef and Chinese broccoli seasoned with oyster sauce, rice wine, and sesame oil, for example (page 237)—these simple dishes are delicious. The Indonesian version is sweetened with tomato paste and sweet soy sauce, and spiced with chilies, shallots, and garlic.

When I make stir-fried noodle dishes like *lo mien* or *bakmie goreng*, I cook extra-big batches. They are wonderful the next day, when I bring them to room temperature and enjoy them, or reheat them in a skillet, crisping them in the process. Either way they are great as brunch, lunch, after-school snack, or light supper. Try adding a dollop of chili and garlic sauce (page 106) if you like a bit of heat against the hearty egg noodles.

In the Philippines, noodle varieties include *bihon* (rice vermicelli); *miswa* (thin dried wheat noodles); *sotanghon* (mung bean thread); and *canton* (egg noodles). Unlike other Asian cooks, the Filipinos cook their noodles until very tender. Like other Asian cultures, they add noodles to soup. *Pancit* (also *pansit*), however, is a sort of Filipino national noodle dish. (The word *pansit* means, roughly, "something that is easily cooked," and is derived from the Hokkien people of China, among whom it may have originated.) *Pancit* starts with any one of a number of noodle types, which are tossed with a sweet and tangy sauce and vegetables, pork, and shrimp, and often topped with shredded egg omelette or crumbled hard-boiled eggs. Served at holiday gath-

erings, birthdays, and other festive occasions, *pancit*, like other noodle dishes (and consistent with Chinese belief systems), symbolizes longevity. Whenever my family is invited to my Filipina sister-in-law's home, or just about any other family gathering, her mother always comes smiling, bearing a large batch of *pancit* for all to share.

A note on slurping noodle soups: In many parts of Asia, noodle soups are slurped loudly. Making a certain amount of noise is acceptable when eating, and is considered a sort of compliment to the chef. (No noise is bad news.) A certain amount of logic is at work here: Some Asian soups are served at the boil. Slurping introduces air into the mouth, mixing with the soup, cooling the liquid to prevent burning or scalding of the mouth and tongue. In terms of taste, the process is not unlike that of wine tasting, i.e., air is introduced into the mouth during tasting, allowing the flavors to develop. I have to admit, to the Western ear, it can seem annoying. When I am in my "French mode," that is, sitting at table expecting Western table manners to prevail, I remember my French grandmother's voice reminding us to sip and eat quietly. Imagine my confusion while growing up! Eating at *Grandmère* Barbet's was noiseless, while eating at *A ma Trang's* was like surround-sound; what was right in one culture was wrong in the other. Sometimes I mildly reprimand my husband when he slurps Asian soups. "Madame," he says smiling, "I am trying to be polite."

One last note on mung bean starch or potato starch (cellophane) noodles. These are generally not regarded as a main starch in a meal, but rather as a vegetable side dish for rice. They might have been properly placed in the vegetable chapter, but they are generally sold as noodles, so they are covered here to minimize confusion. After all, a generous portion of meat and vegetable mixed stir-fry—*chap chae* (page 250)—with cellophane noodles makes for a wonderful single-dish light lunch.

DUMPLINGS, SPRING ROLLS, FLAT BREADS, AND BUNS

THE SUBJECT OF DUMPLINGS, spring rolls, flat breads, and buns is too vast to cover completely in this book. For the cook who wants a general overview of the subject, however, a discussion of fundamentals will illuminate this part of Asian cuisine.

DUMPLINGS

DUMPLINGS ARE ESSENTIALLY A DOUGH that is flattened, cut into a shape, and filled (like Italian ravioli), then steamed, boiled, pan-fried, or deep-fried. The most common—and possibly original—types are based on wheat, but egg, rice, potato, tapioca starch, wheat starch, palm or cassava starch, buckwheat, and other types also occur. Modern kitchens have introduced variations that include colored wrappers derived from vegetable waters (for example, beet or spinach). Other types include sweet dumplings, some of which are mentioned here, but covered as a more developed topic in the "Sweets and Drinks" chapter (page 508).

The origins of dumplings are cloudy. It is known, however, that like the noodles to which they are related, dumplings gained broad culinary significance during the ancient Han dynasty, when the flour mill was first introduced to China from Central Asia, and rice and wheat flour production was ascendant. It is also fairly certain that these items developed in the absence of leavened or yeast-based breads and bread ovens—both of which also came to China from other lands, and which played a minor role in the cuisine until modern times. These are covered in the "Flat Breads, Buns, and Cakes" section, beginning on page 183.

Major Chinese types of dumplings include *hun tun*, widely known as "wonton"; *siu mai*, which are essentially steamed, open-at-the-top wontons; *jaozi*, which are steamed and semicircular in shape; *wortip* or "potstickers," also semicircular but pan-fried; and *haar gao*, or steamed crystal shrimp dumplings.

Wontons (pp. 266–67) are soft, delicate dumplings most often made with shrimp and pork, seasoned with sesame oil, and wrapped in a wheat or wheat and egg dough. Usually bite-size, wontons can be made in three shapes: pouch, pillow, and cloud. Boiled first in water, they are then set afloat in a fragrant ginger-infused chicken broth for the finish. (The word *wonton* derives from the two characters "cloud" and "swallow," and it is believed that these describe the lightness of the dumpling.) A mainstay in Chinese noodle restaurants the world over, they are had as a snack or light lunch in broth, often with thin flat egg noodles for a more satisfying meal. It should be noted that traditional Chinese wontons are unlike the thick, doughy ones commonly served in Chinese-American restaurants. When properly made, the delicate wrapper is balanced with the flavorful filling, so that one does not overwhelm the other. *Siu mai* are steamed circular wonton wrappers. They are formed so that the top is loosely gathered, revealing the filling, often a pork and shrimp mixture.

Jaozi are the familiar dumplings commonly had in Chinese restaurants. Shaped like crescents, they contain meat, seafood, or vegetable, are lightly seasoned, and boiled or steamed. When properly made they are, like wontons, extremely well balanced in flavor and texture. The most common sin here is that the dough dominates. The most common "fix" to this imbalance is dipping sauces, but these should be used as complementary flavor enhancers, and are poor substitutes for proper preparation. *Wortip*, or potstickers, are basically the same crescent-shaped dumplings, but pan-fried. Both types have a wide range of fillings, but the two most popular are beef and garlic chives, and pork and ginger. While they are relatively easy to prepare from scratch, the two main types—and sometimes a seafood or vegetarian version—are also available in the frozen food section of Chinese markets. All you need to do is drop them in boiling water or steam them, and enjoy them with any number of dipping sauces. Two of the best are soy sauce with chili and garlic sauce (page 106), and black vinegar with julienned ginger (page 89). If you wish to fry potstickers using frozen dumplings, I suggest you steam them first, then pan-fry them so they cook all the way through.

Haar gao, crystal shrimp dumplings, have a distinctive thin wrapper made of wheat and tapioca starch. They turn translucent when cooked, revealing their beautiful pink shrimp filling—made with small shrimp, water chestnuts, and bamboo. *Jai gao*, crystal vegetable dumplings, are similar, using green leaf vegetables as a filling. These dumplings are good candidates for the use of color, which is achieved through adding vegetable liquid extract to the dough. Sweet rice dumplings such as *tang yuen* (pp. 526–27) are filled with black sesame seeds and wrapped in sticky rice flour dough, then boiled and served in their cooking liquid. These are covered in the "Sweets and Drinks" chapter (page 508).

Japanese dumplings are generally derived from Chinese precedents. Japanese *siu mai*, for example, are nearly identical to the Chinese version. Somewhat more subtle in flavor than their Chinese counterparts, they nonetheless retain the original Chinese name. One Japanese version I have had in Kyoto was filled with shrimp, sporting a single pea on top, creating a vibrant green on pink color contrast. The Japanese also have dumplings called *gyoza*, which are derived from the Chinese *jaozi*. They have many fillings, but one particularly memorable version I tried in a little snack house in Japan was filled with tofu.

The Japanese also enjoy sweet dumplings called *mochi*. These, too, exist in China, but the Japanese seem to have taken them to heart, having special shops dedicated to their preparation and sale. They are also found on Japanese restaurant dessert menus and can be purchased fresh in Japanese markets. One of my favorites is a sticky and chewy rice flour ball covered with sweet smooth red bean paste and sometimes sprinkled with roasted sesame seeds. Partnered with a cup of green tea (and sometimes served with a tiny wooden fork), *mochi* are absolutely delicious. (See also

"Sweets and Drinks," pp. 524–25.) A third Japanese dumpling style employs buckwheat. Using *soba* dough, the noodle master pinches tiny portions of dough and shapes them into small balls, which he boils and adds to a simple sweet azuki red bean broth. I've enjoyed this dessert—a curious blend of coarse texture and sugary sweet starch—in a lovely teahouse in Tokyo, where it was served at the end of the meal.

Mandu kuk (page 265) is the most popular dumpling in Korea. Based on the Chinese wonton, it is made of wheat flour dough filled with tofu and beef (among other ingredients) and is served in a beef broth (the Chinese, in contrast, use a ginger-infused chicken or pork broth). Koreans also enjoy sweet rice dumplings such as *songp'yon*—firm bite-size rice dumplings shaped as half moons, filled with all sorts of nuts, and sometimes flavored with pine needles or the wild herb mugwort. These tend to be hard, slightly bitter-sweet, and very, very chewy. They are often had as part of social rituals: nibbled with tea while chatting, or during "Korean Thanksgiving," a September ancestor-remembrance and harvest festival. Korean sticky rice dump-

lings, *kyongdan*, resemble the Japanese *mochi* and are based on the Chinese *nor mai chi* (pp. 524–25). Filled with nuts or fruit—including chestnuts, pine nuts, and jujubes—they are boiled in water, drained, and rolled while still hot in a wide range of flavored powders such as sesame powder (blond or black), coconut powder, or pine nut (see "Sweets and Drinks," pp. 526–27).

Any cook aspiring to master Chinese and related dumplings should remember the adage about the emperor who enjoyed a different dumpling dish every day of his long life, never having the same item twice. The thrust of this story is, of course, that dumplings can be as varied, as complex, as creative, and as diverse as ingredients that can be chopped, seasoned, and cooked.

In Southeast Asia, dumplings are perhaps not as developed as they are in China and its northern culinary colonies. In Thailand, street hawkers sell deep-fried wontons with a sweet chili sauce. In Vietnam's central region, crescent-shaped steamed crystal shrimp and pork dumplings, and deep-fried sesame and sticky rice and potato dumplings called *dau xan vung* (page 523) are sold; these are essentially what the Chinese call *jien doy*.

Sticky sweet rice flour balls are also a popular snack served all over Southeast Asia, these also adapted from the Chinese. Boiled in water, and served in syrups or sweet soups, in Southeast Asia they often appear as morsels in a sweet and savory coconut milk soup. Like the Chinese, the Southeast Asians occasionally like to color rice balls with red or green food coloring for festive occasions.

WRAPPERS AND ROLLS

NEARLY EVERYONE KNOWS egg rolls as they are served in Chinese-American take-out restaurants, but these are rather poor versions of a whole host of delicate and beautifully balanced food items generally described as wrappers or rolls. A parallel development to dumplings and noodles, they most likely emerged around 2,000 years ago, during the Han dynasty. Fillings wrapped in a thin, square, or round pancake, they include spring rolls, several types of pancakes, and other types, including those unique to Southeast Asia. The key in these seemingly simple foods is balance in all ingredients, that is, the filling must be balanced so that all its ingredients can be tasted, and balanced also in terms of texture and color. The filling must in turn be balanced with its wrapper. Simple in their conception, and complex in their subtleties, the classic recipes have persisted for hundreds of years with only minor changes.

Two basic types of roll wrappers exist, with a few significant variations. The egg-wheat type is essentially large wonton wrappers (page 253). Most popular in Cantonese Chinese-American restaurants, it is used to make Cantonese egg rolls (dahn guen). These are filled with stir-fried cabbage, carrot, celery, and often leftover Cantonese roast pork (page 454). The wrappers are made like Italian ravioli by kneading together wheat flour, egg, and salt until an elastic, smooth dough is achieved. Rolled out, the dough is cut into large five- to six-inch squares. The filling is rolled up neatly in the raw dough, then deep-fried.

The wheat-type wrapper (chun juan pi) is paper thin and somewhat translucent. Having originated in Shanghai, it is used to make Shanghainese spring rolls (chun juan—literally, "spring roll"). Originally a vegetarian item associated with spring harvest festivals, it is deep-fried and can include stir-fried bean sprouts, napa cabbage, carrots, and other delicate morsels. Modern ver-sions may also include pork, chicken, or shrimp with the vegetable mix.

The Shanghainese spring roll wrapper is made by pressing a ball of wheat dough against the surface of a dry pan over low heat. With a circular motion—and good timing—the dough is pulled away so as to leave a thin film on the pan. This cooks just until its edges separate from the surface, and the paper-thin silky "skin" can be lifted away. (I love to watch this wrapper "birthing ritual"—at once vaguely magical, yet marvelous in its simplicity and rigor.) While you can do this at home, it is much simpler to buy ready-made wrappers. These are used in Thailand, the Philippines, and China and are available fresh or frozen in Chinese markets. My favorite brand, which is consistent in its texture, thinness (ideally paper thin and see-through), flavor, and flexibility, is TYJ Spring Roll Pastry from Singapore. For those of you who cannot find these, or who enjoy a minor challenge, I have included a recipe for spring roll wrappers (page 258).

Mandarin wheat flour pancakes, po ping, are also known as mu shu pancakes (pp. 254–55). They are used to wrap Peking duck slices seasoned with sweet hoisin sauce and pungent, julienned scallions. Also made from wheat dough balls, they require a special preparation technique. Wheat flour is kneaded with hot water, so the flour undergoes an initial cooking process. The dough is then separated into an even number of pieces, and rolled into perfect balls. Two balls at a time are flattened together with the palm of the hand, then lightly brushed on a single side with sesame oil. The two oiled sides are pressed together and rolled out into very thin disks and cooked in pairs in a wok or nonstick pan until they puff up. They are then separated into single pancakes, and—just prior to serving with Peking duck or mu shu pork—are steamed. When made in the traditional manner, mandarin pancakes are delicate and thin, perfect for refined foods. Some Chinese restaurants, however, use readily available Mexican wheat tortillas as a substitute. I find them a bit thick, but in a pinch they will do.

Another wrapper (or noodle sheet) known as cheung fan is made from a wheat starch, rice flour, and tapioca starch. The batter is poured into a square pan, steamed, and peeled off when done. It is used to make soft, tender steamed Chinese rice rolls called *cheung fan guen*, filled with savory shrimp, pork, or beef, which I like to serve with a spicy soy sauce dip infused with cilantro and scallions (page 88). *Cheung fan* are available fresh in Chinese or Southeast Asian markets.

South Asian, and particularly Southeast Asian, countries have a strong tradition of rolls. Using the Chinese spring roll as a point of departure, cooks in Vietnam, Thailand, Cambodia, Indonesia, and the Philippines have developed distinctive variations on the Chinese item as well as arguably unique foods such as the summer roll. As in China, Southeast Asian rolls use a thin to thickish wheat or rice dough wrapper with a filling made of finely chopped poultry, meat, seafood, vegetables, herbs, and occasionally cellophane noodles. These fillings are commonly combined, and when used in spring rolls they are often stir-fried first. Like the Chinese, the filling is rolled in its wrapper and eaten deep-fried or "fresh" (unfried). The similarities end there, however, as a myriad of variations exists, some as subtle as minor differences in the fillings, others as profoundly different as employing unique ingredients and curing techniques.

In Vietnam, deep-fried spring rolls (*cha gio*, pp. 284–85) are quite different from their Chinese counterparts. The key here is understanding the delicate *banh trang*, or rice papers: a rice paper tree pith (or rice flour), salt, and water dough that is flattened and air-cured on bamboo mats. (The pith is technically not from rice, but from a shrub related to the ginseng family and native to southern China.) Both versions of *banh trang* are air, sun, and salt (which is in the dough) cured. The pith version, which may be eaten fresh, is predominant in Vietnam. It is similar to phyllo sheets in texture: delicate, thin, and dry to the touch, yet pliable enough to be used as wraps. When made with rice flour— as they are for commercial use and for export—*banh trang* are slightly thicker than the pith version and always require soaking in water to be made pliable before use.

Whether using one or the other wrapper, the most classic Vietnamese spring roll usually has as much as or more meat (ground pork, sometimes with crab or shrimp meat) than vegetable, and also contains cellophane noodles, eggs, and cloud ear mushrooms. It is wrapped into a distinctively tiny (usually no longer than 1½ inches)

form, deep-fried, and served with *nuoc cham* (page 100), the sweet, tangy, salty, sour, and spicy fish sauce–based dip. In another distinctively Vietnamese gesture, it is often served with copious amounts of lettuce and herbs such as mint or *rau ram* (Vietnamese coriander), which are, in turn, used to wrap and embellish the roll.

The summer roll known as *goi cuon* (pp. 286–87)—and sometimes called fresh spring roll, but literally "salad roll"—is unique to Vietnam. Round rice paper is water softened and filled with cooked shrimp, pork, rice vermicelli, carrots, mint, lettuce, and scallion and wrapped into a moderately thick and long (four to five inches) shape, and served with a light smooth peanut sauce flavored with coconut milk and chicken stock referred to as *nuoc cham dau phong* (page 99). The resulting fresh summer roll is, unlike the crispy deep-fried spring roll, soft and tender.

Another delicious Vietnamese rice roll uses freshly made rice sheets called *banh uot*, similar to Chinese *cheung fan* (pp. 262–63). Called *banh cuon* (page 296), and containing stir-fried ground pork and mushrooms, they are mildly seasoned and are served with *nuoc cham*.

Thai spring rolls, *paw pia taud* and *paw pia saud* (pp. 274–75)—deep-fried and fresh, respectively—are also enjoyed as snacks or at the beginning of a meal. Like the Chinese item, they use Shanghainese-style spring roll wrappers and are filled with stir-fried vegetables and meat. Generally, cellophane noodles are added to the stir-fry—and will become the filling—for texture and their ability to absorb seasonings.

Filipino spring rolls, called *lumpia*, appear in several versions. They use the ultra-thin "skin" wrappers (as for Chinese and Thai spring rolls), are filled with stir-fried vegetables and meat or seafood, and are served fresh or deep-fried. *Lumpia siriwa* (pp. 282–83) are made with a wrapper prepared like a French crêpe: a loose batter is cooked initially over a low flame, filled with a stir-fry mix, rolled, and served "fresh."

While in Cebu, the Philippines, I visited Jessica Avila, cooking teacher and chef of Tiya Nena's, a top-rated restaurant that is also a cooking school. Here I sampled all sorts of Filipino specialties, among them the special *lumpia ubod* (pp. 280–81), fresh, soft crêpes filled with delicately julienned coconut palm heart.

Fresh coconut palm heart is literally the heart of a three- to five-year-old tree, a marvelously tender, mildly sweet, and flavorful treat. Seeing it in *lumpia ubod* was a great surprise. The only other time I had eaten coconut palm heart was in Martinique, where it was considered a rare delicacy taken only from storm felled trees or trees cut for a special occasion. (Because Martinique is an island with limited landmass, the taking of an entire tree for a salad item would be a bit of an indulgence.) When I expressed my surprise to Jessica, she explained: "In the Philippines, coconut palm trees grow in great abundance. As an agricultural product, certain ones are grown specifically for the heart, but all the parts—fruit, juice, shell, trunk, even the leaves—are used in some way or another, so nothing is wasted."

She went on to describe the fine points of making the batter for the wrapper. "You need a low heat, so that the crêpe stays a consistent creamy white even as it cooks through. Browning it, or even having brown spots in it, is wrong." She further explained that some batters are made with egg as the binder, while others are made with tapioca starch. "Either will do as long as there are no brown spots." If you ever have a chance to enjoy this or other coconut palm heart items, jump at the chance. You will always remember the experience.

Indonesian fried spring rolls known as *lumpia goreng* are also stuffed with stir-fried vegetables and meat. Unlike the Chinese, Thai, and Filipino versions, Indonesian fried spring rolls use a soft wrapper made from a loose egg-wheat batter (similar to the Filipino fresh *lumpia* batter) as opposed to a dough. One that I particularly liked in Bali was made from a soft crêpe stuffed with stir-fried cabbage, carrots, leeks, and shredded chicken. Rolled into a bundle and sealed with an egg wash, the soft, rather thick roll was deep-fried and served with a sweet soy sauce containing thinly sliced fresh red chilies. The effect was a semi-crispy, immensely satisfying roll . . . or rolls. Once you get started, it's hard to stop.

Cambodia has essentially adopted Vietnamese deep-fried spring rolls as its own and calls them *lhord*. Made exactly like the Vietnamese *cha gio* (pp. 284–85), *lhord* sometimes omit seafood in the filling. They are served with *tuk trey*—the Cambodian equivalent of the Vietnamese *nuoc* cham (page 100), but with crushed peanuts added. Cambodian restaurants also occasionally serve fresh summer rolls with tuk trey as well.

FLAT BREADS, BUNS, AND CAKES

THE EARLIEST FORM OF BREAD in China dates from the seventh century. Introduced by northern street hawkers, who sold all sorts of steamed or fried pastries, a wheat flour flat bread called tsung yu ping (page 264)—containing scallions, and seasoned with salt and sesame oil—was pan-fried with a generous amount of oil. Most likely derived from similar pan-fried items in Persia and elsewhere in Central Asia, these rich "pancakes" were particularly well adapted to the appetites of northerners, who endured a cold climate. Generally associated with northern cities such as Beijing in modern times, they are also widely available in Chinese restaurants the world over as scallion pancakes.

Despite their simplicity, these pancakes are a wonderful blend of earthiness and pungency, best when not too oily and served very hot. When I was fifteen or so, I remember going with my family to meet a Beijing couple visiting New York for a few months. Arriving at their apartment on a cold winter's day, I was struck by the smell of something marvelous but unfamiliar frying in the kitchen. The couple soon welcomed us with tea and chung yau biang. Cut up into triangular wedges, the pancakes were perfectly done: crispy on the outside, soft on the inside, with hints of scallion and sesame seeds.

Buns, or yeast-leavened breads, emerged in China much later than in the West, and in a centuries-old noodles, dumplings, and flat bread culture have never really achieved the importance they are awarded in the West. Known broadly as bao (page 259), they start with a dough of wheat flour, yeast, water, and salt (and sometimes egg and lard). Initially steamed over woks, eventually they were baked in wood-burning open ovens (likely derived from India's tandoor ovens). Both steamed and baked buns are still made, whether as plain small breads, twists with sesame oil and scallions or powdered sugar, or buns stuffed with meats and vegetables.

One of the most classic and still popular stuffed buns is char siu bao, Cantonese roast pork buns. Originally steamed, the "two-bites" tiny buns (still offered in dim sum restaurants) are today made much larger (perhaps four to six bites), baked, and glazed with sugar water. Mildly curious, perhaps, to the Western palate at first, bao can have fillings ranging from a simple hot dog and ham and egg (two of the most modern adaptations), to stir-fried vegetables and meat combinations. Very inexpensive, they are often eaten in modern circumstances as a quick breakfast item with a cup of coffee or tea. The Vietnamese have a similar steamed bun called banh beo (page 295), which is filled with ground pork, mushrooms, and eggs.

Baked breads after the European style are rare in Asian cuisines. They were introduced as the result of a specific colonial past, wartime occupation, or a modern openness to things foreign. The Vietnamese and Cambodians bake breads that are essentially adaptations of the crispy French baguette, but shorter—approximately the size of American hero, hoagie, or submarine sandwich breads. Made of plain wheat flour, or a combination of both wheat and rice flour, they are used for making hearty sandwiches filled with meat, exotic herbs, and chili paste, or used to scoop up curry. The Philippines has pan de sal, a Spanish-derived salt, sugar, and wheat flour spongy baked bun that is dipped into hot coffee at breakfast. It seems to be both the indicator in determining the quality of a baker (*panadero*), and the barometer of the Filipino national economy: a too-small *pan de sal* indicates a poor economy in which the ingredients are getting expensive.

In Hong Kong, British bread types persist from the early colonial period; in Korea and Japan, some American-style breads and sandwiches can also be found, but they have never become part of the national diet in any meaningful way. Thailand and Indonesia have also largely eschewed Western-style breads, with the possible exception of a few sweet buns.

Asian cakes are not necessarily sweet dessert items, and include gummy, glutinous-based items that may or may not be sweet. Wheat gluten cakes (*mien gu*) are an important example. Created by Chinese Buddhist monks who were strict vegetarians, they were a way to get high-protein food into their seafood- and animal-free diet. Wheat gluten cakes are made by kneading wheat flour and water until great elasticity is achieved. The dough is then left to rest for some time before being kneaded under cold running water to wash out the starch, leaving a highly concentrated glutinous mass, which is sliced, braised, stir-fried, deep-fried, or added to soups. I once shared a wonderful meal with Buddhist monks at a temple in New York's Chinatown. "Mock" dishes were offered; wheat gluten cake slices in thick sauces artfully contrived to mimic chicken, duck, and pork. These dishes are also sometimes offered in Asian vegetarian restaurants.

In Kyoto, Japan, the home of Zen Buddhism, shops making traditional wheat gluten cakes similar to those of the Chinese have been popular for centuries. The most common versions are made from a combination of wheat flour and sticky rice flour and are generically called *fu*. Influenced by Chinese Buddhist culinary traditions, the Japanese add *fu* to soups, braised dishes, and stir-fries. During *shojin-ryori* (a traditional Zen buddhist vegetarian meal), however, it is also pan-fried and called *yaki fu* (page 289). I enjoyed it this way at a special meal in Kyoto, where it was served sashimi-style, and dipped in soy sauce spiced with *wasabi*. Modern versions of *fu* include items flavored with a wide range of ingredients, including herbs, tea, chocolate, and cheese. Cakes made from pure high-gluten flour (cake flour) are also made, and are known as *nama fu*.

During the Chinese Lunar New Year, two specific cake specialties (sometimes referred to as puddings) are prepared: *lok bak go* (pp. 292–93), a savory item made from radish and rice flour, and *nin gao*, or New Year's cake, a sweet item made from sticky rice flour. Both are steamed until set, left to rest overnight, then sliced and pan-fried the next day. (Occasionally, if you can't wait, the overnight part doesn't happen. . . .)

STICKY "GLUTINOUS" SHORT-GRAIN RICE

SERVES 4

2 cups STICKY RICE

STICKY RICE is often referred to as "glutinous" rice even though there is not an ounce of gluten in it. The stickiness comes from the specifics of its starch content: all rice has two starches, amylose and amylopectin; stickier varieties have a higher proportion of amylopectin. Many brands are available and often mislabeled as "glutinous." My favorite is the Rice King brand because it is uniformly high in quality and usually fresh. Sticky rice nearly doubles in volume after soaking and tends to be a bit filling. Sticky rice is especially fun to eat by hand. I like to roll small portions into bite-size balls to dip in sauces. Black sticky rice, an interesting and delicious variation of white sticky rice, is covered in the "Sweets and Drinks" chapter (page 508).

Invest in an inexpensive Thai or Indonesian rice set, a conical woven bamboo basket with a metal pot, or use the wok and bamboo steamer method in step 2.

For 4 generous portions of rice or to serve 6 to 8 persons, prepare 3 cups rice, soaking it in 6 cups water, and then proceed with the same instructions as below.

1. Soak the sticky rice in 4 cups water (2 cups water if using only 1 cup of sticky rice), refrigerated, for at least 4 hours. Drain, then rinse and drain two more times (you can do this step before you soak the rice and refrigerate it if you prefer; either will work).

2. Fill the bottom third of a wok with water (about 6 cups) and place a bamboo steamer covered with a lid on top. Bring the water to a boil over high heat. Lift the lid, then place a damp cheesecloth over the bamboo rack and spread the rice on it, leaving a 1-inch border all around to let the steam through. Fold the cheesecloth over the rice, cover the steamer with the lid again, and steam until the rice is tender but firm, about 25 minutes.

LONG-GRAIN JASMINE RICE

SERVES 4

1 cup JASMINE RICE

JASMINE-SCENTED LONG-GRAIN RICE—rice scented with jasmine leaves—is my favorite rice, and I serve it with most Chinese or Southeast Asian meals. Because so much depends on the subtle fragrance of the rice, try to purchase it from an Asian market where there is high turnover. (Rice kept after six months will, like Italian pasta, go stale, losing its flavor and texture when cooked.) For best results, use a Chinese sand pot, which retains moisture during the cooking process and allows it to dissipate very slowly and evenly, yielding fluffy, tender, and separated rice grains. If using an enameled cast iron or stainless steel pot, you may have to adjust the water and heat. Following the Japanese tradition of sprinkling food tidbits on rice, I sometimes sprinkle jasmine rice with fried scallions and ginger (page 108) for visual effect and added flavor.

For 4 generous portions of rice or to serve 6 to 8 persons, cook 2 cups rice with 3 cups water, following the same instructions as below.

1. Put the rice in a medium pot with a few cups of water. Gently swirl your fingers in the pot to allow the starch to separate from the grains. Once the water becomes white, tilt the pot over the sink to drain out the water. Be careful not to let your rice go into the sink; hold it back with your hand while the water seeps through your fingers. Repeat this process twice more. Each time, the water will get less cloudy. The idea is not to get rid of all the starch, just enough so that the rice will not be too sticky or too dry when cooked. Three times has always given me the best results.

2. After you have drained the rice a third time, add 1¾ cups water. Swirl your fingers in the pot once to ensure the rice is leveled and place the lid on the pot. Cook the rice over medium-low heat until it has absorbed all the water, 20 to 25 minutes. Remove the pot from the heat, stir the rice with a wooden spoon a few times, then let rest, covered, for 10 minutes before serving.

RICE HAS BECOME so deeply ingrained in Asian culture that in the warm southern and southeastern areas where it is widely cultivated, it has come to define the landscape. When in my early twenties I traveled from France to Hong Kong and southern China by train, I noticed decidedly "non-French" cultural activity in the railroad station. People were traveling with large bags, selling rice wrapped in bamboo leaves. Not twenty minutes into the trip, the splendors of China's rice terraces appeared in the hilly, lusciously green countryside north of Hong Kong. Men worked alongside their water buffalo, preparing the paddies for planting. Not far behind, the women came with bushels of rice plants. Holding them in one arm, they used the other to plunge a single rice plug at a time into the wet soil, creating perfectly straight rows of rice plants. For over an hour, I watched as my train traveled cross-country to Guangzhou, crossing the wet paddies and passing the toiling men, women, and water buffalo.

SHORT-GRAIN RICE

SERVES 4

1 cup SHORT-GRAIN RICE

SHORT-GRAIN RICE is preferred by Japanese and Koreans and accompanies most meals. The Japanese also use this semi-sticky rice for sushi, and as such it is often referred to as *sushi-meshi*, or sushi rice. Somewhat confusingly, this short-grain rice is sometimes labeled medium-grain rice. Kakuho Rose, my favorite brand, a California-grown rice believed by many Japanese chefs to be as good as or better than Japanese-grown rice, labels its rice bags "authentic sushi rice," while the ingredient is listed as "medium-grain rice." After comparing the size of these grains to my sticky rice grains, I found they were the same length and just as round. I concluded that this rice is the perfect rice for all sorts of Japanese or Korean side dishes, as well as for making sushi. It is also the brand of choice for making the Chinese rice porridge called *jook* (page 192).

Some distributors, including Kakuho Rose, recommend that you do not rinse your rice because nutrients are washed away in the process. Asians disregard this warning because they know that the sum total of all foods served during a meal makes for a healthy diet. Rinsing is necessary and results in perfectly cooked rice. If you do not rinse, the grains will be mushy and gummy when cooked.

For 4 generous portions of rice or to serve 6 to 8 persons, cook 2 cups rice with 2½ cups water, following the same instructions as below.

1. Put the rice in a medium pot with a few cups of water. Gently swirl your fingers in the pot to allow the starch to separate from the grains. Once the water becomes white, tilt the pot over the sink to drain out the water. Be careful not to let your rice go into the sink; hold it back with your hand while the water seeps through your fingers. Repeat this process twice more. Each time, the water will get less cloudy. The idea is not to get rid of all the starch, just enough so that the rice will not be too sticky or too dry when cooked. Three times has always given me the best results.

2. After you have drained the rice a third time, add 1½ cups water. Swirl your fingers in the pot once to ensure the rice is leveled and place the lid on the pot. Cook the rice over medium-low heat until it has absorbed all the water, 20 to 25 minutes. Remove the pot from the heat, stir the rice with a wooden spoon a few times, then let rest, covered, for 10 minutes before serving.

Variation: To make sushi-meshi rice, follow the recipe, but add a 2-inch square piece of kelp to the rice in step 2. When the rice comes to a boil, remove and discard the kelp, and continue cooking the rice as instructed. Meanwhile, whisk together 2 tablespoons rice vinegar, 2 tablespoons granulated sugar, and a teaspoon of kosher sea salt in a bowl until both sugar and salt have dissolved completely. Transfer the cooked rice to a wooden or plastic container and spread it out in a thick layer. Work the vinegar mixture into the rice with a spatula, making horizontal cutting strokes. At the same time, fan the rice to keep it from getting wet and sticky. You should repeat the strokes and fan the rice for about 10 minutes, until the rice cools down to room temperature.

IN SERVING RICE, presentation counts for a lot. The Koreans and Japanese, especially, are famous for their artistic arrangements of everything from produce at the market, to flowers, to food presented at table. Rice is no different. While some cooks serve plain rice in a bowl, others go a step further and sprinkle it with green tea powder, julienned nori (laver, a sea vegetable dried in sheets and used to make sushi), green or purple *shiso* (perilla) leaves, black or toasted white sesame seeds, blanched and chopped daikon leaves, or green peas. The possibilities are endless, but the purpose is to please both the eye and palate, and to evoke a mood of aesthetic awareness. I encourage you to sprinkle tasty tidbits of choice on your rice prior to serving.

BROWN RICE OR BHUTANESE RED RICE

SERVES 4

1 cup LONG-GRAIN BROWN RICE;
or BHUTANESE RED RICE

BROWN RICE is typically long- or medium-grain rice with its bran left intact. Bhutanese red rice grows in melted glacier water from the highlands of Tibet. While Asian kitchens in general tend to avoid both brown and red rice, I find them to be crunchy in texture, rich and nutty in flavor, and nutritious—ideal complements to vegetarian meals. When I have leftover brown or red cooked rice, I refrigerate it overnight and stir-fry it the next day with vegetables for a simple lunch, as in Japanese stir-fried brown rice (page 213) flavored with shiitake mushrooms and scallions.

For 4 generous portions of rice or to serve 6 to 8 persons, cook 2 cups brown or red rice with 4 cups water following the same instructions as below but increasing the cooking time by 5 minutes. There is no need to rinse these varieties of rice as you would with white rice. No starch will come loose, and the water will not get cloudy. Rinse brown or red rice only once.

1. Put the rice in a medium pot with a few cups of water. Gently swirl your fingers in the pot to clean the grains. Tilt the pot over the sink to drain out the water. Be careful not to let your rice go into the sink; hold it back with your hand while the water seeps through your fingers.

2. After you have drained the rice, add 2 cups water (1½ cups for red rice). Swirl your fingers in the pot once to ensure the rice is leveled and place the lid on the pot. Cook the rice over medium-low heat until it has absorbed all the water, 35 to 40 minutes (20 to 25 minutes for red rice). Remove from the heat, stir the rice with a wooden spoon a few times, then let rest, covered, for 10 minutes before serving.

KALIJIRA RICE

SERVES 4

1 cup KALIJIRA, or "PRINCE" RICE

KALIJIRA RICE grains are the tiniest white whole grains you will ever see. Grown in India, kalijira, also known as "prince rice," is the most delicate rice you can serve and makes your food presentation visually light. Its sweet aroma pairs well with all sorts of spicy to lightly seasoned dishes. I first discovered this rice while testing all sorts of rice for a food article. I especially love to serve the delicate grain when making a vegetarian meal, where it complements the vegetables and is never too filling.

For 4 generous portions of rice or to serve 6 to 8 persons, cook 2 cups rice with 2 ½ cups water following the same instructions as below.

1. Put the rice in a medium pot with a few cups of water. Gently swirl your fingers in the pot to allow the starch to separate from the grains. Once the water becomes white, tilt the pot over the sink to drain out the water. Be careful not to let your rice go into the sink; hold it back with your hand while the water seeps through your fingers. Repeat this process twice more. Each time, the water will get less cloudy. The idea is not to get rid of all the starch, just enough so that the rice will not be too sticky or too dry when cooked. Three times has always given me the best results.

2. After you have drained the rice a third time, add 1 ½ cups water. Swirl your fingers in the pot once to ensure the rice is leveled and place the lid on the pot. Cook the rice over medium-low heat until it has absorbed all the water, 20 to 25 minutes. Remove the pot from the heat, stir the rice with a wooden spoon a few times, then let rest, covered, for 10 minutes before serving.

Variation: Broken rice, left over from processing long-grain rice, can be cooked using the same grain-to-water ratio as for the kalijira rice. The broken pieces are just as tiny.

JOOK (CONGEE)
BASIC RICE PORRIDGE

SERVES 4 TO 6

1 cup SHORT-GRAIN RICE

4 tablespoons BANCHA (green tea leaves; optional)

2 teaspoons SESAME OIL (optional)

BASIC (OR PLAIN) rice porridge is eaten all over Asia, usually as a breakfast or snack item, occasionally replacing a bowl of rice during lunch or dinner. Short-grain rice, sometimes referred to as "sushi" rice, is excellent for making porridge. In Asia, including China, Vietnam, Japan, and Korea, porridge is called *jook*, *chao*, *okayu*, and *chuck*, respectively. These porridges are usually served with all sorts of complementary side dishes to nibble on. In my family we love to serve steamed salt-cured fish (or oil-packed sardines drizzled with soy sauce and sprinkled with dried red chili flakes), fermented bean curd cubes straight from the jar, Chinese sweet pork and liver sausages pan-fried until crispy, omelettes flavored with salted Tientsin cabbage and scallions, and crunchy pickled daikon.

Variations on plain porridge also exist. They include Japanese *cha-gayu*, green tea rice porridge, and Korean *huin chuck*, sesame rice porridge. Both the Japanese and Korean porridges are basic and elegant, and appropriate for serving with side dishes such as preserved daikon, *kimchi*, or deep-fried dried fish.

When making rice porridge, do not rinse the starch from the rice grains prior to cooking. Starch gives the porridge the necessary soft velvety texture. This semi-thick soup can be refrigerated. Reheat over medium-low heat, adding about 1 cup of water to loosen it.

1. For plain rice congee: Put the rice and 2 quarts water in a pot, and bring to a boil over high heat. Reduce the heat to medium-low, stir, cover, and simmer until the grains break down, about 2 hours.

2. For Japanese *cha-gayu*: Steep 4 tablespoons green tea leaves with 2 quarts hot water for 4 minutes. Strain over a pot, discard the leaves, and add the rice to the pot of hot tea. Bring to a boil over high heat. Reduce the heat to medium-low, stir, cover, and simmer until the grains break down, about 2 hours.

3. For Korean *huin chuck*: Soak the rice with water to cover for 1 hour and drain. Heat the sesame oil in a pot over medium heat, add the rice, and stir-fry until golden, about 5 minutes. Add 2 quarts water, reduce the heat to medium-low, stir, cover, and simmer until the grains break down, about 2 hours.

CHONBOK CHUK
ABALONE RICE PORRIDGE

SERVES 4 TO 6

1 cup SHORT-GRAIN RICE

8 ounces ABALONE (boiled in
    water for 2 minutes if canned;
    or soaked overnight if dried),
    julienned

1 teaspoon SESAME OIL

1 tablespoon KOREAN or JAPANESE
    DARK SOY SAUCE

1 teaspoon GRANULATED SUGAR

2 SCALLIONS, root and dark green
    ends trimmed, and 6-inch stalks
    thinly sliced into rounds

KOSHER SALT

Freshly ground BLACK PEPPER

IN KOREA some rice porridges are made quite differently from the Chinese version. Rather than boil whole rice grains with water, the Koreans soak the rice, grind it finely, then cook it down into porridge. The porridge, or gruel, is finer in consistency and thicker than the Chinese jook. While the Koreans enjoy adding abalone, you can also add shredded chicken, beef, or pork. As in many parts of Asia, this porridge is most often enjoyed for breakfast.

Abalone is expensive and is available fresh, frozen, dried, or canned. If using the canned version, I suggest boiling it in water for a couple of minutes to get rid of any tin flavor it has absorbed from the can. The chewy-textured dried version should be soaked overnight.

1. Soak the rice in a cup of water for 30 minutes. Grind the rice with the water in a mortar and pestle (or a blender) until finely ground, not pasty. Transfer the rice and soaking liquid to a pot with 2 quarts water and bring to a boil over high heat. Reduce the heat to medium-low, cover, and cook, stirring occasionally, until thickened, about 2 hours. Ladle the porridge into large individual soup bowls.

2. About 15 minutes before serving the porridge, marinate the abalone with the sesame oil, soy sauce, and sugar for 10 minutes. Heat a nonstick pan over medium heat, add the abalone, and stir-fry until cooked and slightly caramelized, 5 minutes. Spoon 1 to 2 tablespoons of abalone on top of each serving of rice porridge. Garnish each with scallions, and instruct your guests to season their individual servings with sea salt and black pepper as desired.

CHINESE FISH CONGEE is a delicious variation on similarly simple congees. When I go to Chinatown, I stop at one of my favorite Chinese restaurants and order *yueh jook*. A bowl of congee shows up at the table topped with salt and pepper–seasoned bite-size fish chunks (cod, flounder, or bass) that have been added raw to the congee during the last few minutes of preparation. Garnished with generous amounts of julienned ginger and thinly sliced scallions, and drizzled with some sesame oil, it is a very satisfying meal. Roasted peanuts are sometimes added for extra flavor and texture.

DAHN JOOK
EGG RICE PORRIDGE

SERVES 4 TO 6

3 SALTED EGGS (page 17)
3 THOUSAND-YEAR-OLD EGGS,
   shelled and finely diced
   (pp. 17–18)
1 teaspoon VEGETABLE OIL
2 large EGGS (optional)
KOSHER SALT
Freshly ground BLACK PEPPER
BASIC RICE PORRIDGE (page 192)
2 SCALLIONS, root and dark green
   ends trimmed, and 6-inch stalks
   thinly sliced into rounds
SESAME OIL
CHINESE LIGHT SOY SAUCE

I N ADDITION to the more familiar vegetables, seafood, poultry, and meat, the Chinese preserve eggs as well. *Dahn jook* is a celebration of *haam dahn*, salty eggs, and *pei dahn*, the so-called thousand-year-old eggs, balanced with regular eggs (a personal preference). Used with a simple morning rice porridge (or congee), the salty egg provides a savory note, while the thousand-year-old egg—which is brownish-black in color with a greenish-yellow yolk in the center—acts as a nominal sweet. In comparison the regular egg has a neutral flavor, which brings together the sweet and salty notes. A dash of nutty sesame oil and a generous sprinkling of freshly sliced scallions round out all the flavors and lift the palate. Although unfamiliar to most Westerners, this is a delightful dish.

1. Place the salted eggs in a pot with water to cover and bring to a gentle boil over medium heat. Wait 3 minutes, drain, and run the eggs under cold water until cool enough to handle. Crack the shells and peel the eggs. Rinse the eggs under cold water to make sure no shell is left behind. Finely dice the eggs. Transfer the salted eggs to one bowl, and the thousand-year-old eggs to another.

2. Optionally, heat the oil in a nonstick pan. Meanwhile beat the regular eggs with a tablespoon of water and a pinch of salt and pepper, until loosened and well combined. Pour the eggs into the pan and make a thin, dry (not runny) omelette. Transfer the omelette to a cutting board, julienne, and transfer to a bowl.

3. If you have just made the congee, ladle it into large individual soup bowls. If you have made the congee ahead of time and refrigerated it, put it in a pot, stir in a cup of water, and bring it to a gentle boil over medium heat. Serve the congee with the eggs and scallions in their individual serving bowls. Instruct your guests to add a heaping tablespoon of salted and thousand-year-old eggs and some omelette to their congee, then garnish with a generous amount of scallions and a dash or two of sesame oil. Adjust the seasoning with soy sauce, salt, and pepper as desired.

While I was in Hong Kong, I stayed at the Shangri-La, where my Chinese friend Patsy Chan and I loved to sit by the window and discuss food over breakfast. Our favorite dish was *dahn jook,* simple egg congee. Easy to digest, this congee is a perfect example of how something simple can be extremely flavorful. Because subtle flavoring is often favored by the Chinese for the morning meal, this dish is a favorite. It is very subtle in flavoring, and you can adjust the seasoning with soy sauce, although I encourage you to hold back, giving this delicious porridge a chance to stand on its own. If, after tasting, you need to season further, use freshly ground sea salt rather than the soy sauce bottle. Allow the eggs—rather than masking them with salty soy—to shine through and you will not be disappointed.

GAI JOOK
CHICKEN RICE PORRIDGE

SERVES 4 TO 6

6 dried medium to large SHIITAKE
    MUSHROOMS

¼ cup dried SHRIMP (optional)

1 cup SHORT-GRAIN RICE

8 cups BASIC CHICKEN STOCK
    (page 116)

2 cups shredded CHICKEN (from
    making the chicken stock; dark
    or white meat)

2 ounces fresh GINGER, peeled and
    julienned

1 bunch CILANTRO, leaves only

2 SCALLIONS, root and dark green
    ends trimmed, and 6-inch stalks
    thinly sliced into rounds

FRIED GARLIC OIL (page 108)

MAGGI SAUCe (optional)

KOSHER SALT

Freshly ground BLACK PEPPER

G AI JOOK, CHICKEN CONGEE, is a family favorite. The generous amounts of ginger and cilantro are refreshing, making this soup suitable for any time of the year, or whenever you're feeling a little under the weather. Sometimes we add julienned abalone during the cooking for extra flavor, but you can substitute fresh fish or beef, or roast duck or pork for the chicken. For a clear rice soup, see the variation for *chao ga* (Vietnamese), *kao dtom gai* (Thai), or *babah* (Cambodian), Southeast Asian versions of *gai jook*.

1. Put the shiitakes in a bowl with hot water to cover, then set a plate over the bowl to prevent steam from escaping. Let stand until the mushrooms rehydrate and soften, about 30 minutes (or longer, depending on the size of the mushrooms). Squeeze the mushrooms between the palms of your hands to get rid of the excess water. Using a paring knife, remove any hard stems from the mushrooms. Julienne the caps. If using, soak the dried shrimp in water for 20 minutes and drain.

2. Put the rice and chicken stock in a pot and bring to a boil over high heat. Reduce the heat to medium-low, cover, and cook until the rice breaks down and the soup has thickened as a result, about 1½ hours. Add the shredded chicken, shiitakes, dried shrimp, and ginger, and continue to cook until the flavors develop, about 30 minutes

more. Ladle the rice porridge into individual soup bowls. Garnish each serving with some cilantro, scallions, and fried garlic oil. Adjust the seasoning with a dash or two of Maggi sauce, or salt and pepper to taste.

Variation: To make a brothy rice soup, substitute 2 cups cooked long-grain rice for the raw short-grain rice. Bring the chicken stock to a boil in a pot over high heat. Reduce the heat to medium-low, add the chicken, shiitakes, dried shrimp, and ginger, and simmer for 20 minutes. Put some rice into large individual soup bowls and ladle a generous amount of hot broth over each serving. Garnish each bowl as described in step 2, substituting soy sauce for Maggi sauce, or not.

ASIANS OCCASIONALLY USE Maggi sauce as a last-minute flavoring for noodle soups, rice soups, and congees. The sauce has an interesting flavor, combining the extracts of various vegetables. As a child I was addicted to Maggi sauce, its sweet and salty flavor being more interesting to me than soy sauce. Some days I would come home from school and go straight to the kitchen to cook up an afternoon snack of plain rice congee topped with an egg cooked over easy. A drizzle or two of Maggi sauce and I was in heaven. I still make this simple meal once in a while in a pinch.

SAMGYET'ANG
CHICKEN, GINSENG, AND JUJUBE SUMMER RICE SOUP

SERVES 4 TO 6

One 2- to 2½-pound CHICKEN
KOSHER SALT
Freshly ground BLACK PEPPER
2 ounces GINSENG, fresh,
    preserved in alcohol, or dried
    and sliced
8 small GARLIC CLOVES, crushed
    and peeled
½ cup WHITE SHORT-GRAIN
    STICKY ("glutinous") RICE
8 CHESTNUTS, boiled and peeled
    (if dried, soaked overnight)
8 JUJUBES, soaked in water to
    soften
2 SCALLIONS, root and dark green
    ends trimmed, and 6-inch stalks
    thinly sliced into rounds

SAMGYET'ANG, a popular Korean chicken soup flavored with bitter ginseng and sweet jujubes (red dates), is a cooling soup that is traditionally served during *sambok*, the three hottest days of summer in Korea. Often served as a one-dish meal accompanied by cabbage kimchi (page 359), it employs ginseng for its distinctive bitter note. Fresh ginseng is preferred, alcohol-preserved ginseng is fine, and the dried version, which is slightly more bitter but readily available, can also be used (see sidebar). When I was in Seoul, my Korean hosts often talked about this soup so passionately that it was as if they were tasting it right there and then. In my estimation, it is subtle compared to most other Korean foods, which tend to be flavored with chilies and very assertive.

1. Rinse the chicken, pat dry, and season with salt and pepper, inside and out. Stuff the chicken cavity with the ginseng, garlic, and rice. Truss the chicken so none of the ingredients can come out while cooking.

2. Place the chicken in a pot and add 2 quarts water, the chestnuts, and jujubes. Bring to a boil over high heat. Reduce the heat to medium-low and simmer until the chicken is cooked through and fork tender, about 1½ hours. Present the whole chicken at the table, then dispense chunks of it in individual bowls with a little of everything. Instruct your guests to adjust the seasoning to taste with salt and pepper and garnish their servings with scallions if they wish.

THE SEVERAL TYPES of ginseng are generally categorized as either wild or cultivated. Long appreciated by both the Koreans and Chinese, ginseng is sold fresh, preserved in alcohol, dried in its whole form, or sliced, and used for cooking or simply chewing. If you can get your hands on the more expensive fresh ginseng (cultivated costs much less than wild), I highly recommend it because it tends to be mild in flavor and delightfully crunchy. The second best choice is the fresh root preserved in alcohol (usually brandy). The alcohol overtone will dissipate in cooking, and the crunch of the root itself will still be present. When dried, the root's bitter essence becomes much more concentrated, and when cooked the root becomes chewy. Ginseng is also available in powdered form and as an extract for making tea, or in capsule form as a dietary supplement. Believed to retard the ageing process, this root—also known as "man root" because it resembles a human body—is grown in Asia, as well as New York State and Wisconsin. (Surprisingly, perhaps, the American versions are of such excellent quality that they are imported by the Chinese.) The wild varieties are very flavorful, but increasingly rare and too expensive for use in cooking. "Cultivated wild" varieties are grown from wild root stock under controlled conditions. The less expensive cultivated varieties are perfectly suitable for cooking, however, having wonderful flavor. While fresh ginseng of any sort would always be preferred, either the alcohol-preserved or the dried roots will make a very tasty *samgyet'ang*. You can find ginseng in tea or herbal medicine shops. Jujubes, sometimes called Chinese red dates, also have medicinal properties. A sweet and nutritious fruit, it is said that jujubes are a tonic for the spleen and stomach. While often added to both savory and sweet soups, they can also be added to sweet rice cakes such as the Chinese jujube crêpes (page 535). Jujubes can be purchased in Asian markets or medicinal shops.

SAMLAW TRAPEANG
BAMBOO AND FISH
RICE SOUP

SERVES 4 TO 6

½ cup LONG-GRAIN RICE

8 cups BASIC CHICKEN STOCK
(page 116); or BASIC FISH
STOCK (page 123)

1 cup unsweetened COCONUT
MILK (optional, page 77); or
commercial equivalent

1 to 2 tablespoons FISH EXTRACT
(page 76)

2 LEMONGRASS STALKS, root ends
trimmed, outer leaves and tough
green tops removed, and 6-inch-
long inner bulb slightly crushed

1 ounce fresh GALANGAL, thinly
sliced

2 or more THAI CHILIES (optional)

4 GARLIC CLOVES, crushed and
peeled

1 tablespoon GRANULATED SUGAR

2 small ZUCCHINI, halved
lengthwise and sliced diagonally

1 medium fresh BAMBOO SHOOT,
peeled and boiled in water for
10 minutes; or canned whole
BAMBOO SHOOT, boiled in
water for 5 minutes

12 ounces CATFISH or CARP
FILLETS, skinned and cut into
½-inch-thick pieces

4 to 6 ounces dried FISH STEAK or
FILLETS, soaked in water for
1 hour, then flaked (optional)

12 fresh CHILI LEAVES; or THAI
BASIL LEAVES

2 LIMES, quartered (optional)

WITH MORE CAMBODIANS settling in the United States each year, restaurants offering delectable Khmer foods can be found. A few years ago, I met mother-daughter team Longteine and Nadsa De Monteiro, the chefs and partners of the acclaimed Cambodian restaurant The Elephant Walk, in Boston. *Samlaw trapeang* is a refreshing Cambodian freshwater fish soup featuring a small amount of long-grain rice in a pungent broth, which is found in both Siem Reap—home of the world treasure Angkor Wat—and Phnom Penh, where I was raised by my grandparents. Nadsa explained that there are two principal versions of this soup. In Siem Reap coconut milk is used to enrich the broth, and in Phnom Penh the broth is clear with no hint of coconut. Longteine pointed out that you can add sliced pork along with the fish for a more satisfying meal. On a recent trip to Cambodia I had the pleasure of tasting this wonderful rice soup in its place of origin. Preserved fish is used along with fresh fish in the soup, and although the preserved item is an acquired taste, it gives a smoky flavor and complements the fresh fish perfectly. Like many recipes in Southeast Asia, the exact ingredients of the soup are somewhat open to interpretation. In fact, I've added freshly squeezed lime juice to counterbalance the richness of the coconut milk, and on occasion I add whole chilies to lift the palate.

When choosing the zucchini, make sure it is firm and small to medium in size; when zucchinis are too big they have too many seeds and tend to be full of water. If you cannot find fresh or frozen galangal, use the young rhizomes often sold preserved in brine and packed in glass jars.

1. Put the rice with water to cover in a medium pot. Gently swirl your fingers in the pot to allow the starch to separate from the grains. Once the water becomes white, tilt the pot over the sink to drain out the water. Be careful not to let your rice go into the sink; hold it back with your hand while the water seeps through your fingers. Repeat this process twice more. Each time, the water will get less cloudy. The idea is not to get rid of all the starch, just enough so that the rice will not be too sticky or too dry when cooked. Three times has always given me the best results.

2. Pour the stock in the pot containing the rice and bring to a boil over high heat. Reduce the heat to medium-low and add the coconut milk (if using), fish extract, lemongrass, galangal, chilies (if using), garlic, and sugar. Simmer, stirring occasionally, until the sugar has dissolved, and allow the flavors to develop, about 10 minutes.

3. Add the zucchini and cook for 3 minutes. Add the bamboo shoots and catfish and dried fish (if using). Continue to simmer until the zucchini is tender and the fish is cooked through, about 5 minutes. Stir in the chili or Thai basil leaves and simmer for 1 minute more. Remove the lemongrass and galangal and ladle the soup into large individual soup bowls, making sure to divide the ingredients evenly. As an option, serve with a lime wedge on the side of each serving and have your guests squeeze the juice into their soups if they wish, especially if using coconut milk.

Variations: If you wish to add meat or poultry, simply bring a pot of water to a boil and cook an 8-ounce piece of pork butt or tenderloin, or chicken breast, until cooked through, about 15 minutes. Drain, allow the meat to cool, thinly slice the meat against the grain, and add to the soup just before serving.

For those who are strict about not eating meat or poultry, use fish stock (page 123).

If you are a strict vegetarian, skip the fish, add more bamboo and zucchini to the soup, and use vegetable stock (page 126).

CHAO XA GA
LEMONGRASS-INFUSED
CHICKEN RICE SOUP

SERVES 4 TO 6

8 cups BASIC CHICKEN STOCK
(page 116)

2 LEMONGRASS STALKS, root ends
trimmed, outer leaves and tough
green tops removed, and 6-inch-
long inner bulbs cut into 1-inch
pieces, lightly crushed

2 to 3 RED THAI CHILIES,
stemmed, seeded, and very
thinly sliced

2 tablespoons FISH SAUCE

1 cup SHORT-GRAIN RICE

2 cooked CHICKEN LEGS, skinned,
deboned, and shredded (from
making the stock)

KOSHER SALT

½ cup julienned SAW LEAVES;
or whole CILANTRO LEAVES

2 LIMES, quartered

LEMONGRASS AND CHICKEN rice soup, called *chao xa ga* in Vietnamese and *shnor chrook* in Cambodian, is delicious and refreshing. Citrus fruits such as lime or lemon, and refreshing herbs such as lemongrass and saw leaf or cilantro are not just accents but foreground notes, making this rice soup a light meal perfectly suited for any time of the year, but for hot summer days especially. Unlike most Southeast Asian rice soups, this one is rather thick, with the rice grains having broken down all the way in the same fashion as classic Chinese congee. While chicken is the more popular version, the soup can also be made using pork (see variation), the most commonly eaten meat in both Vietnam and Cambodia.

While the recipe calls for hot chilies to be sliced and added as a garnish, if you would like a milder version of this soup, leave the chilies whole and add them in step 1 of the recipe to flavor the stock. To be on the safe side (sometimes chilies break open during extended cooking periods), you can also slice the chilies open and scrape off all the seeds prior to adding them to the stock. Put them in with the lemongrass.

1. Bring the chicken stock to a boil in a pot over high heat. Reduce the heat to medium-low, add the lemongrass, chilies, and fish sauce, and simmer for 30 minutes. Add the rice and cook, uncovered, stirring occasionally, for 1¼ hours more. (At home we remove the lemongrass as we eat the soup. You can, however, remove it prior to adding the rice to the soup, but you may lose some of the wonderful lemongrass flavor in the process, as it won't have steeped as long.)

2. Add the shredded chicken, season to taste with salt, and cook until heated through, about 5 minutes.

Ladle into large individual soup bowls, and instruct your guests to garnish with saw leaves or cilantro, and to squeeze a lime wedge over their soup.

Variation: Substitute basic pork stock (page 118) for the basic chicken stock, and 1½ to 2 cups shredded pork rib meat (from making the stock) for the chicken leg, and proceed with the recipe. This soup can also be made using shredded beef meat and basic beef stock, or fresh fish (cut into 1-inch cubes and added just 5 minutes prior to serving) with basic fish stock as well.

COMING ACROSS A STREET market early one morning in Vietnam, I happened to spy on a busy vendor surrounded by cardboard barrels full of rice. The rice vendor of Saigon was open for business, and what a business it was. His rice is reputed to be the best in town, so as soon as he opened, eager buyers thronged his modest stall. The rice was incredibly fresh, having come directly from the Mekong River Delta, the "rice bowl" of Vietnam. The starchy rice aromas had never seemed so sweet, and there were all sorts of varieties to choose from: long-grain, short-grain, sticky long-grain, sticky short-grain, red, black, brown, scented, and broken. I watched as the vendor scooped up his rice, filling large bags, always selling in bulk. A twenty-five-pound bag of rice, eaten every day for two to three meals, will feed an entire family for three months. "And three months is just about right. After that it turns stale," he told me, smiling while he worked. He was more than happy to point out specifics about each type of rice he sold. "Long-grain rice is good for everyday, especially scented with a few mint or cilantro leaves while boiling," he offered. This is an inexpensive way to scent rice, for true scented varieties such as jasmine are costly. "Sticky rice is good for making sweet or savory snacks," he went on. These are the items you see wrapped in bamboo or banana leaves, virtual serving containers that also lend their subtle flavors to the rice. Broken rice, actually the damaged bits left over from processing, is the least expensive variety. Tasting just as delicious as any unbroken grain, and considered inferior in the East, this rice is marketed as an exotic rarity in the United States, and sold at high prices. I am sure he would have been amused if I had told him.

ARROZ CALDO AT BABOY
PORK RICE SOUP

SERVES 4 TO 6

1 teaspoon VEGETABLE OIL

1 large GARLIC CLOVE, crushed, peeled, and minced

1 small YELLOW ONION, peeled and minced

1 ounce fresh GINGER, peeled and grated

12 ounces PORK BUTT, thinly sliced against the grain

1 cup SHORT-GRAIN RICE

8 cups BASIC PORK STOCK (page 118)

2 tablespoons FISH SAUCE

KOSHER SALT

Freshly ground BLACK PEPPER

2 SCALLIONS, root and dark green ends trimmed, and 6-inch stalks thinly sliced into rounds

RICE HAS ALWAYS held an important place in Filipino cuisine, as testified to by the famous rice terraces of Banaue in the northern Luzon region of the Philippines. Built thousands of years ago, the terraces are supported by rock retaining walls, which act as an irrigation system. They carry water down from the mountaintops, serving each paddy on the way. Today, as in centuries past, the terraces are maintained by the Ifugaos, a northern tribe that has lived in the mountains for millennia. *Arroz caldo at baboy* reflects both this deep rice culture and the European colonial traditions superimposed upon it. In making it, you will notice a Spanish influence in the preparation techniques, particularly in the initial sautéing of garlic and onions in oil and browning of the meat.

1. Heat the oil in a medium stockpot over medium heat. Add the garlic, onion, and ginger, and sauté until fragrant and light golden, about 5 minutes. Add the pork and sauté until lightly browned, about 10 minutes.

2. Add the rice, stock, and fish sauce. Stir well, season with salt and pepper to taste, and cook partially covered until the rice is tender, 30 to 45 minutes. Ladle into large individual soup bowls and garnish each serving with scallions.

NASI KUNING
YELLOW RICE

SERVES 4 TO 6

2 cups MEDIUM-GRAIN or
    LONG-GRAIN RICE
1½ cups unsweetened COCONUT
    MILK (page 77); or commercial
    equivalent
1½ cups BASIC CHICKEN STOCK
    (page 116)
1 teaspoon TURMERIC POWDER
1 LEMONGRASS STALK, root end
    trimmed, outer leaves and tough
    green top removed, and 6-inch-
    long inner bulb halved crosswise
    and bruised
1 ounce GALANGAL, peeled and
    cut into thin slices
KOSHER SALT

DURING FESTIVE OCCASIONS, yellow rice, called *nasi kuning* in Indonesia, is always part of the meal. Cooked in a combination of coconut milk and chicken stock, it not only has a rich flavor but literally glistens from the fat of the coconut milk. Its striking deep yellow color comes from turmeric, a natural dye used all over Asia. *Nasi kuning* is usually served heaped up high for effect, like a mountain peak on a plate. Although it is rich, it is also subtle in flavor and so can certainly replace a simple bowl of steamy white rice at any meal.

The Indonesians use medium-grain rice for everyday meals. Its texture is between that of long-grain and short-grain rice. This medium-grain rice can be found in Indonesian or Malaysian food markets, but if you cannot find it, long-grain rice makes a good substitute. Short-grain rice would be much too sticky.

1. Put the rice in a medium pot with a few cups of water. Gently swirl your fingers in the pot to allow the starch to separate from the grains. Once the water becomes white, tilt the pot over the sink to drain out the water. Be careful not to let your rice go into the sink; hold it back with your hand while the water seeps through your fingers. Repeat this process twice more. Each time, the water will get less cloudy. The idea is not to get rid of all the starch, just enough so that the rice will not be too sticky or too dry when cooked. Three times has always given me the best results.

2. Mix together the coconut milk, chicken stock, and turmeric until well combined. Add to the drained rice and stir to level the rice. Add the lemongrass and galangal, and season lightly with salt. Place the pot, covered, over medium-low heat until the rice is cooked through, about 25 minutes. Remove from the heat, discard the fragrant herbs, stir the rice with a wooden spoon a few times, then let rest, covered, for 10 minutes. Mound the rice into a cone in the center of a plate and serve with the side dishes you have selected for your meal.

KHAO MAN
COCONUT RICE

SERVES 4 TO 6

2 cups MEDIUM-GRAIN or
  LONG-GRAIN RICE
1½ cups unsweetened COCONUT
  MILK (page 77); or commercial
  equivalent
1½ cups BASIC CHICKEN STOCK
  (page 116)

COCONUT-FLAVORED RICE is a specialty of Thailand, where it is called *khao man*, and Indonesia, where it is referred to as *nasi gurih* or *nasi uduk*. Long-grain rice cooked in coconut milk is so rich that it is a wonderful complement to tangy and cool vegetable dishes such as green mango or papaya salad, or banana blossom salad. Because the coconut milk can be overwhelmingly rich, I sometimes cut it with either water or a light ginger-infused chicken stock.

1. Put the rice in a medium pot with a few cups of water. Gently swirl your fingers in the pot to allow the starch to separate from the grains. Once the water becomes white, tilt the pot over the sink to drain out the water. Be careful not to let your rice go into the sink; hold it back with your hand while the water seeps through your fingers. Repeat this process twice more. Each time, the water will get less cloudy. The idea is not to get rid of all the starch, just enough so that the rice will not be too sticky or too dry when cooked. Three times has always given me the best results.

2. Mix together the coconut milk and chicken stock until well combined. Add to the drained rice and stir to level the rice. Place the pot, covered, over medium-low heat until cooked through, about 25 minutes. Remove from the heat, stir the rice with a wooden spoon a few times, then let rest, covered, for 10 minutes before serving.

COM GUNG TUONG
GARLIC AND GINGER RICE

SERVES 4 TO 6

2 cups LONG-GRAIN RICE,
preferably JASMINE

1 tablespoon VEGETABLE OIL

2 large GARLIC CLOVES, crushed,
peeled, and finely chopped

1 ounce fresh GINGER, peeled and
minced

3 cups BASIC CHICKEN STOCK
(page 116)

1 bunch CILANTRO, stems
trimmed

STIR-FRIED CRISPY GINGER and garlic, rich chicken stock, and fragrant jasmine rice make for a simple but exceptionally delicious combination. Cooked in a clay pot and infused with a generous amount of cilantro, the rice boils, absorbing and mediating the herbal notes. This dish is an excellent complement to virtually any vegetable, seafood, poultry, or meat item.

1. Put the rice in a medium pot with a few cups of water. Gently swirl your fingers in the pot to allow the starch to separate from the grains. Once the water becomes white, tilt the pot over the sink to drain out the water. Be careful not to let your rice go into the sink; hold it back with your hand while the water seeps through your fingers. Repeat this process twice more. Each time, the water will get less cloudy. The idea is not to get rid of all the starch, just enough so that the rice will not be too sticky or too dry when cooked. Three times has always given me the best results. Put the rice in a sieve and drain until the rice is fairly dry again.

2. Heat the oil in a medium clay pot or heavy-bottomed pot over medium heat. Add the garlic and ginger and stir-fry until golden and crisp, 5 to 7 minutes. Add the rice and stir with a wooden spoon until lightly golden, 3 to 5 minutes. Add the chicken stock and stir to level the rice. Scatter the cilantro across the top, cover, and cook until the rice has absorbed all the stock, about 25 minutes. Turn the heat off and, with a wooden spoon, stir the rice a few times, thoroughly mixing in the cilantro. Allow to rest, covered, for 10 minutes before serving.

CHOW FAN
FRIED RICE

SERVES 4 TO 6

3 CHINESE SWEET PORK
  SAUSAGES, diced; or 1½ cups
  diced CANTONESE ROAST PORK
  (page 454) or ham

4 large NAPA or GREEN CABBAGE
  LEAVES, julienned

12 or more small SHRIMP, heads
  and shells removed (freeze and
  reserve for stock, page 123),
  and deveined

4 cups day-old cooked LONG-
  GRAIN RICE (page 186),
  refrigerated overnight and
  crumbled

1 tablespoon VEGETABLE OIL
  (optional)

2 tablespoons CHINESE LIGHT
  SOY SAUCE

2 large EGGS

½ cup fresh GREEN PEAS (if frozen,
  blanch in salted water for a few
  seconds)

KOSHER SALT

Freshly ground BLACK PEPPER

CLASSIC CHINESE FRIED RICE is made with leftover white rice and fresh or leftover vegetables, shrimp, chicken, or pork. Sometimes sweet pork sausage is added. Unlike the fried rice served in many Chinese-American restaurants, it should never be dark brown in color. These inferior versions use Chinese thick soy sauce, a shortcut that masks flavors and allows for imprecise cooking. The dish should be lightly seasoned with small amounts of regular thin (or "light") soy sauce and adjusted with salt. The grains should be white to yellowish from being coated with eggs during the stir-frying process. Good fried rice should have enough oil so that the rice grains stay fluffy and separate, but not so much so that they are greasy.

The Chinese generally prefer unadulterated white rice at meals. In traditional kitchens, fried rice would not be served as part of a meal, directly contradicting the common, and somewhat uninformed, Western practice. Fried rice is actually a rather delicate dish, most often served as a snack.

1. Heat a greased wok or a nonstick pan over high heat. Stir-fry the sausage until the fat is rendered and the sausage is lightly crisped. With a slotted spoon, transfer the sausage to a plate.

2. Stir-fry the cabbage and shrimp in the pork fat until the shrimp turn pink, about 1 minute. With a slotted spoon, transfer the cabbage and shrimp to a plate.

3. Stir-fry the rice in the same pork fat (adding the oil if necessary), making sure it is evenly coated. Season and dampen with soy sauce and continue to stir-fry until the rice becomes dry again, about 5 minutes. Add the eggs, and stir-fry to break

the yolks and spread them along with the whites throughout the rice. The rice grains should be evenly coated with the eggs. Keep stir-frying until the rice becomes dry again and is heated evenly throughout, about 15 minutes.

4. Add the stir-fried pork, cabbage, shrimp, and green peas, and stir-fry until evenly distributed. Adjust the seasoning with salt and pepper to taste. Serve hot.

IN VIETNAM AND THAILAND, fried rice is made using the same approach as in China, transforming day-old rice into something so delicious that the idea of "leftover" is somehow ennobled. Influenced by both Chinese culinary traditions and practicality, the Southeast Asian cook chops up fresh or leftover vegetables, meat, and/or seafood, and stir-fries them with the rice. Fish sauce may be used as an alternative to soy sauce, and hot peppers (in Indonesia, for example) may be added. Chinese sweet pork sausages may also find their way into Vietnamese and Thai stir-fried rice if leftover meat is not available. The next time you order fried rice in a Vietnamese or Thai restaurant, remember that you are ordering a dish that begins with day-old items and finishes as something completely different.

I'VE MADE FRIED RICE with rice cooked in the morning and allowed to rest for a few hours until cool, and rice cooked a day ahead of time and refrigerated overnight. The best result has always been with the day-old rice. Generally, Chinese pork sausage has enough fat that you can stir-fry it without adding oil to the dish. Use 1 tablespoon vegetable oil if using roast pork or ham.

SINANGAG
GARLIC FRIED RICE

SERVES 4 TO 6

1 or more tablespoons VEGETABLE
OIL

2 large GARLIC CLOVES, crushed,
peeled, and minced

4 cups day-old cooked LONG-
GRAIN RICE (page 186),
refrigerated overnight and
crumbled

FISH SAUCE

KOSHER SALT

Freshly ground BLACK PEPPER

VEGETABLE OIL for deep-frying

12 or more small dried FISH such
as DANGGIT

4 small links CHORIZO or
LINGUIÇA, thinly sliced
diagonally

4 to 6 large EGGS

2 cups CHINESE BEEF or PORK
JERKY, shredded

COCONUT or CHINESE WHITE RICE
VINEGAR

ONE OF MY FAVORITE BREAKFASTS in the Philippines was rice stir-fried with garlic. Called *sinangag*, it is served with side dishes making for a hearty first meal of the day. Among the most common accompaniments are sunny-side-up eggs, fried fish that has been previously air-dried then deep-fried, *tapa* (beef or pork jerky similar to Chinese jerky), and mild to spicy pork sausage known as *longaniza* (also spelled *longanisa* and closely related to the Spanish *chorizo* or Portuguese *linguiça*). A side of coconut vinegar is also served as a dip to cut the richness of the fish and other items. At home I occasionally prepare the rice and side dishes for Sunday brunch. This garlic rice also works wonderfully with other dishes such as chicken *adobo* (pp. 496–97) or beef *kare-kare* (page 474).

1. To make the rice: Heat the oil in a wok or nonstick skillet over high heat. Stir-fry the garlic until golden, about 3 minutes. Add the rice and stir-fry, breaking down any lumps with the back of a spatula or spoon until the grains separate. Season to taste with fish sauce and/or salt and pepper. Continue stir-frying until well mixed and hot. Shut off the heat and place a cover on top of the rice to keep warm.

2. To make the dried fish: Pour enough vegetable oil in a pot (2 to 3 inches deep) over medium-high heat. When the oil has reached 360° to 375°F, add the dried fish and fry until crisp, about 2 minutes. Remove the fish with a slotted spoon and drain on paper towels. Set aside.

3. To make the sausage: Pan-fry the sausage in a dry nonstick skillet over medium-high heat. Cook until the edges are crispy on both sides, about 2 minutes. Drain on paper towels. Set aside.

4. To make the eggs: Feel free to cook your eggs any style: sunny-side up, over easy, poached, or scrambled. In my opinion, sunny-side-up or over-easy eggs with soft yolks in the center are the most delicious with this particular dish.

5. To serve *sinangag* and side dishes: Place the fried fish, sausages, jerky, eggs, and rice on individual serving platters so your guests can choose whatever they want and how much. Or, on each plate, mound a cup or less of garlic fried rice in the center and surround with individual piles of fried fish, sausages, and jerky. Place an egg on top of each serving of rice or on the side as preferred. Serve the vinegar for dipping the fried fish on the side.

DRIED FISH, VERY POPULAR in the Philippines, is typically eaten at breakfast. The local markets feature many different kinds, from the familiar salted sardines and anchovies to *danggit,* a small fish measuring two inches long on average and found in the waters surrounding Cebu. Because *danggit* can be up to four times the price of other dried fish, it is somewhat uncommon in cooking, even in Cebu. Chef Ding R. Rodenas at the Shangri-La Resort proudly serves *danggit* to his guests, as he did to me when I visited. Butterflied and gutted, *danggit* is sun-dried. (Salted naturally from the Pacific Ocean, it requires no added salt during the drying process.) Deep-fried whole directly from the package, they are deliciously crisp. Dipped in vinegar and chased with a spoonful of garlic fried rice topped with the runny yolk and crispy white of a sunny-side-up egg, they are superb. And while you might have a glass of sweet grapefruit or orange juice as an accompaniment, I urge you to try something a little tangier such as sour and refreshing green mango juice. *Kalamansi* (also *calamansi*), a citrus fruit no larger than a pinball and similar to lime, is also sour, but with a subtle sweet finish, and without lime's bitterness. (In the United States *dayap,* or lime, serves as a reasonable substitute.) Also try freshly squeezed lemon juice in water, as in the French *citron-pressé;* sugar is usually served on the side and added to taste, if at all. These somewhat adventurous departures from the usual orange or grapefruit juices nicely counterbalance the hearty fish, meat, and garlicky rice breakfast. Ripe seasonal fruit such as sliced mango, papaya, and pineapple, or other more exotic fruit such as lychee, rambutan, and longan also make for a great finish.

DRIED-FISH MARKETS ARE SEEN ALL OVER SOUTHEAST ASIA. MANY FILIPINOS ENJOY TINY DRIED FISH SUCH AS *DANGGIT* DEEP-FRIED AND SERVED WITH A SIDE OF COCONUT VINEGAR FOR BREAKFAST.

NASI GORENG
CRAB FRIED RICE

SERVES 4 TO 6

⅓ cup or more SAMBAL TERASI
  (page 79)
6 ounces ground PORK or BEEF
  (70 percent lean)
12 ounces lump CRABMEAT
4 cups day-old cooked LONG-
  GRAIN RICE (page 186),
  refrigerated overnight and
  crumbled
KOSHER SALT
Freshly ground BLACK PEPPER
FRIED SHALLOTS (page 108)

LUCIA ONG, AN INDONESIAN WOMAN of Chinese heritage whom I met in New York, taught me how to make this delicious crab nasi goreng. I must say it is one of the best—if not the best—and most interesting versions I have ever had the pleasure of eating. I have made it over and over again, never tiring of its flavor combinations. It makes a great single-dish meal for lunch, dinner, or brunch. You'll see that with your friends and family, it will become a quick favorite as it has with mine.

While Lucia enjoys an especially savory and spicy version of this dish, she sometimes makes a second batch with far fewer chili peppers for those who can't take the heat. Do not hesitate to adjust the chilies in the sambal terasi to your taste. (Skip the protein for a simple nasi goreng.)

1. Heat the sambal terasi in a wok over high heat until fragrant, about 2 minutes. Add the ground pork or beef and stir-fry, breaking up the meat with the back of a spatula, until cooked through, about 5 minutes. Add the lump crabmeat and stir-fry, breaking it down to heat it through evenly.

2. Add the cooked rice and stir-fry, breaking down any lumps, until all the ingredients are combined evenly and the rice is heated through, about 20 minutes. Adjust the seasoning with salt and pepper if necessary. Serve garnished with fried shallots.

Variation: Having lived in the United States for quite some time now, Lucia occasionally incorporates slab bacon into her crab fried rice, giving the dish a smoky flavor. If you wish to try this version, simply add 6 ounces finely diced slab bacon and stir-fry it along with the sambal terasi, then proceed with the recipe as described.

A BALINESE WOMAN once said to me that the Indonesians invented a grain of rice that was unique, and further research proved her not incorrect. Referred to as javanica (from the word Java), it is a medium grain, fat and dry with a subtle sticky character. The Indonesians steam this rice in the same conical woven bamboo basket used to collect the rice grains from the paddies. Nutty and tender, it is subtly different from other rices, and often used in the traditional rijsttafel, or rice table—an assortment of Balinese specialties served in small amounts with copious amounts of rice. To date, I have found javanica available only in Indonesia.

GENMAI
FRIED BROWN RICE

SERVES 4 TO 6

2 tablespoons VEGETABLE OIL

12 fresh medium SHIITAKE
MUSHROOMS, stems removed,
caps julienned

4 SCALLIONS, root and dark green
ends trimmed, and 6-inch stalks
thinly sliced into rounds

4 cups day-old cooked BROWN
RICE (page 190), refrigerated
overnight and crumbled

1 to 2 tablespoons JAPANESE DARK
SOY SAUCE

1 tablespoon MIRIN

KOSHER SALT

Freshly ground BLACK PEPPER

BLACK SESAME SEEDS; or 1 large
NORI PAPER, julienned into
1-inch-long strips

I N JAPANESE, the word *genmai*, literally "dark rice," is used to describe brown rice. While the Japanese generally prefer white rice over brown, this recipe is inspired by a similar one from the celebrated Japanese cooking teacher Hiroko Shimbo-Beitchman. Delicate yet hearty, brown rice makes for a more satisfying vegetarian meal than white rice. Here I use day-old brown rice stir-fried with a generous amount of both fresh shiitake mushrooms and thinly sliced scallions.

You can also use red Bhutanese rice (page 190) to make this dish.

1. Heat 1 tablespoon oil in a wok over high heat. Stir-fry the shiitakes and scallions until just wilted, about 2 minutes. Transfer them to a plate.

2. Add the remaining oil and the rice to the wok, then the soy sauce and mirin, and stir-fry until the grains are heated through, dry and separate, about 20 minutes.

3. Return the mushrooms and scallions to the wok, adjust the seasoning with salt and pepper, and stir-fry to distribute evenly. Divide among plates or bowls, and garnish each serving with a sprinkle or two of black sesame seeds or julienned nori.

BIMBIM PAP
KOREAN MIXED RICE
IN STONE BOWLS

2 tablespoons KOREAN or JAPANESE
   DARK SOY SAUCE
1 tablespoon GINGER EXTRACT
   (page 74)
Freshly ground BLACK PEPPER
2 teaspoons GRANULATED SUGAR
1 SCALLION, root and dark green
   ends trimmed, and 6-inch stalk
   minced
1 large GARLIC CLOVE, crushed,
   peeled, and minced
12 ounces BEEF SIRLOIN,
   julienned into 2-inch-long strips
   against the grain
2½ teaspoons SESAME OIL
3½ to 4½ teaspoons VEGETABLE
   OIL, plus extra
4 small CARROTS, ends trimmed
   and peeled, julienned into about
   2-inch-long sticks
KOSHER SALT
2 small ZUCCHINI, ends trimmed,
   julienned into 2-inch-long sticks
2 cups MUNG BEAN SPROUTS, root
   ends trimmed
1 bunch SPINACH, stems trimmed,
   leaves separated
4 to 6 EGGS
4 to 6 cups freshly cooked SHORT-
   GRAIN RICE (page 188)
SWEET AND SOUR CHILI DIPPING
   SAUCE (page 105)

A CLASSIC AND POPULAR Korean dish is *bimbim pap*, rice mixed with all sorts of colorful blanched or stir-fried vegetables, beef, an egg, and sweet chili paste called *ch'o koch'ujang*. This dish is served two ways, either in a special hot stone bowl (the most popular method) or in a regular ceramic bowl. Either version has freshly cooked rice at the bottom of the bowl, with julienned carrot and zucchini, spinach, mung bean sprouts, and shredded beef arranged on top of the rice in small, individual piles. The egg is usually raw when served in the hot stone bowl; it cooks when mixed with the other ingredients. When served in a ceramic bowl, the egg's white and yolk are separated and cooked into thin omelettes. These are then julienned and arranged in individual piles, with the other ingredients, on top of the rice. In a simpler version, the egg can also be pan-fried sunny-side up.

For best results, be sure to cook the rice just as you are heating the stone bowls, or just a few minutes before serving in a regular bowl. This will keep the rice hot enough to cook the egg and otherwise blend the flavors. The Korean stone bowls used for *bimbim pap* are wonderful additions to your table, and can be purchased at Korean markets or on the Internet (page 563).

1. Whisk together the soy sauce, ginger extract, black pepper to taste, and sugar in a bowl until the sugar is completely dissolved. Stir in the scallion and garlic, then add the beef. Mix thoroughly and marinate for 10 minutes.

2. Meanwhile, mix the sesame oil with 2½ teaspoons vegetable oil in a bowl. Heat 1 teaspoon of the mixed oil in a wok or nonstick pan over high heat. Stir-fry the carrots with a pinch or two of salt (so they retain their bright orange color), until tender but still firm, about 2 minutes. Repeat this process, using the same cooking vessel, to cook the zucchini (about 2 minutes), mung bean sprouts (15 seconds), spinach (15 seconds), and, lastly, the beef (2 to 3 minutes, until fairly dry but tender).

3. Heat the remaining 1 to 2 tablespoons oil in a nonstick pan over medium heat, and fry the eggs, sunny-side up or over easy, until the whites are slightly crispy and the yolks are still raw. Or separate the whites from the yolks and cook them separately (with half the oil each) into two thin omelettes and julienne them.

For coating the hot stone bowls with oil, I dip a paper towel in oil and, holding it with tongs, spread the oil inside the bowl's surface. (Brush bristles can easily melt.)

BIMBIM PAP is one of my favorite dishes. I never tire of it, especially when it is served in a hot stone bowl and comes to the table sizzling. It is served throughout Korea, and I have even enjoyed it on Asiana Airlines, the Korean carrier. It came without the stone bowl, of course, but had a tube of sweet chili paste, a side of cabbage *kimchi* (page 359), and basic beef stock (page 120). Bimbim pap and an in-flight movie; what a perfect way to fly.

WOMEN ENJOYING *BIMBIM PAP* AT AN OUTDOOR MARKET LUNCH COUNTER IN SEOUL, KOREA

4. If using ceramic bowls, put 1 cup of rice in each individual bowl and arrange some vegetables and beef in individual piles on top. Add a sunny-side-up egg, over-easy egg, or julienned yolk and white in the center. Instruct your guests to mix their rice with 2 to 3 tablespoons of sweet and sour chili dipping sauce.

5. If using stone bowls, heat them over low heat, increasing the heat to medium over the span of 10 to 15 minutes until they're very hot. Remove from the heat and, working quickly, lightly coat with oil, put 1 cup of cooked rice in each bowl, and arrange the vegetables and beef in individual piles on top. Add a raw egg* in the center and serve. Instruct your guests to mix their rice quickly (this is necessary to cook the egg) with 2 to 3 tablespoons of sweet chili paste. (The stone bowls should come with wooden blocks to set them on when it is time to serve. Be sure to use good quality thick cooking gloves to handle the bowls when transferring them from the burners to the wood blocks.)

* Consuming raw eggs carries the risk of contracting salmonella. Dishes containing raw eggs should not be eaten by the very young, the very old, pregnant women, or anyone with a compromised immune system. Consider using pasteurized eggs.

OGOK PAP
KOREAN FESTIVE
FIVE-GRAIN RICE

SERVES 4 TO 6

¼ cup AZUKI RED BEANS, soaked
for 4 hours and drained

1 cup SHORT-GRAIN RICE, soaked
for 4 hours and drained

1 cup STICKY RICE, soaked for
4 hours and drained

¼ cup BLACK BEANS, soaked for
4 hours and drained

¼ cup SORGHUM, soaked
overnight in several changes of
water and drained

¼ cup MILLET

KOSHER SALT

THE KOREAN FIVE-GRAIN rice dish called *ogok pap* is filling. A possible culinary reference to the time of Central Asian cultural dominance of China and the Korean peninsula, it uses the millet and sorghum grown on those windy steppes. Served during the first full moon of the lunar New Year (usually from mid-January to early February), it is composed of rice, azuki red beans, black beans (not to be confused with fermented black beans), sorghum, and millet. Visually, the deep rosy color of the cooked rice and the accompanying grains makes for a beautiful presentation, especially apt for festive occasions. For the perfect sticky consistency the dish exhibits when properly prepared, Korean cooks use one part short-grain rice to one part sticky rice. I especially like to serve *ogok pap* when preparing a vegetarian dinner.

1. Put the red beans and 2¼ cups water in a pot and bring to a boil over high heat. Reduce the heat to medium and cook the beans until just cooked, about 45 minutes. Drain the beans, but reserve the reddish cooking liquid.

2. Put the short-grain rice, sticky rice, black beans, red beans, sorghum, millet, and red bean cooking liquid in a sand pot. Season with salt, and stir to mix and level the ingredients thoroughly. Cover the pot and bring to a boil over high heat. Reduce the heat to medium-low, and continue to cook until the water is fully absorbed and the rice is tender but firm, about 25 minutes. Serve with stir-fried or braised vegetables.

TEMAKIZUSHI
SALMON SKIN HANDROLLS

SERVES 4 TO 6

1 tablespoon VEGETABLE OIL
1 pound SALMON SKIN with about
    ⅛ inch of underside flesh
    attached
6 NORI SHEETS, quartered
SUSHI-MESHI RICE (pp. 188–89)
2 SCALLIONS, root and dark green
    ends trimmed, and 6-inch stalks
    very thinly sliced into rounds
2 small to medium CARROTS,
    peeled and julienned into
    2-inch-long matchsticks
1 small CUCUMBER, peeled,
    seeded, and julienned into
    2-inch-long matchsticks
TOASTED SESAME SEEDS
WASABI
JAPANESE TAMARI SAUCE
PICKLED GINGER (page 355)

WHEN WE THINK of Japanese food we often focus on sushi rolls, vinegared rice rolled in a nori sheet, often complemented by vegetables such as cucumber, carrot, and avocado; or raw seafood. Sushi handrolls can be prepared with only minimal skill, assembled within minutes, and eaten immediately. *Temakizushi* are delicious dipped in tamari.

1. Heat the oil in a nonstick pan over high heat. Pan-fry the salmon skin side down until golden crisp, 3 to 5 minutes. Flip the salmon skin and crisp on the other side, 1 to 2 minutes. Blot the skin with a paper towel to remove excess oil. Slice the skin into 2-inch-long by ¼-inch-wide strips.

2. Place a piece of nori on a clean work surface. Leaving about ½ inch all around, spread a heaping tablespoon of rice on top of the nori. In the center scatter some scallions, and layer some carrots and cucumber. Arrange 3 pieces of crispy salmon skin, in one direction, vertically. Shape the nori with its contents into a cone. Sprinkle a few sesame seeds on top. Repeat the process with the remaining ingredients. Place the cones folded side down on individual plates with *wasabi*, tamari, and pickled ginger on the side.

JENG
STICKY RICE IN
BAMBOO LEAVES

MAKES 12

2 cups WHITE STICKY RICE

¼ cup peeled split MUNG BEANS

6 dried SHIITAKE MUSHROOMS

2 tablespoons small dried SHRIMP

2 SCALLIONS, root and dark green
ends trimmed, and 6-inch stalks
sliced into thin rounds

2 CHINESE SWEET PORK SAUSAGES
(or 1 SWEET PORK SAUSAGE
and 1 CHINESE LIVER SAUSAGE),
thinly sliced into rounds

24 BAMBOO LEAVES (fresh or
dried)

2 SALTY EGGS (page 17) or
commercial equivalent, hard-
boiled, shell removed, and each
cut into 6 slices lengthwise

CHILI AND GARLIC SAUCE
(page 106); or commercial
equivalent

CHINESE THIN SOY SAUCE

KITCHEN STRING

A BUNDLE OF STICKY RICE filled with sweet pork sausage and salty egg and meticulously wrapped in bamboo leaves, jeng originated in China. It is enjoyed as a snack or light meal, and is also found in various forms in Vietnam, Thailand, Indonesia, and Cambodia, where it appears with subtle variations in ingredients and spices. Once the ingredients are assembled, the resulting bamboo packet is boiled in water for four to five hours, after which it is ready to eat.

Wrapping the rice in narrow and long bamboo leaves takes practice and there are several ways to do it, using two to four leaves at any given time. Here I use the two-leaf technique, the easiest, which resembles Mexican tamales.

1. Mix together the sticky rice and mung beans in a bowl and soak in 4 cups water for at least 4 hours. Meanwhile, put the shiitakes in a bowl with hot water to cover, then set a plate over the bowl to prevent steam from escaping. Let stand until the mushrooms rehydrate and soften, about 30 minutes (or longer, depending on the size of the mushrooms). At the same time, soak the dried shrimp in a bowl with water to cover to get rid of excess salt, about 20 minutes.

2. Squeeze the shiitake mushrooms between the palms of your hands to get rid of the excess water. Using a paring knife, remove any hard stems from the mushrooms and julienne the caps. Drain and coarsely chop the shrimp. Mix together the mushrooms, shrimp, scallions, and sausages in a bowl. Drain the rice and mung beans and set aside in a separate bowl.

3. Bring a pot of water to a boil over high heat. Meanwhile make the rice bundles. Overlap two bamboo leaves (if using dried leaves, soak them for a few minutes first) lengthwise by about 1 inch (the rounded edge of one leaf should be about ¼ inch away from the center rib of the other leaf). Spread 3 tablespoons of rice mixture in the center (on top of overlapping leaves) and along the length of the leaves. Shape the rice to form a 1¼-by-6-inch rectangular shape. (Be sure to leave 1 inch of leaf free of rice, uncovered, on each side.) Spoon about 2 tablespoons of sausage and mushroom mixture on top of the rice, being careful to spread the mixture on top of the rice equally. Add

2 slices of egg, one next to the other following the length of the rice pile. Cover with 3 more tablespoons of rice and mung bean mixture. Carefully fold in the sides of the leaves over the rice. Take each end and fold them over the top to form a tamale. Secure the bundle with kitchen string: starting at one end of the rectangular bundle, tie a string around it, continue to make a loop and tie it every ½ inch or so. Repeat this process until you have 12 completed bundles. Reduce the heat under the boiling water to medium-low and gently boil the rice bundles for 3 hours. Serve with chili and garlic sauce or soy sauce, or both on the side.

EVERYWHERE YOU GO in Asia, you will find rice wrapped and cooked in leaves. The wonderful thing about cooking in leaves is that they give off a delicious flavor to the rice. I remember having *jeng* as a school lunch. As I unwrapped bamboo leaves and broke through the translucent rice, the fragrance of rich sweet and savory sausage, pungent scallions, and salty shrimp and eggs would emerge. It was a great lunch, not only for the flavors, but for the reactions on my Western friends' faces as I enthusiastically bit into the "weird" gummy rice.

NEM DZEM FEN STIR-FRIED SILVER PIN NOODLES

SERVES 4 TO 6

6 tablespoons VEGETABLE OIL

3 whole CHICKEN LEGS, skinned, deboned, and thinly sliced

6 SCALLIONS, root and dark green ends trimmed, and 6-inch stalks cut into 1½-inch-long pieces and julienned

1½ pounds fresh SILVER PIN NOODLES; or commercial equivalent

6 tablespoons CHINESE LIGHT SOY SAUCE, plus extra

CHINESE DARK THICK SOY SAUCE

6 large EGGS

CHILI AND GARLIC SAUCE (page 106); or commercial equivalent (optional)

N
EM DZEM FEN, or silver pin noodles, look like thick pins. Made of rice flour, tapioca starch, and water, they are thick, pointed at both ends, two to three inches long, white, and slightly chewy when cooked. I eat these when I visit my family in Paris and my uncle Ming makes a sizzling batch of stir-fried silver pin noodles with bits of chicken, scallion, egg, and a bit of soy sauce. Because the noodles tend to stick together, my uncle usually makes them in small batches so every portion is perfectly cooked. (No matter how good they are, my mother always declines the dish; they remind her of big worms.)

Do not overcrowd your wok or nonstick pan when cooking. There should be enough room so that when using the wok spatula, all the ingredients can be lifted comfortably and tossed without spilling over the top. This rule applies to all stir-fries, and especially rice noodles, which tend to stick together. Be sure to add enough oil to keep these noodles separate when cooking. Fresh silver pin noodles are available in the refrigerated food section of Chinese or Southeast Asian markets. Unlike most noodles, these need no preboiling; just add them to the stir-fry.

1. Working in 6 batches, heat a tablespoon of the oil in a wok or nonstick pan over high heat. Stir-fry the chicken and scallions until the chicken is cooked through, about 3 minutes. Transfer to a plate. Add the noodles to the wok, 1 tablespoon light soy sauce, and a dash or two of the dark soy sauce. Stir-fry to coat the noodles evenly. Transfer to a plate.

2. Break an egg in the center of the wok or pan, and scramble it lightly with your spatula, so the whites are still visible in some spots. Cook the egg through, about 2 minutes, and break it up into small to medium pieces with your spatula. Add the noodles, chicken, and scallions back into the wok, and stir-fry for a minute or so to mix all the ingredients evenly.

3. Transfer to an individual plate and repeat the process 3 to 5 more times. Eat while hot with chili paste and more light soy sauce if you like.

CHOW MI FEN
STIR-FRIED RICE VERMICELLI
SINGAPORE-STYLE

SERVES 4 TO 6

8 ounces dried RICE VERMICELLI

2 or more tablespoons VEGETABLE OIL

4 NAPA CABBAGE LEAVES, cut crosswise into ¼-inch-wide strips

18 SNOW PEAS, julienned

1 medium to large CARROT, peeled and julienned into 2-inch-long matchsticks

2 cups diced CANTONESE ROAST PORK (page 454)

1 cup BASIC CHICKEN STOCK (page 116); or BASIC PORK STOCK (page 118)

2 or more teaspoons INDIAN CURRY POWDER

1 to 2 tablespoons FISH SAUCE; or CHINESE THIN SOY SAUCE

12 sprigs CILANTRO

ONE OF THE MOST POPULAR stir-fried rice vermicelli dishes sold in Chinese restaurants is the so-called Singapore-style noodles. The reference to "Singapore-style" reflects the use of Indian curry powder in the dish; Singapore and Malaysia exhibit significant Indian influence in their cooking. The name is somewhat arbitrary, however, because the dish also includes leftover Cantonese roast pork.

Dried rice vermicelli is available at Asian or health food markets all year long. The best type for making this dish is the very fine Erawan brand imported from Thailand. When stir-frying be sure to have enough oil to keep the rice noodles from sticking.

1. Place the dried rice vermicelli in a dish with water to cover. Let stand until pliable, about 30 minutes, and drain.

2. Heat 2 teaspoons oil in a nonstick skillet over high heat. Stir-fry the napa cabbage, snow peas, carrot, and roast pork until the vegetables are tender but firm, 2 to 3 minutes. Transfer the stir-fry to a plate. Heat the remaining oil in the same skillet, add the vermicelli, 1 to 1½ cups stock, curry powder, and fish sauce or soy sauce, and stir until the vermicelli is tender but firm, the stock is completely absorbed, and the strands become dry and separate easily; add more oil if necessary. Return the stir-fry to the vermicelli and toss to distribute evenly. Divide among individual plates and garnish with cilantro.

MI KROB
SWEET AND CRISPY
RICE VERMICELLI

SERVES 4 TO 6

VEGETABLE OIL for deep-frying,
  plus 2 tablespoons

4 ounces dried RICE VERMICELLI
  (¾ of a package); or 1.4 ounces
  CELLOPHANE NOODLES

3 large GARLIC CLOVES, crushed,
  peeled, and minced

6 ounces PORK BUTT, cut into thin
  strips

6 ounces CHICKEN, skinless, cut
  into thin strips

12 small SHRIMP, heads and shells
  removed, halved lengthwise, and
  deveined

2 large EGGS, beaten

1 to 2 tablespoons FISH SAUCE

¼ cup TAMARIND EXTRACT
  (page 75); or juice of 1 lime

2 tablespoons CHINESE WHITE
  RICE VINEGAR

2 tablespoons YELLOW BEAN
  SAUCE

½ teaspoon CHILI POWDER

3 to 4 tablespoons PALM SUGAR;
  or GRANULATED SUGAR

4 SCALLIONS, root and dark green
  ends trimmed, and 6-inch stalks
  julienned into 1½-inch-long
  strips

1 cake pressed TOFU, thinly sliced

⅓ cup FRIED SHALLOTS (page 108)

½ cup CILANTRO LEAVES

2 RED THAI CHILIES, seeded and
  very thinly sliced crosswise

P ERHAPS NOT QUITE as popular as *pad Thai* (pp. 224–25), the sweet and crispy rice vermicelli (sometimes cellophane noodles) dish mi krob comes in at a close second. Stir-fried chicken, pork, and prawns are combined with noodles that have been deep-fried until slightly puffed up and crispy. Pungent chili, shallots, and garlic are tossed with the mixture. Its distinctive reddish-gold color comes from a sweet sauce that stains the white vermicelli strands, making them look somewhat candied. The sweet and spicy flavors of mi krob are lifted when accompanied by fresh mung bean sprouts and cilantro.

For a leaner version of the dish, use chicken white meat (rather than the thigh) and pork tenderloin (rather than pork butt). While you can use cayenne pepper powder in a pinch, for a more authentic flavor use store-bought Chinese dried red pepper, or make your own by drying Thai chilies and grinding them finely, as I do.

1. Pour enough oil for deep-frying in a wok or pot until it reaches 360° to 375°F over medium heat. Break the rice vermicelli or cellophane noodles a bit and deep-fry them in batches until they puff up (cellophane noodles will puff up more than the rice vermicelli) and turn a light golden color. This happens in a matter of seconds. Using a slotted spoon, transfer the fried vermicelli to a paper towel–lined plate to drain them well.

2. Heat 2 tablespoons oil in a wok or nonstick skillet over high heat. Stir-fry the garlic until golden, about 3 minutes. Add the pork, chicken, and shrimp, and stir-fry until opaque, about 3 minutes. Transfer to a plate.

Add the eggs, scrambling and breaking them up until cooked, about 2 minutes. Return the meat and shrimp to the skillet, add the fish sauce, tamarind extract, vinegar, bean sauce, chili powder, and sugar, and continue to stir-fry until the ingredients are well coated. Add the scallions, tofu, and fried shallots, and continue to stir-fry until well combined. Add the crispy rice vermicelli and stir-fry to mix thoroughly without breaking up the vermicelli too much more. Divide among individual plates and garnish with cilantro leaves and a few fresh chili slices.

BUN TOM NUONG XA LEMONGRASS SHRIMP AND RICE VERMICELLI

SERVES 4 TO 6

8 ounces dried RICE VERMICELLI

24 jumbo SHRIMP, heads and shells (except the tip of the tail) removed, butterflied, and deveined

GARLIC AND LEMONGRASS MARINADE (page 83)

¼ cup SCALLION OIL (page 108)

1 small CUCUMBER, peeled, halved lengthwise, seeded, and thinly sliced into crescents

2 medium CARROTS, peeled and finely julienned

1 head BOSTON LETTUCE, ribs removed and leaves shredded

1 bunch MINT, leaves only, julienned at the last minute

½ cup roasted unsalted PEANUTS, finely crushed (not peanut butter)

NUOC CHAM (page 100)

OFTENTIMES PEOPLE ASK me if they can reduce an Asian marinade and serve it as a sauce. It is not traditional to do so, and you'll find that most Asian foods are accompanied by specific dipping sauces. Reducing a marinade and using it as a dipping sauce would generally be redundant.

RICE VERMICELLI with grilled lemongrass shrimp—this is a classic Vietnamese recipe. The base of the dish—rice vermicelli with delicate julienned tender lettuce and crisp carrots, and cucumber sliced paper thin—is constant in all versions, though beef, pork, or chicken can be used instead of shrimp (see variation). Tossing the noodles with scallion oil helps them stay separate and gives them a nutty flavor. When ready to serve, set the grilled shrimp atop the noodle mixture and drizzle with Vietnamese *nuoc cham*, the wonderful sweet, spicy, and tangy fish sauce mixture. Garnished with freshly torn mint leaves and crushed roasted peanuts, *bun tom nuong xa* is a refreshing one-dish meal any time of the day.

If you're grilling on a barbecue, soak bamboo skewers in water for 20 minutes before skewering the shrimp or pork prior to grilling.

1. Place the dried rice vermicelli in a dish with water to cover. Let stand until pliable, about 30 minutes, and drain.

2. Meanwhile, toss the shrimp with the lemongrass and garlic marinade to coat evenly. Set aside for an hour, refrigerated.

3. Bring a pot of water to a boil over high heat. Divide the rice vermicelli into individual portions. Working with one portion at a time, place the vermicelli in a sieve and lower into the boiling water. Cook for 3 to 5 seconds only, then shock under cold running water to stop the cooking. Drain the vermicelli completely and place in a bowl. Toss with the scallion oil (including scallions) until well combined. Add half the cucumber, carrots, and lettuce and toss until evenly distributed. Divide among individual large bowls or deep plates.

4. Heat a well-oiled grill pan over high heat and grill the shrimp until they turn pink and caramelize on the outside, a minute or so on each side, depending on the size of the shrimp. Place an equal amount of shrimp on top of each serving of rice vermicelli and garnish with mint and peanuts. Have your guests drizzle *nuoc cham* over their bowls of vermicelli and shrimp. Serve any remaining cucumber, carrots, lettuce, mint, peanuts, and *nuoc cham* on the side.

Variation: Substitute pork tenderloin, beef, or chicken for shrimp. Slice them against the grain, ⅛ inch thick, then proceed with the recipe.

PAD THAI
SWEET AND SAVORY
STIR-FRIED RICE NOODLES

SERVES 4 TO 6

8 ounces dried small or medium
  RICE STICKS

2 tablespoons FISH SAUCE

3 tablespoons TAMARIND EXTRACT
  (page 75)

2 tablespoons GRANULATED SUGAR

2 tablespoons or more VEGETABLE
  OIL

1 large GARLIC CLOVE, crushed,
  peeled, and minced

⅓ cup small dried SHRIMP

1 pressed TOFU cake, thinly sliced
  crosswise

1 cup BASIC CHICKEN STOCK
  (page 116)

12 small BLUE TIGER SHRIMP,
  shells and heads removed, halved
  lengthwise, deveined, and
  blanched (optional)

3 large EGGS

3 SCALLIONS, root and dark green
  ends trimmed, and 6-inch stalks
  cut into 1-inch-long pieces, and
  julienned

2 cups MUNG BEAN SPROUTS,
  root ends trimmed

3 tablespoons roasted unsalted
  PEANUTS, crushed (not peanut
  butter)

2 LIMES, each sliced into 6 wedges

PERHAPS THE MOST FAMOUS of all Thai noodle dishes, *pad Thai*, with its numerous sweet and savory flavors, is addictive. When served in Thailand it is offered as a stir-fried noodle dish, commonly available from street hawkers. In the United States and elsewhere in the West, however, it has suffered terribly; restaurant cooks use ketchup both to sweeten and color the noodles, and other compromises have rendered the dish much less interesting than the original. This recipe is adapted from one that Thai cooking expert Sompon Nabnian shared with me when I visited his cooking school, Chiang Mai Thai Cookery School, in northern Thailand. The classic recipe for *pad Thai* uses dried shrimp. Feel free to use fresh shrimp if you prefer their meaty texture, or use them in combination with the chewy dried shrimp. Either version is delicious.

1. Place the dried rice noodles in a dish with water to cover. Let stand until pliable, about 30 minutes, and drain.

2. Whisk together the fish sauce, tamarind extract, and sugar in a bowl until the sugar is completely dissolved. Set the sauce aside.

3. Heat 1 tablespoon oil in a wok or nonstick skillet over high heat. Stir-fry the garlic, dried shrimp, and tofu until the garlic turns golden, about 3 minutes. Add the rice noodles and chicken stock, and stir until the noodles have absorbed all the liquid, about 3 minutes. Add the sauce and blanched shrimp (if using) at this time. Continue to stir-fry until the ingredients are well combined and the noodles are starting to crisp, about 1 minute. (Add more oil to noodles as necessary to keep them separated.)

4. Meanwhile, heat the remaining oil in a nonstick skillet and add the eggs. With a spatula loosely mix the yolks and whites as they are cooking, without making an omelette, about 3 minutes. (The loosely scrambled eggs should be partly white, partly yellow, and partly mixed. It is also necessary to cook the eggs all the way, rather than have them runny.) With the spatula, shred the eggs. Divide and distribute the noodles among individual plates and garnish with some shredded egg, scallions, mung bean sprouts, peanuts, and 2 lime wedges for each plate.

Variation: At Chiang Mai's Regent hotel, I was served *pad Thai* covered in an egg net. It was so beautiful and delicate that I asked the chef to show me the secret of her decorative embellishment. She was kind enough to explain the process to me and I share it with you here. Whisk 3 eggs and a tablespoon of water until the mixture is loose. Heat an oiled nonstick pan. Gather 16 bamboo chopsticks vertically with the thick ends on top, using a rubber band to hold them in place as a bundle. Dip the pointy ends in the beaten egg mixture and immediately drizzle over the hot pan, quickly moving the egg-laden stick bundle left to right and top to bottom across the surface of the cooking vessel. Dip the stick bundle in the egg mixture as many times as necessary to keep it covered lightly with the eggs. You are looking for a net that is similar to a delicate crêpe, with an open weave in which the strands are fairly close to one another, approximately ⅛ inch apart. Cook the egg through, and carefully lift the edges with the help of a spatula, then transfer the net to a plate. Continue until you have one net for each serving. Toss the stir-fried noodles with all the garnishes, except the lime wedges. Divide the noodles among the individual plates and drape each mound of noodles with a single egg net, tucking the edges under on all sides. Garnish with lime wedges.

SOMPON NABNIAN, OF THE CHIANG MAI THAI COOKERY SCHOOL, SELECTS FRESH RICE SHEETS, WHICH HE WILL SLICE INTO NOODLES FOR SOUPS AND STIR-FRIES.

K'TIAO
RICE NOODLES WITH
PORK AND SHRIMP SOUP

SERVES 4 TO 6

8 ounces small or medium dried
RICE STICKS; or 1 pound fresh
RICE NOODLES or SHEETS

10 cups SOUTHEAST ASIAN PORK
STOCK (page 119)

12 ounces PORK TENDERLOIN

16 to 24 medium SHRIMP, shelled
and deveined

2 to 3 cups MUNG BEAN SPROUTS,
root ends trimmed

1 cup CILANTRO LEAVES

3 SCALLIONS, root and dark green
ends trimmed, and 6-inch stalks
thinly sliced into rounds

½ cup PRESERVED CHINESE
CABBAGE

6 red THAI CHILIES, stemmed,
seeded, and thinly sliced

FRIED GARLIC OIL (page 108)

2 LIMES, each sliced into 6 wedges

FISH SAUCE

KOSHER SALT

C AMBODIAN K'TIAO and Vietnamese *hu tieu* are basically the same classic noodle soup. Both sweet and savory, it is eaten at any time of the year. It consists of light rice noodles with thinly sliced pork, shrimp, and mung bean sprouts, all served in a rich pork broth, and garnished with fried garlic oil, scallions, cilantro, and chilies. A drizzle of lime juice adds a refreshing finishing note. Sometimes the dish is also garnished with preserved Chinese cabbage, which you can find in Asian markets packaged in reddish-brown-glazed ceramic jars. The soup can also be served as a "dry" mixture in two separate bowls: the rice noodles, protein, and garnish placed in one; the clear broth placed in another and used for sipping throughout the meal.

Fresh rice sheets (page 262) and fresh rice noodles of all sizes can be found in Chinese or Southeast Asian markets. These do not need any soaking or boiling, as they are already cooked. Simply place fresh rice noodles in each bowl, or cut the sheets into thin strands and place an equal portion in each bowl. The heat from the steaming broth will warm them sufficiently.

1. Place the dried rice noodles in a dish with water to cover. Let stand until pliable, about 30 minutes, and drain.

2. Pour the pork stock into a pot and bring to a gentle boil over medium heat. Reduce the heat to medium-low, add the pork tenderloin, and cook through at a simmer, 20 to 30 minutes. Transfer the pork to a cutting board and continue simmering the broth, partially covered. When cool enough to handle, thinly slice the pork, place it in a bowl, and cover with plastic wrap.

3. Bring a pot filled with water to a boil over high heat. Divide the rice sticks into individual portions. Place one portion at a time in a sieve and lower it into the boiling water. Untangle the rice sticks with chopsticks and boil until tender but firm, about 7 seconds. Remove, drain, and place each portion in a large individual soup bowl.

4. Cook the shrimp in the same pot of boiling water until they turn opaque, about 1 minute. Drain, divide, and place atop each serving of noodles, along with slices of pork and mung bean sprouts. Pour a generous amount of hot stock over each serving and serve. Instruct your guests to add cilantro leaves, scallions, preserved cabbage, chili slices, and fried garlic (with some of its oil) as desired, without forgetting to squeeze a wedge of lime over their noodles. Adjust the seasoning at the table with fish sauce or salt if you wish.

Variation: Substitute 10 ounces ground pork (70 percent lean) and 1 cup small to medium dried shrimp for the pork tenderloin and raw shrimp, respectively. Follow the recipe, making an adjustment as follows in step 2: add the dried shrimp (soaked in water for 20 minutes, and drained) to the stock. After reducing the heat to medium-low, place some ground pork in a ladle and slowly lower it into the stock. Allowing some stock into the ladle, and using a pair of chopsticks, stir the ground pork until it cooks and separates, then release it into the stock. Continue this process until you have added all the ground pork to the stock, and continue to simmer until ready to serve, as described in the recipe.

You can also make the soup using chicken breast (thinly sliced) with chicken stock (page 116).

PHO
RICE NOODLE SOUP

SERVES 4 TO 6

8 ounces dried small or medium
RICE STICKS

10 cups SOUTHEAST ASIAN BEEF
STOCK (page 121)

2 to 3 cups MUNG BEAN SPROUTS,
root ends trimmed

12 ounces BEEF EYE OF ROUND,
slightly frozen, sliced paper thin

1 small YELLOW ONION, sliced
into thin wedges

12 SAW LEAVES; or 1 cup
CILANTRO LEAVES

30 THAI BASIL LEAVES

3 SCALLIONS, root and dark green
ends trimmed, and 6-inch stalks
thinly sliced crosswise

6 RED THAI CHILIES, stemmed,
seeded, and thinly sliced; or
CHILI AND GARLIC SAUCE
(page 106)

FRIED SHALLOTS (page 108)

2 LIMES, each sliced into 6 wedges

HOISIN SAUCE

FISH SAUCE

WHILE PHO, RICE NOODLE SOUP, was originally made famous in Vietnam's northern capital of Hanoi, it is now enjoyed throughout Vietnam. This soup, which used to be served exclusively as a breakfast item, is now eaten at any time of the day, and is made with beef, chicken, pork, or seafood. The two most popular versions are *pho bo*, beef, and *pho ga*, chicken (see variation). While the beef is spicy and sweet with fragrant items such as star anise, cloves, and cinnamon, the chicken version is rather light with a gingery broth. Both are absolutely delicious.

1. Place the dried rice noodles in a dish with water to cover. Let stand until pliable, about 30 minutes, and drain.

2. Meanwhile, pour the beef stock into a pot and bring to a gentle boil over medium heat. Reduce the heat to medium-low, partially cover, and simmer until ready to use.

3. Bring a pot filled with water to a boil over high heat. Drain and divide the rice noodles into individual portions (about one good handful). Place them, one portion at a time, in a sieve and lower into the boiling water. Untangle the noodles with chopsticks, and boil until tender but firm, about 7 seconds. Remove and drain the noodles, then place them in large individual soup bowls containing ⅓ to ½ cup mung bean sprouts.

4. Add the onion to the stock and cook for 5 minutes. Set a few slices of raw beef (if you prefer, cook them first, using the same strainer and boiling water as in step 3) on top of each mung bean sprout and rice noodle serving. Ladle a generous amount of hot beef stock and some onion into the bowls. Instruct your guests to garnish their soups with freshly torn saw leaves (or cilantro) and Thai basil, scallions, chilies (or some chili-garlic paste), and fried shallots as desired, without forgetting to squeeze a wedge of lime over their noodles. They should sweeten their soups with hoisin sauce and adjust the seasoning with fish sauce if desired.

Variations: To make *pho ga*, the chicken version of this soup, replace the Southeast Asian beef stock with basic chicken stock (page 116), and beef eye of round with chicken breast, thinly sliced against the grain. It is absolutely necessary to cook the chicken first. After you

have cooked the rice noodles in the boiling water in step 3, then cook the chicken in the same water until the pieces turn opaque, a minute or two. Then proceed with the recipe as directed.

Another variation is made with seafood. Substitute shrimp and squid (about 5 small shrimp and 1 medium squid per person) for the beef or chicken. Shell the shrimp, remove the heads (reserve for making stock, page 123), butterfly along the back, and remove the vein. The squid should be cleaned (tentacles reserved if you wish) and the body cut into ½-inch-thick rings. Cook the seafood in boiling water for 30 seconds to 1 minute and drain. Top the bean sprouts and noodles with an equal amount of seafood, pour the stock on top, and garnish as in the main *pho* recipe.

MOHINGA
FISH AND RICE
NOODLE SOUP

½ cup skinless split MUNG BEANS

4 ounces dried RICE VERMICELLI

2 cups MUNG BEAN SPROUTS,
root ends trimmed

¼ cup VEGETABLE OIL

2 medium YELLOW ONIONS,
peeled and minced

5 large GARLIC CLOVES, crushed,
peeled, and finely grated

1 ounce fresh GINGER, finely
grated

1 LEMONGRASS STALK, root end
trimmed, outer leaves and tough
green top removed, and 6-inch-
long inner bulb finely grated

1 or more tablespoons
INDONESIAN or THAI
SHRIMP PASTE

1 teaspoon TURMERIC POWDER

1 teaspoon PAPRIKA

¼ cup TOASTED RICE FLOUR
(pp. 24–25)

¼ cup roasted unsalted PEANUTS,
pulverized to a fine powder
(not peanut butter)

3 quarts FISH STOCK (page 123) or
BASIC CHICKEN STOCK
(page 116)

KOSHER SALT

Freshly ground BLACK PEPPER

1 large BAMBOO SHOOT, thinly
sliced lengthwise

1 pound skinless CATFISH FILLET,
cut in 1-inch pieces

4 hard-boiled EGGS, shelled and
cut into ¼-inch-thick slices
lengthwise

1 bunch CILANTRO, leaves only

4 fresh RED THAI CHILIES,
thinly sliced; or 1 tablespoon
or more crushed dried RED
CHILIES

FRIED SHALLOTS (page 108)

2 LIMES, quartered

FISH SAUCE

MOHINGA, A SPICY FISH SOUP, is the national dish of Burma (also known as the Union of Myanmar). No day should pass without this rich peanuty soup full of tasty bits of catfish, strands of delicate rice vermicelli, and hard-boiled eggs, topped with fragrant herbs such as cilantro, scallions, and chilies, and a squeeze of fresh lime juice. Stalls and small eateries abound in the streets of Burma, and they specialize in mohinga. This once-favorite breakfast item is now eaten throughout the day, much like Vietnam's pho (pp. 228–29), or China's jook (page 192). While mohinga is traditionally made with catfish, you can use cod, halibut, or similar white fish. Unfortunately, the heart of the banana tree trunk, which is part of this delicious soup, is close to impossible to find unless you live near a banana plantation and the owner is willing to get rid of one of his trees. I call for bamboo shoots in my version. As with most recipes, there are as many variations as there are cooks. Quantities may vary; some may fry the mung bean paste into crispy wafers and use these as a garnish, or stir the paste into the soup itself as part of its base; regardless of the technique, mohinga is well worth taking the time to make.

If you buy whole fish, reserve the bones and head after filleting. These, combined with 3 quarts water, can be used for making a quick forty-five-minute light fish stock. Be sure to strain the stock through a paper towel–lined sieve to hold back fine fish bones.

1. Put the mung beans in a bowl with 2 cups water and soak until the beans are softened and have almost doubled in size, about 2 hours. Drain.

2. Place the dried rice vermicelli in a dish with water to cover. Let stand until pliable, about 30 minutes, and drain. Bring a medium pot filled with water to a boil and cook the noodles for 5 seconds. Drain and divide the noodles among individual large soup bowls.

3. In the same pot, blanch the mung bean sprouts for 5 seconds. Drain and set aside. Still in the same pot, reserve 1½ cups of the boiling water, reduce the heat to medium-low, and add the split mung beans. Cook until soft, about 20 minutes. Mash the split mung beans to a paste consistency.

4. Heat the oil in a large stockpot over medium heat. Stir-fry the onions, garlic, ginger, and lemongrass until golden, 5 to 10 minutes. Add the shrimp paste and stir-fry, breaking up the paste, until darkened, about 3 minutes. Add the turmeric, paprika, roasted rice powder, and ground peanuts and, stirring constantly, continue to cook the paste, until rich golden in color, about 3 minutes. Add the mung bean paste and fish stock (or chicken stock) and bring to a boil. Adjust seasoning with salt and pepper. Add the bamboo shoots and fish chunks, lower the heat to medium-low, and simmer until the fish chunks are cooked through, about 5 minutes. Ladle the soup over each serving of noodles, making sure to add a bit of everything in the process. Garnish with mung bean sprouts, egg, cilantro, chilies, and fried shallots. Squeeze some lime juice over the soup and adjust the seasoning with fish sauce if you wish.

DAN DAN MIEN
WHEAT NOODLES WITH
PORK-AND-CABBAGE SAUCE

SERVES 4 TO 6

1 tablespoon CHINESE DARK THICK
SOY SAUCE

1 tablespoon SHAOXING WINE

1 tablespoon SESAME OIL

8 ounces GROUND PORK
(70 percent lean)

2 cups or more BASIC CHICKEN
STOCK (page 116)

3 tablespoons GRANULATED SUGAR

3 tablespoons CHINESE LIGHT SOY
SAUCE

2 tablespoons SESAME PASTE

1 tablespoon CHILI OIL

2 tablespoons CHINESE WHITE
RICE VINEGAR

1 tablespoon TAPIOCA STARCH or
CORNSTARCH

1 pound fresh WHEAT NOODLES
(or 8 ounces dried WHEAT
NOODLES)

2 tablespoons VEGETABLE OIL

3 large GARLIC CLOVES, crushed,
peeled, and minced

½ small NAPA CABBAGE, finely
chopped

5 SCALLIONS, root and dark green
ends trimmed, four 6-inch stalks
minced, one cut into 1½-inch
pieces and julienned

SOME OF THE TASTIEST noodle dishes in Asia began in food stalls or with street vendors, and this Szechwan wheat noodle and ground pork specialty, *dan dan mien*, is no exception. The earliest vendors carried their wares and serving dishes on bamboo poles set across their shoulders. When walking though the crowded streets, they made a fair amount of noise, their plates and baskets swinging, dinging, and banging against one another. The noise of that banging is remembered in the name of the dish, *dan dan*, while *mien* means noodle. Complex, with a fragrant combination of rice wine and vinegar, sesame oil, soy sauce, and fresh herbs, the sweet and salty ground-pork-and-cabbage sauce is balanced against the wheat noodles, roughly the size of thin to medium Italian linguine. The noodles are available fresh or dried in Chinese markets.

1. Place the thick soy sauce, Shaoxing wine, and sesame oil in a bowl. Add the pork, mix thoroughly until well combined, and allow to marinate for 20 minutes.

2. Whisk together the chicken stock, sugar, light soy sauce, sesame paste, chili oil, vinegar, and tapioca starch in a bowl, until the sugar is completely dissolved, and set aside.

3. Bring a pot of water to a boil over high heat. Add the noodles to the pot and untangle them with a pair of chopsticks or tongs. Bring the water to a boil once again, and cook the noodles until tender but still firm, about 5 minutes. Drain the noodles and divide among large individual bowls.

4. Meanwhile, heat the vegetable oil in a wok or nonstick skillet over high heat. Stir-fry the garlic and scallions until fragrant. Add the pork, breaking it up. Add the cabbage and stir-fry, until the water from the cabbage evaporates, about 20 minutes. Stir and add the sauce and toss. Reduce heat to medium-low and allow to thicken, about 1 minute. Remove from heat, and top each serving of noodles with the sauce. Garnish with julienned scallions.

UDON NOODLES IN MUSHROOM BROTH

SERVES 4 TO 6

12 dried medium SHIITAKE
  MUSHROOMS

6 cups KONBU DASHI (pp. 124–25)

⅓ cup JAPANESE DARK SOY SAUCE

⅓ cup MIRIN

4 SCALLIONS, root and dark green
  ends trimmed, and 2 6-inch
  stalks cut into 1½-inch-long
  pieces, 2 sliced paper-thin
  crosswise

8 ounces dried UDON NOODLES

2 ounces fresh GINGER, peeled and
  finely grated

6 ounces DAIKON, peeled and
  finely grated

6 fresh SHISO LEAVES, julienned
  just before serving

Roasted SESAME SEEDS

SHISHIRI PEPPER POWDER

UDON, THE THICK JAPANESE wheat noodles, are a specialty of southern Japan. They can be stir-fried, served in a steaming broth, or chilled and eaten with a dipping sauce. Like buckwheat noodles, they are cooked until tender but firm, but not quite as firm as Italian pasta al dente. In this recipe, I serve the udon in a rich broth made using dried shiitakes and konbu dashi (kelp stock). I also use the reserved mushroom soaking liquid, which lends a smoky note. The key here is to rinse the mushrooms very well prior to soaking in water; it is very important to remove all visible soil and other detritus. When the mushrooms have given their deep amber color to the water, filter it through a coffee filter or paper towel–lined sieve. The resulting smoky liquid becomes the basis for the fragrant mushroom-scented dashi that is the core of this soup and a perfect complement to udon noodles. It is a light yet "beefy" dish for any time of the year.

1. Put the shiitakes in a bowl with 3 cups hot water to cover, then set a plate over the bowl to prevent steam from escaping. Let stand until the mushrooms rehydrate and soften, about 30 minutes (or longer, depending on the size of the mushrooms). Squeeze the mushrooms between the palms of your hands to get rid of the excess water. Using a paring knife, remove any hard stems from the mushrooms and julienne the caps. Filter and reserve the mushroom water.

2. Bring the dashi, mushroom water, soy sauce, mirin, shiitakes, and 1½-inch-long pieces of scallion to a boil in a pot over high heat. Reduce the heat to medium-low and simmer until ready to serve.

3. Bring a pot of water to a boil over high heat. Cook the udon noodles, untangling them occasionally, until done, 3 to 5 minutes. Drain and divide among individual large soup bowls. Ladle the mushroom broth (holding back the large pieces of scallion) over each serving, taking care to include mushrooms in each bowl. Serve with sliced scallion, grated ginger, daikon, shiso, sesame seeds, and shishiri powder on the side. (I usually shape the ginger, daikon, and shiso into individual mounds on a plate and put the sesame seeds and shishiri powder in individual bowls.) Instruct your guests to add a little of each garnish as desired to their bowls of soup.

SEUNG HOI SIK LANG MIEN SHANGHAINESE COLD EGG NOODLES

SERVES 4 TO 6

2 cubes fermented BEAN CURD
with 2 to 3 tablespoons BRINE

2 SCALLIONS, root and dark green
ends trimmed, and 6-inch stalks
thinly sliced into rounds

1 cup MUNG BEAN SPROUTS, root
ends trimmed

½ cup roasted unsalted PEANUTS,
finely ground (not peanut
butter)

½ cup FERMENTED BLACK BEAN
AND GARLIC SAUCE (page 86);
or commercial equivalent

⅓ cup CHINESE LIGHT SOY SAUCE

¼ cup CHINESE WHITE RICE
VINEGAR

¼ cup SESAME OIL

¼ cup HOT CHILI OIL

1 pound fresh thin round EGG
NOODLES; or 8 ounces dried
thin EGG NOODLES

NOTHING COULD BE EASIER than making this classic Shanghainese thin egg noodle dish. All you have to do is buy and cook fresh thin round egg noodles and present them in individual bowls with an assortment of sauces, pastes, oils, and chopped scallions and peanuts. The fresh noodles are available in Chinese and Southeast Asian markets or via the Internet. If you cannot find the fresh version, use dried thin egg noodles, such as ramen.

If you have leftover condiments, do not put them back into the jars or you'll risk bacterial contamination. Instead, place plastic wrap over each bowl and save for later use. Fresh thin egg noodles feel semi-dry or semi-fresh to the touch, and are flexible. Sold in one-pound plastic bags, they are somewhat curly and have a vibrant yellow color.

1. Crush together the fermented bean curd and its brine to a paste consistency in its own small serving bowl. Place the scallions, mung bean sprouts, peanuts, black bean paste, soy sauce, vinegar, sesame oil, and hot chili oil in individual serving bowls with a spoon in each. Arrange the condiments in the center of the table.

2. Bring a pot of water to a boil over high heat. Add the noodles and cook until tender but firm, 2 to 3 minutes. Transfer to a strainer and rinse under cold running water. Place a portion of noodles in each individual bowl and instruct your guests to season their servings with some of the condiments offered, then toss well to distribute the flavors evenly. The sesame and hot chili oils will prevent the noodles from sticking together.

LIANG MIEN HWANG DOUBLE-FRIED EGG NOODLES WITH SEAFOOD

SERVES 4 TO 6

12 ounces fresh thin round EGG
NOODLES

2 tablespoons VEGETABLE OIL

2 large GARLIC CLOVES, crushed,
peeled, and minced

1 ounce fresh GINGER, peeled and
julienned

2 SCALLIONS, root and dark green
ends trimmed, and 6-inch stalks
cut into 1-inch-long pieces and
julienned

12 fresh medium SCALLOPS

12 fresh medium BLUE TIGER
SHRIMP, heads and shells
removed, butterflied, and
deveined

12 BABY SQUID, cleaned, halved
lengthwise

1 cup SNOW PEAS

1 medium CARROT, peeled and
thinly sliced diagonally

1 tablespoon CHINESE LIGHT SOY
SAUCE; or FISH SAUCE

KOSHER SALT

Freshly ground BLACK PEPPER

¾ cup BASIC CHICKEN STOCK
(page 116)

2 teaspoons TAPIOCA STARCH or
CORNSTARCH

4 to 6 sprigs CILANTRO

L IANG MIEN HWANG (meaning "two sides brown") was originally developed in China; Chinese thin egg noodles are shaped into a thick round pancake. One side is pan-fried until golden brown, then flipped, and the noodles are pan-fried until the other side is equally golden brown. Crispy on the outside and soft on the inside, the noodles can be topped with any number of stir-fried vegetables, meat, or seafood. The Vietnamese have adopted this noodle dish and serve it with a seafood stir-fry. They call it *mi xao don do bien*, which means (very straightforwardly) "fried noodles with seafood."

These curly yellow thin egg noodles are packaged in plastic bags and sold by the pound in the refrigerated section of Chinese or Southeast Asian markets, or by Chinatown street vendors specializing in fresh noodles. They expand a bit when cooked, so eight ounces is good for four servings.

1. Bring a pot of salted water to a boil over high heat and cook the noodles, untangling them with chopsticks, until tender but firm, 2 to 3 minutes. Drain and arrange in a single round layer on a plate. Allow to dry out, about 30 minutes.

2. Heat 2 teaspoons of the oil in a nonstick skillet over medium heat. Slide the noodles from the plate to the skillet, retaining the pancake-like shape of the noodles. Allow the noodles to become golden crisp, 3 to 5 minutes. Slide the noodles back onto the plate. Add another 2 teaspoons oil to the skillet, carefully flip the noodles, and crisp the other side until deep golden, 3 to 5 minutes more. Slide onto a plate.

3. Heat the remaining oil in a wok over high heat. Stir-fry the garlic, ginger, and scallions until fragrant and slightly golden, about 3 minutes. Add the scallops, shrimp, and squid, and stir-fry until opaque, about 5 minutes. Add the snow peas and carrots, season with soy sauce (or fish sauce), and adjust the seasoning to taste with salt and pepper. Stir-fry to distribute the ingredients evenly. Whisk together the stock and tapioca starch until fluid and free of lumps, and add to the wok. Cook until thickened, about 1 minute. Ladle over the crispy noodles, garnish with cilantro sprigs, and serve.

PRESERVED DUCK AND
EGG NOODLE SOUP

SERVES 4 TO 6

3 CANTONESE DRIED DUCK LEGS

2 ounces fresh GINGER, thinly
sliced lengthwise and lightly
crushed

3 SCALLIONS, root and dark green
ends trimmed, and 6-inch stalks
halved and lightly crushed

Freshly ground BLACK PEPPER

Pinch of SUGAR

8 ounces CHOY SUM, stems
trimmed, flower buds removed
if any; or BABY BOK CHOY or
SPINACH, stems trimmed and
leaves separated

1 pound fresh thin flat EGG
NOODLES

FRIED GARLIC OIL (page 108)

CHILI AND GARLIC SAUCE
(page 106; optional); or
commercial equivalent

ONE OF MY FAVORITE THINGS to do is to go to a Chinese butcher in
New York City's Chinatown, where specialty dried meats—duck legs,
as well as whole ducks, duck wings, whole quail, sweet pork sausages,
duck liver sausages, and pork belly—are hung on the wall behind the counter.
Marinated principally in salt and sugar, and air-dried for months, dried duck
legs add wonderful flavor to braised dishes, stir-fries, and soups such as this
one. If you have no access to dried specialty meats, use Smithfield Virginia
ham to replace the duck leg. The fresh thin flat egg noodles used in this dish
are beautifully packaged in four neat bundles and sold in one-pound clear
plastic bags. Oftentimes they are labeled as wonton noodles, for they are
sometimes added to wonton soup.

Dried meats keep well in the freezer for up to three months. To avoid freezer
burn, wrap each item in several layers of plastic wrap, then place it in a plastic bag.

1. Place the duck legs, ginger, and scallions in a stockpot, cover with 3 quarts water, and bring to a boil over high heat. Reduce the heat to medium-low, season with pepper and sugar, and simmer until the stock is reduced by half, about 1½ hours. With a slotted spoon, remove the duck legs. When cool enough to handle, shred the meat with your fingers or a fork, or slice very thin with a knife. Put the bones back into the stockpot. Place the meat in a bowl and cover with plastic wrap.

2. Bring 2 pots of water to a boil over high heat. Add some salt to one and blanch the *choy sum* until tender but firm, about 2 minutes. Drain and transfer to a plate. Use the second pot to cook the noodles.

3. Divide the noodles into individual portions. Cooking one portion at a time, place the noodles in a sieve. Lower the sieve into the boiling water, and loosen the noodles with a pair of chopsticks so the strands cook evenly, until tender but firm, about 3 minutes. Place a portion of noodles in each individual large soup bowl. Put duck meat on top of each noodle mound and surround with an equal amount of *choy sum*. Ladle a generous amount of broth on top of each serving and garnish with a teaspoon of fried garlic (with its oil if you wish) prior to serving. For a spicy version of the noodle soup, stir a teaspoon of chili and garlic paste into your bowl.

LO MIEN
STIR-FRIED EGG NOODLES
WITH BEEF AND BROCCOLI

SERVES 4 TO 6

3 tablespoons CHINESE LIGHT SOY SAUCE

3 tablespoons OYSTER SAUCE

2 tablespoons SHAOXING WINE

2 teaspoons GRANULATED SUGAR

2 teaspoons TAPIOCA STARCH or CORNSTARCH

2 teaspoons SESAME OIL

12 ounces BEEF SIRLOIN, thinly sliced against the grain

1 pound fresh thick round EGG NOODLES

2 tablespoons VEGETABLE OIL

2 large GARLIC CLOVES, crushed and peeled

1 bunch CHINESE BROCCOLI, leaves separated, stems trimmed, then sliced on the diagonal

1¼ cups BASIC CHICKEN STOCK (page 116)

KOSHER SALT

Freshly ground BLACK PEPPER

L O MIEN IS ONE of the most popular Chinese take-out foods in the West. Thick round egg noodles, often stir-fried with beef and broccoli and darkened with Chinese dark soy sauce, is what you usually get when ordering this dish in Chinese-American restaurants. This is a poor rendition of the classic dish and a misuse of the soy sauce. The noodles should never be dark when cooked but should retain their natural color.

While beef and Chinese broccoli are often combined for making lo mien, you can certainly use your favorite ingredients instead. For a vegetarian version, try julienned carrots, cabbage, and scallions, for example. Chicken, pork, or shrimp with spinach or bok choy make a delicious lo mien as well. Fresh thick round egg noodles are found in the refrigerated section of Chinese or Southeast Asian markets or from Chinatown street vendors. These are the same noodles used in making Thailand's curried noodle soup, khao soi (pp. 240–41).

1. Whisk together the soy sauce, oyster sauce, wine, and sugar in a bowl until the sugar is dissolved completely. Stir in the tapioca starch until well combined. Add the sesame oil and beef, mixing well to coat evenly. Allow to marinate for 20 minutes.

2. Meanwhile, bring a pot of salted water to a boil over high heat and blanch the noodles, untangling them with chopsticks, for a few seconds. Drain.

3. Heat 1 tablespoon oil in a wok or nonstick pan over high heat. Stir-fry the garlic until golden, about 3 minutes. Add the Chinese broccoli and stir-fry until tender but firm, about 5 minutes. Transfer to a plate. Add the remaining oil to the wok and stir-fry the beef until cooked through, about 3 minutes. Transfer to a plate. Bring the stock and any remaining marinade to a boil in the wok. Adjust the seasoning with salt and pepper as desired and add the noodles. Cook until the noodles absorb the stock and are cooked through, 3 to 4 minutes. Add the beef and broccoli, and toss to distribute the ingredients evenly. Divide among individual plates and serve.

PANCIT PALABOK
BIRTHDAY NOODLES
WITH SAUCE

SERVES 4 TO 6

2 tablespoons VEGETABLE OIL

2 large GARLIC CLOVES, crushed, peeled, and minced

1 small YELLOW ONION, peeled and minced

12 ounces PORK BUTT, cut into 2-inch-long thin strips

18 small BLUE TIGER SHRIMP, shells and heads removed, halved lengthwise, and deveined

4 medium CARROTS, peeled, halved crosswise, and julienned

Leaves of half a small GREEN CABBAGE, julienned (2 to 2½ cups)

1 cup or more BASIC PORK STOCK (page 118)

¼ cup CHINESE LIGHT SOY SAUCE

1 tablespoon BROWN SUGAR

1 pound fresh thick Chinese round EGG NOODLES

3 hard-boiled EGGS, yolks crumbled, whites finely diced

2 LIMES, each sliced into 6 wedges

PANCIT IS ARGUABLY the national dish of the Philippines. Many variations exist, usually based on regional ingredients or the cook's personal preferences. As in China, noodles create an association with the idea of good luck and longevity; *pancit* is served at special occasions and, most important, at birthday celebrations. I have had the dish prepared in several different ways, each using a different type of Chinese noodles, including thick round egg noodles, thin egg noodles, or rice vermicelli (called *pancit bihon*; see variation). One of the most traditional renditions of this dish is called *pancit palabok*, which is served with a crumbled or sliced egg garnish. While the Filipinos tend to cook their noodles until soft, I prefer mine tender but firm, in the Chinese manner.

Heat 1 tablespoon oil in a large nonstick pan over medium heat. Stir-fry the garlic and onion until fragrant and lightly golden, about 5 minutes. Add the pork and shrimp and stir-fry until they are cooked through, 2 to 3 minutes. Transfer the stir-fry to a plate. Add the remaining oil to the same pan and stir-fry the carrots and cabbage until cooked through but still firm, 3 to 5 minutes. Transfer to the plate. Add the stock, soy sauce, and brown sugar to the same pan and stir until the sugar has dissolved completely. Add the noodles, untangle them with chopsticks, and cook through, 3 to 4 minutes. Add the vegetable, pork, and shrimp stir-fries back in the pan and toss with the noodles until well combined. Transfer the noodles to a serving platter and scatter the eggs across the top. Place the lime wedges around the noodles and serve.

Variation: For *pancit bihon*, substitute rice vermicelli for the egg noodles. Place 8 ounces rice vermicelli in a dish with water to cover. Let stand until pliable, about 30 minutes, and drain. Proceed with the recipe, using 1 cup stock or more until the noodles are tender but firm and soak up all the stock.

BAKMIE GORENG
STIR-FRIED EGG NOODLES

SERVES 4 TO 6

1 pound fresh thick round EGG
   NOODLES
2 tablespoons VEGETABLE OIL
2 large GARLIC CLOVES, crushed,
   peeled, and minced
2 medium-large SHALLOTS, peeled
   and minced
3 SCALLIONS, root and dark green
   ends trimmed, and 6-inch stalks
   finely chopped
3 fresh RED THAI CHILIES,
   stemmed, seeded, and minced
1 tablespoon INDONESIAN or THAI
   SHRIMP PASTE
2 teaspoons TOMATO PASTE
1 tablespoon INDONESIAN SWEET
   SOY SAUCE
KOSHER SALT
Freshly ground BLACK PEPPER
6 large EGGS
Half a CUCUMBER, peeled, halved
   lengthwise, seeded, and thinly
   sliced in crescents
1 large vine-ripe TOMATO, stem
   removed and sliced into thin
   wedges
FRIED SHALLOTS (page 108)

WHILE STIR-FRIED NOODLES, like stir-fried rice, originated in China, many Asian countries have adopted the concept, including Indonesia, where some of the most delicious versions are made. Depending upon what is available at market on any given day, or the mood of the cook, each restaurant will prepare the dish somewhat differently. This is the *bakmie goreng* I had for breakfast in a small bed-and-breakfast in Ubud, Bali. The dish is basically savory but the sweet soy sauce and tomato paste give this noodle dish its unique sweet character. Often, fried herbal-infused chicken, called *ayam goreng* (page 490), or grilled meat satay (page 421) is served along with a sunny-side-up egg on top of the noodles.

1. Bring a pot of water to a boil and cook the fresh egg noodles, untangling them with chopsticks, until tender but firm, about 2 minutes. (If using dried egg noodles, cook for 3 minutes or as directed on the package.) Drain and rinse under cold running water to stop the cooking.

2. Heat 1½ tablespoons oil in a wok or large nonstick skillet over medium-high heat. Stir-fry the garlic, shallots, scallions, and chilies until fragrant and the garlic becomes golden, the shallots translucent, and the chilies darken a bit, 5 to 10 minutes. Add the shrimp paste and continue to stir-fry until the paste darkens and all the ingredients are well combined. Add the noodles and stir-fry until all the ingredients are combined evenly and heated through, about 2 minutes. Mix together the tomato paste and sweet soy sauce in a small bowl until well combined, then add to the noodles and continue to stir-fry until the noodles are evenly coated. Adjust the seasoning with salt and pepper if necessary. Divide the noodles among individual plates.

3. Heat the remaining oil in a non-stick skillet over high heat and cook the eggs sunny-side up until the whites are opaque, but yolks still soft, 1 to 2 minutes. (You can cook the eggs over easy, or poach them if you like.) Place an egg on top of each serving of noodles and garnish with cucumber, tomato slices, and fried shallots.

Variation: Substitute 4 cups cooked day-old medium-grain rice for the noodles. Proceed with the recipe.

KHAO SOI
CHIANG MAI EGG NOODLE
CURRY SOUP

SERVES 4 TO 6

VEGETABLE OIL for deep-frying,
   plus 1 tablespoon
1 to 1½ pounds fresh thick round
   EGG NOODLES
3 medium GARLIC CLOVES,
   crushed and peeled
2 large SHALLOTS, peeled,
   1 minced, 1 sliced paper thin
1½ tablespoons or more RED
   CURRY PASTE (page 82); or
   store-bought
1½ tablespoons THAI or
   INDONESIAN SHRIMP PASTE
2 tablespoons HAENG LEI POWDER;
   or INDIAN MADRAS CURRY
   POWDER
2 or more tablespoons PALM
   SUGAR
5 cups unsweetened COCONUT
   MILK (page 77); or commercial
   equivalent
5 cups BASIC CHICKEN STOCK
   (page 116)
4 large KAFFIR LIME LEAVES; or
   zest of 2 LIMES
3 LEMONGRASS STALKS, root
   ends trimmed, outer leaves
   and tough green tops removed,
   and 6-inch-long inner bulbs
   crushed
6 or more whole fresh RED THAI
   CHILIES
Juice of 1½ to 2 small LIMES
   (about ⅓ cup)

K HAO SOI IS A CLASSIC NOODLE curry soup from Chiang Mai in
northern Thailand, which is located in the foothills of the beautiful
Mae Rim mountains. Soup stalls abound in the city, each vendor offering his own version of this mildly spicy, reddish-yellow curry soup. The
dish represents classic Thai food at its complex, refined, and subtle best. At
the base of each soup are garlic and shallots stir-fried until golden, giving off
a delicious sweet and nutty character. Shrimp paste, called *kepi*, is then added
to the stir-fried mixture, which is further cooked, yielding an assertively
salty note. Palm sugar is added to tame the flavors a bit prior to the addition
of the *haeng lei* powder (similar to Indian curry powder) and Thai red curry
paste. Rich coconut milk and light chicken broth bring all the flavors together. Fresh lemongrass and kaffir lime leaves are bruised to release their
essence and are added to the pot. Served over soft yet firm egg noodles with
bits of chicken, the soup's sweet, salty, spicy, and bitter notes are complemented with a squeeze or two of sour lime juice. The delicate, sliced Chinese
mustard cabbage provides a wonderful crunch against the tender egg noodles. Topped with crispy egg noodles, Thai basil leaves, and some sliced red
chilies, this soup exemplifies the Chinese principle of *yin yang*, the art of balanced opposites.

Kaffir lime leaves are naturally attached in pairs and resemble a figure 8.
There is no real substitute, although I suggest lime zest, which will give you
a slight bitter note without the complex sweetish essence of the kaffir lime
leaves, and it will do in a pinch.

---

1 pound CHICKEN THIGHS or
   BREASTS, skinned, deboned, and
   thinly sliced against the grain
1 cup CHINESE PRESERVED
   MUSTARD CABBAGE, thinly sliced
   crosswise
12 sprigs THAI BASIL
12 sprigs CILANTRO
2 LIMES, each sliced into 6 wedges

1. Bring a pot of vegetable oil to a
deep-frying temperature of 360° to
375°F over medium-high heat. Take
a quarter of the egg noodles and divide them into individual portions.
Working with one batch at a time,
deep-fry them until they puff up
and become crisp and lightly
golden, about 2 minutes. Drain on
paper towels and set aside.

2. Heat the 1 tablespoon oil in a heavy-bottomed pot over medium-high heat. Stir-fry the garlic and shallots, until the garlic becomes a rich golden color and the shallots caramelize a bit, 5 to 7 minutes. Add the curry paste, shrimp paste, curry powder, and palm sugar and stir-fry until fragrant and slightly darker in color, about 5 minutes. Add the coconut milk, chicken stock, kaffir lime leaves (crushing, not tearing, the leaves in the palms of your hands to release the essential oils), lemongrass, chilies, and lime juice. Bring the broth to a boil, then reduce the heat to medium-low. About 5 minutes before serving, raise the temperature to medium-high once again and add the chicken, cooking it thoroughly, about 3 minutes.

3. Meanwhile, bring a pot of water to a boil and cook the remaining fresh egg noodles, separating them with a chopstick (or a fork) to allow them to cook evenly until tender but firm, about 3 minutes. Drain, rinse under cold running water, and drain once again thoroughly. Divide the boiled noodles equally among individual large soup bowls.

4. Ladle some curry coconut broth with some chicken morsels (holding back the lemongrass and kaffir lime leaves) over each serving of egg noodles with a red chili for color (these can be eaten, small bites at a time, if you wish). Top each serving with a single portion of fried egg noodles and serve with the thinly sliced shallots, the preserved mustard cabbage, basil, cilantro, and lime wedges on the side. Instruct your guests to add a little of everything to their soup, squeezing the lime juice and drizzling it over their dish just before eating.

ASIAN NOODLE SOUPS are versatile, with the noodles more often than not being interchangeable, depending on personal preference. I like fresh rice noodles or sheets for their slightly chewy texture and lightness, for example. I often buy the sheets in Chinatown, where they are sold in one-pound bags for a dollar, then slice them into noodles. The sheets, which are large, are traditionally folded to a manageable size. Without unfolding them, I slice them crosswise into thin strips. Once they're sliced, I place them in soup bowls and ladle the steamy fragrant curry broth and chicken over them. The noodles heat through and untangle into beautiful strands. I serve them with the same garnish as in traditional *khao soi,* substituting deep-fried cellophane noodles (mung bean threads, or mung bean vermicelli) for the fried egg noodle garnish.

KIMCHI AND RAMEN
NOODLE SOUP

SERVES 4 TO 6

12 dried medium SHIITAKE
MUSHROOMS

8 cups BASIC CHICKEN, PORK,
or BEEF STOCK (pp. 116, 118,
120, respectively); or WATER

⅓ cup KOREAN or JAPANESE DARK
SOY SAUCE

2 or more cups CABBAGE KIMCHI
(page 359; or commercial
equivalent), leaves cut into
1½-inch pieces

8 ounces RAMEN NOODLES

12 ounces skinless CHICKEN
BREAST, PORK TENDERLOIN, or
BEEF SIRLOIN, thinly sliced
against the grain

18 medium BLUE TIGER SHRIMP,
heads and shells removed,
butterflied, and deveined

4 SCALLIONS, root and dark green
ends trimmed, and 6-inch stalks
sliced into thin rounds

A DELICIOUS, SPICY, SIMPLE, and healthy meal, this kimchi noodle
soup is one I look forward to any time of the year. To start, cabbage
kimchi and shiitake mushrooms, which are constants in every version
of the recipe, simmer in water or any number of different stocks. (The kimchi
will give up its spicy flavor into the water, rendering it a perfectly acceptable
stock.) Chicken, pork, beef, or shrimp is added, further infusing the soup
base. Ladled over ramen or udon noodles, the soup is then garnished with
sliced scallions just before serving. I call for a generous amount of kimchi, but
if you are sensitive to spicy foods, cut the amount in half and add two to four
fresh napa cabbage leaves instead. Remember that cutting down the amount
of kimchi means that your broth will not be as intense. To make up for this, I
suggest using basic chicken, pork, or beef broth rather than water as the base
for your soup.

1. Put the shiitakes in a bowl with
hot water to cover, then set a plate
over the bowl to prevent steam from
escaping. Let stand until the mushrooms rehydrate and soften, about
30 minutes (or longer, depending
on the size of the mushrooms).
Squeeze the mushrooms between
the palms of your hands to get rid of
the excess water. Using a paring
knife, remove any hard stems from
the mushrooms and julienne the
caps. Reserve the soaking liquid.

2. Bring the stock or water to a boil
in a medium pot over high heat. Reduce the heat to low and add the soy
sauce, kimchi, and shiitakes. Simmer
until the mushrooms are tender and
the broth has taken on a strong kimchi flavor, about 15 minutes.

3. Bring a pot of water to a boil over
high heat. Cook the ramen noodles,
untangling them occasionally with
chopsticks, until done, about 3
minutes. Drain and divide among
individual large soup bowls. In the
same pot (and if using), add the
chicken, pork, or beef, and cook
until opaque and cooked through,
about 2 minutes. Use a slotted
spoon to transfer and divide the
meat equally among individual
bowls. Add the shrimp to the same
pot of boiling water and cook until
opaque but still vibrant pink, 1 to 2
minutes. Drain and divide equally
among each serving. Ladle the
broth, taking care to include kimchi
and mushrooms, over each serving.
Garnish wih scallions and serve.

CLEANING UP AFTER TRIMMING SCALLIONS FOR MAKING LARGE BATCHES OF KIMCHI

ZARU SOBA
COLD SOBA WITH
DIPPING SAUCE

SERVES 4 TO 6

1½ quarts SPRING WATER

2 cups DASHI (pp. 124–25)

¾ cup JAPANESE DARK SOY SAUCE

¾ cup MIRIN

1½ tablespoons GRANULATED
SUGAR

3 ounces DAIKON, peeled and
finely grated

3 SCALLIONS, root and dark green
ends trimmed, and 6-inch stalks
sliced paper thin into rounds

2 tablespoons finely grated fresh
WASABI ROOT or WASABI PASTE

8 ounces dried SOBA NOODLES

1 large sheet NORI, quartered and
julienned

ARU SOBA is the most traditional way to prepare freshly made Japanese *soba* noodles. In the most classic rendition of the dish, exquisite homemade buckwheat noodles are cooked in water, then chilled. They are served on a bamboo mat set over a wooden lacquered box to collect any excess water that may drip from the noodles. Japanese dark soy sauce, mirin, and *dashi* are mixed to create a rich dipping sauce, called *tsuke-jiru*, especially made for this noodle dish; the sauce is chilled and served in a separate cup on the side. Small amounts of spicy *wasabi*, pungent scallion, and refreshing grated daikon are added to the sauce to round out and lift its flavors. A few strands at a time of the nutty *soba* are dipped into the sauce before eating. After the noodles are eaten, the cloudy noodle cooking water is heated and added to the remaining dipping sauce. This is stirred, then drunk as a delicious finishing palate cleanser.

In this recipe I recommend either dried *soba* noodles or the fresh-frozen type occasionally available in Japanese markets. Making *soba* by hand, while rewarding, is difficult to the point of being considered an art form.

1. Pour the spring water in a bowl and refrigerate overnight or at least 12 hours prior to serving this dish.

2. Bring the *dashi*, soy sauce, mirin, and sugar to a gentle boil over medium heat and simmer just long enough for the sugar to dissolve. Remove from the heat, allow to cool, and refrigerate for 2 hours. It should be served slightly chilled. (You can make this a day or more ahead of time, but be sure to take the sauce out of the refrigerator for an hour prior to serving to allow it to come to the proper temperature; it should not be ice cold, just chilled.)

3. Arrange in equal amounts individual mounds of daikon, scallions, and *wasabi* on small individual plates. Loosely cover (so as not to ruin the shaped mounds) each plate with plastic wrap.

4. Bring a pot of water to a boil over high heat and add the *soba* noodles. Bring the water back to a boil. Cook the noodles until tender but firm (but not as al dente as Italian pasta), about 3 minutes. Reserve the cooking water, but transfer the noodles to a strainer and rinse immediately under cold running water until no more steam comes off the noodles. (When boiling noodles, the Japanese shock the noodles by adding a cup of cold water two or three times during the cooking process. This keeps the noodles from overcooking and becoming gummy. But as wonderful as this technique is, I prefer simply to cook the noodles first, and shock them at the very end. Please feel free to experiment.)

5. Remove the spring water from the refrigerator. Place the noodles in a strainer and dip the strainer several times into the water to chill them instantly. Drain the noodles completely. Divide them into equal portions on individual plates and sprinkle some nori over each serving. Serve with the fresh garnishes and dipping sauce on the side. To eat, stir some grated daikon, *wasabi*, and scallion into the dipping sauce. Take some noodles with your chopsticks and dip them. Enjoy every slippery bite. Once you've finished the noodles, pour some of the hot noodle cooking water into the remaining dipping sauce and sip just as you would broth. (You may need to bring the noodle cooking water to a boil while you're eating the noodles, so that it is hot when you pour it into the dipping sauce cups.)

TORI CHA SOBA
TEA SOBA AND
CHICKEN SOUP

SERVES 4 TO 6

½ cup JAPANESE DARK SOY SAUCE

½ cup MIRIN

2 tablespoons JAPANESE SEASONED RICE VINEGAR

1 teaspoon SESAME OIL

1½ tablespoons GRANULATED SUGAR

6 CHICKEN THIGHS, skinned and deboned

8 cups DASHI (pp. 124–25)

8 fresh medium SHIITAKE MUSHROOMS, stems removed, caps peeled and julienned

8 ounces dried CHA SOBA NOODLES

8 ounces BABY BOK CHOY or SPINACH, leaves separated

2 ounces GINGER, peeled and julienned

3 SCALLIONS, root and dark green ends trimmed, and 6-inch stalks thinly sliced on the diagonal

Toasted SESAME SEEDS

T HIS DISH uses thin noodles about the size of Italian cappellini, complemented by sweet soy sauce–marinated chicken, baby bok choy, and fresh shiitake mushrooms. Ginger and scallion provide a refreshing spicy finish. *Cha soba* is a noodle made from a combination of buckwheat flour and green tea powder, or *matcha*. (*Matcha* is also used to make the tea in the Japanese tea ceremony, and for making green tea ice cream; page 546). These rich green noodles have a subtle bitter note, and while the flavor of the tea is very apparent, it is never overwhelming. The subtle sweet and savory *dashi* stock keeps the noodles warm and is a wonderful complement to their bitter flavor.

1. Whisk together 2 tablespoons soy sauce, 2 tablespoons mirin, vinegar, sesame oil, and 1 teaspoon sugar in a bowl until the sugar is dissolved completely. Marinate the chicken thighs, turning the pieces every hour while refrigerated, about 4 hours total.

2. Slowly bring the *dashi* to a boil over medium heat. Reduce the heat to low and stir in the remaining soy sauce, mirin, and sugar. Add the shiitakes and continue to simmer until ready to serve.

3. Bring 2 pots of water to a boil over high heat. Add the noodles to one, untangling them with chopsticks, until cooked, 5 to 7 minutes. Drain and divide among individual large soup bowls. Blanch the bok choy or spinach in the other pot until wilted and cooked through,

about 30 seconds for the bok choy, or 5 seconds for the baby spinach. Drain the greens, divide into individual portions, and place in a circle around the noodles in each bowl.

4. Meanwhile, heat a well-oiled grill pan over medium-high heat. Remove the chicken from the marinade; do not blot the pieces dry, just shake them a little to get rid of the excess marinade. Place the chicken on the grill pan and grill, turning once, until the outside is golden and lightly crisped and the inside is cooked through, about 8 minutes. Remove the chicken from the grill pan.

5. Divide the broth among the individual soup bowls, pouring the broth over each portion of noodles. This will loosen the noodles and heat them up. On a chopping board, slice each chicken thigh into

¼-inch-wide slices and place them on top of each portion of noodles. Garnish with fresh ginger and scallions, sprinkle with sesame seeds, and serve hot.

O' CHAME, A JAPANESE RESTAURANT in Berkeley, California, serves many delicate noodle soups. It is one of the few Japanese restaurants that I have eaten at in the United States that specializes in items other than sushi and sashimi. The noodle menu is extensive, and many people visiting the San Francisco Bay area make a special effort to dine in the restaurant's beautifully appointed Japonesque rooms. The recipe presented here is inspired by many of the wonderful meals I have enjoyed at O' Chame.

SOBA NOODLES WITH THREE MUSHROOMS

SERVES 4 TO 6

8 ounces dried SOBA NOODLES

1 tablespoon VEGETABLE OIL

8 ounces fresh medium SHIITAKE MUSHROOMS, stems removed and caps julienned

8 ounces fresh NAMEKO MUSHROOMS, stems removed and caps julienned

8 ounces fresh ENOKITAKE MUSHROOMS, root ends removed, mushrooms with stems left intact

⅓ cup JAPANESE DARK SOY SAUCE

3 tablespoons MIRIN

3 tablespoons SAKE

1½ tablespoons GRANULATED SUGAR

1 teaspoon SESAME OIL

2 SCALLIONS, root and dark green ends trimmed, and 6-inch stalks cut crosswise into 1½-inch-long pieces and julienned

2 ounces fresh GINGER, peeled and julienned

2 teaspoons toasted SESAME SEEDS

THIS EARTHY DISH combines hearty buckwheat noodles with three different mushroom types. While fresh shiitake mushrooms are readily available, nameko and enokitake mushrooms can usually be found only in Japanese or Korean markets (see mail-order sources, page 563). If you cannot find these special mushrooms, however, you may substitute other delicate mushrooms such as seasonally available oyster mushrooms, or chanterelles. In a pinch, however, you can use shiitakes only, as these are available all year round. For a fuller meal, serve this noodle dish with *yakitori* (page 493), or grilled chicken skewers, which should be placed on top of the noodles before you add the garnishes.

It is important that you prep everything before you start cooking, because you will need to prepare the sauce, mushrooms, and noodles simultaneously. Organizing the ingredients is key to making this dish successfully.

1. Bring a pot of water to a boil over high heat. Add the noodles and cook until tender but firm, untangling them with chopsticks, about 3 minutes. Drain and place in a mixing bowl.

2. Meanwhile, heat the oil in a wok over medium-high heat. (I do not like to use a very hot wok, as the natural water from the mushrooms gives them a certain gloss and keeps them from drying out.) When the wok starts to smoke, stir-fry the shiitakes and nameko mushrooms until just wilted (not shrunken), 1 to 2 minutes. Toss in the enokitake mushrooms and transfer the mushroom medley to the noodles.

3. Whisk together the soy sauce, mirin, sake, sugar, and sesame oil over medium heat until the sugar is completely dissolved and the sauce comes to a boil. Pour the sauce over the noodles and mushrooms and toss to distribute the ingredients evenly. Divide among individual plates. Garnish each serving with scallions, ginger, and sesame seeds, and serve hot.

FUN SI LO HAN JAI
BRAISED CELLOPHANE NOODLES
WITH SHRIMP AND MUSHROOMS

SERVES 4 TO 6

Three .7-ounce packages
  CELLOPHANE NOODLES
½ cup dried SHRIMP
8 dried medium SHIITAKE
  MUSHROOMS
1½ tablespoons VEGETABLE OIL
2 large GARLIC CLOVES, crushed
  and peeled
1 ounce fresh GINGER, peeled and
  sliced paper thin
4 SCALLIONS, root and dark green
  ends trimmed, and 6-inch stalks
  cut into 1-inch-long pieces
8 large NAPA CABBAGE LEAVES,
  halved lengthwise and sliced
  crosswise into 1-inch strips
2 cups BASIC CHICKEN STOCK
  (page 116)
2 tablespoons CHINESE LIGHT SOY
  SAUCE
2 tablespoons OYSTER SAUCE
2 tablespoons SHAOXING WINE
2 teaspoons SESAME OIL

FUN SI, cellophane noodles made of mung bean starch, originated in China. They are also called crystal noodles because they become transparent when cooked. The noodles, when cooked, are springy and slippery. Naturally bland, they absorb a great deal of flavor. For this reason, they have been traditionally used in braised dishes such as this one, incorporated into dumpling stuffing, and added to soups such as Indonesia's classic *soto ayam* (pp. 136–37). These same Chinese cellophane noodles were the inspiration behind Korea's *tang myon*, potato starch noodles, which are used in making *chap chae* (page 250). Although grayish in color, the potato starch noodle becomes transparent when cooked, just like the Chinese cellophane noodle, but with a light grayish hue.

Fun si lo han jai—braised cellophane noodles with dried shrimp, dried shiitakes, and napa cabbage—is a family favorite, and I never get tired of making it.

1. Place the cellophane noodles, shrimp, and shiitakes in 3 separate bowls with water to cover, until soft, about 30 minutes. Drain all three. Place the shiitakes between the palms of your hands and squeeze to get rid of the excess water. With a paring knife remove and discard the stems and julienne the caps.

2. Heat the oil in a sand pot or heavy-bottomed pot over medium heat. Stir-fry the garlic, ginger, and scallions until fragrant and lightly golden, about 5 minutes. Add the shrimp, shiitakes, and cabbage and stir-fry until just cooked, about 5 minutes. Transfer to a plate. To the same pot, add the stock, soy sauce, oyster sauce, Shaoxing wine, and sesame oil and bring to a gentle boil over medium heat. Reduce the heat to medium-low, add the noodles, and cook until they have absorbed all of the stock, 3 to 5 minutes. Return the cabbage stir-fry to the pot and stir to distribute the ingredients evenly. Cover and cook until heated through, about 5 minutes more. Divide among individual plates and serve with a bowl of rice on the side.

CHAP CHAE
STIR-FRIED POTATO
STARCH NOODLES

SERVES 4 TO 6

2 ounces dried SWEET POTATO
STARCH NOODLES; or dried
MUNG BEAN THREADS
(cellophane noodles)

1 or more tablespoons VEGETABLE
OIL

1 large GARLIC CLOVE, crushed,
peeled, and minced

1 medium CARROT, peeled and
julienned into 2-inch-long
matchsticks

8 fresh medium SHIITAKE
MUSHROOMS, stems removed
and julienned

8 ounces BEEF SIRLOIN, thinly
sliced against the grain, then into
thin strips

3 tablespoons KOREAN or JAPANESE
DARK SOY SAUCE

1 to 2 teaspoons SESAME OIL

Pinch GRANULATED SUGAR

1 pound BABY SPINACH

2 SCALLIONS, root and dark green
ends trimmed, and 6-inch stalks
thinly sliced diagonally

Freshly ground BLACK PEPPER

Toasted SESAME SEEDS

CHAP CHAE, literally "stir-fried mixture," is a popular and classic Korean noodle, vegetable, and meat dish. Like cellophane noodles made of mung bean starch, potato starch noodles turn transparent when cooked. Slightly gray in color, they are basically flavorless as stand-alones, but absorb a great deal of flavor. The noodles pick up a golden color from the soy sauce and sesame oil seasonings. Their soft slippery texture is a perfect counterbalance to the crunchy carrots, slightly chewy shiitakes, and tender spinach. A small amount of thinly sliced beef sirloin enriches the dish, making it a perfect first course.

1. Place the dried noodles in a dish with hot water to cover. Allow them to rehydrate, about 30 minutes, and drain. Bring a pot of water to a boil over high heat and cook noodles until transparent, 3 to 5 minutes. Drain.

2. Heat 1 teaspoon of the vegetable oil in a nonstick skillet. Stir-fry the garlic, carrot, shiitakes, and beef along with 1 tablespoon soy sauce, ½ teaspoon sesame oil, and ½ teaspoon sugar, until the vegetables and beef are just cooked, about 3 minutes. Add the spinach and continue stir-frying until just wilted, about 1 minute more. Transfer to a plate. Add the remaining vegetable oil, soy sauce, sesame oil, and sugar to the skillet. Stir-fry the noodles until heated, about 2 minutes. Return the stir-fried vegetables and meat to the skillet, add half the scallions, season with pepper to taste,

and mix the ingredients so they are evenly distributed. Transfer to a platter, sprinkle some sesame seeds across the top, garnish with the remaining scallions, and serve.

Variations: Substitute pork tenderloin or chicken breast for the beef and slice, using the same technique as for the beef.

Omit the meat for a vegetarian version.

GAENG JUED WOON SEN PORK AND CELLOPHANE NOODLE SOUP

SERVES 4 TO 6

Three .7-ounce packages dried
  MUNG BEAN THREADS
  (cellophane noodles)
1½ tablespoons FISH SAUCE
Freshly ground WHITE PEPPER
1½ teaspoons TAPIOCA STARCH, or
  CORNSTARCH
12 ounces GROUND PORK
  (70 percent lean)
10 cups BASIC PORK STOCK
  (page 118)
6 NAPA CABBAGE LEAVES,
  julienned
KOSHER SALT
2 SCALLIONS, root and dark green
  ends trimmed, and 6-inch stalks
  thinly sliced
¾ cup fresh CILANTRO LEAVES
FRIED GARLIC WITH OIL
  (page 108)

FROM THE CENTRAL PLAINS of Thailand comes this tasty ground pork and cellophane noodle soup called *gaeng jued woon sen*. Light in flavor, it is perfect for the spring and summer months. The slippery texture of the noodles is a wonderful counterbalance to the graininess of the ground pork and crunchy napa cabbage. The scallion and cilantro give the soup a refreshing note, while the fried garlic adds a delicious smoky flavor and brings all the flavors together on the palate.

1. Place the cellophane noodles in a dish with water to cover. Let stand until rehydrated and softened, about 30 minutes.

2. Mix together the fish sauce, pepper to taste, and tapioca starch in a bowl. Add the ground pork and combine well. Shape the ground-pork mix into 24 small meatballs.

3. Bring the pork stock to a boil over high heat. Add the meatballs and bring back to a boil. Reduce the heat to medium-low, add the cellophane noodles and napa cabbage, and cook until the cellophane noodles have turned transparent, about 5 minutes. Adjust the seasoning with salt and pepper. Divide the noodles, meatballs, cabbage, and broth among individual large soup bowls. Garnish each serving with scallions, cilantro, and fried garlic oil, and serve.

Variation: For a Thai rice soup, substitute 2 cups cooked long-grain rice for the cellophane noodles. Divide the cooked rice among bowls and ladle the soup with all its ingredients over each serving, and garnish with scallions, cilantro, and fried garlic oil. This dish is most often eaten for breakfast in Thailand.

WHEAT WRAPPERS

MAKES ABOUT 50 WRAPPERS

2 cups all-purpose FLOUR, plus
  extra for kneading and dusting
1 teaspoon KOSHER SALT

FRESH WHEAT WRAPPERS for making Chinese potstickers (pp. 268–71) and Korean *mandu kuk* (page 265) are found in the refrigerated section of Asian markets; they are also easy to make. They must be rolled out thinly, because if made too thick, they will be chewy when cooked.

1. Sift the flour and salt over a mixing bowl. Make a well in the middle and add 1 cup water (more or less) in a steady stream while stirring into the flour with a rubber spatula or wooden spoon. Transfer the dough to a floured work surface and knead it until smooth and elastic, 3 minutes or so, sprinkling some flour on the dough as needed.

2. Divide the dough into 4 sections and transfer a section to each of 4 bowls. Cover with plastic wrap and allow to rest for 30 minutes. Working with one dough ball at a time, form a cylinder about 10 inches long, then cut it into ¾-inch pieces crosswise. Form each piece into approximately ¾-inch-diameter balls. Working on a work surface lightly dusted with flour, flatten each piece of dough with the palm of your hand and, with a dowel, roll out each piece into approximately 2½-inch disks.

WONTON WRAPPERS

MAKES ABOUT 50 WRAPPERS

2 cups all-purpose FLOUR, plus
   extra for kneading
½ teaspoon KOSHER SALT
2 large EGGS, beaten
TAPIOCA STARCH or CORNSTARCH
   for dusting

THESE EGG SKINS are used for making Chinese wontons and siu mai (pp. 266–67), and Cantonese egg rolls (page 288). These wrappers are widely available fresh, square or round, in the refrigerated section of Chinese or Southeast Asian markets; you can make your own if you do not have access to the commercial types.

If you want to make wonton wrappers or egg noodles regularly, invest in an inexpensive pasta machine, as it will make the job go a lot more quickly.

1. Sift the flour and salt over a mixing bowl. Make a well in the middle and add the eggs, stirring with a rubber spatula or wooden spoon until combined. (Add water as needed; no more than ¼ cup.) Then knead until the dough is smooth, stiff, and elastic, about 12 minutes. (You can make the dough using an electric mixer, if you wish.)

2. Divide the dough into 4 sections, cover each piece of dough with plastic wrap, and allow to rest for 30 minutes. Working with one piece of dough at a time, roll it out with a dowel or rolling pin until very thin (thinner than Italian ravioli); dust with tapioca starch on each side to prevent the dough from sticking to the dowel or work surface. If using a pasta machine, shape a piece of dough into a rectangle and pass it through the widest setting. Pass it again, adjusting the machine to a thinner setting every time until you get a sheet that is so thin that you can see your fingers through it. (Every time you pass it through the machine, be sure to dust it with tapioca starch on both sides to prevent sticking.) Cut the strip into 2½-inch squares or rounds, using a cookie cutter. Repeat the process with the remaining pieces of dough. (For egg roll wrappers, cut them into 24 large wrappers, each measuring about 7 inches square.)

PO PING
WHEAT FLOUR PANCAKES

MAKES 36 PANCAKES

2 cups all-purpose FLOUR, plus
    extra for kneading
SESAME OIL

WHEAT FLOUR PANCAKES, *po ping*, are also known as mandarin pancakes or *mu shu* pancakes. They are traditionally used in wrapping Peking duck skin with scallion and hoisin sauce or *mu shu* pork. I love to use these delicate pancakes to make all sorts of healthful Asian wraps for lunch. They are especially good with sauces because they retain texture and do not become soggy. These pancakes can be made a day ahead of time. To reheat them, simply steam for several minutes.

While you can use store-bought fresh Mexican wheat tortillas in a pinch (like some Chinese restaurants do), they are thicker and chewy compared to *po ping*.

1. Bring a cup of water to a boil in a small pot over high heat. Sift the flour over a mixing bowl. While quickly stirring with a rubber spatula or wooden spoon, add the boiling water steadily. Start working the dough with your hands until well combined. Working on a lightly floured work surface, knead the dough until smooth and somewhat elastic, 2 to 3 minutes. Allow the dough to rest for 30 minutes or so, covered with plastic wrap.

2. Divide the dough into 36 pieces and roll them into small balls. Flatten each ball with the palm of your hands and lightly brush each on one side with sesame oil. Take two oiled pieces and press them together, oiled sides facing each other. With your dowel or rolling pin, roll them into 6- to 7-inch pancakes. (They should be thin.) Repeat the process until you have 18 pairs.

3. Heat a wok or nonstick pan over low heat. Add a pair of flattened pancakes. Once the pancakes turn white and begin to puff up with the occasional brown spot, about 2 minutes per side, remove them. Quickly pull the pancakes apart (this is possible because they've been oiled). Repeat the process until you have 36 single pancakes.

HERE ARE SOME COMBINATIONS of delicious Asian sandwich wraps that you can make using *po ping* and leftovers:

• Thai peanut sauce and beef satay (page 98), garnished with shredded lettuce and Thai basil leaves;

• Chili and garlic sauce (page 106) with Vietnamese grilled lemongrass prawns (page 223), and julienned cucumber, carrot, cilantro, and mint leaves;

A DANCER AND HIS HEADDRESS, CELEBRATING THE YEAR OF THE DRAGON

• Hoisin sauce, five-spice roast duck with shiitake mushrooms (pp. 500–1), and julienned scallions;

• Nori-lined wrap with *wasabi* and soy sauce paste with Japanese grilled chicken (page 493), avocado slices, and radish sprouts.

FILIPINO LUMPIA CRÊPES

MAKES 12 CRÊPES

1 cup all-purpose FLOUR
1 tablespoon TAPIOCA STARCH or
 CORNSTARCH; or 2 large EGGS,
 lightly beaten
Pinch of KOSHER SALT
VEGETABLE OIL

F RESH LUMPIA, also called *lumpiang*, are easy to make. Like the Indonesian *lumpia* crêpes (page 257), these are made from a batter resembling French crêpe batter. You can use tapioca starch or eggs as the binder. Either is authentic, but you may get more elasticity from the tapioca starch, while the eggs make for a richer batter in both texture and color.

1. Whisk together the flour, starch or eggs, and salt with 1½ cups water in a bowl until well combined. Allow to rest for 20 minutes.

2. Heat 1 teaspoon oil in an 8-inch nonstick skillet over medium-low heat. While tilting the pan, add ¼ cup of the batter, swirling the pan at the same time to evenly distribute the batter. (Starting from the center of the pan and swirling so the batter moves outward is a good technique, but if you are used to another method, please apply it here.) Once the crêpe starts to bubble gently in the center, loosens itself at the edges, and cooks through, about 3 minutes (it is important that the crêpe have no discoloration, not even light burn spots), do not flip it; instead, transfer it to a plate. Repeat the process with the remaining batter.

INDONESIAN LUMPIA CRÊPES

MAKES 12 CRÊPES

1 cup RICE FLOUR

2 tablespoons TAPIOCA STARCH or CORNSTARCH

2 large EGGS, lightly beaten

1 tablespoon COCONUT OIL (page 77); or VEGETABLE OIL, plus more for cooking

KOSHER SALT

Freshly ground BLACK PEPPER

FRESH LUMPIA (spring roll) crêpes are made from a batter that resembles a traditional, loose French crêpe batter in consistency. There are several variations; my two favorites are made from rice flour, as in Bali, and all-purpose flour, as in the Philippines (page 256). These I learned to make in Bali. The Balinese fill them with a stir-fry such as vegetable and chicken (or whatever ingredient might be available at the market that day), then deep-fry them until golden crisp. They do not have to be fried to be delicious, however.

Because, like all crêpes, the first few pancakes may not be perfect, I usually make enough batter to allow for a few initial tests.

1. Whisk together the rice flour, cornstarch, eggs, 1½ cups water, and the oil. Season with salt and pepper and allow to rest for 30 minutes.

2. Heat 1 teaspoon oil in an 8-inch nonstick skillet over medium-low heat. While tilting the pan, add ¼ cup of the batter, swirling the pan at the same time to evenly distribute the batter. (Starting from the center of the pan and swirling so the batter moves outward is a good technique, but if you are used to another method, please apply it here.) When the crêpe starts to lift at the edges and solidify, about 3 minutes, it is cooked. (Do not brown the wrappers; they should be as spot-free as possible. If the heat is too high, lower it.) Transfer the crêpe to a plate. Continue to make the crêpes with the remaining batter.

SPRING ROLL WRAPPERS

MAKES ABOUT 40 WRAPPERS

1 cup all-purpose FLOUR
1 tablespoon TAPIOCA STARCH or
   CORNSTARCH

VERY GOOD COMMERCIAL brands of spring roll skins (or wrappers) are available round or square in the fresh or frozen sections of Asian markets or through mail-order sources (page 563). If you're up to a challenge, however, these are worth a try. Once you have grasped the technique, you'll enjoy using these lacy spring roll wrappers in making Chinese, Filipino, and Thai fried spring rolls. See-through, light, pliable, and elastic, when freshly made they can be used to wrap all sorts of stir-fried fillings. The wrapped items are most often deep-fried until golden crisp, and, occasionally, enjoyed fresh (meaning unfried). Commercial brands can also be used fresh, but steam them to soften them a bit first.

The amount of dough is plenty to allow for unsuccessful wrappers. If you wind up with more than 40 skins, refrigerate or freeze them, covered in plastic wrap, with an outer layer of aluminum foil.

1. Sift the flour and tapioca starch over a mixing bowl. Make a well in the center and add ½ cup water. With your fingers, start working the flour into the water until it becomes a thick mass. Turn out the dough onto a work surface and start kneading until smooth and elastic, a good 15 minutes. Allow the dough to rest, wrapped in a damp cloth, for 2 to 3 hours at room temperature.

2. Heat a nonstick pan over low heat. Place the ball of dough in your hand, and when the pan is hot, lightly press the dough against the hot surface; move your hand quickly and in a circular motion clockwise, then once counterclockwise, and lift. A thin film should have adhered to the pan. Once the edges start to pull away from the pan, carefully peel off the rest of the skin. Do not let the wrapper turn golden. It should be white. Repeat the process with the rest of the dough. Keep the skins under a damp cloth as you are making them to prevent them from drying out and becoming brittle.

BAO
SPONGY BUNS

MAKES 12 TO 24 BUNS

1 teaspoon active dry YEAST
3½ cups CAKE FLOUR
1 tablespoon GRANULATED SUGAR
1 teaspoon BAKING POWDER
3 tablespoons diced chilled LARD

BAO, ESSENTIALLY SPONGY wheat flour buns, are traditionally filled with savory or sweet classics such as Cantonese roast pork (page 294), Vietnamese ground pork and egg (page 295), or red bean paste (page 544). Spongy buns can also be steamed without any fillings, then sliced in half to make small sandwiches. Make the *bao* bite-size or bigger.

1. Dissolve the yeast in a cup (or more) of lukewarm water in a large bowl and set it aside for about 5 minutes. Whisk together the flour, sugar, and baking powder in a mixing bowl. Add the flour mixture, small amounts at a time, to the yeast while stirring. With your fingertips, work in the lard. Turn the dough out onto a lightly floured surface and knead until the ingredients are well combined and the dough feels smooth, about 2 minutes. Form a ball and lightly dust it with flour. (You can also use an electric mixer, first dissolving the yeast in the mixing bowl. Once the yeast starts to bubble, turn on the mixer at a low speed and start adding the dry ingredients. Increase the speed gradually until a ball of dough starts to form and comes off the sides of the bowl.)

2. Place plastic wrap over the dough and allow it to rise and double in volume at room temperature, about 2 hours.

3. Punch down the dough on a lightly floured surface, then knead until smooth and elastic, about 5 minutes. Shape the dough into 12 to 24 equal-size balls, and cover with plastic wrap until ready to use.

CRYSTAL DUMPLING WRAPPERS

MAKES ABOUT 40 WRAPPERS

1 cup WHEAT STARCH
½ cup RICE FLOUR
2 tablespoons TAPIOCA STARCH
1 tablespoon LARD; or VEGETABLE
OIL

CRYSTAL DUMPLING DOUGH requires the use of wheat starch, not wheat flour. Found in Asian markets, wheat starch has no trace of gluten and is used as a binder or thickener, or in making wrappers for crystal shrimp dumplings (pp. 298–99). Wheat starch is mixed with tapioca starch, rice flour, and water to form a dough, which is kneaded and separated into balls. These are the basis for the final wrappers in which fillings will be enclosed. When steamed, the wrappers turn translucent white and reveal the fillings inside, making it easy to see when the shrimp is done, because you can see its pink color. This dough is also used for crystal vegetable dumplings (pp. 300–1), or jade dumplings, as I like to call them, for their beautiful green color.

It is important to use boiling water when kneading wheat starch.

While this dough is fairly easy to make, you can buy the pre-mixed commercially available version, and you will only need to add the boiling water. The Erawan (Three Elephant) brand is easily recognized by the shrimp dumplings on the package.

1. Sift together the wheat starch, rice flour, and tapioca starch over a mixing bowl. Make a well in the middle and pour in the vegetable oil and 1 cup boiling water in a steady stream while stirring in the starches and flour with a rubber spatula or wooden spoon. The dough will be warm to hot, so be careful as you start to knead. Work the dough with your fingers seconds at a time and eventually longer until the ingredients are well combined. While kneading, you may have to add a tablespoon or two of boiling water, depending on how dry the dough is. What you are looking for is a smooth, somewhat elastic dough that is still warm to the touch. The whole process should take 3 to 5 minutes. (You can also use an electric mixer, adding the dry ingredients first until well combined, then gradually adding the boiling water and canola oil or lard.)

2. Divide the dough into 4 equal-size balls. Then shape each ball into 8-inch-long by 1-inch-diameter cylinders. Cover the dough with plastic wrap until ready to use. Working with one dough ball at a time, form a cylinder about 10 inches long, then cut into ¾-inch pieces. Working on a work surface lightly dusted with flour, flatten each piece of dough with the palm of your hand. With a dowel or rolling pin, roll out each piece into approximately 2½-inch disks. Use when freshly made.

Variation: Crystal vegetable dumplings can be made with colored skins and are sometimes served this way in dim sum restaurants. Bring 1½ cups water to a boil over high heat and blanch a small bunch of spinach leaves. Transfer the spinach and boiling water to a blender and puree until very smooth. Pour the hot thin puree through a very fine mesh sieve and, pressing gently with the back of a spoon, collect the thin green liquid. Discard the solids, and substitute 1 cup hot spinach liquid for the boiling water in step 1 and proceed with the recipe.

CHEUNG FAN
FRESH RICE SHEETS

MAKES 12 SHEETS

1 cup RICE FLOUR
¼ cup TAPIOCA STARCH
Pinch KOSHER SALT
2 tablespoons VEGETABLE OIL

DESPITE THEIR NAME, fresh rice sheets contain not only rice flour but tapioca starch as well. Called *cheung fan* in China, these sheets are used to make *cheung fan guen* (variation) and *haar cheung* (page 297). Called *banh uot* in Vietnam, they are used to make *banh cuon* (page 296). The principal difference between Chinese and Vietnamese rice sheets is the thickness; the Vietnamese *banh uot* is thinner and more delicate.

Rice sheets should be consumed fresh. Once refrigerated they are no longer pliable and tend to stick together. If you have refrigerated the rice sheets, thinly slice them into noodle strands, drop them in boiling water for a few seconds to loosen them up, and add them to any number of stir-fried dishes or soups. While the square pan (see step 2) should be used when making *cheung fan guen*, the round nonstick pan is perfect for making *banh uot*.

1. Whisk together the rice flour, tapioca starch, salt, oil, and 2¼ cups water in a mixing bowl until smooth with no lumps. Cover with plastic wrap and allow to rest for 30 minutes.

2. Meanwhile, set a bamboo steamer with a lid over a wok filled a third of the way up with water and bring the water to a boil over high heat. Oil a nonstick 6-inch-square baking pan and add 3 tablespoons batter, tilting the pan to make sure the bottom is covered with it. When the steamer is filled with hot steam, place the baking pan on top of the bamboo rack (be sure it is level). Secure the steamer lid on top and steam until set, about 5 minutes. Use a spatula to gently lift one corner of the rice sheet, then the entire sheet. Transfer the rice sheet to a plate. Continue this process, whisking the batter prior to ladling it into the pan with each sheet. (When making the Vietnamese version, you can also try making the ultra-thin rice sheets using a round 6-inch nonstick pan over low heat. Add 2 tablespoons batter, swirling it around until the bottom of the pan is covered, then place a lid on top to capture steam.) Repeat this process with the remaining batter.

Variation: For dried shrimp and scallion rice sheet rolls: Soak ½ cup small dried shrimp for 20 minutes and drain. (If using medium or large dried shrimp, be sure to finely chop them.) Thinly slice 5 scallions, white to light green parts only. Proceed with the recipe, but after ladling the batter into the pan, scatter a few dried shrimp and some scallions across the top of the sheet, then steam as directed in step 2 of the recipe. Once steamed, roll up the rice sheets into cylinders and pan-fry in a well-oiled nonstick pan over medium-high heat until golden all around. Serve these dried-shrimp-and-scallion rolls for breakfast or lunch with spicy soy sauce dip (page 88) on the side.

WHEN I WAS A STUDENT and didn't have much money, a dollar went a long way in New York's Chinatown. Street vendors there offer a lot of wonderful foods for very little money. One of my favorites was *cheung fan guen*. Walking down Canal Street, I could smell the rice rolls stuffed with dried shrimp and scallions crisping on their hot griddles. My favorite vendor would always wait until the rolls were perfect. Even if I was hungry or in a hurry, he insisted that they be heated through and lightly golden on the outside. I would wait patiently; his were the best. When they were finished, he would anoint the rice rolls, a soy sauce bottle in one hand and a chili sauce bottle in the other. For a finishing touch, he would include a light sprinkle of toasted sesame seeds. He took great care with his food from beginning to end, and I never left his stand feeling that he had produced anything that was less than perfect.

TSUNG YU PING
SCALLION PANCAKES

MAKES 12 PANCAKES

2 cups all-purpose FLOUR, plus
   extra for kneading

1 teaspoon BAKING POWDER

2 tablespoons LARD, chilled

2 to 3 tablespoons SESAME OIL

2 tablespoons KOSHER SALT

6 SCALLIONS, root and dark green
   ends trimmed, and 6-inch stalks
   thinly sliced into rounds

CHINESE LIGHT SOY SAUCE

WHEAT IS ABUNDANT in northern and northwestern China, and all sorts of wheat flour noodle and bread items are made. *Tsung yu ping*, scallion pancakes, is one of my favorite pancake dishes. Wheat dough—rich with lard and sesame oil and flavored with generous amounts of scallion and kosher salt—is spiraled into thick pancakes and shallow-fried until crispy. A specialty of Chinese street hawkers, these are easily made at home.

When kneaded, the dough should not feel dry and stiff; it should feel soft but not sticky. If you need to add more water, do so in one-tablespoon increments.

1. Sift the flour and baking powder over a mixing bowl. With your fingers, quickly work the lard into the flour. Make a well in the center, and add 1 cup water. With a wooden spoon, gradually combine the flour and water. Turn out the dough onto a floured work surface and knead until smooth and elastic, about 5 minutes. Cover the dough with a plastic wrap and allow it to rest for 30 minutes. Shape the dough into a 12-inch-long cylinder and cut it into twelve 1-inch-long pieces.

2. Roll a piece of dough into a ⅛-inch-thick rectangular sheet measuring about 6 inches long by 2 inches wide. Brush some sesame oil on top of the dough, sprinkle some salt, and scatter about 2 heaping teaspoons of scallions. Roll up the dough lengthwise into a cigar, pinching the ends to enclose the scallions, then roll it up into a thick spiral disk, pinching the end to secure the shape. With a floured rolling pin and surface, roll out the disk and flatten it to about ¼ inch thick. Repeat the process until you have 12 pancakes.

3. Heat 2 tablespoons oil in a nonstick pan over medium heat. Add one or more pancakes and pan-fry until golden crisp, about 2 minutes on each side. Drain on a paper towel–lined plate, and serve with soy sauce on the side.

MANDU KUK
DUMPLING SOUP

MAKES 36 DUMPLINGS

6 ounces GROUND BEEF
(70 percent lean); or GROUND
PORK (70 percent lean)

2 SCALLIONS, root and dark green
ends trimmed, and 6-inch stalks
minced

1 large GARLIC CLOVE, crushed,
peeled, and minced

2 tablespoons KOREAN or JAPANESE
DARK SOY SAUCE

2 teaspoons SESAME OIL

KOSHER SALT

Freshly ground BLACK PEPPER

2 teaspoons VEGETABLE OIL

6 ounces firm TOFU, drained and
crushed

2 large NAPA CABBAGE LEAVES,
blanched, drained, and minced

1 cup MUNG BEAN SPROUTS,
blanched and drained

6 fresh SHIITAKE MUSHROOMS,
stems removed and caps minced

36 round WHEAT WRAPPERS
(page 252); or commercial
equivalent

10 cups BASIC BEEF STOCK
(page 120); or BASIC PORK
STOCK (page 118)

2 large EGGS, beaten with
1 tablespoon WATER

MANDU KUK is the Korean version of the Chinese wonton soup (pp. 266–67). Wheat wrappers are easily made, or you can use commercially produced round wheat Chinese *siu mai* wrappers. *Mandu kuk* can be made with ground beef or pork or a combination of both, with tofu for the filling. *Mandu kuk* is generally accompanied by *kimchi* and a bowl of rice on the side, as many Koreans do not consider noodles (including dumplings) to be a meal.

Slice the tofu in ½-inch-thick slices and place between two double layers of paper towels to drain, refrigerated, overnight.

1. Mix together the ground beef or pork, scallions, garlic, soy sauce, sesame oil, and salt and pepper in a bowl until well combined. Heat 1 teaspoon oil in a nonstick pan over medium heat and add the meat, crumbling it with a wooden or plastic spoon, until cooked through, about 10 minutes. Transfer to a bowl, and add the tofu, napa cabbage, mung bean sprouts, and shiitakes, mixing them until thoroughly combined.

2. Place a wrapper on a clean surface. Center a heaping teaspoon of meat filling on top. Dampen your fingertip with water and run it along the edge of the wrapper. Fold the wrapper in half so it looks like a crescent and pinch the rounded edge to seal. (Be sure to gently press out any air pockets.) Dampen the two folded ends, bringing them around the bulgy center of the dumpling, and pinch them together firmly until they stick. Place the dumpling on a plate and cover with plastic wrap to prevent it from drying out. Repeat this process until you have all 36 dumplings, keeping them under the plastic wrap each time.

3. Bring the stock to a gentle boil in a pot over medium-low heat. At the same time, bring salted water to a boil in a separate pot over high heat and cook the dumplings in batches until they float to the top, about 3 minutes. Drain and divide among individual large soup bowls.

4. Meanwhile, heat the remaining oil in a nonstick pan over medium-high heat. Season the eggs with salt and pepper, and make a thin omelette. Transfer to a cutting board and julienne.

5. Ladle some stock over each serving of dumplings and sprinkle with a generous amount of julienned omelette.

HUN TUN
WONTON SOUP

10 cups BASIC CHICKEN STOCK
(page 116); or SUPERIOR STOCK
(page 117)

2 teaspoons SESAME OIL

2 teaspoons CHINESE LIGHT SOY
SAUCE

Pinch of freshly ground WHITE
or BLACK PEPPER

½ teaspoon CORNSTARCH

8 ounces SHRIMP, shelled,
deveined, and finely chopped

4 ounces GROUND PORK
(70 percent lean)

36 square WONTON WRAPPERS
(page 253); or commercial
equivalent

6 ounces fresh thin EGG NOODLES
(optional)

2 SCALLIONS, root and dark green
ends trimmed, and 6-inch stalks
finely sliced into rounds

ONTONS, OR HUN TUN, are Chinese dumplings traditionally filled with tender pork and sweet shrimp. Boiled, they are then set afloat on a fragrant ginger-infused chicken broth and topped with freshly sliced scallion. As their name suggests (hun means "cloud" and tun means "swallow"), they are delicate on every level, from their shape to their texture and flavor. Noodle shops in China and Chinatowns in the West will offer to add thin fresh egg noodles to any wonton soup for a more satisfying meal. Chinese dumpling-making is an art form that goes back thousands of years. The Chinese pride themselves on making the thinnest skin possible to complement rather than overwhelm the delicious filling. Their creativity in shaping dumplings is demonstrated in this single dish, for three shapes are made: the cloud (the classic), the envelope, and the pouch. Because wontons are so light, it is easy just to keep eating them; when my extended family gets together, the women sit at the table and start making wontons by the hundreds. Also, see the siu mai variation.

1. Bring the chicken stock with 1 teaspoon sesame oil to a gentle simmer in a pot over low heat. Bring water to a boil in a separate pot over high heat. Meanwhile, stir together the remaining sesame oil, soy sauce, pepper, and cornstarch in a mixing bowl. Add the shrimp and pork and mix the ingredients until well combined.

2. Place a wonton wrapper on a clean surface so it looks like a diamond with a pointy side near you. Center a teaspoon of shrimp and pork filling on top. To seal, simply dampen your fingertip and run it across the edge of the wrapper. Fold the wonton wrapper in half so it

looks like a triangle. Be sure to gently press out any air pockets. Dampen the two pointy tips farthest away from each other and bring them together around the rounded center of the dumpling. Press firmly together until they stick. The wonton should be plump in the middle with two pointy sides on opposite ends. (This is the shape of a Chinese gold bar.) Place the wonton on a plate and cover with plastic wrap to prevent it from drying out. Repeat this process until you have 36 wontons, keeping them under the plastic wrap each time.

3. At this time, if using, cook the thin egg noodles in the pot of boiling water until tender but firm, about 3 minutes. Drain and divide among individual large soup bowls. Cook the wontons in the same pot until they float, a minute or two. With a slotted spoon, transfer them in equal amounts to individual bowls (on top of each serving of noodles, if using). Pour the chicken broth over each serving and garnish with scallions.

Variations: To turn wontons into great finger food for any party, heat enough vegetable oil for deep-frying in a wok or pot of your choice over medium-high heat until the oil reaches 360° to 375°F. Working in batches, carefully lower a few wontons at a time into the hot oil and deep-fry, turning them over once, until golden crisp, 2 to 3 minutes. Drain on a paper towel and serve with a spicy soy sauce dip (page 88).

For siu mai (open wontons): Place a round egg wrapper (page 253; or commercial equivalent) in the palm of one hand. Put a heaping teaspoon of wonton filling in the center and push it down, while gathering the wrapper up the sides. Repeat the process for a total of 36 dumplings. Fill the bottom third of a wok with water and bring to a boil over high

heat. Working in batches, line a bamboo steamer rack with 2 napa cabbage leaves (changing the leaves with each batch) and place the siu mai on top (filling—or open—side up), leaving about ¾ inch in between each. Place the bamboo steamer, covered with its lid, on top of the wok and steam dumplings until cooked through, 5 to 7 minutes. Serve with chili and garlic sauce or spicy soy sauce dip.

WHEN I FIRST MOVED to the United States in the late 1970s, the only Chinese restaurants in my neighborhood were chain restaurants serving food adjusted to the Western palate. The first time I ordered wonton soup, I was shocked when a thick whitish dough floating in a neon-yellow broth came to the table. I turned to my father and said, sadly, "I don't think I ordered this." He smiled and told me, "Yes, it's wonton soup, American-style." The so-called wontons were chewy and had almost no filling; they were nothing like the wontons I grew up making and eating. After that meal, I really valued the trips to New York City's Chinatown with my father. He would take us to all sorts of dim sum restaurants and noodle shops where we ate authentic foods, most often regional Cantonese. One of my favorite places was and still is The Wonton Garden on Mott Street. A tiny, noisy place in a busy street, its cooks can be seen deftly preparing wontons and other noodle dishes through the steamed-up front windows. They serve up some of the best wontons I've ever had in a restaurant.

JAOZI

STEAMED GINGER AND

PORK DUMPLINGS

MAKES 36 DUMPLINGS

1 tablespoon CHINESE LIGHT SOY
   SAUCE

½ teaspoon SESAME OIL

1 teaspoon TAPIOCA STARCH or
   CORNSTARCH

Freshly ground BLACK PEPPER

10 ounces GROUND PORK
   (70 percent lean)

1 ounce fresh GINGER, peeled and
   finely grated

2 SCALLIONS, root and dark green
   ends trimmed, and 6-inch stalks
   minced

36 round WHEAT WRAPPERS
   (page 252); or commercial
   equivalent

4 NAPA CABBAGE LEAVES

GINGER-INFUSED VINEGAR
   DIPPING SAUCE (page 89)

CHILI AND GARLIC SAUCE
   (page 106)

I REMEMBER spending time with friends in Chinatown playing Tai-wanese mah-jongg, a tile game played at great speed. We would play for hours, sometimes through the night, and before we knew it, Friday turned into Sunday. Every once in a while, we would take a break, retreat to the kitchen, and make *jaozi* or *kwo tiep*, boiled or pan-fried dumplings, respectively. We all got involved. While one of us chopped and mixed the pork and ginger filling, another kneaded the dough, while yet another made the dipping sauces. We would all shape the dumplings. Steamed, boiled, or pan-fried (see variation), these fragrant items were delicious served with chili paste, cilantro, and scallion soy sauce dip. We would go through them with great enthusiasm until there was not one left on the plate, then return to our game.

1. Whisk together the soy sauce, sesame oil, and tapioca starch in a bowl. Season with pepper, add the pork, ginger, and scallions, and mix thoroughly until the ingredients are well combined. Cover the bowl and place in the refrigerator to allow the flavors to develop, about 2 hours.

2. Place a wrapper on a clean work surface. Center a heaping teaspoon of pork filling on top. Dampen your fingertip with water and run it along the edge of the wrapper. Fold the wrapper in half so it looks like a crescent and pinch to seal. (Be sure to gently press out any air pockets.) Gently press the bottom rounded side of the dumpling onto the work surface to flatten it, so it sits nicely with the pinched side propped up. Repeat this process until you have

formed 36 dumplings. As each dumpling is finished, place it on a plate with plastic wrap to cover so it does not dry out.

3. Fill the bottom third of a wok with water and bring to a boil over high heat. Meanwhile, line a bamboo steamer rack with 2 napa cabbage leaves. Place the pork dumplings, pinched side up, on the rack so they do not touch each other. They should be about ½ inch apart to allow the steam to come through and cook the dumplings evenly. The size of your steamer will determine how many dumplings you are able to steam at a time. Place the bamboo rack in the wok, cover the steamer, and steam until the dumplings are cooked through, about 7 minutes. Serve the dumplings with black vinegar and soy sauce dip and chili and garlic sauce on the side.

Variations: To make *kwo tiep*, potstickers: Heat 2 teaspoons vegetable oil in a nonstick skillet over medium-high heat. Pan-fry the dumplings, pinched side up, until the flattened underside is golden brown. Add ¼ cup water, place a lid on top, and steam the potstickers until the water has almost completely evaporated. Remove the lid and allow the water to evaporate completely and the dumplings to continue crisping, 1 to 2 minutes more. Serve with the dipping sauces.

You can also boil the dumplings in water until they float, about 3 minutes, then drain them as you would raviolis and serve with dipping sauces on the side.

STEAMED BEEF AND CHIVE DUMPLINGS

MAKES 36 DUMPLINGS

1 tablespoon CHINESE LIGHT SOY SAUCE

½ teaspoon SESAME OIL

1 teaspoon TAPIOCA STARCH or CORNSTARCH

Freshly ground BLACK PEPPER

10 ounces GROUND BEEF (70 percent lean)

4 ounces GREEN GARLIC CHIVES (*gau choy*), minced

36 round WHEAT WRAPPERS (page 252); or commercial equivalent

6 NAPA CABBAGE LEAVES

SPICY SOY SAUCE DIP (page 88)

S TEAMED BEEF and chive dumplings are a northern Chinese classic probably inspired by the Mongols, who use beef extensively in their diet. Garlic chives are fascinating in themselves as an ingredient, and here I give recipes for both dumplings and potstickers (see variation) calling for them. Garlic chives, or Chinese chives as they are also known, have a mild garlic flavor with a certain sweetness. Garlic chives come in three versions: *gau choy fa*, or flowering chive, which is dark green, with a tubular stem and a yellow flower bud at the tip; *gau choy*, which is dark green with flat long narrow leaves and has no buds; and *gau wong*, which is yellow and tends to be more delicate and less fibrous than the other types. Although on first impulse you might want to use garlic chives sparingly, they are traditionally used abundantly, often as vegetables, and stir-fried alone or with protein. (*Gau choy* is good as a main stir-fried vegetable dish.) They keep well in a dark and cool area, and I often leave them in the refrigerator in a brown paper bag, perforated plastic bag, or clean, moist cotton kitchen towel. Garlic chives are available almost all year round in Asian markets, although the more expensive yellow chives are more available in spring and summer.

1. Whisk together the soy sauce, sesame oil, and tapioca starch in a bowl. Season with pepper, add the beef and garlic chives, and mix thoroughly until the ingredients are well combined. Cover the bowl and place in the refrigerator to allow the flavors to develop, about 2 hours.

2. Place a wrapper on a clean work surface. Center a heaping teaspoon of beef filling on top. Dampen your fingertip with water and run it along the edge of the wrapper. Fold the wrapper in half so it looks like a crescent and pinch to seal. (Be sure to gently press out any air pockets.)

Gently press the bottom rounded side of the dumpling onto the work surface to flatten it, so it sits nicely with the pinched side propped up. Repeat this process until you have formed 36 dumplings. As each dumpling is finished, place it on a plate with plastic wrap to cover so it does not dry out.

3. Fill the bottom third of a wok with water and bring to a boil over high heat. Meanwhile, line a bamboo steamer rack with 2 or more napa cabbage leaves. Place the beef dumplings pinched side up on the rack so they do not touch each

other. They should be about ½ inch apart to allow the steam to come through and cook the dumplings evenly. The size of your steamer will determine how many dumplings you can steam at a time. Place the bamboo rack in the wok, cover the steamer, and steam until the dumplings are cooked through, about 7 minutes. Serve with spicy soy sauce dip on the side.

Variations: To make potstickers, heat 2 teaspoons vegetable oil in a nonstick skillet over medium-high heat. Pan-fry the potstickers, pinched side up, until the flattened underside is golden brown. Add ⅓ cup water, place a lid on top, and steam the potstickers until the water has almost completely evaporated. Remove the lid and allow the water to evaporate completely and the dumplings to continue crisping, a minute or two more. Serve with the dipping sauces.

You can also boil the dumplings in water until they float, about 3 minutes, then drain them as you would raviolis and serve with dipping sauces on the side.

CHUN GUEN SHANGHAINESE SPRING ROLLS

MAKES 24 ROLLS

10 dried large SHIITAKE
  MUSHROOMS

1 tablespoon VEGETABLE OIL,
  plus oil for deep-frying

2 large GARLIC CLOVES, crushed,
  peeled, and minced

5 SCALLIONS, root and dark green
  ends trimmed, and 6-inch stalks
  thinly sliced in rounds

12 large NAPA CABBAGE LEAVES,
  ribs removed, tender green
  leaves julienned crosswise

1 large BAMBOO SHOOT, julienned
  (about 1 cup)

KOSHER SALT

Freshly ground BLACK PEPPER

24 SPRING ROLL WRAPPERS
  (page 258); or commercial
  equivalent

1 large EGG, lightly beaten

GINGER-INFUSED VINEGAR
  DIPPING SAUCE (page 89)

D URING the Tang dynasty, *chun guen* (or *chun juan* in Mandarin), literally, "spring roll," were created as a celebration of the spring harvest. For this reason the original rolls were filled only with vegetables. Today they are one of the most popular items sold in dim sum restaurants. Fried until crispy, they can be filled with vegetables with or without the addition of shredded or minced chicken, pork, or shrimp. A classic combination of black vinegar and soy sauce infused with fresh julienned ginger is usually served on the side for dipping.

If using a fresh bamboo shoot, peel and boil it for 15 minutes prior to using in the recipe. If using a fresh whole boiled shoot (available in Japanese markets), rinse prior to using. If using a canned whole shoot, boil it for 3 to 5 minutes to get rid of the tin taste.

1. Put the shiitakes in a bowl with hot water to cover, then set a plate over the bowl to prevent steam from escaping. Let stand until the mushrooms rehydrate and soften, about 30 minutes (or longer, depending on the size of the mushrooms). Squeeze the mushrooms between the palms of your hands to get rid of the excess water. Using a paring knife, remove any hard stems from the mushrooms, then cut the mushroom caps into julienned strips.

2. In a wok or nonstick skillet, heat the oil over high heat. Stir-fry the garlic and scallions until the garlic turns just golden, about 2 minutes. Add the shiitakes, cabbage, and bamboo shoot and continue to stir-fry until cooked through, about 5 minutes. Season with salt and pep-

per to taste, toss to distribute evenly, and transfer to a platter. Allow to cool completely.

3. Heat enough oil for deep-frying in a pot over medium heat. Meanwhile, place a round wrapper on a clean work surface in front of you. (If using the square store-bought ones, place the wrapper so it looks like a diamond with a point near you.) Place a heaping tablespoon of filling an inch in from the edge near you. Spread it out so it forms a 4-inch log. (If using the square wrapper, place the filling 1½ inches in from the point and spread it out to form a 4-inch log.) Roll the wrapper over the filling once. Fold in the sides, then fold over twice more, leaving an edge open. Moisten the edge well with some of

the beaten egg, and roll to the end to enclose the filling. Continue until you have 24 spring rolls. While rolling, it is important that you do not make the roll too tight or too loose. If too tight, the roll will crack open while it fries; if too loose, the oil will seep in during the frying process. Be sure to cover the rolls with plastic wrap as you work.

4. When the oil reaches 360° to 375°F, add the spring rolls, a few at a time, and deep-fry until golden crisp all around, about 2 minutes on each side. Drain on a paper towel–lined plate and serve with ginger-infused vinegar dip.

Variation: Preheat the oven to 375°F. Brush the spring rolls lightly with vegetable oil and place them on a baking sheet, about ½ inch apart. Bake until golden on both sides, about 10 minutes per side.

PAW PIA SAUD
FRESH VEGETARIAN
SPRING ROLLS

MAKES 24 ROLLS

6 dried medium SHIITAKE
  MUSHROOMS

One .7-ounce package MUNG BEAN
  THREADS (cellophane noodles)

1 tablespoon CHINESE LIGHT SOY
  SAUCE

1 tablespoon OYSTER SAUCE

1 tablespoon GRANULATED SUGAR

2 teaspoons CANOLA or GRAPESEED
  OIL

10 GREEN CABBAGE LEAVES, core
  removed, leaves julienned

2 medium CARROTS, peeled and
  julienned

1½ cups MUNG BEAN SPROUTS

Freshly ground BLACK PEPPER

24 SPRING ROLL WRAPPERS
  (page 258); or commercial
  equivalent

2 large EGGS, beaten (if deep-
  frying)

SWEET CHILI RELISH

P AW PIA SAUD are delicious rolls available as appetizers in Thai restaurants. Lacy spring roll wrappers are filled with crunchy stir-fried
green cabbage, carrots, mung bean sprouts, shiitake mushrooms, and
mung bean threads (cellophane noodles), and enjoyed as fresh rolls, or unfried. Thai cooks, however, also deep-fry these for a different texture (see
variation). The fried version, paw pia taud, is reminiscent of the Shanghainese
spring roll (page 272), after which it was modeled.

When making fresh rolls, make the wrappers fresh or steam store-bought
wrappers to soften.

1. Put the shiitakes in one bowl and the mung bean threads in another, with hot water to cover, then set a plate over each bowl to prevent steam from escaping. Let stand until the mushrooms rehydrate and soften, about 30 minutes (or longer, depending on size of the mushrooms). Squeeze the mushrooms between the palms of your hands to get rid of the excess water. Using a paring knife, remove any hard stems from the mushrooms, then finely chop or julienne the caps. Drain and coarsely chop the mung bean threads.

2. Whisk together the soy sauce, oyster sauce, and sugar in a bowl until the sugar is completely dissolved. Meanwhile, heat the oil in a wok or nonstick skillet over high heat. Add the cabbage and carrots and stir-fry until just softened, about 5 minutes. Add the mush-rooms, mung bean threads, and soy sauce mixture and continue to stir-fry until the vegetables have cooked through and the cellophane noodles are completely transparent, about 7 minutes. Add the mung bean sprouts and stir-fry until just wilted, about 1 minute more. Transfer to a plate and allow to cool.

3. Meanwhile, place a round wrapper on a clean work surface in front of you. (If using the square ones, place the wrapper so it looks like a diamond with a point near you.) Place a heaping tablespoon of filling an inch in from the edge near you. Spread it out so it forms a 4-inch log. (If using the square wrapper, place the filling 1½ inches in from the point and spread it out to form a 4-inch log.) Roll the wrapper over the filling once. Fold in the sides, then fold all the way. Repeat the process until you have 24 paw pia saud. Be

sure to cover the rolls with plastic wrap as you work and until ready to serve. Serve with sweet chili relish on the side.

Variation: *Paw pia taud* are deep-fried spring rolls. Follow the recipe for making fresh spring rolls, but fold in the sides and roll over twice more, leaving an edge open. Moisten the edge well with some of the beaten egg wash and roll to the end to enclose the filling. While rolling, it is important that you do not make the roll too tight or too loose. If too tight, the roll will crack open while it fries; if too loose, the oil will seep in during the frying process. Meanwhile, heat enough oil for deep-frying in a pot over medium-high heat until it reaches 360° to 375°F. Fry the rolls, turning them once until golden all around, about 2 minutes on each side. Drain on a paper towel–lined plate and serve with sweet chili relish on the side. To bake: Preheat the oven to 375°F. Brush rolls lightly wih vegetable oil, then place them on a baking sheet, about ½ inch apart. Bake until golden on both sides, about 10 minutes per side.

LUMPIA
FILIPINO FRIED
SPRING ROLLS

8 dried medium SHIITAKE
MUSHROOMS

1 ½ tablespoons VEGETABLE OIL,
plus more for deep-frying

2 large GARLIC CLOVES, crushed,
peeled, and minced

1 small ONION, peeled and thinly
sliced

10 ounces GROUND PORK
(70 percent lean); or CHICKEN
BREAST, thinly sliced, then finely
chopped

10 ounces fresh SHRIMP, shelled,
deveined, and finely chopped

2 SCALLIONS, root and dark green
ends trimmed, and 6-inch stalks
finely chopped

2 medium CARROTS, peeled and
finely chopped

8 ounces GREEN BEANS, trimmed
and finely chopped

2 teaspoons GRANULATED SUGAR

KOSHER SALT

24 SPRING ROLL WRAPPERS
(page 258); or commercial
equivalent

2 large EGGS, beaten

LUMPIA COCONUT VINEGAR
DIPPING SAUCE (page 96)

THE FILIPINO *LUMPIA* is a close cousin to the Shanghainese spring roll (pp. 272–73). Filipino cooks often use lacy spring roll wrappers and fill them with a stir-fry of pork, shiitakes, yard-long beans, and carrots. Fragrant with pungent onions and garlic, they are deep-fried and served with a sweet and vinegary dipping sauce.

Because springs rolls are so time-consuming to make, they are generally reserved for special occasions. The filling depends on the cook, but the combination of pork, shrimp, yard-long beans, carrots, and mushrooms is very common. Leftover deep-fried rolls can be kept frozen and reheated in a 375°F oven for 10 minutes; they do not need to be thawed.

1. Put the shiitakes in a bowl with hot water to cover, then set a plate over the bowl to prevent steam from escaping. Let stand until the mushrooms rehydrate and soften, about 30 minutes (or longer, depending on the size of the mushrooms). Squeeze the mushrooms between the palms of your hands to get rid of the excess water. Using a paring knife, remove any hard stems from the mushrooms, then finely chop or julienne the caps.

2. Heat the oil in a nonstick skillet over medium-high heat. Add the garlic and onion, and stir-fry until the garlic is just golden and the onions are translucent, about 5 minutes. Add the mushrooms, pork (or chicken), shrimp, scallions, carrots, and green beans and stir-fry, pressing the ground meat with the back of a spatula to crumble it, until

cooked through, 5 to 7 minutes. Season with the granulated sugar and salt and stir-fry for an additional minute. Transfer to a plate and allow to cool.

3. Meanwhile, place a round wrapper on a clean work surface in front of you. (If using the square store-bought ones, place the wrapper so it looks like a diamond with a point near you.) Place a heaping tablespoon of filling an inch in from the point near you. Spread it out so it forms a 4-inch log. (If using the square wrapper, place the filling 1 ½ inches in from the point and spread it out to form a 4-inch log.) Roll the wrapper over the filling once. Fold in the sides, then fold over twice more, leaving an edge open. Moisten the edge well with some of the beaten egg wash and roll to the end to enclose the filling. Continue until you have 24 *lumpia*. While rolling, it is important that you do not make the roll too tight or too loose. If too tight, the roll will crack open while it fries; if too loose, the oil will seep in during the frying process. Be sure to cover the rolls with plastic wrap as you work.

4. Meanwhile, heat enough oil for deep-frying in a pot over medium-high heat to 360° to 375°F. Fry the rolls, turning them once until golden all around, about 2 minutes per side. Drain on a paper towel–lined plate.

LUMPIA GORENG INDONESIAN FRIED EGG ROLLS

MAKES 12 ROLLS

8 dried medium SHIITAKE
MUSHROOMS

1 tablespoon VEGETABLE OIL,
plus more for deep-frying

2 medium GARLIC CLOVES,
crushed, peeled, and minced

8 ounces CHICKEN BREAST,
skinned and finely chopped

8 ounces SHRIMP, shelled,
deveined, and finely chopped

2 medium-large CARROTS, peeled
and julienned into thin 2-inch-
long sticks

2 medium to large LEEKS, root
ends trimmed, outer leaves
removed, and julienned into
2-inch-long strips

Half a small GREEN CABBAGE,
thinly sliced

2 cups MUNG BEAN SPROUTS, root
ends trimmed

2 tablespoons FISH SAUCE

2 tablespoons INDONESIAN SWEET
SOY SAUCE (kecap manis), plus
1 cup

12 INDONESIAN LUMPIA CRÊPES
(page 257)

1 large EGG, lightly beaten

4 RED THAI CHILIES, stemmed,
seeded, and sliced paper thin
crosswise

I NDONESIAN *LUMPIA GORENG*, deep-fried egg rolls, are large, rich, and delicious. A crêpe batter made with rice flour is used for making the wrappers. Filled with a vegetable and meat stir-fry, the soft wrappers are sealed with egg yolk, deep-fried, and served with *kecap manis*, Indonesian sweet soy sauce, straight from the bottle, and spiced only with freshly sliced red chilies.

Wrappers should be as uniform in color as possible, so be very careful not to let them brown while cooking in the pan.

1. Put the shiitakes in a bowl with hot water to cover, then set a plate over the bowl to prevent steam from escaping. Let stand until the mushrooms rehydrate and soften, about 30 minutes (or longer, depending on the size of the mushrooms). Squeeze the mushrooms between the palms of your hands to get rid of the excess water. Using a paring knife, remove any hard stems from the mushrooms. Julienne the caps.

2. Heat half the oil in a wok or non-stick skillet over high heat. Stir-fry the garlic, chicken breast, and shrimp, breaking them down with the back of a spoon or spatula in the process, until cooked through, about 5 minutes. Transfer to a plate. Heat the remaining oil in the wok and stir-fry the carrots, leeks, cabbage, and mung bean sprouts until tender but firm and the juices have almost evaporated, about 10 min-

utes. Put the chicken and shrimp back into the wok and stir-fry until well combined. Drizzle the fish sauce and 2 tablespoons sweet soy sauce over the stir-fry and continue to stir-fry to coat evenly. Transfer to a plate to cool.

3. Place a *lumpia* wrapper in front of you, and spread a heaping tablespoon of filling on the side nearest you. Shape the filling to look like a single log. Roll the wrapper over the filling once. Fold in the sides, then fold over twice more, leaving an edge open. Moisten the edge well with some egg wash and roll to the end to enclose the filling. Repeat this process until you have made 12 spring rolls, measuring about 4 inches long.

4. Heat enough oil for deep-frying in a wok or pot to 360° to 375°F over medium-high heat. Test the heat of the oil with one spring roll;

the oil should sizzle around the roll but not so vigorously as to destroy the roll. Fry two rolls at a time, turning them once immediately to prevent them from sticking to each other, then turning them occasionally until golden on all sides, 3 to 5 minutes total. Drain on a paper towel–lined plate. Serve spring rolls with the remaining *kecap manis*, topped with a sliced chili on the side. Eat while hot.

LUMPIA UBOD
PALM HEART SPRING ROLLS

MAKES 12 ROLLS

8 ounces HEARTS OF PALM

2 teaspoons VEGETABLE OIL

1 large GARLIC CLOVE, crushed, peeled, and minced

1 medium CARROT, peeled and julienned into 1½- to 2-inch-long matchsticks

2 SCALLIONS, root and dark green ends trimmed, and 6-inch stalks cut into 1½- to 2-inch-long pieces and quartered lengthwise, plus 6 long dark green SCALLION LEAVES, halved lengthwise

Meat of 1 young GREEN COCONUT, julienned into 1½- to 2-inch-long matchsticks as best you can (reserve the coconut water for a different recipe or drink it while cooking!)

12 FILIPINO FRESH LUMPIA CRÊPES (page 256)

12 BOSTON LETTUCE LEAVES or other tender lettuce, ribs removed; or mixed baby greens such as MESCLUN

1 cup unsweetened COCONUT MILK (page 77); or commercial equivalent

½ cup roasted peeled unsalted PEANUTS, finely crushed (not peanut butter)

1 teaspoon FISH SAUCE; or a pinch or two of KOSHER SALT

FILIPINO FRESH *LUMPIA*, also known as *lumpiang*, are filled with fresh coconut palm heart. Unique to the Philippines, the recipe originated in Silay, located in the Visayas region of the country. Harvested from three- to five-year-old coconut trees, the palm hearts are firm to the touch and both tender and crunchy when eaten. Their subtle coconut flavor is what makes these rolls quite wonderful. Coconut palm hearts are not available in the United States, and so I've adapted this recipe to more readily available ingredients. Although re-creating the flavor and texture of coconut palm hearts is impossible, I found that combining regular canned hearts of palm and young green coconut meat was very tasty; julienned carrots can be added for color and texture. The results are wonderful, but if you have the chance to go to the Philippines one day, do try the authentic version.

1. Bring a pot of salted water to a boil and blanch the palm hearts for 5 minutes. Drain and shock them in cold running water to stop the cooking. (The canned hearts are already cooked; the blanching is to get rid of the tin odor they have absorbed.) Julienne the palm hearts into 1½- to 2-inch-long matchsticks and set aside. Heat the oil in a nonstick skillet over medium-high heat and stir-fry the garlic until just golden, about 3 minutes. Add the carrot and scallions and cook until just wilted, about 2 minutes. Add the palm hearts and continue to stir-fry until well mixed, about a minute. Transfer to a bowl and allow to cool. Toss in the coconut meat.

2. Place a crêpe in front of you on a clean work surface. Line the crêpe with a lettuce leaf or some mesclun so it sticks out a little from the rounded edge of the crêpe. Divide the vegetable mixture into 12 equal portions. Place one portion in the center of the crêpe vertically so that the vegetable pile is perpendicular to you. Fold the bottom of the crêpe over once, then fold in the sides. The bundle should look like a wrapped bouquet of flowers with one end open. Take one scallion strand and tie a knot around the *lumpia* a third of the way up from the folded bottom. Repeat the process until you have 12 rolls.

3. Bring the coconut milk and half the crushed peanuts to a boil in a saucepan over medium-high heat. Lower the heat to medium-low and season with fish sauce or salt. Divide

and transfer the sauce among individual sauce dishes. Serve the lumpia sprinkled with some crushed peanuts, with coconut-peanut sauce on the side.

Variation: This recipe will easily make 24 lumpia purses. Make the crêpes half the size. Chop, rather than julienne, the vegetables. Place about 1 teaspoon of the vegetable filling at the center of a crêpe and gather up the sides. Tuck in some mesclun and tie up the purse with a scallion strand. Spoon some of the coconut-peanut sauce on individual plates. Place an equal number of purses on each plate and sprinkle with some ground peanuts. This makes for a beautiful presentation, especially for a sit-down dinner party.

LUMPIA SIRIWA
FRESH SPRING ROLLS

1 teaspoon VEGETABLE OIL

3 large GARLIC CLOVES, crushed, peeled, and minced

1 small ONION, peeled and thinly sliced

3 SCALLIONS, root and dark green ends trimmed, and 6-inch stalks cut into 1-inch-long pieces and julienned; plus 6 long dark green SCALLION LEAVES, halved lengthwise

8 ounces NAPA or GREEN CABBAGE, julienned

4 medium CARROTS, peeled and julienned

1 pound MUNG BEAN SPROUTS, root ends trimmed

½ cup roasted unsalted PEANUTS, peeled and finely crushed (not peanut butter)

12 FRESH FILIPINO LUMPIA CRÊPES (page 256)

1 tablespoon TAPIOCA STARCH or CORNSTARCH

2 tablespoons CHINESE LIGHT SOY SAUCE

3 tablespoons GRANULATED SUGAR

LUMPIA SIRIWA are easy to make; the ingredients for the filling differ, depending on market availability and the individual cook. Although I have used specific ingredients such as cabbage, carrots, and mung bean sprouts, you can substitute your favorite vegetables. Try to choose your ingredients according to color, texture, and flavor, so that the lumpia not only taste great but look beautiful as well. Often shredded, cooked, thinly sliced chicken or pork and shrimp are added to the filling, making the rolls more satisfying as a main dish. Feel free to experiment, because as the relaxed Filipinos say, "Anything goes!"

Roasted unsalted peanuts are widely available, and most of the time they are already peeled. However, if the skin is left on, put them in an oven set at 350°F for about 10 minutes. Then wrap them in a clean kitchen towel and roll them around. The skins should come off easily.

1. Heat the oil in a nonstick skillet over medium-high heat. Add the garlic and onion and stir-fry until the garlic is just golden and the onions are translucent, about 5 minutes. Add the scallions, cabbage, and carrots, and stir-fry until just wilted, about 7 minutes more. Add the mung bean sprouts and continue stir-frying until well mixed, about a minute. Do not overcook the sprouts; they should be just wilted but still firm. If you prefer, stir-fry them separately. Transfer the stir-fry to a bowl and allow to cool. Toss in half the crushed peanuts.

2. Place a crêpe in front of you on a clean work surface. Line the crêpe with a lettuce leaf or some mesclun so it sticks out a little from the rounded edge of the crêpe. Divide the stir-fry into 12 equal portions. Place one portion in the center of the crêpe vertically so that the vegetable pile is perpendicular to you. Fold the bottom of the crêpe over once, then fold in the sides. The bundle should look like a wrapped bouquet of flowers with one end open. Take one scallion strand and tie a knot around the lumpia a third of the way up from the folded bottom. Repeat the process until you have 12 rolls.

3. Dissolve the starch in ½ cup water and transfer to a saucepan. Add the soy sauce and sugar and bring to a boil over medium-high heat. Divide and transfer the sauce among 4 individual sauce dishes. Serve the *lumpia*, sprinkled with the remaining peanuts, with dipping sauce on the side.

Variation: If you wish to add chicken, pork tenderloin, or shrimp, or any combination of these, allow no more than 2 ounces per person. I suggest steaming these ingredients so they stay juicy and tender. Allow to cool and thinly slice the chicken or pork against the grain and halve the shrimp lengthwise, then proceed with step 2.

CHA GIO
VIETNAMESE SPRING ROLLS

MAKES ABOUT 40 ROLLS

One .7-ounce package dried
MUNG BEAN THREADS
(cellophane noodles)
1 ounce dried CLOUD EAR
MUSHROOMS
8 ounces GROUND PORK
(70 percent lean)
8 ounces CRABMEAT; or SHRIMP,
heads and shells removed,
deveined, and finely chopped
1 medium YELLOW ONION, peeled
and minced
1 large GARLIC CLOVE, peeled and
minced
3 CARROTS, peeled; 1 grated,
2 julienned
1 large EGG, lightly beaten
KOSHER SALT
Freshly ground BLACK PEPPER
40 or so triangular RICE PAPERS
VEGETABLE OIL for deep-frying
1 CUCUMBER, peeled, halved
lengthwise, seeded, and thinly
sliced crosswise
1 bunch MINT, leaves only
1 head BOSTON LETTUCE, leaves
separated and ribs removed
NUOC CHAM (page 100)

VIETNAMESE SPRING ROLLS, called *cha gio* in the south and *nem ran* in the north, are smaller than any other type of spring roll in Asia. They are made with rice paper instead of wheat wrappers. Filled with cellophane noodles, cloud ear mushrooms, and pork, they can also include crab or shrimp. These are commonly served with *nuoc cham*. In Cambodia, a similar roll called *lhord* is served with the same fish sauce and lime juice–based spicy dipping sauce garnished with crushed peanuts.

While rolling *cha gio*, stack them on a plate, covering each layer with plastic wrap to keep them from drying out. Deep-fry them a few at a time without crowding your pot. Serve them freshly fried. Any leftover fried rolls can be refrigerated or frozen, then reheated in a single layer on a cookie sheet in the oven at 375°F for 10 to 15 minutes. Turn them once.

1. Soak the cellophane noodles and cloud ear mushrooms in lukewarm water to cover until rehydrated and softened, about 30 minutes. Drain and squeeze the noodles and cloud ears to get rid of the excess water. Finely chop the noodles and cloud ears and put them in a bowl.

2. Add the ground pork, crab or shrimp, onion, garlic, the grated carrot, and egg, and season with salt and pepper. Mix the ingredients with your hands until evenly combined.

3. Pour lukewarm water about an inch deep into a flat square, rectangular, or round dish. Separate (be sure you do this step, or your papers will stick together) and soak three

to four wrappers at a time until pliable, about 5 minutes. Place a clean kitchen towel on your work surface, then place a triangle, rounded side near you, on the towel. With another kitchen towel, blot each wrapper until it is no longer wet but remains sticky. Place about a heaping teaspoon of filling an inch from the rounded edge and shape it like a tiny log. Fold the wrapper once over the filling, then fold in the sides and continue rolling tightly to the pointed end. Repeat this process with the remaining rice papers and filling.

4. Heat the oil in a wok or pot to 360° to 375°F over medium-high heat. Test the oil with one roll; the oil should sizzle around the roll but not so vigorously as to destroy it.

Fry a few rolls at a time, turning them once immediately to prevent them from sticking together, then turning them occasionally until golden on all sides, 3 to 5 minutes. Drain on paper towels.

5. Instruct your guests to wrap a roll with some julienned carrots, cucumber slices, and a few mint leaves inside a lettuce leaf, then dip in *nuoc cham*.

GOI CUON
SUMMER ROLLS

MAKES 12 ROLLS

4 ounces dried RICE VERMICELLI

4 ounces PORK TENDERLOIN

18 small to medium SHRIMP, heads and shells removed

12 round RICE PAPERS (about 8 inches in diameter)

1 head BOSTON LETTUCE, leaves separated and ribs removed

3 medium CARROTS, peeled and julienned

Half a CUCUMBER, peeled, halved lengthwise, seeded, and thinly sliced crosswise

3 SCALLIONS, root and dark green ends trimmed, and 6-inch stalks cut into 1-inch-long pieces and julienned

24 large MINT LEAVES

VIETNAMESE PEANUT SAUCE (page 99); or TUK TREY (page 100)

G OI CUON are a favorite appetizer in Vietnamese restaurants. They are fresh rolls of rice paper filled with tender lettuce, crunchy, sweet carrots, refreshing mint leaves, pungent scallions, and tender pork and shrimp. Some versions include fresh mung bean sprouts and cucumber as well. Goi cuon are served with a light peanut sauce called nuoc cham dau phong (sometimes referred to as nuoc leo). Cambodian restaurants also serve this tasty roll accompanied by a tangy, sweet, and spicy fish sauce dip with crushed peanuts called tuk trey.

While all the ingredients can be prepared ahead of time, the rice papers should be soaked just as you are making the rolls, and the rolls themselves should be made no more than an hour prior to serving for best results. If made too long in advance, the softened rice paper starts to dry out, making the rolls a bit chewy, often the main complaint from customers who order them in restaurants.

1. Place the dried rice vermicelli in a dish with water to cover. Let stand until pliable, about 30 minutes, and drain and squeeze them to get rid of the excess water.

2. Bring a pot of water to a boil over high heat. Place the vermicelli in a sieve and lower it into the boiling water for 5 seconds. Lift up the sieve, shake off the excess water, and transfer the vermicelli to a bowl. When it's cool enough to handle, divide the vermicelli into 12 portions. In the same boiling water, cook the pork tenderloin until well done but still juicy, 10 to 15 minutes. When it's cool enough to handle, thinly slice against the grain. You should have 24 to 36 thin

slices. Add the shrimp to the same pot of boiling water until they turn opaque, 1 to 2 minutes. Drain. When they're cool enough to handle, halve lengthwise and devein.

3. Pour lukewarm water about an inch deep into a flat round dish. Separate (be sure you do this step, or your papers will stick together) and soak three to four wrappers at a time until pliable, about 5 minutes. Place a clean kitchen towel on your work surface, then place each rice paper on the towel. With another kitchen towel, gently blot each wrapper until it is no longer wet but remains sticky. Leaving an inch uncovered on the side closest to you and the adjacent sides, place a lettuce leaf and a portion of vermicelli on top, followed by 2 to 3 overlapped pork slices, 3 overlapped shrimp halves, some carrots, cucumber, scallions, and 2 mint leaves on each rice paper. Fold the wrapper once over the filling, then fold in the sides and continue rolling tightly to the end. Repeat this process with the remaining ingredients to make 12 rolls. Cover the rolls with plastic wrap as you work and until ready to eat. Serve with peanut sauce or tuk trey.

Variation: Vegetarians can replace the pork and shrimp with fresh mung bean sprouts. You can also substitute cooked skinless chicken breast for the pork.

DAHN GUEN
CANTONESE EGG ROLLS

MAKES 24 ROLLS

1 tablespoon VEGETABLE OIL, plus
  more for deep-frying

1 large GARLIC CLOVE, crushed,
  peeled, and minced

3 SCALLIONS, root and dark green
  ends trimmed, and 6-inch stalks
  thinly sliced in rounds

10 large GREEN CABBAGE LEAVES,
  ribs removed, tender leaves
  julienned crosswise

2 medium CARROTS, peeled and
  julienned into 2-inch-long
  matchsticks

2 CELERY STALKS, strings pulled off
  and julienned into 2-inch-long
  strips

2 cups finely diced CANTONESE
  ROAST PORK (page 454)

KOSHER SALT

Freshly ground BLACK PEPPER

24 WONTON WRAPPERS
  (page 253); or commercial
  equivalent

2 EGGS, lightly beaten

SPICY SOY SAUCE DIP (page 88)

PLUM SAUCE (optional)

HEARTY EGG ROLLS are made with what are essentially large wonton wrappers. Filled with stir-fried vegetables—green cabbage, carrots, and celery—they often include finely diced leftover Cantonese roast pork. You can also use chicken, shrimp, or any protein you prefer. *Dahn guen* are great with a spicy soy sauce dip. You can also try the popular plum sauce (often referred to as "duck" sauce), available in any Chinese grocery store or well-stocked supermarket. Lee Kum Kee is a popular brand.

1. In a wok or nonstick skillet heat the oil over high heat. Stir-fry the garlic and scallions until the garlic just turns golden, about 2 minutes. Add the cabbage, carrots, celery, and roast pork, and continue to stir-fry until the vegetables are cooked through, about 5 minutes. Season with salt and pepper to taste, toss to distribute the ingredients evenly, and transfer to a platter. Allow to cool completely.

2. Heat enough oil for deep-frying in a pot over medium heat. Meanwhile, place a wonton wrapper on a clean work surface in front of you. Place the wrapper so it looks like a diamond with a point near you. Place a heaping tablespoon of filling 1½ inches in from the point near you. Spread it out so it forms a 3-inch log. Roll the wrapper over the filling once. Fold in the sides, then fold over twice more, leaving an edge open. Moisten the edge well with some egg wash and roll to the end to enclose the filling. Continue until you have 24 egg rolls. While rolling, it is important that you do not make the roll too tight or too loose. If too tight, the roll will crack open while it fries; if too loose, the oil will seep in during the frying process. Be sure to cover the rolls with plastic wrap as you work.

3. When the oil reaches 360° to 375°F, add the egg rolls a few at a time and deep-fry until golden crisp all around, about 2 minutes on each side. Drain on a paper towel–lined plate and serve with spicy soy sauce dip or plum sauce.

YAKI FU
PAN-FRIED WHEAT GLUTEN

MAKES 20 CAKES

2 tablespoons VEGETABLE OIL
20 fresh boiled WHEAT GLUTEN
   CAKES (pp. 290–91); or
   commercial equivalent
JAPANESE DARK SOY SAUCE
WASABI

Fu, WHEAT GLUTEN, is the protein of vegetarians. There are two types, which are specialties of Kyoto, Japan: *nama fu*, made from raw gluten only; or fu, made by kneading high-gluten flour dough (made with water) under running water to wash away all the starch. Usually sticky rice flour is added to the mix for a stickier texture. Although fu came to Japan by way of Buddhism, and therefore by way of China, the Japanese version is the most refined wheat gluten I have ever had. Walking through the Nishiki-Ichiba market in the old part of Kyoto, my interpreter, Hiroko, who that day had prepared for me the most delicious and colorful *yaki fu*—simply by pan-frying it and serving it sashimi style with soy sauce and *wasabi* on the side for dipping—took me to her favorite fu shop. There we found wonderful pink, green, and yellow squares of wheat gluten, flavored with herbs, tea, and cheese, respectively!

Dehydrated wheat gluten cakes can be purchased in Japanese markets or through mail-order sources (page 563). If using these, put them in a bowl with water to cover until rehydrated and softened. Gently squeeze each cake between the palms of your hands to get rid of excess water and then proceed with the recipe.

Working in batches, heat half the oil in a nonstick pan. Add 10 wheat gluten cakes and pan-fry until golden, 2 to 3 minutes on each side. Repeat with remaining oil and cakes. Divide the cakes among individual plates and serve with soy sauce and *wasabi* on the side.

MIEN GU
WHEAT GLUTEN CAKES

MAKES ABOUT 40 CAKES

4 cups CAKE FLOUR
1 teaspoon KOSHER SALT
VEGETABLE OIL for deep-frying
CHINESE LIGHT SOY SAUCE

WHEAT GLUTEN CAKES are called *mien gu* in China. They've been eaten since ancient times by Buddhist monks who substituted them for seafood, poultry, and meat in their cooking. Cake flour, which has a high gluten content, is preferable for making these chewy morsels. If you're up to the challenge, make this recipe. It will be hard work, for the dough is kneaded for about half an hour nonstop, first on a work surface (for this first step, you may want to use a mixer with dough hook), then under cold running water to wash out all the starch content of the dough, leaving you with a gummy, springy mass, which is the gluten. Occasionally, packaged wheat gluten powder is available in health food stores. If you can find it, use it as per the variation. In China, wheat gluten cakes are most often boiled or deep-fried, then added to soups and braised dishes. Deep-fried is one of my favorite versions, for it forms a somewhat crispy outer shell. I even like these pan-fried and dipped in soy sauce.

Mien gu can be found in the frozen food sections of Chinese markets, or canned, although the latter is less desirable, for it tastes a bit of tin.

1. Sift the flour and salt over a mixing bowl. Make a well in the center and add 1 cup water. With your fingers, slowly work the water into the flour; gradually add 1 more cup water. The dough should be smooth and somewhat firm but most definitely not stiff. Turn it out onto a lightly floured work surface. Knead the dough for about 15 minutes, pulling and punching it down on your work surface. If you have an electric mixer with a hook, you can use it for this step; knead the dough for about 5 minutes, but stop every once in a while so as not to burn out the motor. What you're looking for is a very elastic dough that is smooth to the touch. Return the dough to the bowl, cover it with a damp thin cotton kitchen towel, and allow it to rest to soften the dough and relax the gluten, 2 to 3 hours.

2. Place the dough on a plate or cutting board under cold running water. Press the dough with your hands to extract the starch, letting the starch run off into the sink. Repeat until the water runs clear, about 15 minutes. Left behind will be a springy, soft mass of gluten. Squeeze out any remaining water and roughly shape the gluten dough into a ½-inch-thick rectangle. Pull pieces of dough about ¾ inch in size.

3. Bring a pot of water to a boil over high heat. Add half the wheat gluten cakes, one piece at a time, and cook until they float to the top, about 5 minutes. Drain.

4. Heat enough oil for deep-frying in a wok or pot over medium heat until the temperature reaches 360° to 375°F. Working in batches, pat dry the remaining pieces and gently add them to the oil, one piece at a time. As they start to float, allow them to puff up and crisp all over, 2 to 3 minutes. They should be crispy and golden, not too light and not too dark. With a slotted spoon transfer the cakes to a paper towel–lined plate to drain. Serve hot with soy sauce on the side.

Variation: Mix together 2 cups wheat gluten powder, 1 teaspoon salt, and 1 cup water in the bowl of a mixer until well combined. Pull pieces of dough as per step 2 of the recipe, and follow steps 3 and 4 of the recipe.

LOK BAK GO
SAVORY RADISH CAKE

MAKES 2 OR 3 CAKES

4 dried CHINESE SWEET PORK
  SAUSAGES, quartered
  lengthwise, then finely sliced
  crosswise

5 SCALLIONS, root and dark green
  ends trimmed, and 6-inch stalks
  sliced crosswise into thin rounds

3 pounds DAIKON RADISH, peeled
  and finely shredded, juices
  reserved

¼ cup small DRIED SHRIMP, finely
  chopped

KOSHER SALT

Freshly ground BLACK PEPPER

3 cups RICE FLOUR

CANOLA OIL for pan-frying

CHINESE LIGHT SOY SAUCE

OYSTER SAUCE

CHILI AND GARLIC SAUCE
  (page 106)

EVERY YEAR during the Chinese Lunar New Year we start the celebration at breakfast with this tasty savory radish (daikon) cake, sometimes also called "pudding." The radish is grated and cooked with rice flour and a bit of water to a pastelike consistency. Steamed with dried Chinese sweet pork sausage, scallions, and bits of dried shrimp for added color, texture, and flavor, it rests overnight, refrigerated. The savory lok bak go is sliced and pan-fried until golden crisp and served with a side of soy sauce or oyster sauce and chili and garlic sauce.

This recipe makes three 7-inch-diameter by 2-inch-deep cakes; or two 9-inch-diameter by 1½-inch-deep cakes. If you do not have a triple-tier steamer, you can steam the cakes one at a time.

1. Heat a pot over medium heat. Stir-fry the sausages until the fat is rendered and the sausages are lightly crisped, 5 to 7 minutes. Add the scallions and stir-fry for 2 minutes. Add the daikon with its juices, 1 cup water, and the dried shrimp and stir to distribute the ingredients evenly. Lightly season with salt and pepper. Reduce the heat to medium-low and cook until the daikon becomes translucent, 20 to 25 minutes.

2. Meanwhile, whisk together the rice flour and 2 cups water until you have a smooth batter. Remove the cooked daikon mixture from the heat and stir into the rice flour batter until well mixed.

3. Place a wok filled halfway with water over high heat. Place a triple-tier bamboo steamer with a lid in the wok. While steam fills the steamer, fill three 7-inch-diameter by 2-inch-deep cake pans with the daikon and rice batter mixture. Place a filled cake pan on each of the three bamboo racks, cover with the lid, and steam until the cakes are translucent or a knife inserted in the center comes out clean, 25 to 30 minutes. Remove the cakes from each rack, carefully pour off the excess water from each cake pan, and allow each cake to cool completely. Cover the cakes with plastic wrap and refrigerate overnight.

4. Carefully loosen the edges of the cakes with a knife blade, flip the cakes onto a clean surface such as a cutting board, then cut into ¼-inch-thick slices. As you get to the middle of the pudding, cut the slices in half

crosswise. Heat the oil in a nonstick skillet and pan-fry the slices until golden crisp and heated through, 3 to 5 minutes per side. Serve with soy sauce, oyster sauce, or chili and garlic sauce for dipping.

A PROFESSIONAL CALLIGRAPHER SELLS HIS ART DURING CHINESE NEW YEAR.

CHAR SIU BAO
ROAST PORK BUNS

1 tablespoon VEGETABLE OIL

3 SCALLIONS, root and dark green ends trimmed, and 6-inch stalks thinly sliced

3 cups finely diced CANTONESE ROAST PORK (page 454)

1½ tablespoons GRANULATED SUGAR

3 tablespoons CHINESE LIGHT SOY SAUCE

3 tablespoons OYSTER SAUCE

1 teaspoon TAPIOCA STARCH or CORNSTARCH

1½ tablespoons SHAOXING WINE

12 SPONGY BUNS (page 259)

12 pieces of PARCHMENT PAPER, cut into 2-inch squares

CHAR SIU BAO, Cantonese roast pork buns, are created with the trimmings or leftovers from Cantonese roast pork. Roast pork buns are served steamed, in two-bite-size versions at dim sum restaurants. When served as an afternoon snack, they are made twice the size and baked or steamed. A popular teahouse specialty, both versions are delicious. When steamed, the seam of the dumpling faces up; the bun opens like a flower and the caramelized red pork is revealed. Sometimes the buns are steamed with the seam down and the top snipped with scissors in a crisscross pattern, so when cooked four little dough points puff up. When the buns are baked in a 375°F oven for about 20 minutes, the seam is down and the top is brushed with an egg-yolk-and-sugar-water combination.

1. Heat the vegetable oil in a non-stick skillet over medium-high heat. Add the scallions and stir-fry for a minute. Add the roast pork, sugar, soy sauce, and oyster sauce and continue cooking until the scallions have softened and the pork is heated through, about 3 minutes. Dissolve the cornstarch with the Shaoxing wine and a tablespoon of water in a cup. Add it to the pork stir-fry and continue cooking until the sauce thickens, about a minute. Remove from the heat and allow to cool.

2. Place a ball of spongy bun dough in the palm of one hand and, with the thumb of your other hand, make a well in the center. Fill the well with about 2 tablespoons pork filling, then seal the filling by pinching the dough twice, bringing the two opposite sides together toward the center. Place the bun, pinched side up, on a piece of parchment paper. (Or pinch the dough until the filling is completely enclosed and place the bun pinched side down on the paper. With scissors, snip the smooth top side of the bun twice in a crisscross pattern.) Repeat the process until you have 12 buns.

3. Fill the bottom third of a wok with water and bring to a boil over high heat. Meanwhile, place the pork buns, on their papers, on a bamboo rack so they do not touch one another. They should be 1 inch or more apart to allow the steam to come through and the buns to double in volume. The size of your steamer will determine how many buns you can steam at a time. Place the bamboo rack in the wok, cover securely, and steam until the buns are cooked through, about 12 minutes.

BANH BEO
QUAIL EGG AND
PORK BUNS

MAKES 12 BUNS

1 tablespoon VEGETABLE OIL

2 large GARLIC CLOVES, crushed, peeled, and minced

4 SCALLIONS, root and dark green ends trimmed, and 6-inch stalks thinly sliced

8 ounces GROUND PORK (70 percent lean)

10 NAPA CABBAGE LEAVES, finely chopped

1½ tablespoons FISH SAUCE

1½ tablespoons OYSTER SAUCE

2 teaspoons GRANULATED SUGAR

1 teaspoon TAPIOCA STARCH or CORNSTARCH

KOSHER SALT

Freshly ground BLACK PEPPER

12 QUAIL EGGS, boiled and peeled

12 SPONGY BUNS (page 259)

12 pieces PARCHMENT PAPER, cut into 2-inch squares

BANH BEO are a popular Vietnamese snack similar to classic Chinese *char siu bao* (page 294). Filled with ground pork, cabbage, and hard-boiled egg, they are delicious and satisfying, and often eaten as a quick lunch. You can use regular chicken eggs, but I prefer to use quail eggs, which are available in gourmet markets. When you bite into a quail egg–filled steamed *banh beo*, the whole tiny egg reveals itself, making for an especially refined and delicate presentation.

1. Heat the vegetable oil in a wok or nonstick skillet over medium-high heat. Stir-fry the garlic and scallions until fragrant and lightly golden, about 3 minutes. Add the pork and cabbage and continue to stir-fry, breaking down the pork, until cooked through, about 5 minutes. Stir together the fish sauce, oyster sauce, sugar, and tapioca starch in a bowl until the sugar is completely dissolved and the tapioca is diluted. No lumps should be visible. Add the mixture to the pork stir-fry and continue cooking until the sauce thickens, about a minute. Adjust seasoning with salt and pepper to taste. Remove from the heat and allow to cool.

2. Place a ball of spongy bun dough in the palm of one hand and, with the thumb of your other hand, make a well in the center. Fill the well with about 1½ teaspoons pork filling followed by a quail egg and topped with another 1½ teaspoons pork filling. Seal the filling by pinching the dough toward the center. Place the bun pinched side down on a piece of parchment paper. Repeat the process until you have 12 buns.

3. Fill the bottom third of a wok with water and bring to a boil over high heat. Meanwhile, place the pork dumplings, on their papers, on a bamboo rack so they do not touch one another. They should be 1 inch or more apart to allow the steam to come through and the buns to double in volume. The size of your steamer will determine how many buns you can steam at a time. Place the bamboo rack in the wok, cover securely, and steam until the buns are cooked through, about 12 minutes.

BANH CUON
STEAMED RICE SHEETS WITH
PORK AND MUSHROOMS

MAKES 24 ROLLS

¼ cup dried CLOUD EAR
    MUSHROOMS

12 ounces GROUND PORK
    (70 percent lean)

1 tablespoon FISH SAUCE

1 teaspoon GRANULATED SUGAR

1 tablespoon VEGETABLE OIL

1 large GARLIC CLOVE, crushed,
    peeled, and minced

2 SCALLIONS, root and dark green
    ends trimmed, and 6-inch stalks
    minced

Twenty-four 3-inch-square or
    -round fresh RICE SHEETS
    (page 262); or commercial
    equivalent

FRIED SCALLIONS WITH OIL
    (page 108)

NUOC CHAM (page 100)

A VIETNAMESE CLASSIC, BANH CUON are essentially raviolis. Thin rice sheets are filled with stir-fried ground pork and cloud ear mushrooms and steamed. Drizzled with scallion oil and dipped in nuoc cham, a tangy, spicy fish sauce, banh cuon make for a delicate appetizer.

If you do not want to make the rice sheets yourself, purchase fresh rice sheets from Chinese or Southeast Asian markets.

1. Put the mushrooms in a bowl with hot water to cover, then set a plate over the bowl to prevent steam from escaping. Let stand until the mushrooms rehydrate and soften, about 30 minutes (or longer, depending on the size of the mushrooms). Squeeze the mushrooms between the palms of your hands to get rid of the excess water. Using a paring knife, remove any hard stems from the mushrooms. Mince the mushrooms and transfer them to a bowl with the ground pork, fish sauce, and sugar. Mix thoroughly and allow to marinate for 30 minutes at room temperature.

2. Heat the oil in a wok or nonstick pan over high heat. Stir-fry the garlic and scallions until the garlic turns light golden. Add the pork mixture and continue stir-frying, breaking down the ground pork with a spatula, until cooked, about 5 minutes.

3. If you plan to make the rice sheets yourself, now is a good time, as they should be freshly made, not refrigerated. To assemble banh cuon, spoon a heaping tablespoon of pork filling in the center of each sheet. Fold the sheet over the filling once, fold in the sides, and continue to roll to the end to enclose the filling. Repeat this process until you have 24 rolls. Drizzle with the scallions and their oil and serve nuoc cham on the side for dipping.

4. To reheat banh cuon, fill the bottom third of a wok with water, fit a bamboo steamer with a lid in the wok, and place the wok over high heat. When the water boils, place a plate filled with banh cuon on the steamer rack, cover the steamer, and steam until the filling is heated through, about 5 minutes. Serve with the dips on the side.

HAAR CHEUNG
RICE ROLLS WITH SHRIMP

MAKES 24 ROLLS

1 tablespoon CHINESE LIGHT SOY
  SAUCE
1 tablespoon SHAOXING WINE
2 teaspoons GINGER EXTRACT
  (page 74)
1 teaspoon TAPIOCA STARCH or
  CORNSTARCH
½ teaspoon SESAME OIL
Freshly ground BLACK PEPPER
1 pound BLUE TIGER SHRIMP,
  heads and shells removed,
  deveined, and minced
Twenty-four 3-inch-square fresh
  RICE SHEETS (page 262); or
  commercial equivalent
SPICY SOY SAUCE DIP (page 88)

"HAAR CHEUNG," calls out the woman passing by with her stainless steel cart containing dozens of stacked bamboo steamers. In crowded dim sum restaurants, where strangers share tables, fingers are held high in the air as a sign that her steamed rice rolls are wanted. Before she runs out, I quickly ask for *haar cheung*, rice sheets rolled around plump shrimp—my favorite. Other types are filled with diced Cantonese roast pork or marinated ground beef, and these go quickly. When we're not going to Chinatown for dim sum, my husband often asks me to make *haar cheung* on weekends. I oblige, for they are exquisite, especially with an herb-infused spicy soy sauce dip, a family recipe.

Fresh rice sheets are readily available from Chinese or Southeast Asian markets.

1. Whisk together the soy sauce, wine, ginger extract, and tapioca starch until the starch is diluted and no lumps are visible. Stir in the sesame oil, season with black pepper, and add the minced shrimp. Mix (I suggest using your fingers) to incorporate the ingredients thoroughly. Refrigerate for an hour.

2. Meanwhile, if you plan to make the rice sheets yourself, now is a good time, as they should be freshly made, not refrigerated. To assemble the rolls, spoon 2 heaping tablespoons of shrimp, one next to the other, about 1 inch from the short edge of the sheet in a straight line. Fold the rice sheet over the filling once and continue rolling to the end. Repeat this process until you have all 24 rolls. Cut each roll in half crosswise and arrange an equal amount of small rolls on individual plates in a single layer.

3. Fill the bottom third of a wok with water and bring to a boil over high heat. Arrange the *haar cheung* on a plate set into a bamboo steamer. Place the steamer, covered, over the wok and steam until the filling is cooked through, about 5 minutes. Serve with spicy soy sauce dip on the side.

HAAR GAO
CRYSTAL SHRIMP
DUMPLINGS

MAKES 40 DUMPLINGS

White of 1 medium EGG

1 tablespoon CHINESE THIN SOY
SAUCE

1 tablespoon SHAOXING WINE

1 teaspoon GRANULATED SUGAR

1 teaspoon TAPIOCA STARCH or
CORNSTARCH

½ teaspoon SESAME OIL

KOSHER SALT

Freshly ground WHITE PEPPER

8 ounces fresh BLUE TIGER
SHRIMP, shelled, deveined,
and finely chopped

1 ounce PORK FATBACK, minced
(about 2 tablespoons)

2 ounces BAMBOO SHOOTS,
minced (about ¼ cup)

3 fresh WATER CHESTNUTS, peeled
and finely chopped (optional)

CRYSTAL DUMPLING WRAPPERS
(pp. 260–61)

NAPA CABBAGE or ICEBERG
LETTUCE LEAVES

CHILI AND GARLIC SAUCE
(page 106)

SPICY SOY SAUCE DIP (page 88)

C ANTONESE *HAAR GAO* are the classic crystal shrimp dumpling and a very popular item in dim sum restaurants. When steamed, the skin becomes translucent, revealing the pink color of the shrimp. Traditionally, bamboo, and sometimes water chestnuts, is added to the shrimp filling for their crunchy texture. Unless the water chestnuts are available fresh, I omit them, for the canned versions have not a whit of sweet natural flavor. The translucency and texture of the dumpling skin come from a combination of wheat starch (not flour), tapioca starch, and sticky "glutinous" rice flour. Once you've learned how to make the dough and shape the dumplings, the possibilities are endless. The dough makes about 40 skins, approximately 2½ inches in diameter.

Fresh bamboo shoots are available in Asian markets with their sheath (leaves) on and need to be cleaned; or they are sold already boiled and cleaned. Either is an excellent choice. If you buy fresh shoots, peel them first, then boil them for 10 minutes to get rid of the natural toxins. If only canned are available, buy the whole shoots. As bamboo has the ability to absorb flavors well, canned shoots tend to have a hint of tin when eaten. To get rid of this unpleasant tin taste, boil the shoot for 5 minutes prior to using.

1. Whisk together the egg white, soy sauce, Shaoxing wine, and sugar in a bowl until the egg white loosens and the sugar completely dissolves. Whisk in the tapioca starch, then the sesame oil; season with salt and pepper. (Be sure not to oversalt, as the dumplings are generally eaten dipped in soy sauce.) Add the shrimp, pork fat, bamboo shoot, and water chestnuts (if using), and mix thoroughly. Cover and place the bowl in the refrigerator to allow the flavors to develop, about 2 hours.

2. Take a wrapper and make pleats on one half side, pinching from opposite ends toward the center to form a pouch. Place 1½ teaspoons shrimp filling inside the pouch. Pinch the center of the unfolded half of the skin to the center of the folded half. Fold the pointy ends in front of the pleated side of the dumpling to secure the filling. Repeat this process until you have formed 40 dumplings.

3. Fill the bottom third of a wok with water and bring to a boil over high heat. Meanwhile, line a bamboo steamer rack with 2 napa cabbage or iceberg lettuce leaves. Place the shrimp dumplings about ¼ inch apart on the leaves to allow the steam to come through and cook the dumplings evenly. The size of your steamer will determine how many dumplings you can steam at a time. Place the bamboo rack in the wok, cover securely, and steam until the dumplings become translucent and the shrimp filling turns pink, about 5 minutes. Serve with a selection of dipping sauces such as chili and garlic sauce and spicy soy sauce dip.

MY FAVORITE THING to do on Sundays is to go *yum cha,* or drink tea. Traditionally this means to eat dim sum and sip chrysanthemum-scented tea. While the waitresses push their stainless-steel carts around to crowded tables, flying fingers point to the delicious morsels. We all have our favorites, and my husband's is *haar gao.* He just can't seem to get enough of these crystal shrimp dumplings. Although they seem complicated to make, they're no more difficult than Italian pasta; and they are only a bit more time-consuming. Once I set out to make dumplings, I generally invite friends over to share the work of making these as well as ginger and pork dumplings (pp. 268–69), Shanghainese spring rolls (pp. 272–73), and perhaps the Chinese radish cakes (pp. 292–93). This is the perfect way to spend a Sunday morning for a rewarding afternoon meal.

JAI GAO
CRYSTAL VEGETABLE
DUMPLINGS

MAKES 40 DUMPLINGS

Half a .7-ounce package dried
MUNG BEAN THREADS
(cellophane noodles)

1 pound PEA SHOOTS, leaves only

8 fresh medium SHIITAKE
MUSHROOMS, stems removed
and caps wiped clean

1 tablespoon CHINESE LIGHT SOY
SAUCE

1 tablespoon SHAOXING WINE

½ teaspoon SESAME OIL

1 teaspoon TAPIOCA STARCH or
CORNSTARCH

KOSHER SALT

Freshly ground BLACK PEPPER

CRYSTAL DUMPLING WRAPPERS,
regular or spinach version
(pp. 260–61)

NAPA CABBAGE or ICEBERG
LETTUCE LEAVES

CHILI AND GARLIC SAUCE
(page 106)

GINGER-INFUSED VINEGAR
DIPPING SAUCE (page 89)

SPICY SOY SAUCE DIP (page 88)

EVERY ONCE IN A WHILE, I like to have a vegetarian meal. *Jai gao*, or crystal vegetable dumplings, are filled with shiitake mushrooms and Asian greens such as pea shoots, which happen to be my favorite because the leaves are so tender. Cellophane noodles, used in many parts of Asia, are enjoyed for their texture as well as their absorption capabilities. The Vietnamese call them Chinese noodles.

Mung bean threads come in packages of various sizes, the smallest individual package weighing about .7 ounces, of which you will use only half here. If you cannot find pea shoots, baby spinach is a delicious substitute.

1. Soak the cellophane noodles in lukewarm water to cover in a bowl until rehydrated and softened, about 30 minutes. Drain and squeeze the noodles to get rid of the excess water. Bring a pot of water to a boil over high heat and cook the noodles until they turn transparent, 2 to 5 minutes. Drain, rinse under cold running water, and drain again. Mince the noodles and transfer to a bowl.

2. Bring a pot of salted water to a boil over high heat and blanch the pea shoots until they wilt, less than a minute. In the same pot blanch the shiitakes, about 2 minutes. When cool enough to handle, mince the pea shoots and shiitakes. Add to the noodles and toss to distribute the ingredients evenly.

3. Combine the soy sauce, wine, sesame oil, and cornstarch in a sep-

arate bowl and stir until the cornstarch has dissolved completely and the mixture looks creamy caramel in color. Add to the vegetable and noodle filling and toss to coat evenly. Adjust seasoning with salt and pepper to taste.

4. Place 2 teaspoons vegetable-noodle filling in the center of a wrapper. Fold the skin to form a crescent, but pinch together only one third of it. Take the center of the unsealed edge and with your thumb and forefinger pinch it to the sealed edge at the center of the dumpling. You should have a three-seamed dumpling. Seal the remaining edges to secure the filling. Repeat the process until you have 40 dumplings.

5. Fill the bottom third of a wok with water and bring to a boil over high heat. Meanwhile, line a bamboo steamer rack with 2 napa cabbage or iceberg lettuce leaves. Place the vegetable dumplings on the leaves so that they do not touch each other. They should be about ¼ inch apart to allow the steam to come through and cook them evenly. The size of your steamer will determine how many dumplings you can steam at a time. Place the bamboo rack inside the wok, cover the steamer securely, and steam until the dumplings become translucent, about 5 minutes. Serve with a selection of dipping sauces.

4

VEGETABLES

AND

HERBS

ASIA EN-
JOYS MUCH MORE diversity in its
vegetables than does the West, so
much so that choices can seem
overwhelming. From the indigenous species of the Pacific seacoasts
to those that accompanied historical
influxes from the Central Asian
plains, from those of the ancient
trade routes of the southern island
archipelagoes to those introduced
by international cross-cultural influences from the medieval to the
modern era, the kinds of vegetables
available to cooks are staggering.
Vegetables commonly used in the
Asian kitchen and now available
globally include napa cabbage (*siu
choy*), mustard cabbage (*gai choy*),
water spinach (*ong choy*), white- and
green-stemmed bok choy, Chinese
broccoli (*gai lan*), flowering oil seed
rape (*yau choy*), garlic chives (*gau

choy), mung bean sprouts (*nga choy*),
pea shoots (*dau mui*), yard-long
beans (*bak dau gok*), snow peas (*hoh lan
dau*), winter melon (*tung gwa*), fuzzy
melon (*tseet gwa*), bitter melon (*fu
gwa*), Asian eggplant (*ai gwa*), white
radish (*lok bak*), and bamboo (*chuk
sun*). A myriad more are found only
in Asia but not exported, and still
more are found in limited locales
and used to create specific regional
dishes. The Western cook attempt-
ing to understand the subject need
not feel lost, however. A few key
points of explanation will go a long
way toward understanding.

PREPARATION TECHNIQUES AND VEGETABLE TYPES

ASIAN VEGETABLES are heat-cooked,
cured, and served raw. Heat cooking
is the most familiar to the Western
cook: fresh vegetables are stir-fried,
pan-fried, deep-fried, added to
soups, braised, steamed, or boiled.
Pickling is primarily achieved with
vinegar, together with salt and
sugar, and pickles hold a much
larger place in Asian cooking than in
any Western cuisine. Vegetables are
also preserved by salting, air drying,
or fermentation, with or without
added spices and grains. It is quite

common, for example, to have containers of pickled or fermented vegetables in the Asian pantry, to use
them almost daily, and to integrate
them into an enormously wide
array of dishes.

In this chapter I provide a number
of Asian vegetable recipes and a
sense of the principles underlying
the techniques required to prepare
them. From there, it is possible to
understand regional and national
variations—some of these being as
simple as substituting fish sauce for
soy sauce in the stir-fry, others being
more complex. Specific dishes fo-
cusing on the unique attributes of
particular vegetables are also included.

HEAT COOKING

FIRE UP A WOK, add a little oil, stir-
fry some garlic, add some leafy
green vegetables, season with a bit
of salt or soy sauce, and occasionally
a light sprinkle of sugar. After 5
to 10 minutes (depending on the
vegetable), you will have bright
green, firm yet tender, savory yet
mildly sweet vegetables that complement virtually any Asian meat or
seafood dish. This is not only easy,
but, in fact, the preferred method of
fresh vegetable preparation among
many Chinese cooks. It points to a

ASIAN GREENS LIKE THIS BEAUTIFUL AMARANTH ARE SIMPLY STIR-FRIED WITH OIL AND GARLIC AND SEASONED WITH SALT, FISH SAUCE, OR SOY SAUCE.

traditional celebration of the harvest and is an important part of the fundamental *fan tsai* system of organizing all foods. In this system, grains (*fan*) are seen as a neutral element, while vegetables, meat, poultry, and seafood (*tsai*) have specific *yin yang* attributes that must be balanced (see "Fundamentals" chapter, page 43). In its simplest terms the *fan tsai* system holds that a straightforward stir-fried green will always be seen as balancing a meal, as a chance to experience its natural flavor, and as a buffer to spicy, sweet, and savory seafood or meat dishes. In the larger perspective, every vegetable (indeed, every food) has specific attributes, and in correct combination with other foods, leads to a proper (i.e., nutritious, health-giving/health-preserving, and even "emotionally" balanced) dining experience. As it is in China, so it is in most of Asia.

In Vietnam and Cambodia, for example, vegetables are quickly stir-fried in the Chinese manner. In Korea, mung beans and spinach (a common combination) are often stir-fried with salt and a bit of sesame oil. In Japan, a simple vegetable stir-fry is seasoned with soy sauce, sugar, and mirin (sweet sake). These are, in turn, eaten with rice.

In Indonesia, Thailand, and other countries, vegetable dishes can also be complex, reflecting Indian and other culinary influences. Indonesian *gado gado*, for example, combines vegetables and fruit with peanut sauce. Thai *som tam malako*, green papaya salad, is also eaten in Vietnam (*goi du du*) and the Philippines (*ensal-*

adang papaya). The Chinese-American restaurant concoction of stir-fried mixed vegetables—often including bell peppers, bamboo, carrots, onions, tomatoes, cauliflower, and other similar combinations—is an abomination. Often referred to as Buddha's Delight, it can be described as the name that contains two lies. More is not better; balance is.

Go a bit deeper into the subject of Asian vegetables and the yin yang principle appears. In this system (also expressed as the Chinese "hot-cold" system of food) the majority of vegetables are classified as yin (also female, dark, or cold). Accordingly, other items (such as meat) are understood to be yang (also male, bright, or hot). The idea is to stir-fry items from each of the two categories to achieve a balance, then serve this balanced dish with rice. The Western cook can regard vegetables as a separate dish among many such dishes, or cook them in combination with other food. Either way, they are meant to be an integral part of every meal.

Cultural, regional, and religious differences are manifested in stir-frying, too. The Chinese may stir-fry green vegetables with soy sauce, for example, while Southeast Asians will stir-fry the same items with fish sauce. Strict vegetarian Buddhist monks anywhere must avoid fish-based items, so they use soy sauce or sea salt.

Aside from stir-frying, heat cooking also includes deep-frying, braising, steaming, and blanching/boiling. Stuffed slices of gourds, for example, are sometimes pan-fried so the filling will not fall out during the cooking process. Cooking leafy greens by blanching them in a bath of water with small amounts of vegetable oil is also a popular Chinese method of preparation, the oil lending a beautiful sheen to the vegetables. Prepared this way, greens are usually topped with a drizzle or two of oyster sauce straight from the bottle, or oyster sauce diluted with chicken stock or Shaoxing wine, then thickened with a small amount of tapioca starch.

More developed versions of heat-cooked vegetable dishes also exist, often including a protein in the mix. A bit of pork always adds flavor; so does dried shrimp. (Do not be surprised if you order a vegetable dish other than stir-fried Chinese broccoli and find minced pork in the sauce. This is done both to enrich the dish and to correct its yin aspect.) Other stir-fried greens are sometimes topped with a lobster or crab sauce (a thickened whitish sauce of rich chicken stock, tapioca starch, and finely shredded lobster or crab). In the Asian mind, these are all important aspects of vegetable dishes. Vegetables such as water spinach or pea shoots (pea pod leaves) are also stir-fried with fermented tofu, a favorite among the Chinese and the Vietnamese both.

Wild vegetables and ferns (often collected from the mountains), leafy turnip greens, and other root vegetable tops (sweet potato, for example) are also prepared. With a little imagination, the Western cook can also enjoy these. Red beets, for example, are now often found in Western markets with their delicious broad green leaves intact. (I'm hoping that the turnip tops and sweet potato leaves will follow suit.) These leaves and tops can be simply braised or stir-fried. Served at room temperature or just barely chilled, they are a few of the many accompaniments to a bowl of rice and a bowl of broth.

Bean curd cakes share the same heat-cooking preparation as leafy vegetables. They can be steamed plain, with black bean and garlic sauce, or stuffed with shrimp. They can be sliced and pan-fried, or cubed and deep-fried, and served with dipping sauces.

CURING

AIR-CURED, SALT-CURED, pickled—in vinegar or citrus brine—and preserved or fermented—in salt brines with or without spices and grains—vegetables have been around for millennia in Asia, and at least 3,000 years in China. Lasting for months (and sometimes years!), cured vegetables were historically indispensable for getting through the cold winter months when no fresh vegetables were available. A full accounting of the different types and techniques would fill a book twice the size of this one, but it is possible for the Western cook interested in the tradition to get a sense of the subject without exhaustive study. In Chinese cooking, for example, preserved vegetables in ceramic containers, glass jars, or vacuum-sealed plastic packages may include such common items as black beans (i.e., oxidized soybeans) in salt, bamboo shoots, Asian white radish (daikon), cucumber, garlic, and shallots. These and other items, displayed in huge plastic or metal vats, are sold by the piece or pound to individuals or volume users such as restaurants.

China—especially northern China and northern Central Asia, where long cold winters prevail and growing seasons are limited—was one of the first cultures to experiment with preservation techniques, and a great number of recipes incorporating preserved vegetables are still in common use today. They generally call for out-of-season items in stir-fries, stews, and soups, and serve occasionally as the main ingredient. The very first preserved vegetables were salted and air-dried, then rehydrated and softened in water prior to use. Vegetables preserved in brine do not need to be rehydrated but are soaked in several changes of water to remove excess salt before cooking. Some vegetables are preserved in small to generous amounts of oil, herbs, and spices. They function as convenience foods ("direct from jar to table"), as condiments, and as side dishes.

Classic Chinese recipes employing preserved vegetables include hot and sour soup (page 127), in which both dried and rehydrated cloud ears and lily buds are used for texture; stir-fried Swatow mustard cabbage with beef (page 335); and stir-fried water spinach with fermented bean curd (pp. 324–25), a specialty also enjoyed in Vietnam. These dishes use cured ingredients to emphasize their unique flavors, textures, and other attributes. The fermented bean curd called fu yu, for example, as used in the water spinach stir-fry, has a concentrated flavor, more pronounced than regular bean curd. It is so transformed in the curing process that it is hardly recognizable as tofu and is as pungent as fish sauce.

Red chilies appeared in Asia with the arrival of the colonial Spanish and Portuguese during the sixteenth century. Because Szechwan was already versed in the use of spices, including the mildly hot spice known as fagara (Szechwan peppercorns), the newer, hotter pepper brought from European colonies in the Americas was received with great enthusiasm. Chilies, along with other spices such as ginger, star anise, fennel, and licorice, turned vegetables into delectable spicy preserved items known generically as cha tsai. One of my favorites is the spicy kohlrabi. Salty and covered in red chili powder and flakes, it looks like a wrinkled, roundish knob the size of an orange. Rinsed prior to using like many pickles in China, it is sliced up and added to cold noodles for a pungent note. I've even added some to fried rice for a crunchy texture.

By comparison, only a very few of these preserved vegetables, with the exception of Chinese fermented bean curd, are used in Vietnam, and to a lesser extent in Southeast Asia. In these warmer climates with long growing seasons, lightly pickled items are more the norm. A good

This tsukemono shop in Tokyo offers dozens of pickled vegetables from which to choose.

example is the very standard combination of cucumber, carrot, and daikon, which are sliced, salt-drained, and pickled in rice vinegar and sugar. While these simple pickled vegetables originated in China (you might be served these as something to nibble on and hold you over for the numerous dishes to follow during a Chinese banquet), the Vietnamese and Cambodians also serve them with grilled meat or fish and rice. In Thailand, a sweet cucumber relish is made by boiling vinegar and sugar to a syrupy consistency and adding diced cucumber, chopped chilies, and sliced shallots. This is served alongside deep-fried fish cakes. Lightly pickled items also often accompany the popular Thai satays, available in Western Thai restaurants everywhere. Chinese preserved Swatow mustard cabbage is also popular in Thailand. One of my favorite dishes is the Thai curry soup called khao soi (pp. 240–41). Thinly sliced, the cabbage is served on the side with lime wedges and thinly sliced raw shallots; the garnishes are an integral part of the dish. Other simple salt-brine or vinegar-preserved items include garlic and shallots, which are nibbled on during meals.

JAPANESE AND KOREAN PRESERVED VEGETABLE CULTURES

THE CHINESE and Southeast Asians often have pickled cucumber, daikon, and carrot served with rice and a protein dish for a simple lunch. In Japan and Korea, where a meal comprises dozens of small dishes, preserved vegetables (including pickles) take on a more focused and important role at meals. As such, they have evolved into a separate and distinct part of the culinary culture; a way of cooking as common and integrated into the cuisine as the preparation of any other food item. In other words, pickles and rice are to the Japanese and Korean what cheese and bread are to the French.

TSUKEMONO

THE JAPANESE TECHNIQUES of preserving vegetables started in ancient times as a means to make certain foods last through the harsh winter months. Japanese preserved or pickled vegetables are referred to as tsukemono. As in China, it was not unusual to eat a bowl of rice accompanied by only these preserved vegetables and occasionally a bowl of clear soup. There are hundreds of types to choose from, the most common being napa cabbage, daikon, cucumber, and eggplant (the most desirable of all, and best had in autumn). Traditionally, preserving vegetables was usually done at home or in small shops. Today, however, as is so often the case the world over, artisanal production has been pushed aside for factory-made products produced in mass quantities and compromising quality for lower prices, especially in big cities. Commercial versions of daikon and ginger, for example, are sometimes enhanced with neon-like colors: yellow for daikon, and pink for ginger. (When pickling ginger in salt and rice vinegar, you will notice that the ginger turns a subtle pinkish color naturally.) Packed in large wooden barrels, ceramic jars, or vacuum sealed in plastic packages, tsukemono are preserved mostly in salt brine and rice bran, which encourages the fermentation process.

All vegetables are cured using one (and sometimes two) of several techniques. Shio-zuke is basically salt curing and is the simplest, most common technique. Sliced and sprinkled liberally with salt, vegetables are layered in wooden barrels and weighted down with a ceramic or stone weight. This process draws out the natural juices of the vegetable, which is left to cure for various periods of time. A popular homemade variety is cucumber, curing in an hour or so. If eaten directly from the barrel, salted vegetables must first be rinsed. If they are not eaten at this point, they can undergo a second preservation method called su-zuke (pickling), in which the vegetables are transferred to a low-acidity rice vinegar and sugar liquid. My favorite of these is pickled ginger, which I enjoy in between each bite of sashimi (raw fish) as a palate cleanser and to counteract the oily taste of the fish. Other simple preserving methods are shoyu-zuke in which the vegetables are cured in sweet sake or mirin and soy sauce; and kasu-zuke, using sake, sugar, and salt as the preserving agents.

Still more elaborate techniques of preservation exist. Because they are quite involved, they are now usually left to specialists. In Japan these specialty items are purchased from the pickle shop, where there is an endless array of preserved vegetables to choose from. These shops are usually set up in dark cool places, which generally means the basement level of Japan's food markets.

The more complex types are nuka-zuke, using dry rice bran (nuka, available at Japanese markets), and nukamiso-zuke, employing a combination of rice bran and miso. In the latter, nukamiso is made by mashing together rice bran and soybean paste, which is then left to ferment (or ripen) for about ten days, stirred once a day (or every twenty-four hours). Only after this complex process can the nukamiso-zuke be used. A wide array of vegetables can then be pickled with the paste, usually being ready to serve in only a few hours; afterward, the complex fermented paste can be reused for new batches of vegetables. Nuka-zuke and nukamiso-zuke often include red chili flakes in the mix as well, resulting in more pungent types of preserved vegetables.

I ate many wonderful preserved vegetables in Japan; some of the most memorable ones were at Yoshi-Ima Ryokan, a traditional inn in the heart of Kyoto. My breakfast and dinner consisted of a bowl of rice, broth, and all sorts of side dishes, including two to three kinds of pickles such as eggplant, lotus root, and cucumber. I never thought I would be recommending pickles for breakfast, but they really are extraordinary.

KIMCHI

KIMCHI ORIGINATED over 3,000 years ago in China; the word is derived from two Chinese characters meaning "salted vegetable." Kimchi, preserved vegetables, occasionally contain seafood. It reportedly was used to feed both the Great Wall's workforce and Genghis Khan's armies. It migrated south onto the Korean peninsula, maturing into a Korean mainstay by the twelfth century and becoming spicy via the hot chilies brought to Asia by the colonial Portuguese and Spanish about five hundred years ago.

Traditionally made by women, who used the occasion as a social event, kimchi has mutated to include virtually everything edible, including fish, seafood, fruit, and a large array of cultivated and wild vegetables and herbs. Recently even imported foreign items such as carrots, tomatoes, Brussels sprouts, and Western-style cabbages have emerged, and there is even a sort of "instant" version made with romaine lettuce and a spicy dressing.

Technically, the fermentation process that is crucial in the making of kimchi depends on temperature and air quality, seasonings, and the activities of various micro-organisms that grow in the mixture. Salt is used in every kind of kimchi, but the amount depends on the region and the season, on individual and family tastes, and on eating habits. Essentially a preservative, salt kills the living cells of foods, causing an exchange of materials between the cells and promoting enzymatication, which gives the vegetable mix its overall flavor. It also causes the pectins in the vegetables to harden, giving them a uniquely crispy chewiness.

Introducing toasted sesame seeds or sea vegetables into the kimchi stimulates the taste buds the same way commercial MSG does. The fermentation process emphasizes each core ingredient's fundamental flavor. The garlic that is common to all varieties of kimchi provides a strong flavor note, even more so than the hot chilies. Rehydrated dried radish kimchi, for example, begins with a watery mild radish that is dehydrated, reduced to a bitter essence. It is then rehydrated, mixed with salt, ginger, garlic, and chili, then allowed to ferment for weeks. The result is a chewy distillation of daikon with a bitter background note and a complex spicy overtone accentuated with a pungent garlic finish. The colors are vibrant, from fresh yellow ginger, to white garlic, to green scallion. And the ground hot chili offers a dominant, deep red color.

Today kimchi is virtually synonymous with Korean food. While the most common variety starts with cabbage, garlic, ginger, scallion, fermented baby shrimp, and dried red chilies, kimchi has nearly two hundred variations, including daikon, baby crab, wild fern, and ginseng. It is probably the single Asian food that is as ubiquitous as rice, so much so that it is said in Korea that "a meal without kimchi is not a meal at all." Kimchi is for breakfast, lunch, and dinner. Often used as condiments, it shows up in omelettes, rice and noodle dishes, stir-fries, soups, stews, even pancakes. In fact, the Koreans take special pride in incorporating kimchi into whatever they are eating. At fast-food restaurants in Seoul, Korea, you can order a hamburger or pizza topped with kimchi.

Despite these innovations, Korean classics persist. One I encountered in Korea was made with doragee, the roots of bell flowers found in the mountains, similar in taste to ginseng but less bitter and less expensive. One of my all-time favorites is a kimchi seafood stew. Rich with clams, octopus or squid, and sometimes scallops, enhanced with delicate shiitake mushrooms, and spiced with fiery fermented cabbage and bright green scallions, it tastes of sea and earth, each ingredient having been lifted to its maximum intensity of flavor. On the vegetarian side, a tofu-cabbage kimchi stew transforms the tofu into a fabulous flavor sponge and broth thickener.

You can find oversize jars of napa (or Chinese) cabbage cut in bite-size chunks and exhibiting a light to deep red cast, depending on the specific recipe. Artisanal kimchi (packaged in small plastic containers) ranges from freshly made cabbage to combinations that defy the imagination. Sweet shrimp, for example, is prepared and eaten shells and all. Pan-fried with sugar until caramelized, then dressed with a chili powder glaze, it is sweet like candy yet still tastes of the sea. You can also find baby crab, eaten by sucking the cured spicy flesh out of these tiny but otherwise complete wonders. Or maybe you will find silvery, salty-sweet dried baby anchovies. No longer than a common pin, they pack a wallop of flavor and crunch. Chewy, slippery green sea vegetables, thinly sliced lotus root, and pickled garlic heads, when you find them, are worth a try, too.

SALADS AND RAW ITEMS

SALADS ARE AN IMPORTANT part of Asian cooking, but the term has a somewhat different meaning in Asian usage. Lettuce and other vegetables tossed in a salad dressing in the Western manner, for example, have never been part of the traditional Asian table. Rather, salads include items such as green papaya, green mango, and cucumber. Lettuce and herbs accompany food, however, particularly in Southeast Asia, where they are used as wraps. Modern Korean and Japanese restaurants often offer a Western-style salad with a meal, most likely as a result of the post–World War II American presence in these countries. In Japanese restaurants a version is made with a dressing of sesame oil, vinegar, a bit of mirin, and grated carrot, ginger, or daikon; they are quite good. (A more popular version is made with mayonnaise, which unfortunately is overwhelming.) I especially like to have these salads with miso soup and sushi or sashimi. A spicy salad is sometimes offered in Korean restaurants. It has some of the pungency of kimchi but is an "instant" version that uses fresh instead of fermented vegetables with a spicy-sweet vinegar, soy sauce, ginger, and scallion dressing on romaine lettuce leaves. A transformation of traditional lettuce wraps and dipping sauces, it makes a nice accompaniment to Korean barbecued meat. In this spirit, I have included a few salad dressings here. They can be used with salad greens as a starter when serving the food Western style (i.e., in courses), or when serving a salad with grilled meat or seafood.

LEAFY GREENS

STIR-FRIED LEAFY GREENS such as napa cabbage, mustard cabbage, water spinach, Chinese broccoli, flowering oil seed rape, and white- and green-stemmed bok choy are among the most popularly eaten Asian vegetables in Asia. The preferred method of preparation for leafy greens is stir-frying, with the exception of mustard greens, which are generally prepared as a salt brine–cured dish. Stir-frying allows the tender leaves and contrasting crisp stems to retain not only their character but their natural flavor and vitamins as well. When added to soups, greens are generally blanched for a few seconds prior to being placed atop noodles, for example, broth being ladled over all. Short, quick preparation over a high flame is key. These simply prepared vegetables accompany rather spicy protein dishes, the vegetables acting as a sort of buffer against the complex spicing of curries, for example. Regarded for the most part as a "cold" food in the Chinese hot-cold food system, leafy greens are of great dietary importance, and meals usually do not go without some kind of green being served.

Bok choy is an Asian vegetable, essentially a leafy green, short-stem cabbage that originated in southern China. Moderately familiar in the West, it is increasingly available the world over with each passing year; my local markets carry both white and green stemmed, organic and conventional. Bok choy is usually heat cooked. (Some Western chefs have experimented with adding raw baby bok choy leaves to salads, but this is not customarily done in Asia.) It can be stir-fried with a bit of salt or soy sauce for a quick and tasty dish, added to soups, or steamed or blanched and drizzled with a sauce. The same can be said for Chinese broccoli, pea shoots (essentially pea pod leaves), water spinach, napa cabbage (also known as celery cabbage, or Chinese cabbage), or flowering oil seed rape (a leafy green with tiny yellow floral tips).

Water spinach, also known as "swamp" cabbage, is the most widely eaten vegetable in southern China and southern Vietnam, where it grows in great abundance. There are two types, dry land and wet land; the latter is preferred because it retains water as it matures, making it the more flavorful type. This vegetable is especially loved in southern China because unlike other types of leafy greens, water spinach can withstand summer's humidity and grows with very little effort. It is enjoyed simply stir-fried or added to soups and valued as a culinary item because of the contrasting textures of its crunchy stem and tender leaves, an example of *yin yang* at its best. It has a secondary economic benefit: while the leafy stems are enjoyed by humans, the coarse trimmings are fed to the pigs.

Watercress originated in the West. The Chinese name translates roughly as "Western water vegetable"; the cultivated form was likely brought to China through Hong Kong in the nineteenth century. It can be heat cooked or cured, and the beginner can easily stir-fry it with a little salt or soy sauce and

STANLEY MARKET, HONG KONG

have a satisfying dish. Considered a very "cold" vegetable in the hot-cold food system, peppery watercress is often enjoyed in soups paired with "warm" to "hot" meats as a complement. It is never eaten raw as in the West, where it shows up in many salads.

GOURDS, MELONS, AND CUCUMBERS

GOURD, MELON, AND CUCUMBER are used interchangeably when describing such watery vegetables as winter melon (gourd, squash), fuzzy melon (gourd), and bitter

DRAGON FRUIT ARE BEAUTIFUL. BENEATH THE BRIGHT FUCHSIA IS VERY MILD
TASTING, JUICY WHITE FLESH SPECKLED WITH TINY BLACK SEEDS.

melon (gourd, cucumber). Full of vitamins and minerals, they are used in braised dishes and soups for their ability to absorb flavor easily. They are also stir-fried occasionally, often with protein; and sometimes candied, as with winter melon.

Winter melon and fuzzy melon can be used interchangeably in savory dishes because their flavor is quite similar. I sometimes use conventional cucumber as a substitute in a pinch when I can't get to Chinatown.

Winter melon is most famous for winter melon and ham soup, where it is cooked in a rich stock made from chicken and pork, with bits of Yunnan ham (or Smithfield ham in the United States). A large gourd, it can reach 100 pounds in weight. In its smaller manifestations, skilled Chinese chefs carve its rind and use it as a tureen to serve winter melon and ham soup. During the Chinese New Year, the melon is cubed and sugar-coated; it is often packaged and sold with other sugar-coated items such as lotus root slices and seeds and water chestnuts.

Bitter melon is unique and has no substitute. It is bitter, although many people become accustomed to the taste. It is an ideal example of the Asian idea that food is not only meant to please the palate but all the organs (it is rich in quinine); it is one of those foods that crystallizes the "food is medicine as well as nutrition" principle. Some people eat it like other vegetables, stir-fried with black bean and garlic sauce (page 86), for example. Classic bitter melon recipes have evolved, however, where the *yin yang* philosophy of balance in food is very clear. Sweet pork (neutral) and shrimp (*yang*), for example, are deliberately used to counter the bitterness of the gourd (*yin*), essentially raising the bar in terms of flavor intensity.

FRUIT

THE CHINESE ARE especially fond of consuming oranges after a meal or offering them as food to the ancestral altar. The colors of oranges, tangerines, and kumquats are thought of as a shade of red and are thought to ward off evil spirits and ensure good luck. The Szechwanese are particularly fond of sun-dried tangerine peels, which they reconstitute in water and add to savory and sweet dishes alike. The Cantonese sometimes follow their lead. My favorite tangerine peel–infused dish is the classic sweet red bean soup. The fragrant flowers of certain citrus fruits are added to tea. For entertainment, the Chinese will bet on anything—a fruit vendor and his customers will often make a bet as to how many seeds the orange in question has; the bet is paid after the vendor peels the orange and counts the seeds.

Technically a fruit, eggplant is widely used as a vegetable. It may seem familiar to Western cooks, but it holds a few surprises. It originated in India thousands of years ago and has been popular in Chinese cooking for centuries. There are numerous varieties, including several distinctive Asian types. It appears in several shapes and colors (the most common in Asia is thin, elongated, and light to dark purple). Although it can be heat cooked or cured, it was originally eaten raw. Asian eggplant (also widely known as Japanese eggplant) is used in one of the most popular Chinese eggplant preparations. Double cooked, it is first deep-fried, then stir-fried in a sweet and savory brown garlic sauce, as in Szechwanese eggplant. The deep-frying process ensures that the spongy eggplant will retain its heat throughout the meal. In Japan it is deep-fried and served with miso paste (page 332) or cured in salt brine, a specialty of Kyoto. In Vietnam it is stir-fried with a bit of fish sauce and ground pork (pp. 334 and 462). In Cambodia, pea eggplants (literally pea size) are added to cooked dipping sauces. Still other versions employ elaborate spicing. One of my favorites is Thai eggplant curry (page 333), using either Thai round eggplant (streaky white and green, golf ball size), or Asian eggplant, added to spicy green, red, or yellow curry paste, seasoned with pungent shrimp paste, and rich with coconut milk.

In Southeast Asia, fruits such as *carambola* (star fruit), papaya, and mango are used in their unripe green and sour form as vegetables to be added to soups or fragrant salads. These unripe fruit dishes are often served to counterbalance foods that are herb- or spice-laden and grilled or braised for a cooling effect, which is much needed in tropical climates. Lemon and lime are often used for making dipping sauces or squeezing at the last minute over sweet and savory foods, as a complementary accent.

Finally, exotic fruits such as persimmons, litchi, and longan are eaten fresh, as part of a dessert, or dried and reconstituted in water, resulting in a delicious fruity drink. Jujubes (red dates) are widely used not only in desserts but in savory soups or braised Chinese and Korean dishes as well. They are also used to sweeten medicinal soups. Bananas and coconuts are the most widely used fruits in Southeast Asia. Many if not most desserts contain one or both of these. Coconut is also often used in savory dishes, both in its young green form and mature brown form.

LEGUMES

LEGUMES, INCLUDING TUBERS, nuts, and beans, are covered here as well as in the "Sweets and Drinks" chapter (they are commonly used in making Asian sweets) and in the "Condiments" chapter. Perhaps the most important legume in all of Asia (in the Philippines to a lesser extent) is the soybean. First cultivated in China at least as far back as the Chou dynasty (twelfth century B.C.E. to 255 B.C.E.), they are the source of soy oil, soy sauce, soy milk, bean curd (tofu), bean curd sheets (a by-product of making tofu), and tempeh, a pressed bean curd cake containing whole beans popular in Southeast Asia, especially Indonesia. Fermented soybean products including Chinese fermented bean curd and Japanese soybean pastes (miso) are also important. Used mostly as condiments, they are more than simple flavor enhancers.

A great source of protein and calcium, soybeans are eaten most commonly as tofu, a cheeselike curd. Tofu comes in cake form and varies in texture from silky to soft, medium-soft, firm, pressed (the water having been extracted), or dehydrated (a Japanese specialty), to deep-fried cubes or triangles.

Asian cooks add fresh tofu cubes to soups or braise, steam, stir-fry, or deep-fry them, sometimes adding vegetables, seafood, poultry, and meat to the mix. Freshly made silken tofu is sold by street vendors. Soft in texture, the warm tofu is scooped by the vendor directly from a large metal vat or plastic tub into a small container. Drizzled with a clear to light amber syrup, it is a delicious snack I have enjoyed on many occasions in Hong Kong and New York's Chinatown. A by-product of making this bean curd is bean curd skins. Sold dried, they are known as fu tzook in Chinese and yuba in Japanese. Softened, they are cut in manageable sizes and are used to roll up stir-fried vegetables; the rolls are steamed, deep-fried, or braised. An interesting food made using these sheets is "mock Peking duck" (page 371), a Chinese Buddhist vegetarian dish of braised tofu skin rolls filled with julienned shiitake mushrooms; if you use a little imagination the tofu skin resembles that of the crispy duck. In Japan fresh bean curd sheets are also very much part of a Zen Buddhist diet, simply because they provide a great deal of protein. I go into greater detail on soybeans and related products in the recipe section.

Taro, a tuber, can be grated and deep-fried into edible decorative cups to hold stir-fries. It can also be grated, mixed with wheat flour to make a dough, then turned into individual dumplings stuffed with meat (generally pork) and deep-fried. Like corn or banana, taro is also enjoyed diced and added to sweet coconut and tapioca soup (page 517). Taro, like sweet potatoes (a sixteenth-century Western import), can be eaten boiled, steamed, or roasted as a snack or "fast food," as they often are in the northern provinces of China and other cold-climate countries such as Korea and northern Japan.

Red beans (also azuki red beans) are some of the smallest dried beans available and are most often treated as a sweet item. In Chinese cooking, they are boiled down and served as a sweet red bean soup (page 514), or cooked and mixed with lard to make red bean paste (page 513), a popular filler for steamed red bean buns (page 544) and moon cakes (available during the autumn moon festival). They are similarly reserved for sweet items in Korean and Japanese cooking and throughout Southeast Asia.

Peanuts (also known as "groundnuts" and introduced at the same time as the sweet potato) are popular for making sweets, too, and are occasionally added to savory stir-fries. The Chinese also have tiny peanuts (about half the size of the types found in the West), which are eaten boiled as a snack. Peanuts also play an important role in Southeast Asian foods, where they are crushed and used to garnish numerous dishes or are employed as a main ingredient in several variations of peanut dipping sauces (pp. 97–99).

FUNGI

MUSHROOMS ARE ENJOYED everywhere in Asia. Black mushrooms, also known as shiitakes, range from thin and dark brown to thick and light tan with some dark spots and have numerous variations. For thousands of years, the Chinese have eaten two hundred different types of fresh mushrooms, but one of their favorites is the shiitake, which they seem to prefer dried for their more concentrated flavor. The Japanese and Koreans eat shiitakes both fresh and dried. Two of the most interesting Chinese dishes using mushrooms are braised shiitakes and napa cabbage (page 340), or steamed fish (pp. 386–87). The Japanese grill fresh shiitakes and make broth with

WILD PINE MUSHROOMS, FOUND IN KOREA, ARE AS EXPENSIVE AS THE TRUFFLES OF FRANCE.

dried shiitakes to serve with noodles. In Southeast Asia, shiitakes are used in Vietnamese dishes such as mushroom caps stuffed with ground pork and shrimp, and are sometimes julienned in Chinese-derived stir-fries and soups in other countries.

Straw mushrooms, smallish and tender, are usually sold canned and are available unpeeled (with enclosed stems and resembling tiny brown eggs) and peeled (revealing short stems). They should be rinsed and blanched to get rid of any tin odor. They are popular in soups such as Thai spicy shrimp soup (page 134), or braised as in Vietnamese braised mushrooms in caramel sauce (page 459).

Cloud ears (also known as wood ears or tree ears) are a type of dark brown fungi. The name is derived from their shape, which resembles a cloud. Since the sixth century C.E. they have been harvested from tree trunks, where they grow naturally. Believed to cleanse the blood, they are valued for their medicinal qualities as well as their nutrients. Extremely subtle in flavor, cloud ears are used primarily for their texture and ability to absorb flavors. They are readily available dried in Asian markets, and occasionally fresh in Japanese markets. Choose the thinner and more delicate cloud ear, as the thicker type, which has a tan underside, tends to be overly chewy. Clouds ears are most often added to soups, stir-fries, and fillings.

Suet yee is also eaten by the Chinese. This fungus is generally sold dried and labeled as white fungus or snow fungus. It looks nothing like a typical mushroom yet is technically part of the same family. *Suet yee* is employed in savory dishes including soups for its soft yet crunchy texture and its ability to absorb flavors, but it is most enjoyed in sweet dishes. One of my favorite sweet snacks is white fungus set in a sweet almond-flavored gelatin based on agar-agar (page 529), a dramatic dish that features the flower-like fungi captured in a translucent sea of gel.

SEA VEGETABLES

ALTHOUGH SEA VEGETABLES have been used in China for thousands of years, they play a relatively minor part in the cuisine. It is the Japanese who have excelled in this area of food preparation. Dozens of types of sea vegetables (often referred to as seaweed) appear as raw, salt-preserved, dried, and heat-cooked items. Some types are more worth mentioning than others. *Konbu* (kelp), the main ingredient in making *dashi* (pp. 124–25), is harvested off the coast of Hokkaido. The dark brownish-green leaf can measure yards long and as much as a foot wide. Sun-dried kelp is available in several grades, and a *konbu* shop in Japan has these available in pieces ranging from small to medium and large, to full-length leaves folded and beautifully wrapped in white paper with black hand-painted Japanese characters. In the United States, large cut pieces sold in plastic packaging are the most widely available. As a general rule, the more expensive the *konbu*, the better the quality. Nori is dried algae or laver sold in large paper-thin rectangular sheets, or small rectangular pieces in packages of twenty-five sheets or more. Greenish black in color, nori is most familiar as an element of sushi. In Japan and Korea, however, I have also enjoyed it as a side dish, picking up a small piece of nori with my chopsticks to collect a small amount of rice from my bowl. This is a great way to savor the rice and vegetable morsel and add flavor to a simple bowl of rice. Harvested in spring, *wakame* (sea-tangle) is also widely used in Japanese cooking. While it is available seasonally fresh in Japan, only the dried version is available in the United States. Dark green, *wakame* is often added to *miso* soup (page 128). *Kanten* is processed from a red sea vegetable known in Japan as *tangusa*. This somewhat white, transparent product known to us as agar-agar has been used in Western and Asian cuisines for centuries as a pure gelatin for preparing savory and sweet foods. *Kanten* is also sold in strips, flakes, and powdered form. (The Chinese also sell *kanten*, but the Japanese version is of much better quality.)

In addition to these popular types of sea vegetables in Japan, other varieties are used in making nutritious salads. These include the ever more popular hijiki, a black sea vegetable that looks like black threads and is often tossed with carrot (for color), tofu, and a bit of sesame oil. Sea vegetables are available in Japanese markets and many health food stores.

ASIAN HERBS

THE MOST IMPORTANT HERBS in Chinese cooking are garlic, ginger, scallion, and cilantro (also known as coriander). They are used in Southeast Asia as well, along with other exotic herbs such as Thai basil, Vietnamese coriander, saw leaf, lemongrass, and mint, for example. Herbs in Asian cooking can be used in the same fashion as in Western cooking, that is, as a flavor enhancer in vegetable, seafood, poultry, and meat dishes. They are also eaten in great abundance at meals, however, more like vegetables are eaten in the West.

The Vietnamese, for example, love to add large amounts of freshly torn herbs to rice noodle soups called pho (pp. 228–29). They also stir-fry herbs such as cilantro, Thai basil, and dill to eat with cha ca (pp. 396–97), a deep-fried fish specialty of Hanoi. In this particular dish the fried fish cubes are added to a mound of rice vermicelli and topped with a generous amount of stir-fried herbs. Tossed with peanuts and nuoc cham (page 100), it is absolutely delicious.

Another interesting herb worth a mention is shiso (or perilla leaf), used by Japanese and Korean cooks. Pungent and tender, this heart-shaped green or purple leaf is also slightly bitter. It has a mustard-like character; when you bite it, a hot sensation quickly travels through your sinuses. Fresh shiso leaves are often placed on a sushi or sashimi serving plate next to a mound of grated daikon and under the raw fish. Unfortunately, most people look at the leaf as a plate decoration and forget that it is also a delicious herb. One of the more memorable times I tasted shiso was in a small Okinawan restaurant in New York. The chef stuck a fresh leaf between the vinegar-flavored rice and salty fresh, translucent orange salmon eggs (ikura), then wrapped the whole morsel in nori. I loved the way the leaf set off the richness of the eggs. Asian herbs, including the ones briefly discussed here, are further explained in "Essential Ingredients" (page 5).

SIMPLE STIR-FRIED
LEAFY GREENS

SERVES 4 TO 6

1 pound leafy green vegetable
such as CHINESE BROCCOLI,
BOK CHOY, ASPARAGUS, LEEKS,
or WATERCRESS

1 tablespoon VEGETABLE OIL

2 large GARLIC CLOVES, crushed
and peeled

1 tablespoon CHINESE LIGHT SOY
SAUCE; or FISH SAUCE

KOSHER SALT

Freshly ground BLACK PEPPER

Pinch of GRANULATED SUGAR
(optional)

Dash of SESAME OIL (optional)

LEAFY GREENS or other vegetables are delicious when stir-fried. They retain their vitamins and their firmness, all the while releasing their essence upon quick contact with heat. Use the familiar asparagus, watercress, or leeks, or the more exotic *gai lan* (commonly known as Chinese kale or Chinese broccoli) or bok choy. A minimal amount of seasoning—garlic and sea salt—leaves room for the natural flavor of the vegetable to shine through. Any moisture given up by the stir-fried vegetable evaporates, leaving behind tender yet firm vegetables that are bright green from a sprinkling of sea salt and naturally sweet (or occasionally enhanced with a pinch of sugar). In the case of Chinese broccoli especially, the stems are crunchy while the leaves are tender, a wonderful textural contrast.

Garlic can be chopped or minced, depending on the intensity of flavor you desire. Soy sauce and fish sauce can be added as flavor enhancers along with a touch of sesame oil for an interesting background flavor.

1. Here are ways to prep the vegetables: For the Chinese broccoli, trim the leafy stems and cut them into 1½-inch-long pieces. For the bok choy, trim the stem end and separate the leaves. Depending on the size, keep the leaves whole if using baby bok choy, or halve them lengthwise. For the asparagus, cut the spears into ¼-inch-thick diagonal slices. For the leeks, julienne them into 2-inch-long by ¼-inch-wide strips. For watercress, trim the stem ends.

2. Heat the oil in a wok over high heat. Stir-fry the garlic until golden, 1 to 2 minutes. Add the leafy greens, and soy sauce or fish sauce, and stir-fry until cooked through, 2 to 5 minutes, depending on the veg-

etable. At this time, season with salt, pepper, sugar (if using), a dash or two of sesame oil (if using), and toss well. Transfer to a plate and serve.

IN ASIA garlic is stir-fried until golden but never brown. Doing this brings out the sugars in the garlic, releasing its true essence early on in the cooking process, adding a roasty note only garlic can give to the vegetable, and flavoring the surface of the wok, adding a wealth of taste that wouldn't be there otherwise. That said, be sure not to brown or burn your garlic, because the color means that the natural sugars have burned. As in making caramel, if it goes beyond the color of gold, then it is sure to be unpleasantly bitter.

HOBAK NAMUL
STIR-FRIED ZUCCHINI

SERVES 4 TO 6

2 small to medium ZUCCHINI,
ends trimmed, halved
lengthwise, and cut crosswise
into ⅛-inch-thick slices
1 teaspoon KOSHER SALT
1 tablespoon VEGETABLE OIL
1 teaspoon SESAME OIL
1 large GARLIC CLOVE, crushed,
peeled, and minced
½ teaspoon DRIED RED PEPPER
POWDER
½ teaspoon toasted SESAME SEEDS

WHETHER YOU GO to a regular or vegetarian Korean restaurant, even if you've ordered only meat, many small side dishes containing all sorts of vegetables will be served. The Koreans love their vegetables and not one meal is served without them. They are quickly stir-fried or blanched so as to retain their natural crunch. In this dish, thinly sliced zucchini is tossed with salt to remove any bitterness and drain out its water content. While I use the whole zucchini, it is not unusual to make this dish using only zucchini peel, in which case you'll need at least four zucchini. Julienne the peel, which should be about ⅛ inch thick, into 2-inch matchsticks.

Place the zucchini in a colander, sprinkle with the teaspoon salt, and drain for 30 minutes. Wrap the zucchini in a cotton kitchen towel and squeeze to extract the juices. Heat the vegetable and sesame oils in a wok over high heat. Stir-fry the garlic until golden, 1 to 2 minutes. Add the zucchini and stir-fry until wilted, about 2 minutes more. Sprinkle with the red pepper powder and toasted sesame seeds and stir-fry for a minute more. Transfer to a platter and serve.

STIR-FRIED DAIKON PEEL AND CARROTS

SERVES 4 TO 6

6 cups DAIKON PEELS, cut 2 inches
  long and julienned lengthwise

1 teaspoon KOSHER SALT

1 tablespoon VEGETABLE OIL

½ teaspoon SESAME OIL

3 medium CARROTS, peeled,
  halved crosswise, and julienned

2 tablespoons JAPANESE DARK SOY
  SAUCE

2 tablespoons KONBU DASHI
  (pp. 124–25)

2 tablespoons MIRIN

½ teaspoon GRANULATED SUGAR

1 SCALLION, root and dark green
  ends trimmed, and 6-inch stalk
  sliced paper thin into rounds

¼ teaspoon BLACK SESAME SEEDS

IN JAPAN, STIR-FRIES are usually seasoned with soy sauce, mirin (sweet sake), sugar, and *dashi*. The tricky part is to know how much of each to use for a particular stir-fry. Different vegetables absorb these seasonings differently, so the amount of soy sauce used for eggplant may not be the same amount used for cabbage, for example. The technique is learned over time and once mastered is a good way to grasp how seemingly simple items can in fact be complex and refined. Compared to Chinese stir-fries, where all the liquid must evaporate, Japanese stir-fries tend to be a bit moist (but not wet) as a result of adding *dashi*, soy sauce, and mirin. The vegetables should be tender but firm and ever so slightly moist when done. This delicious stir-fry will accompany virtually any Japanese fish, poultry, or meat dish beautifully.

Place the daikon in a colander, toss with the salt, and allow to drain for 30 minutes. Heat the vegetable and sesame oils in a wok over high heat. Stir-fry the carrots and daikon until just wilted, about 3 minutes. Add the soy sauce, *dashi*, mirin, and sugar and continue to cook until tender but firm, about 2 minutes more. Transfer the vegetables to a platter and garnish with scallion and black sesame seeds.

Variation: Remove and discard the stems from 8 fresh medium shiitake mushrooms and julienne the caps. Follow the recipe, stir-frying the shiitakes along with the carrots and daikon.

FOOD IN JAPAN IS presented perfectly sliced and looks remarkably uniform. For the longest time I couldn't help thinking that a lot of food routinely went to waste for the sake of visual appearance. Traveling in Japan, however, I learned that this was not always the case. While I was visiting cooking teacher and tea master Taeko Fujii in Kyoto, she prepared a Japanese favorite, daikon (also called Asian radish or Chinese radish). As she cooked our meal, she explained, "The daikon has three parts. First the green leafy top, which I will blanch, chop, and mix into my rice for a beautiful decoration. Secondly, I will stir-fry the crunchy peel with carrots. Then I will drain the core with salt, slice it, and stir-fry it with mushrooms to mix with potato starch noodles.

"Presentation is taken very seriously in Japan," Taeko proudly said, handing me a six-page menu on which she had painted in watercolors each of the courses she had so graciously pre-

TAEKO FUJII, AN EXPERT IN ZEN VEGETARIAN COOKING, DOES NOT BELIEVE IN WASTE WHEN COOKING. SHE USES EGGPLANT AND DAIKON TOPS TO CLEAN HER POTS AFTER EACH USE.

pared for me. I noticed that once the daikon's leafy tops were chopped, she used the end—just like that of an eggplant—to clean her pots and pans. She mentioned that in the old days nothing was wasted the way it is now with the new generation. She talked of her love for farmers' produce grown naturally. "The vegetables and fruit were all uneven. This is a good sign. If they all measure the same, they've been injected with something. It's not natural for anything to look and feel exactly the same. I grow my own pumpkins in my backyard and buy my produce direct from the farmer. It is more expensive, but the flavors, textures, and shapes are all worth the money." I can't help agreeing with her. Walking through the aisles of a supermarket in Tokyo, I indeed noticed that all the vegetables were the same size, shape, and color. The fact that there were many varieties was wonderful, but that they were all so uniform seemed sad. While we talked, Taeko's hands moved deftly, and beautiful stir-fried and steamed vegetable dishes were created: fried tofu in kelp stock; pan-fried eggplant; stir-fried daikon peelings with carrots; a marinated daikon and shiitake mushroom dish; and daikon leaves mixed in sushi rice. "This is a Zen Buddhist meal," she said as she served me.

STIR-FRIED PEA SHOOTS OR WATER SPINACH WITH FERMENTED TOFU

SERVES 4 TO 6

1 tablespoon VEGETABLE OIL

2 large GARLIC CLOVES, crushed, peeled, and finely chopped

2 small cubes fermented TOFU (about 1½ tablespoons)

1 pound PEA SHOOTS, leaves only; or WATER SPINACH, stem ends trimmed, and cut into 2-inch-long pieces

KOSHER SALT

Freshly ground BLACK PEPPER

Pinch of GRANULATED SUGAR

PEA SHOOTS, DAU MUI, are a Chinese favorite. Increasingly popular among Westerners, they are clusters of leaves that grow on thin stems. Prevented from flowering or fruiting, the leaves become very tender and wilt just as they're picked. (If you see pea shoots that are a bit wilted, do not be alarmed. Place them in water and they will come back. Overly wilted and dark leaves should be left behind.) While pea shoots should be eaten the day you buy them, you can keep them longer by placing them in a plastic bag and refrigerating them for a day or two. These were once some of the most expensive vegetables in Chinese markets, but owing to increased cultivation they are now more affordable. If you're cooking water spinach, choose well-formed arrowhead-shaped leaves with thin hollow stems. The larger the leaves and the shorter the stem, the more tender the vegetable. Ong choy, as water spinach is called in Chinese, is also very popular in Southeast Asia. In Vietnam it is the preferred vegetable, especially in the south, where it is grown in abundance. Fairly inexpensive, it can be found almost throughout the year but is especially plentiful in the spring and fall. It is enjoyed not only for its refreshing flavor but its balance of tender and firm textures. The tender leaves and crunchy stems are a perfect example of yin yang, or balance of opposites. Both dau mui and ong choy are delicious flavored with pungent fermented bean curd, fu yu (see sidebar).

Heat the oil in a wok over high heat. Stir-fry the garlic until golden, 1 to 2 minutes. Dilute the fermented tofu with 1 tablespoon water, then add to the wok and heat through, about 1 minute. Add the pea shoots or water spinach and stir-fry until well coated with sauce and cooked through, about 3 minutes for the pea shoots, and 5 to 10 minutes for the water spinach. When cooking water spinach, you may have to cover the wok to create some steam and tenderize the stems. Adjust the seasoning with salt, pepper, and sugar (if using), and stir-fry for 2 minutes more.

FU YU IS fermented (or preserved) bean curd. Shaped into approximately 1-inch cubes, it is sold preserved in rice wine or salt brine and is available plain (grayish tan), colored with red food coloring, or spiced with chili. It is packed in glass or ceramic jars, usually imported from mainland China or Taiwan. All versions are delicious and interchangeable, depending on your preferences. Preserved bean curd can be used directly from the jar in tiny amounts as an accompaniment to rice porridge. It is also used as a background flavor in *char siu,* Cantonese roast pork (page 454), or in stir-fries such as this pea shoot or water spinach recipe, always adding a wealth of flavor. While it is pungent at first, *fu yu* quickly transforms itself into a rather pleasant sweet and savory aroma when cooked.

Note: Depending on the brand, you will find that fermented bean curd cubes come in two sizes. The small ones are just shy of ¾ inch all around, while the larger cubes measure approximately ¾ inch thick by 1 inch long and wide. I generally use two of the small cubes or one of the large cubes when making this recipe. Use more or less to taste.

SHIGUMCHI NAMUL
STIR-FRIED SPINACH AND
MUNG BEAN SPROUTS

SERVES 4 TO 6

2 teaspoons VEGETABLE OIL

2 teaspoons SESAME OIL

1 bunch SPINACH, well washed
   and root ends trimmed

½ pound MUNG BEAN SPROUTS,
   root ends trimmed

1 teaspoon KOSHER SALT

¼ teaspoon toasted SESAME SEEDS

¼ teaspoon BLACK SESAME SEEDS

I HAVE EATEN Korean food for the better part of fifteen years, and this simple stir-fry of spinach and mung bean sprouts has always accompanied the meal. It is served at room temperature and seasoned with a touch of salt and sesame oil to bring out the natural flavor of the vegetables. It is pleasingly simple, since the foods served with it, such as barbecued beef (page 480) and kimchi (pp. 357–61), are highly seasoned.

Heat half the vegetable and sesame oils in a nonstick pan over medium heat. Add the spinach, season with salt, and stir-fry until the leaves are wilted and the stems are tender, about 1 minute. Transfer to a plate. Add the remaining vegetable and sesame oils, the mung bean sprouts, season with salt, and stir-fry until tender but firm, about 1 minute. Transfer to a separate plate. Drain both vegetables separately and arrange them in individual piles on a single serving plate or on individual ones, sprinkled with sesame seeds (toasted for the spinach, and black for the mung bean sprouts).

Variation: Another way to make this dish is to bring two pots of salted water to a boil. Put the spinach in one pot, and the mung bean sprouts in the other, and blanch each until just wilted, a few seconds. Keeping the vegetables separate, drain, shock under cold water, and drain thoroughly again. Season each vegetable with 1 teaspoon sesame oil each. Serve garnished with sesame seeds as directed in the recipe.

KAMJA NAMUL
EXOTIC STIR-FRIED
POTATOES

SERVES 4 TO 6

1 tablespoon KOSHER SALT

2 large IDAHO POTATOES, peeled
   and cut into ½-inch cubes

2 tablespoons VEGETABLE OIL

1 teaspoon SESAME OIL

1 large GARLIC CLOVE, crushed,
   peeled, and minced

2 tablespoons KOREAN or JAPANESE
   DARK SOY SAUCE

2 teaspoons SWEET AND SOUR
   CHILI DIPPING SAUCE
   (page 105)

4 SHISO (perilla) LEAVES, julienned

½ teaspoon toasted SESAME SEEDS

P OTATOES ARE VERY MUCH enjoyed in Korea. While in Kyongju, considered to be the historical capital of the country, I ate in several restaurants, one of which offered vegetarian meals. One of the dishes on the table looked very familiar yet exotic. A small celadon bowl of crispy fried potatoes flavored with sesame oil and soy sauce, pungent with garlic, was garnished with julienned *shiso* (perilla leaf). It was unusual, but I loved it. I rarely prepare potatoes Asian style; in fact, I use them only to make chicken curry (page 499) or potato and rice dumpling dough (page 523). Mildly exotic, *kamja namul* and *bulgogi* (barbecued beef, page 480) are a great way to introduce Asian foods through familiar ingredients to a meat-and-potatoes kind of person. I think of this combination as the ultimate "transitional" meal, familiar yet exotic.

1. Whisk the salt with 4 cups water in a bowl until the salt is completely dissolved. Add the potatoes and allow to soak for 20 minutes. Drain.

2. Heat the vegetable and sesame oils in a nonstick pan over high heat. Stir-fry the garlic until golden, 1 to 2 minutes. Add the potatoes and stir-fry until almost tender, about 10 minutes. Stir together the soy sauce and chili paste in a bowl until smooth and add to the stir-fry. Continue to stir-fry the potatoes until any liquid is absorbed and the potatoes become lightly crisp, about 10 minutes more. Transfer to a platter, garnish with julienned *shiso*, sprinkle with toasted sesame seeds, and serve.

TRAVELING THROUGH KOREA, my translator, Sophie Park, and I enjoyed many delicious meals together. At each meal we were served bowls of rice, clear soup, and *kimchi;* then twenty to thirty other dishes to choose from and share came to the table: dried fish, acorn pudding, beef, mushrooms, and *namul* (vegetable dishes). The *namul* were prepared any number of ways: stir-fried, blanched, steamed, and boiled. They were both vegetables and herbs, some cultivated, others wild, some spicy, others mild. Each dish complemented the others perfectly and I cherished each one, a small bite at a time, throughout the meal. The portions were very small, and while it looked like a lot of food, at the end of the meal I didn't feel uncomfortable and full but most definitely satisfied.

BITTER MELON STUFFED WITH SHRIMP AND PORK

SERVES 4 TO 6

¼ cup small dried SHRIMP

1 tablespoon CHINESE LIGHT SOY
SAUCE; or FISH SAUCE

2 teaspoons TAPIOCA STARCH or
CORNSTARCH

½ ounce fresh GINGER, peeled
and finely grated

1 SCALLION, root and dark green
ends trimmed, and 6-inch stalk
minced

10 ounces BLUE TIGER SHRIMP,
heads and shells removed,
deveined, and minced

6 ounces GROUND PORK
(70 percent lean)

KOSHER SALT

Freshly ground BLACK PEPPER

1 teaspoon SESAME OIL

2 small to medium BITTER
GOURDS, ends trimmed, cut into
½-inch round slices, and cored

2 teaspoons VEGETABLE OIL

1 large GARLIC CLOVE, crushed,
peeled, and thinly sliced

CHILI AND GARLIC SAUCE
(page 106)

B ITTER MELON, also known as bitter gourd or bitter cucumber, grows
on climbing vines. It is preferably picked young, when it is less bitter.
Found in Chinese and Southeast Asian markets, it is elongated and has
a light green bumpy exterior. It gets its name from its very pronounced bitter flavor, which for some can be an acquired taste. In China and Southeast
Asia, this vegetable is consumed for its medicinal properties. Containing
quinine and vitamin C, it is believed to aid digestion and strengthen the immune system, among many other things. Because it is rather "cold" in character, it is always counterbalanced with a "hot" item such as ginger. There are
several popular ways to prepare it: sliced, added to clear broth, and served as
a soup; stir-fried with garlic and fermented black beans; or pan-fried stuffed
with pork and shrimp, as it is often enjoyed in China and Southeast Asia.

Always discard the spongy core, which contains seeds that are extremely
bitter. To get rid of some of the bitterness initially, toss the sliced vegetable
with salt and drain for 30 minutes to an hour. You can also soak it in cold
salted water if you wish. Pat the slices dry prior to stuffing.

1. Place the dried shrimp in a bowl with water to cover and allow to soak for 20 minutes to get rid of the excess salt. Drain and lay out to dry out again. Grind the shrimp finely in a mini food processor. Set aside.

2. Meanwhile, whisk together the soy sauce and starch until smooth. Add the ginger, scallion, fresh shrimp, and pork. Season with salt and pepper, add the sesame oil, and mix to combine the ingredients thoroughly. Stuff each bitter melon ring with the shrimp and pork stuffing.

3. Heat half the vegetable oil in a nonstick pan over medium heat. Add half the garlic and stir-fry until golden, 1 to 2 minutes. Pan-fry half the stuffed bitter melon in a single layer until golden on both sides and cooked through, about 3 minutes per side. Repeat the process with the remaining oil, garlic, and stuffed bitter melon slices. Transfer to a platter and garnish each slice with some finely ground dried shrimp. Serve with jasmine rice and chili and garlic sauce on the side.

Variation: Vietnamese stuffed mush-room caps are delicious. Soak 24 small (about 1 inch in diameter) dried shiitakes in water to cover until rehydrated and softened, about 30 minutes (or longer, depending on the size of the mushrooms). Drain and squeeze the mushrooms between the palms of your hands to get rid of any excess water. Cut the stems off and keep the caps whole. Make the pork and shrimp mixture, seasoning it with fish sauce instead of soy sauce. Stuff each mushroom cap with about 1 teaspoon of filling. If cooking in 10 cups of basic chicken or pork stock (pp. 116 and 118, respectively), be sure to place the mushrooms so the stuffing faces up. (At this time you can also add half of a bitter gourd, cored, and thinly sliced, to the stock.) Place the lid on top and cook over medium-low heat until the mushrooms are cooked through, 5 to 7 minutes. If steaming, fill the bottom third of a wok with water and place a bamboo steaming rack with a lid on top. Bring to a boil over high heat. Arrange the stuffed caps on a plate. Place the plate inside the bamboo steamer and cook until done, 5 to 7 minutes. Serve with dipping sauces such as ginger and scallion salt dipping sauce (page 104), spicy soy sauce dip (page 88), or nuoc cham (page 100).

YU HEUNG CARE TZE SZECHWANESE DOUBLE-COOKED EGGPLANT

SERVES 4 TO 6

6 ASIAN EGGPLANTS, stems
  removed, quartered lengthwise,
  and cut into 1-inch-long pieces
KOSHER SALT
4 to 6 dried CLOUD EAR
  MUSHROOMS
3 tablespoons CHINESE LIGHT
  SOY SAUCE
2 tablespoons WHITE RICE
  VINEGAR
2 tablespoons SHAOXING WINE
2 teaspoons CHINESE DARK THICK
  SOY SAUCE
2 teaspoons GRANULATED SUGAR
VEGETABLE OIL for deep-frying
2 teaspoons SESAME OIL
2 large GARLIC CLOVES, crushed,
  peeled, and minced
1 ounce fresh GINGER, peeled
  and minced
8 whole dried RED CHILIES
2 SCALLIONS, root and dark green
  ends trimmed, and 6-inch stalks
  cut into 1-inch-long pieces and
  quartered lengthwise
½ cup BASIC CHICKEN STOCK
  (page 116)
3 tablespoons HOISIN SAUCE
1 tablespoon TAPIOCA STARCH or
  CORNSTARCH
4 or more sprigs CILANTRO,
  stems trimmed

A POPULAR DISH in Chinese restaurants the world over, "eggplant in garlic sauce" is a Szechwanese specialty with a name that translates to "fish-flavored eggplant." Actually this dish contains no hint of fish, but the intensity of all the flavors contained in the sauce—ginger, garlic, scallion, Shaoxing wine, rice vinegar, sesame oil, chilies, soy sauce, and sugar—creates a flavor that is, perhaps, reminiscent of fish. Whatever the reason, it is a popular and delicious dish. I prefer to call it Szechwanese double-cooked eggplant to indicate the way it is prepared: first deep-fried in oil, then stir-fried. Eggplant has a very mild flavor, but its spongy interior is perfect for absorbing flavors. The cloud ears add a crunchy texture, counterbalancing the tender eggplant.

1. Toss the eggplant with the salt and let stand in a colander to drain for an hour. Pat the pieces dry with a clean towel. Meanwhile, put the cloud ears in a bowl with hot water to cover, then set a plate over the bowl to prevent steam from escaping. Let stand until the mushrooms rehydrate and soften, about 30 minutes (or longer, depending on the size of the mushrooms). Squeeze the mushrooms between the palms of your hands to get rid of the excess water. Using a paring knife, remove any hard stems and halve the mushrooms.

2. Whisk together the light soy sauce, vinegar, wine, dark soy sauce, and sugar in a bowl until the sugar is completely dissolved. Set the sauce aside.

3. Heat enough oil in a wok for deep-frying until the temperature reaches 360° to 375°F. Carefully add the eggplant and deep-fry until just soft and lightly crisp, about 2 minutes. With a slotted spoon, transfer the eggplant to a paper towel–lined plate to drain. Transfer the deep-frying oil to a heat-proof jar and keep for another use. Do not wipe the wok; it should be well greased.

4. Place the wok over high heat, add the sesame oil, and stir-fry the garlic and ginger until fragrant and light golden, 1 to 2 minutes. Add the chilies and stir a few times until fragrant. Add the eggplant, cloud ears, scallions, and soy sauce mixture. Reduce the heat to medium, whisk together the chicken stock, hoisin sauce, and tapioca starch in a bowl until smooth, then add the mixture to the wok. Stir-fry to coat

the eggplant with the sauce. Stir-fry until the eggplant is tender and the sauce is thickened, about 2 minutes. Serve garnished with cilantro.

THE CHINESE have been eating eggplant for thousands of years. In ancient times, the Chinese often referred to eggplant as "Malayan purple melon," which suggests that it was introduced to them by way of Southeast Asia. While no one knows for sure, it is almost certain that the eggplant originated in Central Asia, probably Persia, and that it was domesticated in India. It is technically a fruit, and at first the Chinese enjoyed eating it raw, but they soon figured out that the rather mild flavor and spongy texture of the eggplant were perfectly suited to absorb all sorts of delicious seasonings and sauces. The Chinese also believe that eggplant helps prevent diabetes and relieve hypertension. While the Chinese grow several varieties, the most popular is the long and narrow Asian eggplant, sometimes referred to as Japanese eggplant.

NASU NO MISO YAKI
ROASTED EGGPLANT WITH
SWEET MISO SAUCE

SERVES 4 TO 6

3 medium PURPLE EGGPLANTS
    (or 12 baby PURPLE
    EGGPLANTS), halved lengthwise
¼ cup VEGETABLE OIL
1 teaspoon SESAME OIL
⅓ cup SHIROMISO
3 tablespoons GRANULATED SUGAR
3 tablespoons SAKE
2 tablespoons MIRIN
1 tablespoon GINGER EXTRACT
    (page 74)
1 tablespoon toasted WHITE
    SESAME SEEDS

EVERY TIME MY HUSBAND and I go
to a Japanese restaurant, we order
the same appetizers: fried tofu (page
363), sea vegetable salad, and *nasu no
miso yaki*, our favorite eggplant dish. I
enjoy making all of these at home;
they're healthy and incredibly satisfying. This is the only time my husband
does not miss some kind of seafood,
poultry, or meat dish with his meal.

I N JAPANESE COOKING, just as in Chinese, eggplant is usually deep-
fried. This is why when you order it in Japanese and Chinese restaurants,
the eggplant is usually piping hot and, in my opinion, much too oily. I
have found that brushing the eggplant with oil, then roasting it, makes an incredible version of this classic Japanese dish. The thick sauce is a combination of the least salty of all soybean pastes, *shiromiso* or white miso (although
yellow in color), sugar, dry sake, and mirin, a sweet sake. You can use large
Italian eggplants or my favorite baby eggplants for this dish. Either makes for
a beautiful presentation.

1. *For the eggplants:* Preheat the oven to
375°F. Meanwhile, being careful
not to cut through the skin, score
the meaty part of the eggplants, just
until you've almost reached the
skin, every ½ inch in one direction,
then in the other, thus creating a
crisscross pattern. (Not only will
this technique cut the cooking time
by about half; it will also allow the
miso sauce to penetrate the eggplants
evenly and make them easier to eat.)
Mix the vegetable and sesame oils
together. Brush the eggplant halves
with the oil mixture on both sides
and place them on a baking sheet
(or dish) meaty side up. Roast until
golden and cooked through, about
30 minutes. The eggplants should
be very tender.

For the baby eggplants: Pierce the
meaty side all over with a skewer,
then make a crisscross pattern on the
skin side with incisions ¼ inch apart
in both directions, going through

the skin but not the meaty part.
Brush the eggplants with the oil
mixture on both sides. Heat a nonstick skillet over medium heat and
place the eggplant halves meaty side
down. Cook until golden, about 5
minutes. Flip the eggplants and continue to cook through about 5 minutes more. The eggplants should be
very tender.

2. Meanwhile, whisk together the
shiromiso, sugar, sake, mirin, and ginger extract in a double boiler over
medium heat or in a saucepan over
low heat until the sugar is completely dissolved and the sauce is
heated through, about 10 minutes.

3. Serve the eggplant halves meaty
side up, with the sauce spooned
over each eggplant half. Sprinkle
lightly with sesame seeds and serve
hot.

ULTIMATE EGGPLANT CURRY

SERVES 4 TO 6

1 tablespoon VEGETABLE OIL

3 large GARLIC CLOVES, crushed
and peeled

1 large SHALLOT, peeled and sliced
into thin wedges

1 or more tablespoons THAI RED or
GREEN CURRY PASTE
(page 82); or commercial
equivalent

1 tablespoon THAI or INDONESIAN
SHRIMP PASTE

2 teaspoons PALM SUGAR

1½ cups unsweetened COCONUT
MILK (page 77); or commercial
equivalent

1½ cups BASIC CHICKEN STOCK
(page 116); or VEGETABLE
STOCK (page 126)

6 ASIAN EGGPLANTS, stems
removed, quartered lengthwise,
and cut into 1-inch pieces

4 to 6 KAFFIR LIME LEAVES

1 bunch WATERCRESS, stems
trimmed

18 THAI BASIL LEAVES

1 LIME, cut into 4 or more wedges

THERE ARE VARIOUS TYPES of eggplant enjoyed through Southeast Asia. Among the more exotic is the slender purple Asian eggplant; the Thai eggplant, which is the size of a golf ball and streaked white and green; and the pea eggplant, which is uniformly green and as tiny as peas. Other small oblong-shaped ones are white, yellow, or purple in color. For this Thai curry, the eggplant's subtle flavor is enriched with coconut milk and spiced with curry paste, bitter kaffir lime leaves, and sweet licorice-like Thai basil. The watercress adds a delicious peppery and tangy note.

Any type of eggplant (including the large Italian eggplant) will do, but be sure to cut it in approximately 1-inch chunks, unless using Thai round or pea eggplants. Kaffir lime leaves are available at Southeast Asian markets or via the Internet (page 563).

1. Heat the oil in a heavy-bottomed pot over medium heat. Add the garlic and shallot and stir-fry until golden, 3 to 5 minutes. Add the curry paste, shrimp paste, and palm sugar and stir-fry until fragrant and darkened, about 3 minutes. Stir in the coconut milk and stock, picking up any brown bits, then add the eggplants and kaffir lime leaves.

2. Cook the eggplants, partially covered, until tender, 15 to 20 minutes. Add the watercress and basil and continue to cook until wilted and tender, about 5 minutes more. Serve with jasmine rice or sticky rice on the side. If you wish, squeeze a piece of lime over your serving of curry to cut the richness of the coconut milk.

I MUST ADMIT that eggplant is one of my favorite vegetables. I never grow tired of it, whether it is prepared Western or Asian style. Its texture and ability to absorb flavors make it an especially wonderful candidate for Asian seasonings, and while I like mixed vegetable curries, I really enjoy having just eggplant with crunchy watercress and Thai basil for their sweet and peppery aroma. To me this is the ultimate vegetable curry.

HEO TIM NUONG
PAN-FRIED EGGPLANT
AND PORK MEDLEY

SERVES 4 TO 6

6 ASIAN EGGPLANTS, halved
  lengthwise
KOSHER SALT
2 tablespoons FISH SAUCE
1 tablespoon GRANULATED SUGAR
1 LEMONGRASS STALK, root end
  trimmed, outer leaves and tough
  green top removed, and 6-inch-
  long inner bulb finely ground
12 ounces GROUND PORK
  (70 percent lean); or CRABMEAT
1 tablespoon VEGETABLE OIL,
  plus more for greasing pan
2 large GARLIC CLOVES, crushed,
  peeled, and minced
2 SCALLIONS, root and dark green
  ends trimmed, and 6-inch stalks
  thinly sliced into rounds
NUOC CHAM (page 100)
½ cup roasted unsalted PEANUTS,
  crushed (not peanut butter)
¼ cup DRIED SHRIMP, finely
  ground
FRIED SHALLOTS (page 108)
½ cup CILANTRO LEAVES

PAN-FRIED EGGPLANT topped with stir-fried ground pork, *heo tim nuong*, is enjoyed equally by the Vietnamese and Cambodians. For this recipe, I like to use the slender Asian eggplants with the stems on for presentation. Halved lengthwise, they are scored and pan-fried on both sides, then topped with a ground pork stir-fry flavored with lemongrass. Some cooks use crabmeat instead of the pork, but I must admit that the savory crispy ground pork against the sweet, spongy eggplant makes for a sublime combination. The subtle bitterness of the eggplant skin is counterbalanced with the ubiquitous sweet, sour, salty, and spicy *nuoc cham*. At the last minute a sprinkle of finely crushed peanuts, ground dried shrimp, fried shallots, and fresh cilantro makes this eggplant dish a real treat. The medley of flavors, both familiar and exotic, is refreshing.

1. Score the skin side of the eggplants about ⅛ inch deep every ½ inch in one direction, then in the other, creating a crisscross pattern. (Not only will this technique cut the cooking time by about half, it will also allow the sauce to penetrate the eggplant evenly.) Sprinkle with salt and allow to drain in a colander set over a bowl for 45 minutes. Wipe clean.

2. Whisk together the fish sauce and sugar until the sugar is completely dissolved. Stir in the lemongrass and add the ground pork. Mix thoroughly, incorporating the pork and lemongrass.

3. Preheat the oven to 250°F. Heat a well-greased nonstick pan over medium heat. Working in batches, place the eggplants skin side down in the pan until softened, about 10

minutes. Flip the eggplants and pan-fry until golden, about 10 minutes more. Place the first eggplant batch on a cookie sheet, meaty side up, and keep warm in the oven. Place the eggplant halves skin side down on individual plates.

4. Meanwhile, heat 2 teaspoons oil in a wok over high heat. Stir-fry the garlic until golden, 1 to 2 minutes. Add the scallions and ground pork mixture, and stir-fry continuously to break down the pork. Stir-fry until the pork is cooked through and lightly crisp, about 5 minutes. Spoon an equal amount of ground pork over each eggplant half. Drizzle about 2 tablespoons of *nuoc cham* over each serving, sprinkle with some crushed peanuts, dried shrimp, and fried shallots, and garnish with a generous amount of cilantro.

PRESERVED MUSTARD CABBAGE AND MARINATED BEEF

SERVES 4 TO 6

One 12.3-ounce package
 PRESERVED MUSTARD CABBAGE
1 tablespoon CHINESE LIGHT SOY
 SAUCE
1 tablespoon OYSTER SAUCE
1 tablespoon SHAOXING WINE
1 tablespoon GINGER EXTRACT
 (page 74)
1 teaspoon GRANULATED SUGAR
1 teaspoon TAPIOCA STARCH or
 CORNSTARCH
½ teaspoon freshly ground BLACK
 PEPPER
½ teaspoon SESAME OIL
12 ounces SIRLOIN BEEF STEAK,
 thinly sliced against the grain
1 to 2 tablespoons VEGETABLE OIL
3 large GARLIC CLOVES, crushed,
 peeled, and chopped

STIR-FRIED PRESERVED (or pickled) mustard cabbage with beef is a family favorite. Preserved mustard cabbage can be found packed in plastic bags in Chinese or Southeast Asian markets. This vegetable, although found fresh, is most popularly grown for preserving. Tender beef sirloin marinated in nutty sesame oil, Shaoxing wine, and black pepper is a delicious counterpoint to this crunchy, tangy, sweet, and salty vegetable. In the "hot-cold" Chinese food system, the "cool" cabbage and "hot" beef complement each other well.

Silver Leaf Brand from Thailand produces a delicious preserved mustard cabbage sold in 12.3-ounce packages (8.8 ounces when drained).

1. Drain the cabbage, rinse it well, and place in a bowl with water to cover. Drain after 30 minutes and repeat the process. Squeeze the cabbage well to extract any excess water. Slice the cabbage crosswise into thin strips.

2. Whisk together the soy sauce, oyster sauce, wine, ginger extract, and sugar in a bowl until the sugar is completely dissolved. Stir in the starch until the mixture is smooth, then stir in the black pepper and sesame oil. Add the beef and mix well to coat evenly. Allow to marinate for 20 minutes.

3. Heat the vegetable oil in a wok over high heat. Stir-fry the garlic until golden, 1 to 2 minutes. Add the beef and continue to stir-fry until just cooked, about 2 minutes. Add the mustard cabbage and keep stir-frying until heated through, about 3 minutes more. Divide into individual portions and serve with jasmine rice on the side.

MY PATERNAL GRANDPARENTS were born in Chiu Chow, near Fukien, in southern China. This preserved mustard cabbage, *ham suen choi* (literally "salty sour vegetable"), also known as Swatow cabbage, is very much part of the diet in that part of China; it is to the Chinese what sauerkraut is to the Germans. This recipe goes at least as far back as my grandmother, who probably learned it from her mother; she passed it on to her own children, my aunts, who in turn passed the recipe on to their married children.

PINAKBET

VEGETABLE STEW WITH FERMENTED SEAFOOD SAUCE

SERVES 4 TO 6

1 tablespoon VEGETABLE OIL

2 large GARLIC CLOVES, crushed, peeled, and minced

1 ounce fresh GINGER, peeled and finely grated

2 large SHALLOTS, peeled and sliced into thin wedges

CRISPY PORK BELLY (page 457)

2 large ripe TOMATOES, stems removed, each cut into 6 wedges

1 or more tablespoons BAGOONG; or CHINESE ANCHOVY SAUCE

½ cup BASIC PORK STOCK (page 118); or WATER

2 ASIAN EGGPLANTS, stems removed, quartered lengthwise, and cut into 1-inch pieces

1 BITTER MELON, halved lengthwise, cored, and cut into ¼-inch slices crosswise

12 small OKRA, stems removed

KOSHER SALT

Freshly ground BLACK PEPPER

PINAKBET IS A CLASSIC FILIPINO vegetable stew flavored with *bagoong*, fermented seafood sauce, and *bagnet*, deep-fried pork belly. Traditionally it contains eggplant, bitter melon, okra, and tomatoes cooked down with garlic, ginger, and onions. The pork belly is boiled with ginger and garlic, then deep-fried. While it adds a delicious flavor to the stew, it is fatty. You can use ground pork for a leaner variation of *pinakbet* (see variation). What makes this vegetable stew unique is the fermented seafood sauce, which can be made from fish (the most popular being anchovy derived) or shrimp. Using simple fish sauce, *patis*, would be delicious but not as pronounced as *bagoong*, so make an effort to find this item.

Bagoong can be purchased in Filipino markets or by mail order (page 563). For this recipe I like to use *bagoong isda*, made with anchovies. If you cannot find it, substitute Chinese anchovy sauce. Both are light gray in color and rather loose in consistency. You can also use a more pungent shrimp paste called *bagoong alamang*, or substitute shrimp paste from Indonesia or Thailand, in which case I recommend you halve the quantity.

1. Heat the oil in a heavy-bottomed pot over medium heat. Stir-fry the garlic and ginger until fragrant, about 3 minutes. Add the shallots and continue to stir-fry until golden, 2 to 3 minutes more. Add the pork belly, tomatoes, *bagoong*, and stock. Bring to a boil, reduce the heat to medium-low, and simmer, covered, for 10 minutes.

2. Add the eggplants, bitter melon, and okra. Adjust the seasoning with salt and pepper and cook until the vegetables are tender, 15 to 20 minutes. Serve as a main dish with long-grain rice on the side.

THROUGHOUT ASIA, perhaps with the exception of Korea and Japan, many vegetable dishes are not totally vegetarian, unless religious observance dictates it. Often their rich background flavors come from pork (and occasionally poultry or seafood) for added flavor. Pork used to be the only cooking fat, because vegetable oil was far too expensive. As a result, even the simplest vegetable stir-fries always had a meaty flavor. In the Philippines, pork is prepared in any number of ways; as in the rest of Southeast Asia and in China, it is the most popular meat used in cooking. *Pinakbet* is one of the tastiest of all classic Filipino vegetable dishes.

Fast food, Filipino-style. Pointing to the pot with your chin or lips is the way to get what you want.

STEAMED LEAFY GREENS WITH MUSHROOM SAUCE

SERVES 4 TO 6

8 dried small to medium SHIITAKE
MUSHROOMS

2 pounds CHINESE BROCCOLI,
FLOWERING OIL SEED RAPE, or
BOK CHOY

1 tablespoon VEGETABLE OIL

2 large GARLIC CLOVES, crushed
and peeled

2 cups BASIC CHICKEN STOCK
(page 116); or SUPERIOR STOCK
(page 117)

2 tablespoons SHAOXING WINE

2 tablespoons OYSTER SAUCE

1½ teaspoons SESAME OIL

½ teaspoon GRANULATED SUGAR

KOSHER SALT

Freshly ground BLACK PEPPER

1 tablespoon TAPIOCA STARCH; or
CORNSTARCH

4 to 6 sprigs CILANTRO, stems
trimmed

THE CHINESE often steam leafy greens or boil them in oiled water (see variation) until tender yet firm. Boiling them in water that contains some sesame oil not only adds a rich flavor but gives the vegetables a beautiful sheen. Choose from Chinese broccoli (*gai lan*), flowering oil seed rape (*yau choy*), or bok choy (green or white stemmed). Often water-cooked vegetables are topped with a slightly thick sauce incorporating ginger-infused chicken broth, oyster sauce, and Shaoxing wine. For a richer flavor, use superior stock for making your sauce. Sometimes this sauce serves as the braising liquid for dried shiitakes to create a more interesting combination of tender vegetables and slightly chewy mushrooms. Served over jasmine rice, these vegetables successfully complement any number of seafood, poultry, or meat dishes.

1. Put the shiitakes in a bowl with hot water to cover, then set a plate over the bowl to prevent steam from escaping. Let stand until the mushrooms rehydrate and soften, about 30 minutes (or longer depending on the size of the mushrooms). Squeeze the mushrooms between the palms of your hands to get rid of the excess water. Using a paring knife, remove any hard stems from the mushrooms. Keep the caps whole, or halve or julienne them.

2. Trim the leafy stems of the Chinese broccoli and flowering oil seed rape and cut them into 1½-inch-long pieces. Trim the stem end of the bok choy and separate the leaves. Depending on the size, if using baby bok choy, keep the leaves whole, or halve them lengthwise.

3. Set a bamboo steamer with a lid over a wok filled halfway with water, and bring the water to a boil over high heat. When the steamer is filled with hot steam, place the plate containing the leafy greens on top of the bamboo rack. Secure the steamer lid on top and steam the greens until cooked through, about 10 minutes.

4. Meanwhile heat the oil in a wok over high heat. Stir-fry the garlic until fragrant and golden, 1 to 2 minutes. Stir in the stock, wine, oyster sauce, sesame oil, and sugar. Allow the sauce to come to a boil, then reduce the heat to medium-low, add the mushrooms, and cook, covered, until tender, 5 to 7 minutes. Adjust seasoning to taste with salt and pepper. Dilute the tapioca starch with a tablespoon of water and stir into the stock. Boil until thickened, about a minute. Remove the leafy greens from the wok. Pour the sauce with mushrooms over the greens and serve garnished with cilantro.

Variation: Bring a pot of water to a boil over high heat and add 2 tablespoons vegetable oil, and 1 teaspoon sesame oil. Cook the leafy greens until tender but firm, 1 to 4 minutes. The Chinese broccoli will take longer because it has thicker stems and leaves. Proceed with the recipe as directed in step 4.

BRAISED NAPA CABBAGE
AND SHIITAKE MUSHROOMS

SERVES 4 TO 6

12 dried small to medium
SHIITAKE MUSHROOMS

¼ cup dried small to medium
SHRIMP (optional)

1 tablespoon VEGETABLE OIL

1 large GARLIC CLOVE, crushed,
peeled, and finely chopped

2 ounces SMITHFIELD HAM, sliced
paper thin (optional)

18 large NAPA CABBAGE LEAVES,
halved lengthwise and cut into
1-inch-wide strips crosswise

2 SCALLIONS, root and dark green
ends trimmed, and 6-inch stalks
cut into 1-inch-long pieces and
julienned

1 tablespoon CHINESE LIGHT SOY
SAUCE

½ teaspoon SESAME OIL

KOSHER SALT

Freshly ground BLACK PEPPER

NAPA CABBAGE (also known as Tientsin celery, or Chinese cabbage) is naturally sweet. Although delicious stir-fried, in this braised recipe its juices seep out, mingling with the concentrated perfume of the shiitake mushrooms. Soy sauce, garlic, and a small amount of sesame oil make this vegetable dish rich in flavor, especially when dried shrimp and Smithfield ham are added.

Choose a napa cabbage that is not too fat but rather slim, with more yellowish-green leafy tops than stem. Pick small to medium very orange-pink dry shrimp that are meaty rather than full of dried-up shells. Choose darker mushrooms that are thin and small to medium in size. While you can serve them halved, when preserved whole they represent prosperity.

1. Put the shiitakes in a bowl with hot water to cover, then set a plate over the bowl to prevent steam from escaping. Let stand until the mushrooms rehydrate and soften, about 30 minutes (or longer, depending on the size of the mushrooms). Squeeze the mushrooms between the palms of your hands to get rid of the excess water. Using a paring knife, remove any hard stems from the mushrooms. Leave the mushroom caps whole or halve them. In a separate bowl place the dried shrimp with water to cover to get rid of the excess salt. Drain and set aside.

2. Heat the oil in a heavy-bottomed pot over medium heat. Stir-fry the garlic until golden, 1 to 2 minutes. Add the ham (if using), mushrooms, dried shrimp (if using), napa cabbage, scallions, soy sauce, and sesame oil. Season with salt and pepper to taste and stir-fry to toss the ingredients well. Reduce the heat to low, cover with a lid, and cook until the cabbage is tender and the flavors have mingled, about 20 minutes. Transfer to a platter and serve.

SMITHFIELD HAM from Virginia substitutes for Chinese Yunnan ham. It is available in Chinese butcher shops in whole or sliced "steak" form. The full leg is available, but I usually buy the smaller shoulder, which will last me a few months. Soak the ham for 48 hours, changing the water once, to get rid of the excess salt and soften the meat for easy slicing. Keep it refrigerated, wrapped in a cotton kitchen towel. It will keep indefinitely. If you buy this ham by the slice, boil it for 15 minutes. Drain and use as directed in the recipe.

STEAMED FUZZY MELON WITH DRIED SCALLOPS

SERVES 4 TO 6

24 dried medium SCALLOPS

Two 1½-pound FUZZY MELONS, peeled, cut into at least 24 ½-inch-thick and cored slices

2 cups SUPERIOR STOCK (page 117); or BASIC CHICKEN STOCK (page 116)

2 tablespoons OYSTER SAUCE

¼ cup SHAOXING WINE

2 teaspoons TAPIOCA STARCH or CORNSTARCH

4 to 6 sprigs CILANTRO

FUZZY MELON, *tseet gwa*, is a delicious bright green (sometimes blotchy-skinned) gourd with a thin layer of soft fuzz, reminiscent of that of the kiwi fruit. Mild in flavor, it is cooling and can be had throughout the year. *Tseet gwa* range in size from four to eight inches long and from two to three inches in diameter, but the smaller ones are the best and tend to be the firmest. Peeled and cored, they can be thinly sliced and added to soups, stir-fries, or steamed. Cut in ½-inch-thick round slices, the melon can be stuffed with a softened dried scallop called *conpoy*, a Chinese delicacy that ranges in price depending on the size and quality of the scallop. The fuzzy melon slices can be stuffed with anything, however. Try the fresh shrimp paste variation.

A cucumber makes a good substitute for fuzzy melon in this recipe.

1. Place the dried scallops in a bowl with cold water to cover and rehydrate overnight, refrigerated. Drain and place one scallop in the center of each slice of fuzzy melon set on a plate to fit inside a steamer. (The scallops should fit snugly.)

2. Set a bamboo steamer with a lid over a wok filled halfway with water and bring the water to a boil over high heat. When the steamer is filled with hot steam, place the plate with the stuffed fuzzy melon on top of the bamboo rack. Secure the steamer lid on top and steam until cooked through, 15 to 20 minutes.

3. Meanwhile, heat the stock in a pot over high heat. Reduce the heat to medium and stir in the oyster sauce and wine. Dilute the tapioca starch with a tablespoon of water and stir it into the flavored stock until thickened, about 1 minute. Transfer the steamed and stuffed fuzzy melon to individual plates and spoon an equal amount of thickened sauce over and around each serving and garnish with cilantro. Serve with rice on the side.

Variation: Substitute half the recipe of the shrimp balls (page 406) for the dried scallops and use as filling for the center of each slice of fuzzy melon. Proceed with steps 2 and 3 of the recipe.

GADO GADO
MEDLEY OF VEGETABLES
WITH PEANUT SAUCE

GADO GADO, a medley of cooked vegetables (and sometimes fruit) dressed with *sambal kacang*, peanut sauce, is a classic dish enjoyed throughout Indonesia. Vegetables are blanched separately in salted water and tossed together with the sweet, savory, and spicy peanut sauce just before serving. When my uncle Ming Jong visits from Jakarta, after a few days in the States he starts mentioning *gado gado* and how much he loves it. There are probably as many variations of this classic dish as there are cooks in Indonesia, and everyone uses his or her favorite vegetables. I have found that the most delicious versions use tender yet firm yard-long beans, mung bean sprouts, carrots, potatoes, and cabbage. Hard-boiled eggs, pan-fried tofu, and crispy shallots make not only for a colorful presentation but textural contrast as well.

For presentation, I have substituted smaller Brussels sprouts for the cabbage, and added baby red potatoes with their skins on for color. The peanut sauce should be freshly made or reheated with a little water if necessary; the sauce should be thick but fairly loose in consistency.

1. Slice the tofu into ½-inch-thick rectangular slices. In a single layer, place the tofu between a double layer of paper towels. Refrigerate for 12 hours, changing the paper towels when really drenched; about once every 4 hours will do. Heat a well-greased nonstick pan over high heat and pan-fry the tofu slices in a single layer until heated through and golden crisp, about 2 minutes per side. Halve the tofu slices crosswise.

2. Cook each type of vegetable separately in salted water (add about 1 tablespoon salt to 1 quart water) to retain the bright colors. Bring the pot of water to a boil over high heat.

You can have several pots going at the same time, or use the same pot, changing the water each time. Cook the vegetables until tender but slightly firm: Brussels sprouts and yard-long beans can be cooked together, for about 10 minutes; potatoes, about 20 minutes; carrots, about 3 minutes; mung bean sprouts, about 5 seconds. Drain, halve the Brussels sprouts, and quarter the potatoes. Transfer all the vegetables (except the potatoes) to a large mixing bowl. Toss the vegetables with half the peanut sauce.

3. Transfer the tossed vegetables to a serving platter. Arrange the potato quarters (skin facing up), hard-boiled eggs (yolk facing up), and tofu slices, alternating them to create a pattern at the edge of the platter. Drizzle the remaining peanut sauce on top of the mixed vegetables and garnish with a generous amount of cucumber slices and fried shallots. Serve with rice on the side for a complete meal, or shrimp chips for a tasty afternoon snack.

Variation: For a vegetable-and-fruit version of *gado gado*, peel, core, and cut half of a pineapple into bite-size chunks. Peel and cut a mango into bite-sized chunks, removing the pit in the process. Toss with the vegetables called for in the recipe, dress with the peanut sauce, and garnish with cucumber and fried shallots.

SHRIMP CHIPS are made all over Asia, but the best quality come from Indonesia, where they are called *krupuk*. These chips, or wafers, are made of tapioca starch and flavored with fish or shrimp; they are easily found in Asian markets and occasionally in gourmet markets across the United States. My brothers and I have enjoyed eating shrimp chips since we were young. We love them even more than popcorn. Deep-fried in oil, the dried raw chips went from being tiny and translucent to expanding to at least twice their size and turning an opaque almond color. We enjoyed them not only for their delicious shrimp flavor but for the sizzling shrinking sensation they created upon contact with our tongues. Their crunch and flavor are a perfect complement to *gado gado*. If you feel festive, you can find these chips in green and red colors. While the packaged fried chips can be purchased, I do not recommend them. They have less flavor and are not as crispy as when freshly fried.

GULAI PAKIS
FIDDLEHEAD FERNS IN
SPICY COCONUT SAUCE

SERVES 4 TO 6

2 tablespoons VEGETABLE OIL

2 large GARLIC CLOVES, crushed, peeled, and minced

½ ounce fresh GINGER, peeled and finely grated

½ ounce GALANGAL, peeled and finely grated

1 LEMONGRASS STALK, root end trimmed, outer leaves and tough green top removed, inner 6-inch-long bulb finely ground

½ ounce fresh TURMERIC, peeled and finely grated; or ½ teaspoon TURMERIC POWDER

4 or more RED THAI CHILIES, stemmed, seeded, and minced

1½ teaspoons CORIANDER SEEDS, finely ground

1 teaspoon CUMIN SEEDS, finely ground

3 CANDLENUTS or MACADAMIA NUTS, finely crushed

1 tablespoon INDONESIAN or THAI SHRIMP PASTE

3 cups unsweetened COCONUT MILK (page 77); or commercial equivalent

¼ cup or more TAMARIND EXTRACT (page 75); or commercial equivalent

4 KAFFIR LIME LEAVES (2 pairs)

KOSHER SALT

1½ pounds FIDDLEHEADS, well washed and drained, tail base trimmed

GULAI PAKIS, sometimes *gulai paku*, is a delicious Indonesian classic dish of fiddlehead ferns cooked in a rich coconut sauce spiced with chilies, galangal, and ginger. Fiddleheads are available in late spring and throughout the summer in gourmet stores or Asian markets. They look like deep green coils and are technically the stage of a fern before its leaves open fully. Select the tender, smaller ones (no more than about 1½ inches in diameter) with the least amount of tail end. The bigger they are, the more fibrous they are.

Fresh or frozen galangal and turmeric can be found in Southeast Asian markets or on the Internet. If you cannot find fiddleheads, substitute yard-long beans or regular green beans, and cut into 2-inch-long pieces.

1. Heat the oil in a heavy-bottomed pot over medium heat. Stir-fry the garlic, ginger, galangal, and lemongrass until fragrant and lightly golden, about 5 minutes. Add the turmeric, chilies, ground coriander, cumin, and candlenuts, and stir-fry for 2 minutes more. Add the shrimp paste and stir-fry until 1 to 2 shades darker, about 2 minutes. Add the coconut milk and tamarind extract, and bring to a gentle boil.

2. Reduce the heat to low, add the kaffir lime leaves, adjust seasoning with salt, and simmer, partially covered, for 15 minutes. Add the fiddleheads and continue to simmer until they are tender but firm, 5 to 10 minutes. Serve with rice on the side and with any grilled fish or meat.

TEMPURA
DEEP-FRIED VEGETABLES
IN LACY BATTER

SERVES 4 TO 6

VEGETABLE OIL for deep-frying

2 large EGGS

¼ cup CHILLED SAKE (optional)

1 cup ICE WATER (if not using sake, add ¼ cup extra water)

1¼ cups all-purpose or cake FLOUR

1 medium SWEET POTATO, peeled and sliced into ⅛-inch-thick pieces

1 ASIAN EGGPLANT, sliced diagonally into ⅛-inch-thick pieces

1 small LOTUS ROOT, peeled and and sliced into ⅛-inch-thick pieces

12 fresh medium SHIITAKE MUSHROOMS

12 YELLOW STRING BEANS, ends trimmed

12 SHISO LEAVES

TEMPURA DIPPING SAUCE (page 92)

TEMPURA, DEEP-FRIED BATTERED food, goes back approximately to the sixteenth century in Japan and was introduced to the Japanese by the Spanish and Portuguese colonials. Of course, the Japanese took a borrowed concept and made it their own. The result is a light fried food that is lacy and crispy and served with a refreshing gingery dipping sauce unique to Japan. The trick to a good tempura is not to overmix the batter; make sure it is lumpy. It should be made just as you are ready to deep-fry. You can fry all sorts of sliced vegetables from the common broccoli, carrots, cauliflower, eggplant, and sweet potato to the more exotic lotus root, shiitake mushrooms, and shiso (perilla) leaves. I like to add sake (or white wine) to my batter for an interesting subtle flavor. I've listed some of my favorite vegetables, but feel free to choose your own favorites; there are no rules.

This makes a copious vegetarian meal with a bowl of rice on the side. You'll find a recipe for seafood tempura on page 417.

1. Heat enough oil for deep-frying in a pot over medium heat until the temperature reaches 360° to 375°F.

2. Lightly beat the eggs with the sake (if using) and water. Add the flour all at once and give it only a few stirs. Don't whisk it. The batter should be loosely combined and lumpy.

3. Make sure all your vegetables are thoroughly dry. Dip a piece of vegetable into the batter, then carefully lower it into the hot oil. Repeat this process, working with one piece at a time, until you have 5 to 6 pieces in the hot oil, but no more. Deep-fry until crispy and light golden on all sides, about 3 minutes total. Drain on a paper towel–lined plate.

Divide equally among individual plates and serve with dipping sauce on the side.

JEON
PAN-FRIED VEGETABLES

SERVES 4 TO 6

2 small to medium ZUCCHINI,
    ends trimmed and cut into
    ¼-inch-thick slices
2 large ASIAN EGGPLANTS, stem
    end discarded, cut into ¼-inch-
    thick diagonal slices
KOSHER SALT
VEGETABLE OIL for pan-frying
2 small to medium SWEET
    POTATOES, peeled and cut into
    ¼-inch-thick slices
1 cup all-purpose FLOUR
2 large EGGS, beaten
SPICY VINEGAR DIPPING SAUCE
    (page 93)

LIKE THE JAPANESE, the Koreans also love to batter their vegetables. But rather than deep-fry them, the Koreans like to pan-fry them. You can use any vegetable (or fish; see variation), but the most popular is zucchini. I have made this dish using not only zucchini but eggplant and sweet potato. Prior to pan-frying, the Koreans also like to decorate each slice of vegetable with a single cilantro leaf, or bell pepper slice, just to add color to the dish. Feel free to experiment with all sorts of edible decorations, which are usually secured with the egg wash.

1. Toss the zucchini and eggplants separately with salt and drain each in separate colanders for 45 minutes. Drain and pat dry with a cotton kitchen towel.

2. Heat 1 tablespoon oil in a nonstick pan over medium-high heat. Dredge a slice of zucchini, eggplant, or potato with flour, then dip it in the eggs. Place as many pieces as will fit in your pan and pan-fry until golden, 3 to 5 minutes per side. (The sweet potato will take more time to cook through, about 2 minutes more per side.) Serve with spicy vinegar sauce for dipping on the side.

Variation: For fish, *saengson jeon*: Substitute 1 to 1½ pounds skinless, boneless flounder or sole fillets for the vegetables, and cut into approximately 1½-inch-square pieces. Proceed with step 2 of the recipe.

BAMBOO SHOOT AND SHIITAKE SALAD

SERVES 4 TO 6

12 fresh medium SHIITAKE
    MUSHROOMS, stemmed
4 medium whole BAMBOO SHOOTS
¼ cup MIRIN
⅓ cup JAPANESE DARK SOY SAUCE
1 tablespoon JAPANESE RICE
    VINEGAR
1 teaspoon SESAME OIL
Freshly ground BLACK PEPPER
2 SCALLIONS, root and dark green
    ends trimmed, and 6-inch stalks
    thinly sliced on the diagonal

IN JAPAN, bamboo shoots are prized for their crunchy texture and rich flavor and are often prepared so as to emphasize these characteristics. In this delicate salad a well-balanced dressing combines mirin, Japanese soy sauce, tangy rice vinegar, and a small amount of nutty sesame oil. Bamboo shoots are cut lengthwise so that the inner growth rings are partially visible. Shiitake mushroom caps are julienned to expose more of their dark brown and creamy white tones. Scallions are sliced on the diagonal, visually complementing the other ingredients. The result is a beautiful dish, high in fiber, perfect for setting the tone of a sophisticated vegetarian meal or acting as a palate opener for meat and fish dishes to follow.

If using fresh bamboo shoots, be sure to remove the sheath (leaves) completely and boil the shoot for 15 minutes to remove natural toxins. You can buy bamboo shoots already boiled in any Asian market. The best quality are from Japan, found in Japanese markets in tubs full of water or vacuum sealed.

1. Bring 2 small pots of water to a boil over high heat. Blanch the mushrooms in one pot for a minute or so, and blanch the whole bamboo shoots in the second pot for 3 to 5 minutes if canned, or 10 to 15 minutes if raw. Drain both ingredients completely.

2. Halve the shoots lengthwise from the tip toward the wider part, then slice thinly lengthwise. Place in a sieve set over a bowl and drain for about 15 minutes. Finely julienne the shiitakes.

3. In a salad bowl, whisk together the mirin, soy sauce, vinegar, sesame oil, and black pepper to taste. Add the bamboo shoots, shii-takes, and half the scallions, and toss until well combined. Allow to marinate for 10 minutes and divide among individual plates. Garnish each serving with the remaining scallions and serve.

Variation: Add 2 cups thinly sliced or shredded steamed chicken breast to the salad and toss until well combined. Serve with rice for a more complete single-dish meal.

JAPANESE-STYLE ZUCCHINI SALAD

SERVES 4 TO 6

3 small to medium ZUCCHINI, sliced into paper-thin rounds

1 teaspoon KOSHER SALT

1 tablespoon JAPANESE DARK SOY SAUCE

1 tablespoon MIRIN

1 tablespoon JAPANESE RICE VINEGAR

½ teaspoon SESAME OIL

2 teaspoons GINGER EXTRACT (page 74); or finely grated GINGER

½ teaspoon GRANULATED SUGAR

1 tablespoon finely grated CARROT

ONE DAY AT THE MARKET I found beautiful young zucchini. They felt perfectly firm; I thought, why not make a salad with them rather than cook them? I sliced them paper thin and I tossed in a dressing made from soy sauce, mirin, sesame oil, vinegar, and ginger juice to cure for 30 minutes. I drained them and served them with grilled salmon served over sushi rice. They were absolutely delicious; the zucchini had retained all their crispness and vitamins, which they lose to a certain degree upon contact with heat.

1. Toss the zucchini with the salt in a colander set over a bowl. Drain for 30 minutes. Transfer to a cotton kitchen towel and twist it to extract and discard the juices.

2. Stir together the soy sauce, mirin, vinegar, sesame oil, ginger juice, and sugar in a large bowl until the sugar is completely dissolved. Add the zucchini and toss to coat the slices evenly. Allow to rest for 30 minutes, tossing every 10 minutes or so. Drain lightly. Serve on individual plates garnished with finely grated carrot.

KOREAN-STYLE MESCLUN SALAD

SERVES 4 TO 6

2 tablespoons PINE NUTS

1 pound MESCLUN

½ seedless CUCUMBER, peeled,
halved lengthwise, seeded, and
thinly sliced into crescents

½ small YELLOW ONION, peeled
and sliced paper thin
(about ½ cup, loosely packed)

¼ cup SPICY VINEGAR DIPPING
SAUCE (page 93)

MESCLUN MIX will make a beautiful Korean-style salad. This recipe is based on a delicious salad I had in New York City's Woo Lae Oak restaurant in SoHo. My husband, who is sensitive to overwhelming amounts of garlic, and therefore kimchi, was happy to have this alternative to accompany his meal. The delicious sweet, savory, tangy, and spicy dressing complemented everything from our soy sauce–braised black cod (page 393) to the sweet eel cooked on stones, to the chicken and beef slices we grilled on the hibachi.

1. Toast the pine nuts, shaking the pan continuously, in a nonstick pan over medium heat until golden, 3 to 5 minutes. Set aside.

2. Mix together the mesclun, cucumber, and onion in a large bowl, then add the dressing and toss well. Divide among individual plates and garnish each serving with toasted pine nuts. Serve with grilled seafood, poultry, or meat.

Variation: Romaine lettuce makes for a delicious, crunchy alternative. Slice the leaves about ½ inch thick and proceed with the recipe.

COLORFUL CUCUMBER AND SHALLOT SALAD

SERVES 4 TO 6

2 small to medium CUCUMBERS,
  peeled, halved lengthwise,
  seeded, and cut into ¼-inch-
  thick slices diagonally
1 tablespoon KOSHER SALT
1 cup CHINESE WHITE RICE
  VINEGAR
5 tablespoons GRANULATED SUGAR
2 medium SHALLOTS or 1 small
  RED ONION, sliced into thin
  wedges
1 or more THAI CHILIES, seeded
  and sliced into thin rounds

THIS TANGY SALAD is a classic Thai dish; less-spicy versions exist elsewhere in Southeast Asia. Its flavor combinations—salt, sweet, sour, bitter, and spicy—are a wonderful example of the yin yang philosophy of balanced opposites. Although it is sometimes eaten as an impromptu snack over rice, it is most delicious when eaten with grilled meat or seafood. The tanginess of unseasoned rice vinegar tamed by sugar perfectly complements dishes such as grilled beef satay (page 98) served with a rich peanut sauce. Not only do the refreshing cucumber, pungent shallot, and hot chili complement the beef, but the tanginess of the salad cuts the richness of the peanut sauce as well. The textures and colors of the salad are as uplifting as its flavors. The crunchy translucent green cucumber, pungent purple shallots, and hot red chilies are great examples of Southeast Asian flavor combinations manifest in a rich visual array.

1. Toss together the cucumber and salt in a strainer and let stand until the cucumber has drained, about 30 minutes. Discard the water. Rinse the cucumber, then drain thoroughly.

2. Bring the rice vinegar and sugar to a gentle boil over medium heat. When the sugar has dissolved completely and the mixture thickens to a syrup consistency, remove from the heat and allow to cool. Add the cucumber, shallots, and chilies and toss until the ingredients are evenly distributed. Let stand for 30 minutes before serving.

Variation: For less-pungent and softer shallots, toss them in the vinegar-and-sugar marinade, and allow them to cure for about 30 minutes prior to adding the cucumbers and chilies. You can also make this spicy, sweet, and sour salad without preparing a vinegar-and-sugar syrup. Instead, whisk the vinegar and sugar together until the sugar has completely dissolved, and toss all the ingredients together. Let stand for 30 minutes before serving.

GOI DU DU
GREEN PAPAYA SALAD

SERVES 4 TO 6

Juice of 2 LIMES or LEMONS

3 tablespoons FISH SAUCE

3 tablespoons GRANULATED SUGAR

1 pound GREEN PAPAYA or
MANGO, peeled, halved
lengthwise, seeded, and
julienned into 2-inch-long
threads

2 medium CARROTS, peeled and
julienned into 2-inch-long
threads

2 or more RED THAI CHILIES,
stems removed, seeded, and
sliced paper thin crosswise

2 tablespoons roasted unsalted
PEANUTS, finely crushed (not
peanut butter)

⅓ cup CILANTRO LEAVES

YOU WILL ENCOUNTER green papaya salad similarly prepared with a tangy, sweet, and savory fish sauce–based dressing in Vietnam, Thailand, Cambodia, and the Philippines. I strive for balance when making the dressing; some like it sweeter, tangier, or saltier. Feel free to experiment, but be sure to taste your sauce prior to tossing in the papaya, in case you need to adjust the flavors. For color contrast, I occasionally add vibrant orange julienned carrot. A refreshing salad garnished with roasted peanuts and lemony cilantro leaves, it complements grilled or deep-fried seafood, poultry, and meat rather well, aiding the digestion of these rich foods. Green mango, an equally popular unripe fruit, is prepared in the same manner.

Unlike the ripe fruit, green papaya (shaped round or oblong) and green mango are green all the way through from the skin (dark green) to the meat (light to lime green). They are available in Asian or Latin markets, and while there is really no substitute for either one of these, in a pinch you can use the more familiar and equally delicious kohlrabi or jicama, which are mildly sweet in flavor and have a great crunchy texture.

Whisk together the lime juice, fish sauce, and sugar in a bowl until the sugar is completely dissolved. Add the papaya, carrots, and chilies, and toss until well combined. Let stand for 20 minutes. Divide among individual plates, sprinkle each serving with crushed peanuts, and garnish with cilantro leaves.

YUM HUA PLEE
SHRIMP AND BANANA
BLOSSOM SALAD

SERVES 4 TO 6

¼ cup small DRIED SHRIMP

Juice of 1 LEMON

2 BANANA BLOSSOMS, creamy
yellow hearts only, quartered
lengthwise and sliced paper
thin crosswise

8 ounces CHICKEN BREAST
(about half a breast), skinned;
or PORK TENDERLOIN

12 small BLUE TIGER SHRIMP

⅓ cup FISH SAUCE

Juice of 1 LIME (about ⅓ cup)

2 tablespoons CHINESE WHITE
RICE VINEGAR

4 tablespoons PALM SUGAR;
or GRANULATED SUGAR

3 fresh RED THAI CHILIES,
stemmed, seeded, and sliced
paper thin

1 large GARLIC CLOVE, crushed,
peeled, and minced

¼ cup roasted unsalted PEANUTS,
finely crushed (not peanut
butter)

12 THAI BASIL or MINT leaves,
julienned

FRIED SHALLOTS (page 108)

BANANA BLOSSOMS are harvested and enjoyed as a vegetable and as the main ingredient in salads throughout Southeast Asia. The dressing always includes fish sauce, lime juice, and sugar. While this dish can be served without protein, many variations include chicken, pork, or shrimp for a more satisfying dish; most of the time it is a combination of two of these, shrimp being a constant. It is a perfect way to make use of leftover steamed, boiled, grilled, or roasted chicken breast, pork tenderloin, or small shrimp. Remove the purplish-pink sheaths of the banana blossom (often reserved for presentation) and tiny stamen to reveal the creamy yellow, pointy heart. Like artichoke hearts, once cut the blossom hearts tend to turn dark; for this reason they are submerged in lemon juice and water to prevent them from darkening.

Banana blossoms are available fresh at Southeast Asian markets and sometimes, although rarely, in gourmet stores. The flavor is quite distinct, but in a pinch you can use Jerusalem artichokes, blanching these until tender but firm. The texture and flavor are quite different but delicious just the same.

1. Put the dried shrimp in a bowl with water to cover to get rid of the excess salt. Drain, set aside to dry, and grind finely in a mini food processor. Set powder aside

2. Mix the lemon juice with 1 quart cold water and add the banana blossoms. Allow to soak for 30 minutes. Drain well.

3. Bring two pots of water to a boil over high heat. Reduce the heat to medium and add the chicken breast or pork tenderloin to one pot. Cook until the juices run clear, about 10 minutes. Add the shrimp to the other pot; cook until opaque, about a minute. Drain both, put the meat in a bowl, and cover with plastic wrap to prevent it from coloring. Shock the shrimp in ice water. When cool enough to handle, finely shred the chicken (or thinly slice the pork tenderloin against the grain). Remove the shells (and heads, if any) from the shrimp, halve them lengthwise, and devein.

4. Whisk together the fish sauce, lime juice, vinegar, and palm sugar in a bowl until the sugar is completely dissolved. Stir in the chilies and garlic and let stand for 30 minutes to allow the flavors to blend.

5. Put the banana blossoms, chicken or pork, and shrimp in a large bowl and toss with the fish sauce dressing until well coated. Transfer to a serving platter. Garnish with a generous amount of peanuts, basil or mint, fried shallots, and powdered dried shrimp. Serve with sticky rice on the side.

BANANA BLOSSOMS MAKE A DELICIOUS SALAD ENJOYED THROUGHOUT SOUTHEAST ASIA.

RAU CAI CHUA
PICKLED VEGETABLE
NIBBLES

SERVES 4 TO 6

1 pound CARROTS, peeled and cut
into 2-inch-long matchsticks
3 tablespoons KOSHER SALT
1 pound DAIKON, peeled, halved
lengthwise, and cut into thin
crescents
6 tablespoons GRANULATED SUGAR
1 cup CHINESE WHITE RICE
VINEGAR
1½ pounds CUCUMBER, peeled,
seeds removed, cut into 6 thick
stems lengthwise, then cut
crosswise into 2-inch-long sticks

VIETNAMESE AND CAMBODIAN pickled vegetables go particularly well with grilled, roasted, or deep-fried seafood, poultry, and meat. The crunchy white daikon, carrot, and cucumber, macerated in a sweetened rice vinegar–based pickling liquid, help digest rich foods. In many restaurants (including Chinese, where this recipe originates), these colorful orange, white, and green pickles make for a wonderful *amuse-bouche* to nibble on while you wait for your main dishes to arrive. They also make a delicious alternative to stir-fried vegetables. Often I have these pickles for lunch with a bowl of rice and some broth on the side.

1. Toss the carrots in a sieve set over a bowl with 1 tablespoon of the salt. Let stand for about 45 minutes. Gently press the carrots against the sieve to remove any remaining moisture. Rinse and drain. Place the carrots in a clean kitchen towel and twist the towel to squeeze out any excess water.

2. Repeat step 1 with the daikon.

3. Whisk together the sugar and vinegar until the sugar is completely dissolved. Divide this pickling mixture among 3 quart-size plastic bags; set a bag aside to use in step 4. Put the carrots in one bag and the daikon in the other. Seal the bags and shake them to coat the ingredients evenly. Lay the bags flat on a plate and refrigerate at least 24 hours (or overnight), turning the bags over every hour if possible.

4. The next day, repeat step 1 with the cucumbers. After draining, place the cucumbers in the third plastic bag of pickling liquid, seal, and toss to coat evenly. Lay the bag flat on a plate and refrigerate for 4 to 6 hours, turning the bag over every hour if possible.

5. Drain the carrots, daikon, and cucumbers well at room temperature for 30 minutes before serving.

YOUNG PICKLED GINGER

MAKES ABOUT 2 CUPS

1 pound young fresh GINGER,
  peeled
2 teaspoons KOSHER SALT
1½ cups CHINESE WHITE RICE
  VINEGAR
½ cup SPRING WATER
¼ cup GRANULATED SUGAR

GINGER is a rhizome. When young, it has a thin, pinkish-yellow, translucent skin and is juicy and tender; this is the preferred type for making pickled ginger. Older ginger rhizomes have dark yellow-tannish skins and are very fibrous with much less juice in them; they are used in everyday cooking, although when young ginger is available, that is all I use. For this recipe you will need young ginger; there is really no substitute. When pickled, ginger tends to turn creamy pink naturally, a chemical reaction to the vinegar. Some of the commercially available pickled ginger is neon pink; unfortunately, that comes from the use of food coloring. In herbal medicine, ginger is believed to aid digestion and cold symptoms. It is regarded as a cure-all, having a warming effect and being good for the heart, lungs, stomach, spleen, and kidneys.

1. Place the young ginger in a bowl and sprinkle the salt evenly over each knob. Refrigerate for 24 hours, then drain and blot each knob dry with a paper towel.

2. Slice each ginger knob paper thin along the grain, and place the slices in a jar. Whisk together the rice vinegar, water, and sugar in a bowl until the sugar is completely dissolved. Pour the sweetened vinegar over the ginger. Close the jar and allow to pickle for at least a week.

NASU SU-ZUKE
PURPLE PICKLED EGGPLANT

MAKES ABOUT 1 QUART

4 ASIAN EGGPLANTS, quartered
  lengthwise and cut into
  1-inch-long pieces
1 tablespoon KOSHER SALT
1½ cups JAPANESE SEASONED RICE
  VINEGAR
¾ cup SPRING WATER
¼ cup GRANULATED SUGAR

IN AUTUMN, THE JAPANESE go crazy for pickled eggplant. This is the time of year when the fruit is at its best. Preserved in salt brine for several days, the eggplant is then pickled in a seasoned Japanese rice vinegar. It is sweet and salty at the same time and much less acid than Chinese rice vinegar. Slender Asian eggplant (also Japanese eggplant) is used for this recipe. The beautiful purple color of the skin will seep into the pickling liquid, which becomes quite a vibrant color.

1. Toss the eggplant pieces with the salt in a colander set over a bowl. Allow to drain for an hour. Rinse the pieces under cold water and drain. Place in a ceramic jar.

2. Whisk together the rice vinegar, spring water, and sugar in a bowl until the sugar is completely dissolved. Pour the pickling liquid over the eggplant, making sure the pieces are completely submerged. Place a lid on top of the jar and refrigerate for 48 hours before eating.

MUL KIMCHI
PICKLED DAIKON

MAKES ABOUT 1 QUART

2 tablespoons KOSHER SALT

2 tablespoons GRANULATED SUGAR

1 pound DAIKON, peeled, halved
  lengthwise, and thinly sliced
  crosswise

2 large GARLIC CLOVES, peeled and
  sliced paper-thin lengthwise

3 SCALLIONS, root and dark green
  ends trimmed, and 6-inch stalks
  cut into 2-inch-long pieces and
  julienned

1½ ounces fresh GINGER, peeled
  and julienned

2 RED THAI CHILIES, stemmed,
  seeded, and julienned; or
  2 tablespoons DRIED KOREAN
  RED CHILI STRIPS

I N KOREA it is often said that a Korean woman can turn anything into
kimchi. This is a northern-style kimchi; unlike its southern counterparts, it
is quite pungent and spicy. As with all kimchi, however, garlic is never
lacking. Mul kimchi, daikon (radish) water kimchi, is easy to make, and while it
has subtle overtones of ginger and scallion, the garlic is prominent. Feel free
to cut the garlic amount in half if you are sensitive to it. Served slightly
chilled in individual bowls, it is a perfect complement to grilled meats,
especially during the spring and summer.

1. Bring 3 cups water with the salt
and sugar to a boil over high heat.
Remove from the heat and allow to
cool completely. Place the daikon,
garlic, scallions, ginger, and chilies
in a glass jar. Pour the seasoned
water over the ingredients to cover
and place a lid on top without
screwing it on.

2. Allow to ferment for 24 hours at
room temperature in a cool, dark
place. Once fermented, remove the
garlic, tightly cover with the lid, and
refrigerate. Serve individual portions of the daikon with its refreshing herbs and brine for sipping.

WHILE IN KOREA, I was told never
to make *kimchi* using regular iodized
salt. "Natural sea salt crystals are the
only type of salt you should be using
for making *kimchi*," a Korean *kimchi*
master once cautioned. That's great
news to me because it is the only type
of salt I use in cooking. Natural sea
salts are grayish-green in color and
moist and taste of the sea. Once the
bag is opened, transfer the salt crystals to an airtight container to keep
them from drying out. While they used
to be difficult to find, that is no longer
true. Natural sea salts can be found in
all Asian markets and are imported
from China, Korea, and Japan. A one-
pound bag costs less than five dollars.
Fancy gourmet shops sell the French
type, but the same one-pound bag will
cost you an average of ten to twenty
dollars.

Bok Hi Chang teaches the art of making kimchi at Son's Korean Home Culture, in Seoul, Korea.

BAECHU KIMCHI
PICKLED SPICY CABBAGE

MAKES ABOUT 2 QUARTS

½ cup plus 1 tablespoon KOSHER
  SALT

1 large NAPA CABBAGE
  (2 to 4 pounds), halved or
  quartered lengthwise

1 large DAIKON (1½ to 2 pounds),
  peeled and julienned into
  2-inch-long matchsticks

1 cup SPRING WATER

1½ tablespoons RICE FLOUR

6 large GARLIC CLOVES, crushed,
  peeled, and minced

2 ounces fresh GINGER, peeled and
  finely grated

3 SCALLIONS, root and dark green
  ends trimmed, and 6-inch stalks
  cut into 2-inch-long pieces and
  julienned

¼ cup fermented BABY SHRIMP,
  minced; or ⅓ cup FISH SAUCE

¼ cup KOREAN RED CHILI
  POWDER

2 tablespoons KOREAN RED CHILI
  FLAKES

1 bunch WATERCRESS, tough stem
  ends trimmed

CABBAGE KIMCHI is perhaps the most popular *kimchi* of all. Often sold in jars, it is added to soups, stir-fries, and stews. Although there are several ways of making fermented cabbage kimchi, this is the one I learned to make in Seoul. While you can use a water brine to cure the cabbage, I was told that rice water (a combination of rice flour and water) is much better, adding another layer of flavor. The presence of the grain will help push along the fermenting process.

1. Bring 2 quarts water with the ½ cup salt to a boil over high heat. Once the salt has dissolved, remove the pot from the heat and allow to cool completely. Place the cabbage quarters in a container and cover with the salt brine. Let stand overnight in a dark, cool place. Rinse under cold water and drain. Toss the daikon with the remaining tablespoon salt in a colander set over a bowl. Allow the daikon to drain, about 2 hours. Place the daikon in a cotton kitchen towel and twist it to drain out the liquids. Do not rinse the daikon.

2. Whisk together the spring water with the rice flour in a small saucepan and bring to a boil over high heat. Remove from the heat and allow to cool. Stir in the garlic, ginger, scallions, baby shrimp (or fish sauce), chili powder, and chili flakes to form a paste. Transfer the paste to a bowl and mix in the daikon and watercress until well

combined. Place some of the daikon mixture in one of the smallest cabbage leaves. Roll it up and taste. You're looking for a balance of flavor; remember that what you taste now will change through fermentation. All you need to know is that the flavors are balanced.

3. Working with one napa cabbage half or quarter at a time, spread some of the spicy mixture between each napa cabbage leaf until you get to the last leaf. Wrap the last leaf over and around the stuffed cabbage piece to form a bundle. Place the stuffed cabbage inside a ceramic jar (or any nonreactive container you have on hand). The jar should be tightly packed. Screw the lid tightly on top of the container and refrigerate for at least 2 weeks.

OI SOBAEGI KIMCHI
PICKLED CUCUMBER

MAKES ABOUT 1 QUART

4 seedless CUCUMBERS, halved
   crosswise

¼ cup KOSHER SALT

2 cups SPRING WATER

3 tablespoons RICE FLOUR

6 large GARLIC CLOVES, crushed,
   peeled, and finely grated

2 ounces fresh GINGER, peeled and
   finely grated

¼ cup fermented BABY SHRIMP,
   minced; or FISH SAUCE

¼ cup CHILI POWDER

2 tablespoons CHILI FLAKES

2 ASIAN PEARS, peeled, cored, and
   julienned

1 teaspoon GRANULATED SUGAR

3 SCALLIONS, root and dark green
   ends trimmed, and 6-inch stalks
   cut into 2-inch-long pieces and
   julienned

IN THE SUMMER everyone in Korea looks forward to eating cucumber kimchi. Salted and prepared very much the same way as spicy napa cabbage kimchi, this crunchy cucumber treat is refreshing and well suited for the hot summer days of Korea. Seedless cucumbers are best. They tend to be thinner, less watery, and more crunchy. You have to wait only twenty-four hours before being able to enjoy this kimchi.

1. Make a crisscross incision in each cucumber half, going all the way through but leaving ½ inch intact on each end of each cucumber half. Sprinkle inside the incisions liberally with salt and rub salt all over the skins. Place the cucumbers in a colander and allow to drain. Rinse the cucumber halves under cold water, then lightly squeeze the cucumber pieces with your hands to extract any excess water. Pat the pieces dry.

2. Whisk together 1 cup spring water with the rice flour in a small saucepan and bring to a boil over high heat. Remove from the heat and allow to cool. Stir in the garlic, ginger, baby shrimp (or fish sauce), chili powder, chili flakes, and sugar to form a paste. Transfer the paste to a bowl and mix in the Asian pears and scallions until well combined. Taste the mixture and adjust the seasoning. Stuff each cucumber incision generously with the spicy Asian pear mixture. Place the stuffed cucumber halves upright in a large jar, pouring any leftover Asian pear mixture (liquid and all) on top. Swirl the remaining spring water inside the bowl that held the mixture, and pour that liquid into the jar to cover the cucumbers. Allow the vegetables to ferment, refrigerated, for 24 hours before tasting. These are at their best consumed within 7 days. Serve the cucumber with its filling, sliced into 1-inch-long pieces.

Variation: For making *kaji sobaegi*, eggplant *kimchi*, substitute 4 Asian eggplants for the cucumbers and follow the recipe.

KIMCHI IS A PRIME EXAMPLE of Asian food as "health food." It is an excellent source of vitamins, minerals, and dietary fiber; the fermentation produces organic acids that are believed to be cancer preventatives. Fish, seafood, and occasionally meat can be added to the seasoning mix, making *kimchi* a great source of protein and calcium. Garlic is good for your intestines and improves blood flow while cleansing the blood. Ginger is excellent for the heart, lungs, stomach, spleen, and kidneys. Chilies stimulate the appetite.

My understanding of *kimchi* deepened when I recently visited Korea and experienced it in its land of origin. It is literally present in the landscape in the form of *jahng dak*. One of the most distinctive sights in Korea, these black earthenware *kimchi* storage pots line the flat rooftops of apartments and private homes. They are tucked away in corners of houses, and are buried in the garden for winter storage. Made by Korean potters for centuries and still available in various sizes of five, ten, and up to forty gallons, they seem to be everywhere.

KOREAN EARTHENWARE USED TO STORE GRAINS AND KIMCHI

TOFU WITH CRISPY GINGER AND SCALLION

SERVES 4 TO 6

2 pounds firm TOFU, cakes, cut
  into ½-inch-thick slices
¼ cup CHINESE LIGHT SOY SAUCE
1 teaspoon SESAME OIL
FRIED SCALLIONS AND GINGER
  (page 108); 2 tablespoons of
  the frying oil reserved

OFU COMES IN VARIOUS TEXTURES—silken, soft, medium, and firm. It can be fried, steamed, and braised, or included in any number of stir-fries or soups. This recipe is derived from the classic deep-fried soft tofu served with a spicy soy sauce, but when my father complained of too much fat in his diet, I modified the recipe, using firm tofu and pan-searing it. Crispy on the outside and soft on the inside, the pan-seared firm tofu is drizzled with a delicate soy sauce and nutty sesame oil dressing and garnished with beautiful crispy strings of golden ginger and green scallions. The outcome is a light and beautiful first course.

For fried tofu, see page 363.

1. Place a double layer of paper towels on a plate. Gently place the tofu pieces on top and place a double layer of paper towels on top. Refrigerate at least 6 hours, allowing the paper towels to absorb the water from the tofu. Check after 2 hours to see if the paper towels are drenched and need to be replaced.

2. Gently blot dry the tofu pieces. Heat the 1 teaspoon vegetable oil in a nonstick pan over medium-high heat. Pan-fry the tofu slices until lightly golden and heated through, about 2 minutes per side.

3. Whisk together the soy sauce, sesame oil, and reserved frying oil in a small bowl.

4. Place an equal amount of tofu in the centers of individual plates. Top each serving with an equal amount of crispy scallions and ginger. Drizzle with a tablespoon or so of the soy sauce dressing, making sure to stir so the oil and soy sauce blend well. Serve while hot.

TOFU, OR BEAN CURD, is, in essence, soybean cheese. It originated in China as far back as the ancient Han period. Made from soybean milk, it is solidified by gypsum. Easy to digest, low in cost, it is a great source of protein, rich in minerals, especially calcium. The Chinese eat more tofu than anyone in the world, except the Japanese and North Americans.

AGE-DOFU
FRIED TOFU IN
VELVETY SAUCE

SERVES 4 TO 6

VEGETABLE OIL for deep-frying

½ cup ARROWROOT or TAPIOCA
STARCH

1 pound firm TOFU
(about 4 cakes), drained
and quartered

2 cups KONBU DASHI (pp. 124–25)

2 tablespoons JAPANESE DARK SOY
SAUCE

3 tablespoons MIRIN

2 SCALLIONS, root and dark green
ends trimmed, and 6-inch stalks
thinly sliced diagonally

6 ounces DAIKON, peeled and
finely grated

TOFU WAS INVENTED in China thousands of years ago, but it quickly traveled to its neighboring countries. In Japan, there are numerous ways of preparing tofu, including deep-frying it just as the Chinese do and serving it in a delicate sauce. Firm tofu is ideal for deep-frying, but it is necessary to drain it first. I like to wrap it in several layers of paper towels and refrigerate it for 2 hours. You can also place a couple of plates on top of the tofu to press the water out. Either way will work. Most of the packaged tofu is squared off, so you do not have to trim the sides. Prior to deep-frying, be sure the tofu has come to room temperature, and pat it dry.

1. Pour enough oil in a pot for deep-frying and bring the temperature to 360° to 375°F over medium-high heat. Place all but 1 teaspoon of the arrowroot starch in a plastic bag and place a piece of tofu in the bag; shake it to cover it well. Shake the excess starch off the piece and carefully lower it into the hot oil. Continue with the remaining pieces of tofu, dredging each in the starch one piece at a time and deep-frying as many pieces as the pot will allow. Drain on paper towels.

2. Meanwhile, bring the dashi to a boil over high heat. Lower the heat to medium and add the soy sauce and mirin. Dilute the remaining arrowroot starch with 1 tablespoon water and stir in the dashi. Once thickened, about a minute, remove from the heat and divide among 4 shallow bowls. Transfer the tofu to individual plates and garnish each piece with some scallions and grated daikon. Serve while still hot.

PAI HUA NIANG DOFU
SHRIMP-STUFFED TOFU
WITH BLACK BEAN SAUCE

SERVES 4 TO 6

1 pound small BLUE TIGER
SHRIMP, heads and shells
removed, butterflied and
deveined, and minced

2 NAPA CABBAGE LEAVES, minced

1 teaspoon TAPIOCA STARCH
or CORNSTARCH

KOSHER SALT

Freshly ground BLACK PEPPER

1 pound firm TOFU cakes, cut
crosswise into ¾-inch-thick
rectangular slices

⅓ cup FERMENTED BLACK BEAN
AND GARLIC SAUCE (page 86)

1 bunch CILANTRO, tough stems
removed

F IRM TOFU CAKES cut on the diagonal are stuffed with a combination
of minced fresh shrimp and napa cabbage. Flavored with pungent fermented black bean and garlic paste, the steamed "pillows" are beautiful, rich, and delicious. A generous amount of cilantro leaves lift the palate.
Served with jasmine rice, *pai hua niang dofu* makes a very nutritious meal.

Be sure not to overseason the shrimp stuffing, as the fermented black bean
and garlic sauce is already salty.

1. Mix together the shrimp, cabbage, and tapioca starch in a bowl
until thoroughly combined. Season
lightly with salt and pepper. Cut
each tofu slice on the diagonal.
Make an incision along the freshly
cut side of the tofu, scooping out
some of the tofu, and stuff with a
heaping teaspoon of shrimp filling.
Put the tofu on a plate.

2. Drizzle the black bean and garlic
sauce over the tofu and scatter the
cilantro across the top. Meanwhile,
fill a wok halfway with water and
bring it to a boil over high heat.
Place a bamboo steamer on top, and
put the plate containing the tofu inside. Secure the lid and steam until
the shrimp is cooked and the tofu is
heated through, about 10 minutes.
Serve while hot.

A vendor arranges his tofu at Central Market in Hong Kong.

NANZENJI YUDOFU
SPRING WATER TOFU WITH
SWEET SAKE SAUCE

SERVES 4 TO 6

¾ cup TAMARI SAUCE

½ cup MIRIN

1 SCALLION, root and dark green
 ends trimmed, and 6-inch stalk
 sliced paper thin into rounds

1 quart SPRING WATER

2 pounds silken, soft, or firm TOFU,
 about 4 cakes, quartered (if
 using firm tofu, slice off the
 somewhat firmer outer skin, so it
 is uniformly smooth all around)

I ATE ONE OF the most delicious tofu dishes I've ever had during a *kaiseki* meal in Kyoto's Jensei restaurant, set amid beautiful Zen gardens. Everything on the table was meticulously prepared and beautiful. After the twelfth dish, out came a wooden tub with a pipe in the middle to hold hot charcoal. In the tub were white cubes of soft tofu heated in a pool of hot spring water, which were served with a dipping sauce of mirin (sweet sake) and tamari sauce, and thinly sliced scallion. Incredibly satisfying, it tasted pure, light, and rich at the same time.

1. Mix together the tamari and mirin and divide among individual small bowls. Garnish each serving with scallion.

2. Bring the spring water to a boil over high heat. Reduce the heat to medium-low, gently add the tofu cubes, and simmer until heated through, about 5 minutes. Carefully, so as not to break up the tofu pieces, transfer the tofu and spring water to a large ceramic bowl with a ladle. Instruct your guests to help themselves to a piece of tofu and dip it in their sauce.

SOYBEANS, *MAME* IN JAPANESE, play a big role in the Japanese diet, so much so that the farmers do not grow the crop nearly fast enough to satisfy the demand. For this reason, soybeans are often imported from the United States and turned into soy sauce, tamari, bean curd, soy milk, and *yuba* (tofu skin). An incredibly healthy food, soy is full of protein.

During the New Year, black soybeans are eaten in order to have a healthy year.

BRAISED TOFU AND KIMCHI

SERVES 4 TO 6

1½ cups BASIC CHICKEN STOCK
   (page 116); or VEGETABLE
   STOCK (page 126)
1½ cups CABBAGE KIMCHI
   (page 359); or commercial
   equivalent
KOSHER SALT
Freshly ground BLACK PEPPER
2 SCALLIONS, root and dark green
   ends trimmed, and 6-inch stalks
   cut into 1-inch-long pieces
1 pound firm TOFU, cut into
   1-inch cubes

LIKE MANY ASIAN vegetarian dishes, this one is easy to make. The mild tofu is rich and silky, while the crunchy cabbage kimchi is pungent with garlic, ginger, and chilies. Cooked down and served over rice, it makes for a healthful lunch or dinner. In my version, I like to add fresh scallions and sometimes chicken stock for a richer broth. If you have leftover chicken or pork, you can shred the meat and add it as well. If you want to keep it strictly vegetarian, use vegetable broth or add water.

Heat the stock or 1½ cups water in a pot over high heat. Reduce the heat to low and add the kimchi. Season with salt and pepper to taste, then add the scallions. Cover and simmer until heated through, about 15 minutes. Add the tofu and mix carefully so as not to break the tofu too much. Cook to heat tofu through, about 3 minutes. Serve with rice on the side.

PAN-FRIED TOFU WITH SPICY LEMONGRASS STIR-FRY

1 pound firm TOFU, cut into
  ½-inch-thick rectangular slices

2 tablespoons VEGETABLE OIL

2 tablespoons FISH SAUCE

1 tablespoon GRANULATED SUGAR

1 large GARLIC CLOVE, crushed,
  peeled, and minced

1 large SHALLOT, peeled and
  minced

1 stalk LEMONGRASS, root end
  trimmed, outer leaves and tough
  green top removed, and 6-inch-
  long inner bulb finely ground

1 to 2 small RED THAI CHILIES

*Excellent – Light, subtle
I added some stock
to peapods/onion/pepper
to serve over rice*

SOYBEAN PRODUCTS such as soy milk and tofu originated in China. Today, everywhere in Asia you can eat tofu, whether deep-fried, steamed, or in liquid form. You can also buy pressed tofu, firm, silken, soft, medium-firm tofu, and *tempeh* (a tofu cake containing whole yellow soybeans). The soybean is used in making soy sauces (wheat and soybeans) and tamari, made from soybeans only. In Vietnam, deep-fried tofu is very popular, especially served with a stir-fry of finely ground lemongrass and chilies, and shallots. I like to drain the tofu slices overnight and pan-fry them the next day for a lighter version of this delicious vegetarian treat.

1. Place a double layer of paper towels on a plate and arrange the tofu slices in a single layer on top. Cover with a double layer of paper towels and refrigerate overnight. Check every 4 to 6 hours to change any drenched towels.

2. Heat 1 tablespoon oil in a nonstick pan over medium heat. Pan-fry the tofu slices on both sides until golden, 2 to 3 minutes on each side. Drain on paper towels and arrange an equal amount on individual plates.

3. Whisk together the fish sauce and sugar in a bowl until the sugar has completely dissolved. Heat the remaining oil in a small saucepan over high heat. Stir-fry the garlic and shallots until golden, 3 to 5 minutes. Add the lemongrass and chilies and continue to stir-fry until fragrant and lightly golden, about 2 minutes. Add the fish sauce mixture and continue to stir-fry until the ingredients are slightly caramelized, about 1 minute. Top each tofu serving with some spicy lemongrass stir-fry.

Goi Cuon: Summer Rolls (pp. 286–87)

KAENG PHET KAI: THAI CHICKEN CURRY (PAGE 499)

BUBUH INJIN: BLACK STICKY RICE PUDDING (PAGE 519)

HUN TUN: WONTON SOUP (PP. 266-67)

STIR-FRIED PEA SHOOTS WITH FERMENTED TOFU (PP. 324–25)

FRIED POMFRET AND COLORFUL CUCUMBER AND SHALLOT SALAD (PP. 394 AND 350, RESPECTIVELY)

CHAP CHAE: STIR-FRIED POTATO STARCH NOODLES (PAGE 250)

KINILAW: FILIPINO CEVICHE (PAGE 404)

TOFU SKINS STUFFED WITH SHIITAKE MUSHROOMS

24 dried SHIITAKE MUSHROOMS

2 to 3 round sheets dried TOFU skins, cut into 6-inch squares (about 24 pieces)

2 tablespoons VEGETABLE OIL

1 cup VEGETABLE STOCK (page 126)

2 tablespoons CHINESE LIGHT SOY SAUCE

2 tablespoons SHAOXING WINE

2 teaspoons GRANULATED SUGAR

1 teaspoon SESAME OIL

1 SCALLION, root and dark green ends trimmed, and 6-inch stalk thinly sliced diagonally

T OFU SKINS are a by-product of making tofu. When the tofu simmers, a thin skin forms on top (as when boiling cow's milk), and the Chinese, who are fanatical about not wasting food, have devised a way to use the skin. Stuffed with sliced shiitake mushrooms, the skins are rolled up and braised in soy sauce, sesame oil, and Shaoxing wine. This classic dish, which I have had in vegetarian restaurants and with Chinese Buddhist monks, is often referred to as "mock Peking duck," perhaps because the tofu skin resembles the crispy Peking duck skin, and the dark mushrooms the flesh beneath.

Tofu skins are purchased in large round sheets that must be softened by soaking, unless fresh and found in the refrigerated section of Asian markets.

1. Put the shiitakes in a bowl with hot water to cover, then set a plate over the bowl to prevent steam from escaping. Let stand until the mushrooms rehydrate and soften, about 30 minutes (or longer, depending on the size of the mushrooms). Squeeze the mushrooms between the palms of your hands to get rid of the excess water. Using a paring knife, remove any hard stems from the mushrooms and julienne the caps. Soak the tofu squares in water until softened. Drain.

2. Place an equal amount of shiitake mushrooms in each of the 24 tofu skins about 1 inch from the edge closest to you. Shape filling into a 3-inch log. Fold the skin over the filling once. Fold in the sides and roll to the end to enclose the filling. Place the rolls in a heavy-bottomed pot, in layers as necessary. Whisk together the stock, soy sauce, wine, sugar, and sesame oil in a bowl, until the sugar is dissolved completely. Add the sauce to the pot. Place a lid on top and simmer over medium-low heat until cooked through and tender, 10 to 15 minutes. Cut the rolls in half crosswise and drizzle with the sauce remaining in the pot. Garnish with scallion and serve.

5

FISH AND
SEAFOOD

ASIA, with 39,000 MILES of coastline and numerous rivers, is blessed with an abundance of fish, crustaceans, and mollusks. Coastal areas range from the glacial Arctic in the north to tropical, volcanic archipelagoes in the east and south. The Pacific Ocean, the South China Sea, the Gulf of Thailand, the Sea of Japan, and other seas are supplemented by modern fish farms and traditional rice paddies, all of which contribute their bounty to Asia's daily diet. China's vast high plains drain to surging waters such as the Yangtze, Hsi, and the Huang Ho (Yellow) rivers. The Southeast Asian peninsula is a series of mountainous ridges that drain southward to the vast Mekong and its delta, as well as several other rivers. Korea is a rocky,

PREVIOUS SPREAD: ONLY THE MOST HIGHLY TRAINED JAPANESE SUSHI CHEFS CAN BE TRUSTED TO PREPARE FUGU, OR BLOWFISH.

rainy outcropping. Japan, the Philippines, and Indonesia are islands with mountainous spines. Rivers drain the highlands, offering rich harvests as they flow to the sea. For these reasons, as well as the tendency of populations to concentrate near water systems, fish and seafood are readily available, and generally less expensive than beef, duck, and many other types of protein.

In China, the character for fish, *yueh*, is synonymous with prosperity and abundance. A whole fish is always served during special occasions—a wedding, birthday, or New Year's celebration, for instance; in Chinese culture, when fish swim in pairs, they symbolize a blissful marriage. Fishing in China's lakes, rivers, coastlines, and canals goes back at least five thousand years. Hundreds of types of fish are eaten, but the most popular are fish caught in fresh water, because they tend to be more delicate in flavor. Carp is the most prized, but mullet, bream, catfish, and eel are also widely enjoyed. Flounder and sea bass, in particular, are popular for steaming.

Carp, which can taste of soil and is not very popular in the West, is thought of as a kind of "king" fish in China. It is prized by Chinese cooks, who for millennia have been

farming carp, a practice that no doubt started with farmers who filled their house ponds with carp and fed them inexpensive kitchen scraps. Not surprisingly, the Chinese are among the most enthusiastic carp eaters in the world.

Carp's distinctive flavor is best enjoyed when the fish is harvested in fall and spring—water levels are high and the fish are not forced into dry summer's shallow muddy waters. At best, the fish has a tender texture, earthy flavor, and large, easy-to-find bones, making it a pleasure to eat. My family delights in eating carp, especially the sweet flesh of the head. At a dinner at Hong Kong's famous restaurant Fook Lam Moon, we were served shark's fin soup. The base of the dish was superior stock (page 117), fragrant with salt-cured Yunnan ham, meaty chicken and pork bones, ginger and scallion. As the waiter set the soup in the center of our table, everyone looked at the glorious, translucent (and expensive) shark's fin. My father's eyes, however, went directly to the large carp head set in the center. Our host honored my father by offering him the two-pound wonder. My father in turn offered it back to him. This went on several times, until my father finally accepted and set to pulling apart this delectable item, one small piece at a time.

Saltwater fish such as sole, grouper, bass, and pomfret are also eaten, along with mollusks such as oysters, mussels, octopus, and squid, and crustaceans including shrimp, lobster, crayfish, and hairy crab—a Shanghainese specialty best steamed or boiled in autumn, when the heads are full of caviar. The Chinese, in particular, are also very fond of exotic sea creatures, for which they'll often pay exorbitant prices. Mollusks such as abalone and sea slug, also known as sea cucumber or *bêche de mer*, are often prepared and served in thick velvety sauces; reptiles such as turtles and snakes become the main ingredient in medicinal soups; and amphibians such as frogs are stir-fried with herbs. While some of these may not technically fall under the "seafood" category, they are commonly sold by fishmongers and are included here.

Fish enjoyed in Western cuisines, such as tuna, swordfish, and cod, are shunned by the Chinese because they are considered to be rather dry and of poor texture. Salmon heads, especially the giant Alaskan, are an exception, having made their way into soups or been served as special items at banquets. As far as the rest of the fish is concerned, I rarely, if ever, have seen it on a Chinese menu. The Japanese, on the other hand, enjoy tuna and salmon, but mostly raw, or cooked in specific ways (see salmon skin handrolls and salmon teriyaki, pp. 217 and 402, respectively).

While fish is prepared in many ways in Chinese coastal regions, the most refined preparation is that of the Cantonese Chinese of Hong Kong, where the preferred seafood cooking technique is steaming. A fish is never overcooked, the central bone being left pink, the flesh moist yet fully and properly cooked. A gray bone—all too common in Western restaurant cooking—would in Asia be a sign that the fish has been cooked too long and rendered "flaky" and dry. The quick stir-fry technique is also employed, particularly with crustaceans and mollusks. A third, also quick, technique used in preparing fish, crustaceans (mostly shrimp), and mollusks (mostly squid) is deep-frying. When cooked, these golden, crispy sea creatures are often presented as a simple lunch, accompanied by crunchy sweet and sour pickled vegetables. They are enjoyed throughout China and Southeast Asia.

I love steamed sole, carp, or bass simply topped with julienned scallions, ginger, and shiitakes and seasoned with soy sauce. When it first became popular in the United States, I steamed rich and buttery Chilean sea bass in this fashion. It was absolutely delicious. Steamed, a fish retains its delicate character. Infused with herbs, it complements rather than overwhelms other dishes—be they vegetable or meat —at the table.

A small fried butterfish served over rice is perfectly counterbalanced by a medley of tangy, sweet, rice vinegar–pickled carrot, cucumber, and daikon, a favorite light lunch of mine that takes me only minutes to prepare. When deep-fried, the fish is crispy most all the way through, which makes it completely edible, head to tail. Stir-fried razor clams with fermented black beans and garlic sauce (page 86), served with chilies and a generous amount of palate-lifting and refreshing cilantro, are simple and delicious, yet have people guessing about their complex character.

Specialty eel dishes are also worth a mention. Freshwater eels are fish that live most of their lives in fresh water but spawn at sea. True saltwater eels tend to be a bit fatty; they include the conger eel, which the Japanese call *anago* and serve grilled as a specialty.

I must admit that I've never liked eating seafood in heavy sauces, but there are a few delicious classics worth mentioning. Shanghainese freshwater yellow eel, served in a brown sauce that combines superior stock (page 117) and malt-flavored dark thick soy sauce as the base, can be an extraordinary and memorable dish. So can the Cantonese specialty that uses the larger saltwater eel braised with shiitake mushrooms and bamboo shoots in an oyster sauce and Shaoxing wine–based sauce. I also like eel steamed the same way as carp, with ginger and scallions, or deep-fried. One afternoon my husband and I happened into a Korean restaurant in New York's Koreatown. The dining room had the most beautiful and delicately rendered wall paintings, rivaling classical Japanese *ukiyo-e* prints. The place served eels exclusively, displaying them in tanks placed throughout the room, and offering dishes that included eel soup, fried eel spine, and eel in a variety of fragrant sauces. We tried many items, then, awash in the traditional, strong Korean alcoholic beverages, walked off the unforgettable meal.

While the Chinese generally avoid eating raw seafood, there are some exceptions. Live baby shrimp or crabs are drowned in 100-proof (or stronger) rice alcohol to eliminate any impurities and flavor the flesh. They are eaten raw or simply cooked by being flambéed in their alcohol bath at the table, a spectacle that includes a "dance" produced by the exposure of the crustaceans' muscles to intense heat. Another raw item that has come into fashion in Chinese seafood restaurants is thinly sliced giant clam served with *wasabi* and soy sauce. Originally a Japanese specialty, the Chinese enjoy this slightly chewy clam for its texture and pronounced flavor.

In the ritual of eating seafood—whether in a private home or a restaurant—the Chinese and many other Asians share the whole fish at table, wielding their chopsticks to pick bite-size morsels from the carcass. In the most authentic versions of this tradition, fins, heads, and other cartilage-bearing bits are chewed and/or sucked clean; the diners drop the bones and other inedible bits from their mouths onto their plate. Almost nothing goes to waste, so the idea of serving separate fish fillets or fish steaks is rare. This dining ritual is performed

with crustaceans as well. Sucking the delicious tomalley out of a shrimp head with a loud noise is perfectly normal. Dissecting a crab's head for every bit of the sweet flesh, tomalley, and caviar with chopsticks is an art form (the fingers are hardly ever used). The nod to civility here is that you never see your fellow diners' teeth in action; everything happens with the mouth closed.

The Chinese also preserve fish, crustaceans, and mollusks. Air-drying of seafood began hundreds of years ago, employed by Chinese cooks as a method of preservation for times when fresh items were not available. Much to the delight of succeeding generations, the cooks soon learned that this curing process—also referred to as sun-drying—concentrated flavors wonderfully. Taken straight out of the water, fish were gutted, planked (some were heavily salted), then left in the sun to air-dry. Today, all sorts of fish, from the tiniest of anchovies to plump, fatty fish, are dried this way. A humble meal can be based on a chunk of rehydrated dried fish, steamed with oil and served as a side dish when eating plain rice porridge called *jook* (page 192). Because some items are rather salty, the fish is consumed in small bites and followed by a spoonful or two of rice porridge. Dried fish can also be deep-fried until crisp and eaten as a snack or crumbled as a robust garnish for any stir-fry or soup.

Pinkish-orange shrimp is perhaps the most widely eaten dried crustacean in China and Southeast Asia. Reasonable in price, and easy to procure and store, it adds flavor and texture to soups, stir-fries, and stews, and can be used as a garnish when finely ground. Squid is the most popular of all dried mollusks, often dry-roasted over an open flame, then added to stock to deepen its flavor, or torn into thin strips and enjoyed as a snack. My father enjoys dried squid with a cup of green or black tea. Because of their overwhelming abundance, dried fish, shrimp, and squid are available at Chinese and Southeast Asian markets all the time, and at very affordable prices. (Mexican and other Latin cultures also use dried seafood in their cooking, so you may be able to find what you need in these markets as well.)

Other somewhat unusual dried mollusks used in Chinese cooking include oysters, mussels, and jellyfish. The jellyfish is particularly versatile. It is often sliced into linguini-like, translucent, slippery,

Sutukil restaurants in the Philippines offer fish cooked three ways: in soup, grilled, and vinegar-cured.

and crunchy strips, dressed with sesame oil and rice vinegar, and featured at the center of a Chinese cold-cut platter during special banquets. While they might have been humble foods at one point in history, many of these dried mollusks are considered delicacies today.

Available through herbal medicine shops, they can, depending on quality, be very expensive. The dried amber-colored scallop known as *conpoy*, for example—depending on its size and quality—can be as much as nine hundred dollars a pound, more expensive than top-quality shark's fin. This expensive dried seafood is most often used sparingly, principally as a background flavor in elaborate soups and stir-fried or braised dishes. On very special occasions, however, these same expensive items may appear as one of the main (or the main) ingredients in a dish. Cantonese fuzzy melon stuffed with dried scallop (page 341), or battered and deep-fried dried oysters served during formal banquets celebrate the rather bold flavor of these two mollusks, while reflecting the prestige of an honored guest or otherwise emphasizing the importance of a meal.

Even more exotic dried seafood includes the best varieties of shark's fin. Believed to be a medicinal tonic by the Chinese, the fin is harvested from specific species. Fins are usually braised or employed in making the classic shark's fin soup, which sells for upward of a hundred dollars a bowl, depending on where you eat it, how it is prepared, and the quality of the shark's fin. The shredded type sold dried in bags at markets is usually of a lesser quality and much less expensive than the superior quality dried whole fin presented in clear plastic boxes. (Whole fins require a lot more skillful preparation, however, and are usually better left to professional chefs.) Fins provide a generous amount of protein, iron, and calcium, not to mention a rich gelatinous texture (the secret to shark's fin soup's silky-smooth broth). I have not included a recipe for shark's fin, however, and have ceased eating this delicacy for environmental reasons. Sharks, unlike many fish, are not farmed and are being fished to the verge of extinction.

Dried abalone, like the fresh and canned variety, is also very expensive. When softened by soaking in water, dried abalone has a unique flavor and chewy yet tender texture. It is particularly well suited for braised dishes like *hao yau bao pin*, braised abalone with oyster sauce (and sometimes top-quality softened dried shiitake mushrooms), a specialty item served at formal banquets. The Chinese often value display at table, and an acceptable way to show one's wealth is to order an abalone platter for a wedding celebration. A canned whole abalone can easily cost seventy-five dollars; the fresh and dried versions can be much more expensive.

Dried seafood's very concentrated flavor and aroma can be overwhelming, even for those who grew up eating it. Shopping for it can be a bit daunting, especially in summer. Hong Kong's food markets offer hundreds of dried seafoods, each perfectly presented and separated into individual categories and qualities, and each giving up its pungent perfume, peaking in the hottest, most humid months. In New York's Mott and Elizabeth Street markets (which I've dubbed "mini Hong Kong"), the smells can be difficult. Don't let this deter you from trying these items, however, for they are truly remarkable and worth the extra effort and price. Once you start to enjoy the similarly strong flavors of fish sauce or shrimp paste, for example, your enjoyment of dried seafood will follow. Remember that you most likely do not need a pound of *conpoy*, nor do you need to buy the most expensive version of any item. I've bought half a pound of dried scallops (at sixty-five dollars a pound) and made use of them in many dishes over a long period of time. Like Western luxury items such as truffles, dried seafood is most often meant as flavor enhancer, and a small amount will go a long way. While you may be put off by the idea of its intense saltiness, dried seafood is normally soaked in water to get rid of the excess salt and to soften the flesh prior to cooking.

Like China, Southeast Asia is also blessed with abundant waters. Cambodian, Filipino, Indonesian, Thai, and Vietnamese diets have fish as their most abundant protein, with some sort of seafood present in almost every dish. The ubiquitous condiment, fish sauce—tuk trey in Khmer, patis in Filipino, nam pla in Thai, and nuoc mam in Vietnamese—made mostly of fish such as anchovies (and sometimes mollusks), is the "salt" of choice in Southeast Asian kitchens. Made by layering fish and salt in wood barrels for months until extracted juices can be collected and bottled, it shows up in virtually every dish, excepting strict Buddhist vegetarian foods, in which soy sauce is used. Even if you are eating what appears to be a vegetable, poultry, or meat dish, in Southeast Asian cuisines it mostly likely includes seafood, whether obvious or not. Fermented shrimp and fish are other equally important condiments in these cuisines. The most widely known are kepi, a Thai semisoft, purplish-gray shrimp paste sold in round plastic tubs; terasi, an Indonesian brownish-gray shrimp paste shaped in rectangular blocks and sold wrapped in several layers of paper; bagoong, a Filipino loose light gray fish or shrimp sauce sold in bottles; and prahoc, whole fish (or chunks) fermented in rice-based brines, grayish-tan in color, and sold in glass jars; the latter being truly unique to the cuisine of Cambodia. These seafood condiments are what give Southeast Asian cuisines their uniquely bold character.

When it comes to fresh seafood, the Southeast Asians use the same cooking techniques as the Chinese, steaming, stir-frying, braising, and deep-frying. Southeast Asians love to marinate their seafood in herbs such as garlic, ginger, shallots, lemongrass, galangal, and chilies and to grill it as well. Often, when walking through the streets of Denpasar, Chiang Mai, Manila, Phnom Penh, and Saigon, the smell of pungently seasoned fish, shrimp, or squid searing over hot charcoal will no doubt get your attention. The Filipinos grill seafood as much as other Southeast Asian cooks, but their marinades consist of the more familiar garlic, shallots, and ginger. Any of these served with rice and pickled vegetables is a common, satisfying meal.

More elaborate fish dishes exist. Seafood is used as the main ingredient in curries all over Southeast Asia, for example, and other interesting but perhaps not as familiar items are worth a few words. Deep-fried, golden crisp Indonesian fish cakes, otak pipih (page 407), are served with a spicy garlic and chili sambal. Similar fish cakes, referred to as taud man (page 407) in Thailand, are enjoyed with a chunky sweet, vinegary, and spicy cucumber relish. In Vietnam, ca kho (page 392), mackerel braised in coconut water and fish sauce and sweetened with golden caramel, is enjoyed, especially in the north. Cambodian fish and rice soup, called samlaw trapeang (pp. 200–1), employs both fresh and dried fish and is sometimes enriched with coconut milk. Also in Cambodia, amok trey (page 391), white fish steamed in a spice-laden coconut custard held together in a banana leaf packet, is a specialty enjoyed at home and in restaurants alike; a similar dish exists in Thailand. Sour fish soup sweetened with pineapple is also a specialty enjoyed throughout Southeast Asia. Called canh ca chua in Vietnam, samlah m'juu trey in Cambodia, sayur asam ikan in Indonesia, and tom som pla in Thailand, the soup often uses a large fish head to produce a rich flavor. In the Philippines, sour soups are much enjoyed and can be made with any-

sweet, tender, and juicy sugar cane, is a Vietnamese specialty. *Lhord* (pp. 284–85), the Cambodian spring roll filled with or without crab, and pork, is based on the Vietnamese *cha gio* and is served with a sweet, sour, and spicy fish sauce dip also rooted in Vietnam but here garnished with a generous amount of crushed roasted peanuts. In Bali, fish, shrimp, and scallop are minced together, mixed with spices, and grilled, wrapped around lemongrass stalks (a popular skewer throughout Southeast Asia) for a delicious seafood specialty called *sate lilit* (page 421). The Philippines also has delicious seafood dishes such as *ukoy* (page 407), a shrimp and sweet potato fritter, and the more exotic *rellenong pusit* (page 416), stuffed squid served in its own ink.

A few unique specialties merit special mention. While in the Philippines, I tasted one of the most memorable items, raw fish cured in coconut vinegar, a sort of *ceviche* found all over the country. I first encountered it in Cebu, where they call it *kinilaw*; the same dish is called *kilawin* in the Tagalog language. The dish consisted of a medley of cubed raw fish, julienned ginger, shallots, and occasionally coconut palm heart. Tossed with *kalamansi* juice (a

thing from pork to a mixture of various seafoods. One of my favorite Filipino sour soups is *sinigang de isda* (pp. 146–47), which sometimes includes rich coconut milk and spicy chilies, as in the region of Bicol. Abundant fish reflects the trans–Southeast Asian presence of many popular recipes as a counterpoint to

the many unique elements of individual cuisines.

Crustaceans and mollusks are also enjoyed in Southeast Asia, and shrimp and squid are so abundant that they, as in China, are the most widely eaten. *Chao tom* (page 421), fresh shrimp minced to a pastelike consistency and wrapped around pinball-size sour green citrus fruit found in the Philippines and Indonesia) and coconut vinegar, the ingredients were left to cure for twenty minutes, until the fish became opaque, "cooked" by the acid. There are many delicious variations on the theme. For instance, in Bicol, where the food is rather rich and spicy, thinly sliced Thai chilies—referred to as finger chilies by Filipinos—and coconut milk are added to the mix. A rather sophisticated dish, kinilaw had humble beginnings. Centuries ago, fishermen would marinate the whole fish in coconut vinegar for just a few minutes (in fact, they just dipped it a few times) and eat the flesh right off the bones. Until recently, this specialty was considered very primitive. It is now enjoying a sort of revival.

Sutukil is another popular fish specialty sold by street vendors in the Philippines. A coined word, sutukil is derived from su, from sugba (short form of sunugba), meaning to grill; tu, from tinola, meaning soup; and kil, from kinilaw, meaning to marinate in vinegar. Hence, fish-three-ways. First, the center plump fillets are grilled; second, the head is used for making soup; and third, the meaty tail end is marinated in vinegar. (This is somewhat similar to the way Chinese Peking duck is served: crispy skin wrapped in flour pancakes; meat chopped and stir-fried; and bone soup.) In Cebu the markets had restaurants specializing in sutukil, and next to these were street vendors selling such colorfully named meat and poultry items as "helmets," "Adidas," and "Walkmans." For those who can't bear the suspense, fast forward to the "Meat and Poultry" chapter (page 426) for insights into these dishes.

As befits an archipelago comprising hundreds of islands, Indonesia enjoys all sorts of fish. Fish and seafood are generally stewed or grilled, often with intense herbal marinades or pastes, including hot chilies, galangal, and lemongrass. Aside from the Balinese sate lilit mentioned above, the Indonesian sour and spicy fish stew, ikan asam pedes (page 399), is a sort of classic. Fatty white fish such as saltwater mackerel or freshwater catfish is normally used in ikan asam pedes, and I have included an eel variation. Other unexpected variations exist, as well. Recently, I was surprised to see fresh tuna sold in large quantities at some Indonesian markets. Possibly reflecting European colonial tastes, tuna is eaten smoked, added to soups and stews, or used to make pastry filling. If you would like to try Indonesian sour and spicy fish stew using tuna, be sure to select steaks that are fatty, so that the fish will not dry out during cooking.

Gastropods, i.e., snails, are a Southeast Asian delicacy as well as a French one. The Balinese prepare snails out of their shells in a spicy soup or stew called jukut kakul. The Vietnamese mince and combine them with ground pork, cloud ears, and lemongrass, and steam them in their shells before serving (page 423). These are called oc nhoi thit and are served with nuoc cham (page 100) for dipping. Frog's legs are also enjoyed throughout Southeast Asia. My aunt Huoy has told me of the times she caught frogs near my grandparents' home when she was a little girl in Phnom Penh. Bearing her bag of slippery creatures, she would present the frogs to her older sisters, who would clean them and marinate them in fish sauce and sugar with finely chopped lemongrass and garlic. Grilled over hot charcoal, they were served in the manner of the Vietnamese eel dish called ech xao xa ot (page 422), using the legs and torso of the frog, with slices of slightly green *carambola* (star fruit) for flavor balance.

I was always interested in serving frogs at home, but for the longest time I couldn't find anything but frozen, minuscule frog's legs at market. Today, my fishmonger in Chinatown carries fresh plump frogs, which I select live. In just twenty minutes, I get a dozen cleaned ones. I usually separate the torso from the legs, reserving the top part for curries. I have found that adventurous guests, even those unaccustomed to eating frogs, find them to be sweet, tender, subtle, and delicious—but not much like chicken at all.

In Southeast Asia, as in China, dried seafood items are essentially used as flavoring enhancers in stocks, stir-fries, and braised dishes. Cooks in these countries primarily use dried fish, shrimp, and squid, as these are abundant in Southeast Asian waters, and relatively inexpensive.

Dried seafood is occasionally eaten as snacks. In Vietnam I enjoyed dried shrimp tossed with lime juice, fish sauce, sugar, and chilies as a finger food, especially good when chased with a cold beer on a summer's day. It is not unusual to see dried squid hanging on a rod above a food stall anywhere in Southeast Asia. These will be grilled, the sweet aromas used to entice passersby. Dried squid is also roasted until lightly charred, then added to pork stock (see Southeast Asian pork stock, page 119). This gives the stock a sweet seafood flavor and a beautiful amber color; it is the secret to the delicious *hu tieu*, Saigon seafood and rice noodle soup, or Cambodian *k'tiao* (pp. 226–27). Dried fish is also enjoyed deep-fried until golden and crisped from head to tail.

While it is not unique to the Philippines to deep-fry dried fish and eat it with rice, one of the most memorable times I had this delicious combination was on the island of Cebu. A typical breakfast there consisted of fried rice flavored with garlic, a sunny-side-up egg, and deep-fried dried fish. My favorite were *danggit*, tiny roundish fish that were butterflied, gutted, sun-dried, and then dipped in coconut vinegar. Rather expensive, *danggit* is usually not sold by your typical street vendor but is bought in quantity, mostly by restaurateurs. While walking through a street market, I stopped by the dried-fish vendor. Different types of fish from sardines to mackerels were salted and sun-dried. They were loaded with flies, no matter how many times the vendor tried to fan them off; he looked at me, smiled, and said, "The more flies, the more delicious the fish." Perplexed, I looked at my guide, who further explained, "If the flies like the fish so much, it must be of really good quality." I demurred, however.

The waters surrounding Korea and Japan are as bountiful as any in Asia, and part of the fun in visiting these countries is to see their spectacular seafood markets. Large selections of sea creatures are sold, from the familiar to the colorful and exotic to the downright weird, like the sea slug that resembled a twitching hot dog. While I was in Pusan (the main fishing port of Korea), I saw that the fish market vendors not only sold fish but would also prepare it for you on the spot. I selected my fish from a tank, and the vendor cut it up on the spot as I ate each raw piece. Short of being on a fishing boat, you can't get much fresher than that!

In Korea seafood is braised, stir-fried, grilled, added to soups, and pickled. One of the most interesting ways of preparing fish, oysters, clams, mussels, shrimp, or crab, for example, is in the preparation of kimchi (pp. 310–11). Left to ferment for several days with the usual kimchi basics—salt, garlic, ginger, scallions, chilies, and salted (or fermented) baby shrimp—the seafood is packed raw, sometimes between fresh napa cabbage leaves. Too many variations exist to list here, but one of the most memorable seafood kimchi I have ever tasted is spicy baby raw crabs. The only way to eat these tiny things is to assertively suck the meat out of them. The Koreans also eat modum hoe, raw fish slices served with sweet and vinegary chili sauce. A simple but immensely pleasurable way of enjoying fresh fish that dates back hundreds of years, it is the Korean equivalent of Japanese sashimi.

Other delicious Korean seafood specialties include tchigae, spicy seafood stew (page 420), which can include not only fish but squid, scallops, and shrimp, generous amounts of tofu and scallions, and sometimes watercress for a peppery note and crunchy texture; and saengson jeon (page 346), pan-fried fish slices that have been dipped in an egg wash and flour. Eel is also eaten, and in New York City's Woo Lae Oak restaurant, I tasted one of the best eel dishes ever. Basted with sweetened soy sauce, the eel is both cooked and presented on sizzling-hot, rounded river stones. A house specialty, it is incredibly succulent, right down to the skin, which is picked away from the rock after the meat is consumed. Black cod braised in a sweet, savory, and spicy sauce (page 393) with tender daikon is another rich, complex, and flavorful Korean specialty.

Preserved seafood items in Korea are used primarily in flavoring kimchi. The tiny, salted pink baby shrimp mentioned above, for example, deepen the flavor of preserved or pickled vegetables. Pounded with garlic, ginger, and chilies, these salted shrimp are extremely salty, and the key to the best-tasting kimchis. When I asked if I could use fish sauce instead, an avid Korean cook said matter-of-factly, "You can, and some do, but it won't be the same."

Seafood plays an enormously important role in the Japanese diet. Eaten raw as sashimi, or wrapped in rice and nori (laver) as sushi, tuna, yellowtail, fluke, and many other types of fish are enjoyed. Special items at a typical Japanese raw bar include uni (sea urchin), giant clam, octopus, and squid, among many, many others. The Japanese also cook seafood, adding it to clear broths, deep-frying it in batter (tempura; page 417), broiling it as in salmon teriyaki (page 402), or grilling it, such as sardines with a vinegary sauce; still, the most memorable way to eat fish Japanese style is as sashimi (page 403) with a bowl of rice, some pickled ginger, and a mixture of wasabi-laden tamari dipping sauce on the side.

The Japanese prepare fish with a significant emphasis on precision, delicate and refined presentation, deep knowledge of harvesting techniques, enjoyment of particular seasonal or otherwise rare items, and, always, freshness. Fish in Japanese culture enjoys extremely sophisticated rituals and social customs associated with the mastery of sushi preparation, fishmongering, and the extremely hygienic and proper presentation of fish for sale at market. Sushi-grade tuna, for example, can be much more expensive than other good grades of tuna, and there are Japanese restaurants such as Honmura An in New York that fly in special shrimp from Tokyo for inclusion on their menu. Exotic items such as blowfish, or fugu, are eaten as sushi, or taken in hot sake, the enjoyment being heightened by the fact that the fish is considered to be both an aphrodisiac and known to contain deadly toxins in its liver. Indeed, even though the restaurant

A THAI FISHMONGER SCALES FISH FOR HIS CUSTOMERS.

it. "I remember it as being very sweet," he told me. While this can be understood as passion for the freshest seafood and pride in ritualized presentation, the Japanese also have an affinity for items that in today's world can be seen as ethically questionable, as in their consumption of whale meat. Even though the sea mammal appears on endangered-species lists, Japanese fishmongers and restaurants in both Tokyo and Kyoto continue to specialize in whale meat and nothing else. I normally like to try any food once, and though I was curious about how whale tasted, I couldn't bring myself to try it. There is so much diversity in food that as with shark's fin, and with similarly overfished sources of caviar, I do not feel I should indulge at the cost of destroying a species.

For about a thousand years, the Japanese have been particularly fond of *katsuo-bushi* (bonito mackerel) in several forms. Looking much like paper-thin wood chips, cured bonito fillet shavings, with their rich concentrated flavor, are appreciated for their role in making *dashi* (pp. 124–25), the ubiquitous Japanese stock. *Ito-kesuri-katsuo*, bonito threads, are essentially the same product, cut more delicately for a last-minute garnish. The fish, when

sale of *fugu* liver is now banned in Japan, occasional deaths from eating it are still reported.

While not necessarily widely enjoyed or eaten every day, some Japanese culinary traditions may seem not only exotic but cruel. Similar to an experience of mine, my father tells a story of a restaurant sashimi

meal in Tokyo. Live lobsters were presented at table. My father selected one, and the waiter turned to the sushi chef, who in turn cut the thing in half lengthwise with the single whack of a sharp blade; an instant "butterfly" through the hard shell. Served immediately, the lobster was still moving as my father ate raw, is also enjoyed as sashimi and sushi.

There is some evidence that sushi began historically as a way of preserving fish using vinegar and rice, but in modern Japan, sushi and sashimi chefs must study for years before being considered able to practice their now highly evolved art. To suggest that the home cook can easily accomplish anything like their efforts would be a disservice to chefs and readers alike. I include one sashimi dish and a salmon skin handroll (pp. 403 and 217, respectively) by way of example of Japanese raw fish dishes; these are fairly basic and fun to prepare and eat. Generally, though, I focus on cooked and preserved seafood items.

This introduction is merely an overview of seafood in Asia; individual dishes are explained more completely in the recipe section. A cook who has achieved some confidence with seafood should realize that substitutions are common. If you can't find carp, use grouper or sea bass to make the Vietnamese *ca hap bia* (fish steamed in beer, page 390). If you are allergic to mollusks such as squid, you can replace them with shrimp or crab, for example, in many recipes, or vice versa. Always bear in mind that seafood is very delicate and tends to cook rather quickly. Be sure you know your equipment and how it reacts on your stove. Cooking shrimp a minute too long can mean the difference between having a firm yet tender shrimp or a mealy one. One of my tricks when I'm cooking many dishes simultaneously is to select items that are forgiving, such as blue tiger shrimp, which tend to stay firm even when cooked a few seconds too long. I also braise seafoods in traditional Chinese clay pots; these diffuse heat better than any metal cooking vessel and make it more difficult to scorch items. A last note of advice: no matter which seafood you are preparing, don't step away from it for too long, and really tend to it carefully while cooking.

STEAMED FISH
CHINESE-STYLE

4 dried medium SHIITAKE
  MUSHROOMS

One 2-pound whole SEA BASS,
  FLOUNDER, or CARP

KOSHER SALT

Freshly ground BLACK PEPPER

2 SCALLIONS, root and dark green
  ends trimmed, and 6-inch stalks
  cut into 1½-inch-long pieces
  and julienned

1 ounce fresh GINGER, peeled and
  julienned

2 tablespoons VEGETABLE OIL

2 tablespoons CHINESE LIGHT SOY
  SAUCE

1 teaspoon SESAME OIL

6 sprigs CILANTRO, trimmed

T HE CHINESE STEAM all sorts of fish, the most popular being carp, flounder, and sea bass. Most simply, a whole fish is steamed with julienned ginger, scallions, and shiitakes. Seasoned with soy sauce and a touch of sesame oil, the steamed whole fish is drizzled with piping-hot oil at the last minute, ensuring the fish not only stays hot but has a lively flavor and pleasing appearance (proof that the most basic ingredients can turn any fish into a marvelous dish). In many Asian cultures, it is an honor to be served a whole fish, which is a sign of prosperity. If you are offered the fish head, it is more of an honor still. Fish heads in Western cultures are used to make stock. This holds in Asian cultures as well, but the head is also eaten at table, and is perhaps the most delicious part of the fish. Loaded with cartilage and bones, the head tends to be more flavorful than any other part of the fish.

Depending on the fish, cooking times will differ (even if they're all two-pounders). A flat fish such as flounder will cook in less time than a round fish such as sea bass or carp. The fish is cooked when the flesh is opaque all the way through and the central bone is still pink; if the bone is gray, the fish is overcooked.

1. Put the shiitakes in a bowl with hot water to cover, then set a plate over the bowl to prevent steam from escaping. Let stand until the mushrooms rehydrate and soften, about 30 minutes (or longer, depending on their size). Squeeze the mushrooms between the palms of your hands to get rid of the excess water. Using a paring knife, remove any hard stems and discard, and julienne the caps.

2. Fill the bottom third of a wok with water, and set a metal steaming rack in the center. Cover with a lid

and place the wok over high heat. Lightly season the fish with salt and pepper on both sides, place it on an oval plate, and score it with a knife at ¾-inch intervals. Evenly scatter the shiitakes, scallions, and ginger over the fish. When the steamer is filled with hot steam, place the plate with the fish on top of the rack. Steam, securely covered, until the fish is cooked through, 15 to 20 minutes, depending on the fish. (You should not uncover the fish while it is steaming, but after 15 minutes start testing for doneness for a flounder, and about 20 minutes for sea bass or carp.) Insert a skewer in the thickest part of the fish. If it goes through easily, the fish is done. If it shows any resistance at all, let the fish cook for an additional 3 to 5 minutes.

3. Meanwhile, heat the oil in a small saucepan over medium heat. Carefully remove the fish from the steamer and drizzle the soy sauce and sesame oil across the length of the fish. Drizzle the hot oil all over the fish. (The oil should sizzle for a few seconds.) Garnish with the cilantro sprigs and present the fish at the table.

4. To carve, carefully run the edge of a spoon down the middle of the fish. To separate and detach the two fillets from the central bone, use the edge of the spoon again to carefully push one of the fillets to the side, while using a second spoon to push the other fillet to the opposite side, revealing the central bone. Break the bone just below the head and carefully lift the central bone, being careful to leave the bottom fillets intact. If you need to, run the edge of the spoon under the bone as you are lifting it to ensure that no flesh sticks to the bone and that the flesh remains intact on the plate. Use the two spoons to divide the fish among individual plates, drizzle with the juices, and serve with rice and stir-fried greens on the side.

STEAMED FISH WITH HAM

6 dried small to medium SHIITAKE
  MUSHROOMS

One 2-pound whole SEA BASS or
  GROUPER

Freshly ground BLACK PEPPER

GRANULATED SUGAR

4 ounces SMITHFIELD HAM,
  soaked and sliced paper thin

1 tablespoon GINGER EXTRACT
  (page 74)

1 tablespoon SHAOXING WINE

2 or more tablespoons SCALLION
  OIL (page 108)

2 tablespoons CHINESE LIGHT SOY
  SAUCE

1 teaspoon SESAME OIL

6 sprigs CILANTRO, trimmed

IN THIS RECIPE, the fish is scored every ½ inch on the top, and a slice of ham, followed by a shiitake mushroom half, is inserted into the skin. Not only does the ham add a robust flavor to the fish, it adds texture as well. Smithfield ham, a very good substitute for the Yunnan ham used in China, can be bought at Chinese butcher shops. For this recipe I like to use a round fish like sea bass or grouper.

Because it can be chewy and incredibly salty if not soaked properly, Smithfield ham needs to be soaked prior to using in any recipe (see "Essential Ingredients," page 17). To ensure that it has maximum tenderness, slice it paper-thin against the grain. The scallion oil must be made at the same time that the fish is cooking so the oil is fresh and piping hot.

1. Put the shiitakes in a bowl with hot water to cover, then set a plate over the bowl to prevent steam from escaping. Let stand until the mushrooms rehydrate and soften, about 30 minutes (or longer, depending on the size of the mushrooms). Squeeze the mushrooms between the palms of your hands to get rid of the excess water. Using a paring knife, remove any hard stems and discard, and halve the caps.

2. Fill the bottom third of a wok with water and set a metal steaming rack in the center. Cover with a lid and place the wok over high heat. Lightly season the fish with pepper and sugar to taste on both sides. On the top (select the best-looking side) slice the fish crosswise every ½ inch. Cut all the way to the central bone, leaving the bone intact. Place the fish on an oval plate, and insert 1 or 2 slices of ham, overlapping the slices, across the width of each slit, followed by 1 or 2 mushroom halves, also overlapping the slices. Drizzle the ginger extract and wine down the length of the fish. When the steamer is filled with hot steam, place the plate with the fish on top of the rack. Steam, securely covered, until the fish is cooked through, about 20 minutes.

3. Meanwhile, make the scallion oil. Carefully remove the fish from the steamer and drizzle the soy sauce and sesame oil down the length of the fish. Drizzle the hot scallion oil (making sure to include a generous amount of scallions) all over the fish. (The oil should sizzle for a few seconds.) Garnish with the cilantro sprigs and present the fish at the table.

4. To serve, use spoons to lift single sections of fish, ham, and mushrooms. Divide the fish among individual plates. Once the top is served, break the central bone just below the head and carefully lift the central bone, being careful to leave the bottom fillets intact. Divide the bottom fillets among each serving, placing them next to the top pieces. Drizzle the juices on top and serve with jasmine rice and stir-fried greens on the side.

Variation: On rare occasions, Chinese cooks use fish fillets, rather than whole fish, in certain recipes. This is one of them: Cut 2 pounds of white fish fillets into ½-inch-thick "scallop" slices. To achieve scallop-like slices, simply tilt your blade on an angle rather than straight down when cutting. Then, following the recipe, insert a slice of ham and a mushroom half in between each slice of fish, making sure to keep the shape of the fillets intact. Proceed with the rest of the recipe.

A SAMPAN—A FISHING AND TRANSPORTATION BOAT—IN THE BAY OF HONG KONG

CA HAP BIA
FISH STEAMED
WITH BEER

SERVES 4 TO 6

4 cups BLOND BEER, such as
HEINEKEN or SAPPORO

2 LEMONGRASS STALKS, root ends
trimmed, outer leaves and tough
green tops removed, and 6-inch-
long inner bulbs thinly sliced
diagonally

One 2-pound SEA BASS or
GROUPER, or any whole FISH,
cleaned

KOSHER SALT

Freshly ground BLACK PEPPER

2 SCALLIONS, root and dark green
ends trimmed, and 6-inch stalks
cut into 1½-inch-long pieces
and julienned

1 ounce fresh GINGER, peeled and
julienned

2 tablespoons VEGETABLE OIL

2 THAI CHILIES, stemmed and
seeded, and sliced paper thin
in rounds

1 tablespoon FISH SAUCE

⅓ cup VIETNAMESE CORIANDER
LEAVES; or CILANTRO LEAVES

THE VIETNAMESE sometimes prepare seafood by steaming it in beer. Pick any type of white fish, or substitute large prawns, for this dish, and steam it in any light-flavored, blond beer with herbs such as lemongrass and scallions. The herbed beer both replaces water as the steaming liquid and enhances the flavor of the fish. For a more pronounced flavor I like to drizzle a small amount of beer directly on the fish during the cooking process. As with the other steamed fish dishes, I serve *ca hap bia* with simple stir-fried greens and jasmine rice.

1. Fill the bottom third of a wok with all but ¼ cup of the beer and set a metal steaming rack in the center. Add the lemongrass to the beer, cover with a lid, and place the wok over high heat. Lightly season the fish with salt and pepper on both sides, place it on an oval plate, evenly scatter the scallions and ginger over the fish, and drizzle it with the remaining beer. When the steamer is filled with hot steam, place the plate with the fish on top of the rack. Steam, securely covered, until the fish is cooked through, about 20 minutes.

2. Meanwhile, heat the oil in a small saucepan over medium heat. Add the chilies and fry for a minute. Turn off the heat. Remove the fish from the steamer and carefully tilt the plate to drain it. Drizzle the fish sauce over the fish so that it is evenly distributed. Drizzle the hot oil with the chilies all over the fish. The oil should sizzle for a few seconds. Garnish with a generous amount of Vietnamese coriander or cilantro, and present the fish at the table.

3. To carve, carefully run the edge of a spoon down the middle of the fish. To separate and detach the two fillets from the central bone, use the edge of the spoon again to carefully push one of the fillets to the side, while using a second spoon to push the other fillet to the opposite side, revealing the central bone. Break the bone just below the head and carefully lift the central bone, being careful to leave the bottom fillets intact. If you need to, run the edge of the spoon under the bone as you are lifting it to ensure that no flesh sticks to the bone and that the flesh remains intact on the plate. Divide the fish among individual plates, drizzle with the juices, and serve.

AMOK TREY
FISH IN COCONUT CUSTARD

SERVES 4 TO 6

2½ cups unsweetened COCONUT
MILK (page 77); or commercial
equivalent

3 large EGGS

⅓ cup KROEUNG (page 78);
or 2 tablespoons THAI RED
CURRY PASTE (page 82); or
commercial equivalent

1 tablespoon FISH SAUCE

1 teaspoon GRANULATED SUGAR

2½ pounds fresh skinless thick
COD fillet, cut into 6 pieces

EATERIES ABOUND in Phnom Penh, and at one of its small family-owned restaurants I ordered Khmer foods such as sour soup, green mango salad, and delicious *amok trey*, fish steamed in herbal-infused coconut custard. Flavored with the ubiquitous *kroeung* herbal paste, the fish, set in the center of the custard, was fragrant with hints of galangal, garlic, shallot, and lemongrass. Wrapped in tiny banana leaf cups, it was beautifully presented. *Amok trey* is also found in the central plains of Thailand, where it is called *haw mok*, and the coconut custard is looser and richer. It is also spicy hot, with red curry paste replacing the *kroeung* paste.

1. Fill the bottom third of a wok with water and set a bamboo steamer with a lid over it. Bring the water to a boil over high heat.

2. Whisk together the coconut milk, eggs, *kroeung* (or red curry paste), fish sauce, and sugar in a bowl until the sugar is completely dissolved. Place a piece of fish in each of 6 small bowls. Divide the coconut milk mixture equally among each serving of fish. When the steamer is filled with hot steam, transfer the bowls to the steamer, cover it, and lower the heat to medium so the custard does not curdle. Cook until the custard sets, about 15 minutes. Remove from the steamer and serve with jasmine rice and stir-fried greens on the side.

ONE DAY, I turned this rich steamed fish into a braised lobster-tail dish. Using my favorite cooking vessel, the clay pot, I heated some canola oil to brown the *kroeung* paste and release its herbal essence. Once the paste had darkened slightly, I stirred in the coconut milk and 1 cup of seafood broth made with the heads and shells of 4 small lobsters. Once the rich broth reached a gentle boil, I added the lobster tails, which I had halved lengthwise, and the whole claws. A handful of Thai basil leaves added a nice licorice-like aroma. I piled rice in the center of each of 4 serving plates and topped it with lobster tails and claws, forming a reconstituted whole (but headless) lobster. Drizzled with the rich coconut and lobster broth, it was delicious when served with long beautiful baby eggplant halves I had scored, brushed with sesame oil, and grilled.

CA KHO
MACKEREL BRAISED IN
CARAMEL SAUCE

SERVES 4 TO 6

8 dried small to medium SHIITAKE
   MUSHROOMS

2½ pounds MACKEREL fillets, cut
   into large pieces; or EEL,
   bone-in, cut into 1½-inch-long
   pieces

KOSHER SALT

Freshly ground BLACK PEPPER

3 tablespoons GRANULATED SUGAR

1 cup young COCONUT WATER; or
   BASIC FISH STOCK (page 123);
   or WATER

1 teaspoon CHINESE DARK THICK
   SOY SAUCE (optional)

2 tablespoons FISH SAUCE

2 large GARLIC CLOVES, crushed
   and peeled

2 SCALLIONS, root and dark green
   ends trimmed, and 6-inch stalks
   halved crosswise and lightly
   crushed

3 to 5 dried RED CHILIES

FRIED GINGER AND SCALLIONS
   (page 108)

THIS DISH ORIGINATED in northern Vietnam but is now enjoyed throughout the country. Sweet and savory, the fish simmers in co-conut water collected from young green coconuts and is seasoned with caramel and fish sauce. Mackerel is one of my favorite fish. It is rich and incredibly flavorful, stronger than mild-flavored fish like sole but wonderful when fresh. A nice way to counterbalance the pungent taste of mackerel is to add a generous amount of ginger and scallions during the cooking. For a more satisfying meal, I also like to add dried shiitake mushrooms while cooking, keeping these whole for presentation. To deepen the color of the braising liquids, add Chinese thick soy sauce.

Eel is also perfect for this dish; select large, mature eel.

1. Put the shiitakes in a bowl with hot water to cover, then set a plate over the bowl to prevent steam from escaping. Let stand until the mushrooms rehydrate and soften, about 30 minutes (or longer, depending on the size of the mushrooms). Squeeze the mushrooms between the palms of your hands to get rid of the excess water. Using a paring knife, remove any hard stems and discard. Keep the caps whole, or halve them if you wish.

2. Season the fish pieces with salt and pepper on both sides and set aside.

3. Make a caramel by combining the sugar and 2 tablespoons water in a clay pot or heavy-bottomed pot over medium-low heat. When the sugar melts and turns golden, about 10 minutes, remove the pot from the heat and stir in the coconut water (or fish stock, or water), thick soy sauce (if using), and fish sauce. Reduce the heat to low and add the shiitakes, garlic, scallions, chilies, and fish pieces. Cover and simmer until the fish is cooked through, 10 to 15 minutes. Divide among 4 plates and garnish each serving with a generous amount of fried ginger and scallion threads. Serve with jasmine rice on the side.

MAEUNT'ANG
BRAISED BLACK COD
WITH DAIKON

SERVES 4 TO 6

¼ cup KOREAN or JAPANESE DARK
   SOY SAUCE

2 tablespoons SAKE

3 tablespoons GRANULATED SUGAR

1 teaspoon SESAME OIL

1 pound DAIKON, peeled and
   cut into 1-inch-thick rounds
   (4 to 5 slices)

2½ pounds BLACK COD or
   MACKEREL fillets (preferably
   thick), cut into 6 large chunks

2 ounces fresh GINGER, sliced
   lengthwise and lightly crushed,
   plus 2 paper-thin slices of
   GINGER julienned into delicate
   strings

6 SCALLIONS, root and dark green
   ends trimmed; four 6-inch stalks
   halved crosswise and lightly
   crushed, and 2 thinly sliced
   diagonally

1 cup BASIC BEEF STOCK
   (page 120); or BASIC FISH
   STOCK (page 123); or WATER

8 large GARLIC CLOVES, crushed
   and peeled

1 or more teaspoons KOREAN RED
   CHILI POWDER (or fine flakes)

THIS IS A TRADITIONAL KOREAN spicy fish stew that is made using fatty fish such as black cod. Sweet, spicy, and savory, the fish is incredibly rich and is perfect as a follow-up to a raw beef and Asian pear salad (page 471). The black cod sits on thick slices of tender daikon and simmers in a sweetened broth made from beef stock seasoned with soy sauce, garlic, ginger, and scallions. You will notice that while the fish practically falls apart when served, the generous amount of braising liquid and the natural fat of the fish keep it wonderfully moist.

I like to use Chinese sand pots for braising, but a heavy enameled cast iron or similar type pot will do. Be sure to select fatty fish when making this dish to ensure that the fish will remain moist when cooked. The result should be a tender fish that comes apart easily without being dry. You may substitute fish stock for beef stock if you prefer.

1. Whisk together the soy sauce, sake, and sugar until the sugar is completely dissolved. Add the sesame oil.

2. Place the daikon slices in the bottom of the pot in one single layer. Add the fish fillets skin side down to cover the daikon. Scatter the crushed ginger slices and scallion halves on top of the fish, and pour the marinade and stock or water over the whole thing. Add the garlic and chili powder, cover the pot, place over medium-low heat, and gently cook until the fish falls apart easily, about 20 minutes. Using a spatula, carefully lift a layered daikon and fillet portion and transfer it to a plate. Repeat this process for each individual serving. Garnish each serving with julienned ginger and sliced scallion. Serve with short-grain rice on the side.

I MUST have died and gone to heaven when I first tasted this dish. Cooked perfectly, the black cod was soft and moist, and the daikon was tender enough to yield upon contact with my chopsticks. (I remember going back to the restaurant four times in one week with friends to share the good news.) The waiters, different ones each time, all said, "This is my favorite dish." Back home, I tested the recipe over and over again, trying to re-create this succulent fish dish. I used all kinds of fatty fish such as Chilean sea bass and mackerel and even tried bluefish. All had a slightly different texture, but they were delicious nonetheless.

FRIED OR GRILLED WHOLE FISH

SERVES 4 TO 6

VEGETABLE OIL for deep-frying

12 whole POMFRET or
 BUTTERFISH, about 3 ounces
 each, cleaned, heads and tails
 left intact

INDONESIAN SWEET SOY SAUCE

2 or more THAI CHILIES,
 stemmed, seeded, and thinly
 sliced

COLORFUL CUCUMBER AND
 SHALLOT SALAD (page 350)

NUOC CHAM (page 100)

D EEP-FRIED WHOLE FISH are adored everywhere in China and South-east Asia. Simply grilled or fried, they can be found at any number of restaurants and often at street vendors' stalls. While in the West dredging a whole fish in flour is common, in Asia this step is either omitted, or, occasionally, cornstarch is used. The undredged cooked fish is ultra-crispy and has a somewhat dry texture, which is adjusted with any number of dipping sauces. In China, a simple soy sauce might do; in Indonesia, it's the thick sweet soy sauce, *kecap manis*, with a few chili slices added. In Vietnam and Cambodia, a concoction of fish sauce, lime juice, sugar, garlic, and chili is the norm; the Cambodians add crushed peanuts to their version. In Thailand, it is enjoyed with a sweet and spicy cucumber salad. In the Philippines, people love fried foods, or fish grilled over hot wood coals, accompanied by rice and pickled vegetables (page 354).

1. IF DEEP-FRYING: Blot fish dry. Heat enough vegetable oil for deep-frying in a pot over medium heat. When the temperature reaches 360° to 375°F, working in batches, carefully lower the fish into the hot oil. Cook until very crispy on both sides, about 4 minutes.

IF GRILLING INDOORS: Oil both the fish and grill pan. Place the pan over medium-high heat. When the pan starts to smoke, grill the fish until cooked through, about 5 minutes per side.

IF GRILLING OUTDOORS: Brush some oil over the fish. Grill over a barbecue (make sure the flames have subsided and the coals are red with white ashes) until the fish is cooked through and the skin is crisp, about 5 minutes per side. (If the fish sticks to the grill, place aluminum foil over the grill and cook the fish on top of the foil, or buy a nonstick fish rack, which will hold the fish in place.)

2. Serve the fried or grilled fish with jasmine rice and pickled vegetables on the side with condiments such as a mixture of Indonesian soy sauce and chilies, a sweet and spicy cucumber salad, or *nuoc cham*.

A Filipino fisherman grills and sells his catch of the day.

CHA CA
HANOI FRIED YELLOW FISH

SERVES 4 TO 6

12 ounces dried RICE VERMICELLI

VEGETABLE OIL for deep-frying,
plus a tablespoon for stir-frying

1 cup all-purpose FLOUR or
TAPIOCA STARCH

1 teaspoon TURMERIC POWDER

2½ to 3 pounds FLOUNDER fillets,
cut into 1-inch cubes; or BABY
FISH (about 2 inches long)

2 SCALLIONS, root and dark green
ends trimmed, and 6-inch stalks
cut into 1½-inch-long pieces
and julienned

½ cup THAI BASIL LEAVES

1 bunch CILANTRO, stems
trimmed, sprigs separated

1 bunch DILL, stems trimmed,
sprigs separated

⅓ cup roasted unsalted PEANUTS,
finely crushed (not peanut
butter)

NUOC CHAM (page 100)

FRIED FISH NUGGETS have never tasted better than when mixed with rice vermicelli, stir-fried exotic herbs, and crunchy peanuts, then drizzled with *nuoc cham*, the delicious Vietnamese sweet and spicy lime and fish sauce table condiment. In Hanoi this fried specialty, *cha ca*, is found along the aptly named Cha Ca Street in the old French Quarter of the capital. The fish, dredged in flour and turmeric powder, turns a vibrant yellow color. Set atop the rice vermicelli and garnished with a generous amount of stir-fried scallions, cilantro, dill, Thai basil, and peanuts, the golden fish cubes look beautiful.

I realize that calling for a "bunch" of herbs is hard to visualize, especially when markets have their own definition of what constitutes a "bunch." Use your judgment, and be sure that when stir-fried, the herbs amount to a good one-third cup per serving.

1. Place the dried rice vermicelli in a dish with water to cover. Let stand until pliable, about 30 minutes, and drain. Bring a pot of water to a boil over high heat. Divide the vermicelli into 4 equal portions. Working with one portion at a time, place in a sieve. Lower the sieve into the boiling water and use chopsticks to untangle the noodles so they cook evenly, about 5 seconds. Remove immediately, drain, and place in a bowl. Repeat this step with the remaining vermicelli portions. Transfer the vermicelli portions to individual bowls or plates.

2. Pour the oil in a pot (about 3 inches deep) and heat over medium heat to 360° to 375°F. Meanwhile, mix the flour and turmeric in a plastic bag. Put the fish in the flour mixture, seal the bag, and shake it to coat each piece evenly. Put the fish pieces, a few at a time, in the palms of your hands and shake off the excess flour. Working in batches, deep-fry the fish until golden crisp all around, 3 to 4 minutes total. Drain on paper towels, then divide the fish pieces among the servings of the rice vermicelli.

3. Heat 1 tablespoon oil in a wok or nonstick pan over high heat. Stir-fry the scallions for a minute. Add the Thai basil, cilantro, and dill and continue to stir-fry until just wilted, about 30 seconds. Divide and arrange the stir-fried herbs in a mound over each serving of fish and rice vermicelli. Have your guests drizzle some *nuoc cham* and scatter some peanuts over their servings.

WHEN I WAS A CHILD in France, my family lived with my French grandmother, Jeanne Barbet, in the Loire Valley for quite some time. We thought we were twice blessed because she is a sweet woman who really knows how to cook. Every once in a while my uncles would come back from fishing trips, having caught dozens of the tiniest fish, no more than 2 inches long and about ½ inch wide. My grandmother would gut them, leaving the heads on, and dredge them in flour. I could smell the sizzling fish as they went into a large pot of hot oil. Once they were deep-fried, she would sprinkle them with sea salt and black pepper and serve them with lemon wedges on the side. Known as *fritures,* they were crispy and sweet, and we always ate every single one (including the crunchy heads). Occasionally my fishmonger in Chinatown has baby fish. When he does, I buy a couple of pounds and make Vietnamese-style *fritures,* dredging the fish in a combination of flour and turmeric and deep-frying them until they turn a rich golden color. Then I toss them with freshly ground sea salt and some cayenne pepper. Served with lime wedges, they make a delicious finger food for cocktails. I have also served my *fritures* with *nuoc cham* on the side as a starter for a Vietnamese meal. If you don't like the tiny crunchy heads, pinch them off!

LUON CUON XA
GRILLED LEMONGRASS EEL

SERVES 4 TO 6

2 tablespoons FISH SAUCE

1 tablespoon GRANULATED SUGAR

1 LEMONGRASS STALK, root end
trimmed, tough green top and
outer leaves removed, and
6-inch-long inner bulb finely
ground

1 ounce fresh GINGER, peeled and
finely grated

1 large GARLIC CLOVE, crushed,
peeled, and minced

1 small SHALLOT, peeled and
minced

1 tablespoon VEGETABLE OIL

Freshly ground BLACK PEPPER

3 pounds EEL (about 2 eels), cut
into 2-inch pieces, butterflied,
and deboned

8 ounces CAUL FAT, cut into
2-inch-square pieces

NUOC CHAM (page 100)

EEL IS A WONDERFUL FISH with a rich flavor and firm texture. When it is available live (usually in Chinatown), I select large ones an inch or more in diameter to make *luon cuon xa*, grilled eel flavored with lemongrass, garlic, and ginger, which is absolutely delicious dipped in *nuoc cham*.

Some cooks blanch the eel for a few seconds before butterflying it, making it easier to handle.

1. Whisk together the fish sauce and sugar in a large bowl until the sugar is completely dissolved. Stir in the lemongrass, ginger, garlic, shallot, and oil and season with pepper. Add the eel pieces, rubbing them thoroughly with the marinade. Marinate for 1 hour, refrigerated.

2. Wrap each piece of eel with caul fat. Heat a well-oiled grill pan or nonstick pan over high heat, and grill the eel until crispy on both sides, about 2 minutes per side. If grilling outdoors on a barbecue or hibachi, place the eel pieces in a fine wire fish holder to keep them in place. Serve *nuoc cham* for dipping and jasmine rice and green papaya salad (page 351) on the side.

WHEN BUYING EEL, ask your fishmonger to gut it, remove its head, spine, and bones, and, if possible, to butterfly it for you. If he or she will not oblige, do not be alarmed if the "dead" eel seems to wake up and bite at its plastic bag. This happened to me once when I had a whole gutted eel in a bag while in a taxi. The ride was a bit uncomfortable as I watched eel teeth coming through the side of the bag. Remembering how my Asian aunts had handled these muscular fish, when I got home I hit the eel a few times, then chopped its head off with a cleaver. (If you're going to do this, I suggest you wear thick rubber gloves; eel teeth are sharp and nasty.) Don't be alarmed by the twitching; the fish is dead but its muscles are reacting to temperature changes. Anyway, we had a great meal.

IKAN ASAM PEDES
PAN-FRIED CATFISH WITH SPICY COCONUT MILK

SERVES 4 TO 6

½ cup TAPIOCA STARCH or CORNSTARCH

12 small CATFISH fillets

2 to 3 tablespoons VEGETABLE OIL

½ cup COCONUT CREAM

1 cup unsweetened COCONUT MILK (page 77); or commercial equivalent

½ cup or more BASE GEDE (page 80)

2 LIMES, cut into 6 wedges

A FAVORITE FRESHWATER fish in Southeast Asia, catfish is grilled and flavored with *base gede*, the basic spice paste used to season all sorts of fish, seafood, poultry, and meat in Indonesia. Cooked in coconut milk, the fish is also flavored with hints of lemongrass, galangal, garlic, and chilies. I prefer to pan-fry the fish fillets, but you can certainly deep-fry them, as many Indonesians like to do. Serve ikan *asam pedes* with pickled vegetables (page 354) on the side and jasmine rice.

1. Place the tapioca starch in a large plastic bag. Pat dry the fish fillets, put them in the starch, seal the bag, and shake to coat the fillets evenly. Remove the fillets from the bag and shake off the excess starch.

2. Heat the oil in a nonstick skillet over high heat and pan-fry the fillets until golden, about 3 minutes per side.

3. Meanwhile, heat the coconut cream and milk and the *base gede* in a saucepan over medium-high heat, and boil until the coconut separates, leaving behind its oil and the *base gede* paste, 20 to 30 minutes. Most of the white coconut milk should have evaporated; mostly remaining should be a fragrant oily paste. Place 2 fish fillets on each individual plate, and top with some of the spicy paste and a lime wedge.

MISO-MARINATED BLACK COD

SERVES 4 TO 6

½ cup SHIROMISO
3 tablespoons SAKE
3 tablespoons MIRIN
⅓ cup GRANULATED SUGAR
2½ pounds BLACK COD, regular
COD, or MACKEREL from the
thick side of the fillet, cut into
approximately 12 equal pieces
YOUNG PICKLED GINGER
(page 355)

PART OF COOKING'S PLEASURE is being inspired by people in your family, people you meet in your travels, or restaurants you visit. I once was served miso-marinated broiled black cod. It was so delicious that I decided to experiment with this recipe on my own. Black cod is not always available. Accordingly, I have tried this recipe using other fish such as regular cod, mackerel, and Chilean sea bass (although this variety is now overfished, so I hesitate to recommend it), and all were very tasty. Marinated in a combination of sake, mirin (sweet sake), and shiromiso (white miso) for a day, the fish takes on a sweet salty flavor and caramelizes while broiling.

If you can find black cod (sometimes it is a matter of asking your fishmonger ahead of time), it is well worth trying.

1. Whisk together the shiromiso, sake, mirin, and sugar in a bowl until the sugar is completely dissolved and the marinade is smooth. Add the fish pieces to the marinade and mix well to coat evenly. Cover with a plastic wrap and refrigerate for 24 to 48 hours, turning the pieces 4 to 6 times.

2. Position an oven rack in the center of your oven, about 8 inches from the broiler. Preheat the broiler. Transfer the fish pieces to a baking sheet and broil until the fish caramelizes, turning a rich golden hue, about 10 minutes. Turn the pieces over and cook for another 4 minutes. Place a piece of broiled fish in the center of individual plates. Squeeze a few slices of pickled ginger to get rid of their excess pickling liquid and set atop each piece of fish. Serve with short-grain rice and stir-fried daikon.

WHEN I FIRST ATE black cod prepared this way, I was surprised at how the texture of the fish had changed after 48 hours of marination. The curing process had actually made the fish firmer! I thought this might be specific to the black cod, so I tested the recipe using Chilean sea bass, which resulted in an equally firm fish. When cooked, the fish has a curious yet pleasantly firm texture and candy-like flavor. Although I love to sip Japanese green tea with Japanese meals, for this dish I recommend something chilled, such as a light Japanese beer or sake or a dry white wine to cut the richness of the sweet and salty marinade as well as the natural fat of the fish.

SAKANA YAKIMONO
SKEWERED SWORDFISH

SERVES 4 TO 6

2½ pounds ¾-inch-thick
SWORDFISH steaks, skin
removed, and cut into
1-inch cubes

KOSHER SALT

1 tablespoon VEGETABLE OIL

YAKITORI SAUCE (page 91)

YOUNG PICKLED GINGER
(page 355)

12 or more BAMBOO SKEWERS,
soaked in water for 20 minutes

*S*AKANA means food served with sake, but it also means fish. *Yakimono* means grilled foods, which are skewered to form what are essentially Japanese kebabs. In Japan, these snack foods are eaten with beer and sake. For this recipe I use swordfish, a wonderful fish that is usually sold in steak form. Cut into bite-size morsels and skewered, they are grilled and basted with a sweet soy sauce. The dish is absolutely delicious, especially with a shot of sake chased with cold beer. Do not hesitate to experiment with this wonderful recipe, using all sorts of fish, seafood, poultry, meat, and vegetables.

If grilling on a hibachi, be sure to soak the bamboo skewers for at least twenty minutes prior to skewering the fish. The wet bamboo will not burn while the fish cooks.

1. Season the fish pieces with salt on all sides and set aside for 30 minutes, refrigerated. Skewer 3 to 4 pieces of fish on each bamboo skewer.

2. Heat the oil in a nonstick grill pan over high heat. Dip each piece of fish in the yakitori sauce and place it on the grill pan for a minute. Dip the fish in the sauce again and return it to the pan, this time grilling the other side for a minute. Repeat this process until the fish is cooked through but juicy, 2 or 3 more times. Place 2 to 3 skewers of swordfish on individual plates, garnished with pickled ginger. Serve with short-grain rice or vinegared sushi rice on the side and grilled vegetables such as eggplant or leeks.

YAKIMONO IS WONDERFUL served at home. I skewer all sorts of fish—tuna, swordfish, and salmon; seafood such as shrimp and baby squid with the tentacles. I also skewer poultry such as chicken and duck, and meats such as beef sirloin and pork tenderloin. Although I often cook these skewered items ahead of time, when the weather allows for outdoor entertaining I like to involve my guests in the cooking. This is fairly simple to do: place a brazier or hibachi in the center of a picnic table (be sure you've placed it on a trivet so as not to burn your table) and have your guests grill their own food.

SAKE TERIYAKI
SALMON TERIYAKI

SERVES 4 TO 6

Three 1-pound SALMON fillets,
 skin on, each cut into 3 pieces
KOSHER SALT
1 tablespoon VEGETABLE OIL
TERIYAKI SAUCE (page 87)
YOUNG PICKLED GINGER
 (page 355)

TERIYAKI IS PERHAPS one of the most famous dishes on Japanese menus, next to sashimi and sushi. In this recipe, the teriyaki sauce—soy sauce, sake, and sugar—is heated at the very end and used to coat the fish just before serving. Salmon is a fatty fish and perfect for cooking at high temperatures because the melting fat keeps the flesh moist. Grilled vegetables such as leeks brushed with sesame oil complement salmon teriyaki nicely. You can also serve a refreshing bamboo shoot and shiitake salad (page 347).

I generally buy 7 to 8 ounces of fish per person because it is less filling than meat, and I find that people tend to eat a little more.

1. Season the fish pieces with salt on both sides and set aside for 30 minutes, refrigerated.

2. Heat the oil in a nonstick pan over high heat. Pan-fry the fish skin side down until golden crisp, about 5 minutes. Flip the fish pieces so the skin side is up and continue to sear until the fish is cooked through but moist, about 2 minutes more. Transfer the fish pieces onto a paper towel–lined plate to drain the excess oil. Add the teriyaki sauce to the pan and bring it to a boil. Return the fish pieces to the pan and cook in the sauce for 20 seconds on each side to coat evenly. Divide the fish among individual plates and drizzle some of the sauce over each serving. Garnish with pickled ginger and serve with short-grain rice on the side.

SASHIMI
RAW FISH PLATTER

SERVES 4 TO 6

8 ounces DAIKON, peeled and
   julienned into threads
12 ounces TUNA, thinly sliced into
   8 pieces
12 ounces FLUKE, thinly sliced on
   the diagonal into 8 pieces
8 SHISO LEAVES, green or purple
   or both
1 CUCUMBER, peeled and cut into
   8 pieces crosswise
12 ounces SALMON ROE
3 cups SUSHI-MESHI RICE
   (pp. 188–89)
2 tablespoons MATCHA
   (green tea powder)
YOUNG PICKLED GINGER
   (page 355)
JAPANESE TAMARI SAUCE or DARK
   SOY SAUCE
WASABI

I LOVE RAW FISH and often eat it in Korean and Japanese restaurants. Served lightly chilled, the fish—tuna, fluke, and salmon roe—makes for a colorful presentation. To prepare this dish, get your fish at a Japanese market that offers sushi-quality fish. The fish will be more expensive, but you can generally be sure that it is of the highest quality. These portions are adequate for an appetizer. Garnished with julienned daikon and green and purple *shiso* leaves, the delicate slices of raw fish tease the palate for the main course that follows. The sushi rice balls sprinkled with green tea powder add texture and a pungent vinegary and bitter note to the dish that nicely complement the raw fish.

If you wish to serve this as a main course, double the quantities.

1. Arrange a mound of daikon on each of 4 plates. Place the fish on top, fanning the slices of both tuna and fluke. Place two *shiso* leaves between the tuna and the fluke, making a colorful separation.

2. Scoop out the seeds from each of the cucumber pieces, leaving some at one end. They should look like cups. Fill each cup with a generous amount of salmon roe and place these next to the slices of fish.

3. Make small, equal-size balls (each one no bigger than a Ping-Pong ball) out of the sushi rice, and sprinkle each lightly with *matcha*. Divide these among individual servings. Serve with pickled ginger, tamari, and *wasabi* on the side.

MY FAVORITE RAW FISH to order in Korean restaurants is tuna, which Koreans call *ch'amch'ihoe*. They may not offer the pickled ginger, soy sauce, and *wasabi* with the raw fish (as would the Japanese), but they do serve an addictive sweet and sour chili dipping sauce (page 105) instead. Often served at the beginning of a meal, raw fish is a perfect introduction for the spicy main courses that follow.

KINILAW
FILIPINO CEVICHE

Juice of 1 LIME

½ cup COCONUT VINEGAR; or
CHINESE WHITE RICE VINEGAR

¼ cup unsweetened COCONUT
MILK (page 77); or commercial
equivalent (optional)

1 ounce fresh GINGER, peeled and
julienned

1 large SHALLOT or small YELLOW
ONION, peeled and sliced into
thin wedges

1 SCALLION, root and dark green
ends trimmed, and 6-inch stalk
cut into 1-inch-long pieces and
julienned

1 GREEN MANGO, peeled and
julienned; or 1 cup julienned
GREEN PAPAYA

2 THAI CHILIES, stemmed, seeded,
and thinly sliced (optional)

2 pounds skinless MACKEREL fillets,
cut into bite-size cubes

KOSHER SALT

Freshly ground BLACK PEPPER

⅓ cup CILANTRO LEAVES

K INILAW, OR KILAWIN, is basically a Filipino *ceviche*, or raw fish cured in sour, acidic juices. The acid usually comes from a combination of coconut vinegar and *kalamansi* (also *calamansi*) juice, which you can occasionally find in the United States. Most of the time, however, I use the more readily available rice vinegar and lime juice. There are many variations on *kinilaw*, using many types of fish, from mild-flavored white fish to those with more pronounced flavors such as *tanguige*, or mackerel, a favorite among fishermen. (You can also use scallops or octopus.)

Be sure the fish you use is very fresh; buy it from a trusted fishmonger or get sushi-quality fish. If you cannot find unripe green mango or papaya, use pickled mango or kohlrabi. The latter has a pleasant, subtle flavor and is also crunchy.

Whisk together the lime juice, vinegar, and coconut milk (if using) in a bowl until well combined. Add the ginger, shallot, scallion, mango, chilies (if using), and mackerel. Season with salt and pepper and let stand for 15 to 20 minutes. Divide the *kinilaw* among individual bowls and serve garnished with cilantro leaves.

DRUNKEN SHRIMP

SERVES 4 TO 6

6 dozen live or very fresh small
SHRIMP, head and shells intact
1 cup RICE ALCOHOL, at least
100 proof
SPICY SOY SAUCE DIP (page 88)

DRUNKEN SHRIMP is one of those Chinese specialties you either love or hate. Live baby shrimp are drowned in 100-proof rice alcohol, eliminating any impurities while allowing the shrimp meat to absorb the flavor of the alcohol. In Taiwan they are eaten raw just after they have been drained. In New York's Chinatown, I've had them flambéed in rice alcohol after being drained. Cooked in the flames, they retain their firmness; the delicious rice alcohol that collects in the shrimp heads mixes nicely with the sweet tomalley. It's a delicacy that's easy to make at home. If you can't get live or very fresh head-on shrimp, don't let that stop you from cooking this easy-to-make delicacy. Simply use the freshest raw shrimp available. Be careful with the flames: always use a dish with a lid to suppress the flames if they get too high.

1. Rinse the shrimp and blot them thoroughly dry. Place them in a dish and add ⅓ cup of the rice alcohol. Place a lid or plate on top and shake the dish three times during a 15-minute period. Drain the shrimp and repeat the process once more, using another ⅓ cup rice alcohol. Drain.

2. Pour the remaining rice alcohol in a ladle and ignite it (have a cover handy to smother the flames if necessary). Disperse the flames over the shrimp. Using slotted spoons, gently toss them until they turn opaque and lightly crisp, about 5 minutes. Divide the shrimp among individual plates and serve with spicy soy sauce dip on the side.

JAR HAR YUEN
FRIED SHRIMP BALLS

MAKES ABOUT 50 PIECES

VEGETABLE OIL for deep-frying

3 pounds BLUE TIGER SHRIMP, shelled, deveined, and minced

1 teaspoon SESAME OIL

2 ounces fresh GINGER, peeled and finely grated

3 SCALLIONS, root and dark green ends trimmed, and 6-inch stalks minced

1 tablespoon TAPIOCA STARCH or CORNSTARCH

KOSHER SALT

Freshly ground BLACK PEPPER

SPICY SOY SAUCE DIP (page 88)

IN THE STREETS of New York's Chinatown, street hawkers sell stir-fried noodles, fried chicken wings, stuffed bell pepper wedges, and these deep-fried shrimp balls called *jar har yuen*. Easy to prepare, these shrimp balls can be served as cocktail party food, skewered on decorative picks, or set out on small endive leaves for a complementary bitter note. The sweet shrimp, flavored with nutty sesame oil, spicy ginger, and pungent scallions, are delicious dipped in any number of sauces. I especially like them with herb-infused spicy soy sauce. If you do not like to deep-fry, they are delicious pan-fried or steamed. I also have added them to seafood noodle soups.

I prefer blue tiger shrimp for making this recipe, because they are flavorful and mildly salty and keep their firm texture when cooked. Remember that the shrimp balls will be served with a spicy soy sauce dip, so do not overseason the shrimp mixture.

1. Heat enough oil for deep-frying in a pot over medium-high heat until the temperature reaches 360° to 375°F.

2. Mix together the shrimp, sesame oil, ginger, scallions, and tapioca starch in a bowl until evenly combined. Lightly season with salt and pepper and mix again thoroughly. Shape into small balls, about ¾ inch in diameter. Working in batches, deep-fry the shrimp balls (making sure they float separately) until they are golden all around, about 2 minutes total. Drain on a paper towel–lined plate and serve with spicy soy sauce dip on the side.

UKOY

FRIED SHRIMP AND SWEET POTATO CROQUETTES

SERVES 4 TO 6

KOSHER SALT
1 large SWEET POTATO
1 large IDAHO POTATO
½ teaspoon CAYENNE PEPPER,
  or more to taste (optional)
1 teaspoon BAKING POWDER
Freshly ground BLACK PEPPER
VEGETABLE OIL for deep-frying
3 dozen medium headless BLUE
  TIGER SHRIMP, shelled and
  deveined, but tails left intact for
  presentation
2 LIMES, each cut into 8 wedges

TRADITIONALLY, THE FILIPINOS make ukoy, shrimp and sweet potato fritters, by wrapping shrimp (heads and shells intact) with julienned sweet potato. These are delicious but hard to eat. I have devised a croquette version of this classic dish, which is perfect finger food for cocktail parties or appetizers. The shrimp are peeled and minced, and the potatoes are cooked, peeled, and mashed through a ricer. The resulting mixture is seasoned with salt and pepper. Deep-fried, these are delicious drizzled with lime juice or garlic vinegar dipping sauce (page 95).

Classic ukoy are made using only sweet potato, but when mashed, this root vegetable becomes a very sweet foreground note, rather than the crispy subtly sweet background note. As a personal preference, I have combined sweet and plain potatoes to balance the flavor of the croquettes.

1. Bring a pot of salted water to a boil over high heat. Add both the sweet and Idaho potatoes and cook until soft, 30 to 45 minutes. Peel and cube the potatoes, then put through a fine ricer. Stir in the cayenne pepper, baking powder, and season with salt and pepper. Allow the mashed potatoes to cool. Stir in the baking powder.

2. Heat enough oil for deep-frying in a pot over medium-high heat until the temperature reaches 360° to 375°F.

3. Wrap about 1 tablespoon of mashed potato around each shrimp, leaving the tail exposed for presentation. Working in batches, deep-fry the shrimp until golden all over, about 3 minutes total. Drain on a paper towel–lined plate and serve with lime wedges on the side.

Variation: To make Thai taud man or Indonesian otak pipih, fried fish cakes, substitute 1½ pounds skinless and boneless white fish fillets for the shrimp. In the bowl of a mixer, place the fish, ½ ounce peeled and grated galangal, ½ ounce ginger, 2 tablespoons finely grated lemongrass, 1 teaspoon sesame oil, 2 large peeled and grated garlic cloves, ⅓ cup potato starch, 1 teaspoon baking powder, and 2 trimmed and finely chopped scallions, and season lightly with salt and pepper. Process to a paste-like consistency and shape the paste into 1½-inch diameter by ½-inch-thick patties. Deep-fry until golden, and serve with Colorful Cucumber and Shallot Salad (page 350) on the side.

UDANG KUNING
BALINESE YELLOW
PRAWN CURRY

SERVES 4 TO 6

2 tablespoons COCONUT OIL
(page 77); or VEGETABLE OIL

2 large GARLIC CLOVES, crushed,
peeled, and minced

1 large SHALLOT, peeled and
minced

1 ounce fresh GINGER, peeled and
minced

1 LEMONGRASS STALK, root end
trimmed, outer leaves and tough
green top removed, and 6-inch-
long inner bulb finely ground

2 to 3 RED THAI CHILIES,
stemmed, seeded, and
minced

2 CANDLENUTS or MACADAMIA
NUTS, finely crushed

2 teaspoons INDONESIAN or THAI
SHRIMP PASTE

½ ounce fresh TURMERIC, peeled
and finely grated; or 1 teaspoon
TURMERIC POWDER

1 large PLUM TOMATO, blanched,
peeled, seeded, and finely
chopped

1 cup unsweetened COCONUT
MILK (page 77); or commercial
equivalent

1½ cups SHRIMP STOCK
(page 123)

2 to 3 tablespoons TAMARIND
EXTRACT (page 75)

2 KAFFIR LIME LEAVES

1 SALAM LEAF (optional)

I N INDONESIA, *udang* means prawns or shrimp, and *kuning* means yellow. "Yellow prawns," however, does not convey the dish's complexity. *Udang kuning* is an example of Indonesian curry, similar to other curries but fragrant with distinctive flavors such as candlenut, tamarind, and salam leaf. The yellow paste, which is the spice and herbal base of the dish, can also be used to flavor chicken, pork, beef, or fish. All versions are delicious, including the pork-stuffed baby squid variation. "Yellow prawns" are especially popular in Bali.

Coconut oil is the preferred oil in Indonesia, and it can be made easily at home by gently boiling coconut cream until the milk evaporates and leaves behind the oil.

36 medium BLUE TIGER SHRIMP,
heads and shells removed
(optional), butterflied, and
deveined

FRIED SHALLOTS (page 108)

Heat the oil in a medium pot over medium-high heat. Stir-fry the garlic, shallot, ginger, lemongrass, and chilies until fragrant and golden, 5 to 10 minutes. Add the candlenuts and shrimp paste, and continue to stir-fry until the ingredients brown a bit more, about 2 minutes. Add the turmeric and tomato, and stir-fry until the tomato releases its juices, about 5 minutes. Cook the paste down until it is concentrated and semi-thick, about 5 minutes more. Stir in the coconut milk, stock, and tamarind extract, add the kaffir lime leaves and salam leaf, and bring to a boil over high heat. Add the prawns and cook until pink and opaque, about 2 minutes. Divide among individual plates and garnish with a generous amount of fried shallots. Serve with jasmine rice and green papaya salad on the side.

Variation: For a squid and pork variation: Finely chop the tentacles of 36 baby squid and mix with 8 ounces ground pork (70 percent lean). Stuff the squid bodies with the pork mixture, and use wooden toothpicks to enclose the filling. Proceed with the recipe, adding the stuffed squid instead of the shrimp, cooking them for 5 to 7 minutes.

CUA FARCI
FRENCH-VIETNAMESE
STUFFED CRAB SHELLS

SERVES 4 TO 6

6 dried CLOUD EAR MUSHROOMS
One .7-ounce package dried
  MUNG BEAN THREADS
  (cellophane noodles)
1½ pounds lump CRABMEAT
8 ounces GROUND PORK
  (70 percent lean)
2 large EGGS
1 large SHALLOT, peeled and
  minced
1 large GARLIC CLOVE, crushed,
  peeled, and minced
KOSHER SALT
Freshly ground BLACK PEPPER
6 to 8 ATLANTIC BLUE CRAB
  SHELLS, cleaned and about the
  same size
VEGETABLE OIL; or UNSALTED
  BUTTER
SCALLION OIL (page 108)
NUOC CHAM (page 100)
SPICY SOY SAUCE DIP (page 88;
  optional)

STUFFED CRAB SHELLS look beautiful and are delicious with soy sauce or fish sauce–based dips. Crabmeat, ground pork, cellophane noodles, cloud ears, and garlic are mixed together and stuffed into the crab shells, then deep-fried or baked. The Vietnamese call this classic dish dating from the mid-1800s *cua farci* (note the half-Vietnamese, half-French name). Traditionally this dish is served with *nuoc cham* as the dipping sauce, but I have also tried it with the spicy soy sauce dip, a delicious option.

When you steam Atlantic blue crabs (pp. 418–19), clean and save the shells for this recipe. When it is available, buy lump crabmeat at the fishmonger's. It is much easier than picking the meat out yourself. I prefer stuffed crab shells baked, but you can deep-fry them in vegetable oil if you wish.

1. Preheat the oven to 375°F. Put the cloud ears in a bowl with hot water to cover, then set a plate over the bowl to prevent steam from escaping. Let stand until the mushrooms rehydrate and soften, about 30 minutes (or longer, depending on the size of the mushrooms). Meanwhile, place the cellophane noodles in a dish with water to cover. Let stand until pliable, about 30 minutes. Squeeze the noodles and cloud ears between the palms of your hands to get rid of the excess water. Using a paring knife, finely chop the noodles and cloud ears (removing hard knobs, if any) and put them in a bowl.

2. Add the crabmeat, pork, eggs, shallot, and garlic to the bowl and season with salt and pepper. Mix the ingredients thoroughly. Divide the

mixture into 4 to 6 equal portions and stuff the shells with them. (Push the stuffing in if necessary.) Place the stuffed crab shells, stuffing side up, on a baking sheet. Brush with oil or place thin shavings of butter on top and bake until the stuffing is cooked through, browned, and crispy, about 20 minutes. Place the crab shells on individual plates and serve with scallion oil and *nuoc cham* or spicy soy sauce on the side.

Variation: For Filipino stuffed crab shells: Heat a tablespoon of vegetable oil over high heat and stir-fry a large crushed, peeled, and minced garlic clove, ½ ounce peeled and minced ginger, and a small peeled and minced onion until fragrant and slightly golden, about 5 minutes. Add 2 stemmed, seeded, and minced Thai red chilies, 2 cups julienned young coconut meat (or a cup of finely grated fresh coconut), and a cup of coconut cream. Lower the heat to medium, stir, and cook until the sauce thickens, 5 to 10 minutes. Add a pound of lump crabmeat, a tablespoon of fish sauce, and freshly ground sea salt and black pepper to taste. Continue to stir-fry to evenly distribute the ingredients. Transfer to a platter and allow to cool completely. Add a beaten egg to the cooled stir-fry and mix well. Stuff each crab shell and bake in a 375°F oven. If you wish, wrap the shells individually in banana leaf, securing at both ends, and grill on the barbecue.

CUA FARCI is a French-influenced Vietnamese classic dish, but there are other variations of stuffed crabs in Asia with European influence, notably the Filipino *pinais na alimasag* (see variation) and the Chinese *gook hai goi*. In the Filipino version, shells are stuffed with a combination of crabmeat, julienned young coconut meat, and coconut cream, flavored with ginger, garlic, onion, and a small amount of chili. Wrapped in banana leaves, the stuffed shells are grilled and enjoyed as is. In China, a roux made with all-purpose flour, Indian curry powder, and coconut milk is used to season the crabmeat. The shells are stuffed and baked with butter. A similar interpretation, often served at Cantonese banquets, uses conch shells (page 413).

STIR-FRIED LOBSTER WITH GINGER AND SCALLIONS

SERVES 4 TO 6

Three 1¼-pound LOBSTERS
(heads on)
1 tablespoon VEGETABLE OIL
½ teaspoon SESAME OIL
2 large GARLIC CLOVES, crushed,
peeled, and coarsely chopped
1 ounce fresh GINGER, peeled,
halved, and sliced paper thin
lengthwise
3 SCALLIONS, root and dark green
ends trimmed, and 6-inch stalks
cut into 1½-inch-long pieces
and julienned
KOSHER SALT
Freshly ground BLACK PEPPER
6 sprigs CILANTRO

ANY GOOD CHINESE seafood restaurant will have this simple dish on the menu or be able to serve it upon request. Fresh lobster, ginger, and scallions are a winning combination. If you add side dishes such as stir-fried baby bok choy (page 320), soy sauce chicken (pp. 488–89), or winter melon and ham soup (page 143) to your menu, two to three lobsters will be more than enough. However, if the lobsters are the only thing you are serving with rice, add two more lobsters to the dish and a little more ginger and scallions as well.

1. Halve the lobsters lengthwise, then separate the heads from the tails. Halve the tails crosswise, so you have a total of 6 pieces from each lobster, including the heads. Separate the claws at the joints and chop the large claws in half lengthwise.

2. Heat the vegetable and sesame oil in a wok over high heat. Add the garlic and stir-fry until fragrant, about 1 minute. Add the ginger and scallions and continue to stir-fry until fragrant, about 1 minute more. Add the lobster and toss to coat the pieces evenly with the fragrant herbs. Season with salt and pepper, cover with a lid, and cook, tossing the pieces occasionally, until the lobsters turn pink and opaque, about 10 minutes. Serve hot, garnished with cilantro.

CURRIED CONCH SHELLS
CANTONESE BANQUET–STYLE

SERVES 4 TO 6

KOSHER SALT

12 CONCHS with shells intact,
4 inches long

2 tablespoons UNSALTED BUTTER

2 tablespoons all-purpose FLOUR

1 tablespoon VEGETABLE OIL

1 large GARLIC CLOVE, crushed,
peeled, and minced

1 small ONION, peeled and
minced

1 cup SUPERIOR STOCK (page 117)

2 teaspoons INDIAN CURRY
POWDER

½ cup unsweetened COCONUT
MILK (page 77); or commercial
equivalent

Freshly ground BLACK PEPPER

1 bunch CILANTRO, stems
trimmed

SERVED OFTEN AT CANTONESE BANQUETS, stuffed curried conch shells are a favorite among the Chinese. A Portuguese-influenced dish, it most likely originated in Macao, an island near the coast of Hong Kong that was a Portuguese colony from 1557 until recent times. The Portuguese were great borrowers themselves, as you will notice when making this recipe. For example, the roux, a cooked flour paste, is a French technique adopted by the Portuguese, while the curry-based flavor comes from Indian Madras curry powder. These beautiful stuffed conch shells require fresh conch and take a bit of time to prepare. When you want to eat this specialty in Chinatown restaurants, you may need to order it up to three days in advance.

1. Preheat the oven to 375°F. Bring a pot of salted water to a boil and boil the conchs in their shells for 5 minutes. When cool enough to handle, pry out the conchs and remove the dark brown tails. Rinse the conch shells well and drain until dry. Cut the conch meat into ½-inch dice and set aside.

2. To make the roux, melt the butter in a saucepan over medium heat. Whisk in the flour and stir vigorously until smooth and cooked, but not browned, about 2 minutes. Remove from the heat and allow the roux to cool.

3. Heat the oil in a wok over high heat. Stir-fry the garlic and onion until golden, about 5 minutes. Stir in the stock, curry powder, and coconut milk, and add the diced conch. Stir-fry to distribute the ingredients evenly. Adjust the seasoning with salt and pepper and stir in the roux, mixing the ingredients thoroughly. Transfer the conch and curry sauce to a bowl to cool. Stuff each conch shell equally with filling and place the shells on a baking sheet. Bake until cooked through, 10 to 15 minutes. Serve the shells on individual plates (2 to 3 per person), garnished with cilantro.

MOLLUSKS STIR-FRIED IN BLACK BEAN AND GARLIC SAUCE

SERVES 4 TO 6

36 small RAZOR CLAMS or medium MUSSELS; or SCALLOPS
1 tablespoon VEGETABLE OIL
½ cup FERMENTED BLACK BEAN AND GARLIC SAUCE (page 86)
Freshly ground BLACK PEPPER
1 bunch CILANTRO, stems trimmed
2 SCALLIONS, roots and dark green ends trimmed, and 6-inch stalks thinly sliced on the diagonal

BLACK BEAN AND GARLIC SAUCE is a classic Chinese flavoring for seafood. For this stir-fry use mollusks such as razor clams or mussels in the shell, or scallops, and a generous amount of scallions and cilantro. I like the smaller razor clams, which are more tender. Large bay scallops are delicious, but if you can find them on the shell with the coral intact (at a fish wholesaler or by special order), they're even more delicious. If you can find only shell-free scallops, you will need about a pound and a half.

1. Put the clams in a bowl with water to cover and soak for 30 minutes. Drain, and repeat the process twice more. (This should get rid of any sand that may be in the shells; if not, continue soaking them until they release the sand.)

2. Heat the oil in a wok over high heat. Add the black bean and garlic sauce and stir-fry until fragrant, about a minute. Add the clams, mussels, or scallops and stir-fry to coat evenly. Season with black pepper and scatter the cilantro on top, cover with a lid, reduce the heat to medium, and cook until the shells open up, about 7 minutes. Discard any that do not open. Transfer the mollusks to a serving dish, garnish with scallions, and serve hot.

FERMENTED BLACK SOY BEANS, preserved in salt, are sold in thin cardboard containers or are vacuum packed. They are dry but moist to the touch and should be soaked prior to using to get rid of the excess salt. At the Chinese market, and even in the international aisles of some supermarkets, you will find garlic and black bean sauce that can be used right from the bottle. Just stir-fry 2 tablespoons of the sauce with oil until fragrant, and proceed with the recipe. I suggest that you make your own black bean sauce if you have the time. Like anything homemade, it will taste better.

DEEP-FRIED SALTY SQUID

SERVES 4 TO 6

3 pounds baby or medium SQUID
(tentacles optional), skinned and
cleaned (page 40); or BLUE
TIGER SHRIMP, shelled and
deveined, heads and tail ends
left intact (optional)

VEGETABLE OIL for deep-frying

1 to 1½ tablespoons KOSHER SALT

1 teaspoon freshly ground BLACK
PEPPERCORNS; or 1 teaspoon
CAYENNE PEPPER

¼ teaspoon FIVE-SPICE POWDER
(optional)

½ teaspoon TURMERIC POWDER

½ cup TAPIOCA STARCH or
CORNSTARCH

3 LIMES, each cut into 8 wedges

WHETHER IN CHINA or Southeast Asia, you'll find delicious salt-and-pepper-flavored deep-fried squid. Easy to make, it requires no batter—only good-quality sea salt, black pepper or cayenne pepper, and oil. I sometimes add five-spice powder. I like to use baby or medium-size squid, with tentacles, if possible. While frying, the tentacles curl up, making for a beautiful presentation. Salt-and-pepper squid makes for an excellent appetizer or great finger food with cocktails. This recipe is equally good using shrimp.

1. Rinse the squid under cold water and separate the tentacles from the bodies. Drain and pat the pieces thoroughly dry, making sure to dry the insides. Slice the bodies into ¼-inch rings. Leave the tentacles intact.

2. Heat the vegetable oil in a wok over medium heat to 360° to 375°F. Meanwhile, mix the salt, pepper, five-spice powder (if using), turmeric, and tapioca starch in a plastic bag. Add the squid, seal the bag, and shake it to coat each piece evenly. Put a few squid pieces at a time in the palms of your hands and shake off the excess tapioca starch mix. Working in batches, deep-fry the squid until the rings turn golden and crisp, a minute or two. Drain on paper towels and serve with lime wedges on the side.

RELLENONG PUSIT
STUFFED SQUID IN INK

SERVES 4 TO 6

1 cup dry WHITE WINE

36 baby SQUID, cleaned, bodies
 intact; ⅓ cup ink reserved;
 tentacles finely chopped

2 teaspoons VEGETABLE OIL

2 large GARLIC CLOVES, crushed,
 peeled, and minced

1 large SHALLOT, peeled and
 minced

10 ounces GROUND PORK
 (70 percent lean)

2 ripe small to medium PLUM
 TOMATOES, blanched, peeled,
 seeded, and minced

4 ounces SERRANO HAM, minced

¼ cup minced FLAT LEAF PARSLEY

KOSHER SALT

Freshly ground BLACK PEPPER

1 cup VEGETABLE STOCK
 (page 126)

1 BAY LEAF

¼ teaspoon or more CAYENNE
 PEPPER

6 sprigs CURLY PARSLEY, stems
 trimmed

36 wooden TOOTHPICKS

I F YOU LIKE SQUID and do not mind cleaning it and collecting its ink, then you're in for a treat with this Filipino specialty. Bread crumbs are used to stuff the squid in the Philippines, but I use ground pork. All other ingredients—garlic, onion, tomatoes, and cured ham (such as Spanish Serrano ham)—are classic. Try to find baby squid: not only is it more tender than mature squid, it is also more delicate and beautiful for presentation. If you cannot find ink, skip it altogether; there is no substitute. To enclose the filling, use sturdy wooden toothpicks and thread the opening of the squid bodies shut.

For cleaning squid, see page 40.

1. Put the wine in a bowl and add the squid ink.

2. Heat the oil in a nonstick pan over medium heat. Stir-fry the garlic and shallot until golden, about 5 minutes. Add the ground pork (stir-frying continuously to break it up), the tomatoes, ham, squid tentacles, and parsley, and continue to stir-fry until cooked through, about 5 minutes. Season to taste with salt and pepper and stir-fry until the ingredients are evenly distributed and the liquid evaporates, about 2 minutes more. Transfer to a bowl or plate and allow to cool.

3. Stuff the squid bodies with about 1 tablespoon of stuffing and enclose the filling by threading a toothpick through the flesh around the opening. Heat the stock and ink-and-wine liquid in a heavy-bottomed pot over medium-high heat. Add the bay leaf and cayenne pepper and bring to a gentle boil. Reduce the heat to low, carefully layer the stuffed squid, and adjust the seasoning with salt and pepper. Cook the squid, covered, until cooked through, about 5 minutes. Transfer the squid with the sauce to a platter and garnish with parsley sprigs.

TEMPURA
DEEP-FRIED SEAFOOD
IN LACY BATTER

SERVES 4 TO 6

VEGETABLE OIL for deep-frying

2 large EGGS

¼ cup chilled SAKE (optional)

1 cup ICE WATER (if not using
SAKE, add ½ cup extra ICE
WATER)

1¼ cups cake FLOUR

18 headless SMELTS, gutted

18 medium headless BLUE TIGER
SHRIMP, shelled and deveined

1½ cups PANKO (optional)

12 SHISO LEAVES

TEMPURA DIPPING SAUCE
(page 92)

WHEN WELL MADE, tempura is crispy and light even though it is deep-fried. The batter is loose, making for a very lacy result. "The trick is to use self-rising cake flour in combination with ice water. And to loosely mix the two. The batter should be lumpy, not smooth," explained Elizabeth Andoh, an authority on Japanese cuisine, while I was in Tokyo. Her trick makes for a delicious tempura. I'm not a big fan of foods that are battered and fried, but I must admit that here the Japanese excel. If you want a very crispy-textured tempura, after dipping the seafood in the batter, roll it in panko, Japanese bread crumbs. Feel free to use any type of fresh fish, crustaceans, or mollusks in this recipe. I prefer to stick to smelts and prawns. Be sure to select fresh smelts; when cooked, the frozen ones tend to become mealy.

You'll find a recipe for vegetable tempura on page 345.

1. Heat enough oil for deep-frying in a pot over medium heat until the temperature reaches 360° to 375°F.

2. Meanwhile, lightly beat the eggs with the sake and ice water. Add the flour all at once and give it only a few stirs. Don't whisk it. The batter should be loosely combined and lumpy.

3. Pat the smelts and prawns thoroughly dry. Dip a smelt or prawn in the batter, shake, coat with panko if you wish, and carefully lower it into the hot oil. Continue this process, working with one or two pieces at a time, until you have 5 or 6 pieces in the hot oil, but no more. Deep-fry until crispy and light golden on all sides, about 3 minutes total. Drain on a paper towel–lined plate. Divide the fried seafood among individual plates, garnish with shiso leaves, and serve with tempura dipping sauce on the side.

STEAMED SEAFOOD WITH FAVORITE DIPPING SAUCES

SERVES 4 TO 6

Six 1-pound whole LOBSTERS

12 medium BLUE CRABS

24 WHELKS

24 steamer CLAMS

24 PERIWINKLES

24 MUSSELS

24 large BLUE TIGER SHRIMP (heads on)

1 cup CHINESE WHITE RICE VINEGAR

12 large CLOVES GARLIC, crushed, peeled, and coarsely chopped

6 SCALLIONS, root and dark green ends trimmed, and 6-inch stalks cut into 1½-inch-long pieces and julienned

2 ounces fresh GINGER, peeled, halved, and sliced paper thin lengthwise

Freshly ground BLACK PEPPER

ONCE IN A WHILE I steam crabs and lobsters and serve them with different types of dipping sauces, ranging from Vietnamese to Chinese, Japanese, and Korean, letting my guests try whatever they like. It's a relaxed meal; I layer craft paper on the table and put out a few wooden or rubber mallets and nutcrackers. You can also steam shrimp, clams, and mussels in addition to or instead of the crabs and lobsters. Served with rice and various salads such as green papaya salad (page 351), or bamboo shoot and shiitake salad (page 347), steamed seafood makes for a great Sunday brunch.

My favorite dipping sauces to serve are Vietnamese fish sauce and lime-based *nuoc cham*, Chinese spicy soy sauce dip, and Korean spicy vinegar sauce. Feel free to select any others from the "Condiments" chapter (page 64). For example, if you like a richer sauce, try any of the peanut sauces. The Vietnamese sauce is particularly suitable because it is the lightest of the three peanut types, not too thick, and easy to dip into. When choosing the blue crabs, be sure to select those that are uniform in size so you can reuse the shells for making *cua farci* (pp. 410–11). Choose any or all of the seafood listed here (or your favorites) for your meal. If you wish to boil rather than steam, that is fine, too.

(Depending on the size of your stock pots and ingredients, you may have to double up on the pots and every ingredient, except for the seafood, to cook everything.)

1. Scrub the crustaceans and mollusks clean under cold running water, being especially careful to clean the lobsters and crabs well. Whelks, steamer clams, periwinkles, and mussels should also soak in several changes of water to get rid of any sand.

2. To steam the seafood: Fill the bottom of 2 large stock pots with 2 inches of water. Divide the rice vinegar, garlic, scallions, and ginger equally between the pots. Season with pepper, cover each pot, and bring the water to a boil over high heat. When the water starts to boil and the pots are filled with steam, add the lobster and crabs to one pot, and cook for 8 to 12 minutes. Add the whelks, steamer clams, periwinkles, mussels, and shrimp (in that order so the shrimp are the top layer) to the second pot, cover, and

cook for about 5 minutes. Proceed to step 4.

3. To boil the seafood: Fill 2 large pots halfway with water, and divide the rice vinegar, garlic, scallions, and ginger equally between the pots. Season with salt and pepper, and bring the water to a boil over high heat. Add the crabs and lobsters to one pot and boil until cooked through, 5 to 10 minutes. Add the whelks, steamer clams, periwinkles, mussels, and shrimp to the other pot and boil until cooked through, about 2 minutes.

4. Transfer the seafood to several large platters and serve with a selection of Asian dipping sauces.

THE FISH LADY CLEANS FISH FOR HER CUSTOMERS, THE PHILIPPINES.

TCHIGAE
SPICY SEAFOOD STEW

SERVES 4 TO 6

2 teaspoons VEGETABLE OIL

2 large GARLIC CLOVES, crushed, peeled, and minced

2 ounces fresh GINGER, peeled and julienned

2 SCALLIONS, root and dark green ends trimmed, and 6-inch stalks cut into 1-inch pieces crosswise

2 cups BASIC CHICKEN STOCK (page 116); or SEAFOOD STOCK (page 123)

1 to 2 teaspoons KOREAN CHILI POWDER

12 medium SQUID (tentacles optional), cleaned, halved lengthwise, cut into 1-inch-wide pieces, and scored in a crisscross pattern on one side

18 medium BLUE TIGER SHRIMP (head-on optional), peeled, butterflied, and deveined

18 BAY SCALLOPS

8 NAPA CABBAGE LEAVES, halved lengthwise and cut into 1-inch-wide pieces

1 bunch WATERCRESS, stems trimmed

KOSHER SALT

Freshly ground BLACK PEPPER

8 ounces firm TOFU, drained and cut into ¾-inch cubes

THIS KOREAN SEAFOOD STEW, which combines squid, shrimp, and scallops, is pleasantly spicy. I like to use firm shrimp such as blue tiger shrimp or pink shrimp from the Florida gulf. (Gray shrimp are delicious but tend to turn mealy if cooked for a second too long.) Large bay scallops require more time to cook; the stew picks up their flavor and the scallops cook perfectly without becoming tough. Medium squid is preferred here because it is tender and cooks at an even pace. Baby squid, although delicious, cooks too quickly, while large squid generally tends to be chewy. Spooned over short-grain rice, this dish makes for a pungent and delicious meal, if spicy foods are what you like.

This stew is often made with octopus and clams.

1. Put the oil, garlic, ginger, and scallions in a sand pot and stir-fry over medium heat until fragrant and golden, about 5 minutes. Add the stock and the chili powder, reduce the heat to medium-low, and add the squid, shrimp, scallops, napa cabbage, and watercress. Season with salt and pepper and stir.

2. Cover with a lid and cook until the seafood turns opaque, 5 to 7 minutes. Adjust the seasoning, add the tofu, and continue to cook, covered, until heated through, 5 minutes more. Transfer to a serving dish and serve with short-grain rice on the side.

Variation: Cabbage kimchi (page 359) can be substituted for the chili powder and fresh napa cabbage leaves in the recipe.

ALTHOUGH I LOVE TO EAT this stew with octopus and clams, they are harder to prepare. The octopus must be dipped in boiling water three to four times to tenderize it, and the clams need to be soaked in several changes of water to get rid of the sand—if you *can* get rid of it all. When making the stew at home, it is much easier to use seafood like squid, shrimp, and scallops, all of which require very little preparation.

SATE LILIT
SPICY SEAFOOD SATAY

SERVES 4 TO 6

8 ounces skinless WHITE FISH fillets, such as COD or FLOUNDER, cut into small chunks

8 ounces headless BLUE TIGER SHRIMP, shelled and deveined, coarsely chopped

8 ounces SCALLOPS, coarsely chopped

½ cup or more BASE GEDE (page 80)

2 tablespoons POTATO STARCH

1 teaspoon BAKING POWDER

36 LEMONGRASS STALKS, root ends trimmed, outer leaves removed; or 6 BANANA LEAVES, cut into 6-inch squares

72 wooden TOOTHPICKS, soaked in water for 20 minutes (if using banana leaves)

T HE INDONESIANS make a tasty seafood satay, which combines fish, shrimp, and scallops. Minced to a fine paste, the seafood is flavored with *base gede*, a spicy herbal paste, and wrapped around stalks of lemongrass, or wrapped in banana leaves. Grilled on the barbecue, these morsels make a delightful dish that goes well with rice and pickled vegetables. (Using the same recipe, substitute 1 to 1½ pounds ground duck breast or chicken breast, pork butt, or beef sirloin for the seafood to make a meat version of this satay.)

Use sugar cane as a skewer instead of lemongrass, as the Vietnamese do for *chao tom* (see variation).

---

1. Put the fish, shrimp, and scallops in a food processor and pulse to a fine paste. Add the *base gede*, potato starch, baking powder, and continue to pulse to mix thoroughly into a paste. Refrigerate for 1 hour.

2. Wrap an equal amount of paste around each lemongrass skewer, or place it in the center of each of the banana leaf squares and fold each side (one over the other) toward the center to form a small log. Thread a toothpick on each end of the bundle to enclose the filling.

3. Grill in a lightly oiled nonstick pan over medium heat or outdoors on a barbecue grill. If using skewers, cook the satay until golden (or charred) all over, 3 to 5 minutes. If using banana leaves, grill for 3 to 5 minutes per side. Serve hot.

Variation: The Vietnamese wrap fresh shrimp paste on sugar cane, a specialty called *chao tom*. It is delicious when grilled and dipped in *nuoc cham* (page 100). Place 1½ pounds headless, shelled, and deveined blue tiger shrimp, 2 ounces pork fatback, 1 teaspoon granulated sugar, 1 teaspoon baking powder, and 2 chopped, trimmed scallions in a food processor and pulse to a smooth paste. Quarter lengthwise six 3-inch-long fresh sugar cane sticks. Wrap an equal amount of paste around one end of each stick, tapering the paste so that it is thinner as you work toward the middle of the stick. Grill in a well-oiled nonstick pan over medium heat or on a barbecue grill until golden (or lightly charred) all over and cooked through, 3 to 5 minutes.

ECH XAO XA OT
STIR-FRIED FROG'S LEGS
WITH HERBAL PASTE

SERVES 4 TO 6

1 tablespoon VEGETABLE OIL

¼ cup or more KROEUNG PASTE
(page 78); or GARLIC AND
LEMONGRASS MARINADE
(page 83)

2 or more THAI CHILIES,
stemmed, seeded, and minced

1 tablespoon FISH EXTRACT
(page 76); or 1 tablespoon THAI
or INDONESIAN SHRIMP PASTE;
or FISH SAUCE

1 tablespoon PALM SUGAR

12 pairs of FROG'S LEGS, separated
into single legs

2 unripe CARAMBOLA (star fruit),
thinly sliced into stars

12 sprigs CILANTRO

FROG'S LEGS, eaten all over Southeast Asia, can be prepared any number of ways. Using Vietnamese *nuoc mam tuong xa* (garlic and lemongrass marinade) or Cambodian *kroeung* paste, rich with lemongrass, galangal, and kaffir lime leaves, I stir-fry them until lightly crispy. They make for an excellent appetizer or a tasty light meal served with jasmine rice and pickled vegetables (page 354) on the side. If you have a Chinatown near you, chances are some of the fishmongers in the neighborhood will carry live frogs, which yield plumper, tastier, and more tender legs than frozen frogs. The entire body of the frog, excepting the head, is edible, so the fishmonger will probably return cleaned, skinned, headless frogs to you. I use the upper part for a Thai curry. If you do not like the upper part—which, by the way, tastes the same as the legs—have the fishmonger chop it off.

1. Heat the oil in a nonstick pan over medium heat. Stir-fry the *kroeung* paste, chilies, and *prahoc* extract until fragrant and lightly darkened, about 3 minutes. Add the palm sugar and stir-fry until the sugar is melted. Add the frog's legs and stir-fry to coat evenly with the paste. Arrange the legs in a single layer and pan-fry for 3 minutes. Turn the legs over and pan-fry for 3 minutes more. Cover the pan and continue to cook for 2 minutes.

2. Meanwhile, arrange the star fruit slices, overlapping, in a circle in the center of each individual plate. Center an equal amount of frog's legs on each plate and garnish with cilantro.

OC NHOI THIT
STEAMED LEMONGRASS-INFUSED SNAILS

SERVES 4 TO 6

2 fresh LEMONGRASS STALKS, root ends trimmed, outer leaves removed and reserved, and 6-inch-long inner bulbs finely ground

12 ounces GROUND PORK (70 percent lean)

Two 7-ounce cans large BURGUNDY SNAILS, drained, rinsed, patted dry, and minced

1½ ounces fresh GINGER, peeled and finely grated

3 RED THAI CHILIES, stemmed, seeded, and minced

1½ teaspoons SESAME OIL

KOSHER SALT

Freshly ground BLACK PEPPER

NUOC CHAM (page 100)

SPICY SOY SAUCE DIP (page 88)

48 SNAIL SHELLS

THIS IS PERHAPS one of the most exotic Vietnamese dishes I have ever tasted. Very different from French snail preparation—which requires a total of five hours from the time you buy the live snails to the time you eat them—the Vietnamese version eliminates purging, cutting preparation time by about two-thirds. The Vietnamese prepare the snails quickly, removing them from their shells, then rinsing, chopping, and mixing them with ground pork, lemongrass, ginger, chili, and sesame oil. Because snails are rarely available fresh, I often buy Burgundian snails imported from France. These have been purged and cooked and are a wonderful substitute. For an exotic presentation, the Vietnamese gently bend a yellowish-green lemongrass sliver and place it in each shell. The filling is then set between the slivers, rounded off at the shell rim, and steamed. The dish is enjoyed in a memorable ritual: each guest pulls out the bite-size morsels, using the lemongrass slivers as "handles." Perfect as an appetizer or a snack, dipped in *nuoc cham* or spicy soy sauce, this snail delicacy is delicious.

Canned snails from France's Burgundy region, which are of particularly high quality, can be purchased through mail-order sources or at select gourmet markets. They're often sold with real, reusable shells, ready to be stuffed.

1. Tear the lemongrass leaves into 3-inch-long thin slivers and put aside. Mix together the pork, snails, lemongrass bulbs, ginger, chilies, and sesame oil in a bowl until thoroughly combined. Season lightly with salt and pepper.

2. Bend a lemongrass sliver in half and stick it inside a snail shell, bent side in, with the 2 ends sticking out. Stuff the shell with 2 teaspoons of the snail and pork filling, gently pushing it between the two lemongrass ends. (The stuffing should be almost flush with the shell opening.) Repeat this process until all 48 shells are stuffed.

3. Fill the bottom third of a wok with water and bring to a boil over high heat. Meanwhile, arrange the stuffed snails, open side up, on a bamboo steamer rack. Place the lid securely on the steamer and set the steamer inside the wok. Steam until the stuffed snails are cooked through, about 5 minutes. Serve with *nuoc cham* or spicy soy sauce dip on the side.

6

MEAT AND POULTRY

IN TRADITIONAL CHINESE CULTURE (and, by inference, in much of Asia), one's wealth is measured by how much protein is included in one's diet and, especially, how much is offered to guests. This perception is rooted in the historic fact that for many in densely populated Asia, even the most humble portions of pork, chicken, and eggs were a luxury. It is further reinforced by the fear of starvation, a harsh reality that persisted well into the twentieth century in parts of China. Where animal protein is widely available, or where income levels and proximity to areas of agricultural production allow it, swine and poultry products are the mainstay animal proteins of the daily diet. Other, more expensive types—beef, lamb, duck, squab, and quail—are

generally reserved for formal meals and celebrations. Island nations and coastal regions tend to favor fish and other seafood over meat, reflecting millennia-old patterns of harvest, relatively undeveloped transportation networks, and strict governmental control of trade.

Asians eat proportionally more vegetables and less meat than do Westerners. In the "Vegetables and Herbs" chapter and elsewhere in this book, I mention that a simple lunch may consist of pickled vegetables and boiled rice, accompanied by broth or tea for sipping and clearing the palate. Protein holds a secondary place in the diet, and animal protein is often second to seafood. This holds true in China, Korea, and Japan, as well as Southeast Asia. Where fish is abundant, for example, small deep-fried fish such as pomfret are added to the rice-based lunch. An exception is the northern Mongolian steppes, where cattle and other hoofed animals, herded by nomads, compose the core of the diet. There, vegetables are scarce and cooking techniques relatively simple, often involving boiling and, on occasion, marinating of "green" or un-aged meat and quick barbecuing. These "portable cuisines" were perfectly suited to

cultures based on constant travel, temporary settlement, and basic cooking techniques such as open fires and heated rocks. Through ancient patterns of conquest, trade, and modern transportation and communication, these meat-based cultures have contributed wonderful meat dishes to China and the rest of Asia. The lamb- or beef-based Mongolian hot pot (pp. 152–53) and its variants are enjoyed in China's modern coastal cities, in Korea (which has racial, cultural, and historical connections to Mongolia), and indeed in many "theme" restaurants throughout Asia and the world. I have had good Mongolian hot pot in Silicon Valley south of San Francisco, for example.

The limited use of meat in the diet has been reinforced by religious beliefs, particularly those of Buddhism, which discourages or forbids eating animals; Islam, which forbids the consumption of pork; and Hinduism, which forbids eating beef, as in the proverbial "sacred cow." Like certain meat, milk-based dairy products are not commonly used and are often completely absent in the Asian diet. There is little agreement as to why Chinese, particularly southern and eastern Chinese, avoid dairy products in the form of milk and cheese. (These products, enormously important in the north, include yak and mare's milk, for example.) It is true that the vast majority of Asia's northern milk- and lamb- and beef-based cuisines were historically far away from the governmental, economic, and cultural centers of China's coasts and trade routes. This geographical reality was exacerbated by the construction of the Great Wall, nearly four thousand miles of a military barrier, and thus a cultural and culinary barrier between China and its northern neighbors. It was further reinforced by the centuries-long strict control of internal and external trade by China's rulers. Despite the contravening influence of the thirteenth-century Mongol conquest and seventeenth-century Manchu conquest—and their beef-, lamb-, and goat-based food cultures—however, the de-emphasis of certain meat in the Asian diet remained intact. Even Mongol rulers of China, who had known about Buddhism for centuries, were eventually deeply influenced both by the sophistication of southern culinary traditions and their Buddhist precepts. The most compelling modern fragment of this evolution in belief systems is now seen in that Mongol remnant of the Middle Ages we now know as Tibetan Buddhism.

"Can you imagine," my father noted while holding forth on the subject over dinner one evening, "the Mongols coming on horseback, at first killing and taking whatever they see, but eventually noticing the complex governmental administration, the culture of refinement, the balanced diets, the use of medicinal herbs, the curatives, the complex flavors, the sophisticated dishes prepared by their so-called vassals? The Mongols came from a nomadic culture that was basically still in the Bronze Age. They rode by horse to the future, to a culture advanced by thousands of years. Eventually, even they were influenced by the land they occupied, by its religion, its customs. Even they came to rely less on meat in the diet." As Rome conquered Greece militarily, Greece conquered Rome culturally; a parallel exists relative to the kitchens of China and their limited use of meat, for their patterns of food preparation dominate most of Asia even today.

One of the first things a Westerner notices upon entering an Asian meat market is that nearly all the parts of every animal are available for sale (see "Offal in Asian Cooking," pp. 439–41). Familiar pork loin and pork belly sit beside pig's feet, slabs of fresh pig liver, ears, tail, and snout. Beefsteaks are displayed adjacent to neatly sorted tripe, tongue, liver, kidneys, and other offal. Frozen cow's foot is readily available, as is chopped bull's penis. Chicken heads (including the combs) and feet are as common as breast and drumstick, while duck tongue and duck feet (webs intact) are also offered. Split dried quail and duck (heads on) are displayed next to cured bacon, while fresh halved armadillo in its own blood appears seasonally on street carts. What a friend of mine refers to as "Chinatown mystery ingredients" are traditionally anything but mysterious to Asian cooks. Each animal and all its parts are treasured, harkening both to the Buddhist-influenced belief that if you must kill the animal, you should show respect by using all of its parts; and to the folk and Taoist beliefs that something whole is superior to something incomplete. Thus, as a steamed whole fish is traditionally preferred to a fillet, a wok-fried five-spice-flavored squab is served with its head on. Additionally, the animal is understood in terms of its nutrients and, as with the armadillo, for its medicinal properties. While much of this "knowledge" is valid (liver is good for growing kids, for example, because of its iron content), in the most extreme manifestations it descends into little more than superstition. Exotic parts from rare and endangered species such as bear and tiger paws, rhino penis, and monkey brains, for example, are seen as beneficial to men, sometimes as a medicinal tonic, sometimes offering the promise of sexual prowess or longevity. Dog is occasionally eaten in southern China, the Philippines, and Vietnam as part of a sort of male bonding ritual. While offensive to the Western sensibility, the consumption of dog is ultimately less damaging to the planet and our legacy as a species than the relentless, wholesale destruction of endangered animals for the perceived benefit of an ignorant, callous, and prosperous few. I sincerely hope that a younger, more worldly generation will see the folly in these practices and stop them, if, indeed, the impending extinction of species at the hands of their parents even affords them a choice.

PORK

PORK IS THE MOST COMMONLY eaten animal in China, the Pacific, and Southeast Asia. A light, eminently versatile meat, it can be grilled, roasted, stir-fried, and braised, made into sausage and other charcuterie, or added to soups. Pork is considered "neutral" in the traditional Chinese hot-cold food system (page 45), mixing well with other protein such as chicken eggs, shrimp, or squid, for example. Pork is not only eaten as a main dish but often appears as a flavor enhancer in broths and soups and may even lurk in so-called fish or vegetable dishes as an ingredient. Notwithstanding the northern and western regions of China, where Islamic law is followed, Indonesia (which has the largest Muslim population of any nation on earth), and the strict vegetarian practices of Buddhist monks, there is otherwise no historical prohibition against the consumption of pork in Asian culture. This and the favorable economic realities of small-scale swine production have conspired to make it a staple in the Asian diet, particularly in southern and eastern China and throughout Southeast Asia.

A basic barnyard animal, the pig requires a small amount of land, minimal fencing, little maintenance, and a diet of forage and kitchen scraps. It is not unusual for families throughout China and Southeast Asia to own a pig or two and raise them until slaughter. The pig is traditionally considered a symbol of prosperity, and indeed, if you have one, you will not starve. In recognition of the nature of this bountiful animal, a whole, roasted, crispy pig is central to many Asian religious food offerings and is served on special occasions, especially the marriage celebration.

On the most basic level, the pig is valued because it can feed many people many meals and can do so for months if preserved. This is usually accomplished by salt- and air-curing, as in Chinese Yunnan ham, bacon, or sweet pork sausage. Innards such as heart, liver, spleen, kidneys, and blood are all valued as food items; intestines are used as sausage casings; and the gelatinous snout, ears, and tails are delicious, especially when braised. What might be considered exotic to Westerners (excepting, perhaps, the French and Italians) is a mainstay in many Asian cultures. The open-air markets in Hong Kong, Chiang Mai, Hanoi, Bali, Manila, and Phnom Penh all have butchers who feature all manner of offal, including head, tail, reproductive organs, and innards, as well as Western-style tenderloin, loin, ribs, legs, and shoulders.

In Chinese and many other Asian cuisines, fatty, inexpensive cuts of pork such as pork belly (also referred to as fresh bacon), shank, and pork butt are prized. Sweet and tender when cooked, their fat keeps the lean meat moist throughout the cooking process. Fatty cuts also present well at table, with a moist, glistening surface—a characteristic many Asians find appetizing—and can form the basis for complete, satisfying, and nutritious meals. When rendered from these cuts, pork fat, or lard, is used as a substitute for cooking oils and is employed in savory and sweet dishes alike—lard is added to red bean paste (page 513), for example, and used for making pastry shells (page 539). Fatty or lean ground pork can be added to vegetable or noodle dishes as a background note or flavor enhancer.

Pork belly can be stuffed with preserved vegetables, as in mui choi ju yook, a specialty of the Hakka people of China. In this dish, the pork belly is molded around and over a mound of chopped preserved mustard cabbage, and the whole is slow-cooked in a sweet soy sauce–based liquid for a couple of hours until tender. Once braised, the molded

pork is thinly sliced to reveal its marbled, fatty character. Essentially braised bacon, this dish is extremely rich, and when I eat it, I stop after perhaps two thin slices. Unlike American bacon, which is smoked, then pan-fried until crispy, in this recipe the meat simmers. The result is a minimal amount of tender lean meat, with lots of soft fat and skin. Oddly enough, fatty pork is relatively easy to digest. Chinese braised pork shank (also often made with pig's feet or hock, pp. 458–59; see hong sieu ju yook below), flavored with star anise and served with boiled eggs, is rich but balanced with white rice and sides of vegetables when served. It is often eaten as a mid-winter dish, when fat is traditionally required as a bulwark against the cold.

Pork butt is about 70 percent lean and can be used as a substitute for very fatty cuts mentioned here. It is especially desirable for making a Cantonese specialty called char siu (page 454), a dish popularly known in the West as Cantonese roast pork. Cut into thick strips, the pork butt is marinated for several hours in ingredients such as soy sauce, fermented bean curd, honey, Shaoxing wine, and a few drops of red food coloring (the secret behind its fes-

tive and distinctive ruby red color). Typically roasted in vertical ovens and brushed with a bit more honey as it is finished, Cantonese roast pork butt is thinly sliced and served over a mound of rice. An inexpensive dish that is filling and delicious, char siu fan (roast pork rice) may be ordered in Chinese restaurants specializing in Cantonese cuisine.

Leftover char siu is usually diced and used as a filling for buns. Roast pork buns, or char siu bao (page 294), can be found either steamed in dim sum restaurants or golden-baked from bakeries. Leftover char siu is also diced and added to stir-fried rice for a quick lunch or afternoon snack. You'll recognize this sort of "candied" pork butt hanging in long strips in the windows of authentic Chinese restaurants and shops in Chinatowns around the world.

The Filipinos make a fatty pork belly dish called humba (page 455). I first encountered the dish while walking through the marketplace near a church on the island of Cebu, where I observed a woman preparing food on the side of the road. She crushed garlic cloves and left the skins on, then added sliced shallots and minced ginger to her mixing bowl. After stirring in some soy sauce, coconut vinegar, and sugar, she added thinly sliced pork belly. She smiled at me and said, "Come back in a couple of hours, when it's cooked." Filipinos, like many other Asians, often prefer pork to other meats, and fatty pork especially, because of its tenderness. They also have historical ties to the Hakka of China, as well as to the Spanish who colonized the country, as is evident in their preparation of braised pork dishes. Humba, as I would soon learn on Cebu, is a particularly good example of the type. After several hours of braising, the dish gives off a sweet, salty, tangy aroma, and the bay leaf and Chinese fermented black beans added during cooking lend a curious and delicious Eurasian character. Sometimes the dish is made with less fatty cuts such as shoulder, shank, or pork butt.

The Filipinos also prepare a fatty, crispy pork belly that is extremely appetizing and easy to make. Called bagnet (page 457), the fresh pork belly is always prepared with the skin on, seasoned with salt and pepper, and deep-fried until the meat curls slightly and becomes very crispy. It is so crispy, in fact, that the skin resembles pork cracklings. Sliced bagnet is added to a traditional savory vegetable dish called pinakbet (page 336). Although rich, the pork

bagnet adds a wonderfully crunchy texture to the dish, complementing the tender vegetables. I must caution anyone who attempts it, however—it is addictive!

The Japanese do not eat much meat but usually prefer fish as a protein source. They make certain memorable pork dishes, however, and certain recipes from the port city of Nagasaki are especially good. Deriving—perhaps uniquely deriving—from Chinese influences, the specialty pork belly dishes of Nagasaki are found nowhere else. Perhaps this is traceable to the fact that the city, from the seventeenth to the nineteenth centuries, was the only Japanese port open to foreign trade. These dishes combine a Chinese penchant for fatty pork with the Japanese philosophy of wabi sabi (pp. 53–54).

The renowned Japanese cookbook author Shizuo Tsuji's Nagasaki-style pork belly, buta kaku-ni, is a good example. The pork is sweet, savory, and spicy from being braised in mirin, soy sauce, dashi (pp. 124–25), and ginger. The secret to its distinctive character, however, is that the pork undergoes a "flavor removal" process. This makes the already mild-tasting meat even milder. Simmered in soy milk for close to an hour, the

pork is then drained and added to a pot with its seasonings. Blanched pearl onions and snow peas are added, and the meat is braised for an additional half hour. The resulting dish is succulent, rich, and spicy with gingery notes. The pearl onions are mild but still pungent, a nice counterbalance to the fatty pork. The peas pop as you eat them. Mouthwatering, it is a perfect winter dish.

In the same vein, Japanese cooking teacher Hiroko Shimbo-Beitchman slow-cooks pork shoulder with sweet carrots and pungent pearl onions with the same mirin, soy sauce, dashi, and ginger seasonings but adds fermented miso paste to enrich the stew. Rather than boil the pork in soy milk, she steams it over water. The result is rich but not as fatty as pork belly; it is accompanied by blanched, unseasoned spinach.

Inspired by these two master cooks, I have taken the liberty of fusing their approaches, developing my own interpretation, which I call twice-cooked pork (pp. 468–69). Soy milk (or regular whole milk if you wish) is used to remove any strong flavors from the meat. More important, it tenderizes the meat, especially when using pork butt (pork belly has so much fat in it that tenderizing it is not much of an

BARNYARD ANIMALS LIKE THIS VIETNAMESE BLACK PIG ARE COMMON IN ASIA. PIGS EAT KITCHEN SCRAPS AND, ONCE SLAUGHTERED, CAN FEED AN ENTIRE FAMILY FOR WEEKS.

issue). Adding *miso*, as does Shimbo-Beitchman, gives the dish a nutty, robust flavor when added to the braising liquid. Absolutely delicious, this pork dish will surely be a winner when entertaining meat eaters, especially when served with boiled short-grain rice.

The Japanese often cook food twice, boiling the ingredient once, then draining it prior to additional cooking by a different method. This is true not only for the Nagasaki-style pork but also for vegetables such as bamboo. When cooked in this way, the food tastes incredibly mild and clean but still distinctive and flavorful.

Southeast Asian cuisines also display a penchant for pork dishes, and one of my favorite Southeast Asian–influenced family recipes uses cubed pork butt slow-cooked in pork stock, fish sauce with a bit of sugar to tame the saltiness, garlic, and lots of freshly cracked black pepper (page 461). This is a dish my Cambodian aunts made at home, and one my mother also eventually learned to make. I loved this tender, spicy, salty pork over rice when I was a child and still crave it today.

Another Southeast Asian dish my mother learned to cook when we lived in Phnom Penh was thinly sliced pork stir-fried with lots of ginger (page 492). Stir-fried with fish sauce (or sometimes oyster sauce, which has a subtly sweet character), the dish contains almost as much ginger as pork. If the amount of ginger is overwhelming for your palate, you can cut the amount by half, substituting julienned scallions. For a contrasting texture and added flavor, rehydrated and halved dried shiitake mushrooms add a wealth of flavor and texture.

Gaeng haneg lei muu (page 463) is a northern Thai curry specialty of pork shoulder or butt cut up into large cubes and cooked in water or basic pork stock. Tangy with tamarind extract and sweet with palm sugar, this fish sauce–seasoned curry is spiced with fresh ginger, *haeng lei* powder (a combination of ground cumin, coriander, mace, and turmeric), and red curry paste. During the cooking process, crushed, roasted unsalted peanuts are also added. While some cook this stew until the meat is tender but still somewhat firm, I prefer to braise the pork a bit longer so it can be pulled apart effortlessly. I garnish this curry with a generous amount of sweet, crispy, fried shallots, as is traditional, and serve it with steamed white sticky rice.

Ground pork shows up in many Chinese and Asian specialties. Sold either plain or seasoned and mixed with other ingredients, ground pork is commonly used in making all sorts of dumplings, especially Chinese potstickers (pp. 268–69) or wontons (pp. 266–67). The Japanese use it in making dumplings such as pork *shumai* and *gyoza*, and the Southeast Asians use ground pork as part of the filling for fried spring rolls (pp. 284–85). The Chinese use it to enrich dishes such as pork and preserved mustard cabbage relish (page 452), or the Szechwanese tofu specialty called *ma po dofu* (page 368). A hint for those venturing into Chinese butcher shops: you will observe that the pork is coarsely ground and arranged in piles by its fat content. The whiter the pork, the more fat it contains. I choose ground pork that is 70 percent lean, like pork butt. I find that there is enough fat in it to create succulent dishes.

While traveling in Bali, Indonesia, I tried all sorts of spicy satays, including shrimp, duck, and pork. (Hinduism, which allows the consumption of pork but not beef, is the predominant religion in Bali.) They were all delicious, and unlike elsewhere in Asia, nothing was ever sliced and threaded on skewers. Instead, the ground meat was mixed with spice pastes—which included lemongrass, galangal, *kencur*, turmeric, garlic, and chili—then wrapped around lemongrass stalks or molded inside small pieces of banana leaves. The satays were grilled over long, narrow, and shallow wood charcoal–fired barbecue pits,

usually employing two long, parallel metal spits as supports. The lemongrass skewers were balanced over this arrangement, allowing the meat to grill slowly. The aroma was enticing, the spice paste having really penetrated the ground meat. The ground pork versions were spicy, their herbal bouquet unforgettable.

Another interesting Indonesian ground pork dish is *piong duku babi* (page 464). In this preparation, the pig—meat, offal, and blood—is finely chopped or ground, mixed with a spice paste, and stuffed inside two-foot pieces of bamboo culm. The culms are then roasted over an open fire and are turned occasionally so that the contents are evenly cooked. I have included a version of the recipe using only ground pork and liver. You can use fresh bamboo culms if you can find and know how to prepare them. I wrap the spiced meat in the more readily available banana leaves and grill it in a similar way.

"Meaty bone" cuts of pork, ranging from the gelatinous foot to the delicate rib, are also relatively inexpensive and can be used creatively to achieve maximum flavor. In Chinese and Southeast Asian cooking, ribs, like other meaty bones, are often used for making stocks because the

amount of bone, meat, and fat is perfectly balanced, resulting in deep-flavored stocks. When cooked as meat, however, the ribs benefit from spices, sauces, and pastes. One of the most classic ways of preparing ribs is steaming them, as in the Cantonese specialty *jing pai gwat* (page 455), steamed spareribs. As served at dim sum restaurants, the pork ribs are cut into one-inch pieces and marinated with fermented black bean and garlic sauce (page 86), soy sauce, sugar, and rice wine for a couple of hours. They are then steamed with ginger and scallions for a second hour. The steam keeps the meat moist while cooking; the result is succulent bits that are savored with tea and other small items such as dumplings. If you want to try making these at home, you can find precut pork ribs in Chinese butcher shops, or ask your butcher to cut the ribs into one-inch pieces crosswise through the bone.

Using the same basic ingredients as in *jing pai gwat*, you can also braise the spareribs, as my family likes to do. When braised, the flavors are concentrated, the meat having absorbed the robust flavor of the fermented black bean paste. Ribs are also grilled, usually brushed with a sweet and savory sauce and sometimes made spicy. Another family favorite based on a Vietnamese recipe parboils the ribs prior to marinating them in hoisin sauce, fish sauce, and minced garlic. The parboiling rids the meat of any impurities, including loose bone bits, and tenderizes it. The sauces and the garlic add sweet, salty, and pungent notes. When barbecued (or broiled in the oven), the sweet, juicy, flavorful rib meat is so tender that it literally falls off the bones.

The Koreans have wonderful pork rib dishes, their bold spicing bringing out the best in the mild meat. Braised in soy sauce, garlic, ginger, and chili paste, the remarkably tender Korean pork rib stew called *toeji kalbi kangjong* (page 481) is sweet, spicy, and salty at the same time. Its sauce is made thick and velvety as it cooks down slowly over low heat. Served with water *kimchi* on the side, it makes for a great dinner. I also love *toeji kalbi* and *toeji kogi kui* (page 465), broiled or grilled pork ribs and sliced pork. Both the ribs or very thinly sliced pork (I like to use pork butt or any well-marbled cut of meat) are marinated in sake, sesame oil, soy sauce, chili paste, and sugar. Flavored with aromatic herbs such as garlic, ginger, and scallions, both are incredible when grilled just long enough for the edges to crisp and eaten dipped in a spicy vinegar sauce (page 93).

PRESERVED PORK

AIR-CURED PORK in the form of ham, bacon, and sausages is also widely employed in Asian cooking, enhancing the flavor of numerous dishes with its sweet and savory character. Yunnan ham (or shoulder), especially important in Chinese cooking, is air-cured with lots of salt. This exact ham is not available in the United States, but a very similar type called Smithfield ham is often used as a substitute, and you will have no trouble finding it in Chinese butcher shops. This type of air-cured "raw" ham is harder and much saltier than Italian prosciutto, for example. The secret to many fragrant foods, including Chinese superior stock (page 117), winter melon and ham soup (page 143), and steamed fish with ham (pp. 388–89), Smithfield ham can also be shredded (or ground to a stringy powder-like consistency) and used to garnish stir-fried or steamed greens. It is always soaked and drained prior to using. Soaking for at least twenty-four hours softens the meat for easy slicing and, most important, gets rid of the excess salt, which can be overwhelming. You can buy Smithfield ham by the slice (usually vacuum-packed) or the shoulder or ham. I prefer to buy the shoulder, as it is small enough to handle easily and fits in a conventional refrigerator. The piece usually lasts me at least six months when wrapped in a cotton kitchen towel and refrigerated after soaking.

Pork belly seasoned with sugar, soy sauce, and other spices and hung to air-cure can be thought of essentially as Chinese bacon. I like to braise it with shiitake mushrooms and bamboo shoots. Robust in flavor, the sweet and savory dish is perfect for a cold day. You will find dried dark-brown bacon strips with the rind still intact in Chinese butcher shops. Be sure to select a piece from behind the counter. It usually hangs next to Chinese red sweet pork sausages and brown pork (or duck) liver sausages. These are artisanally made and are the best you can possibly buy. The mass-produced, commercial types sold vacuum-packed are not as tasty and usually have more fat than lean. Thinly sliced Chinese bacon (or sweet pork sausages) can be added to any stir-fry as well as fried rice. Chinese sweet pork sausages are used throughout Southeast Asia, in a similar way, often stir-fried with rice. Generally the diced or sliced pork belly or sausage is the first item added to the hot wok to render the fat. Once the crispy meat is scooped out, the remaining fat is used to stir-fry and flavor the rice and other ingredients. The dish is finished by returning the crispy pork and stir-frying it with the rice for a few minutes prior to serving the fried rice. You can stir-fry vegetables the same way.

ROAST WHOLE PIG

PERHAPS THE CROWNING achievement of Asian pork preparation (and certainly the most dramatic) is the traditional whole roast suckling pig. The Chinese have a special vertical roasting oven to accommodate the animal, roasting it steadily and slowly, until the skin turns golden and very crisp. Unlike their adult counterparts, suckling pigs are only milk fed, and, as a result, very lean and tender. When carved, the meat falls right off the bones; the skin crackles; virtually everything is eaten. The leftovers make for delicious stews, soups, or stir-fries. Perhaps the most complete expression of this dish occurs in Canton and its sur-rounding areas, where it has evolved as a specialty. In the Philippines and Vietnam, as in China, whole suckling pigs are roasted for special occasions such as weddings and occasionally for birthday celebrations.

While it is not practical (and nearly impossible) to roast an entire pig in a standard home oven, there is no reason that the adventurous cook cannot produce a version of the roast suckling pig using a pork section. I have included a recipe for crispy pork belly (page 456), in which a large piece of well-marbled fresh pork belly (skin on) is employed. This cut is about 50 percent lean. When brushed with some sesame oil, five-spice powder, and soy sauce, and having had holes poked in it, the skin bubbles in the hot oven until golden crisp. Thinly sliced and served with the reduced sweet, savory, and spicy pan juices, the tender and crispy pork is delicious when served over rice, or with thin, flat egg noodles set in steamy rich superior stock (page 117).

BEEF

THE LIMITED USE of beef in Chinese cuisine probably relates to the ascendancy of Buddhism during certain historical periods (fourth to twelfth centuries, especially), as well as the possible influence of Indian Hinduism, the lack of available and adequate grazing land in much of the country, and the usefulness of the animal in plow-based farming. When it comes to traditional Chinese medicine, beef holds little or no importance. It is not well regarded in terms of health benefits, possibly because of its high cholesterol content, and no doubt reflects prevailing emotional and religious values as well. There is some evidence that China enjoyed significant beef consumption during the Han Dynasty, 206 B.C.E. to 221 C.E., but most of its history has seen both cattle and water buffalo revered and protected from slaughter. It may seem curious to Westerners that the same people who eat cats and dogs would have reverence for any animal, but this is the case with beef. Beef butchers are sometimes equated with families who practice female infanticide, reviled for their cruelty and insensitivity to what is generally regarded as a friend and benefactor of the family. Perhaps the closest parallel to these beneficent feelings toward large animals in the West is the North American respect for and statutory protection of the horse.

Protective feelings and laws are, as

we have seen, almost completely absent in beef-eating northern regions such as Mongolia and the Manchu areas. These nomadic peoples practice very little agriculture, preferring to raise and slaughter not only cattle but yaks, goats, sheep, and camels, among other animals. Even the horse, the primary means of transport and essential component of military conquest, is eaten here. The vast grazing lands and harsh climate of the north allow for relative ease in herding large- and medium-size animals when compared to the travail of trying to farm these cold, barren, and wind-whipped lands. It is also very likely that beef is consumed because significant amounts of protein are needed to fend off winter cold and prevent one from freezing to death. Indeed, in the traditional system of hot and cold foods, beef, unlike neutral pork, is considered "hot" or *yang*.

China is vast, however, and its history is long. Despite the predominant negative feelings about beef, beef dishes do have a place in Chinese gastronomy and are enjoyed in areas that have had significant contact with the West, especially in modern times. Even in traditional cultures, there comes a time when the family cow or water buffalo

(considered cattle in the south of China) is too old to perform its farming chores. Consistent with the Chinese aversion to wasting anything, it is slaughtered for food. One such dish is oxtail (sometimes considered offal) and lotus root soup (page 120). The lotus root in Chinese medicine is considered a sedative that relieves headaches and heaviness in the chest. The oxtail is sweet and rich with flavor, making it a delicious medicinal soup. The same soup is eaten in northern Vietnam, which has national beef dishes, and where the influence of its thirteenth-century Mongol invaders and the Chinese in general remains particularly strong.

The foods of Guangdong (Kwangtung) province and its capital, Guangzhou (Canton), are widely regarded as masterful. Known as Yue or Guangdong cuisine, it is a mixture of dishes from Canton, Chaozhou (Chaochow), and Dhanjiang, with a tendency toward the fresh, tender, delicate, and refined. It has been recorded in literature dating back to the second century C.E. Cantonese chefs generally prefer the delicacy of good cuts of beef to the stronger flavors of lamb, mutton, or goat and may have gravitated to this meat when first presented with the

"new" foods that arrived in southern China with the beef-eating Mongols and Manchus. They have evolved dishes with thinly sliced, tender cuts of beef, including wok-fried beef in oyster sauce, and iron plate beef, twice-cooked and served with winter bamboo shoot and two types of mushrooms. Beef is also ground for dumplings, as in the popular beef and chive dumplings. Other less specific uses of beef also occur, of course, such as beef thinly sliced or shredded and stir-fried with vegetables; shredded beef with rice noodles; and beef congee.

Hong Kong chefs are often seen as modern and innovative, influenced by the Western, especially British, love of meat, as well as by their city's requirements for international business entertaining and global tourism. Many Hong Kong chefs are from Canton, which is eighty miles to the north, and they often bear its culinary preferences. Equally important, however, is the impulse to fuse cuisines, both regional Chinese to regional Chinese, and Chinese to Western. Take, for example, T-bone steak marinated in soy sauce and sugar, dredged in cornstarch, and pan-fried. Crispy on the outside and medium on the inside, it is found both in Hong

there are hundreds of traditional recipes for pork, there exists only a fraction of that number for beef. This may be somewhat of a surprise to Westerners who have eaten beef dishes in Cantonese, Mongolian, Vietnamese, or Korean restaurants in Asia or the West, or who have heard of or tasted the extraordinary Japanese Kobe beef. It is most likely that in all these cases, the menus have been skewed to what are observed or assumed to be the tastes (and budgets) of the Asians' Western clientele.

In Vietnam, especially in the cold north, there is a deep appreciation for beef, although it can be costly and is sometimes regarded as a luxury. The classic beef and rice noodle soup, pho, uses relatively small amounts of beef eye of round sliced paper thin and often many of the lesser-priced parts such as tendon and navel. While it used to be eaten mostly for breakfast, it is now eaten at any time of the day. Beef pho has become popular all over the country and can be found at small indoor or outdoor restaurants, including those in the south, where fish and pork generally dominate. I have even seen it prepared on the side of the road, ad hoc and al fresco, by vendors balancing baskets full of

Kong and in the more sophisticated Chinese (Canton or Hong Kong–style) restaurants in the West. Another such dish commonly found in Chinese restaurants in the West is beef (often sirloin) and broccoli over rice. The dish is usually accompanied by Western broccoli, but the best beef and broccoli is made with Chinese broccoli (page 237). The tender, wide leaves and firm, thick stems are a great complement to the sweet, savory, and tender sirloin.

It should be emphasized, however, that beef, even to this day, is not widely eaten in most of Asia. While fresh noodles and fragrant lemony herbs on one shoulder and a stockpot full of delicious sweet beef stock on the other.

Another Vietnamese beef dish is beef seven ways, bo bay moon, in which beef is literally prepared and eaten seven different ways, including beef fondue (pp. 158–59), beef congee, and several others. Variations exist, but generally this ritual is quite expensive and usually eaten only on special occasions and in restaurants that specialize in bo bay moon. The Vietnamese also prepare a dish akin to the French boeuf aux carottes, a traditional beef and carrot stew. In Vietnam, however, it is manifested as bo kho ca rot (page 482), a spicy dish perfumed with exotic flavorings such as star anise, five-spice powder, cassia bark, and lemongrass.

Beef is rarely eaten in Cambodia, where cost, culture, and religion dictate against it. When it is eaten, it appears in fairly small quantities, especially in spicy Khmer dishes. Cambodian spicy beef soup, samlaw machou kroeung (pp. 150–51), is out of this world. Fragrant with an herbal paste consisting of galangal, turmeric, lemongrass, kaffir lime leaves, garlic, and shallots, it is cooked down with water or beef stock. The flavors are further enhanced with a few red-hot chilies and pungent prahoc, fish extract (page 76). Simmered with Thai eggplant, the soup is rich from the sweet beef juices having intermingled with the herbal paste over several hours. I am not much of a beef eater, but I must say this particular way of preparing beef makes me question my tendencies. Served with a bowl of jasmine rice on the side, it really is spectacular.

I am also very fond of loc lac (page 475), a beef dish I enjoyed at Phnom Penh's Hotel Le Royal near Monivong Boulevard, which happens to face the school my older brother attended when we were kids. Loc lac uses cubed sirloin marinated in mushroom soy sauce, sugar, garlic, and lots of freshly cracked black pepper. It is stir-fried over high heat or skewered and grilled on a barbecue. The spiciness is well rounded and nutty, rather than sharp, as might be expected from the generous amount of black pepper. A squeeze or two of lime juice makes for a wonderful complement. When making beef loc lac at home, I often sprinkle it with finely crushed peanuts before serving. The Cambodians also make a raw-beef salad (page 470) that is similar to the Thai version; both are discussed on page 438.

The Filipinos have been eating beef only since the early 1500s. The date corresponds to the arrival of the Spanish. The Philippines lacks vast grazing land, so Filipinos raise water buffalo (thought of here, as in China, as beef) in pens. One of my favorite Filipino beef recipes is the rich, Malaysian-influenced kare kare (page 474), oxtail and vegetables cooked in a peanut sauce; the stew sometimes includes tripe as well. When I visited Filipina food expert Glenda Rosales Barretto in Manila, we talked about the proper way of preparing kare kare, specifically her rendition of the classic. "Be sure to grind your own roasted unsalted peanuts because store-bought peanut butter is full of salt and margarine," she cautioned. (I couldn't agree more.) "Oxtail, a fatty, meaty bone cut, is perfect for braising, and after several hours the meat is so tender it falls right off the bones." Annatto seeds give the dish a beautiful red hue, while onions, garlic, and bay leaves lend a mildly spicy character. Classic vegetable ingredients include eggplant, tomatoes, string beans, bok choy, and, if you can find it, banana bud. (I also make the dish using daikon or turnips instead of banana bud.) An equal amount of toasted sticky rice flour (pp. 24–25) and ground peanuts are added to slightly thicken the sauce and add a robust, nutty flavor. Four hours of simmering render a succulent meat dish that is perfect for a cold winter's day.

Cambodia's raw-beef salad, *pleah saiko* (page 470), is seasoned with *prahoc*, fish extract (page 76), lime juice, and sugar. Thailand's version is seasoned with fish sauce. In both these recipes, paper-thin slices of tender sirloin, eye of round, or filet mignon are lightly cured with the spice mixtures, then tossed with mung bean sprouts, freshly torn Thai basil, and lemongrass and red chilies sliced paper thin. Served with steamed sticky rice, it makes for a relatively light meal on a hot day. In a Vietnamese variation, the beef is seared lightly to brown the edges before it is sliced for the recipe.

Descendants of the Mongol and Manchu peoples who live in a cold climate, Koreans have a cultural predisposition toward eating relatively more beef than other Asians. Cost is a factor here as it is elsewhere, however, and beef dishes are more likely to be eaten on special occasions, or as a way of honoring guests when entertaining. Korean beef dishes can be amazing. I have had wonderful examples such as braised short ribs, *kalbi tchim* (page 481), which are slow-cooked with bold flavorings, including soy sauce, rice wine, sesame oil, garlic, and scallions. Sugar is added to round out and sweeten the beef and its braising liquid. The dish is rich, and often daikon, fresh shiitakes, chestnuts, and ginkgo nuts are added to the pot for a great fall or winter meal.

Korean barbecue is known the world over, and while pork, chicken, and seafood are used, the most popular form is *bulgogi* (page 480), broiled or grilled marinated beef wrapped in fresh lettuce leaves. Dabbed with small amounts of sweet and sour chili dipping sauce (page 105) and dipped in a spicy vinegar dipping sauce (page 93), this is a meal you will not soon forget. Another popular barbecue item, *kalbi gui*, uses beef short ribs. Here, the rib meat is sliced down the middle and spread so that it is still on the bone, but it can be flattened for grilling. I have found grilling *kalbi gui* on a hibachi results in a slightly chewy texture. To correct this, I lower the temperature of my grill by removing some charcoal, lowering the gas flame, or raising the grill. Slow-grilling cooks the ribs through and makes them a little more tender.

Ground beef is employed for making *mandu kuk* (page 265), a Korean version of wontons. Relatively light, the dish wraps beef and tofu in wheat flour wrappers and is served in a clear beef broth. It is eaten as an appetizer, quick lunch, or afternoon snack. Raw beef also is enjoyed in Korean cuisine, as in *yuk hoe* (page 471): sirloin or eye of round is lightly frozen, then sliced into thin strips, tossed with juicy peeled and julienned Asian pear, and drizzled with a tangy, sweet sesame oil dressing.

Cattle were introduced to Japan in the second century C.E., most likely through trade with China, and principally as plow animals. Warriors were sometimes fed beef before battle, but the practice was generally discouraged and held by some to be an insult to the ancestors when eaten indoors. It is said, in fact, that *sukiyaki* (see below), or "plow-cooked beef," derives its name from the practice of soldiers who prepared beef outdoors on iron plowshares. The reluctance to eat beef was strongly linked to the prevalence of Buddhist thought in Japan, specifically the precept that four-legged animals should not be used for food. It may also have been reinforced by the defeat in the thirteenth century of the beef-eating Mongol invaders whose fleet and army were completely destroyed in a typhoon. This event was of great importance to the Japanese sense of themselves as a nation and gave rise to their image of themselves as a chosen people protected by the "divine wind" (*kamikaze*); it also led to an extended period of proud isolation from the rest of world. The advent of beef largely resulted from contact with the West in the 1850s and the Meiji or "enlightened rule" period that followed. Today the Japanese enjoy dishes such as beef *negimaki*, or scallions wrapped in thin slices of beef; beef *sukiyaki*; and beef teriyaki. They are known the world over for their special cattle, which are fed beer during the summer months and massaged with sake. This special technique fattens the animal and tenderizes its flesh. The beef bears the name of its city of origin, Kobe, where it was traditionally produced. Japanese Kobe beef is available in the United States and is very expensive, costing more than a hundred dollars a pound, depending on the cut. This beautifully marbled and incredibly tender beef

is extremely flavorful and perfectly suited for *nabemono* items, which are essentially dropped in a cooking utensil and retrieved by each diner at the table. Types of *nabemono* include *shabu-shabu* (page 160), the traditional Japanese hot pot in which beef is cooked in broth, and *sukiyaki* (page 480), in which beef is cooked in a shallow pan in suet and melted, caramelized sugar, sake, and soy sauce. (Japanese *sukiyaki*, or a close version of it by the same name, is a popular street hawker food specialty in Thailand.)

OFFAL IN ASIAN COOKING

OFFAL—INCLUDING ORGAN MEATS, head, snout, ears, tail, and other parts usually not considered "meat"—is often considered exotic in Western, particularly modern American, cuisine but is rather common in the traditional cuisines of Asia. Some people may have trouble with the idea, but offal is common in French, Italian, British, and other European cuisines, such as the delicatessen tongue sandwich, meat (often calf brain) ravioli, sausages, and any number of liver-based items, including the familiar liverwurst. In Asia offal appears both in specific dishes and as items that are

interchangeable with meat in protein-based recipes. They are also traditionally associated with Chinese medicine and have attributes as preventatives, curatives, and tonics. Like any meat, organic farmed products are best, especially for organ meats, which filter and retain impurities from the animal's blood.

White pork offal is literally white and includes pig's feet and tail, which are believed to increase blood flow. Red pork offal is, obviously, red, and includes gallbladder, which is supposed to help cure hernias, and heart, which is regarded as a mild sedative. Pork liver, also red, is high in iron and used to treat anemia. Commonly eaten beef offal includes tripe, tongue, and heart, although these (like the meat) are not regarded as having any particular health benefits.

White pork offal contains large amounts of skin, fat, and cartilage, which give them the gelatinous character that is particularly popular among the Chinese. I am not crazy about overly fatty foods, but I do enjoy white pork offal. Firm in texture, these parts—snout, ears, tail, feet—require long cooking hours. The Chinese braise pig's feet in a sweet and savory sauce for at least four to six hours, until the meat is easily separated from the bones. Referred to as *hong sieu ju yook* (pp. 458–59), or red-cooked pork, the pig's feet slow-cook over low heat in a caramel, soy sauce, and black vinegar–based braising liquid. Star anise is added to give the braised dish a licorice-like back note, while ginger and scallions add a refreshing herbal character. The result is succulent and incredibly tender, sweet and savory, with the gelatinous pork rind and cartilage acting as a natural thickening agent for the sauce. The same caramelized pork dish can be made with other gelatinous pig parts such as tail or ears, or leaner but still fatty cuts such as fresh hocks or shanks, which I use when cooking this dish for Western friends. No matter which part you pick, be sure you never cut away the skin or trim the fat. These important elements enrich and thicken the sauce and make it glisten. (You can always skim the melted fat that surfaces when you have finished braising the dish.)

The northern Vietnamese like to braise pig's feet, too. Their caramelized pig's feet and fresh hocks, *thit heo kho nuoc dua* (pp. 458–59), are derived from the Chinese classic *hong sieu ju yook*, described above. In the Vietnamese version, however,

fish sauce is substituted for soy sauce, and young green coconut water (rather than plain water or stock) is used for braising pig's feet, pork shank, fresh hock, or even meaty pig's cheeks (sometimes considered offal). The Vietnamese add dried red chilies and five-spice powder in addition to the star anise. Both the Chinese and Vietnamese add hard-boiled eggs (preferably duck eggs) to the dish. The Chinese shell and add hard-boiled eggs to the braising liquid, which turns the egg whites deep brown; the Vietnamese deep-fry the shelled hard-boiled eggs until golden crisp, then halve them and add them to the dish upon serving. In either version of the dish, the twice-cooked eggs tend to be a little dry, but when drizzled with the rich, sweet, savory, and spicy pork sauce, they are very tasty.

The red pork heart is lean and properly cooked only by being stir-fried or grilled until just cooked, or braised for several hours until it comes apart easily. When I was a kid in Paris, I learned to appreciate its possibilities when my extended Asian family got together for a barbecue. The gatherings would be large, with a lot of great cooks—the perfect opportunity to

learn about and share a lot of different foods. We would have *brochettes* (a French word used to describe skewered meats) with pork or beef heart and chicken gizzards, along with the more familiar cuts of meat. These were usually marinated in a combination of soy sauce, sesame oil, five-spice powder, garlic, ginger, and rice wine for a Chinese flavor; and fish sauce, garlic, and lemongrass for a Southeast Asian flavor. After marinating for an hour or so, all the cubed items were slid onto skewers, then cooked over redhot charcoal until the edges were crisp all around, leaving the insides tender and juicy. Served with refreshing salads and rice, the offal brochettes took no time to prepare, and the cook never had to call anyone to the table more than once.

A few years back, while celebrating Tet with a family in Hanoi, I was served pork heart with caramelized clams. Thinly sliced, the heart was stir-fried with lots of thin onion wedges and sliced carrots, then seasoned with fish sauce and cracked black pepper and topped with the caramelized clams. The tender, savory pork heart worked incredibly well against the crispy, sweet clams. I never forgot the dish, and I sometimes make it at home. Beef heart, like pork heart, is sometimes used in similar stir-fry recipes, or marinated and grilled on skewers and barbecued. The key is to cook it quickly; long cooking will toughen the meat.

Spleen is not often used in cooking, but I assure you that if you like liver, you'll also enjoy spleen, as they are closely related in flavor. The spleen, a bit grainy in texture, can be boiled in vinegared water (a sort of court bouillon—vinegar and water bath—using rice vinegar, ginger slices, salt, and pepper). When it is cooked, the spleen is thinly sliced and added to noodle soups such as the Cambodian k'tiao (or Vietnamese hu tieu), a rice noodle soup with pork and seafood (pp. 226–27). Garnished with some freshly sliced hot red chilies, herbs, and fried garlic oil (page 108), this is a soup that can be enjoyed all year round. You can also add some thinly sliced pork tenderloin that has been either steamed or boiled.

If you know a butcher who sells fresh pork blood (usually preserved with a bit of vinegar), or you have access to frozen blood from a specialty store or Asian market, the Filipino pork blood stew, which is called dinuguan baboy (page 460), is well worth a try. Be sure to bring a large jar containing a couple of tablespoons or so of vinegar to preserve the blood if bought fresh (vinegar prevents the blood from coagulating). A dish with Malaysian influences, dinuguan is pork meat, liver, and sometimes stomach, simmered in pork blood and coconut vinegar. Fragrant with garlic, onions, and chilies, the dish has lively savory and tangy flavors.

Beef tripe is delicious and used in any number of Asian dishes. It can be steamed or stir-fried so that it is chewy, or slow-cooked for several hours so that it is very tender. (I prefer it very tender and will eat it only braised.) It sometimes appears as an item on Chinese dim sum carts, and is enjoyed with the dumplings and other bite-size items, and tea. When shopping, always look for tripe that is bright and white, never dull or yellow. Butchers will usually have done the required initial parboiling in vinegar so that the tripe is ready to be prepared. Do not hesitate to ask about the parboiling, and try to get honeycomb tripe, as it is the preferred type in most dishes.

Beef tripe is often used as a substitute for pork in dishes such as caramelized Chinese or Vietnamese pig's feet or shank (pp. 458–59) and is sometimes added to the pork dish for a different texture and flavor note. Tripe also appears in the Balinese spicy herbal soup called soto babat (page 161), fragrant with lemongrass and kaffir lime leaves. In Korea, raw tripe and pork liver are cut into thin slivers and wrapped around pine nuts. These are served with salt, black pepper, and sesame oil for dipping and are often accompanied by strong alcoholic drinks. Pork tripe is also used in dishes, often in ways similar to beef tripe, or in regional dishes such as braised pork kidney and pork tripe from Szechwan.

While pig's and lamb's tongue are sometimes prepared, the best, most flavorful, tender, and preferred type of tongue is ox. Ox or beef tongue is a popular item the world over; the French cook it in vinegared water with a bouquet garni (bay leaf, parsley, and thyme, for example); and the Chinese in soy sauce with five-spice powder, sesame oil, ginger, scallions, and garlic until tender (page 472). Chilled and thinly sliced, it is often served as part of the cold cut platter at Chinese wedding banquets. Korean cooks also prepare oxtail using similar spices, minus the five-spice powder.

MUTTON, LAMB, GOAT, AND GAME

MUTTON, LAMB, AND GOAT have been enjoyed by the northern Mongols and Manchurians for thousands of years. These small domesticated animals are relatively easy to care for and simple to herd, requiring a minimal amount of grazing land; they are a generally affordable form of dietary protein. Mutton, lamb, and goat are often prepared in the style of Mongolian hot pot (pp. 152–53), in which guests cook the sliced meat in boiling water or broth. The meat is then dipped in a spicy rich soy sauce. Double-cooked five-spice lamb (page 483) is another northern specialty, which has the cook boil lamb breasts (to get rid of the strong flavor) until tender, then drain and deep-fry them until crisp.

Paralleling the southern Chinese resistance to beef, the more sophisticated Chinese cooks have historically avoided lamb, mutton, and goat, finding them too strong in flavor and odor and lacking in the delicacy they expect from meat. These items do not appear very often in complex or subtle recipes and, aside from the hot pot, and occasional stew, are generally not part of the southern and eastern Chinese tables. They do occur in Beijing cooking, however, reflecting that city's role as host to the Manchu dynasty that ruled China from the seventeenth to the twentieth century. In addition to developing refined versions of hot pot cooking, Chinese cooks also make a Peking barbecue lamb with scallions, dipping sauce, and, as in Peking duck, wheat flour pancakes. There are also specialty dishes such as lamb cooked with honey, and dishes that reflect regional preferences in vegetables, such as lamb with leeks.

Categorized as warm in the hot-cold food system, lamb and mutton have a place in Chinese medicine and are sometimes cooked with garlic to cure body aches, pain, fatigue, and weakness. This meat is also eaten by China's Muslim populations in the western and northwestern provinces, as their religious beliefs forbid the consumption of pork. All three meats appear in stews such as the Filipino *kaldareta* (also *caldareta*), or marinated goat meat and goat liver stew, but are more often than not thought of as one item among many, simple substitutes for one another, based on availability and taste, and often interchangeable with chicken, beef, and pork.

There are cooking techniques, however, that can address the character of these strong-tasting meats. I once prepared a lamb dish for my aunt Chou, who prefers the southern cuisine of her familial Chiu Chow and tends to avoid "northern" meats. After initially hesitating a bit, she eventually ate and enjoyed every bite of the lamb I served her. She was surprised at herself and could not figure out why the meat was so mild in flavor. I explained that I had boiled the lamb not in one but two changes of water for fifteen minutes each time, prior to braising it. I also skimmed the lamb fat while the dish was braising, because much of the lamb's strong flavor comes from its fat. These little tricks will help those who do not generally like lamb, mutton, or goat but would like to try them in a new dish.

Indonesian curried lamb, *kambing kare* (page 484), is prepared with a medley of dry spices—coriander, fennel, green cardamom, cumin, and cloves—and aromatic herbs such as lemongrass, ginger, garlic, and shallots. Cooked in rich coconut milk, it can be served as part of an elaborate *rijsttafel*. It can also be made with mutton or goat, as is traditional.

Game such as antelope, venison, and hare are also eaten in northern

China. Wild boar is enjoyed in the south, particularly in Canton, where special recipes for it have been developed. Domestication of rabbit and emphasis on its commercial production have increased significantly in the twentieth century, but these are recent developments, and the animal has no distinctive presence in refined cuisine. I have not experienced much game in Asian cuisine because few Asian cooks are willing to experiment with meat that is not part of their tradition. In the countryside, however, hunters kill and eat game just as they do in the West. I have not included specific game recipes in this chapter, but if you enjoy game, you can substitute venison in beef dishes and hare for pork or chicken. Different yet similar in terms of flavor intensity and texture, they would be used as substitutes in rural areas where they are part of family cooking traditions.

CHICKEN, DUCK, SQUAB, QUAIL, AND OTHER FOWL

CHICKEN IS AS POPULAR in Asian cooking as it is in the West, and duck shares an almost equal place. Small birds such as squab and quail are also common, and the eggs of all these birds are eaten in a variety of ways. In certain very refined cuisines exotic birds are also used, sometimes including, as in French haute cuisine, songbirds. Goose dishes occur occasionally in southern and eastern provinces but are not common. Turkey, which enjoys great popularity in the West, is used even less, the Chinese considering it dry and too big for a single dish, and subject to waste.

Chicken is at least equal to pork in terms of consumption and is popular for the same reasons that the pig is. The small bird is useful in almost all of its parts with minimal waste; it's a basis for stocks; and it can be used for more than a single dish or meal. Chicken is also inexpensive, delicious, and simple to prepare in any number of ways. Healthy, and mild in flavor, it will please even fussy eaters, including children and, on occasion, some vegetarians. A versatile food, it is categorized as warm or neutral (like pork) in the hot-cold system of Chinese food classification. Like pork, chicken is both rich and light at the same time, and its flesh has the ability to absorb flavorful sauces and fragrant herbs easily. Considered a tonic, it is, as in the West, believed to relieve cold symptoms, especially when prepared as a broth with gin-ger. It has a mild yet assertive flavor that complements rather than overwhelms dishes and allows it to marry well with seafood or other animal protein.

Chickens and ducks have been domesticated in China and many parts of Asia for millennia. Chickens were likely descended from wild jungle fowl and held great importance in ancient Asia, having been associated with folk beliefs, rituals, and, as is still the case in most of Asia, with sports. Roosters were seen as symbols of sexual prowess and sometimes thought of as sacred animals. Cock fighting, in particular, remains an important part of many Asian cultures even today. Eggs were also important ritual objects in ancient cultures, and even modern culinary art in much of Asia includes symbolic whole eggs in meat dishes and ceremonial cakes such as the moon cake, in which a whole salted egg yolk is embedded as a reference to the full moon. Ducks, also domesticated from wild fowl, were also afforded significance beyond their function as food. They were used to control insects and valued because they could be raised in rice fields, where they would forage without disturbing the crop.

Because chickens and ducks are easy to raise—they live on insects, worms, kitchen scraps and other waste, as well as on what remains in fields after harvest—many Asians still raise their own. Valued initially for their eggs, when slaughtered the birds not only provide food for the table but feathers and down for clothing and furnishings. Black-skinned chickens, which also have dark flesh, are small (not much bigger than squabs), are prepared as medicinal items, and in the eastern province of Fukien, they are sometimes preferred over white-fleshed chickens as food.

Asian cuisine celebrates these birds and you will find delicious chicken dishes in almost every country. Unlike beef or pork, there are few religious prohibitions against eating them, excepting the strict vegetarian Buddhists, who eat wheat gluten or tofu in "mock" chicken dishes. Asian chickens tend to be smaller, tougher, stringier, and more flavorful than the ones sold in the United States. An Asian bird weighs an average of a pound and a half, while, in the United States, roasters of three or more pounds are not unusual. I have come to prefer the smaller birds. In New York City, vendors at the Union Square

farmers' market sell organic, grain-fed, hormone-free poultry. The birds tend to be smaller than factory-produced items, each two and a half pounds or less, but the birds are more flavorful. Chicken (and duck) dishes are often marinated, wine-soaked, or braised, both to tenderize and otherwise "correct" the bird.

As with other meat, the Asians sell chicken and duck with parts that many Westerners might not think of as edible. In addition to the familiar chicken breasts, thighs, and drumsticks, whole chickens (with head and feet), chicken blood, and offal such as chicken feet, hearts, gizzards, and the reddish combs from the head, as well as the head itself, are all ready for purchase. You can also purchase duck blood that has been steamed and cut into small rectangular cakes, which can then be braised or stir-fried.

When preparing Asian chicken dishes, you'll find a single chicken goes a long way. Small amounts of meat are used because other dishes such as vegetables, rice, and clear soups are also present at every meal. I can get at least four meals for two people from a two-pound chicken, for example. A simple half chicken breast, thinly sliced, stir-fried with vegetables, and served over rice

makes for a more than reasonable lunch. Chicken wings are great deep-fried and are often spiced and served this way from street carts or shops that sell snacks. The wings, when served with simple vegetable and shrimp dishes, soup, and rice, can make for a good meal. Whole legs are delicious when braised in curry, as they often are in Southeast Asian cooking. Chicken hearts and gizzards are delicious stir-fried and served as part of a more elaborate dinner. My father has always maintained that the best stock is made with chicken, and the meaty bones, including the back and other parts often discarded in Western cooking, can be made into a great palate-cleansing broth for sipping during the meal.

Popular Chinese chicken dishes include boiled (or steamed) chicken, cut up and served with a ginger and scallion salt dipping sauce (page 104); chicken braised in soy sauce spiced with ginger, scallions, and sweetened with sugar (pp. 488–89); "drunken" chicken, steamed and marinated in rice wine and salt (page 486); and chicken rubbed with five-spice powder and salt and deep-fried until golden crisp (page 487). These are all fairly simple to make, inexpensive, varied in flavor, and versatile. You will find them anywhere from a street cart to a restaurant to a formal banquet. The chicken, cut into small pieces, and served over rice with a bowl of chicken stock for sipping, makes for a great quick lunch. More complex, indeed legendary, dishes, such as beggar's chicken, also exist. This is prepared by encasing a seasoned pork-sausage-and-cabbage-stuffed bird in clay (contemporary cooks use dough), and presenting it with great fanfare (and a hammer) at table, traditionally removing the feathers with the clay. Similarly, the Hakka dish known as salt-baked chicken reputedly began as a dish cooked in a pit in the ground, covered with a salt "baking oven" that was cracked open to reveal the bird when served. These dishes are time-consuming and demanding to prepare and generally best eaten in a restaurant when prepared by a chef. Salt-baked chicken is the least time-consuming of the two recipes and can be re-created at home, if you have a clay pot large enough to hold a whole chicken and salt—lots of it. Here is a modern interpretation of the classic dish. Fill a pot one-third full with coarse salt. Place a two-and-a-half-pound chicken wrapped in parchment paper, breast side up,

on top of the bed of salt. Fill the pot with more coarse salt to cover the bird completely. Bake in a 375°F oven for about two hours, and you will have a golden chicken, ever so slightly salted, ready for eating.

Southeast Asian chicken dishes include Thai coconut chicken curry (page 499) made with spicy hot Thai curry paste, or with milder Indian curry powder for the Vietnamese version. The Thai serve their curry with regular long-grain rice or sticky rice, while the Vietnamese serve theirs with a French baguette. In Cambodia, chicken is stir-fried in the same manner as pork with a generous amount of julienned ginger. It is also marinated in mushroom soy sauce, a generous amount of chopped garlic, and freshly cracked black pepper, then spit-roasted. This marinade is often used for quail and other small birds and prepared by street vendors. In Vietnam and Thailand, these small birds are used for offerings at temples.

An Indonesian specialty, *ayam goreng* (page 490), or fried chicken, cooks the chicken twice. The chicken is first braised with a spice paste, including fragrant herbs such as garlic, galangal, and coriander seeds diluted with a bit of water.

Cooked through but still firm, the chicken is considered done when the water (or any juices) evaporates completely and the spices cling to the pieces. These are deep-fried until crisp and golden. The fried chicken is served with a simple rice dish such as *nasi goreng* (page 239, variation) or as part of an elaborate buffet-style *rijsttafel* (pp. 57–58).

Inasal na manok (pp. 494–95) is a Filipino national chicken dish. Marinated with garlic, ginger, soy sauce, and lime juice, the chicken is either spit-roasted whole, or cut up and skewered for grilling. It can be purchased from local street vendors, who usually sell the drumstick and thigh. Another popular dish in the Philippines is *adobong na manok*, or chicken *adobo* (pp. 496–97). A whole chicken is braised in soy sauce and a generous amount of coconut (or rice) vinegar and flavored with pungent herbs such as ginger and garlic. The chicken cooks until the liquid has just about evaporated, leaving behind the fat to crisp the chicken prior to serving. Some cooks braise the chicken in the vinegar, remove it from the pot with a slotted spoon, further reduce the sauce, then put the chicken back in to finish. Others leave the chicken in the pot throughout the whole cooking process, or until the meat falls off the bones. I prefer the latter for a more concentrated flavor, but you have to be careful about the bones, especially when serving it to children.

In addition to these dishes—which betray, to a greater or lesser extent, their Chinese and Spanish roots—a number of dishes traditionally prepared by indigenous tribal peoples also persist in modern Filipino cooking. While the techniques are ancient, the names are curiously modern, often reflecting American advertising and mass-market culture. While visiting a friend in Manila, for example, I learned of a dish named after the American popular song "Killing Me Softly." Originally from the highlands, the preparation technique involves slowly beating a young chicken until it is black and blue, and eventually killing it, using a cane. "*Pinik pikan,*" my friend emphasized, literally "beaten up." Other oddly named Filipino chicken items are often sold by *sunugba* (street food vendors), who grill specialties such as: "IUDs," "Adidas," and "helmets," or chicken intestines, feet, and heads, respectively.

The Japanese prefer chicken to be bite-size when served. In *yakitori* (page 493) the chicken is separated into its various parts—breast, thigh, drumstick, gizzard, liver, heart, and skin—and cut into small pieces, then threaded three to four pieces to a single bamboo skewer and grilled. The meat is basted repeatedly until cooked and very lightly charred. *Yakitori* in Japan is typically offered by restaurants specializing in skewered grilled meat and seafood. It is also considered a bar snack food and often enjoyed with a beer or sake. The Japanese do not particularly like duck, finding it a bit heavy for their tastes and overpowering when cooked with other foods. It is sometimes stewed with tofu and onions. It is also served as a sauced teriyaki (page 87), but some pains are taken to remove all the fat before cooking. (Ironically, many Western cultures and, in fact, the Chinese, actually savor duck fat, rendering it for use in other dishes, considering it to be rich with essential flavors.) Quail and their eggs are widely eaten in Japan. Originally reserved for the nobility, they are now in commercial production and more reasonable in price. They are often seasoned with salt or *miso* paste, or dusted with *sansho* powder (page 13) and grilled, or simmered whole in soy sauce.

In Korea, chicken is prepared like pork and beef. Marinated in soy sauce, sugar, garlic, scallion, and ginger and grilled on a hibachi, then dipped in vinegary ginger-infused soy sauce, it can be eaten as is or wrapped in lettuce leaves. In *samgyet'ang* (pp. 198–99), a Korean specialty chicken and rice soup, the bird is cooked with ginseng, jujubes, and "glutinous" rice. It is served as a complete meal and traditionally eaten for three days during the hottest period of the lunar summer. The Koreans, like the Chinese, eat chicken offal. Gizzards, hearts, and livers, for example, are seasoned with salt, pepper, and sesame oil (for a nutty flavor), then grilled. Braised giblets are also popular, often cooked with garlic, scallions, bamboo, and mushrooms. Chicken is also prepared by simply boiling it in the Chinese fashion, adding scallion, ginger, or garlic to the broth, and serving the meat with pear, cucumber, carrot, and eggs dressed lightly with soy sauce. Duck, paralleling Japanese tastes, is not widely eaten, although it may sometimes be grilled. As in Japan, quail eggs are an ingredient in dishes such as a simple pork and vegetable stir-fry.

In addition to being used as a sort of occasional alternate for chicken, duck is also prepared in ways that celebrate its unique aspects. Duck meat is all dark meat, flavorful, somewhat gamey, and perhaps more interesting than chicken when properly prepared. In areas where it is plentiful, such as the countryside in the southern and eastern provinces of China, duck is often valued more for its eggs than its meat and so is kept until old and too tough for anything but braising. More expensive than chicken, when slaughtered young it is often reserved for festive occasions and presented in special dishes such as the Chinese classic, Peking duck. Originally from Beijing (Peking), the dish is offered by Chinese restaurants the world over. Relatively few serve it properly, however. When prepared in the traditional way, it involves several complex preparation steps and three different serving courses, and it requires more than twenty-four hours of preparation.

The bird is cleaned, treated with boiling water, stuffed, massaged with flavorings, hung to air-dry, then roasted until crisp. When done, the bird is presented with great fanfare, displayed to the diners on a cart, often by a gloved waiter who will attend during the entire dining and serving ritual. First, the golden, incredibly crispy skin is carved into squares and served as a first course, with diners taking a piece or two and placing it in the center of a thin and delicate *po ping* (or *mu shu*) pancake, or wheat flour crêpe. Dabbed with some sweet hoisin sauce and with fresh scallions and cucumber added, the crêpe is folded over to enclose the ingredients and eaten like a sort of flat spring roll. The crispy skin against the tender crêpe, and the pungent scallions and crunchy cucumber, complemented by the sweet sauce, is exquisite in flavor and texture. After the waiter finishes carving the skin, the meaty carcass is taken back to the kitchen. When the first course is complete, the now twice-cooked (stir-fried) shredded duck meat is brought back to the table. It is served with tender lettuce leaves that are used to wrap the duck and its seasonings. After this course, a clear broth made with the duck bones is drunk to clear the palate. Peking duck is the ultimate three-for-one dish and a perfect example of the sophistication and ceremony of Chinese cooking at its best.

When I crave the rich flavor of roast duck and especially its crispy skin, I make five-spice roast duck (pp. 500–1), a recipe that references the classic Peking duck but is simple to make at home. After carefully separating the skin from the flesh with my fingers, I fill the gap with a layer of plump shiitake mushrooms. The duck then marinates overnight in a combination of sugar, five-spice powder, and soy sauce. Roasted in a high-temperature oven until crisp, this dish is nothing less than superb. When carved, each slice of duck reveals, from top to bottom, crispy skin, mushroom, and meat, just like a beautiful layer cake.

Duck is somewhat costly in Southeast Asia, and, after the Chinese fashion, it is served on special occasions. Duck and bitter flavors go well together, and a wonderful example of this combination is the Cambodian duck and preserved lime soup (pp. 140–41). In this recipe, the duck is usually served whole in the same clay pot in which it was cooked, or in a soup tureen, with the preserved bitter limes intact. Traditionally, diners pick sweet bits from the bird and sip the lightly bitter broth during the meal. In Bali, I observed the day-long process of creating the smoked-duck dish called *bebek betutu* (pp. 502–3). After being slaughtered and cleaned, the fresh duck is marinated with an herbal paste for twelve hours, then wrapped in large salam leaves (banana or lotus leaves can be used instead), and smoked in a low-tamped rice husk fire for twelve hours. The next day the bird has been transformed, its incredibly tender and succulent meat falling off the bones. (The recipe I give has been adjusted for Western kitchens.)

The Vietnamese make a wonderful version of the French classic *canard à l'orange*, a caramelized, braised duck seasoned with fish sauce, sugar, and flavored with freshly squeezed orange juice. After a couple of hours of slow-cooking, the duck is tender and savory and offers a rich orange note, both sweet from the pulp and bitter from the zest.

The Filipinos prefer duck eggs to the meat, as do rural Chinese cooks. At the end of their useful life, mature ducks are usually braised adobo style with soy sauce and lemon juice and flavored with ginger in a dish called *pato tim*.

Squab, and smaller birds such as quail, are a delicacy in China, generally reserved for special banquets. Flavorful, rich in protein, and having virtually no fat, these birds are regarded as being very healthy food. Squab is prepared in many different ways, including braising, and as meat in soups. One of the most classic dishes is twice-cooked squab, in which the bird is first poached in ginger-infused chicken stock, then brushed with soy sauce and deep-fried in peanut oil. Quail is cooked by rubbing the cleaned bird with salt, pepper, and five-spice powder, then simply deep-frying it, a method used in China and throughout Southeast Asia. Southeast Asian cooks also marinate various small birds in special mushroom soy sauce, sugar, black pepper, and garlic, and spit-roast them on thick bamboo skewers. You can smell the aroma of quail grilling as you walk through the streets of Vietnam, Cambodia, or Thailand. These roasted, golden birds are a constant enticement to passersby on the routes to temples, where they are symbolically offered to the ancestors, then eaten.

EXOTIC MEATS: DOGS, CATS, RATS, AND INSECTS

I MENTION THESE MEATS because they are a source of myth and misinformation about Asian cooking, and because they deserve to be considered thoughtfully by cooks who are serious about understanding Asian cooking. In my opinion, preparation of these animals and insects is in decline, except where food shortages are a problem, or where it has particularly deep cultural roots. They are more the subject of interesting conversation and novelty than recipes, but I feel they warrant some examination here.

For millennia, dog, cat, rat, and other meat now considered exotic were eaten in many countries. Dog, for example, was eaten in Europe, specifically Germany and Switzerland, into the twentieth century. While many of these foods have faded from consumption in the West, they persist to a certain extent in Asia, which is generally less dynamic and slow to modernize than the West, poorer than the West, more in touch with the realities of famine and starvation (which persisted well into the twentieth century), and accustomed to using these animals as tonics and medicines.

Restaurants in modern southern and eastern China and Vietnam still specialize in dog and rat. The "rat" is a field rat and closer, perhaps, to rabbit or muskrat than the urban rats that come to mind. Dogs were historically raised for hunting and as guards; they were favored over pigs for sacrificial rituals and provided a ready source of meat. Mus-

A VENDOR SELLS ROASTED EXOTIC MEAT AT AN OUTDOOR MARKET IN HANOI.

lims and Buddhists did not eat dog, however, and indeed, it was never universally favored by all Chinese peoples.

Although dog is generally considered an inferior meat, the custom of eating it is, however, still practiced in and around Canton and northern Vietnam and eaten primarily by men, often as a display of strength or character. Dog is considered a "hot" food, according to the cold-hot food system, and is often eaten roasted in winter, along with wild game parts and other tonic foods. Similarly, in ancient China, cats, both wild and domesticated, were eaten in all their parts and used for medicinal purposes. The practice persists today in and around Canton, where the meat is considered tasty and sometimes combined with other exotics such as snake.

Insects, too, are sometimes eaten. Crickets and locusts, for example, have a good amount of protein and are considered a delicacy in many parts of Southeast Asia. I have to say, even though I grew up in these cultures and have eaten some exotic food in my life, Filipino cricket dishes were a real challenge. While in Manila, I had the pleasure of meeting restaurateur Larry Cruz. A cultured man, he has a soft spot for traditionally prepared cricket dishes. "They're delicious sautéed with chopped onions, garlic, and chilies, with just a touch of vegetable oil," he said. I tried them, and while they were nicely flavored, I found the texture a bit difficult. From what I understand, they are a special delicacy because they are seasonal. Captured in large quantities, they are prepared, as my host explained, by "plucking off the wings." While traveling elsewhere in Asia, I also found grilled locusts and large, furry spiders, notably in the markets of Phnom Penh. These I politely declined.

SPICY PORK WITH SHIITAKE MUSHROOM STIR-FRY

12 dried medium to large SHIITAKE MUSHROOMS

2 tablespoons OYSTER SAUCE

2 tablespoons CHINESE LIGHT SOY SAUCE

2 tablespoons SHAOXING WINE

2 teaspoons GRANULATED SUGAR

2 teaspoons TAPIOCA STARCH or CORNSTARCH

1 pound PORK BUTT, sliced thinly against the grain

2 tablespoons VEGETABLE OIL

2 large GARLIC CLOVES, crushed, peeled, and minced

1 ounce fresh GINGER, peeled and julienned

3 SCALLIONS, root and dark green ends trimmed, and 6-inch stalks cut into ½-inch pieces

5 or more dried RED CHILIES

A GOOD CHINESE COOK—one who understands his or her ingredients—can turn almost anything into a delicious stir-fry. Many are based on what is at market, or what leftovers are available, or simply the mood of the cook. In my mind, however, this spicy pork-and-mushroom dish is less a spontaneous stir-fry and more a classic. It is also a fond memory, because my mother used to serve it to my brothers and me when we came home from school.

1. Put the shiitakes in a bowl with hot water to cover, then set a plate over the bowl to prevent steam from escaping. Let stand until the mushrooms rehydrate and soften, about 30 minutes (or longer depending on the size of the mushrooms). Squeeze the mushrooms between the palms of your hands to get rid of the excess water. Using a paring knife, remove any hard stems from the mushrooms, then quarter the mushroom caps.

2. Whisk together the oyster sauce, soy sauce, wine, sugar, and tapioca starch, until the sugar is completely dissolved and the tapioca is smooth and well incorporated. Add the pork to the marinade and mix well to coat the meat evenly. Allow to marinate for 30 minutes.

3. Heat the oil in a wok over high heat. Stir-fry the garlic until fragrant and lightly golden, about 1 to 2 minutes. Add the ginger, scallions, and chilies and continue to stir-fry.

Add the pork and mushrooms and stir-fry until cooked through, about 10 minutes.

SOME PEOPLE ARE SURPRISED to learn that schoolchildren will eat hot foods such as this stir-fry. Like many Asian children, my brothers and I started eating spicy foods when we were very young and never had a problem with chilies. If you like to eat spicy foods but are hesitant to use chilies or other "hot" spices when cooking for your children, try working in the spices in small amounts at a time to get them used to the flavors. A good method and one used in many Asian families is to build the children's taste buds by using fresh black pepper, increasing the amount a little at a time, then switching over to a single chili, then two, and so forth. After a while, they will have developed a taste for more complex and challenging flavors, and you will have less need to prepare separate dishes for them. Just do not rush the process.

PORK AND CABBAGE RELISH

SERVES 4 TO 6

1 tablespoon VEGETABLE OIL

3 large GARLIC CLOVES, crushed,
   peeled, and minced

8 ounces GROUND PORK
   (70 percent lean)

½ teaspoon FIVE-SPICE POWDER

One 10.5-ounce package
   PRESERVED SOUR MUSTARD
   CABBAGE

1 small NAPA CABBAGE, finely
   chopped

2 tablespoons CHINESE LIGHT SOY
   SAUCE

Freshly ground BLACK PEPPER

I FIRST HAD THIS SIMPLE PORK-AND-CABBAGE dish in a small Chinese restaurant in New York City's Chinatown, where it was served as a rich sauce over rice with a deep-fried five-spice chicken leg (page 487). For the lack of a better name, I call it a "relish." Fragrant with five-spice powder, it is usually fried in rendered pork fat and some of the reserved frying oil. I offer a less fatty version here, using ground pork with just enough fat to cook down the vegetables, and without extra frying oil. A slight tanginess from the preserved mustard cabbage (ham suen choi) counterbalances the richness of the pork, and the mild napa cabbage rounds out the flavors. While I can eat a bowl of rice topped only with this pork-and-cabbage relish, I have to say that the addition of Chinese fried five-spice chicken really makes for a wonderful meal.

1. Heat the oil in a wok over high heat. Stir-fry the garlic until golden, 1 to 2 minutes. Add the pork and cook, breaking down the pork with the back of a wooden spoon, until the pork is well separated and has cooked through and rendered its fat, about 7 minutes.

2. Reduce the heat to medium-low, add the preserved mustard and fresh napa cabbages, season with soy sauce and pepper, and cook, covered, to a chunky sauce consistency, 30 to 45 minutes.

Variation: You can substitute ground beef for the pork. You can also use ground turkey, but you will need to increase the oil by 1 tablespoon when stir-frying to make up for the lack of fat in the bird.

CHINESE MENU IN A SMALL, FAMILY-STYLE EATERY, HONG KONG

CHAR SIU
CANTONESE ROAST PORK

SERVES 4 TO 6

7 tablespoons HONEY

2 tablespoons HOISIN SAUCE

1 tablespoon PRESERVED RED or
WHITE BEAN CURD

¼ cup CHINESE SOY SAUCE

¼ cup GRANULATED SUGAR

1 tablespoon SHAOXING WINE

2 large GARLIC CLOVES, crushed,
peeled, and minced

3 dashes of RED FOOD COLORING

2 pounds PORK BUTT, cut into
long strips, about 1½ inches
thick

SOME OF THE MOST ARRESTING sights in any Chinatown are the windows of Chinese restaurants serving cooked meats. All sorts of delicious items from soy sauce chicken to roast duck, crispy suckling pig, or ruby-red Cantonese roast pork hang side by side in the front windows to entice passersby. Very inexpensive, they make delicious quick meals when served sliced over rice. Cantonese roast pork, called *char siu*, is marinated in the savory and sweet flavors of preserved bean curd, soy sauce, rice wine, and honey. To achieve good-quality *char siu*, it is important to use pork that is slightly fatty, pork butt being the best.

Two pounds of pork butt may seem like a lot for four people, but the leftovers make for a delicious fried rice, or roast pork buns, called *char siu bao* (page 294).

1. Whisk together 4 tablespoons of the honey, the hoisin sauce, bean curd, soy sauce, sugar, wine, garlic, and red food coloring in a baking dish. Add the pork butt, coating it well on all sides, and allow to marinate for 6 hours, refrigerated, turning the meat over several times (about once every hour).

2. Preheat the oven to 450°F. Pour about ½ cup water into a baking dish fitted with a flat roasting rack. Place the pork butt strips on the rack and roast for about 45 minutes, basting with the marinade every 15 minutes and turning the meat after 15 minutes. When the strips are cooked, brush the remaining honey on all sides of the strips and allow to rest for 15 minutes before thinly slicing against the grain. Serve over rice with pan juices on the side for dipping, if you wish.

Variation: Substitute 2 to 3 pounds pork ribs (regular, baby back, or country cut) for the pork butt, and barbecue these on the grill until crisp.

JIN PAI GWAT
PORK RIBS WITH BLACK
BEAN AND GARLIC SAUCE

SERVES 4 TO 6

2 tablespoons VEGETABLE OIL

2 pounds PORK SPARERIBS,
separated and halved crosswise

½ cup FERMENTED BLACK BEAN
AND GARLIC SAUCE (page 86)

2 ounces fresh GINGER, sliced
lengthwise and lightly crushed

6 SCALLIONS, root and dark green
ends trimmed, and 6-inch stalks
cut into 1-inch-long pieces

1 or more tablespoon GRANULATED
SUGAR

KOSHER SALT

Freshly ground BLACK PEPPER

1 tablespoon CHINESE DARK SOY
SAUCE (optional)

A POPULAR DISH in dim sum restaurants, *jing pai gwat* are pork ribs with black bean and garlic sauce and pungent garlic, ginger, and scallion. While this dish can be steamed, our family likes to braise it (see variation) for a really deep flavor. Variations on ingredients (which always include those in the list here) do exist. For a pronounced amber color, Chinese dark (also referred to as "thick") soy sauce can be used. Filipino cooks make a similar dish with pork belly instead of pork ribs. Their version, which is soured with coconut vinegar, is called *humba* (see variation).

Have your butcher halve the ribs through the bone, crosswise. If this is not possible, just separate the ribs.

1. Heat the oil in a wok over high heat. Add the spareribs and stir-fry until crispy on the edges, about 10 minutes. Add the black bean and garlic sauce, ginger, scallions, and sugar, and season with salt and pepper as desired. Add the dark soy sauce (if using) and continue to stir-fry for a minute or so to coat the pieces evenly. Transfer the pork to a plate.

2. Set a bamboo steamer with a lid over a wok filled halfway with water and bring the water to a boil over high heat. When the steamer is filled with hot steam, place the plate with the pork on top of the bamboo rack. Secure the steamer lid on top and steam until the pork is fork-tender, about 1 hour. Serve with rice and stir-fried vegetables on the side.

Variations: To braise the ribs, follow step 1, using a clay pot or heavy-bottomed pot. After adding the dark soy sauce, add ¼ cup water and ¼ cup Shaoxing wine, and simmer over low heat until the pork is fork tender, about 1 hour.

To make Filipino *humba*, substitute 1½ pounds skin-on pork belly, cut into ¼-inch-thick slices for the ribs. Stir together 2 tablespoons coconut or rice vinegar, 2 tablespoons Chinese light soy sauce, and 1 tablespoon sugar, until the sugar is completely dissolved. Stir in the black bean and garlic sauce and a peeled and sliced large shallot. Add the pork, toss to coat evenly, and marinate for an hour at room temperature. Transfer the pork and marinade with a cup of basic pork stock to a heavy-bottomed pot and bring to a boil over high heat. Reduce the heat to medium-low and simmer, covered, until the pork becomes very tender, 1 to 1½ hours.

FIVE-SPICE
ROAST PORK BELLY

SERVES 4 TO 6

¼ cup CHINESE LIGHT SOY SAUCE

2 tablespoons GRANULATED SUGAR

1 teaspoon FIVE-SPICE POWDER

1 teaspoon SESAME OIL

2 pounds PORK BELLY with rind
intact

FIVE-SPICE ROAST PORK BELLY is my approach to ovens that will not hold a whole pig. Buy one to two pounds of pork belly with the skin still on. Be sure it is at least 50 percent lean. Fresh pork belly, also known as fresh (as opposed to smoked) bacon, can be purchased at any Chinese butcher shop. Western butcher shops occasionally carry it, but because it is not a popular item, it may be best to order it a few days in advance.

1. Make the basting liquid by mixing the soy sauce, sugar, and five-spice powder in a bowl until the sugar is completely dissolved. Stir in the sesame oil. Marinate the pork belly for 4 hours, refrigerated, and turn occasionally.

2. Preheat the oven to 450°F. Pierce holes every inch through the pork skin with a metal skewer. Place it skin side up on a rack set over a baking dish containing about ½ inch water. Place in the oven and roast until golden and crispy, for about 1 hour, basting the top side (skin) with the soy sauce mixture every 15 minutes. Remove from the oven and let rest for 15 minutes before slicing.

WHEN YOU BUY a crackling whole roast pig in Chinatown, the collected juices of the roast pig flavored with soy sauce and spices come with the purchase. The pan juices of the five-spice roast pork belly can be reduced for about 10 minutes with the remaining basting liquids. Not as concentrated as the juices from a whole pig, the flavorful drippings from the smaller pork belly are sufficient to produce a perfectly good dipping sauce.

BAGNET
CRISPY PORK BELLY

SERVES 4 TO 6

2 large GARLIC CLOVES, crushed,
   peeled, and minced
1 ounce fresh GINGER, peeled and
   finely grated
KOSHER SALT
Freshly ground BLACK PEPPER
2 BAY LEAVES
2 pounds PORK BELLY with rind
   intact, cut into 4 slabs
VEGETABLE OIL for deep-frying

THE FILIPINOS USE BAGNET, deep-fried pork belly, for salad and for their classic vegetable stew called *pinakbet* (page 336). It is absolutely delicious, even addictive, with the extra-crispy skin as the result of being deep-fried. The pork is flavored with garlic, ginger, and bay leaf and simmered in water for about an hour prior to deep-frying. The simmering allows the essence of each herb to penetrate the meat and tenderizes it prior to being deep-fried until very, very crispy. *Bagnet* can be sliced and eaten as a main meat dish, or added to vegetable stews or soups for flavor and texture.

1. Mix the garlic and ginger together, adding salt and pepper to taste. Rub the mixture over the pork belly and allow to marinate for 1 hour, refrigerated.

2. Bring a pot of water to a boil over high heat. Reduce the heat to medium-low and add the bay leaves and pork. Do not wipe off the herb rub. Cook until tender but firm, about 1 hour. Drain and let dry about 30 minutes.

3. Meanwhile, heat enough oil in a pot for deep-frying over medium heat. Let the temperature reach 360° to 375°F. Deep-fry the pork, turning it every 5 minutes or so, until very crispy and deep golden all around, about 15 minutes total. Serve, thinly sliced.

HONG SIU JU YOOK BRAISED CARAMELIZED PORK

SERVES 4 TO 6

8 CHICKEN or DUCK EGGS

½ cup GRANULATED SUGAR

8 cups BASIC PORK STOCK
(page 118); or WATER

¾ cup CHINESE LIGHT SOY SAUCE

¼ cup CHINESE DARK THICK SOY
SAUCE

¼ cup CHINESE BLACK VINEGAR
(optional)

4 pounds PORK (shanks, hocks, or
pig's feet)

8 SCALLIONS, root and dark green
ends trimmed, and 6-inch stalks
halved crosswise and lightly
crushed

3 ounces fresh GINGER, thinly
sliced lengthwise

8 large GARLIC CLOVES, crushed
and peeled

5 or more CHINESE DRIED RED
CHILIES

7 STAR ANISE

BRAISED CARAMELIZED PIG'S FEET (also hocks or shanks) are a favorite with the Chinese, who call them *hong siu ju yook*, and the Vietnamese, who refer to their version as *thit heo kho nuoc dua* (see variation). Both start with a caramel made by melting sugar with a small amount of water until it turns a rich amber color. Soy sauce or fish sauce is added to the pot along with ginger, garlic, scallions, and star anise. The pork is braised until it falls off the bones and has taken on a deep reddish-brown color from the caramel and Chinese dark soy sauce. Duck or chicken eggs are boiled, shelled, and added to the pot; they pick up a beautiful golden hue. The Chinese sometimes add their pungent black vinegar to counterbalance the sweet and savory flavors of the dish.

The more gelatinous the meat, the more velvety the sauce. If you plan to use the meatier shanks, be sure to add a pig's foot to thicken the sauce. The stew is so delicious that it is worth making in large quantities. Like many braised dishes, it always tastes better reheated.

1. Gently place the eggs in a pot with water to cover. Bring to a gentle boil and cook until hard-boiled, about 5 minutes. Rinse under cold water and allow to cool completely before peeling off the shells. Set aside in the refrigerator.

2. Combine the sugar with ¼ cup water in a heavy-bottomed pot over medium heat. When the sugar is melted and turns a rich golden color, about 8 minutes, remove the pot from the heat and carefully stir in the stock or water, light and dark soy sauces, and vinegar (if using). Return the pot to the burner over medium-low heat. Stir the stock until the caramel melts completely.

Add the pork, scallions, ginger, garlic, chilies, and star anise and bring to a boil. Reduce the heat to low and simmer, covered, until the meat is fork-tender, about 4 hours. Skim most of the fat off the top and add the eggs. Continue to simmer, ladling the sauce over the eggs occasionally (or turning them), until the eggs turn golden, about 10 minutes. Serve hot with jasmine rice and stir-fried watercress.

Variations: For a Vietnamese version of the dish, substitute fish sauce for the Chinese light soy sauce and add 1 teaspoon five-spice powder when adding the scallions and other seasonings to the pot. The Vietnamese also like to deep-fry the hard-boiled and shelled eggs. To do this, heat enough oil for deep-frying in a pot over medium heat. When the oil reaches 360° to 375°F, carefully lower the eggs (they should be thoroughly dry; pat them with a paper towel to make sure) into the oil and fry, rolling them, until golden crisp all over. Add them to the pot to cook with the sauce before serving.

Braised Carmelized Mushrooms: Put 12 medium to large dried shiitake mushrooms in a bowl with hot water to cover, then set a plate over the bowl to prevent steam from escaping. Let stand until the mushrooms rehydrate and soften, about 30 minutes (or longer, depending on the size of the mushrooms). Squeeze the mushrooms in the palms of your hands to get rid of the excess water. Using a paring knife, remove and discard any hard stems. Leave the caps whole, or halve them. Add the mushrooms along with 12 shelled, hard-boiled quail eggs to leftover Chinese or Vietnamese pork-flavored caramel sauce and braise for 30 minutes, allowing the flavors to mingle. Another option is to add the mushrooms to the Chinese or Vietnamese braised caramelized pork recipe when you add the pork to the pot in step 2.

You can use canned straw mushrooms instead of the shiitakes, but be sure to rinse them, and blanch them in boiling water for 1 to 2 minutes prior to proceeding with the recipe. Also, braise for 15 minutes only.

DINUGUAN BABOY
PORK BLOOD STEW

SERVES 4 TO 6

1 tablespoon VEGETABLE OIL

3 large GARLIC CLOVES, crushed, peeled, and minced

1 large SHALLOT, peeled and minced

1 pound PORK BUTT, cut in ¾-inch cubes

8 ounces PORK LIVER, diced

2 tablespoons or more FISH SAUCE

1 tablespoon or more GRANULATED SUGAR

4 fresh RED THAI CHILIES

¾ cup COCONUT or CHINESE WHITE RICE VINEGAR

2 cups BASIC PORK STOCK (page 118)

2 cups fresh or frozen PORK BLOOD (thaw completely if frozen)

LIKE TRADITIONAL EUROPEAN culinary cultures, many Asian cultures employ cooked animal blood in meat dishes. One of the most interesting Filipino dishes I have ever tasted is *dinuguan baboy*, pork cooked in its own blood. Diced pork butt and liver simmer in this tangy, spicy blood sauce until fork-tender. Coconut vinegar cuts the richness, and herbs such as garlic, shallot, and finger chilies (also known as Thai chilies) lift the palate. Referred to—in its short form—as *dinuguan* ("that which has been bled on"), this pork stew is delicious served over rice. This recipe is derived from one served at family gatherings when my sister-in-law Melinda's mother presides. She sometimes adds eight ounces pork intestines cut into small pieces.

If you cannot find coconut vinegar, Chinese white rice vinegar is a good substitute. Be sure to simmer this stew; the blood should not boil.

Heat the oil in a heavy-bottomed pot over medium heat. Stir-fry the garlic and shallot until fragrant and lightly golden, 3 to 5 minutes. Add the pork butt, liver, fish sauce, sugar, and chilies and stir-fry until the meat is cooked, 25 minutes. Add the vinegar and cook until the acidity is reduced, about 20 minutes. Add the pork stock, and bring to a gentle boil. Reduce the heat to low and stir in the pork blood. Continue to cook, stirring occasionally, until the blood turns black and the sauce is thickened, about 10 minutes more. Serve with rice.

COOKING IN PORK or duck blood has been a practice for centuries in Asia but is not unique to that part of the world. In fact, cooking an animal in its own blood is thought of as being quite a delicacy in many parts of Europe. In France, *civet de lapin* is a classic dish of rabbit cooked in its own blood; and a fish version of the dish, using eel and its own blood, *civet d'anguille,* is made as well. Sausages or "puddings" of blood encased in pork intestines are poached in simmering *court bouillon* (a vinegar-water bath), then pan-fried or grilled. *Boudin noir,* as the French call these blood sausages, are found not only in France but with variations in Ireland and England, where they are referred to as blood puddings.

CAMBODIAN BRAISED BLACK PEPPER PORK

SERVES 4 TO 6

4 cups BASIC PORK STOCK
(page 118); or WATER

2 tablespoons or more FISH SAUCE;
or CHINESE LIGHT SOY SAUCE

1 tablespoon GRANULATED SUGAR

3 large GARLIC CLOVES, crushed
and peeled

1 ounce fresh GINGER, thinly sliced
lengthwise, or peeled and
julienned

1 tablespoon freshly ground BLACK
PEPPER

1½ pounds PORK BUTT, cut into
1-inch cubes

BRAISED PORK BUTT in fish sauce, pork stock (or water), and lots of black pepper is a family classic that my grandmother and aunts taught my mother when we lived in Phnom Penh. Easy to make, it is perfect for a quick lunch or dinner. For a mildly spicy flavor, I often add crushed garlic and sliced ginger, the latter sometimes julienned for a more assertive character. The dish is very satisfying when served over jasmine rice, and all you need on the side for a balanced meal is some pickled crunchy vegetables or stir-fried tender greens.

Bring the pork stock and fish sauce to a boil over high heat. Reduce the heat to medium-low. Add the sugar, garlic, ginger, black pepper, and pork, cover the pot, and simmer for about 1½ hours. The pork should be fork-tender. Serve the pork over rice, drizzling each serving with some of the braising liquid.

CA PHAO KHO
BRAISED PORK AND
EGGPLANT

SERVES 4 TO 6

6 ASIAN EGGPLANTS or 2 medium
   to large PURPLE EGGPLANTS
1 tablespoon VEGETABLE OIL
3 large GARLIC CLOVES, crushed,
   peeled, and minced
1 large SHALLOT, peeled and
   minced
12 ounces GROUND PORK or BEEF
   (70 percent lean)
2 tablespoons FISH SAUCE
KOSHER SALT
Freshly ground BLACK PEPPER

PORK AND EGGPLANT are used in nearly equal quantities in this South-east Asian dish. The charred eggplant lends a delicious smoky flavor, breaking down to a chunky puree consistency not unlike Middle Eastern baba ghanoush. This recipe is enjoyed both by Cambodians, who call it *cha traop dot*, and Vietnamese, who call it *ca phao kho*.

You can use Asian eggplants or the larger, meatier eggplants. My mother makes a version of the dish with beef rather than pork. Try both.

1. Char the eggplants over an open flame on medium-high heat until the skin turns black all around. Enclose the eggplants in a paper bag or aluminum foil until cool enough to handle. Peel off the skin and cut the eggplants into 1-inch chunks.

2. Heat the oil in a clay pot or heavy-bottomed pot over medium heat. Add the garlic and shallot and stir-fry until golden, 3 to 5 minutes. Add the ground meat and stir-fry, breaking up the meat, about 7 minutes. Reduce the heat to medium-low; add the eggplants and fish sauce. Braise, partially covered, until the eggplants have cooked down but are still slightly chunky, 45 minutes to 1 hour, stirring occasionally so nothing sticks to the bottom. Adjust seasoning to taste with salt and pepper, and serve with rice on the side.

GAENG HAENG LEI MUU
CHIANG MAI PORK CURRY

SERVES 4 TO 6

1 tablespoon VEGETABLE OIL

1 large GARLIC CLOVE, crushed, peeled, and minced

1 large SHALLOT, peeled and minced

1½ teaspoons HAENG LEI POWDER

1 tablespoon THAI RED CURRY PASTE (page 82); or commercial equivalent

1 tablespoon THAI or INDONESIAN SHRIMP PASTE

1 tablespoon PALM SUGAR

2 pounds PORK BUTT or SHOULDER, cubed

4 cups BASIC PORK STOCK (page 118)

4 KAFFIR LIME LEAVES, lightly bruised

1 LEMONGRASS STALK, root end trimmed, outer leaves and tough green top removed, and 6-inch-long inner bulb crushed

2 ASIAN EGGPLANTS, quartered lengthwise and cut into 1-inch-long pieces

4 YARD-LONG BEANS, ends trimmed and cut into 1-inch-long pieces

24 THAI BASIL LEAVES

I HAVE ALWAYS ASSOCIATED Thai curries with coconut milk, but I recently discovered that cooks in Chiang Mai (northern Thailand) also make simple water- or stock-based curries such as *haeng lei* curries. In this dish red curry paste is combined with a *haeng lei* spice powder, which is easily made by finely grinding equal amounts of the following dried spices: coriander, cumin, turmeric, and mace. (In a pinch you can use Indian curry powder.) Following the same principle as in making coconut curries, the spice base (powder and paste) is stir-fried with shrimp paste and palm sugar prior to adding any water, stock, or meat.

You can use chicken, beef, or duck instead of pork if you wish.

1. Heat the oil in a clay pot or heavy-bottomed pot over medium heat. Stir-fry the garlic and shallot until golden, 3 to 5 minutes. Add the *haeng lei* powder and stir-fry until fragrant, about 2 minutes. Add the curry paste, shrimp paste, and palm sugar and continue to stir until the paste darkens, 2 to 3 minutes more. Add the pork, stir-frying to coat the pieces evenly, then add the stock, kaffir lime leaves, lemongrass, eggplant, and beans.

2. Reduce the heat to medium-low and braise until the pork is fork-tender, 1 to 1½ hours. Add the Thai basil leaves, cover the pot for 5 minutes, and serve hot with jasmine rice on the side.

PIONG DUKU BABI
SPICED PORK IN LEAVES

MAKES 24 ROLLS

1 tablespoon VEGETABLE OIL

3 large GARLIC CLOVES, peeled and minced

2 large SHALLOTS, peeled and minced

½ ounce fresh GINGER, peeled and finely grated

½ ounce GALANGAL, peeled and finely grated

3 RED THAI CHILIES, stemmed, seeded, and minced

1 teaspoon CORIANDER SEED POWDER

2 ripe PLUM TOMATOES, blanched, peeled, seeded, and minced

2 tablespoons unsweetened COCONUT CREAM (page 77); or commercial equivalent

8 ounces GROUND PORK (70 percent lean)

8 ounces PORK LIVER, finely chopped

KOSHER SALT

Freshly ground BLACK PEPPER

24 medium GRAPE LEAVES, soaked, rinsed, drained, and any hard stems trimmed

VEGETABLE OIL for grilling

INDONESIAN SWEET SOY SAUCE

BAMBOO SKEWERS, soaked in water for 20 minutes

I N BALI, PORK IN ALL ITS PARTS is widely used. Indonesian food expert Sri Owen writes about *piong duku babi*, a recipe that combines pork meat, offal, and blood with crushed tomatoes, onion, garlic, chilies, ginger, and galangal, which is cooked inside a bamboo culm over an open fire. Bamboo culms for cooking are difficult to find, and the papaya leaves included as an alternative in the recipe are not readily available in the United States. In fact, I have never seen them anywhere. I use grape leaves, but rather than chop these and mix them with the ground pork, as the original recipe suggests, I use the leaves to wrap the pork. The results are a very reasonable adaptation of the admittedly exotic *piong duku babi*.

Grape leaves are easily found in the international section of any supermarket. They are usually imported from Greece. Be sure to soak the leaves for 30 minutes to get rid of the salty brine flavor prior to using them. Repeat the process if the leaves are still briny.

1. Heat the oil in a wok over high heat. Stir-fry the garlic, shallots, ginger, galangal, chilies, and coriander powder until the garlic and shallots are golden, 5 to 7 minutes. Add the tomatoes and coconut cream and cook until any liquid has evaporated, about 10 minutes more. Transfer the mixture to a plate and allow to cool completely.

2. Mix together the ground pork and liver with salt and pepper to taste until well combined. Add the tomato mixture and combine well.

3. Place a grape leaf so the pointy end faces you. Put a heaping tablespoon of the meat mixture in the center and fold the pointy end of the leaf over the meat. Fold in the sides and continue to roll to enclose the filling. (It should look like a spring roll.) Repeat the process, using up the leaves and meat. You should have roughly 24 rolls, depending on the size of the leaves. Try to select leaves of the same size for presentation.

4. Depending on the length of the skewers, slide 4 to 6 grape leaf rolls crosswise onto each skewer. Grill over a barbecue, or on a well-oiled nonstick pan (or grill pan) over medium-high heat, about 3 minutes per side. Serve with Indonesian sweet soy sauce on the side for dipping.

TOEJI KOGI KUI
SPICY GRILLED PORK

3 tablespoons KOREAN or JAPANESE
  DARK SOY SAUCE

3 tablespoons SAKE

3 tablespoons GINGER EXTRACT
  (page 74)

2 tablespoons SWEET AND SOUR
  CHILI DIPPING SAUCE
  (page 105)

1 SCALLION, root and dark green
  ends trimmed, and 6-inch stalk
  minced

1 large GARLIC CLOVE, crushed,
  peeled, and minced

2 teaspoons SESAME OIL

Freshly ground BLACK PEPPER

2 pounds PORK BUTT, sliced paper
  thin against the grain

I NEVER GET TIRED OF KOREAN barbecued meat. The beef known as *bulgogi* may be the most popular barbecued (or broiled) meat ordered in Korean restaurants, but the pork versions described here are also absolutely delicious. Like the beef, the thinly sliced pork butt is marinated with sweet and sour chili sauce, in addition to soy sauce and herbs such as garlic, ginger, and scallions. Pork ribs, called *toeji kalbi kui*, are similarly prepared (see variation). These, however, are roasted to render the fat prior to broiling or barbecuing. Both versions of the pork (thinly sliced butt or ribs) are barbecued until crispy on the edges, then served with tender lettuce leaves for wrapping the morsels. Use a spicy vinegar sauce (page 93) for dipping. Serve with kimchi and rice on the side, as well as a basic pork stock garnished with thinly sliced scallion and flavored with a dash of sesame oil for sipping during the meal.

To slice the meat paper thin, freeze it for 30 to 45 minutes. While you may think the amount of marinade to be insufficient, I assure you it is fine; all you want to do is stain the meat, as with many Asian recipes that season meat or seafood with marinades.

1. Whisk together the soy sauce, sake, ginger extract, chili sauce, scallion, garlic, sesame oil, and black pepper. Add the pork, tossing it with your hands to make sure it is evenly coated on all sides. Cover the bowl with plastic wrap and refrigerate for 30 minutes.

2. Grill the pork slices flat on a table hibachi. If using a grill pan, brush a generous amount of oil on the cooking surface and heat it over medium-high heat. When it starts to smoke, add the pork slices and grill to your preferred doneness, but probably no more than a minute on each side, so the pork remains tender.

Variation: For pork country ribs, preheat the oven to 450°F. Mix 2 tablespoons Korean or Japanese dark soy sauce and 2 tablespoons ginger extract and rub over ribs. Refrigerate, covered, for 30 minutes. Place the ribs on a rack over a roasting pan containing about ½ inch of water. Roast for about 20 minutes to render the fat. Score the ribs; brush with the marinade (step 1). Roast until tender, about 30 minutes, basting every 10 minutes.

JAPANESE PULLED PORK

SERVES 4 TO 6

2 pounds cooked PORK RIBS
    (from BASIC PORK STOCK,
    page 118), finely shredded

3 tablespoons MIRIN

3 tablespoons JAPANESE DARK SOY
    SAUCE

3 tablespoons JAPANESE SEASONED
    RICE VINEGAR

1 teaspoon SESAME OIL

2 teaspoons VEGETABLE OIL

1½ ounces fresh GINGER, peeled
    and julienned

3 SCALLIONS, root and dark green
    ends trimmed, and 6-inch stalks
    thinly sliced into rounds

WHENEVER I MAKE A PORK STOCK, I usually discard all the solids, but, remembering the recipe for Japanese double-cooked pork (pp. 468–69), I was inspired to shred the succulent cooked meat off the bones. The Japanese love subtlety, and so I thought I would try to make use of pork that had already lent much of its flavor to a stock. At this point the meat was incredibly tender and very mild in flavor—particularly well suited to a Japanese meal. Tossed with some mirin (sweet sake), soy sauce, rice vinegar, and a dash of sesame oil, then stir-fried with ginger and scallion, the crispy pork is delicious served over Japanese sushi rice with a side of pickled daikon.

If you have not made a pork stock, then simply cook the ribs in gently boiling water until the meat is fork-tender, about 1½ hours, in which case you might as well reserve the mild stock for other uses.

1. Toss the pork with the mirin, soy sauce, rice vinegar, and sesame oil in a bowl until well combined.

2. Heat the oil in a nonstick pan over medium-high heat. Add the pork, scatter the ginger and scallions, and stir-fry until slightly crispy, about 10 minutes. It is important to keep stir-frying so the pork does not burn. The high heat will crisp the meat and allow the excess juices to evaporate while creating a concentrated flavor.

WITH THIS RECIPE I had a chance to open a new bottle of Japanese dark soy sauce I had brought back from a trip to Japan. Brewed the old-fashioned way, in oak barrels, the soy sauce is velvety thick and rich, with a deep fermented soybean flavor, not to mention hints of oak on the finish. It is superb and unlike any other soy sauce I have ever tasted. A gift from Masuhiro Fukaya, a fifth-generation master brewer of organic soy sauce, the soy sauce is made at Sakae Soy Sauce Brewing in rural Osuka-cho, located between Tokyo and Kyoto. Describing the company founded by his family back in 1861, Fukaya said, "The formula for brewing my ancestors' soy sauce has never changed. The barrels I use are over a hundred years old. I use organic whole soybeans grown in Japan with no preservatives." When visiting the factory, I noticed the brewing soybeans were ebony black, grainy, soft, and thick, with a pungent aroma. "After the soybeans have undergone a steaming process," he explained, "mashed wheat, *kouji* [yeast], and salt brine are added, and the soybean mixture is barrel-fermented for no less than the period of one year before bottling." (By comparison, many mass-produced Japanese soy sauces are made with soy milk or tofu by-products—soybeans that have been crushed, then dried again—brewed in large stainless steel vats for only four months. The result is a thin, poorly flavored soy sauce.) The robust flavor of artisanal soy sauce is reminiscent of a vintage wine. Fukaya makes several types of soy sauces, including *koikuchi,* or dark soy sauce, for all-purpose use (this is the one I used in cooking the pulled pork); *usukuchi,* a light soy sauce that is the saltiest of all soy sauces and can be used for seasoning soups; and *saishikomi,* a twice-fermented soy sauce, which tends to be more expensive than other soy sauces. Tamari, made only of soybeans (no trace of wheat), has a sweet *miso*-like flavor that is perfect for eating with raw fish. In fact, Fukaya explained, "Tamari is the only true complement to sashimi, and it was the first soy sauce ever produced in Japan."

SAKAE SOY SAUCE BREWING, OWNED BY MASUHIRO FUKAYA, USES 100-YEAR-OLD OAK BARRELS TO PRODUCE A RICH ORGANIC SOY SAUCE SOUGHT AFTER BY MANY CONNOISSEURS.

JAPANESE SWEET AND SAVORY DOUBLE-COOKED PORK

SERVES 4 TO 6

1 quart pure SOY MILK; or whole COW'S MILK

2 pounds PORK BUTT, cut in 1½-inch cubes

1 DAIKON (about 1½ pounds), cut into ¾-inch-thick rounds

2 cups KONBU DASHI (pp. 124–25)

¼ cup SAKE

¼ cup HATCHOMISO (rice-free), or SHIROMISO (white miso)

1 tablespoon JAPANESE DARK SOY SAUCE

¼ cup MIRIN (sweet sake)

1 tablespoon GRANULATED SUGAR

1 ounce fresh GINGER, peeled and julienned

12 PEARL ONIONS, peeled

1 large bunch SPINACH, leaves only

3 medium to large CARROTS, peeled

S TEWS ARE MY FAVORITE FOODS because the ingredients have a chance to mingle slowly, creating very rich flavors. Served hot, braised dishes or stews, like soups, are a comfort food perfect for the cooler days of the year. In this pork dish, the pork is simmered in soy milk; this process eliminates any strong flavors, adds a mild soy flavor to the meat, and tenderizes it a bit. The pork butt or shoulder is then braised in *shiromiso*, or white *miso*, and sake, kelp *dashi*, ginger, and pearl onions. It is full of savory and sweet accents. The daikon rounds out the flavors of the cooking liquid and pork while taking on a beautiful golden color. The pearl onions, star-carved carrots, and rolled-up spinach leaves make a delicate presentation. While two pounds of pork is a lot of meat, when braising I often double the ingredients; the next day the meat tastes even better.

Pure soy milk can be found in the refrigerated food section of Asian markets. Soy milk available in health food stores tends to have added ingredients, particularly sugar, and therefore does not make a good substitute. If you do not have access to pure soy milk, use whole cow's milk instead.

1. Bring the soy milk to a gentle boil over medium heat. Add the pork and simmer for 20 minutes. Drain the pork.

2. Place the daikon slices in one layer across the bottom of a heavy-bottomed pot. Whisk together the *dashi*, sake, *shiromiso*, soy sauce, mirin, and sugar in a bowl until the sugar is completely dissolved. Add the pork, ginger, and pearl onions to the sauce and mix well, then scatter everything in an even layer on top of the daikon slices. Add ¼ cup water to the bowl and stir to collect the remaining bits of the sauce; add to the pot. Cover the pot with a lid and bring to a gentle boil over medium heat. Reduce the heat to low and simmer until the meat is fork tender, 1½ to 2 hours. There should be just enough liquid for braising the pork; the daikon should not turn into mush, although both will be very tender. Check every once in a while to see that the liquids have not completely evaporated. If they have, add ¼ cup water at a time.

3. Forty-five minutes before serving the pork, bring two pots of salted water to a boil over high heat. Blanch the spinach in one for about 5 seconds, and the carrots in the other until tender, about 3 minutes.

Drain the spinach completely and divide the leaves into 6 piles, rolling each into tight bundles, then halve crosswise. You should have 12 small rolls. Cut the carrots into ⅛-inch-thick diagonal slices. You can also cut carrots into ¼-inch rounds and carve these into 5-point stars if you wish.

4. With a spatula, carefully lift a thick and very tender slice of daikon with some pork and pearl onions onto each of 4 plates. Arrange 3 spinach bundles upright next to the pork with a few slices of carrot for each serving. Serve with short-grain rice on the side.

PLEAH SAIKO
RAW BEEF SALAD

Juice of 3 LIMES (about ½ cup)

¼ cup FISH EXTRACT (page 76); or
   FISH SAUCE

4 tablespoons GRANULATED SUGAR

1 LEMONGRASS STALK, root end
   trimmed, outer leaves and tough
   green top removed, and 6-inch-
   long inner bulb sliced into
   paper-thin rounds

1 large SHALLOT, peeled and thinly
   sliced

1 medium GARLIC CLOVE,
   crushed, peeled, and minced

1 pound TOP ROUND or FILET
   MIGNON, sliced paper thin
   against the grain (approximately
   ⅛-inch-thick by 1-inch-wide by
   2-inch-long slices)

1 cup MUNG BEAN SPROUTS, root
   ends trimmed

8 fresh MINT LEAVES, torn or
   julienned

8 fresh THAI BASIL LEAVES, torn or
   julienned

¼ cup roasted unsalted PEANUTS,
   finely crushed (not peanut
   butter)

THERE ARE MANY VERSIONS of raw beef salad made throughout Southeast Asia. What makes this one distinctly Khmer is *tuk prahoc*, Cambodian fermented fish extract, as opposed to milder fish sauce used in Vietnam, Laos, or Thailand. Technically, the beef is not exactly raw but cured and rare. (Curing is cooking without heat; acid from the lime juice and salt from the fermented fish sauce are curing agents.) If you feel uneasy about eating cured meat, simply sear the beef on all sides until brown outside and rosy red inside. Then slice it and proceed with the recipe. I encourage you to try the recipe the way it was intended, however.

Ask your butcher to slice the beef paper thin for you. If this is not possible, wrap the beef in plastic and place it in the freezer for thirty to forty-five minutes; this will allow you to slice the beef paper thin. If you use a Chinese cleaver instead of a chef's knife, the cleaver blade is so large you will only need to make one motion, top to bottom, instead of slicing back and forth.

1. Whisk together the lime juice, fish extract, and sugar in a bowl until the sugar is dissolved completely. Add the lemongrass, shallot, and garlic and allow the flavors to blend for 30 minutes. Divide the dressing into 2 portions. Toss the beef with one portion and allow to cure for 10 minutes at room temperature. Drain, pressing the beef gently between the palms of your hands.

2. Return the beef to the bowl. Add the bean sprouts, most of the mint and basil, and half the peanuts. Add the reserved portion of the dressing and toss well. Transfer the beef salad to a serving platter and garnish with the remaining mint, basil, and peanuts. Serve.

YUK HOE
RAW BEEF AND
ASIAN PEAR SALAD

SERVES 4 TO 6

2 tablespoons KOREAN or JAPANESE DARK SOY SAUCE

1 tablespoon GRANULATED SUGAR

1 or more teaspoons SESAME OIL

1 medium GARLIC CLOVE, crushed, peeled, and minced

1 SCALLION, root and dark green ends trimmed, and 6-inch stalk thinly sliced crosswise

12 ounces TOP ROUND or FILET MIGNON, lightly frozen and cut into 2-inch-long strips

4 ROMAINE LETTUCE LEAVES (young green ones)

1 ASIAN PEAR, peeled and julienned into 2-inch-long matchsticks

1 QUAIL EGG; or small CHICKEN EGG

1 tablespoon PINE NUTS, lightly roasted and finely crushed; or ½ teaspoon toasted SESAME SEEDS

SURPRISINGLY SIMPLE TO MAKE, this delicious salad is a refreshing and memorable appetizer. The beef, usually eye of round, is sliced into thin strips and marinated with a soy sauce, sesame oil, sugar, garlic, and scallion dressing. Asian (also Korean) pear adds a contrasting crisp and juicy character with a subtle floral note. The dish is often topped with a single raw quail egg (like the French *steak tartare*) and sprinkled with crushed pine nuts or toasted sesame seeds.

Sesame oil is often used sparingly in Asian cookery; in this recipe it is a foreground note. Add as desired, but in small increments. If you want a slightly more elegant dish, strain the sauce after it has steeped for 20 minutes and discard the solids, then use it to marinate the beef. If your Asian pear is juicy but not so sweet, julienne and marinate it in a bowl with equal amounts of sugar and water.

1. Whisk together the soy sauce and sugar in a bowl until the sugar is completely dissolved. Stir in the sesame oil, garlic, and scallion and allow the flavors to blend for about 20 minutes. (At this time, strain the dressing if you wish.) Add the beef and toss to coat evenly. Allow to marinate for 10 minutes, refrigerated.

2. Drain the beef completely. To serve, line a plate with the lettuce leaves, pointing the ribs toward the center. Mound the beef in the middle of the plate on top of the leaves. Around the beef scatter the julienned Asian pear, or toss the beef and pear together. Make a small well in the center and break the raw egg in it.* Sprinkle the pine nut powder or toasted sesame seeds and serve chilled.

* Consuming raw eggs carries the risk of contracting salmonella. Dishes containing raw eggs should not be eaten by the very young, the very old, pregnant women, or anyone with a compromised immune system. Consider using pasteurized eggs.

HONG SIU NGAW YOOK
SWEET BRAISED
BEEF OXTAIL AND TRIPE

SERVES 4 TO 6

⅓ cup GRANULATED SUGAR

½ cup CHINESE LIGHT SOY SAUCE

¼ cup CHINESE BLACK VINEGAR

3 ounces fresh GINGER, thinly
sliced lengthwise

4 large GARLIC CLOVES, crushed
and peeled

5 SCALLIONS, root and dark green
ends trimmed, and 6-inch stalks
halved crosswise and lightly
crushed

5 whole dried CHINESE RED
CHILIES

7 STAR ANISE

½ teaspoon FIVE-SPICE POWDER

2 pounds BEEF OXTAIL, cut in
1-inch-thick pieces; or SHORT
RIBS, cut in 2-inch-long pieces
through the bone

2 pounds HONEYCOMB BEEF
TRIPE, cut into 1-inch-square
pieces (optional)

THIS DISH IS DELICIOUSLY sweet and spicy. Braised for six to eight hours at a low heat in caramel and soy sauce, the meats are fork-tender. The Chinese black vinegar (somewhat reminiscent of Italian balsamic vinegar) gives a subtle tanginess to the dish. Served over rice with sautéed greens such as baby bok choy (page 320) on the side, this hearty dish is perfect, especially during the cooler months of the year.

Tripe and fatty beef tend to shrink quite a bit during the cooking process. For this reason I call for what might seem to be large quantities. In any case, leftovers are even better the next day. This stew is equally delicious when made with beef short ribs.

1. To make caramel, heat the sugar with 2 tablespoons water over medium heat until the sugar melts and becomes a rich golden color, 5 to 7 minutes. Remove the pot from the heat and carefully add the soy sauce, vinegar, and 1 quart water. Return the pot to the heat and allow the caramel to melt completely, about 5 minutes. Add the ginger, garlic, scallions, chilies, star anise, and five-spice powder. Reduce the heat to low, add the oxtail (or short ribs) and tripe (if using), and simmer until the meat and tripe are tender, about 6 hours; stir occasionally to expose the ingredients equally to the simmering juices. Skim most of the fat as it renders. Cool completely and refrigerate overnight.

2. Remove and discard the fat from the braised beef and tripe (and the loose large bones, if using short ribs), then reheat over low heat until hot, about 1 hour. Serve over steamy white rice with any sautéed green vegetable on the side.

Variations: For sweet braised beef tongue, follow the recipe, substituting one 4-pound beef tongue for the oxtail and tripe. Add 1 teaspoon sesame oil to the pot and braise the tongue until tender, about 4 hours. Transfer the tongue to a cutting board. Remove the tough skin and thinly slice the meat. Arrange the tongue on a platter and drizzle with braising liquid.

Dried shiitake mushrooms can be added to the dish for extra flavor and texture. Put about 12 small mushrooms in a bowl with hot water to cover, then set a plate over the bowl to prevent steam from escaping. Let stand until the mushrooms rehydrate and soften, about 30 minutes (or longer, depending on the size of the mushrooms). Squeeze the mushrooms between the palms of your hands to get rid of the excess water. Using a paring knife, remove any hard stems from the mushrooms, discarding the stems, and leave the caps whole (a sign of prosperity). Add to the pot at the same time as the meat and proceed with steps 1 and 2 of the recipe.

HAVING GROWN up in a French-Chinese family, I've enjoyed quite a few unusual foods. More and more, however, I see restaurants in major American cities offering dishes I once thought of as too exotic for mainstream dining. On the menus of New York City restaurants, for example, I see tripe (stomach) with increasing frequency. I've eaten it French style, cooked with onion, garlic, and *bouquet garni;* Italian style, in a tomato-based stew; and Chinese style, braised with soy sauce and sweetened with a caramel sauce. When you buy tripe from the butcher, be aware that there are various kinds. The one used in this recipe is the most common—honeycomb tripe. It is soaked in lime, then boiled, often in a vinegar-infused water called *court-bouillon,* a French technique employed to get rid of impurities. By the time you buy it, the tripe is white, and all you need to do is rinse, slice, and cook it as you like. If you are not confident that the butcher has done a good job of blanching, boil 2 quarts water and ½ cup vinegar over high heat, then add the tripe, reduce the heat to low, and simmer for an hour. Drain and proceed with step 1 of the recipe. No matter what the recipe, tripe must be cooked long enough to be tender. If it is still chewy, it isn't ready to be eaten.

KARE KARE
OXTAIL BRAISED IN
PEANUT SAUCE

SERVES 4 TO 6

4 pounds OXTAIL, cut into 1-inch-thick pieces; or BEEF SHORT RIBS, cut into 2-inch-long pieces through the bone

4 large GARLIC CLOVES, crushed and peeled

2 large SHALLOTS, peeled and quartered

3 ripe PLUM TOMATOES, blanched, peeled, halved, seeds removed, and diced

8 cups BASIC BEEF STOCK (page 120)

1 BAY LEAF

2 tablespoons FISH SAUCE

KOSHER SALT

Freshly ground BLACK PEPPER

¼ cup toasted RICE FLOUR (pp. 24–25)

1 cup roasted unsalted PEANUTS, powdered

12 YARD-LONG BEANS, cut into 1-inch-long pieces

MUCH FILIPINO FOOD is hearty, and this dish of oxtail braised in peanut sauce is a great example. *Kare kare*, like many Filipino dishes, is based on garlic and shallots. Bay leaves are added for a pungent floral note, while tomatoes add a beautiful reddish hue. If you think oxtail is too rich, you can use another meaty bone such as short ribs.

Be careful not to turn the peanuts into peanut butter when processing them. One cup of whole peanuts will yield about ¼ to ⅓ cup when finely ground. Powdered roasted peanuts are available in Asian markets.

1. Heat a heavy-bottomed pot over medium heat. Working in batches, add the beef and brown on all sides, about 20 minutes per batch. (I use no fat to brown the beef, as the oxtail renders enough fat to do the job; if using the leaner short ribs, however, you may want to add a tablespoon of oil.) Transfer the meat to a platter.

2. Stir-fry the garlic and shallots in the beef fat until golden, 3 to 5 minutes. Add the tomatoes to the pot and return the beef. Add the stock to cover and bring to a boil. Reduce the heat to medium-low, add the bay leaf and fish sauce, season with salt and pepper, and cook until the beef is fork-tender, about 6 hours.

3. Skim as much fat as you want off the top. With a slotted spoon, transfer the beef to a platter. Add the rice flour and peanuts to the pot and whisk until smooth. Add the yard-long beans and simmer until just tender, about 5 minutes. Return the beef to the pot. Mix to coat the pieces evenly. Simmer 10 minutes more, until the beans are tender and the sauce thickens. Serve with rice on the side.

LOC LAC
BEEF WITH LIME SAUCE

SERVES 4 TO 6

¼ cup MUSHROOM SOY SAUCE

1 teaspoon CHINESE DARK SOY
  SAUCE

¼ cup GRANULATED SUGAR

3 large GARLIC CLOVES, crushed,
  peeled, and minced

1 tablespoon freshly cracked
  BLACK PEPPER

1 tablespoon VEGETABLE OIL

1½ to 2 pounds BEEF SIRLOIN or
  FILET MIGNON, cut into ¾-inch
  cubes

Juice of 4 LIMES or LEMONS

3 tablespoons roasted unsalted
  PEANUTS, finely crushed (not
  peanut butter)

1 head BOSTON LETTUCE, leaves
  separated

BAMBOO SKEWERS, soaked for
  20 minutes (optional)

THIS REMARKABLE SKEWERED beef recipe is popular in both Cambodia and Vietnam. The cubes of sirloin or filet mignon marinate in mushroom soy sauce, cracked black pepper, sugar, and lots of pungent garlic. (This marinade is also used for quail; page 505). Sautéed or grilled, the fragrant, tender beef morsels are wrapped in tender lettuce leaves and dipped in tangy lime juice that has been sweetened with sugar and spiced with more black pepper and garlic. In Phnom Penh I enjoyed loc lac at Hotel Le Royal, where the specialty was served in a deep-fried taro basket (page 109) for a beautiful presentation.

If grilling on a barbecue, be sure to soak the bamboo skewers in water for twenty minutes prior to skewering the beef cubes.

1. Whisk together the mushroom and dark soy sauces, and 2 tablespoons of the sugar in a bowl until the sugar is completely dissolved. Stir in half the garlic and black pepper. Add the oil and the beef and toss to coat the meat thoroughly. Allow to marinate for 20 minutes. Heat the oil in a nonstick grill pan over high heat and grill the beef cubes for 15 to 30 seconds on each side.

2. Meanwhile, whisk together the lime juice with the remaining sugar in a bowl until the sugar is completely dissolved. Add the remaining garlic and black pepper and the crushed peanuts. To serve, place the beef cubes on a plate (or in one large or several small individual fried taro cups, if you wish) and the lettuce leaves on a separate plate, and divide the sauce among individual small bowls. Eat, wrapping some meat with a lettuce leaf and dipping the bundle in the sauce.

BO LA LOT
BEEF GRILLED IN LEAVES

12 ounces GROUND BEEF
  (70 percent lean)
1 large SHALLOT, peeled and
  minced
1 large GARLIC CLOVE, crushed,
  peeled, and minced
2 tablespoons finely ground
  LEMONGRASS BULB
2 teaspoons GRANULATED SUGAR
1 tablespoon FISH SAUCE
24 GRAPE LEAVES (choose leaves
  that are approximately the same
  size; medium is best)
VEGETABLE OIL for grilling
NUOC CHAM (page 100)

BAMBOO SKEWERS, soaked for
  20 minutes

WILD BETEL LEAVES, called *la lot* in Vietnamese, are vibrant green and heart-shaped and are used in a variety of brothy soups for a refreshing note. They are also used in the delicious northern specialty called *bo la lot*. Here, marinated ground beef is wrapped in *la lot* leaves prior to grilling, like tiny spring rolls. *La lot* leaves are occasionally but rarely found in Southeast Asian markets; as a result, many Vietnamese home cooks and restaurant chefs in the West use grape leaves as a substitute. These can be found packed in glass jars filled with brine in Middle Eastern markets or in the international food section of many supermarkets. Be sure to rinse the grape leaves in several changes of water to get rid of the salty brine flavor prior to using. Soak the bamboo skewers for twenty minutes before skewering the beef rolls.

Bo la lot is delicious grilled over natural wood charcoal, as is traditionally done in Vietnam.

1. Mix together the beef, shallot, garlic, lemongrass, sugar, and fish sauce in a bowl.

2. Rinse, drain, and pat dry the grape leaves. Put about 2 teaspoons beef mixture in the center of a leaf, slightly closer to the wider end. Fold the wider end over the filling, fold in the sides, then roll up carefully, making sure the filling is completely and tightly enclosed. Repeat the process with the remaining leaves and beef mixture.

3. Depending on how long the skewers are, slide 3 to 5 beef rolls crosswise onto each skewer. Heat a well-oiled nonstick grill pan over medium-high heat, and grill until cooked through, about 2 minutes per side. Serve with *nuoc cham* for dipping.

SAYUR BEBANCI
SPICY BEEF STEW WITH
GREEN COCONUT

SERVES 4 TO 6

1½ tablespoons VEGETABLE OIL

4 large SHALLOTS, peeled and minced

4 large GARLIC CLOVES, crushed, peeled, and minced

1 ounce fresh GINGER, peeled and finely grated

1 ounce GALANGAL, peeled and finely grated

1 ounce fresh TURMERIC, peeled and finely grated; or 2 teaspoons TURMERIC POWDER

4 to 6 THAI CHILIES, seeded (optional) and minced

5 CANDLENUTS or MACADAMIA NUTS, finely ground

1 tablespoon INDONESIAN or THAI SHRIMP PASTE

1 to 1½ tablespoons PALM SUGAR; or 1 tablespoon GRANULATED SUGAR

2 pounds BEEF CHUCK or SHIN, cut into 1-inch cubes

2 cups unsweetened COCONUT MILK with cream (page 77); or commercial equivalent

1 young GREEN COCONUT, juice reserved (usually 1½ to 2 cups), meat scraped with a teaspoon, then cut into ½-inch-wide by 1½-inch-long strips

KOSHER SALT

Freshly ground BLACK PEPPER

I DISCOVERED this Indonesian spicy beef and coconut stew in my travels to Jakarta a few years ago. It may have, in fact, originated there, where it is served at street-side food stalls and is considered by some to be an expression of the melting-pot culture centered in the city. It is called a soup (sayur), but its consistency is more like that of a stew. Laden with herbs including shallots, garlic, ginger, galangal, and chilies, and spices including cumin and coriander seeds, the stew is also seasoned with vibrant terasi (fermented shrimp paste). Rich with creamy coconut milk, and sweetened with palm sugar to tame its spiciness and saltiness, sayur bebanci offers beef garnished with strips of young green coconut meat. The coconut makes for a beautiful contrast against the tender beef and adds a texture that is velvety and crunchy at the same time.

1. Heat the oil in a large heavy-bottomed pot over medium heat. Stir-fry the shallots and garlic until lightly golden, 3 to 5 minutes. Add the ginger, galangal, turmeric, chilies, and candlenuts, and continue to stir-fry until fragrant and lightly golden, about 3 minutes. Add the shrimp paste and stir-fry to break it up and toast it, about 2 minutes. Add the palm sugar and stir to melt it thoroughly. Add the beef, stirring to coat the pieces evenly, and pour in the creamy coconut milk and young coconut juice. (You should have equal parts coconut milk to juice; make up the lack of coconut juice with regular water if necessary.)

2. Reduce the heat to medium-low, partially cover, and simmer until the meat is fork-tender and easily pulls apart, and the sauce has evaporated almost completely, leaving behind a thick sauce, about 6 hours. Adjust the seasoning with salt and pepper to taste.

3. Transfer the stew to a platter or individual plates and garnish with young coconut strips. Serve with rice and stir-fried yard-long beans on the side.

GYUNIKU NO NAGANEGI
BEEF AND SCALLION ROLLS

SERVES 4 TO 6

KOSHER SALT

16 SCALLIONS, root and dark green
  ends trimmed

1 cup DASHI (pp. 124–25)

½ cup MIRIN (sweet sake)

⅓ cup JAPANESE DARK SOY SAUCE

¼ cup SAKE

1 pound well-marbled BEEF, sliced
  paper thin into wide, long strips

VEGETABLE OIL for grilling

SANSHO PEPPER

Toasted SESAME SEEDS

KITCHEN STRING

RELATIVELY EASY TO MAKE, these beef and scallion rolls are flavored with soy sauce, sake, and mirin (sweet sake). The paper-thin slices of beef should be well marbled to keep the meat and the scallions moist while cooking. To cut the beef into thin slices, partially freeze the meat, or buy pre-sliced marbled beef at Asian markets (Japanese, Korean, and Chinese). You will most likely find this item in the frozen foods section, next to chicken or pork sliced in a similar manner; either the chicken or the pork can be used as a substitute for the beef. Beef, however, will be the best complement for the generous amount of pungent scallions.

1. Bring a pot of salted water to a boil and blanch the scallions for 1 minute. Shock the scallions in an ice-water bath. Stir together the *dashi*, ¼ cup of the mirin, and 2 tablespoons of the soy sauce in a deep dish and add the scallions. Allow to marinate for 4 hours, refrigerated.

2. Stir together the remaining mirin, soy sauce, and sake in a bowl and set aside. Lay flat 4 strips of beef, overlapping them slightly to form a sheet 5 to 6 inches across. Pat dry the scallions and place 4 in the center of the beef sheet. The scallions should be roughly the length of the beef sheet. Roll the beef over the scallions until a uniform roll is formed. Repeat this process until you have finished the beef and scallions to make about 6 rolls. Tie the rolls with kitchen string so they do not fall apart. Place the rolls in a deep dish and pour the beef marinade on top.

3. Heat a well-oiled nonstick grill pan over high heat and grill the beef rolls until lightly crisp all around, about 6 minutes total. To serve, cut each roll into 5 or 6 equal pieces and stand them up (so the scallion is visible) on a plate. (You can also divide them among individual plates.) Sprinkle lightly with *sansho* pepper and toasted sesame seeds just before serving.

GYUNIKU NO MISO-ZUKE
MISO-MARINATED BEEF

SERVES 4 TO 6

½ cup AKAMISO (red miso)
⅓ cup MIRIN (sweet sake)
One 1½-pound, ¾-inch-thick
    SIRLOIN STEAK (Kobe beef
    optional)
3 medium GARLIC CLOVES,
    crushed and peeled
1 tablespoon VEGETABLE OIL
1 tablespoon SAKE
4 to 6 SHISO LEAVES, julienned

KOBE BEEF IS THE FATTIEST, most expensive, and arguably the tastiest beef in the world; the cows are fed beer and massaged with sake to render the meat tender and sweet. I've indulged in Kobe beef cut in bite-size chunks and simply grilled on a hibachi at Tokyo's Four Seasons Hotel, and I've enjoyed it marinated in the red miso called akamiso, a traditional way to prepare beef that goes back to the nineteenth century. I must say that beef marinated in miso is by far one of the most exciting beef dishes I have ever tried, and, surprisingly, it is simple to execute. Serve this dish with pickled or grilled eggplant and sushi rice on the side.

1. Whisk together the akamiso and ¼ cup of the mirin in a bowl until well combined. Rub the steak generously all over with garlic. Place half the marinade evenly across the bottom of a rectangular dish big enough for the steak to fit in. Place a double layer of cheesecloth on top. Place the steak on top and cover with another double layer of cheesecloth. Spread the remaining marinade on top of the cheesecloth. Cover the dish with plastic wrap and allow the steak to marinate for 4 hours, refrigerated.

2. Remove the steak from the refrigerator and allow to come to room temperature, about 1 hour. Heat the oil in a large skillet over high heat (tilt the skillet or use a brush to spread the oil evenly). Lift the cheesecloth with the miso marinade, reserving 3 tablespoons in a bowl and discarding the rest. Sear the steak until crisp on the outside and rare to medium rare on the inside, 2 to 5 minutes on each side. Or cook steak to desired doneness. Transfer the steak to a cutting board and allow to rest for 10 minutes.

3. Deglaze the skillet with the remaining mirin and a tablespoon of water over medium heat. Add the sake and cook until the alcohol evaporates, about 2 minutes. Stir in the reserved miso marinade, bring to a boil, and stir for a minute. Remove from the heat. Thinly slice the steak against the grain and divide among individual plates. Serve with sauce on the side, and garnish with julienned shiso.

BULGOGI
BARBECUED BEEF

SERVES 4 TO 6

¼ cup JAPANESE or KOREAN DARK
 SOY SAUCE

3 tablespoons GRANULATED SUGAR

1 tablespoon VEGETABLE OIL, plus
 more for grilling

1 teaspoon SESAME OIL

1 teaspoon toasted SESAME SEEDS

3 medium GARLIC CLOVES,
 crushed, peeled, and grated

3 SCALLIONS, root and dark green
 ends trimmed, and 6-inch stalks
 minced

2 pounds marbled SIRLOIN or RIB
 STEAK, sliced paper thin against
 the grain

BESIDES KIMCHI (PICKLED VEGETABLES), *bulgogi* (barbecued beef) is perhaps one of the most popular Korean foods in the West. A soy and herbal marinade is the key to this tasty beef dish, but like many Asian marinades, only a small amount of liquid is used to flavor the meat. Grilled over a hibachi or in a grill pan, or stir-fried, until crisp (or to preferred doneness), the beef is wrapped in a tender lettuce leaf and may be eaten with a dab of pungent fermented Korean bean paste.

You will find thinly sliced beef, chicken, or pork in Japanese, Korean, and Chinese butcher shops. If you do not have these near you, ask your local butcher if he or she can slice the meat for you. If not, buy a large chunk and place it in the freezer for forty-five minutes to facilitate the slicing. Slice against the grain while the meat is still frozen.

1. Whisk together the soy sauce and sugar in a bowl until the sugar is dissolved completely. Stir in the vegetable and sesame oils, sesame seeds, garlic, and scallions until well combined. Add the beef, tossing it with your hands to make sure it is evenly coated on all sides. Cover the bowl with plastic wrap and refrigerate it, allowing the meat to marinate for 30 minutes. Drain the beef, shaking off the excess liquid and scraping off the scallion and garlic.

2. Grill the beef, laying the slices flat on a table hibachi. If using a grill pan, brush a generous amount of vegetable oil on the cooking surface and heat it over medium-high heat. When it starts to smoke, add the beef slices and grill to your preferred doneness, but no more than

5 seconds on each side, so the beef remains tender.

Variation: Japanese *sukiyaki*, pan-seared beef, is similar to *bulgogi*. Mix together in a bowl 1 teaspoon tapioca starch, 2 tablespoons Japanese dark soy sauce, 1 teaspoon sesame oil, 1 tablespoon sake, and 1 tablespoon sugar. Add 1 pound thinly sliced beef sirloin and mix well. (There is just enough marinade; the beef should not be drowning.) Marinate for 30 minutes. Heat 1 tablespoon beef suet in a pan over high heat. Sear the beef until done, about 5 seconds per side.

KALBI TCHIM
BRAISED BEEF SHORT RIBS
WITH WINTER NUTS

SERVES 4 TO 6

⅓ cup KOREAN or JAPANESE DARK
   SOY SAUCE

¼ cup SAKE

¼ cup GRANULATED SUGAR

2 tablespoons HONEY

1 tablespoon SESAME OIL

1 small ONION, peeled and minced

6 SCALLIONS, root and dark green
   ends trimmed, and 6-inch stalks;
   1 minced, and 5 quartered
   crosswise

6 large GARLIC CLOVES; 5 crushed
   and peeled, 1 minced

Freshly ground BLACK PEPPER

3 pounds BEEF SHORT RIBS, cut
   crosswise into 2-inch pieces
   through the bone

½ pound DAIKON, peeled and cut
   into 1-inch cubes

12 CHESTNUTS, boiled long
   enough to facilitate peeling

12 GINGKO NUTS, shelled

12 large fresh SHIITAKE
   MUSHROOMS, stems removed,
   caps quartered

Toasted SESAME SEEDS

THIS SUCCULENT KOREAN braised-beef short-rib dish is delectable and perfect for lunch or dinner. The meat is flavored with soy sauce, sugar, scallions, honey, sake, and sesame oil, making for a well-rounded salty, sweet, spicy, and nutty dish. The short rib (the trimmed part of English-cut prime rib) is a delicious cut of meat, with enough fat to tenderize during the slow cooking process, and enough bone to deepen the flavor of the dish. Chestnuts and gingko nuts make *kalbi tchim* a perfect fall or winter item. The fresh shiitake mushrooms and daikon offer a tender and crunchy texture, complementing the starchiness of the nuts.

1. Whisk together the soy sauce, sake, and sugar in a bowl until the sugar is completely dissolved. Stir in the honey and sesame oil and continue to stir until smooth. Add the onion, minced scallion and minced garlic, and season with black pepper to taste. Score the beef ribs every ½ inch, place them in a deep dish, and pour the marinade over them. Be sure each piece of rib is well coated with marinade, especially between the cuts. Allow to marinate for 4 hours, refrigerated.

2. Transfer the beef ribs into a heavy-bottomed pot with the marinade and 1 quart water. Add the cut scallions and crushed garlic. Cook over medium-low heat, partially covered, for 6 hours. Add the daikon, chestnuts, and gingko nuts and continue to cook for 30 minutes. Add the mushrooms and cook for an additional 15 minutes. At this point both the beef and daikon should be fork-tender. Transfer to a serving platter or serve on individual plates garnished with toasted sesame seeds.

Variation: For making *toeji kalbi kangjong*, the pork version of this dish, substitute for the beef 2 pounds pork country ribs or butt cut into 2-inch pieces. Follow the recipe, but do not score the meat in step 1, and skip the chestnuts and gingko nuts entirely. Instead, add 3 or more tablespoons of sweet and sour chili dipping sauce (page 105) to the braising liquid.

BO KHO CA ROT
SPICY BEEF AND
CARROT STEW

SERVES 4 TO 6

¼ cup FISH SAUCE

¼ teaspoon FIVE-SPICE POWDER

2 tablespoons GRANULATED SUGAR

3 to 4 pounds SHORT RIBS or SHIN,
cut crosswise into 2-inch pieces;
or OXTAIL, cut into 2-inch-wide
round pieces by a butcher

1 tablespoon VEGETABLE OIL

4 large GARLIC CLOVES, crushed
and peeled

6 large SHALLOTS, peeled

3 ounces fresh GINGER, thinly
sliced lengthwise

2 cups young GREEN COCONUT
WATER; or BASIC or SOUTHEAST
ASIAN BEEF STOCK (pp. 120
and 121, respectively)

2 LEMONGRASS STALKS, root ends
trimmed, outer leaves and tough
green tops removed, and 6-inch-
long inner bulbs lightly crushed

5 STAR ANISE

1 piece of CASSIA BARK (or
CINNAMON STICK), about
4 inches long

6 dried RED CHILIES

2 tablespoons ANNATTO SEED
WATER (page 12; optional)

3 large CARROTS, peeled and cut
crosswise into ½-inch-thick
diagonal slices

MODELED AFTER THE CLASSIC French dish called *boeuf aux carottes*, this Vietnamese spicy beef and carrot stew is sweet, savory, and spicy with ginger, garlic, lemongrass, cinnamon, star anise, and chilies. Perfectly balanced, it is especially delicious when made with oxtail or beef short ribs, in which the meat, fat, and bone each contribute to the dish's rich flavor. *Bo kho ca rot* is especially wonderful with jasmine rice and stir-fried greens such as peppery watercress.

Do not be alarmed at the amount of meat used; much of it is bone. Ask your butcher to cut the oxtail or short ribs into the manageable-size pieces called for here.

1. Whisk together the fish sauce, five-spice powder, and sugar in a dish until the sugar is completely dissolved. Add the beef pieces, rubbing them well with the marinade to coat evenly. Allow to marinate for 4 to 6 hours, refrigerated.

2. Heat the oil in a heavy-bottomed pot over medium heat. Stir-fry the garlic, shallots, and ginger until fragrant and golden, 5 to 10 minutes. Add the meat and its marinade to the pot, with the coconut water (or beef stock). Reduce the heat to medium-low, add the lemongrass, star anise, cassia bark, chilies, and annatto seed water, and simmer, covered, for 4 to 6 hours. Add the carrots and continue braising until the meat falls off the bones and the carrots are tender, about 30 minutes more. Transfer to a platter and serve hot.

NG HEUNG YEUNG YOOK DOUBLE-COOKED FIVE-SPICE LAMB

SERVES 4 TO 6

¼ cup CHINESE LIGHT SOY SAUCE

2 tablespoons CHINESE DARK THICK SOY SAUCE

1 tablespoon FIVE-SPICE POWDER

2 tablespoons GRANULATED SUGAR

3 to 4 pounds LAMB BREASTS

2 ounces fresh GINGER, thinly sliced lengthwise

5 SCALLIONS, trimmed and halved

1 large YELLOW ONION, peeled

1 pound DAIKON, peeled and cut into 1-inch-thick rounds

3 CARROTS, peeled and halved

VEGETABLE OIL for deep-frying

4 to 6 sprigs CILANTRO

THIS FIVE-SPICE-FLAVORED lamb recipe is Mongol–northern Chinese in origin. The wonderful spices—star anise, cassia bark, Szechwan peppercorns, fennel, and cloves, among others—are a perfect complement to the strong-tasting meat. A generous amount of ginger is included to aid digestion. In this recipe, lamb breast is marinated overnight, boiled, then deep-fried, a process that both flavors and tenderizes the meat.

1. Whisk together the light and dark soy sauces, five-spice powder, and sugar in a bowl until the sugar is completely dissolved. Rub the marinade on both sides of the lamb breasts and refrigerate, covered, for at least 12 hours or overnight.

2. Place the meat in a pot and add the ginger, scallions, onion, daikon, and carrots. Cover with water to about an inch above the ingredients and bring to a boil over high heat. Reduce the heat to medium-low and gently boil until the meat is fork-tender, 1 to 1½ hours. Use tongs to retrieve the lamb breasts and place them on a cutting board. Separate each rib with a cleaver or knife. Place the ribs in a colander set over a plate to drain the meat completely.

3. Heat enough oil for deep-frying over medium heat. When the temperature reaches 360° to 375°F, deep-fry the lamb pieces until crisp all around, about 3 minutes. Serve hot, garnished with cilantro.

KAMBING KARE
SPICE ISLAND CURRIED GOAT

SERVES 4 TO 6

2 pounds GOAT or LAMB, boneless leg or shoulder, cut into 1-inch cubes

1 tablespoon VEGETABLE OIL

½ cup BASE GEDE (page 80)

1 teaspoon CORIANDER SEEDS, finely ground

½ teaspoon freshly grated NUTMEG

¼ teaspoon CLOVE POWDER

Freshly ground BLACK PEPPER

2 LEMONGRASS STALKS, root ends trimmed, outer leaves and tough green tops removed, and 6-inch-long inner bulbs halved crosswise and lightly crushed

1 cup unsweetened COCONUT MILK (page 77); or commercial equivalent

KOSHER SALT

I ALWAYS THOUGHT OF CURRIED GOAT as a Jamaican specialty, but the Indonesians also have a delicious version called *kambing kare* (sometimes *gulai kambing*) in Java, and *kambing mekuah* in Bali. You will most likely have to order the goat from your butcher several days in advance, or you can use lamb as a substitute. The leg and shoulder are perfect parts for the recipe, as they tend to stay tender after long periods of cooking. *Base gede*, the Indonesian meat spice paste—fragrant with herbs including lemongrass, shallots, garlic, and chilies, and spices such as coriander and turmeric—is key to this delicious stew. The turmeric lends a beautiful yellow color to the dish, and the coconut adds richness to the sauce.

1. Bring a large pot of water to a boil over high heat and add the goat or lamb. Bring back to a boil and cook for 15 minutes. Drain the meat. This process gets rid of any impurities and strong smell often associated with the meat.

2. Heat the oil in a clay pot or heavy-bottomed pot over medium heat. Add the *base gede*, coriander, nutmeg, clove powder, and pepper to taste, and stir-fry until fragrant and darkened, about 5 minutes. Add the goat (or lamb), lemongrass, coconut milk, and 2 cups water. Adjust seasoning with salt and pepper. Cover the pot, reduce the heat to medium-low, and cook until the meat falls off the bones or shreds easily, 4 to 6 hours. (Stir the meat once in a while to make sure it is coated with sauce.)

KALDARETA
SPICY FILIPINO-STYLE
LAMB STEW

SERVES 4 TO 6

2 pounds boneless LEG OF LAMB, cut into 1½-inch cubes

2 cups good dry RED TABLE WINE; or 1 cup dry SHERRY

½ cup COCONUT VINEGAR or CHINESE WHITE RICE VINEGAR

2 tablespoons VEGETABLE OIL

6 large GARLIC CLOVES, crushed and peeled

1 medium YELLOW ONION, sliced into thin wedges

6 ripe PLUM TOMATOES, blanched, peeled, seeded, and chopped

2 GREEN BELL PEPPERS, charred, peeled, stems and cores removed, and julienned

1 teaspoon CAYENNE PEPPER

1 BAY LEAF

2 teaspoons PAPRIKA

2 tablespoons TOMATO PASTE

1 cup small GREEN OLIVES, with or without pits, rinsed

KOSHER SALT

Freshly ground BLACK PEPPER

THE MOUNTAIN TRIBES of Luzon in the northern Philippines are responsible for some of the heartiest traditional Filipino stews. The most classic are *pinakbet* (page 336), a crispy pork belly and vegetable stew; and this spicy lamb stew, *kaldareta*. This is the only way Filipino cooks traditionally prepare lamb, mutton, or goat. The meat is first marinated in alcohol—some cooks use red wine, others use dry sherry—and coconut vinegar or rice vinegar. The acidity tames the strong flavors associated with the meat. The meat is browned prior to braising it with tomatoes, which give the stew a nice reddish hue; green olives; bell peppers; and the ever-present pungent garlic and onion. The result is a delicious and rich braised lamb dish that is perfect served in winter.

There are various types of small green olives to choose from; my favorite are the French Picholines. If using wine, remember that if it is not good enough to drink, it is not good enough for cooking. To prepare the bell peppers, char the peppers over an open flame until blackened. Place in a paper bag or wrap them in foil for twenty minutes to facilitate peeling.

1. Marinate the lamb with the red wine or sherry and vinegar at least 12 hours or overnight, refrigerated. Drain the meat but reserve the marinade. Heat the oil in a heavy-bottomed pot over high heat. Working in batches, brown the lamb pieces on all sides, about 15 minutes total for each batch. Transfer the meat to a plate.

2. Add the garlic and onion and cook until golden, about 5 minutes. Reduce the heat to medium-low, add the tomatoes, bell peppers, cayenne pepper, bay leaf, paprika, tomato paste, and olives. Add 2 cups water, place the lid on top, and braise, stirring the meat occasionally. Adjust the seasoning to taste with salt and pepper, and continue to braise until the meat is fork-tender, 4 to 6 hours.

JIEU GAI
DRUNKEN CHICKEN

SERVES 4 TO 6

1½ pounds CHICKEN BREAST
  (on or off the bone), whole
  breasts split in half
1 tablespoon KOSHER SALT
Freshly ground WHITE PEPPER
1 ounce fresh GINGER, peeled and
  julienned lengthwise
2 SCALLIONS, root and dark green
  ends trimmed, and 6-inch stalks
  cut into 1½-inch-long pieces
  and julienned
1 cup SHAOXING WINE, or more
4 sprigs CILANTRO, stems trimmed

THIS CHICKEN AND RICE wine recipe takes no time to make, yet it packs a lot of flavor. I usually use only the breast meat for this dish, as it looks beautiful when sliced. The chicken is steamed with ginger, scallions, and salt, "drowned" in wine, then chilled. The salt is especially wonderful against the sweet character of the wine. *Jieu gai* is often served along with Chinese cold cuts during special banquets.

When selecting Shaoxing wine, be sure the label does not read "cooking wine," which is seasoned and will alter the recipe. Use the rice wine that is fit for drinking (e.g., Pagoda brand), and season as indicated. I usually follow tradition and keep the skin on the chicken; feel free to remove it if you prefer.

1. Set a bamboo steamer with a lid over a wok filled halfway with water and bring the water to a boil over high heat. Meanwhile, season the chicken with half the salt and some pepper, place the chicken, skin side up, on a plate, and scatter the ginger and scallions across the top to cover the breasts. When the steamer is filled with hot steam, place the plate with the chicken on top of the bamboo rack. Secure the steamer lid on top and steam until the juices run clear, about 20 minutes.

2. Discard the ginger and scallions and place the chicken breasts on a cutting board. Season the chicken with the remaining salt and cut the breast halves crosswise into ½-inch-wide pieces. Reconstitute the breasts and place them skin side down inside a small rice bowl. They should fit very snugly, one on top of the other, the skin always facing down. Place the bowl on top of a plate and pour the Shaoxing wine over the chicken to cover. Place another bowl on top of the chicken with a foil-wrapped brick (or can) to weight the chicken down.

3. Refrigerate for 24 hours. To serve, turn the chicken out onto a plate; hold the bowl in place and in the center of the plate while draining the wine marinade over a sink. Place the plate on a flat surface and lift the bowl to reveal the chicken mound with the skin facing up. With a clean kitchen towel, blot any wine marinade remaining on the plate and around the chicken. Garnish with cilantro sprigs.

SHANGHAINESE FIVE-SPICE FRIED CHICKEN

SERVES 4 TO 6

VEGETABLE OIL or PEANUT OIL for
  deep-frying
2 teaspoons FIVE-SPICE POWDER
2 teaspoons KOSHER SALT
2 teaspoons freshly ground BLACK
  PEPPER
¼ cup TAPIOCA STARCH or
  CORNSTARCH
4 to 6 CHICKEN LEGS, thighs and
  drumsticks joined

DURING THE WINTER I like to go to one of my favorite hole-in-the-wall restaurants in New York City's Chinatown. With its six tables set snugly against the wall of a long, narrow room, and a tiny kitchen and take-out cash register in an adjoining corridor, you would miss it completely if you did not know it was there. Its menu is limited, but it has two stellar dishes: deep-fried chicken legs; and pork chops seasoned with five-spice powder, salt, and pepper. These are cooked in a vat of boiling oil until very crispy and served over a great big bowl of white rice topped with pork and cabbage relish (page 452). Whether you sit shoulder-to-shoulder with the Asian patrons in the restaurant or scurry home with overflowing take-out containers, you are eating what I call Chinese soul food.

1. Heat enough vegetable oil for deep-frying in a pot over medium-high heat. Meanwhile, mix together the five-spice powder, salt, pepper, and tapioca starch in a bag. Add the chicken legs and seal and shake the bag until the pieces are evenly coated.

2. When the oil reaches 360° to 375°F, carefully add the chicken legs and fry until golden crisp on all sides, 15 to 20 minutes. Drain on paper towels. Serve with jasmine rice topped with pork and cabbage relish.

Variation: Substitute four to six ½-inch-thick pork chops (bone-in) for the chicken legs and proceed with the recipe, deep-frying until crispy and golden, about 5 minutes per side. I have also used squab for this recipe and it is absolutely delicious. If you wish to try it, substitute 4 to 6 small squabs for the chicken, and cook until crispy, 15 to 20 minutes.

HONGZAO GAI
RED-COOKED CHICKEN

SERVES 4 TO 6

1 ounce dried TIGER LILIES

12 dried medium to large SHIITAKE
MUSHROOMS; or 24 small ones

2 tablespoons CHINESE LIGHT SOY
SAUCE

2 tablespoons CHINESE DARK SOY
SAUCE

2 tablespoons OYSTER SAUCE

2 tablespoons SHAOXING WINE

1 teaspoon SESAME OIL

2 tablespoons GRANULATED SUGAR

One 2½-pound CHICKEN

1 tablespoon VEGETABLE OIL

3 large GARLIC CLOVES, crushed
and peeled

2 ounces fresh GINGER, thinly
sliced lengthwise

3 SCALLIONS, root and dark green
ends trimmed, and 6-inch stalks
halved crosswise

3 or more dried CHINESE RED
CHILIES

2 whole medium BAMBOO
SHOOTS, cut lengthwise into
¼-inch-thick wedges

RED-COOKED FOOD is a specialty of southern China and refers specifically to food (mostly meat and poultry) that has been cooked in a generous amount of soy sauce, giving the food a reddish-brown tone. This braised chicken dish, *hongzao gai*, is a family favorite. Because it includes copious amounts of shiitake mushrooms and bamboo shoots, it is not necessary to cook an additional vegetable dish to make a balanced meal. The chicken is simmered whole in its own juices accented by Shaoxing wine and soy and oyster sauces, and spiced with garlic, ginger, scallions, and chilies. Serve with jasmine rice.

This dish can easily be made only with chicken legs, but I also love to use a whole chicken, which makes for a beautiful presentation. This way, the chicken breast never dries out; the braising over low heat allows the bird's fat to moisten the meat throughout the cooking process. While red sticky rice paste is traditionally used in this dish for its deep red color, the soy sauces and the long braising result in a bird with a beautiful reddish-brown hue.

1. Put the tiger lilies and shiitakes in two separate bowls with hot water to cover, then set a plate over each bowl to prevent steam from escaping. Let stand until the lilies and mushrooms rehydrate and soften, about 30 minutes (or longer, depending on their size). Drain and rinse. Squeeze the lilies and mushrooms between the palms of your hands to get rid of the excess water. Using a sharp paring knife, remove any hard stem ends of the lilies and any hard stems of the mushrooms and discard. Tie each lily in a knot and cut the mushroom caps in half, using the medium to large ones, or leave whole if using the small ones. They should be bite-size.

2. Whisk together the light and dark soy sauces, oyster sauce, wine, sesame oil, and sugar in a bowl until the sugar dissolves completely. Add the chicken and marinate for 1 hour, turning the bird over every 15 minutes.

3. Place the oil with the garlic, ginger, and scallions in a heavy-bottomed pot over medium-low heat and stir-fry until the ingredients become fragrant and turn slightly golden, about 10 minutes. Increase the heat to medium, then add the mushrooms, marinade, chilies, a cup of water, and the bamboo shoots and bring to a boil. Reduce the heat to low and put the

chicken, breast side down, on top of the mushrooms and bamboo shoots. Cover the pot and braise for 45 minutes. Turn the chicken over (breast side up) and add the lilies. Cover and continue to braise, basting every 15 minutes, until the juices of the chicken run clear, about 1 hour more.

TIGER LILIES, also known as golden needles, are the unopened bud of a lily flower. They are packaged dried. When purchasing them, be sure to pick bright yellow lilies, as opposed to dark brown ones. The beautiful yellow or "golden" lily will impart a subtle flowery fragrance to your food; the dark brown ones are simply too old and rather bitter. Once you open the package, keep it refrigerated for extended freshness. I enjoy adding these buds to all sorts of soups, stir-fries, and stews. Not only do they lend a subtle flavor, they also add a crunchy texture to many dishes. Chinese take-out restaurants include tiger lilies in hot and sour soup, so you may already have enjoyed them without knowing it. Chinese chefs tie the lilies in a knot for aesthetic reasons.

AYAM GORENG
WORLD'S BEST
FRIED CHICKEN

SERVES 4 TO 6

6 whole CHICKEN LEGS, thighs
and drumsticks separated (if
you wish)

2 medium-large GARLIC CLOVES,
crushed, peeled, and minced

1 large SHALLOT, peeled and
minced

1 ounce fresh GINGER, peeled and
minced

1 ounce GALANGAL, peeled and
minced

1 LEMONGRASS STALK, root end
trimmed, outer leaves and tough
green top removed, and 6-inch-
long inner bulb finely ground

1 ounce fresh TURMERIC, peeled
and sliced; or 1 teaspoon
TURMERIC POWDER

1 tablespoon INDONESIAN SWEET
SOY SAUCE

KOSHER SALT

Freshly ground BLACK PEPPER

VEGETABLE OIL for deep-frying

I RARELY EAT FRIED FOODS, but there are times when it would be a shame not to indulge. Indonesian fried chicken is out of this world—one of those dishes that is nearly impossible to resist. It is first simmered with a medley of spices, including coriander, garlic, ginger, and galangal, and then, just before serving, deep-fried until crisp. Although palm sugar is traditionally added to the simmering chicken, I like to use sweet soy sauce. It not only sweetens but imparts a deep golden-reddish hue to the meat. This is a good dish to serve when entertaining because the simmering can be done ahead of time, even the night before. Also, unlike many fried chicken dishes, there is no heavy batter and the chicken is not dredged in flour prior to deep-frying. This helps to lighten the dish on the palate. Deep-frying without batter or dredging in flour is not unusual in Southeast Asia. In fact, in many places you'll find that fish is fried without having been dredged in flour or dipped in batter. When I visited my aunt in Indonesia, she served this delicious chicken with rice and sautéed greens on the side. I've also had it served with a simple *nasi goreng* (page 212; or page 239, variation) or as one of the side dishes at a *rijsttafel* meal (pp. 57–58).

1. Place the chicken, garlic, shallot, ginger, galangal, lemongrass, turmeric, sweet soy sauce, and ½ cup water in a pot over medium heat. Cook the chicken, turning the pieces a few times, until the chicken is cooked through but still firm and the liquid has completely evaporated, 20 to 30 minutes. It is important that the liquid evaporates completely and the chicken pieces be dried prior to deep-frying. Any moisture will result in spitting oil. If you're nervous, gently blot the pieces dry without rubbing away the delicious spices prior to frying. Season the chicken to taste with salt and pepper.

2. Heat enough vegetable oil for deep-frying in a pot over medium-high heat. When the oil reaches 360° to 375°F, carefully add the chicken pieces and fry until golden crisp all over, about 10 minutes. Drain on paper towels. Serve with white or yellow rice (page 205) and any number of vegetables on the side.

AYAM PELALAH
SHREDDED CHICKEN SALAD

SERVES 4 TO 6

2 large GARLIC CLOVES, crushed, peeled, and chopped

3 large SHALLOTS, peeled and chopped

4 RED THAI CHILIES, stemmed and seeded

4 CANDLENUTS

½ ounce KENCUR ROOT, peeled and chopped (optional)

½ ounce GALANGAL, peeled and chopped

½ ounce fresh TURMERIC, peeled and chopped; or ½ teaspoon TURMERIC POWDER

1 LEMONGRASS STALK, root end trimmed, outer leaves and tough green top removed, and 6-inch-long inner bulb chopped

3 to 4 tablespoons VEGETABLE OIL

1 tablespoon PALM SUGAR

1½ teaspoons INDONESIAN or THAI SHRIMP PASTE

2 SALAM LEAVES (optional)

2 large ripe PLUM TOMATOES, skinned, seeded, and minced

Juice of half a LIME

1½ to 2 pounds cooked CHICKEN, steamed, boiled, or roasted; shredded or thinly sliced

1 RED BELL PEPPER, stemmed, seeded, and julienned

1 LIME, cut into 8 wedges

I DISCOVERED THIS MEMORABLE chicken salad dish while traveling in Bali. Although it is normally made with freshly boiled or steamed chicken, you can also make it with any leftover, mildly seasoned roasted chicken. (Obviously leftover *coq au vin*, chicken cooked in wine sauce, would not do!) Candlenuts have a distinctive flavor. Used widely in Indonesia, they can be found in most Malaysian or Indonesian food markets. If you cannot find them, however, macadamia nuts, which have a very similar texture and are just as rich, make a good substitute. Roots such as *kencur* and galangal (also known as lesser ginger) are available in Southeast Asian markets. If you cannot find them, replace both with fresh ginger. (Although ginger does not have the same flavor, it will add its own equally refreshing aroma to the paste.) In Indonesia a mortar and pestle would be used to grind the various fresh spices and herbs, but you can certainly use a mini-grinder. Your shallots may get frothy and mushy, but the water they contain will evaporate when you stir-fry the paste.

Salam leaves have a unique flavor, and there is no substitute.

1. Grind together the garlic, shallots, chilies, candlenuts, *kencur* (if using), galangal, turmeric, and lemongrass with a mortar and pestle until fine; or place these ingredients in a mini-grinder and grind until very fine and pasty. Heat the oil in a pot over medium-high heat, add the herbal paste, and stir-fry until fragrant, about 5 minutes. Add the palm sugar and shrimp paste and continue to stir-fry, breaking down the shrimp paste and melting the palm sugar completely. Allow the paste to brown slightly, about 5 minutes. Add the salam leaves (if using), tomatoes, and lime juice, and cook until thick, 5 to 10 minutes. Remove the paste from the heat.

2. If not using freshly cooked chicken, be sure that any leftover chicken comes to room temperature. In a bowl toss together the chicken with the paste until well combined. Toss in the julienned red pepper and serve with lime wedges on the side.

MUAN CHHA K'NEI
STIR-FRIED CHICKEN WITH YOUNG GINGER

SERVES 4 TO 6

2 tablespoons VEGETABLE OIL

2 medium GARLIC CLOVES,
crushed, peeled, and minced

2 ounces fresh GINGER, peeled and
julienned

4 SCALLIONS, root and dark green
ends trimmed, and 6-inch stalks
cut into 1-inch-long pieces and
quartered lengthwise

2 pounds CHICKEN LEGS, skinned,
deboned, and sliced ¼-inch
thick

1 to 2 tablespoons FISH EXTRACT
(page 76); or FISH SAUCE

2 RED THAI CHILIES, stemmed,
seeded, and julienned (optional)

1 or more teaspoons GRANULATED
SUGAR

Freshly ground BLACK PEPPER

¼ cup fresh CILANTRO LEAVES,
tightly packed

GINGER PLAYS an important role in Cambodian stir-fries. Used in great quantities, it is almost always julienned. The stir-frying here is a direct influence from the Chinese, but the fish sauce seasoning is what makes this dish especially Southeast Asian in spirit. I prefer to use chicken legs for this recipe, because the dark meat tends to stay moist, but you can certainly use white meat, thinly sliced against the grain, if you wish. Cambodian cuisine is not an exact science, so feel free to experiment with the quantities. You can also use the very pungent *prahoc* extract instead of the fish sauce if you prefer. Chilies are optional, as I have had this stir-fry with and without them.

Be sure to select young pinkish-yellow ginger, which is juicier, less fibrous, and more pungent than the older and darker yellowish-beige root.

Heat the oil in a nonstick skillet or wok over high heat. Stir-fry the garlic until golden, 3 to 5 minutes. Add the ginger and scallions, and continue to stir-fry until fragrant, about a minute more. Add the chicken, fish sauce, and chilies (if using), sprinkle sugar across the top, and stir-fry until the chicken is cooked through, 5 to 10 minutes. Adjust the seasoning with pepper to taste. Transfer to a serving platter and top with cilantro leaves. Serve with jasmine rice on the side and a green vegetable such as stir-fried yard-long beans (page 320).

Variation: Substitute pork butt or beef sirloin sliced thinly against the grain for the chicken.

THESE QUICK STIR-FRIES are so easy to make and require very little time to prepare. My mother always had stir-fries ready for me and my brothers when we came home from school. She would prepare jasmine rice and pile it up on our plates, then top it with this gingery chicken. She'd also make thinly sliced pork butt with shiitake mushrooms (page 451). Both dishes made it worth skipping the lunch at school.

YAKITORI
GRILLED SKEWERED
CHICKEN

SERVES 4 TO 6

One 2½-pound CHICKEN; heart, liver, and gizzard included, if possible

6 to 8 SCALLIONS, root and dark green ends trimmed, and 6-inch stalks cut crosswise into 1-inch pieces

VEGETABLE OIL for grilling

YAKITORI SAUCE (page 91)

BAMBOO SKEWERS, soaked in water for 20 minutes

YAKITORI, LITERALLY "GRILLED CHICKEN," is a Japanese specialty so popular in Japan that there are restaurants dedicated solely to serving the dish. Morsels of chicken in all its parts—including meat, skin, gizzards, and livers—are cut into bite-size pieces and skewered separately. A long and narrow brazier holds a multitude of skewers lined up perfectly, and a tiny space is reserved between each skewer, allowing the heat to distribute evenly. Yakitori's flavor comes from basting it with a special yakitori sauce made from chicken bones, dark soy sauce, a generous amount of sake, mirin, sugar, and tamari sauce. The dish is simple to execute and can easily be made indoors at home, or outside for a picnic, where guests can grill and baste their own Japanese kebabs. A light Japanese beer such as Kirin or Sapporo or sake served at room temperature is a perfect accompaniment. If you do not drink alcohol, green tea is always appropriate.

1. Remove the skin from the chicken and cut into 1-inch-square pieces. Debone the chicken and cut the meat into approximately ¾-inch cubes. (Reserve the bones and wings for making stock.) Cut the heart, liver, and gizzard in half. Skewer 3 to 5 pieces of chicken, inserting a piece of scallion between each piece of chicken for color and texture. Skewer the skin pieces together (if you wish to eat this part), the white meat together, dark meat together, and offal together; this way the chicken pieces will cook evenly.

2. Place a well-oiled grill pan over medium-high heat. Baste the chicken with the yakitori sauce and place the skewers on the grill pan (or hibachi). Grill for 15 seconds, dip the skewers in the marinade, and put back (preferably a different side of the chicken) on the grill for 15 seconds. Continue this process until the chicken is grilled on all sides and cooked through, 3 to 5 minutes total.

INASAL NA MANOK
GRILLED HERBED CHICKEN

SERVES 4 TO 6

¼ cup LIGHT CHINESE SOY SAUCE
Juice of 1 LIME
2 tablespoons BROWN SUGAR
3 ounces fresh GINGER, peeled and
  chopped (optional)
3 large GARLIC CLOVES, crushed
  and chopped
2 LEMONGRASS STALKS, root ends
  trimmed, outer leaves and tough
  green tops removed, and 6-inch-
  long inner bulbs chopped
Freshly ground BLACK PEPPER
One 2½-pound CHICKEN

THIS HERB-MARINATED GRILLED CHICKEN is a specialty of the Visayan Islands region of the Philippines, and variations are enjoyed throughout the country. In Cebu, which is in the Visayan chain, street vendors often add ginger, garlic, and lemongrass to the bird's cavity throughout the spit-roasting process. This is a curious regional practice because, while lemongrass grows wild in the Philippines, aside from this dish, the herb is rarely, if ever, used in cooking. Although the spit-roasted chicken is particularly delicious, oven roasting works just fine. Rather than fill the cavity with crushed ginger, garlic, and lemongrass, however, I turn these ingredients into a paste and smear it over and under the skin of the chicken, as well as inside its cavity. To roast more effectively and do away with turning the bird, you can also butterfly and flatten the chicken. If you are not good at splitting fresh fowl through the breast bone, ask your butcher to do it for you.

1. Whisk together the soy sauce, lime juice, and brown sugar in a bowl until the sugar is completely dissolved. Place the ginger, garlic, and lemongrass in a mini-grinder and pulse until the ingredients turn into a paste. (If you do not have a mini-grinder, mince.) Transfer the paste to the soy sauce mixture and whisk until well combined. Add pepper to taste.

2. Butterfly the chicken by cutting through the breast bone lengthwise. With your hands spread it open so it sits flat in a deep dish. Loosen the skin with your fingers, being careful not to tear it. Massage the chicken all over with the marinade; massage under the skin as well. Transfer the chicken to a large plastic bag with the marinade and refrigerate it for 2 hours.

3. Preheat the oven to 450°F. Drain the chicken (but do not wipe off the marinade) and place the chicken skin side up on a flat roasting rack set over a baking dish containing ¼ inch water. Roast until golden and the juices run clear, about 45 minutes to 1 hour.

Variation: As much as I love oven roasting, in spring, summer, and fall I prefer to grill outside on the barbecue. This chicken is perfect when grilled over direct heat. Wait until the flames have subsided and the natural wood charcoals turn red with a coating of white ash (embers). Lightly brush your marinated chicken with a little vegetable oil and place it skin side down on the grill. Once the skin is crispy and lightly charred, turn it over several times, in order not to burn it too much, until done. The whole process should take 30 to 45 minutes. I have also tried this wonderful herbal marinade on pork, beef, and shrimp and am pleased to report that the results were very tasty. Feel free to experiment with other foods such as swordfish or tuna steaks, or other fleshy items.

YOU CAN FIND *inasal na manok* all over the Philippines, often sold directly from street vendors' grills, not unlike the way barbecued ribs are sold directly from the cooking pit or barbecue barrel in many parts of Texas. The recipe is consistent in its basics everywhere in the Philippines, but the addition of ginger and lemongrass is typical only of the Visayan Islands region. As is traditional in the Philippines, I complement the chicken with white steamy long-grain rice, and a side of green papaya salad seasoned with a rice vinegar (a good substitute for the coconut vinegar used in Filipino cooking) and sugar dressing.

ADOBONG NA MANOK
CHICKEN ADOBO

SERVES 4 TO 6

1 tablespoon VEGETABLE OIL

1 large head of GARLIC, cloves crushed

2 ounces fresh GINGER, thinly sliced lengthwise

6 CHICKEN LEGS (1½ to 2 pounds), separated at the joint, thighs and drumsticks halved through the bone crosswise

½ cup COCONUT VINEGAR or CHINESE WHITE RICE VINEGAR

¼ cup CHINESE LIGHT SOY SAUCE

5 SCALLIONS, root and dark green ends trimmed, and 6-inch stalks cut into 1-inch-long pieces

1 tablespoon BLACK PEPPERCORNS

2 fresh BAY LEAVES

THE FIRST THOUGHT that comes to mind when I hear the word *adobo* is the delicious Mexican stew of meat cooked in wine. Adobo, however, is not specific to Mexico. Filipinos have a dish by the same name, although it is most often referred to by its (possibly adapted) name, *adobong*. While Filipino food has been largely influenced by Spanish, Spanish colonial, and, to a lesser extent, Chinese cooking cultures, Filipino cooks believe that *adobong* originated with them. Arguably the national dish of the Philippines, *adobong* also refers to the entire style of cooking in vinegar and is made with seafood and vegetables as well as meat. Regardless of the specific national origin of the technique, *adobong* cooking probably had its roots in necessity. Cooking in vinegar is a way of preserving food because it inhibits bacterial growth, allowing food to be stored at room temperature.

Peeling the garlic cloves and ginger is optional.

1. Heat the oil in a large clay or heavy-bottomed pot over medium-high heat. Stir-fry the garlic and ginger until fragrant and golden, about 5 minutes. Add the chicken, vinegar, soy sauce, scallions, peppercorns, bay leaves, and ¼ cup water, reduce the heat to medium-low, and simmer until the chicken is fork-tender and the juices have reduced by half, about an hour. You can serve the chicken over rice with a sautéed vegetable on the side now, or refrigerate it overnight.

2. Take the *adobong* out of the refrigerator and allow to come to room temperature. Place the pot, uncovered, over medium heat and, stirring occasionally, reheat the stew until a little more of the juices have

evaporated. The more the juices evaporate, the more the fat surfaces and crisps the chicken pieces, making them very delicious.

Variation: You can make this with a whole 2½-pound chicken. This is what I call "family style" *adobong*. Remove the legs from the chicken, and split them at the joint. Chop the drumsticks and thighs in half through the bone. (Use a cleaver to do this, but if you are uncomfortable using a cleaver for chopping, slice the pieces in half lengthwise so some of the halves retain the bone, while the others are bone-free.) Separate the back from the breast side of the chicken. Use kitchen shears or a cleaver. Quarter the backbone. Separate the wings from the breast at the joint, and discard the tips. Halve the breast through the bone, then quarter each half through the bone crosswise. Enjoy, but be very careful of the small bones.

I HAVE EATEN MANY TYPES of *adobong,* some in the Philippines and others at my sister-in-law's house. Typical of home cooking, *adobong* cooks rarely follow set recipes, preferring to be guided by inspiration, touch, smell, and sight. Or, as my mother says, "It depends on the weather!" This stew almost always includes generous amounts of garlic, black peppercorns, and vinegar; ginger and soy sauce are sometimes added as well. These last two ingredients are direct influences from the Chinese, and they are, in my opinion, wonderful additions that bestow a wealth of flavor on the dish. Some cooks put the chicken and its marinade in a pot, let it marinate for an hour or so, then cook it. While Filipino cooks would tend to use coconut vinegar (sometimes available in Southeast Asian markets), I sometimes use Chinese white rice vinegar, a perfectly good substitute. Japanese rice vinegar, which is slightly amber in color, is not a good substitute because it is already seasoned and tends to be on the sweet side. *Adobong manok* is delicious when just made, but, as with anything stewed, it is well worth letting it rest overnight and reheating it the next day. By that time, the flavors have had the chance to develop, and the results are superb. No discussion of chicken *adobong* would be complete without examining what my husband refers to as "the bone problem." In traditional versions of the dish, a whole chicken is coarsely cleaver-chopped through the bones into one- and two-bite pieces. When eating the dish in the Philippines, I was caught up in the fun of eating the dish *al fresco,* and however inconvenient it may have been to pick around the bones, I enjoyed every bit of caramelized shredded chicken. When I made the dish at home, my husband loved it, but he felt it would be better adapted to Western dining if the pieces were not so shattered. The next time, only the legs went into the pot, and the dish was just as delicious but much easier to eat.

DAK KUI
KOREAN
BARBECUED CHICKEN

SERVES 4 TO 6

2 pounds skinless CHICKEN
  BREASTS (2 whole breasts)
2 tablespoons KOREAN DARK SOY
  SAUCE
1 tablespoon GRANULATED SUGAR
½ ounce fresh GINGER, peeled and
  grated
1 large GARLIC CLOVE, crushed,
  peeled, and minced
1 SCALLION, root and dark green
  ends trimmed, and 6-inch stalk
  minced
½ teaspoon SESAME OIL
Freshly ground BLACK PEPPER
VEGETABLE OIL for grilling
1 head BOSTON LETTUCE, leaves
  separated and ribs removed
SWEET AND SOUR CHILI DIPPING
  SAUCE (page 105)
SPICY VINEGAR DIPPING SAUCE
  (page 93)

D AK KUI, KOREAN BARBECUED CHICKEN, is more delicate than *bulgogi*,
the classic barbecued beef dish (page 480). Marinated for a short period in a combination of soy sauce, sugar, ginger, garlic, scallion,
sesame oil, and black pepper, it absorbs just the right amount of flavoring.
For this dish the breast meat is usually employed, cut up into medium-size
chunks. It is best when made on the grill or a special Korean table hibachi,
but a well-oiled grill pan will also do a beautiful job. Like all Korean barbecues, *dak kui* is served with a side of tender lettuce leaves for wrapping, as-
sorted *kimchi* (pp. 357–61), short-grain rice (page 188), sweet and sour chili
sauce, and spicy vinegar sauce on the side. It is also often accompanied by a
clear broth for sipping during the meal.

1. Halve the chicken breasts so you
have 4 half breasts. Cut them into
1-inch pieces and flatten them
slightly with the side of a cleaver
blade.

2. Whisk the soy sauce and sugar in
a bowl until the sugar is completely
dissolved. Stir in the ginger, garlic,
scallion, sesame oil, and black pepper. Add the chicken and toss with
your hands until each piece is
evenly coated with the marinade.
Cover with plastic wrap and allow
to marinate for 30 minutes, refrigerated.

3. Place a well-oiled grill pan over
medium-high heat. When it starts to
smoke, add the chicken pieces. Turn
them every so often until cooked
through, 3 to 5 minutes, depending
on the size of the pieces.

KAENG PHET KAI
THAI CHICKEN CURRY

SERVES 4 TO 6

1 tablespoon COCONUT OIL or
VEGETABLE OIL

1½ to 2 tablespoons THAI RED or
GREEN CURRY PASTE (page 82);
or commercial equivalent

2 teaspoons THAI or INDONESIAN
SHRIMP PASTE

2 LEMONGRASS STALKS, root ends
trimmed, outer leaves and tough
green tops removed, and 6-inch-
long inner bulbs sliced paper-
thin crosswise

1 cup unsweetened COCONUT
MILK (page 77); or commercial
equivalent

1 cup BASIC CHICKEN STOCK
(page 116)

1 tablespoon THAI FISH SAUCE

2 pounds CHICKEN THIGHS, bone-
in or -out, with or without the
skin, halved crosswise; or WINGS

2 medium WAXY POTATOES or
YAMS, peeled and cut into
approximately 1½-inch cubes

6 YARD-LONG BEANS, trimmed
and cut into 2-inch pieces

12 THAI EGGPLANTS

20 THAI BASIL LEAVES

THAILAND HAS LONG BEEN FAMOUS for its spicy coconut curries, which include red, green, and yellow curries. This dish uses the red curry, and is one of the simplest to prepare and serve as a single-dish meal. If you do not have the time to make your own curry paste, you can use the excellent Thai curry pastes available in Asian markets. If you don't have the time to make fresh unsweetened coconut milk, you can use the canned version, cutting preparation time of the dish by half. Although making a Thai curry from scratch helps you understand the food better, sometimes this sort of involved preparation is a bit of a hindrance. Either way, you'll have a memorable meal. Serve over steamy jasmine rice or sticky rice.

I like to use the dark meat of the chicken when making curry because breast meat cooks too quickly in the sauce and dries out. Drumsticks and thighs hold together better when cooked for long periods of time in sauces, so the curry can cook long and slow, allowing the flavors to blend.

1. Heat the oil in a heavy-bottomed pot over medium-high heat. Add the Thai curry and shrimp pastes and the lemongrass, and stir until lightly toasted, about 3 minutes.

2. Reduce the heat to medium-low, add the coconut milk, chicken stock, fish sauce, chicken, potatoes, beans, and eggplants, and simmer for 30 minutes. Add the Thai basil and cook for an additional 10 minutes. Serve over jasmine rice.

Variation: Add 4 to 6 shelled hard-boiled chicken eggs to the pot 10 minutes prior to serving. Curried chicken eggs or duck eggs are eaten in Indonesia and are often part of the rijsttafel, or rice table.

CANTONESE FIVE-SPICE ROAST DUCK

SERVES 4 TO 6

⅓ cup CHINESE LIGHT SOY SAUCE
¼ cup GRANULATED SUGAR
1 teaspoon FIVE-SPICE POWDER
Freshly ground BLACK PEPPER
One 4- to 5-pound LONG ISLAND
   DUCK
2 ounces fresh GINGER, thinly
   sliced lengthwise
4 SCALLIONS, root and dark green
   ends trimmed, and 6-inch stalks
   halved crosswise and lightly
   crushed
6 large GARLIC CLOVES, crushed
   and peeled

KITCHEN STRING
METAL SKEWER

THE MOST CELEBRATED and famous Chinese duck dishes are Peking duck and Cantonese roast duck. Peking duck is a complex restaurant dish that requires twenty-four hours of cold-weather air-drying (or an industrial fan) to tighten the skin so it becomes very crispy; this is a signature regimen that is just shy of impossible for all but the most ambitious home cooks. Cantonese roast duck is also wonderful; it requires much less preparation (it is often seen hanging in the windows of Chinese restaurants) but has a much less crispy skin. This recipe is my family's version of Cantonese roast duck, made with skin crisped to a degree that is somewhere between that of Cantonese roast duck and Peking duck.

I have prepared squab in the same manner. Substitute 6 squabs for the duck and roast for a total of forty-five minutes.

1. Whisk together the soy sauce, sugar, and five-spice powder in a large dish. Season with black pepper. Carefully loosen the skin of the duck by gently running your fingers between the skin and the meat (breast and legs). You may need a paring knife to help you separate the skin from the central bone area. Try not to tear the skin in the process. Place the duck in the marinade and rub the marinade over it, inside and out and between the flesh and the skin. Drain and refrigerate the duck, uncovered, turning it occasionally, for 24 hours.

2. Preheat the oven to 450°F. Place the ginger, scallions, and garlic inside the cavity of the duck, then truss it with kitchen string. With a metal skewer, poke the skin a few times on the breast, legs, and back. Place the duck breast side down on a rack set over a baking dish filled with ¼ inch water. Roast the duck for 45 minutes, basting it every 15 minutes with the drippings. Turn the duck breast side up and continue roasting (basting every 15 minutes) until the juices run clear, about 45 minutes more.

Variations: The Vietnamese have a version of this roast duck, vit quay. To try it, substitute fish sauce for the Chinese light soy sauce.

Another variation of the dish (and a personal favorite) is to add shiitake mushrooms under the skin for an earthy and nutty flavor. Put 18 to 24 small to medium dried shiitake mushrooms in a bowl with hot water to cover, then set a plate over the bowl to prevent steam from escaping. Let stand until the mushrooms rehydrate and soften, about 30 minutes (or longer, depending on the size of the mushrooms). Squeeze the mushrooms between the palms of your hands to get rid of the excess water. Using a paring knife, remove any hard stems from the mushrooms. After rubbing the duck with the marinade, place the shiitake caps in any remaining marinade and toss to coat well. Place the shiitakes under the skin of the duck over the breast in a single layer. Proceed with the recipe.

BEBEK BETUTU
SMOKED DUCK

SERVES 4 TO 6

4 large GARLIC CLOVES, crushed, peeled, and sliced

8 large SHALLOTS, peeled and thinly sliced

3 LEMONGRASS STALKS, root ends trimmed, outer leaves and tough green tops removed, and 6-inch-long inner bulbs finely ground

4 KAFFIR LIME LEAVES, finely ground

4 CANDLENUTS or MACADAMIA NUTS, finely ground

1 ounce fresh GINGER, peeled and minced

2 ounces fresh TURMERIC, peeled and minced; or 1½ tablespoons TURMERIC POWDER

2 ounces KENCUR ROOT, peeled and minced

4 or more THAI CHILIES, stemmed, seeded, and minced

1 teaspoon CORIANDER SEEDS, finely ground

1 tablespoon INDONESIAN or THAI SHRIMP PASTE

KOSHER SALT

Freshly ground BLACK PEPPER

One 4- to 5-pound LONG ISLAND DUCK

1 large BANANA LEAF; or 1 large LOTUS LEAF; or 3 layers PARCHMENT PAPER and 1 layer heavy-duty ALUMINUM FOIL

METAL SKEWER/NEEDLE
KITCHEN STRING

I

N BALI, BEBEK BETUTU, smoked duck, is reserved for special occasions, as it is expensive and quite an indulgence for most Indonesians. Rubbed and stuffed with a medley of spices, the duck is wrapped in banana leaves and smoked twelve hours in rice husks until the meat falls off the bones. In this modern adaptation, the duck is rubbed with spices, wrapped in the banana leaves (to impart flavor and hold the duck together while it cooks), and slow-roasted in an oven at 275°F for 6 hours.

Because the meat is cooked for a long time until very tender, the skin will not be crispy, and the duck may look a little dull. While the spices rubbed into the bird lend a nice golden-yellow hue, for presentation I cut the banana leaf wrapping at the table. If you do not have banana leaves, the next-best thing is lotus leaves. These are sold dried and need to be rehydrated in water until softened completely prior to use. Both types of leaves are available in Asian markets and through some mail-order sources. If you simply cannot get the leaves, wrap the duck in three layers of parchment paper, then in heavy-duty aluminum foil, as explained below.

Preheat the oven to 275°F. Meanwhile, place the garlic, shallots, lemongrass, lime leaves, candlenuts, ginger, turmeric, kencur, chilies, coriander, shrimp paste, salt, and 1 to 2 tablespoons water in a food processor and process to a paste consistency. Adjust seasoning with salt and pepper to taste. Pat the duck dry inside and out and rub the herbal and spice paste all over the duck, putting all the remaining rub inside the cavity. Use a skewer or needle and kitchen string to sew up the duck. Place the duck in the center of the banana or lotus leaf. Bring up the long sides of the banana leaf and fold them over the duck. Fold over the short sides of the leaf. Use kitchen string to tighten the leaf in place. If using the parchment paper, do the same thing, enclosing the duck in the parchment first, then wrapping it in aluminum foil. Place the wrapped duck in a roasting pan and cook until very tender, 6 to 8 hours. When finished, the duck meat should fall off the bones.

I DISCOVERED *BEBEK BETUTU* (sometimes *bebek tutu*), smoked duck, in Bali a few years ago. Walking through a deserted outdoor market in the afternoon one day, I stumbled upon a man with his teenage son and daughter preparing something that looked interesting. While the boy was grinding fresh herbs with a mortar and pestle made of lava stone, the girl was slaughtering and cleaning ducks. The man was walking back and forth, in and out of a modest hut, shuffling around some warm, smoking rice husks. Before I could ask what he was doing, he pulled out of the fire a bundle that was wrapped in large pandan leaves. As he opened the package, the aromas were a delicious medley of pungent herbal notes. I later learned that the leaf-wrapped package was *bebek betutu*. The man explained that he had been selected by the president of Indonesia to prepare the representative dish of his area for presentation at meals in Jakarta. He later showed me the entire cooking process from start to finish over a period of two days. The duck was remarkable, its pungent, spicy, moist meat falling off the bones. It still ranks as one of the most delicious dishes I have ever eaten anywhere.

IN INDONESIA, LONG TREE TRUNKS ARE CARVED TO RECEIVE SEAWATER. LEFT IN THE SUN, THE WATER WILL EVENTUALLY EVAPORATE, LEAVING BEHIND SALT FOR PRESERVING OR COOKING FOODS.

VIT NAU CAM
DUCK IN SPICY
ORANGE SAUCE

SERVES 4 TO 6

One 4- to 5-pound LONG ISLAND
DUCK; or 6 DUCK LEGS

8 large GARLIC CLOVES, crushed
and peeled

2 ounces fresh GINGER, thinly
sliced lengthwise

4 cups fresh-squeezed ORANGE
JUICE

Juice of 2 LIMES

¼ cup FISH SAUCE

1 tablespoon GRANULATED SUGAR

½ teaspoon FIVE-SPICE POWDER

5 STAR ANISE

4 or more fresh RED THAI CHILIES;
or CHINESE DRIED RED CHILIES

6 SCALLIONS, root and dark green
ends trimmed, and 6-inch stalks
halved crosswise and lightly
crushed

2 LEMONGRASS STALKS, root ends
trimmed, outer leaves removed,
and 6-inch-long inner bulbs
finely ground

KOSHER SALT

Freshly ground BLACK PEPPER

THE INFLUENCE of the French colonial kitchen is evident in the cuisines of Hanoi and Saigon. *Canard à l'orange*, duck flavored with the essence of orange, is a classic French dish adapted by the Vietnamese, who call their version *vit nau cam*. Although the French dish is traditionally cooked with orange juice, it is very rich with butter. The Vietnamese version is much lighter. This is achieved by eliminating the butter and cooking the duck in its own fat, then braising it in orange juice and seasoning it with fish sauce, five-spice powder, star anise, and chilies. The result is a delicious Asian rendition of the French classic—and a great conversation piece.

1. Place the duck legs in a single layer, skin side down, in a nonstick pot over medium heat, and cook until golden and crisp, about 20 minutes. Transfer to a plate. Add the garlic and ginger, stirring these occasionally, until golden brown, 5 to 10 minutes.

2. Add the orange juice, lime juice, fish sauce, sugar, five-spice powder, star anise, chilies, scallions, and lemongrass. Return the duck pieces to the pot, and add 1 quart water. Adjust seasoning with salt and pepper to taste. Cover the pot, reduce the heat to medium-low, and braise the duck until fork tender, about 6 to 8 hours. Skim the fat off the top prior to serving.

MOULARD DUCKS ARE RAISED for their *foie gras*, fat liver, a delicacy made famous in France; they are the meatiest, most tender of all ducks. For this reason, once the fat liver, reaching well over a pound at times, is extracted, the *magrets* (breasts) are sold fresh, and the legs are used for making *confit*, a process in which the duck legs are salted, then cooked in duck fat. Needless to say, moulard ducks are very fatty, but they are also the tastiest ducks you will eat. In Vietnam, ducks are much thinner, and while I prefer the moulard ducks for this recipe because the finished dish has a much richer flavor, Long Island ducks are more widely available.

CHIM NUONG TOI
GARLIC-ROASTED QUAIL

SERVES 4 TO 6

¼ cup MUSHROOM SOY SAUCE

2 tablespoons GRANULATED SUGAR

4 medium to large GARLIC
CLOVES, crushed, peeled, and
minced

2 tablespoons freshly cracked
BLACK PEPPER

1 tablespoon VEGETABLE OIL

12 QUAILS; or 6 BABY CHICKENS
(*poussins*)

KITCHEN STRING

STREET VENDORS ABOUND in Southeast Asia. They often offer foods cooked over an open fire. In Vietnam, in particular, quail is the most popular grilled bird because it is small, tasty, and cooks quickly. Marinated in a combination of mushroom soy sauce, garlic, and freshly cracked black pepper, this grilled dish makes a delicious light lunch, especially in warm weather, when it can be cooked outdoors. Chicken is also used in this recipe, and I usually prefer *poussins*, or baby chickens, which weigh between ten and twelve ounces and are juicier and more tender than larger, older birds. The Cambodians make similar versions of this dish, and I saw Thai variations on my way to Doi Su Tep, a Buddhist temple in Chiang Mai, Thailand.

This is also a recipe worth trying using squab. A serving is usually a bird per person.

1. Whisk together the mushroom soy sauce and sugar in a bowl until the sugar is completely dissolved. Stir in the garlic, black pepper, and the oil. Carefully loosen the skin of the bird by gently running your fingers between the skin and the meat (breast and legs). Try not to tear the skin in the process. Put the birds in a plastic bag, add the marinade, seal the bag, and shake it a few times. Marinate the birds, refrigerated, for 2 hours, shaking the bag every 30 minutes or so. Drain the birds, discarding the marinade.

2. Place a rack in the middle of the oven and preheat the oven to 450°F. With a cleaver, cut through the center bone of the breast lengthwise and flatten the birds. Place skin side up on the rack set over a roasting pan containing ½ inch water, and roast until the juices run clear, about 20 minutes for quail, and 40 minutes for baby chickens.

3. To roast the chickens whole, tie the drumsticks together with kitchen string and roast the chickens breast side down for 15 minutes, then breast side up for 30 minutes. Serve with rice and pickled vegetables.

7

SWEETS AND

DRINKS

ASIANS TEND TO PREFER fresh fruit over pastries and other heavier items for dessert, because they feel their dishes have been balanced in terms of sweet, savory, bitter, sour, and spicy throughout the meal. Many Asian foods served any time of the day or night, alone or in combination with other dishes, have a sweet character. Accordingly, a simple platter of fruit is likely to be appreciated to complete the dining experience. This might include citrus fruits such as oranges or tangerines, or other fresh fruit in season such as litchi, longan, rambutan, or watermelon. The idea is that fresh fruit aids digestion, clears and refreshes the palate, and is understood as being healthful. The many varieties of oranges, in

particular, are associated with good luck and are often used in ritual offerings. One often sees them at the base of Buddha statues, where they are presented as gifts.

What Westerners think of as "dessert"—small, sweet pastries in the form of tarts, pies, cakes, and puddings, and so forth—is traditionally enjoyed in Asia both informally as snacks, or in a more structured manner at teatime. In this chapter, I have included several types of sweet foods, which you can serve either as snacks or desserts; and I have included sweet drinks, which are generally served as snacks as well.

Sweet soups are also popular in Asia. They can be hot, warm, room temperature, or chilled, depending on the season or mood. The Chinese love *hong dau sah*, a red bean soup (page 514) often made with creamy-white lotus seeds and flavored with tangerine peel. The Japanese enjoy a similar version of the soup that omits the lotus seeds and tangerine peel altogether. Enjoyed throughout China and Southeast Asia, banana and coconut soup (page 517) is lightly thickened with tapioca pearls. The same soup is also made with taro, sweet potato, or corn instead of banana. Some cooks add more tapioca pearls than

others, turning the soup into a pudding. The Vietnamese are especially fond of mung beans, which show up in a dessert called *che dau xanh*, a smooth yellow mung bean and coconut soup (page 516), which is sometimes cooked down to a pudding consistency. (Other mung bean–based desserts are mentioned below.) My favorites of many sweet rice porridges are the Korean black sesame or pine nut–flavored porridges (page 518). These soups and porridges make for wonderful snacks and are particularly good when eaten as hot breakfast dishes on a cold day.

Southeast Asia's plentiful coconuts, bananas, and sticky rice appear in a good number of the region's sweet snacks. In Thailand, *khao tom mat* (page 522), sticky rice cooked in coconut milk, combined with chunks of sweet Asian bananas, and wrapped in banana leaves, is steamed until tender, yet lightly chewy. This sweet snack is found virtually everywhere in Southeast Asia in one form or another, often adapted to local tastes. In the Philippines, for example, I saw a similar sweet snack called *budbud*, but over the rice was drizzled a small amount of melted bitter chocolate. Another Thai dessert, *khao neow mamuang* (pp. 520–21), is sticky white rice steamed, topped with a warm sweet and savory coconut cream sauce, and garnished with ripe mango slices or durian. (The latter is a large, prickly, hard-shelled tropical fruit that has a famously offensive odor, a creamy-yellow flesh with rich avocado-like texture, and a pleasant sweet flavor.) This same sticky rice specialty can be found in Vietnam, where it is called *che dau trang* (page 521); it is topped with stewed, sweetened red azuki beans or black-eyed peas. Yet another version exists in Cambodia, where it is called *baw samdaik ankoy*. Here the rice is not steamed but cooked in coconut milk to a pudding-like consistency, with boiled sweetened black-eyed peas stirred in. All of these are delicious. Indonesia's *bubuh injin* and Thailand's *kao niow dam* (page 519) are both made with sticky black rice, coconut milk, and palm sugar. When cooked, black sticky rice turns a beautiful deep purple color, and Indonesia's version mixes both black and white sticky rice for a lighter but still very purple appearance. Once cooked, the sticky rice is topped with a rich coconut sauce that is sweet with a salty back note. The pudding can be made loose or dense.

In China and Southeast Asia, white sticky rice flour is mixed with hot water to form a dough. Shaped into balls ranging from the size of BB pellets to the size of pinballs, they are often stuffed with mung bean paste and boiled in water until they float to the surface. These rice dumplings are then served with a hot, warm, or chilled sweet ginger broth. Called *banh troi nuoc* (pp. 524–25), these festive items are popular at weddings, where they are sometimes colored red to symbolize good luck.

The same dough is used to make *mochi* (page 525) in Japan, where a small amount of boiled rice dough is covered with sweet red bean paste and sprinkled with sesame seeds. When you bite into one of these, the textural contrast of the soft red bean paste against the chewy sticky rice is wonderful. In Korea the same rice dough is used to make *kyongdan* (pp. 526–27), rice balls filled with minced jujube or red bean paste, boiled, drained, then rolled in any number of powdered items such as black sesame, soybean flour, and pine nuts for flavor and an attractive presentation. I also use green tea powder (*matcha*) because I like the bitterness against the sweet bean paste. Cassia bark, which is similar

in flavor but sweeter and less harsh than common cinnamon, is a good choice for a pungent but never overwhelming note.

The Chinese and Vietnamese combine rice flour, sticky rice flour, and boiled, mashed potato to make a dough. Formed into small balls filled with sweet black sesame paste, coconut-flavored mung bean paste, sweet and salty finely crushed peanuts, rich and sweet red bean paste, or ripe banana, they are rolled in white sesame seeds, then deep-fried until crisp. These classic deep-fried sesame balls, called *jien doy* in Chinese and *dau xanh vung* in Vietnamese, are best with tea in the afternoon, as they are very rich and the tea aids in their digestion.

While cow's milk is not part of the daily diet in China, it is necessary to make the light Chinese, and more specifically Cantonese, specialty called *geung nai* (page 528), a steamed ginger-infused egg-white custard. Other popular cow's milk–based desserts include all sorts of ice creams with exotic flavors ranging from green tea to red bean, black sesame, and anything else you would want. I have experimented with lemongrass, star anise, white pepper, and saffron, for example, and my toasted coconut ice cream (page 548), which uses the fruit as flavoring and texture, is a favorite among friends and family. The Chinatown Ice Cream Factory in New York's Chinatown features a wide array of very good quality Asian-flavored ice creams, and going there for an ice-cream cone for an afternoon snack is a ritual for the locals on hot summer days.

While cow's milk is used in making some custards, Southeast Asians tend to prefer the flavor of coconut and use it in making both savory and sweet foods. Following the same principle for making French custards, they substitute coconut milk, as in the Vietnamese version of the classic French crème caramel, for example. Called *banh gan* (page 534), it looks like its French counterpart but has a richer texture and wonderful coconut flavor. Steamed coconut custard served in small pumpkins, buttercup squash, or acorn squash is popular in Cambodia and Thailand, where it is called *sankiah l'poh* and *sankaya fuk thong* (pp. 530–31), respectively. *Hung yan dofu* (page 529) is a dessert of cubed almond-flavored white jelly served with fruits in syrup. Curiously, this so-called *dofu* (tofu) custard has no soybeans in it.

French-style tartlets are popular in Asia. The Chinese love *dahn tot* (page 539), small egg custard tarts often enjoyed in dim sum restaurants, while the Vietnamese love *banh dua* (page 539), a shredded coconut tart. The latter is also enjoyed in the Philippines, where the tender meat of young coconuts called *buko* is used instead of the drier meat of mature coconuts. Both the egg custard tarts are available in miniature or small individual sizes in Asian bakeries but can easily be reproduced at home. Other tasty pastries include *cho lie woo pan* (page 535), which is essentially a thin layer of red bean or red date (jujube) paste sandwiched between two rectangular crepes (spring roll wrappers). Pan-fried until crisp, the crepe is sprinkled with both toasted sesame seeds and black sesame seeds for a beautiful presentation, then cut up into bite-size squares. In the Philippines, spring roll wrappers are also used for making sweets. *Turon de saba* is a banana and jackfruit spring roll (pp. 536–37) that is served with a light crème anglaise, or lightly dusted with confectioners' sugar. I generally prefer to end my meals with fresh fruit, but I was served *turon de saba* several times each day when I was in the Philippines (it is offered as a snack when you visit people's homes), and I must admit that I really came to love it.

The Balinese make French-style crêpes filled with toasted and candied shredded coconut, called *dadar* (page 538). Deep-fried battered bananas, called *chien chuoi* (page 542) in Vietnam, are modeled after the French beignet, and are enjoyed throughout Southeast Asia. Doused with rice alcohol or rum, then set aflame (usually at the table for dramatic effect), the blue-hot flames caramelize the sugar as the beignet crisps further. Vietnamese restaurants in France almost always serve them as *bananes flambées* for dessert. In Korea, rice wine–flavored, deep-fried dough tossed in honey is popular as a tea snack. Called *maejakgwa*, it requires little effort to make. Flour, water, honey, and oil for deep-frying are all you'll need.

All over Southeast Asia you will find what I call "rainbow drinks," yellow mung beans and red beans layered between shaved ice and coconut milk, and topped with jelly sticks and/or fresh fruit such as longan or litchi. These filling drinks are called *che ba mau* and *halo halo*, in Vietnamese and Filipino, respectively. The Koreans make all sorts of sweet beverages using fresh or dried fruit such as dried persimmon or pear simmered in water with ginger and sugar. The infusion is drunk, and the fruit can be eaten, too. Pine nuts are often added as a garnish.

In contrast to many Western cultures, the Chinese do not sweeten their tea. Having raised tea preparation to an art, they emphasize its freshness, its proper brewing, its specific intensity, and the flavor of its individual leaf type: green, which is unfermented; oolong, which is semifermented; and black, which is fermented. Rather, they take sweets in the form of main dishes or snacks and use pure infusions of tea leaves as fragrant counterpoints that also aid digestion. In Southeast Asia, Korea, and Japan, where tea growing, harvesting, preparation, presentation, and serving compose a culture unto itself, tea is also drunk unsweetened.

Tea is regarded as having health benefits. Not only does it aid digestion, but in its green stage, it is believed to help prevent or cure cancer, decrease blood pressure, and decrease cholesterol, to name a few benefits. As such, whether part of an elaborate ceremony or not, tea is always made with great care. First, the water must be heated but never to the boiling point. The loose tea leaves must never be touched by

GREEN TEA IS SERVED ALL DAY LONG AT THE YOSHI-IMA RYOKAN IN KYOTO. THE TEA IS BELIEVED TO HELP PREVENT OR CURE CANCER.

hands; instead, they are scooped up with special bamboo spoons. Once the leaves are transferred to the brewing pot (Yixing pots are small, holding about 8 fluid ounces), hot water is poured over the leaves, and poured instantly into the serving (as opposed to brewing) pot and individual cups, which are the size of shot glasses. This process not only loosens the leaves, releasing their essence, but heats the serving pot and cups. The first draining can then be sniffed, much like one sniffs wine to determine its nose. The hot water is then poured out of the serving pot and cups and discarded. Now it is time to brew the tea leaves. More hot water is poured into the brewing pot, which contains a heaping teaspoon of leaves. The tea will brew for no more than a minute, then be poured into the serving pot, and immediately into individual cups. The same tea leaves can be brewed up to three times. The second serving will brew for two minutes, the third serving will brew for three minutes. You can follow these instructions when you are brewing any type of loose tea leaves. While loose tea bags are convenient, they certainly do not compare to freshly brewed loose tea leaves.

There are many teapots from which to choose. I prefer the old-fashioned Yixing teapots. These unglazed red-clay pots retain the heat of the water beautifully, but more important, they cure with time, taking on the flavor of the many tea leaves that have brewed in them. Teapots should not be washed with soap but simply rinsed under hot water after each use. The same holds true for teacups.

There are exceptions, of course. With the arrival of the French in Southeast Asia came *café au lait*, coffee with milk. During that period the Southeast Asians developed their own version, using condensed milk to sweeten the coffee (which includes chicory) and, having developed a taste for it, to sweeten black teas. These sweetened caffeinated drinks seldom accompany meals and are mostly enjoyed in the afternoon as a pick-me-up.

SWEET PASTES

MAKES ABOUT 2 CUPS EACH

1 cup RED AZUKI BEANS, soaked
for 4 hours and drained
or

1½ cups dried LOTUS SEEDS,
soaked for 12 hours, then
drained
or

3 cups JUJUBES, soaked until
softened and pitted
or

1 cup peeled split MUNG BEANS,
soaked for 3 hours, then drained
or

1 cup BLACK SESAME SEEDS, rinsed
and drained, then finely ground
or

1½ cups peeled roasted unsalted
PEANUTS, finely ground (not
peanut butter)

¼ cup or more GRANULATED
SUGAR

2 tablespoons LARD; or VEGETABLE
OIL

I N ASIA, SWEET PASTES are used as fillings in desserts such as rice dumplings and pastries. The most popular are red bean, lotus, sweet peanut, and mung bean pastes. Others include jujube (red date) paste and black sesame paste. While I may call for certain pastes in specific recipes, experiment with others. Generally, pastes made from red bean, lotus, and jujube contain lard; you may substitute vegetable oil for the lard if you prefer.

While red bean and lotus pastes are available canned, I find that they absorb a tin flavor, and so whenever possible I make my own, which is a fairly simple procedure. Prior to using these starchy pastes, be sure to refrigerate them so they solidify, which makes them easier to handle. The colors of freshly made pastes are not as dark as those of the canned versions.

For the red bean paste: Put the red beans with 4 cups water and the sugar in a pot and bring to a boil over high heat. Reduce the heat to medium-low and cook the beans, covered, until they are tender and have absorbed all the water, about 2 hours. Transfer the beans to a food processor with the lard. Process until smooth. (Pass through a fine mesh sieve, discarding the skins, if you wish.) Chill before using.

For the lotus paste: Put the lotus seeds with 2 cups water and the sugar in a pot and bring to a boil over high heat. Reduce the heat to medium-low and cook the lotus seeds, covered, until they are tender and have absorbed all the water, about 1 hour. Transfer the seeds to a food processor with the lard; process until smooth. Chill before using. (Repeat for the mung beans.)

For the jujube (red date) paste: Put the jujubes with water to cover in a pot and bring to a boil over high heat. Reduce the heat to medium-low and cook the jujubes until they are plump and tender, about 30 minutes. Drain and transfer to a food processor with the sugar and lard. Process to a smooth paste. Chill before using.

For the black sesame paste: Place the black sesame seeds in a food processor with the sugar and process to a smooth paste. Chill before using.

For the peanut paste: Place the peanuts in a food processor with the sugar and process to a very fine powder.

HONG DAU SAH
SWEET RED BEAN SOUP

SERVES 4 TO 6

¾ cup dried RED AZUKI BEANS,
soaked for 4 hours or overnight,
then drained

⅓ cup or more GRANULATED
SUGAR

6 TANGERINE PEELS, soaked until
softened and pith removed

20 LOTUS SEEDS, soaked for
12 hours or overnight, then
drained

THE CHINESE LOVE RED. It is a vibrant color that signifies happiness and luck and is believed to ward off evil spirits. For this reason, the color is always used at celebrations such as weddings, birthdays, and, especially, the Chinese New Year. For this dessert red azuki beans are used along with ivory-white lotus seeds for contrast in both color and texture. This can be served as a dessert, but because it is a bit starchy, it makes a better afternoon snack. It can be served hot, at room temperature, or chilled. It is particularly good served hot in the winter, because it has a distinct warming effect. Once this soup is chilled, the beans, which continue to soak up the liquid, can be used as a topping for vanilla ice cream, or used as an ingredient for making red bean ice cream (page 545).

Some cooks like to add tapioca pearls to thicken the soup and give it more texture. You can add about ¼ cup tapioca (or sago) pearls to the soup and stir them until they turn transparent.

Place the red azuki beans and sugar in a pot with 7 cups water over medium heat, cover with a lid, and cook until the beans are tender and the liquids have reduced by about 3 cups, about 1½ hours. (Adjust the heat if boiling too vigorously.) Add the tangerine peels and lotus seeds and cook until tender, about 30 minutes more.

Variations: I have had red bean soup in a Japanese restaurant made of nothing but red beans, sugar, and water. Follow the recipe, omitting the lotus seeds and tangerine peels, for the Japanese version of this red bean soup.

For a red bean sauce, often used as an ice cream topping, cook the soup until the water has completely evaporated. Mix in a tablespoon of sugar syrup for every cup of cooked red beans in order to give a light sheen to the beans and sweeten them further.

In Hong Kong, a man burns incense at the Yuen Yuen Institute and Temple to invite his ancestors to join in the New Year celebration.

CHE DAU XANH
SWEET MUNG BEAN SOUP

SERVES 4 TO 6

1 cup peeled split MUNG BEANS,
    soaked for 3 hours, then drained
3 cups unsweetened COCONUT
    MILK (page 77); or commercial
    equivalent
⅓ cup or more GRANULATED
    SUGAR
Toasted SESAME SEEDS

MUNG BEANS ARE WIDELY USED in Vietnam in both savory and sweet dishes, and in this dessert the mung beans are cooked and mashed, then diluted with coconut milk. The result is a creamy yellow mung bean soup called *che dau xanh*, which you can also serve hot for breakfast on a cold day.

Some Vietnamese chefs like to cook the beans down with the coconut milk until the liquids evaporate, turning a light soup into a pudding. I prefer the soup, but you can certainly try the pudding. To facilitate things, be sure to buy dried peeled split yellow mung beans, rather than whole green (skin on) mung beans, or you'll need to spend time soaking and removing every bit of skin.

1. Bring 2 cups water to a simmer in a pot over medium heat. Add the mung beans and cook, stirring constantly, until the water is completely absorbed and the beans are tender, about 20 minutes.

2. Transfer the beans to a fine mesh sieve set over a pot. With the back of a spoon or ladle, press the beans through the sieve. Add the coconut milk, 1 cup water, and sugar to the pot. Stir with the mung bean soup until smooth. Bring to a simmer over medium-low heat. Ladle some soup into individual bowls and garnish each serving with some sesame seeds.

CHE CHUOI
SWEET BANANA AND
COCONUT TAPIOCA SOUP

SERVES 4 TO 6

2 cups unsweetened COCONUT
MILK (page 77); or commercial
equivalent

⅓ cup TAPIOCA PEARLS

½ cup GRANULATED SUGAR

Pinch or two of KOSHER SALT

6 small ripe ASIAN BANANAS,
or 2 large ripe ones, peeled
and diced

Toasted SESAME SEEDS

COCONUT MILK AND SUGAR serve as the base for this delicious sweet banana and coconut tapioca soup, *che chuoi*. As in all Vietnamese (or Southeast Asian) desserts, a pinch of salt counterbalances the sweetness of the soup, while water is added to lighten the rich coconut milk. Any ripe bananas can be used here, but I prefer the tiny Asian kind, which are sweet with an amazing floral flavor note.

You can also use sweet fresh yellow corn, or diced taro or sweet potato, which the Chinese prefer instead of the banana, for a different yet equally delicious version of the soup. You can also adjust the tapioca pearl, coconut milk, and water quantities to create a pudding version of the recipe.

1. Bring the coconut milk and 2 cups water to a boil in a pot over high heat, reduce the heat to medium-low, stir in the tapioca pearls, sugar, and salt, and cook until the tapioca pearls are translucent, about 30 minutes.

2. Stir in the bananas, turn off the heat, cover the pot, and allow the bananas to steam, about 15 minutes. Serve hot. Ladle some soup into individual small bowls and garnish each serving with some toasted sesame seeds.

Variations: For the corn version, add 2 cups fresh corn kernels instead of the bananas and follow the recipe exactly.

For the root vegetable version, peel and dice a large sweet potato or an equivalent amount of taro. Follow the recipe, adding the root vegetable of choice at the same time as the tapioca pearls, and then proceed with the recipe. Taste to be sure the root vegetable is tender prior to serving.

HUGIMJAJUK
BLACK SESAME
SWEET RICE PORRIDGE

SERVES 4 TO 6

1 cup short-grain RICE, soaked in
2 cups water for 3 hours, then
drained

½ cup BLACK SESAME SEEDS,
rinsed

¼ cup or more GRANULATED
SUGAR

½ teaspoon KOSHER SALT

¼ cup roasted PINE NUTS,
finely ground

IN KOREA RICE PORRIDGE is enjoyed as a sweet food as well as a savory item. I especially enjoy this nutty gruel for breakfast, as it is warming and mildly filling. A generous amount of black sesame seeds is ground and added to the porridge, giving it a distinctive grayish-black color. The porridge is often garnished with ground pine nuts for a contrasting color.

Place the short-grain rice and black sesame seeds in a blender with 1½ cups water, and process until smooth. Pour the mixture in a pot, add 7 cups water, the sugar, and salt, and cook until smooth and thick, about 2 hours. Ladle some of the porridge into individual bowls and garnish with ground pine nuts.

Variation: For *chatjuk*, the pine nut version of this porridge, use ¼ cup black sesame seeds and ½ cup ground pine nuts. Cook the porridge with the pine nuts and garnish with the whole black sesame seeds. Pine nut porridge is often garnished with jujubes: Soak 8 jujubes until completely softened. Remove the pits, finely julienne the fruit, and sprinkle on top of the porridge just before serving.

BUBUH INJIN
BLACK STICKY
RICE PUDDING

SERVES 4 TO 6

1 cup BLACK STICKY ("glutinous") RICE, rinsed, soaked for at least 4 hours, then drained

½ cup WHITE STICKY ("glutinous") RICE, rinsed, soaked for at least 4 hours, then drained (if not using, increase the amount of black sticky rice by ½ cup)

3 tablespoons PALM SUGAR or BROWN SUGAR, or more to taste

2 PANDAN LEAVES (optional)

1½ cups unsweetened COCONUT MILK (page 77); or commercial equivalent

Pinch of KOSHER SALT

CALLED BUBUH INJIN in Indonesia, or *kao niow dam* in Thailand, black sticky ("glutinous") rice pudding topped with sweet coconut cream sauce is enjoyed as a snack. Black sticky rice is sometimes confused with the "wild" or whole-grain version of white sticky rice, but it is actually a different item with a similar shape and more pronounced nutty flavor. Because of its mysterious appearance, black sticky rice is sometimes referred to as "the forbidden rice"; and because it is widely consumed in Indonesia, it is also often called Indonesian black rice. The dry grains appear black with brown streaks, but when soaked and cooked, they become purple. Like white sticky rice, black rice needs to soak for at least 4 hours prior to cooking. (I usually soak the rice overnight in the refrigerator.)

In this version, the black sticky rice is combined with white sticky rice for a lighter purple color, and it is boiled rather than steamed.

1. Place both the black and white sticky rice in a pot with 1 cup water. Bring to a boil over high heat, then reduce heat to low; stir in 1 tablespoon palm sugar and add the pandan leaves (if using). Cover and cook until all the water is absorbed, about 20 minutes. Divide among individual dessert bowls.

2. Bring the coconut milk to a boil in a pot over high heat. Reduce the heat to medium-low, add the remaining palm sugar and a pinch or two of salt, and simmer until both the sugar and salt have dissolved completely, about 2 minutes. Spoon some coconut sauce over each serving of sticky rice pudding.

Variation: For *kao niow dam*, the Thai version of the pudding, substitute ½ cup black sticky rice for the white sticky rice, omit the pandan leaves, and proceed with the recipe. For a looser version of the pudding, add an extra cup of water to the rice when cooking it.

KHAO NEOW MAMUANG
DIVINE COCONUT STICKY
RICE WITH MANGO

SERVES 4 TO 6

1 cup WHITE STICKY
("glutinous") RICE (yields about
2 cups cooked)

1¾ cups unsweetened COCONUT
MILK (page 77); or commercial
equivalent

3 tablespoons PALM SUGAR; or
GRANULATED SUGAR

Pinch of KOSHER SALT

1 tablespoon TAPIOCA STARCH
or CORNSTARCH

1 ripe MANGO, peeled and sliced
into 12 wedges

Toasted SESAME SEEDS

CHEESECLOTH, about 12 inches
square (or a thin cotton kitchen
towel)

A STICKY RICE AND MANGO SNACK, *khao neow mamuang* is one the most popular Thai sweets. Like many such Thai dishes, it appears in one form or another in several other Asian cultures. The Thai also have a version of the recipe that uses red beans rather than mango. The Vietnamese version of the dish uses black-eyed peas and is called *che dau trang*; the Cambodians version, *bay damneoub*, is sticky rice topped with durian sauce (see variations).

Traditionally the coconut sauce is made using coconut cream or a combination of coconut cream and coconut milk. I find coconut cream to be much too heavy and use only coconut milk thickened with tapioca starch. You may also use any other starch you have on hand (use only 1½ teaspoons diluted with 1 tablespoon of water). If you like a rich coconut flavor, simply use coconut cream.

1. Rinse the sticky rice in cold water twice, gently swishing the grains with your fingers each time, and drain. Soak the sticky rice in 2 cups water, refrigerated, for at least 4 hours or overnight. Drain when ready to use.

2. Fill the bottom third of a wok with water and place a bamboo steamer with a lid inside it. Bring the water to a boil over high heat. Place a dampened cheesecloth (or towel) over the bamboo rack and spread the rice on it, leaving a 1-inch border all around to let the steam through. Fold over the cheesecloth or towel, cover the steamer securely with the lid, and steam until the rice is translucent and tender but firm, about 20 minutes.

3. Bring the coconut milk to a boil in a small pot over high heat. Reduce the heat to medium-low, add the sugar and salt, and stir until both are completely dissolved. Dissolve the tapioca starch with 2 tablespoons water and, using a whisk, quickly stir it into the coconut milk. Allow the coconut milk sauce to thicken, about 1 minute. Remove from the heat. Pour half the coconut mixture into a serving bowl. Transfer the sticky rice to the remaining coconut milk in the small pot and stir to coat the grains evenly. Cover with the lid and let stand until the rice has completely absorbed the coconut milk, about 15 minutes. Divide the rice among individual plates and spoon a bit more coconut sauce over each serving of rice. Gar-

DURIAN IS A LARGE PRICKLY FRUIT WITH AN AROMA THAT MANY FIND OFFENSIVE.
HOWEVER, ITS YELLOW FLESH IS CREAMY, LIKE A RIPE AVOCADO, AND SWEET.

DURIAN IS A FRUIT NATIVE to the tropics of Southeast Asia. It is expensive in Asia, and you can find it in the United States in Asian markets for about thirty dollars per fruit. Look for a large brownish-green prickly fruit the size of a football (one durian easily serves six), sometimes hung in plastic netting. The durian has a rich creamy flesh with a pleasantly sweet flavor. Be forewarned, however, that the fruit has a notoriously powerful and offensive odor. People enjoy it despite (or perhaps because of) its reputation for what can only be described as stinkiness.

nish with an equal amount of sliced mango, sprinkle with sesame seeds, and serve while still warm or at room temperature.

Variations: To make Vietnamese *che dau trang*, soak ½ cup black-eyed peas overnight. Drain, then place the beans in a pot with 4 cups water and 2 tablespoons granulated sugar. Bring to a boil, reduce the heat to medium-low, and cook until the beans have absorbed most of the liquid and are tender but firm,

about an hour. Spoon over the sticky coconut rice with extra coconut sauce as desired.

To make the Cambodian *bay dam-neoub*, place 1 cup durian flesh (crushed with a fork until smooth), 2 cups coconut milk, 2 tablespoons sugar, and a pinch of salt in a pot over medium heat, and stir until heated through. Stir in the steamed sticky rice and mix well. Cover the pot with a lid for 15 minutes, then serve.

KHAO TOM MAT
STICKY RICE WITH BANANA WRAPPED IN LEAVES

MAKES 8 RICE BUNDLES

1 cup WHITE STICKY
("glutinous") RICE (yields about
2 cups cooked)

1¾ cups unsweetened COCONUT
MILK (page 77); or commercial
equivalent

3 tablespoons PALM SUGAR; or
GRANULATED SUGAR

Pinch of KOSHER SALT

Eight 6-inch-square BANANA
LEAVES; or 16 BAMBOO LEAVES,
soaked in water until softened

4 small ripe ASIAN BANANAS; or
2 regular ripe BANANAS, peeled
and thinly sliced diagonally

CHEESECLOTH, about 12 inches
square

KITCHEN STRING

THROUGHOUT SOUTHEAST ASIA, sticky rice cooked in a sweet coconut milk with a salty back note is often wrapped in banana leaves
with ripe banana slices and steamed until set. In Thailand and Cambodia, where it is known as *khao tom mat* and *nom nsahm chaek*, respectively, it is
sold in markets or by street vendors. In the Philippines, it is known as *budbud*
(meaning "cracking at the seams") and sometimes has bitter chocolate drizzled on top.

You can also use bamboo leaves, which may be easier to find. Bamboo
leaves are dried, and will need to be soaked until pliable prior to using.

1. Rinse the sticky rice in cold water twice, gently swishing the grains with your fingers each time, and drain. Soak the sticky rice in 2 cups water, refrigerated, for at least 4 hours or overnight. Drain when ready to use.

2. Fill the bottom third of a wok with water and place a bamboo steamer with a lid inside it. Bring the water to a boil over high heat. Place a dampened cheesecloth over the bamboo rack and spread the rice on it, leaving a 1-inch border all around to let the steam through. Fold over the cheesecloth, cover the steamer with the lid, and steam until the rice is translucent and tender but firm, about 20 minutes.

3. Heat the coconut milk, sugar, and salt in a pot over medium heat. Stir in the steamed sticky rice and mix well. Cover the pot and remove it from the heat. Allow the rice to ab-sorb the coconut milk, about 10 minutes. Spread about 2 tablespoons sticky rice in the center (so it looks like a narrow white rectangle) of each of the banana leaves. Top with 2 to 3 banana slices, overlapping them as necessary. Top with 2 table-spoons sticky rice. Fold in the short sides of the leaves, then the larger sides. Use kitchen string to secure the bundles. They should look like large spring rolls.

4. Replenish the water in the wok and remove the bamboo steamer. Place the tied rice bundles inside the wok, cover, and gently boil over medium-low heat until the rice is very sticky and molded, about 45 minutes. Serve hot or at room tem-perature. Once refrigerated, the rice hardens, so you will need to re-steam the bundles before serving.

DAU XANH VUNG
DEEP-FRIED
SESAME DUMPLINGS

MAKES ABOUT 30 DUMPLINGS

¾ cup peeled split MUNG BEANS,
    soaked for 3 hours, then drained

¾ cup GRANULATED SUGAR

2½ cups STICKY ("glutinous")
    RICE FLOUR

½ cup RICE FLOUR

1 flaky medium POTATO such as an
    Idaho, boiled, peeled, and
    mashed

½ cup raw BLOND SESAME SEEDS

VEGETABLE OIL for deep-frying

IN VIETNAM, DEEP-FRIED sticky rice balls covered in sesame seeds are popular, especially when filled with mung bean paste. The Vietnamese love mung beans as a filler, but these dumplings can be made with all sorts of sweet pastes (page 513), so feel free to experiment. The Chinese call these *jien doy*, and they often fill them with red bean paste. A good Chinese bakery carries *jien doy*, as does a dim sum restaurant, where the morsels are sometimes filled with savory ground pork.

1. Bring 2 cups water to a simmer in a pot over medium heat. Add the mung beans and ¼ cup of the sugar. Cook, stirring constantly, until the water is completely absorbed, about 20 minutes. (If the beans are still firm, add a little water and continue cooking until tender.) Remove the pot from the heat and allow to cool. Crush the beans with a fork to form a fairly smooth paste. Refrigerate to cool.

2. Mix together the sticky rice flour, rice flour, potato, and remaining sugar in a bowl. Add a cup of water and mix until all the ingredients are well combined and the dough detaches from the side of the bowl. Knead for 2 to 3 minutes; the dough should feel moist and slightly sticky. Roll the dough into a long rope and cut it into 30 equal pieces. Form each piece of dough into a ball, then flatten each into a disk. Cover with plastic wrap.

3. Divide and shape the cooked mung beans into 30 balls. Enclose each mung bean ball in a rice flour disk and shape into a smooth ball. Scatter sesame seeds on a plate and gently roll the balls in the seeds until they are evenly coated.

4. Heat the oil in a wok or pot over medium heat to 360° to 375°F. Working in batches, carefully lower the dumplings into the hot oil. Use chopsticks to roll them around, while keeping them apart, so they crisp and turn golden evenly, 3 to 5 minutes. Drain on paper towels and serve with tea.

Variation: While these dumplings are traditionally presented as balls, my students have had fun shaping the dumplings into crescents, squares, and logs. Have fun with shapes!

BANH TROI NUOC
RICE PEARLS
IN GINGER BROTH

MAKES ABOUT 150 PEARLS

1 cup STICKY ("glutinous") RICE
FLOUR
¾ cup boiling WATER
2 ounces fresh GINGER, thinly
sliced lengthwise
1 cup RAW SUGAR, or more
to taste
Toasted SESAME SEEDS

I N VIETNAM, STICKY RICE DUMPLINGS—plain or filled with sweet
ground mung beans—are sometimes served in a ginger-infused broth.
Derived from a similar Chinese dessert called *nor mai chi*, my aunt Loan's
rice dumplings are plain and look like pearls. Sometimes, for a festive occasion, she will color half the dough red (see variation). Pinched and shaped
into tiny balls, the rice pearls are served in a sweet ginger-infused broth or a
light sweet coconut broth with a salty backnote (see variation). The trick to
making this dough properly is to stir boiling water into the sticky rice flour,
making the dough easier to knead while partially cooking it. When cool
enough to handle (but still warm), the dough is kneaded until smooth. The
same dough is used to make Japanese *mochi* (see the third variation).

I like to use raw sugar, which gives the ginger broth a beautiful amber
color. You can also use palm sugar. The broth will not be as clear, but it will
have a subtle palm flavor.

1. Put the flour in a mixing bowl
and form a well in the middle. Stir
in about ½ cup boiling water until
well combined. Transfer the dough
to a work surface. The dough may
feel hot; if you can't take the heat,
wait until the dough cools a bit, but
it must still be warm while you
knead it. Knead 2 to 3 minutes, until
the dough feels moist without sticking to your hands. Pinch small
amounts of dough to form ½-inch-
diameter pearls.

2. Bring 8 cups water to a boil over
high heat. Add the ginger slices and
sugar, reduce the heat to medium,
and gently boil until spicy, 30 to 45
minutes. Strain and discard the
ginger.

3. Meanwhile, bring another pot of
water to a boil over high heat. Working in batches, add the dough balls
and cook until they come up to the
surface and float, about 3 minutes.
Transfer about a dozen rice balls to
individual bowls. Ladle some sweet
ginger broth into each bowl, sprinkle with toasted sesame seeds, and
serve.

Variations: For red-colored pearls,
stir 2 dashes of red food coloring
into the boiling water prior to
adding to the rice flour. If you wish,
you can split the recipe in half, stain-
ing a portion with red food coloring.

In China and Southeast Asia small
rice balls are served in a sweet coconut broth. In the Philippines, they

call the soup *ginataang bilo-bilo*. Bring 4 cups unsweetened coconut milk (page 77; or commercial equivalent), 4 cups water, 1 cup raw sugar, and a pinch or two of salt to a gentle boil in a pot over medium heat. Add the boiled rice balls to individual bowls. Ladle some coconut broth over each serving and sprinkle with toasted sesame seeds.

For Japanese *mochi* (rice and red bean dumplings), shape the balls so they are about ½ inch in diameter. After boiling them until cooked, about 5 minutes, refrigerate to chill. Cover each rice ball with about 1 teaspoon red bean paste (page 513). Refrigerate to chill, at least 4 hours. Present them sprinkled with toasted sesame seeds or black sesame seeds, or a combination of both.

KYONGDAN
RAINBOW RICE DUMPLINGS

MAKES ABOUT 48 DUMPLINGS

1 cup STICKY ("glutinous") RICE
FLOUR

¾ cup boiling WATER

⅓ cup SWEET RED BEAN PASTE
(page 513), chilled

⅓ cup SWEET PEANUT PASTE
(page 513), chilled

⅓ cup SWEET BLACK SESAME PASTE
(page 513), chilled

⅓ cup SWEET MUNG BEAN PASTE
(page 513), chilled

⅓ cup MATCHA (green tea powder)

⅓ cup dried unsweetened
COCONUT FLAKES, finely
ground or powdered

⅓ cup SOYBEAN FLOUR, lightly
toasted

⅓ cup BLACK SESAME SEEDS, finely
ground or powdered

KOREANS ENJOY RICE DUMPLINGS, called *kyongdan*, made from sticky rice flour. The chewy dumplings are shaped like pinballs and filled with all sorts of sweet pastes, made from peanuts, red beans, jujubes, or other things. Once boiled, they are rolled in colorful and flavorful powders made from black sesame, soybean flour, and pine nuts. I love making these little delights; my favorite powder is Japanese *matcha*, green tea powder. The bitter essence and bright-colored green powder are quite wonderful when the rice ball is filled with sweet red bean paste. While the Koreans enjoy all sorts of colorful variations on these rice dumplings, they actually originated in China, where they are called *tong yuen*. There they are filled with black sesame paste or peanut paste and served in their cooking water as a broth for sipping. They are also boiled, drained, and rolled in finely shredded dried coconut; they are sold in Chinese or Southeast Asian markets. The Vietnamese enjoy a version filled with mung bean paste, while the Cambodians like them filled with palm sugar.

For coconut powder, simply process coconut flakes in a spice grinder until very fine. Do the same for the black sesame seeds. Toast the soybean flour in a dry skillet over low heat, stirring continuously, until just golden.

1. Put the flour in a bowl and form a well in the middle. Stir in about ½ cup boiling water until well combined. Transfer the dough to a work surface. The dough may feel hot; if you cannot take the heat, wait until the dough cools a bit, but it should still be warm while you knead it. Knead 2 to 3 minutes, until the dough feels moist without sticking to your hands. Cut the dough in 2 equal portions and roll out into ropes. Cut the dough into 48 equal pieces, shape them into balls, and flatten them into thin disks. Divide the disks into 4 piles.

2. Fill a dough disk with 1 teaspoon red bean paste. Enclose the filling and reshape the dough into a ball. Continue until you have 12 red bean paste balls. Repeat the process, making 12 peanut paste balls, 12 sesame paste balls, and 12 mung bean paste balls. Be sure to keep the balls separated by type of filling.

3. Bring a pot of water to a boil and, working in batches, cook the balls until they float to the top, 5 minutes (keep them separated by type of filling). Drain and allow to cool a bit on a lightly oiled plate. When the balls are cool, roll the red bean paste balls into the green tea powder; the peanut paste balls into the coconut powder; the black sesame paste balls into the soybean flour; and the mung bean paste balls into the black sesame powder. Place them on a platter, arranging them in concentric circles, or in rows, or however else you may prefer.

GEUNG NAI
DELICATE GINGER CUSTARD

SERVES 4

1 1½ cups whole MILK

3 tablespoons GRANULATED SUGAR

2 large EGG WHITES

or more tablespoons GINGER
  EXTRACT (page 74)

THIS WONDERFULLY LIGHT GINGER custard is popular in Hong Kong, where it is served in a few shops specializing in custards and herbal jellies. The Chinese enjoy this delicate egg-white-and-ginger custard in the afternoon, often served warm and right out of the bamboo steamer; it can also be served chilled after dinner. The ginger flavor is a nice refreshing finale to a meal and aids digestion.

1. Fill a wok halfway with water and bring to a boil over high heat. Put a bamboo steamer inside it and reduce the heat to medium-low. (The water should remain at a gentle simmer or the custard will curdle.)

2. Whisk together the milk, sugar, egg whites, and ginger extract in a bowl until the egg whites are smooth (no discernible transparent globs anywhere) and the sugar is completely dissolved. Divide the custard among four ½-cup dessert bowls or soufflé ramekins. Transfer the bowls to the steamer, cover, and cook until the custards set, about 20 minutes. Remove from the steamer and allow to cool completely. Cover with plastic wrap and refrigerate at least 12 hours or overnight. Serve hot, at room temperature, or chilled.

HUNG YAN DOFU
ALMOND CUSTARD WITH FRESH FRUIT

SERVES 4 TO 6

3 cups whole MILK
2 teaspoons ALMOND EXTRACT
¼ cup GRANULATED SUGAR
1 tablespoon AGAR-AGAR POWDER
2 PEACHES, poached, peeled, pitted, and diced
1 cup fresh GOOSEBERRIES
12 MARASCHINO CHERRIES

HUNG YAN DOFU is one of my favorite snacks. Served chilled, this almond-flavored custard (which has not an ounce of tofu in it) is cubed and topped with diced fruit in syrup. When I make it at home, I like to take advantage of ripe fruit such as peaches, cherries, and gooseberries, which cook in a light sugar syrup.

1. Heat the milk, almond extract, 2 tablespoons sugar, and the agar-agar to a gentle boil over medium heat; stir until the sugar and agar-agar are completely dissolved, about 5 minutes. Pour into a 9-inch nonstick square cake pan and chill, refrigerated, until completely set, about 4 hours, or overnight.

2. Place the remaining sugar with a cup of water in a pot and bring to a boil over high heat; reduce until lightly thickened, about 10 minutes. Pour over the peaches and gooseberries. Allow to cool, then refrigerate.

3. To serve, cut the almond jelly into approximately ½-inch cubes and gently toss with the chilled peaches and gooseberries. (I usually drain these of their sugar syrup, but this is entirely up to you.) Spoon some of the cubed custard into individual dessert bowls. Garnish with 2 or 3 cherries each.

SANKIAH L'POH
COLONIAL-ERA SQUASH
WITH COCONUT CUSTARD

SERVES 4 TO 8

1½ cups unsweetened COCONUT
   MILK (page 77); or commercial
   equivalent
3 large EGGS
2 tablespoons PALM SUGAR
Pinch of KOSHER SALT
2 ACORN SQUASH, halved
   lengthwise, seeds removed

M Y FAMILY BROUGHT BACK this delicious acorn squash and coconut custard recipe from Cambodia in the late 1960s. Known as *sankiah l'poh*, it is most likely a French-Cambodian fusion dish from the colonial era. Its earthy squash flavor and texture are a perfect complement to the sweet, silky custard. Traditionally, small pumpkins are used to steam the custard, but these are not always readily available; acorn squash makes a good substitute. As in many Southeast Asian sweets, a pinch of salt counterbalances the sweetness of the custard, which in this case comes from palm sugar. A dessert or snack, *sankiah l'poh* is traditionally steamed, but I also love it baked (see variation). Baking allows the natural sugars from the pumpkin or acorn squash to surface and caramelize. You can brush some melted butter on the rim of the squash for extra flavor and a glistening finish. At the table, the green, orange, and white colors of *sankiah l'poh* evoke autumn, when pumpkins and acorn squash are in season. When done cooking, the custard-filled pumpkin can be served at room temperature or chilled. This custard-filled pumpkin can also be found in Thailand, where it is called *sankaya fuk thong*. Just before serving the pumpkin, a sweet coconut sauce, much like the one made for the coconut sticky rice and mango dessert (pp. 520–21), is drizzled on top.

1. Fill the bottom half of a wok with water, fit a bamboo steamer with a lid inside it, and place the wok over high heat. Meanwhile, whisk the coconut milk, eggs, palm sugar, and salt in a bowl until the palm sugar and salt have dissolved completely and the custard is perfectly smooth.

2. Using aluminum foil, make 4 rings. Place an acorn squash half, rounded side down, on top of each foil ring. (The ring will stabilize the acorn squash.) Fill each half with

the custard. Place in the steamer and steam until cooked through and very tender, 30 to 45 minutes, depending on the size. To check for doneness, simply insert a skewer into the acorn squash and the custard. The custard should not feel wet; the squash should feel tender. Allow to steam for a few extra minutes if necessary. Serve hot, at room temperature, or chilled.

Variation: Preheat the oven to 375°F. Fill the acorn squash with custard and sprinkle some palm sugar across the top. Place the pumpkin or acorn squash in a baking dish, scatter some butter shavings on the rim of each squash, place on a baking sheet, and bake until cooked through, about 30 minutes. Check for doneness as in step 2. Serve hot, at room temperature, or chilled.

NOM L'POH

PUMPKIN PUDDING IN BANANA LEAVES

MAKES 12 PUDDINGS

KOSHER SALT

1 small BUTTERNUT SQUASH, peeled, seeded, and cubed

2 tablespoons PALM SUGAR

1 cup unsweetened COCONUT MILK (page 77); or commercial equivalent

1 tablespoon TAPIOCA STARCH or CORNSTARCH

Twelve 6-inch square BANANA LEAVES; or CUPCAKE PAPERS

24 round TOOTHPICKS (not flimsy flat ones), if using banana leaves

N OM L'POH is a delicious pumpkin pudding native to Cambodia. The owners of Cambodiana Restaurant in Berkeley, California (who were originally from Phnom Penh), serve this wonderful dessert cooked in banana leaves. Because it is not always possible to know whether the pumpkin you choose is going to be sweet, I prefer to use butternut squash for this dessert, as it has never disappointed me.

1. Bring a pot of salted water to a boil over medium heat and add the butternut squash. Cook until very tender, about 20 minutes. With a slotted spoon transfer the butternut squash pieces to a blender. Add the palm sugar and salt with the coconut milk to a pot over medium heat. Dilute the tapioca starch with 1 tablespoon water and add to the pot. Do not let it come to a boil. Add the mixture to the squash in the blender and puree to a smooth, thick consistency.

2. Place an equal amount of squash purée in the center of each of the 12 banana leaves, folding in the sides. Thread a toothpick at each open end to enclose the puree. The leaves should look like flat spring rolls.

3. Fill the bottom third of a wok with water and place a bamboo steamer with a lid inside it. Working in batches, if necessary, place the stuffed banana leaves, folded side facing up, inside the steamer. Cover the steamer securely. Steam over high heat until set, about 15 minutes. Allow to cool. Serve hot, at room temperature, or chilled.

A CAMBODIAN WOMAN WEAVES BEAUTIFUL RAW SILK, USED FOR MAKING TRADITIONAL CLOTHING SUCH AS THE SARONG.

BANH GAN
COCONUT CRÈME CARAMEL

SERVES 4

½ cup GRANULATED SUGAR

3 large EGGS

1 cup unsweetened COCONUT
MILK (page 77); or commercial
equivalent

½ cup WHOLE MILK or HALF AND
HALF

4 fresh MINT LEAVES of equal size

THIS FRENCH-INFLUENCED Southeast Asian dessert is found in Vietnam. The French use cow's milk for making this creamy custard; in Southeast Asia, rich coconut milk is used. For a lighter version, I like to cut the rich coconut milk with whole cow's milk. In the Philippines, a similar dessert, called *leche flan*, is made with condensed milk; this is a Spanish influence.

1. Melt ¼ cup of the sugar with a tablespoon of water in a saucepan over medium-low heat, occasionally swirling the pan, until the sugar starts to bubble and turn a rich golden color, 3 to 5 minutes. Remove from the heat and divide the caramel among four ½-cup soufflé ramekins. Tilt the ramekins so the bottoms and sides are covered with the caramel.

2. Preheat the oven to 275°F. Meanwhile, whisk the remaining sugar and the eggs until well combined. Add the coconut milk and whole milk, and continue to whisk until smooth and the sugar is completely dissolved. Divide the mixture among the ramekins. Create a water bath by filling a baking dish halfway with water. Place the ramekins in it and bake until the custards set, about 45 minutes. Remove from the oven and allow to cool in the water bath. Cover with plastic wrap and refrigerate at least 12 hours. To serve, loosen the *banh gan* with a knife and turn onto plates so the caramel is on top, and drizzle any remaining caramel on the plates around the custard. Served chilled, garnished with a mint leaf.

CHO LIE WOO PAN
SWEET RED BEAN OR
JUJUBE CRÊPES

MAKES ABOUT 24 SMALL
SQUARES

½ cup RED BEAN PASTE or JUJUBE
   PASTE (page 513), chilled
8 SPRING ROLL WRAPPERS
   (page 258); or commercial
   equivalent
1 or 2 large EGGS, beaten
2 tablespoons VEGETABLE OIL
BLACK SESAME SEEDS
Toasted SESAME SEEDS

SOLD BY STREET VENDORS in northern China, cho lie woo pan are thin crêpes filled with a thin layer of rich, sweet red bean or jujube paste. I have enjoyed this as a dessert many times at my neighborhood Shanghainese restaurant. Easy to make, cho lie woo pan are essentially flat paste-filled spring rolls, pan-fried until crispy and cut into bite-size squares. For an authentic presentation, sprinkle black sesame seeds and toasted sesame seeds on top before serving.

1. Spread about 2 tablespoons red bean paste on each of 4 wrappers, leaving a 1-inch border all around. Brush some egg wash around the 1-inch border and place a second wrapper on top. Press the edges and middle to make sure the filling is securely enclosed.

2. Heat 2 teaspoons oil in a nonstick pan over medium heat. When the pan is hot, pan-fry 1 pancake until golden all around, about 2 minutes per side. Transfer to a paper towel-lined plate to drain. Repeat the process with the remaining oil and pancakes. Sprinkle each pancake with black and toasted sesame seeds. Cut into small squares and serve while hot.

TURONES DE SABA
BANANA AND JACKFRUIT SPRING ROLLS

MAKES 24 ROLLS

VEGETABLE OIL for deep-frying
24 SPRING ROLL WRAPPERS
   (page 258); or commercial
   equivalent
3 ripe BANANAS, peeled and thinly
   sliced on the diagonal
2 cups fresh JACKFRUIT, thinly
   sliced
2 tablespoons BROWN SUGAR
3 large EGGS, 1 beaten
1½ cups unsweetened COCONUT
   MILK (page 77); or commercial
   equivalent
1 tablespoon PALM SUGAR; or
   BROWN SUGAR

T URONES DE SABA, fried sweet banana and jackfruit spring rolls, are enjoyed throughout the Philippines. Street vendors sell these items all day long; they're a particular favorite of schoolchildren when it's time for recess. "Turon turon," the vendors call, using the nickname for the item, and the children come running. I must admit that I, too, was hooked on the first bite and continued to enjoy them at least once a day while in the Philippines. They are especially delicious with coconut cream sauce drizzled on top. I sometimes cut down on the amounts of sugar in Filipino recipes (they are often a bit too sweet for my taste). I prefer to rely on the sweetness of the bananas and jackfruit and add only a sprinkle of sugar, but you can make your own judgment call.

Fresh jackfruit is occasionally available in Chinatowns. If using canned jackfruit in syrup, be sure to drain and rinse the fruit prior to using.

1. Heat enough oil for deep-frying in a pot over medium-high heat to a temperature of 360° to 375°F. Meanwhile, place a spring roll wrapper on a clean work surface in front of you. (If using the square store-bought ones, place the skin so it looks like a diamond with a point near you.) Place 2 to 3 slices of bananas overlapping each other with 2 to 3 slices of jackfruit on top, an inch in from the edge of the skin near you. Sprinkle the fruit lightly with brown sugar and roll the wrapper over the filling once. Fold in the sides, then fold over twice more, leaving an edge open. Moisten the edge well with some of the beaten egg wash and continue rolling all the way to enclose the filling. Repeat the process until you have 24 turones

de saba. It is important that you do not make the rolls too tight or too loose. If too tight, the roll will crack open while it fries; if too loose, the oil will seep into it during the frying process.

2. Working in batches, deep-fry the rolls, turning them once until golden all over, about 3 minutes. (If the oil is too agitated, lower the heat. If the oil is too calm, either it is not hot enough and you need to wait, or your burner is not powerful enough and you need to increase the heat.) Drain on a paper towel–lined plate.

3. Meanwhile, whisk together the remaining egg yolks (reserve whites for other use), coconut milk, and palm sugar until the sugar dissolves

completely. Warm the mixture over a double-boiler set over medium heat. Whisking constantly, be sure the mixture thickens to a loose custard consistency resembling that of *crème anglaise* (it should stick lightly to the back of a spoon), 15 to 20 minutes. The egg should not scramble; if it does, your heat is too high. All is not lost—pass the custard through a very fine mesh sieve and discard any solids. Serve the crispy *turones de saba* with the coconut sauce on the side or drizzled on top.

ABOUT A DOZEN SPECIES of bananas are grown in the Philippines, and in this recipe *saba,* a short and fat yellowish-green skinned banana, is traditionally used. While some Filipinos enjoy eating *saba* fresh, it is generally considered a cooking banana, like a plantain, but sweet. *Saba* is difficult to find in the United States, so I use regular bananas here. Jackfruit, known as *nangka* in Tagalog, is one of the largest fruits in the world, weighing up to forty pounds. An oblong thick fruit protected by a green bumpy skin, with yellow flesh and seeds that are generally eaten, it is enjoyed throughout Southeast Asia and China. Because the fruit is so large, it is usually sold at the market in slices, or with its flesh and seeds

JACKFRUIT IS THE LARGEST FRUIT IN THE WORLD; IT CAN WEIGH AS MUCH AS FORTY POUNDS. SOUTHEAST ASIANS ENJOY IT RIPE AS A DESSERT OR SNACK AND UNRIPE IN SALADS, STIR-FRIES, OR SOUPS.

separated. Sometimes available fresh in the United States, it is still a relative rarity, and you may have to use canned jackfruit. You can also grind the fruit into a pulp and make pudding or ice cream. Smooth in texture, with a wonderfully sweet aroma, jackfruit can be eaten as is or used in cooking. In its unripe stage, it is consumed as a vegetable.

DADAR
TOASTED COCONUT ROLLS

MAKES ABOUT 12 ROLLS

2 cups finely grated COCONUT
  MEAT
⅓ to ½ cup PALM SUGAR
Pinch of KOSHER SALT
12 INDONESIAN LUMPIA CRÊPES
  (page 257)

THESE WONDERFUL SWEET ROLLS are the essence of simplicity. Called *dadar*, they are made by filling *lumpia* crêpes with finely grated coconut that has been toasted with palm sugar until sticky and caramelized. Served as afternoon snacks with tea or coffee, they are popular in Bali, Indonesia, where I first discovered them.

1. In a nonstick pan, toast the fresh coconut with palm sugar and salt over medium-low heat, stirring until caramelized evenly, 3 to 5 minutes. Transfer the mixture to a dish and allow to cool.

2. Place a crêpe on a clean work surface. Place about 2 heaping tablespoons of filling in the center of the crêpe and fold the side closest to you over the filling. Fold in the sides of the crêpe, then continue rolling to form a roll. Continue making the rolls with the remaining crêpes and coconut filling until you have 12 altogether. Serve hot or at room temperature.

DAHN TOT
EGG CUSTARD TARTLETS

MAKES ABOUT 12 SMALL PASTRIES

1½ cups all-purpose FLOUR

Pinch of KOSHER SALT

⅓ cup chilled solid LARD or VEGETABLE SHORTENING, diced

2⅓ cups WHOLE MILK

2 to 3 tablespoons GRANULATED SUGAR, to taste

4 large EGGS

1 tablespoon VANILLA EXTRACT

A TRADITIONAL PASTRY served in dim sum restaurants or found at Chinese bakeries, these egg custard tartlets are sold in small and miniature sizes. To re-create these light custard pies, I use two-and-a-half-inch-diameter fluted tins, or the miniature version, which are about half the size. Light and mildly sweet, this flaky egg custard pastry is best eaten freshly made, at room temperature. The same pastry dough is used to make coconut turnovers (see variations).

Lard is the secret to the flaky character of the pastry shell, but vegetable shortening, butter, or a combination of the two can also be used. In a pinch, you can use commercial puff pastry.

1. To make the pastry shell: Sift the flour and salt over a bowl. With your fingers quickly work the lard into the flour until well combined. You should have a loose grainy consistency. Stir in ⅓ cup of the milk and knead for 30 seconds. The more you work the dough, the tougher it gets. You're not looking for a smooth elastic dough, but rather a dough that holds together but is still somewhat crumbly. Refrigerate until chilled. Once it's chilled, roll out until ⅛ inch thick. Using a round cookie cutter or a glass, cut out circles about 2½ inches in diameter.

2. Preheat the oven to 375°F. Grease and flour two tins and then line each with a thin layer of pastry dough. Whisk together the remaining 2 cups milk and the sugar until the sugar is completely dissolved. Whisk in the eggs and vanilla until the mixture is smooth. Fill each pastry-lined tin almost to the very top with the egg mixture. Bake until the blade of a knife inserted in the center of the custard comes out clean, about 30 minutes. Cool the tarts on a rack and pry them up carefully with a knife so as not to break the pastry shell.

Variations: To make *banh dua* shredded coconut tarts: Make the pastry shells. Mix together 1½ cups finely shredded fresh coconut, 3 eggs, and 3 tablespoons palm sugar in a bowl until well combined. Fill the pastry shells with the coconut mixture and bake in a 375°F oven until golden, about 25 minutes.

You can also shape these into half-moon turnovers, sealing the edges with egg wash.

FOI THONG
GOLDEN THREADS

MAKES ABOUT 2 CUPS

2 cups GRANULATED SUGAR
1 tablespoon ROSE WATER
  (optional)
12 large EGG YOLKS
Pinch of KOSHER SALT

THE RECIPE FOR GOLDEN THREADS, or *foi thong*, as they are called in Thailand, goes back about five hundred years. Made from egg yolks and a simple sugar syrup, these egg strands are believed to have originated with the Portuguese, who were actively involved with trade in Siam, as Thailand was then known. Since then, *foi thong* have remained a favorite sweet. Because they are very sweet, they are often used to garnish less-sweet desserts and various snack items, such as sticky rice with coconut sauce (pp. 520–21). Although *foi thong* are most often associated with Thailand, you will also find them in Cambodia, where they are sold by street vendors in Phnom Penh and are called *vawee*.

The trick to making these golden threads successfully is to make sure the syrup is fluid. If it is too thick and does not flow, the threads will not be delicate and smooth but crinkly and unusable.

1. Put the sugar in a saucepan with 2 cups water and bring to a boil over high heat. Reduce the heat to medium-low and continue at a gentle boil until the sugar has completely dissolved and the liquid starts to thicken, about 10 minutes. Add the rose water (if using) and continue to boil for 5 minutes more.

2. Press the yolks through a very fine mesh sieve set over a bowl and discard the membrane. Give the eggs a quick stir with a whisk to ensure they are loose.

3. Pour the eggs into a funnel with the smallest opening, about 1⁄16 inch in diameter. Control the funnel opening with your fingertip, and work in small batches. Carefully open the funnel tip and allow the eggs to drip into the gently boiling syrup while you quickly move the funnel back and forth to form long threads. Allow the strands to cook for 30 seconds, pushing them gently into the syrup. Using chopsticks, or a small strainer, lift the threads out of the syrup and place them on a dish. Continue until you have cooked the entire egg mixture. After each batch it may be necessary to add a couple of tablespoons of water to loosen the thickening syrup; this is a judgment call. You can garnish all sorts of desserts with these beautiful golden threads, or make little nestlike bundles and serve with shredded and toasted coconut on top or small melon balls such as honeydew or cantaloupe.

IT TOOK ME SEVERAL TRIES to get *foi thong* right, so figure that you will have to consider the first dozen eggs or so as an offering to the culinary gods. Once you get a handle on the process, however, the coordinated drip-in-a-circular-motion process is quite simple. The trick is to work quickly, carefully, and, most of all, deliberately, with total control. This is especially important when moving the funnel back and forth quickly.

CHIEN CHUOI
BANANA FRITTERS

1½ cups unsweetened COCONUT
    MILK (page 77); or commercial
    equivalent
2 extra-large EGGS
1 or 2 tablespoons GRANULATED
    SUGAR, to taste
Pinch of KOSHER SALT
1 cup all-purpose FLOUR
1 teaspoon BAKING POWDER
½ cup grated COCONUT (optional)
6 small ripe ASIAN BANANAS,
    peeled and halved lengthwise; or
    3 large ripe BANANAS, peeled,
    halved lengthwise, and again
    crosswise
VEGETABLE OIL for deep-frying
CONFECTIONERS' SUGAR
    (optional)
RICE ALCOHOL or RUM (optional)

BANANES FLAMBÉES is a dessert that's found on many Vietnamese restaurant menus in France. Ripe bananas are dipped in batter and deep-fried, then sprinkled with sugar and set aflame using rice alcohol or rum. Banana fritters are not only popular with the Vietnamese, who call them *chien chuoi*, but are widely eaten in Thailand and the Philippines, where they are called *kluay khek* and *maruya*, respectively. In Thailand, grated coconut is often added to the batter for extra flavor and crispy texture.

If you plan to flambé the fritters, be sure to sprinkle some sugar on them prior to doing so. Otherwise, dust the *chien chuoi* with confectioners' sugar.

1. Whisk together the coconut milk, eggs, a tablespoon or more of the sugar, and the salt in a bowl until the sugar and salt have completely dissolved. Sift the flour and baking powder over the bowl, whisking at the same time. The consistency of the batter should be similar to that of American pancake batter, i.e., semi-thick and smooth. At this time add the grated coconut, if using. Add the banana pieces and mix to coat evenly.

2. Heat the oil in a wok over medium heat to 360° to 375°F. Working in batches, with chopsticks or tongs, pick up the banana pieces one at a time, shaking off the excess batter. Carefully lower them into the hot oil and fry until golden and crisp, 2 to 3 minutes per side. Drain the fritters on a paper towel–lined plate, then transfer to a heatproof platter if you plan to flambé. Otherwise, just before serving, dust with confectioners' sugar.

3. To flambé, sprinkle granulated sugar on top, drizzle with spirit, and light with a match. With a spoon, baste the fritters with the burning spirit until the fritters start to darken just a bit, or the sugar starts to caramelize. Have a lid near you to smother the flames if necessary. Serve hot.

HONG KONG SPONGE CAKE

SERVES ABOUT 12

VEGETABLE OIL
¾ cup all-purpose FLOUR
½ cup GRANULATED SUGAR
6 extra-large EGGS, separated
1 teaspoon BAKING POWDER
1 tablespoon VANILLA EXTRACT

PARCHMENT PAPER

THE CHINESE have never been highly regarded for their pastries, but there are a few Chinese bakery cakes that are worth a mention. This Hong Kong cake is as light as air, its consistency being somewhere between an angel food cake and a sponge cake. Baked or steamed at a very high heat, the cake batter triples in volume and becomes extraordinarily light as a result. Delicious for breakfast or as an afternoon snack with tea or coffee, it is sometimes garnished with thin almond slices prior to cooking.

1. Preheat the oven to 425°F. Oil a 10-inch angel-food-cake tube pan, sprinkle the sides with 1 tablespoon flour, and shake it to coat evenly. Turn the mold over to shake out the excess flour. Line the bottom of the pan with parchment paper cut to fit.

2. Whisk together all but one tablespoon of the sugar and the egg yolks in a bowl to a thick pale yellow consistency. In a separate bowl, beat the egg whites with the remaining tablespoon of sugar to a stiff peak.

3. Whisking the egg yolk mixture with one hand, sift the remaining flour and the baking powder over the mixture, making sure it is well combined and the batter is smooth. Whisk in the vanilla extract. At this time gently fold in half the stiffened egg whites to lighten the batter, then fold in the remaining egg whites. Pour the smooth and frothy batter into the cake pan and place it in the oven. Bake undisturbed until golden, 15 minutes. Remove the cake from the oven and immediately turn it over. This will prevent the cake from deflating. When cooled completely, run a knife blade around the edge and unmold.

STEAMED RED BEAN
AND LOTUS BUNS

MAKES 24 BUNS

1 recipe SPONGY BUNS (page 259)
1½ cups RED BEAN PASTE
  (page 513)
1½ cups LOTUS PASTE (page 513)
RED FOOD COLORING

24 pieces of PARCHMENT PAPER,
  cut into 2-inch squares

STEAMED SPONGY BUNS filled with sweet red bean paste or lotus paste make for a tasty breakfast. They are made with the same dough that is used to make Cantonese roast pork buns. During the Chinese New Year, I like to brush or dot the sweet buns with red food coloring as a symbol of good luck. Once the buns are steamed, the shiny smooth skin is peeled and discarded, or eaten, as preferred.

Leftover steamed buns can be refrigerated or frozen. To reheat, simply steam the buns for about 5 minutes or so.

1. Divide the dough into 24 equal pieces and shape them into balls. Place a ball of dough in the palm of one hand and, with the thumb of your other hand, make a well in the center. Fill the well with about 1 tablespoon of either red bean or lotus paste, then seal the filling by pinching the dough twice, bringing two opposite sides together toward the center. Pinch well to secure the filling. Place the bun, pinched side down, on a piece of parchment paper. Repeat until you have 24 small buns. Dip the thick tip of a chopstick in red food coloring and dot each red bean paste bun on top.

2. Set a bamboo steamer with a lid over a wok filled halfway with water and bring the water to a boil over high heat. Meanwhile, place the dumplings on a bamboo rack on their papers, leaving about an inch all around. The size of your steamer will determine how many buns you can steam at a time. Secure the steamer lid on top and steam until cooked through, about 10 minutes.

RED BEAN ICE CREAM

MAKES ABOUT 1½ QUARTS

4 cups plus 2 tablespoons HALF-
AND-HALF

½ cup GRANULATED SUGAR

4 extra-large EGG YOLKS

1½ tablespoons TAPIOCA STARCH
or CORNSTARCH

2 cups RED BEAN PASTE
(page 513)

RED BEAN ICE CREAM is served in Japanese restaurants and at New York City's Chinatown Ice Cream Factory, an establishment famous for its multitude of exotic ice cream flavors. Many inferior versions of this recipe contain too little red bean paste, resulting in a creamy but rather bland ice cream. This recipe contains enough paste so that the bean flavor is dominant. In Japan, red bean ice cream is often served with a sweet red bean sauce as a topping (page 514).

1. Pour the 4 cups half-and-half into the top of a double boiler over medium heat.

2. Meanwhile, whisk together the sugar and egg yolks in a bowl until the yolks turn thick and pale. Temper the yolks by gradually adding the hot half-and-half mixture a cup at a time while whisking vigorously so as not to scramble the eggs.

3. Return the mixture to the top part of the double boiler and whisk over simmering water until slightly thickened and heated through, 10 to 15 minutes. Dilute the tapioca starch with the remaining 2 tablespoons half-and-half and add it to the mixture. Continue whisking to a custard consistency that coats the back of a spoon, about 2 minutes. Transfer the custard to a heat-proof bowl and whisk in the red bean paste. Set over an ice bath and refrigerate overnight (or at least 12 hours).

4. The next day, pour the custard into an ice cream maker and process the custard according to the manufacturer's instructions, 30 to 35 minutes. Transfer the ice cream to a container and freeze until ready to serve.

GREEN TEA ICE CREAM

MAKES ABOUT 1½ QUARTS

4 cups plus 2 tablespoons HALF-
   AND-HALF

⅓ cup or less MATCHA (green tea
   powder)

½ to ¾ cup GRANULATED SUGAR

4 extra-large EGG YOLKS

1½ tablespoons TAPIOCA STARCH
   or CORNSTARCH

MY FAVORITE GREEN tea ice cream is the one served at New York City's Omen Japanese restaurant. Its version is very dark green, particularly creamy, with an especially pronounced bitter note. I have modeled the flavor and texture of this recipe after the wonderful Omen version. Another popular ice cream flavor in Japan is black sesame (see variation).

Lacking such stabilizing agents as the carob gum typically found in commercially made ice creams, the homemade versions tend to melt quickly. I add tapioca starch to combat this.

1. Pour the 4 cups half-and-half into the top of a double boiler over medium heat. Add the green tea powder and stir until the half-and-half has become uniformly green.

2. Meanwhile, whisk together the sugar and egg yolks in a bowl until the yolks turn thick and pale. Temper the yolks by gradually adding the hot half-and-half mixture a cup at a time while whisking vigorously so as not to scramble the eggs.

3. Return the mixture to the top part of the double boiler and whisk over simmering water until slightly thickened and heated through, 10 to 15 minutes. Dilute the tapioca starch with the remaining 2 tablespoons half-and-half and add it to the mixture. Continue whisking to a custard consistency that coats the back of a spoon, about 2 minutes. Transfer the custard to a heat-proof bowl set over an ice bath and refrigerate overnight (or at least 12 hours).

4. The next day, pour the custard into an ice cream maker and process the custard according to the manufacturer's instructions, 30 to 35 minutes. Transfer the ice cream to a container and freeze until ready to serve. Lightly dust each portion of ice cream with some of the remaining green tea powder before serving.

Variation: For a black sesame seed version of the ice cream, substitute 1 cup finely ground sesame seeds for the green tea powder. This makes for a very rich but very delicious ice cream.

I ENJOY BLACK SESAME SEEDS both as a main ingredient and a garnish for sweets. I find their rich nutty flavor particularly delicious and was delighted when I had the opportunity to try them on ice cream in Tokyo. The ice cream was a gray, nutty, and somewhat buttery item. Elizabeth Andoh, a celebrated cookbook author and authority on Japanese cuisine, suggested that I include the recipe here. For a touch of *yin yang* contrast, I sprinkle the ice cream with toasted blond sesame seeds.

TOASTED COCONUT
ICE CREAM

MAKES ABOUT 1½ QUARTS

¾ cup finely ground unsweetened
   fresh COCONUT

3 cups unsweetened COCONUT
   MILK (page 77); or commercial
   equivalent

1 cup plus 2 tablespoons HALF-
   AND-HALF

Pinch of KOSHER SALT

½ to ¾ cup GRANULATED SUGAR

4 extra-large EGG YOLKS

1½ tablespoons TAPIOCA STARCH
   or CORNSTARCH

I HAVE MADE THIS TOASTED coconut ice cream over and over again and never gotten tired of it. Ground coconut is toasted until nutty, then folded into a rich, chilled-egg-and-coconut-milk custard as it is processed into ice cream. As with many Southeast Asian desserts, the sweet element of the ice cream is counterbalanced by a pinch or two of salt. The dessert is a wonderful example of textural contrast—smooth against slightly crunchy and grainy.

If making your own coconut milk, be sure to use the combined coconut cream and milk for this recipe.

1. In a nonstick pan, toast the fresh coconut over medium heat, stirring to brown evenly, 3 to 5 minutes. Transfer the toasted coconut to a dish and allow to cool.

2. Pour the coconut milk, the 1 cup half-and-half, and the salt into the top of a double boiler and bring to a simmer over medium heat. Meanwhile, whisk together the sugar and egg yolks in a bowl until the yolks turn thick and pale. Temper the yolks by gradually adding the toasted coconut and half-and-half mixture a cup at a time while whisking vigorously so as not to scramble the eggs.

3. Return the mixture to the top part of the double boiler and whisk over simmering water until slightly thickened and heated through, 10 to 15 minutes. Dilute the tapioca starch with the remaining 2 tablespoons half-and-half and add it to the mixture. Continue whisking to a custard consistency that coats the back of a spoon, about 2 minutes. Transfer the custard to a heat-proof bowl set over an ice bath. Stir in ½ cup toasted coconut and refrigerate overnight (or at least 12 hours).

4. The next day, pour the custard into an ice cream maker and process the custard according to the manufacturer's instructions, 30 to 35 minutes. Transfer the ice cream to a container and freeze until ready to serve. Sprinkle each serving of ice cream with some of the remaining toasted coconut prior to serving.

CHE BA MAU
RAINBOW DRINK

SERVES 6

¾ cup peeled split MUNG BEANS, soaked for 3 hours, then drained

¾ cup GRANULATED SUGAR

½ cup RED AZUKI BEANS, soaked for 4 hours, then drained

1½ cups unsweetened COCONUT MILK (page 77); or commercial equivalent

¼ cup TAPIOCA PEARLS

1 cup LITCHI or LONGAN, peeled and pitted; if using canned, drain

THIS VIETNAMESE ICED DRINK is a good example of the so-called rainbow drinks of Southeast Asia, which are enjoyed as afternoon snacks. The idea here is to layer various types of fruits, legumes, and root vegetables with coconut milk (with or without tapioca pearls) and shaved ice in between. Containing tender yellow mung beans, red azuki beans, and slightly chewy and transparent tapioca pearls cooked in rich coconut milk, che ba mau is sometimes also topped with exotic fruit such as litchi, longan, or jackfruit. Refreshing and filling, it quenches thirst and satisfies hunger at the same time. In the Philippines, a version of the drink called halo halo can include cooked and diced purple yam, sweet potato, banana, and taro. Either as che ba mau or halo halo, the recipe here is open to interpretation. Feel free to follow the lead of Asian cooks, and experiment.

1. Bring 2 cups water to a simmer in a pot over medium heat. Add the mung beans and ¼ cup of the sugar. Cook, stirring constantly, until the water is completely absorbed, about 20 minutes. The beans should be tender but still somewhat intact. Remove from the heat and allow to cool. Refrigerate until ready to use.

2. Bring 3 cups water to a simmer in a pot over medium heat. Add the red beans and another ¼ cup of the sugar. Reduce the heat to medium-low, cover, and simmer until the beans are cooked through, about 1½ hours. The beans should be tender but still somewhat intact. Remove from the heat and allow to cool. Refrigerate until ready to use.

3. Bring the coconut milk and 1½ cups water to a boil. Reduce the heat to low, add the remaining ¼ cup sugar and the tapioca pearls, and simmer until the tapioca pearls have become completely transparent, about 10 minutes. Remove from the heat and allow to cool. Refrigerate until ready to use.

4. In an ice cream soda glass, working in layers, layer 2 tablespoons shaved ice alternately between 2 heaping tablespoons of each of the ingredients starting with the coconut tapioca, then the mung beans, azuki beans, and finally the coconut tapioca again. Garnish with a few litchis or longans on top. Use ice cream spoons to eat and a straw to sip.

FRUIT, HERB, AND SPICE INFUSIONS

¼ cup or more GRANULATED
   SUGAR
2 tablespoons HONEY
1 ounce fresh GINGER, peeled and
   thinly sliced lengthwise
1 ripe ASIAN PEAR, peeled, sliced
   into 8 wedges, and cored
1 CINNAMON STICK (about
   2 inches long)
1 tablespoon BLACK PEPPERCORNS
2 dried PERSIMMONS
PINE NUTS

IN KOREA, FRUIT INFUSIONS enhanced with herbs and spices are often drunk after a meal. Honey-sweetened, they can be served hot, at room temperature, or chilled. Here the fruits are Asian pear and dried persimmon flavored with ginger, cinnamon, and black peppercorns. Pine nuts are usually added as a garnish. I have also made an infusion using apples complemented by lemongrass and star anise to complete a Southeast Asian meal. Feel free to experiment with your own favorite fruits and spices.

1. Pour 1½ quarts water in a pot and add the sugar, honey, ginger, Asian pear, cinnamon, black peppercorns, and persimmons. Bring to a boil over high heat, then reduce and simmer until the drink is fragrant, about an hour.

2. Strain the liquid (discarding the solids) and serve hot, at room temperature, or chilled, in individual glasses garnished with a few pine nuts.

SOUTHEAST ASIAN SWEET COFFEE

SERVES 4

¼ cup or more sweetened
  CONDENSED MILK
4 DOUBLE ESPRESSOS; or brewed
  THAI COFFEE

VIETNAMESE AND THAI COFFEE are both made by combining strong brewed coffee with sweet condensed milk. Thai grocery stores sell a ground coffee mix that contains herbs and chicory. You can brew it as an everyday coffee, with or without the sweet condensed milk. But I must say that particular type of coffee is delicious sweetened. If you cannot find this coffee, don't let this stop you from making this Southeast Asian coffee using espresso. The results will still be delicious. The coffee can be served hot, at room temperature, chilled, or on ice.

Add a tablespoon of condensed milk to each of four 8-ounce cups or glasses. In each pour 2 shots of espresso and stir until the coffee and milk are well combined. Add a few ice cubes to each serving, if you wish.

Variations: Make enough sweet coffee to fill a pitcher by combining 4 parts espresso to one or more parts sweetened condensed milk (if too sweet, cut with whole milk). Stir to combine and refrigerate until well chilled.

To make sweet Vietnamese or Thai tea, brew 1 teaspoon gunpowder tea for every cup of water. Let steep for no more than 5 minutes. Proceed with the recipe, using condensed milk to sweeten each tea drink.

FOOD RITUALS AND SAMPLE MENUS

W HENEVER I EAT with my family, we discuss the meal. The ingredients—freshness, flavor, texture, shape, and color—and the combinations—the way the food tastes and feels on the palate, the way it reacts to our broth, tea, or wine—are of great importance. Was the food undercooked or overseasoned? Are the textures balanced? Where did the item originate? Was it Mongol or Manchu? We often sit at the table for three hours, evaluating. My husband was shocked when we first met and ate together, never having seen food subjected to such scrutiny. He now understands, however, that these examinations are for learning, expanding one's understanding, and for bonding. He understands them as family rituals, and he has joined in the fray.

Every country has activities that can be loosely described as food rituals. Some are an everyday thing, others are specific to a special occasion, others are unique to a culture, and still others are confined to small family groups and individuals. Here I include a cross-section of food rituals I have gathered while traveling in Asia, followed by sample menus intended to encourage any cook who is curious or wants to try the food described. All menu items are culled from this book and cross-referenced by page numbers.

THIS GEISHA MAY REPRESENT THE LAST GENERATION OF THE MYSTERIOUS WOMEN ENTERTAINERS OF KYOTO.

chinese tea and dim sum: Teatime in China involves much more than tea. The words *yum cha*, which literally mean "drink tea," are spoken when one wants to go have tea and *dim sum*, or dumplings. The Chinese ritual of taking tea goes back two thousand years. In the early days, the teahouse was meant for men. It was a place where they would talk about business and personal affairs over tea without the enthusiastic vocal interruptions of women. As teahouses started opening all over China, a need developed for small bites to accompany the patrons' tea. *Dim sum*, figuratively meaning "delights of the heart," were created, and as the name suggests, they are quite delightful, both visually and in terms of flavor. Some Chinese chefs say that there are over three hundred kinds of savory and sweet *dim sum* today. Others claim the number reaches to over a thousand, and even today, innovative versions of *dim sum* are being added to the carts. (The number doesn't matter as much as how well the item is executed.)

While *dim sum* are most often enjoyed in the morning, they can also be eaten throughout the day. Early Sunday morning is perhaps the best time to see the ritual, when the savory and sweet tidbits come out of the restaurant kitchen at their freshest, the turnover is fast, and the rooms are noisy with animated conversation and seemingly random activity. Especially in Hong Kong and Singapore, the art of making dumplings is taken to very high levels; presentation exceeds by far that of the *dim sum* restaurants in New York's and San Francisco's Chinatown dumpling houses, which are already quite good. The delicate dough wrappers are exquisitely thin and the filling-to-dough ratio, flavors, and textures are perfectly balanced. The highly trained chefs of Hong Kong and Singapore are masters, meticulously creating shapes with mechanical precision, offering the exotic with the classic, surprising with the occasional innovation or revived item once seemingly forgotten.

The young serving women call out *"haar gao, char siu bao, dahn tot!"* as they push their stainless steel carts, offering crystal shrimp dumplings (pp. 298–99), roast pork buns (page 294), egg custard tart (page 539), and a myriad of other items, all of which they know by heart. They move from kitchen to dining room, offering a sort of endless parade of tiny delights that appear and then vanish as they are rolled along their busy way.

korean *kimjang*: One of the most important food-based activities for Korean women is kimjang, or kimchi making, which takes place in autumn. Women gather and grate, slice, and chop garlic, ginger, and radish mixed with salt, sugar, and fine and coarse chili powder to form a chunky paste that is spread between leaves of a salted cabbage. The paste-and-cabbage combination is placed in large ceramic crocks and allowed to ferment for several weeks before eating. Originally large amounts of food were preserved in this way, ensuring steady supplies for long winters without harvests. Today, with the markets full and ingredients available all year round, this autumn ritual is becoming a lost tradition, and women make kimchi as they need it throughout the year. Aficionados all over Korea still say, however, that the best kimchi is made in autumn.

While in Seoul, I was invited to visit the Son family and participate in kimchi making. Dressed in a traditional Korean hemp costume called the hanbok, I learned to make and taste kimchi in the age-old artisanal manner. Bok Hi Chang, who was the mother of the family and produced the best kimchi I have ever eaten, taught me the ritual behind the techniques. While Bok Hi made the kimchi from start to finish, salting the cabbage and prepping and mixing the ingredients, her sister's only job was as official "taster" of the family. "The kimchi maker never tastes her own kimchi while she is making it, perhaps for the fear of biasing her work," explained Yeon Sook, Bok Hi's eldest daughter. "Instead, Mother pinches an inner tiny leaf of the cabbage and wraps the kimchi paste she has just finished making. She rolls it up tightly and feeds it to her sister." After a few chews, the sister answered by nodding conditional approval, perhaps, and Bok Hi responded by adding more salt, chili, or any other ingredients that might need adjusting. When the mixture was done, it was stuffed into ceramic jars and left to ferment in the traditional way.

Invited for lunch, I sat on the lacquered yellow mulberry-paper floor and was presented with a traditional Korean meal in small celadon bowls and plates filled with delicious morsels of pan-fried fish (page 346), stir-fried spinach and mung bean sprouts (page 326), and many other dishes. Not surpris-

MAKING MULBERRY PAPER, WHICH WILL BE USED TO WRAP GIFTS OR COVER FLOORS

ingly, the most memorable was the kimchi. It was crunchy, and I could taste the salt, the ginger, the chilies, and the garlic. All the complex flavors were in perfect harmony.

japanese *kaiseki*: An outgrowth of the tea ceremony, kaiseki is the grand cuisine of Japan, the highest form of Japanese dining, and, perhaps, the closest thing to dining as an art form in world gastronomy. Kaiseki food is selected according to the season and is presented in a series of small dishes with an artful simplicity that brings out the unique natural tastes of foods from the nearby mountains and sea. Perhaps the key to the composition of the *kaiseki* meal lies in the word *aishoh*, compatibility. The form was developed and perfected in Kyoto, Japan, and dates back to the seventeenth century. Dozens of small fish and vegetable dishes are served over a period of hours in exquisitely beautiful settings with highly ritualized presentation techniques.

While I find that most Asian foods can be created at home, *kaiseki* preparation requires all the discipline and study that it takes to master any art form. I have included the wonderful *nanzenji yudofu*, poached tofu, and other non-*kaiseki* items that will make for simple and wonderful Japanese meals.

While in Kyoto I was invited to experience *kaiseki* at the Junsei restaurant. Set in beautiful traditional Zen gardens, it has, since 1839, offered some of the most refined *kaiseki* in the city. *Kaiseki* chefs are incredibly skillful, selecting, slicing, and presenting foods with the utmost attention to detail. Nothing is left to chance. Their great precision goes beyond the preparation of food, however. They also decorate the plates according to the season, using leaves (not always edible), shaved ice, and other food items to represent seasons and to evoke feelings in the diner.

While I sat on my heels at a lacquered low table overlooking one garden, two Japanese women dressed in traditional kimonos brought out small bowls and plates in succession. Each dish had enough seafood or vegetables for one, maybe two bites. Luckily, the chef sat with me to give me a sign as to which of the delicate decorations were edible and which were not.

There were grilled sardines set on small narrow fresh bamboo leaves; gingko nuts with arrowroot pudding topped with *uni* (sea urchin) and caviar; squid liver set delicately inside a scooped-out green lime; fresh chrysanthemum flower petals with pine mushrooms; grilled barracuda set on top of *sancho* leaves; eel pudding rolled in nori and topped with fern; vinegared abalone on freshwater sea vegetables; potato stems with *miso*; pan-fried wheat gluten with freshly grated *wasabi*. Dishes kept coming, followed by a bowl of perfectly cooked white rice, and a delicate clear mushroom broth at the finish.

While everything was absolutely delicious and fresh, my favorite item was the specialty of the house, *nanzenji yudofu*, the one item I felt was easy enough to reproduce at home comfortably. It was the most delicate tofu dish I have ever eaten. Brought to the table in a wooden tub, the tofu sat in steaming spring water and was accompanied by a savory sweet dipping sauce of tamari and mirin. After a couple of hours of savoring my meal, I felt wonderful, not full, not hungry, but sated.

filipino fiestas: In the Philippines one always finds a reason to celebrate. Whenever there is a festive occasion—be it a wedding, birthday, christening, job promotion, or someone's homecoming—there is likely to be music, dancing, and lots of food and drink.

I was always greeted with great generosity by my Filipino hosts, no matter where I ventured in their country. Foods such as the crispy roast pork called *lechon*; oxtail in peanut sauce, or *kare kare*; *lumpia*, or fried spring rolls; and longevity noodles, or *pancit*, were always part of the feast, and every time my plate was empty, it was replenished. Served buffet style, food is set out so that guests eat as they wish, the only rule being that they enjoy themselves.

Usually, after a meal, there is music and dancing, often American-style line dancing, or Spanish classics such as the cha-cha. In Cebu, I attempted the traditional stick dance, in which one attempts to jump between snapping bamboo culms without getting caught in the process. Afterward, I was escorted to the dessert table and rewarded with such sweet items as *halo halo*, coconut milk with shaved ice and fruit; and *turones de saba*, sweet spring rolls filled with banana and jackfruit.

indonesian rice table: I have visited Bali several times and have always looked forward to enjoying the delicious Balinese food. *Rijsttafel*, or rice table, is one of my favorites, a wonderful way to enjoy Indonesia's fragrant foods. Ibu Wayan's restaurant, Cafe Wayan, is on Monkey Forest Road in Ubud, a small village known for its wood carvers, batik artists, and painters. When it comes to food, however, the main attraction is Cafe Wayan and its *rijsttafel*. My husband and I have enjoyed this ritual, which begins with richly flavored foods arranged on a beautiful round, banana leaf–lined plate. The food ranges from mild to very spicy and often includes *ayam goreng*, chicken legs braised with an herbal

paste and fried; duck smoked in rice husk called *bebek betutu*; *sate lilit*, seafood sate; *gado gado*, vegetables with peanut sauce; and more.

Served bowls of fluffy white rice topped with crispy-fried shallots, we ate in the traditional way, with our fingers. The Indonesians hold that food eaten this way tastes better than when eaten with utensils. My husband was only too happy to oblige, saying he felt a closer connection to the food, which was exactly what he was after. In the case of Ibu Wayan's *rijsttafel*, I couldn't blame him. We could taste the richness of the coconut, the spiciness of the chilies, and the deep aroma of lemongrass, galangal, and garlic. Turmeric lent a beautiful yellowish color to some of the foods, notably the hard-boiled eggs, turning them into something extraordinary. A sour soup was served to complement the herbal character of the food.

thai street hawker food: One of my favorite things to do in Thailand is to eat "fast" or street hawker food. Restaurants abound, of course, but I, like most people, enjoy sitting on a stool in front of a food stand, watching the vendor prepare a Thai specialty right in front of me. In

Bangkok I experienced fast food on the decks of several boats. The floating market affords food vendors the opportunity to sell their goods—fresh vegetables, fruit, and freshly prepared snack foods—from their small boats, where you are welcome to come and have a quick bite. These harbor-bound food sellers, so famous they are considered part of the landscape, are a destination for locals and visitors alike. To see Bangkok without having experienced this curious little culinary subculture is to have missed the city at its most fascinating.

In Chiang Mai, arguably the most important food city in Thailand, the ritual involves sampling these foods at night, so like everyone else, I went to the night bazaar. Famous worldwide, these shopping arcades, which stay open all night, are complemented by hard-working food hawkers who stand ready to serve. They also provide stools for perching while your food is prepared, and the aromas are so enticing it is hard to pass up an empty stool.

Visitors come from all over the world to sample spicy beef or chicken satay, the sweet rice noodle stir-fry called *pad Thai*, sticky rice wrapped in banana leaves, coconut pudding cooking in cast iron skil-

A VEGETABLE STAND AT AN OUTDOOR MARKET IN THE PHILIPPINES

lets, grilled bananas, sour shrimp soup called *tom yum goong*, spring rolls known as *paw pia taud*, curries, and even Chinese fried wontons. The choices are too numerous to name here, but one is worth a special mention: if you are in the mood, and sated from shopping, you can try the fried insects.

khmer noodle soup: I lived in Phnom Penh as a very young child, and no particular food rituals were brought to mind when I visited as an adult. The country is now focused on trying to rebuild its economy. For many, to have enough food to survive is ritual enough. Indeed, I found it difficult to discuss cuisine, when people, including my own family, were starved or summarily executed for eating as little as a rice worm or beetle without permission.

While I did enjoy wonderful food in Cambodia, and have often eaten Cambodian dishes prepared by my family in Paris, I also cherish a recurring dream of my grandmother Huong making and serving noodle soup we call *k'tiao*. In the dream, I am at my grandparents' home in Phnom Penh, where my parents, brother William, and I lived with several of my aunts and uncles. The dream is extremely simple and would be unremarkable save for the fact that it, along with the dreams and memories of other Cambodian genocide survivors, is all that is left on which to rebuild an ancient culture that all but perished from the earth just a few short years ago.

The dream goes something like this: It is a beautiful day, with the sun shining through the open windows, and my grandmother is at her stove. She plunges rice noodles into boiling water for a split-second, just to warm them through, then drains and divides them among the several large soup bowls, enough to feed her extended family.

Her broth, fragrant with roasted

dried squid, pork bones, ginger, and fish sauce, steams in the background as she slices the pork and shrimp she has just poached in the same water as her noodles. She takes great care in arranging the delicate slices of pork and shrimp over each serving of noodles, then ladles a copious amount of broth into each bowl. This is served with lime wedges and the freshly torn fragrant herbs from the pots on her balcony. As I was the youngest in the family, my grandmother Huong would have me sit on my heels in front of a red stool so that I would come up to the bowl's height comfortably, without having to reach. She would watch me eat, picking up my noodles with chopsticks, slurping loudly as was appropriate. She smiled, as if to say, "I taught you well!"

vietnamese rice in red clay: The best part about visiting Vietnam is that I keep discovering new foods. At Hanoi's Metropole hotel, a renovated establishment dating back to the turn of the twentieth century and a perfect example of French colonial architecture, the chefs pride themselves on preserving northern Vietnamese cuisine. Chef Didier Corlou (a Frenchman whose heart is truly in Hanoi) works with an all-Vietnamese kitchen staff and his wife, a native of Hanoi, to re-create the city's most classic foods. Chef Corlou explains that in contrast to the country's other culinary centers, Hue and Saigon, "the cooking of Hanoi, and the north in general, is mild yet refined, and the rice cooked in red clay embodies the spirit of the cuisine."

In the red clay ritual, the waiter brings rice in a red clay pot with its bottom facing up. With a wood mallet, he strikes the pot once, splitting it in half and revealing perfectly molded rice. The orangey-red clay imparts a beautiful reddish color to the outer, crusty shell of the rice, and a curiously pleasing earthy, even subtly clay-like back note.

Corlou explains: "This recipe goes back over several hundred years; and uniquely in any recipe I know, it is the clay that makes the dish." Because it is expensive to break handmade rice pots after a single use, Metropole Chef Corlou is the only person who offers this dish presented in the classic way.

S A M P L E
M E N U S

WHEN you want to eat Asian style, put all the food dishes in the center of the table and let everyone share, picking up the food with their chopsticks. Give an individual bowl of rice or noodles and a brothy soup, chicken or pork, to clear the palate, to each diner on the side. You can add freshly torn herbs such as cilantro, Vietnamese coriander, Thai basil, or freshly sliced scallion as garnishes, and adjust the seasoning with salt, fish sauce, or soy sauce. Even if you're planning to serve dessert, be sure to have fresh fruit such as sliced oranges, watermelon, Asian pear, or any type of watery fruit to finish the meal on a pleasant, refreshing note.

CHINESE DIM SUM MENU
Cantonese Roast Pork Buns
   (page 294)
Crystal Vegetable Dumplings
   (pp. 300–1)
Shanghainese Spring Rolls
   (pp. 272–73)
Beef and Chive Dumplings
   (pp. 270–71)
Deep-Fried Sesame Dumplings
   (page 523)
Egg Custard Tarts
   (page 539)

CHINESE LUNCH MENU
Wheat Noodles with Pork and
   Cabbage Sauce (page 232)
Steamed Ginger Custard (page 528)

CHINESE DINNER MENU
Winter Melon and Ham Soup
   (page 143)
Cantonese Five-Spice Roast Duck
   (pp. 500–1)
Stir-Fried Leafy Greens (page 320)

KOREAN LUNCH MENU
Korean Mixed Rice (pp. 214–15)
Cabbage Kimchi (page 359)

KOREAN DINNER MENU
Basic Beef Stock (page 120)
Braised Black Cod with Daikon
   (page 393)
Stir-Fried Spinach and Mung
   Bean Sprouts (page 326)
Cabbage Kimchi (page 359)

THAI LUNCH MENU
Pad Thai (pp. 224–25)
Chicken Satay (page 98)

THAI DINNER MENU
Spicy Shrimp Soup (page 134)
Chiang Mai Pork Curry (page 463)
Pickled Vegetable Nibbles
   (page 354)
Banana Fritters (page 542)

JAPANESE LUNCH MENU
Miso Soup (page 128)
Raw Fish Platter (page 403)
Black Sesame Ice Cream
   (pp. 546–47)

JAPANESE DINNER MENU
Japanese Bubbling Beef Hot Pot
   (page 160)
Bamboo Shoot and Shiitake Salad
   (page 347)
Japanese Rice and Red Bean
   Dumplings (page 525)

INDONESIAN LUNCH MENU
Crab Fried Rice (page 212)
Sweet Banana and Coconut Tapioca
   Soup (page 517)

INDONESIAN DINNER MENU
Medley of vegetables with Peanut
   Sauce (pp. 342–43)
World's Best Fried Chicken
   (page 490)
Fiddlehead Fern in Spicy Coconut
   Sauce (page 344)
Black Sticky Rice Pudding
   (page 519)

VIETNAMESE LUNCH MENU
Grilled Lemongrass Shrimp with
   Rice Vermicelli (page 223)
Rainbow Drink (page 549)

VIETNAMESE DINNER MENU
Summer Rolls (pp. 286–87)
Caramelized Pork Shank
    (pp. 458–59)
Stir-Fried Water Spinach with
    Fermented Tofu (pp. 324–25)
Rice Pearls in Ginger Broth
    (pp. 524–25)

FILIPINO LUNCH MENU
Pinakbet (page 336)
Toasted Coconut Ice Cream
    (page 548)

FILIPINO DINNER MENU
Filipino Ceviche (page 404)
Chicken *Adobo* (pp. 496–97)
Stir-Fried Watercress (page 320)
Banana and Jackfruit Spring Rolls
    (pp. 536–37)

CAMBODIAN LUNCH MENU
Fried or Grilled Whole Fish
    (page 394)
Pickled Vegetable Nibbles
    (page 354)

CAMBODIAN DINNER MENU
Duck and Preserved Lime Soup
    (pp. 140–41)
Pan-Fried Eggplant with Crabmeat
    (page 334)
Squash with Coconut Custard
    (pp. 530–31)

DRIED RED CHILIES, AN ESSENTIAL SPICE IN MAKING KIMCHI

WASABI ROOTS ARE FRESHLY GROUND AND SERVED WITH COLD SOBA NOODLES AND RAW FISH, GIVING A REFRESHING SPICY FINISH TO EVERY BITE.

SOURCES

These mail-order sources carry most of or all the ingredients you need to re-create the recipes.

For Asian vegetables and exotic fruit

Diamond Organics
P. O. Box 2159
Freedom, CA 95019
Tel: 888-ORGANIC (674-2642)
Fax: 888-888-6777
Website: www.diamondorganics.com

Melissa's World Variety Produce, Inc.
P. O. Box 21127
Los Angeles, CA 90021
Tel: 800-588-0151
Fax: 323-588-9774
Website: www.melissas.com

For Asian herbs and ingredients in general

ImportFood.com
P. O. Box 2054
Issaquah, WA 98027
Tel: 425-392-7516
Fax: 425-391-5658
Website: www.importfood.com

Kalustyan's
123 Lexington Avenue
New York, NY 10016
Tel: 212-685-3451
Fax: 212-683-8458
Website: www.kalustyans.com

Penzeys Spices
P. O. Box 933
Muskego, WI 53150
Tel: 414-679-7207
Fax: 414-679-7878
Website: www.penzeys.com

The Spice Merchant
P. O. Box 524
Jackson Hole, WY 83001
Tel: 307-733-7811
Tel: 800-551-5999
Fax: 307-733-6343
Website: www.email.com/spice

Uwajimaya
519 Sixth Avenue South
Seattle, WA 98104
Tel: 206-624-6248
Tel: 800-889-1928
Fax: 206-624-6915
Website: www.uwajimaya.com

Pacific Mercantile Company
1925 Lawrence Street
Denver, CO 80202
Tel: 303-295-0293
Fax: 303-295-2753

The CMC Company
P. O. Drawer 322
Avalon, NJ 08202
Tel: 800-CMC-2780 (262-2780)
Fax: 609-861-3065
Website: www.thecmccompany.com

To grow your own herbs

Shepherd's Garden Seeds
30 Irene Street
Torrington, CT 06790
Tel: 860-482-3638
Fax: 860-626-0865

For squab, baby chickens, and quail

D'Artagnan, Inc.
280 Wilson Avenue
Newark, NJ 07105
Tel: 800-327-8246
Fax: 973-344-0565
Website: www.dartagnan.com

Travel information

This is the best travel agency for organizing trips to Asia. The staff is very knowledgeable, each having traveled to Asia to inspect hotels and seek out interesting destinations. They will handle everything from organizing your itinerary, with guides and drivers if you like, to handling all necessary paperwork for obtaining visas where required.

Absolute Asia
180 Varick Street
New York, NY 10014
Tel: 800-736-8187
Fax: 212-627-4090
Website: www.absoluteasia.com

Here are some of the most helpful government organizations. They will send you any information on any destination in their countries.

Hong Kong Tourism Association
Tel: 800-282-HKTA
Website: www.hkta.org and
  www.discoverhongkong.com

Korean National Tourism
  Organization
Tel: 1-800-868-7567
Website: www.visitkorea.or.kr

Japan National Tourist
  Organization
Tel: 212-757-5641
Website: www.japantravelinfo.com

Tourism Authority of Thailand
Tel: 212-432-0433

The Royal Embassy of Cambodia
Tel: 202-726-7742
Fax: 202-726-8381
Website: www.embassy.org/
  cambodia

Cooking schools in Asia
LEARN TO COOK and drink tea while visiting Asia. Here are some of the places that offer lessons in cooking and culture as well.

Son's Home
740-8 Yeoksam-dong
Kangnam-gu Seoul
135-080, Korea
Tel: 82-2-562-6829
Fax: 82-2-565-6829
Website: www.sons-home.com

Han Jung Hea's Cooking Academy
55-1 Nakwon-dong
Jongro-ku Seoul
Korea
Tel: 82-2-742-3567
Fax: 82-2-766-0737

Panyaro Institute for the Way of Tea
31-39 Gahoidong
Jongrogu Seoul
110-260, Korea
Tel: 82-2-763-8486
Fax: 82-2-763-8976

Chiang Mai Thai Cookery School
1-3 Moonmuang Road
Opp. Tha Phae Gate
Chiang Mai 50200
Thailand
Tel: 053-206-388
Fax: 053-206-387
Email: nabnian@loxinfo.co.th

The Regent Chiang Mai
Maerim-Samoeng Old Road
Maerim, Chiang Mai 50180
Thailand
Tel: 66-53-298-181
Fax: 66-53-298-189

A Taste of Culture Japanese
  Culinary Arts Program
1-22-18-401 Seta, Setagaya-ku
Tokyo 158-0095 Japan
Tel & Fax: 03-5716-5751
Email: aeli@gol.com

Urasenke International Association
610-0121 87-11 Terada Hijiri
  Joyo-city
Kyoto, Japan
Tel & Fax: 0774-52-1851
Email: thm5116@gold.ocn.ne.jp

WAK (Women's Association of
  Kyoto)
4-6-67 Kaguraoka-cho, Yoshida
Sakyo-ku, Kyoto 606-8311
Japan
Tel: 075-752-9090
Fax: 075-752-9092

Sakae Soy Sauce Brewing
Tel: 0537-48-2114
Fax: 0537-48-3168
Email: fukaya@po.across.or.jp

Ryokan Yoshi-Ima (traditional
  Japanese inn)
Shinmonzen St.
Gion, Kyoto 605
Japan
Tel: 075-561-2620
Fax: 075-541-6493

Hotel Sofitel
17 Le Duan Blvd., Dist 1
Ho Chi Minh City, Vietnam
Tel: 84-8-824-1555
Fax: 84-8-824-1666

Sofitel Metropole Hanoi
15 Ngo Quyen Street
Hanoi, Vietnam
Tel: 84-4-826-6919
Fax: 84-4-826-6920

Asian cooking schools in the United States

THAI CUISINE:
Kasma Loha-unchit
P.O. Box 21165
Oakland, California 94620
Tel: 510-655-8900
Website:
  www.thaifoodandtravel.com

CAMBODIAN CUISINE:
Longteine and Nadsa De Monteiro
The Elephant Walk
900 Beacon St.
Boston, MA 02215
Tel: 617-247-1500

2067 Massachusetts Ave.
Cambridge, MA 02140
Tel: 617-492-6900
Website: www.elephantwalk.com

Carambola
663 Main Street
Waltham, MA 02154
Tel: 781-899-2244

CHINESE AND SOUTHEAST ASIAN
CUISINES:
Corinne Trang
Drexel University
Hospitality Management Dept.
Academic Building
33rd and Arch Streets
Philadelphia, PA 19104
Tel: 215-895-2411

A Hong Kong specialty food shop offering dried or salt-cured food such as fish, meat, and vegetables

SELECTED BIBLIOGRAPHY

Alegre, Edilberto, et al. *Kinilaw, A Philippine Cuisine of Freshness.* Manila: Bookmark, 1991.

Alejandro, Reynaldo. *The Philippine Cookbook.* New York: Perigee Books, 1982.

Andoh, Elizabeth. *An American Taste of Japan.* New York: William Morrow, 1985.

————. *An Ocean of Flavor.* New York: William Morrow, 1988.

Baker, Demaz Tep. *Cambodian Cuisine.* Waseca, Minn.: Walter's Publishing, 1999.

Bladholm, Linda. *The Asian Grocery Store Demystified.* Los Angeles: Renaissance Books, 1999.

Blasdale, Walter C. *Some Chinese Vegetable Food Materials.* Washington, D.C.: U.S. Department of Agriculture, 1899.

Boun Thuy, Sovan. *Cambodian Cooking, Authentic Recipes.* N.p. 1992.

Chan, Henry, et al. *Classic Deem Sum.* New York: Holt, Rinehart and Winston, 1985.

Chandler, David P. *A History of Cambodia.* Boulder: Westview Press, 1992.

Chang, K. C. *Food in Chinese Culture.* New Haven: Yale University Press, 1977.

Chang, Sun-young. *A Korean Mother's Cooking Notes.* Seoul: Ewha Woman's University Press, 1997.

Le Chant du Riz Pile. Paris: Les Editeurs Français Réunis, 1974.

Chin, R. D. *Feng Shui Revealed.* New York: Clarkson Potter, 1998.

Choi, Trieu Thi. *The Food of Vietnam.* Singapore: Periplus Editions, 1997.

Chong, Elizabeth. *The Heritage of Chinese Cooking.* New York: Random House, 1993.

Cordero-Fernando, Gilda. *Philippine Food & Life.* Manila: Anvil Publishing, 1992.

Cultures of the World, Cambodia. Singapore: Times Editions, 1996.

Davidson, Alan. *The Oxford Companion to Food.* New York: Oxford University Press, 1999.

De Monteiro, Longteine, et al. *The Elephant Walk Cookbook.* New York: Houghton Mifflin, 1998.

Duong, Binh, et al. *Simple Art of Vietnamese Cooking.* New York: Prentice Hall, 1991.

Fernandez, Doreen G. *Fruits of the Philippines.* Manila: Bookmark, 1997.

————. *Tikim, Essays on Philippine Food and Culture.* Manila: Anvil Publishing, 1994.

Gelle, Gerry G. *Filipino Cuisine.* Sante Fe: Red Crane Books, 1997.

General, Honesto C. *The Coconut Cookery of Bicol.* Manila: Bookmark, 1994.

Han, Chung Hea. *Korean Cooking.* Seoul: Chung Woo Publishing, 1998.

Hau, Vu Cong. *Arbres Fruitiers du Vietnam.* Hanoi: The Gioi Publishers, 1999.

Homma, Gaku. *The Folk Art of Japanese Country Cooking.* Berkeley: North Atlantic Books, 1990.

Honda, Kyoko. *Tofu & Soybean Cooking.* Tokyo: Graph-sha Ltd, 1997.

Hyun, Judy. *The Korean Cookbook.* Chicago: Follett Publishing, 1970.

Kim, Man-Jo, et al. *The Kimchee Cookbook.* Singapore: Periplus Editions, 1999.

Kongpan, Sisamon, et al. *The Elegant Taste of Thailand.* Berkley: SLG Books, 1990.

Lai, T. C. *Hong Kong & China Gas Chinese Cookbook.* Hong Kong: Hong Kong & China Gas, 1978.

Lam, Kam Chuen. *The Personal Feng Shui Manual.* New York: Owl Books, 1998.

Larkcom, Joy. *Oriental Vegetables.* New York: Kodensha, 1991.

Lee, Chun Ja, et al. *The Book of Kimchi.* Seoul: Korea Information Service, 1998.

Lee, Florence C. *Facts About Ginseng.* Elizabeth, N.J.: Hollym, 1992.

————, et al. *Kimchi, A Korean Health Food.* Elizabeth, N.J.: Hollym, 1998.

Lie, Sek Hiang. *Indonesian Cookery.* New York: Crown, 1963.

Lin, Hsiang Ju, et al. *Chinese Gastronomy.* New York: Pyramid Publications, 1972.

Lo San Ross, Rosa. *Beyond Bok Choy.* New York: Artisan, 1996.

Lo Yin-Fei, Eileen. *The Dim Sum Book.* New York: Crown, 1982.

Loha-Unchit, Kasma. *It Rains Fishes.* San Francisco: Pomegranate Artbooks, 1994.

Lu, Henry C. *Chinese System of Food Cures, Preventions & Remedies.* New York: Sterling Publishing, 1986.

———. *Chinese System of Natural Cures.* New York: Sterling Publishing, 1994.

Mark, William. *The Chinese Gourmet.* San Diego: Thunder Bay Press, 1994.

La Médecine Traditionnelle Vietnamienne. Hanoi: The Gioi Publishers, 1993.

Nabnian, Sompon. *A Passion for Thai Cooking.* Chiang Mai: Chiang Mai Thai Cookery School, 2000.

Ngo, Bach, et al. *The Classic Cuisine of Vietnam.* New York: Plume, 1986.

Nguyen, Ngoc Tu. *A Guide to Typical Vietnamese Cookery.* Dong Nai: Dongnai Publishing, 1998.

Nguyen, Thu Tam. *Vietnamese Dishes.* Ho Chi Minh: Mui Ca Mau, 1997.

Noh, Chin-hwa. *Practical Korean Cooking.* Elizabeth N.J.: Hollym, 1985.

Omae, Kinjiro, et al. *The Book of Sushi.* Tokyo: Kodansha, 1981.

Owen, Sri. *Indonesian Regional Cooking.* New York: St. Martin's Press, 1994.

———. *The Rice Book.* New York: St. Martin's Press, 1993.

Pinsuvana, Malulee. *Cooking Thai Food in American Kitchens.* Bangkok: Thai Watana Panich Press, 1976.

Poladitmontri, Panurat, et al. *Thailand, The Beautiful Cookbook.* San Francisco: Collins, 1992.

Reid, Daniel P. *Chinese Herbal Medicine.* Hong Kong: CFW Publications, 1987.

Rosales-Barretto, Glenda. *Flavors of the Philippines.* Manila: Via Mare Catering Services Inc., 1997.

Routhier, Nicole. *The Foods of Vietnam.* New York: Stewart, Tabori & Chang, 1989.

Schneider, Elizabeth. *Uncommon Fruits & Vegetables, A Commonsense Guide.* New York: Harper & Row, 1986.

Simoons, Frederick J. *Food in China, A Cultural and Historical Inquiry.* Boca Raton: CRC Press, 1991.

So, Yan-Kit. *Classic Food of China.* London: Macmillan, 1992.

Son, Ly Van. *Vietnamese Cookery Book.* Dong Nai: Dongnai Publishing, 1995.

Trang, Corinne. *Authentic Vietnamese Cooking: Food from a Family Table.* New York: Simon & Schuster, 1999.

Tsuji, Shizuo. *Japanese Cooking, A Simple Art.* Tokyo: Kodensha International, 1980.

———, et al. *Practical Japanese Cooking.* Tokyo: Kodensha International, 1986.

von Holzen, Heinz, et al. *The Food of Bali.* Singapore: Periplus Editions, 1994.

———. *The Food of Indonesia.* Singapore: Periplus Editions, 1994.

Young, Grace. *The Wisdom of the Chinese Kitchen.* New York: Simon & Schuster, 1999.

Windridge, Dr. Charles. *The Fountain of Health.* Edinburgh: Mainstream Publishing, 1994.

A TOFU AND BEAN SPROUT VENDOR AT CENTRAL MARKET IN HONG KONG

TABLE OF EQUIVALENTS *

LIQUID AND DRY MEASURES

U.S.	METRIC
¼ teaspoon	1.25 milliliters
½ teaspoon	2.5 milliliters
1 teaspoon	5 milliliters
1 tablespoon (3 teaspoons)	15 milliliters
1 fluid ounce (2 tablespoons)	30 milliliters
¼ cup	65 milliliters
⅓ cup	80 milliliters
1 cup	235 milliliters
1 pint (2 cups)	480 milliliters
1 quart (4 cups, 32 ounces)	950 milliliters
1 gallon (4 quarts)	3.8 liters
1 ounce (by weight)	28 grams
1 pound	454 grams
2.2 pounds	1 kilogram

LENGTH MEASURES

U.S.	METRIC
⅛ inch	3 millimeters
¼ inch	6 millimeters
½ inch	12 millimeters
1 inch	2.5 centimeters

OVEN TEMPERATURES

FAHRENHEIT	CELSIUS	GAS
250	120	½
275	140	1
300	150	2
325	160	3
350	180	4
375	190	5
400	200	6
425	220	7
450	230	8
475	240	9
500	260	10

* The exact equivalents in the above tables have been rounded off for convenience.

INDEX

chicken (*cont.*)
  stir-fried, with young ginger, **492**
  in summer rolls, **287**
  and tea *soba* soup, **246–47**
  Thai curry, **499**
  twice-cooked, 445
  and young coconut soup, **138–39**
chicken blood, 444
chicken feet, 444, 446
chicken heads, 444, 446
chicken livers, 446
chicken wings, 444
chien chuoi, 510, **542**
chilies, 361, 451
  Chinese red, 13
  how to seed, 40
  Thai, 21, 55, 151, 222
chili oil, 6–7
chili sauces:
  fried black, **107**
  garlic and, 12, **106**
  sweet, 12
  sweet and sour, **105**
chim nuong toi, **505**
Chinese broccoli, 22, 338, 339, 436
Chinese cabbage, 23, 340
Chinese cuisine:
  beef, 435–36
  black vinegar, 11
  cakes, 184
  categories of, 49–52
  chicken, 444–45
  drinks, 510–12
  dumplings, 177–78
  eastern (Shanghainese), 52
  fish, 374–78
  fish congee, **193**
  hot pot, 114–15, **156–57**
  influence of, 43–44, 48–60, 427
  key to, 44–45

liver sausage, 17
marinades, 67–68
menus, 453, 560
noodles, 171–73, 174, 176
northern (Beijing), 50
outside influences on, 49–50
pastes, 65–66
pork, 428–29
red chilies, 13
soups, 113
southern (Cantonese), 50–52, 435–36
soy sauces, 7
steamed fish, **386–87**
stir-frying, 322
sweet pork sausage, 17, 169, 209, 434
sweets, 508, 509–10
tea and dim sum, 554, 560
vegetables, 307, 309
western (Szechwanese), 52
Chinese parsley, 19
Chiu Chow *ling mown dun ngap*, 140, 141
Chiu Chow region, 51
chive and beef steamed dumplings, **270–71**
ch'o kanjang, **93**
ch'o koch'ujang, **105**, 214
cho lie woo pan, **535**
chonbok chuk, **193**
chopping, 39
chopsticks, 34–35
chow fan, 208–9
chow mi fen, **221**
choy sum, 23
chun guen, **272–73**
chung yau biang, 183
cilantro, 19
  cure-all, and pork soup, **145**
citronella, 20
citrus zests, 71

clams:
  in *miso* soup, **128**
  spicy seafood stew, **420**
clay pots, 35
clay pot-steamed chicken soup, **135**
cleavers, 35–36
  cutting techniques with, 39, 470
cloud ears, 15, 127, 318
cock's combs, 444
coconut, 56, 139, 316, 508–9
  and banana soup, sweet, **517**
  cracking, 77, 142
  crème caramel, **534**
  curry paste, Thai red or green, 82
  green, 77, 138, 142
  green, spicy beef stew with, **477**
  spicy sauce, fiddlehead fern in, **344**
  sticky rice with mango, divine, **520–21**
  sweet broth, rice balls in, **525**
  toasted, ice cream, **548**
  toasted, rolls, **538**
  young, and chicken soup, **138–139**
coconut custard:
  colonial-era squash and, **530–31**
  crème caramel, **534**
  fish and, **391**
coconut milk, 24, 65, 548
  fresh, **77**
  spicy, pan-fried catfish with, **399**
coconut oil, 7, 77, 408
coconut palm heart, 182
coconut powder, 526
coconut rice, **206**
coconut vinegar, 11, 460
coconut water, 10–11, 62, 64, 142
cod, black:
  braised, with daikon, 383, **393**
  miso-marinated, **400**

miso, 8, 66, 316
marinated beef, **479**
marinated black cod, **400**
soup with tofu and *wakame,* **128**
sweet sauce, roasted eggplant with, **332**
mi xao don do bien, 59
mochi, 178–79, 509, **525**
mock Peking duck, **371**
mohinga, **230–31**
mollusks:
stir-fried in black bean and garlic sauce, **414**
see also seafood
Mongolian lamb hot pot, 115, 122, **152–53,** 442
Mongols:
beef-eating, 435, 436, 438
influence of, 54, 270, 438, 442
influences on, 427–28
moon cakes, 316, 443
mortar and pestle, 36, 82
mouan chha k'nei, **492**
MSG, 64
mulberry paper, making, 555
mul kimchi, **357**
mung bean noodles, 29–30, 172, 176–77
mung beans, peeled split, 18, 516
mung bean soup, sweet, **516**
mung bean sprouts, 23
spinach and, **326**
in summer rolls, 287
mung bean threads, 29–30, 176, 241, 300
mung bean vermicelli, 241
mushrooms, 317–18
black, 14–15
broth, *udon* noodles in, **233**
canned, straw, 24
fresh, 24
fresh autumn, soup, **129**

sauce, steamed leafy greens with, **338–39**
and shrimp-braised cellophane noodles, **249**
steamed rice sheets with pork and, **296**
straw, 24, 134
stuffed caps, **328–29**
three, *soba* with, **248**
wild pine, 317
see also shiitakes
mushroom soy sauce, 8
mu shu pancakes, 180, **254–55,** 447
mussels, dried, 377
mustard cabbage, preserved, and marinated beef, **335**
mustard paste, hot, 11
mustard sauce, **94**
mutton, 442

nabemono, 53, 439
Nabnian, Sompon, 224, 225
nama fu, 184, 289
nam jim sate, **98**
nam pla, 379
nam prik pow, **107**
namul, 327
nanzenji yudofu, **366**
napa cabbage, 23
and shiitake mushrooms, braised, **340**
nasi goreng, 57–58, 169, **212,** 445
nasi gurih or *nasi uduk,* **206**
nasi kuning, **205**
nasu no miso yaki, **332**
nasu su-zuke, **356**
negimaki, 439
nem dzem fen, 173, **220**
nem ran, 59, **284–85**
New Year's cake, 184
ng heung yeung yook, **483**
niban dashi, **124**

nin gao, 184
nom l'poh, **532**
nom nsahm chaek, **522**
noodles, 28–31, 164, 171–77
birthday, with sauce, **238**
cellophane, *see* cellophane noodles
cooking techniques, 172–73
crystal, 249
double-cooked, 172–73
dried, 175
egg, *see* egg noodles
hand-rolled, 173
potato, stir-fried vegetable, meat and, **250**
ramen, 30, 174
ramen, and *kimchi* soup, **242**
recipes, 220–51
rice, *see* rice noodles
rice vermicelli, *see* rice vermicelli
soba, see soba noodles
soups, 241, **226–31, 233, 236, 240–43, 246–51,** 558–59
spicy pickled cabbage soup with, **130**
stir-fried silver pin, **220**
transparency of, 250
udon, in mushroom broth, **233**
wheat, 30–31, 172, 173, 174, 176
wheat, with pork and cabbage sauce, **232**
noodle soups, 172, 174–77
egg, **236, 240–43**
Khmer, 558–59
rice, **226–31**
wheat, **233**
nori, 17
nori and rice, 170–71
nuoc cham, **100,** 334, 418
nuoc cham dau phong, **99**
nuoc mam, 379
nuoc mam tuong xa, **83**

ABOUT THE AUTHOR

Corinne Trang is an award-winning author. She has published articles in such distinguished magazines as *Food & Wine*, *Bottom Line Personal*, CITY, *Organic Style*, and *Saveur*. Her first book, *Authentic Vietnamese Cooking: Food from a Family Table*, won Best Asian Cuisine Book in English and Best Book on Asian Cuisine in the World from Salon International du Livre Gourmand in 2000, and was awarded Best of the Best of 1999 by *Food & Wine*.

Trang is a faculty member at Drexel University in Philadelphia, where she teaches Culinary Arts and Tourism. She has also been a guest critic and lecturer at Massachusetts Museum of Contemporary Art in North Adams; California College of Arts & Crafts in San Francisco; University of the Arts in Philadelphia; Rhode Island School of Design in Providence; University of Applied Sciences in Cologne, Germany; and New York University in New York City.

She has appeared on numerous radio and television shows, including Bloomberg radio's *Executive Dining*; Business Talk Radio's *America's Dining & Travel Guide*; NBC-TV's *B. Smith with Style*; CBS-TV's *Martha Stewart Living*; Discovery Channel's *Home Matters*; and TV Food Network's *Cooking Live*.

In addition to writing, Trang has styled and photographed food for various publications. She lives in New York City.

For more information visit www.corinnetrang.com online.